PEOPLE OF INDIA

# PUNJAB

VOLUME XXXVII

# PEOPLE OF INDIA

## NATIONAL SERIES

| | | |
|---|---|---|
| VOL. I | PEOPLE OF INDIA | AN INTRODUCTION |
| VOL. II | PEOPLE OF INDIA | THE SCHEDULED CASTES |
| VOL. III | PEOPLE OF INDIA | THE SCHEDULED TRIBES |
| VOL. IV | PEOPLE OF INDIA | INDIA'S COMMUNITIES (A-G) |
| VOL. V | PEOPLE OF INDIA | INDIA'S COMMUNITIES (H-M) |
| VOL. VI | PEOPLE OF INDIA | INDIA'S COMMUNITIES (N-Z) |
| VOL. VII | PEOPLE OF INDIA | IDENTITY, ECOLOGY, SOCIAL ORGANIZATION, ECONOMY, DEVELOPMENT, PROCESS AND LINKAGES: A QUANTITATIVE PROFILE |
| VOL. VIII | PEOPLE OF INDIA | COMMUNITIES, SEGMENTS, SYNONYMS SURNAMES AND TITLES |
| VOL. IX | PEOPLE OF INDA | LANGUAGES AND SCRIPTS |
| VOL. X | PEOPLE OF INDIA | THE BIOLOGICAL VARIATION IN INDIAN POPULATIONS |
| VOL. XI | PEOPLE OF INDIA | AN ANTHROPOLOGICAL ATLAS |

## STATE SERIES

| | |
|---|---|
| VOL. XII | ANDAMAN AND NICOBAR ISLANDS |
| VOL. XIII | ANDHRA PRADESH |
| VOL. XIV | ARUNACHAL PRADESH |
| VOL. XV | ASSAM |
| VOL. XVI | BIHAR |
| VOL. XVII | CHANDIGARH |
| VOL. XVIII | DADRA AND NAGAR HAVELI |
| VOL. XIX | DAMAN AND DIU |
| VOL. XX | DELHI |
| VOL. XXI | GOA |
| VOL. XXII | GUJARAT |
| VOL. XXIII | HARYANA |
| VOL. XXIV | HIMACHAL PRADESH |
| VOL. XXV | JAMMU AND KASHMIR |
| VOL. XXVI | KARNATAKA |
| VOL. XXVII | KERALA |
| VOL. XXVIII | LAKSHADWEEP |
| VOL. XXIX | MADHYA PRADESH |
| VOL. XXX | MAHARASHTRA |
| VOL. XXXI | MANIPUR |
| VOL. XXXII | MEGHALAYA |
| VOL. XXXIII | MIZORAM |
| VOL. XXXIV | NAGALAND |
| VOL. XXXV | ORISSA |
| VOL. XXXVI | PONDICHERRY |
| VOL. XXXVII | PUNJAB |
| VOL. XXXVIII | RAJASTHAN |
| VOL. XXXIX | SIKKIM |
| VOL. XL | TAMIL NADU |
| VOL. XLI | TRIPURA |
| VOL. XLII | UTTAR PRADESH |
| VOL. XLIII | WEST BENGAL |

PEOPLE OF INDIA

# PUNJAB

VOLUME XXXVII

*General Editor*
K.S. SINGH

*Editors*
I.J.S. BANSAL
SWARAN SINGH

ANTHROPOLOGICAL SURVEY OF INDIA

MANOHAR
2003

ISBN 81-7304-123-7

*Published on behalf of ASI by Ajay Kumar Jain*
*Manohar Publishers & Distributors, 4753/23 Ansari Road, Daryaganj,*
*New Delhi-110 002*

*Typeset by AJ Software Publishing Co. Pvt. Ltd, New Delhi-110 005*

*Printed at Lordson Publishers Pvt. Ltd., Delhi-110007*

# CONTENTS

# ILLUSTRATIONS

# A NOTE ON THE SERIES

There exists an information gap on a very large number of communities in India, and whatever information exists on them is scanty or needs to be updated. The Anthropological Survey of India (ASI) launched a project on the People of India on 2 October 1985. The objective of the project was to generate a brief, descriptive anthropological profile of all the communities of India, the impact on them of change and development processes and the links that bring them together. This was in accordance with the objectives of the ASI, established forty-five years ago in December 1945. The ASI has been pursuing bio-cultural research among different population groups from its eight regional centres. Its objectives have been redefined in the policy resolution, adopted in 1985, which commits this organization to the survey of the human surface of India.

The identification of the communities and their listing have had a long history which started from the early period of our history, with Manu. Regional lists of communities figured in Sanskrit works. Medieval chronicles contained a description of communities located in various parts of the country. Listings in the colonial period were undertaken on an extensive scale after 1806. The process gathered momentum in course of the censuses from 1881 to 1941. In our compilation of the lists of the communities of India under the People of India project, we drew upon ethnographic surveys, the lists of Scheduled Castes and Scheduled Tribes drawn up by the Government of India, the lists of backward classes prepared by Backward Classes Commissions set up by various state governments, and the list that exists in the Mandal Commission Report. We were able to put together about 6,748 communities at the start. This list was taken to the field, tested and checked, and finally 4,635 communities were identified and studied.

Unlike surveys in the colonial period, which covered British India and a few princely states, our project covers the whole country, bringing within its ambit such areas that had not been ethnographically surveyed earlier or where the survey had been done in a perfunctory manner. Each state and union ter ritory was treated as a unit of study. It was decided to start with the investigation of the least known communities, and then move on to a field study of the lesser-known and better-known ones. Investigators for the survey were identified for each area on the basis of their experience and expertise. Teams of investigators of the Survey, as well as local scholars, were set up for each state and union territory to plan the surveys, seek the cooperation of local scholars, generate and evaluate findings, etc. Later, editorial boards consisting of local scholars—one or more of these were nominated as co-editors for each local volume—were set up for each state and union territory. We sought the cooperation of the state governments in implementing the project, and this we received in ample measure, particularly from the welfare and backward classes departments of the state governments, local officers of the Census of India, tribal research institutes, university departments of anthropology, other departments of local universities, etc. Local scholars participated enthusiastically in our project as well as in the seminars held by us.

The progress in the investigation and coverage of communities from 2 October 1985 to 31 March 1992 was steady and impressive. We were able to identify, locate and study 4,635 communities in all the states and union territories of India, out of the 6,748 listed initially. As many as 600 scholars participated in this project, including 197 from 26 institutions. About 100 workshops and rounds of discussions were held in all the states and union territories, and in these about 3,000 scholars participated. The investigators spent 26,510 days in the field, which works out to 5.5 days per community studied in the various states and Union Territories of India. Our scholars interviewed a large number of people, out of whom we have recorded only the key informants, i.e. 24,951. This works out to about 5 'informed' informants per community. Of the informants, 4981 were women. Our instruction to the investigators was to study a community at two or three places, and in at least two or three cultural regions into which the larger states of India ware divided. Interviews were conducted in connection with the study of the communities in 3,581 villages, mostly multi-community villages, and in 1,011 towns and cities spread over almost all the districts of India, i.e. 421 districts and 91 cultural regions. We were able, thus, to study on an average a community at about two places. It should be noted that most of the smaller communities could be studied at only one place since they are not located in more than one area.

A major achievement of this project was the preparation of cartographic maps showing the distribution of the communities and the location where they were studied. About 4,000 maps were prepared. Yet another achievement was the visual documentation of the people of India as part of the field operations. About 21,362 photographs were generated, most of them in black & white, and a substantial number in colour, by amateur photographers.

An early stage of our project in March 1985 we decided to transfer the data to a computer. We were subsequently able to develop probably the first software in the country—and one of the first in the world—in ethnography, in close collaboration with the National Informatics Centre. From 28 May 1988 we started transferring the quantitative data collected in computer format to floppies. Simultaneously, the transfer of descriptive data (abstracts, etc.) on to the computer also started at almost all the regional centres. We succeeded in computerizing an enormous mass of data, and also in producing the first results of univariate analysis, by March 1990.

The descriptive material, running into 120 manuscript volumes, and the quantitative data contained in 157 diskettes, were released on 1 October 1990 by Sri Chimanbhai Mehta, Minister of State for Human Resource Development, in the presence of a distinguished audience in Delhi, for use by scholars at the Nehru Memorial Museum & Library, and at eight regional centres of the ASI.

The phase of more elaborate analysis started in July 1991, in collaboration with the Centre for Ecological Sciences, Indian Institute of Science, Bangalore. This resulted in a voluminous output of analysed data, which have been presented in a comprehensive matrix consisting of the four categories of populations, the constitutional, religious, occupational and locational. These sets of data, together with a map, were released by Shri Arjun Singh, Minister of Human Resource Development, on 24 December 1991. The last workshop on the People of India project was held at the Indian Institute of Social and Economic Change in Bangalore, where the preliminary results of the analysis presented by the ASI were discussed by distinguished scholars.

It should be noted that the study of communities has been conducted in 3,581 villages and 1,011 towns situated in 421 districts of the states and union territories of India. The information was collected from about 25,000 of the 'learned' informants by our scholars, 500 of them, over the period 1985 to 1992. Therefore, the observations relate to this limited time frame and to the universe of the ethnographic project titled People of India. The percentages relate strictly to the responses made by the informants to the questionnaire contained in the schedule guideline and computer format, and to the queries made by the investigators at the places of investigation. The responses have been supplemented with the observations of the investigators, the secondary material has been checked and cross-checked at many levels with other sources of information by scholars, particularly local scholars.

We are presenting the material published under the People of India project in two parts which are interrelated. The first consists of the ten-volume national series, five of which contain an abstract on all communities across the length and breadth of the country. The data generated in this respect has been strengthened by the addition of information from census and other secondary sources. These volume include two on the Scheduled Castes and Scheduled Tribes, prepared as part of the celebration of Dr. B.R. Ambedkar's birth centenary; three on all the communities of India, and two containing data on the languages and biological structures of Indian population. The remaining volumes contain description of the quantitative profile, communities and their segments, community-specific languages and the biological structure of Indian populations.

The second part comprises the state/union territory volumes based on a detailed write-up on each community of India. The contributors of the national volumes on the SC, ST and all communities are listed in the last volume, Volume VI. The Glossary given in Volume VI is common to all the national volumes. At the end of each account we have given references to the texts from which we have quoted, or references for further reading. This is only illustrative. An exhaustive bibliography appears at the end of the national volumes, in Volume VI.

Oxford University Press are publishing the national volumes. A consortium of publishers has been set up to publish the material on states and union territories. Seven volumes each for the northern states, southern states and the islands, the central and western states are being published respectively by M/s Manohar Publishers & Distributors (New Delhi), M/s Affiliated

East-West Press Private Limited (Madras) and M/s Popular Prakashan Pvt. Ltd. (Bombay). The eleven volumes on the north-eastern and eastern states are being published by M/s Seagull Books Private Limited (Calcutta), which has already published the introductory national volume. This is bring republished as a revised edition by Oxford University Press.

I trust the series on the People of India, which is based on a comprehensive anthropological survey of the country, will be found useful by all sections of our people, including students, researchers, teachers, social activists, administrators and political leaders. I hope we have laid the groundwork for a comprehensive ethnography of the people of India which needs to be continually updated and built upon by successive generations of researchers and scholars.

K.S. SINGH

# FOREWORD

The land of the five rivers, Puṇjab, known as *panchanad* in the ancient Sanskrit texts derives its identity from the Persian compound comprising the words *panj* (five) and *ab* (water), watered by the Jhelum, Chenab, Ravi, Beas and Satluj rivers. Of these rivers only the last three now flow in India's Punjab. Yet our informants insist that the Indian Punjab is still a land of the five rivers as they add Ghaggar and another river Baiene—it could be any other—to the three rivers.

The eco-cultural zones in of Punjab are known as Malwa, Majha and Doaba. Malwa consists of the four districts, namely, Ludhiana, Patiala, Sangrur and Ropar which are situated between the rivers Satluj and Ghaggar; Majha of the districts of Gurdaspur, Amritsar, Ferozepur, Faridkot and Bhatinda, while the Doaba covers the districts of Hoshiarpur, Jalandhar and Kapurthala lying between the rivers Beas and Satluj. The dialects of Punjabi language define regional identities, Malwa is defined by Malwai, Majha by Majhia and Doaba by Doabi. Historically the people of Malwa, Majha and Doaba, were isolated as there were no bridges on the rivers. There is high concentration of Ramdasia Sikhs in Malwa, Ad-Dharmis in Doaba and Majhabi Sikhs in Majha. There are also stereotypes about the people in general and about the people of each region. Malwa is looked down upon Majha, and both are looked down upon Doaba. All this has changed and is changing. While the Jats are spread through all regions, the Khatris were traditionally concentrated in Amritsar of Majha and other towns. Malwa is considered the most important of the regions, followed by Majha and Doaba. The last is known for the migrants it has sent out to different countries.

## II

The prehistory of Punjab is still to be reconstructed. The Siwalik hills have emerged as one of the theatres of human evolution in the sub-continent, with the discovery of the fossil of a hominoid. The Indo-Aryan languages like Sanskrit interacted with non-Indo-Aryan lanugage families, and there are Mundari words in Punjabi like *kuri* (girl), *munda* (boy), etc. The Tibeto-Burman languages are spoken in Punjab hills. A DNA based study will help in establishing the pattern of the peopling of Punjab.

As a frontier region of India, Punjab has faced invading hordes and absorbed peoples coming from Western and Central Asia such as the Indo-Scythian, etc. A Central and Western Asian connection is seen in the bio-anthropological profile of the state. The historians trace the surnames of many communities to the Central Asian natal groups and to the ancient territories. The surnames, *hoon*, *sur*, *sobthi*, are originally Central Asian but are now integrated with the ethnic mozaic of Punjab. The *bahal* derive their origin from the ancient territory of Punjab, known as *vahilik*.

The Jats are among the ancient people in Punjab. They are referred to as Jety by Pliny and Ptolemy. We studied a pastoral community called Jat Muslim in Gujarat which provides a link of the Jat with the pastoral past. The transformation of the Jats from a pastoral people into peasants is one of the most fascinating stories waiting to be reconstructed. As Jats settled down as peasants, they set up a most elaborate system of relationship based on family, kinship, and a set of patriarchal norms. Wherever they acquired political power, they founded states. They chafed at their status as Shudras in the Brahmanical order inspite of their control over land and their dominance. It is estimated that one third of the Jats became Muslims, one third became Sikhs and one third remained Hindus some of whom entered the fold of Arya Samaj.

In the medieval period, following repeated invasions there was conflict and violence. Bulhe Shah (1680-1758) in his well known composition describes the condition of Punjab as topsy turvy.

'Other adverse times have come. The crows have beaten the hawks and falcons have been eaten by sparrows. The horses are being whipped and the asses are being fed on green wheat plants. Who can change the orders of the highest authority?' Says Bulhe.

'The Mughals have drunk the cups of poison. The Jats with blankets have been made the kings. All the gentle persons walk silently, and they have been slighted by you. O love, you may stay away, you have put me to grief. Tell me whom you have ferried across?' (cited in Kohli, pp. 28-9)

Bulhe further speaks of hatred and fear between Hindus and Muslims. A translation 'slightly' modified says 'The Muslim fears the flame, and the Hindu the tomb, Both die in this fear, such is the hatred between them' (Subrahmanyam, p. 44 ).

There was large scale conversion to Islam, of pastoral tribes, higher castes, artisan groups bound by the *jajmani* system. That the upper castes had converted extensively to Islam and Sikhism, is shown by

1931 census which records 51 per cent population as of Muslims which contained 4.57 lakh Muslim Rajputs, a substantial portion of artisans and lower castes, Jats, etc. This was however only one side of the picture. Punjab probably presents one of the finest examples of syncretisim that emerged in the medieval period and shaped policies of liberarlism particularly followed by the local rulers including Sikhs. Punjabi emerged as a language that became the most important identity marker. Hindu and Islamic traditions mingled; the Sufi and the Bhakti traditions blended. There were endearing examples of how people mixed together. A branch of the Saraswats, Mohiyal recall having travelled all over the medieval world of Arabia, Iraq, Persia and sacrificed seven sons in trying to save the grandsons of the Prophet in the battle field of Karbala. They came to be known as Hussaini Brahman. Folklores reflect the inter-community linkages that developed as a result of the people living together in the space called Punjab. Apart from the common heritage built upon by the saints and sufis, there was a great deal of interaction, and mutual accommodation in political and administrative spheres. And yet there was the devastating experience of partition, with 5 lakh people killed and 10 lakh people uprooted, and thousands of women dishonoured of which Punjab bore the brunt. However Malerkotla remained an island of communal harmony because it represents a unique expression of the continuing gratitude of a people for the descendants of a ruler belonging to another religion who dared to defend the tenth Guru's sons before his co-religionists.

The flowering of this syncretic process could best be seen in the rise of Sikhism. Sikhism as a religion was life-affirmative, renouncing 'renunciation'; it frowned upon the caste system, inequality and untouchability. For our purposes, it is interesting to recall that Sikhism stressed collective action through *sangat* (congregation), and *pangat* (inter-dinning). Later *kar-sewa* was added, a feature of the religion that at one stroke did away with the taboo on working with hand and with a culture that excluded many classes of people from touching the plough and treated those who worked with hand as 'menial classes'. The opposition between manual and non-manual labour brokedown. Sikhism was the most comprehensive assault on the caste system. It was not as radical in its attempts at eradication of endogamy as attempted by the movement led by Basava in twelfth century in Karnataka. Sikhism was however more enduring with its repeated declaration of the values of social equality, abolition of untouchability, inter-dining and community living. The holy *Guru Granth Sahib* compiled by the fifth Guru is a compilation of the compositions not only of the Sikh Gurus and Hindu and Muslim Bhagats, Brahmans (Gita Govind and Surdas), Sheikh Farid, and Bhikan (Sufis), but also of the subalterns, belonging to different castes-tailor (Namdev), butcher (Sadhan), vaisya (Trilocan), barber (Sain), Jats (Dhanna), weaver (Kabir) and cobbler (Ravidas),

Sikhism stressed identity for its followers by prescribing the five K's, surname monogamy, and abstaining from the use of tobacco, drinks, and meat by *halal.* The tenth Guru, Gobind Singh (A.D. 1668-1708), organized the Sikhs into a distinct fratenity by ordaining them to keep the five symbols—(i) uncut hair, (ii) comb, (iii) iron bangle, (iv) underwear and (v) the sword for both men and women. The turban as the head gear of the Khalsa Sikh was also added later. The Guru laid stress on the equality of various castes, symbolically by choosing the Five Beloved from all castes in an assembly of thousands of Sikhs gathered at Anandpur to celebrate the Baisakhi festival. When these five chosen ones drawn from different castes (Khatri, Jat, Nai, Jheewar, Chhimba) were initiated into the new fraternity of the Khalsa 'the pure', others followed drinking from the same bowl and eating from the same plate, adopting the surname Singh for men and Kaur for women signifying one common brotherhood. This ceremony, known as *amrit chakna*, that is the practice of eating from the same plate and drinking from the same bowl is followed at the time of initiation of a Sikh into the Khalsa. The holy book of the Sikhs, the *Granth*, succeeded the tenth Guru and was recognized as the Guru of the Sikhs.

Many castes accepted Sikhism. The great Sikh Gurus themselves belonged to the Khatri caste and married within the caste. However, Sikhism started as the religion of the oppressed, emancipated the lower orders and galvanized the peasants, artisans, leather workers, scavengers and others. Sikhism mobilized the 'lowly' castes such as Tarkhans (later called Ramgarhias), Kalals (now called Ahluwalis), Sansis (a Dalit caste), and the Jats. The newly formed Sikh community consisted of the Shudra castes that emerged at the top of the new hierarchy (Judge, 'Religion, Caste, and Communalism in Punjab', 2001) and acquired political power. The Jats who had already emerged as prosperous peasants now largely formed the leadership of political formations such as *misl* (confederation)—the majority of the chiefs of the *misl* were Jats—and went on to constitute the largest group of the followers of Sikhism from the eighteenth centuary onward. The 1931 population of the Jat stood at 60.7 lakh and of Jat Sikh at

15.31 lakh. It is said that the entry of the Jat into Sikhfold 'created a major difference in the caste structure among the Sikhs due to three reasons. First, as evidence suggests, the Jats converted to Sikhism after they had achieved economic prosperity [due to the adoption of water wheel that augmented production]. From this perspective, the conversion of Jats to Sikhism took place due to status dissonance. Secondly, they constituted more than half the population of the Sikhs, which implies that the Jats were central to the affairs of the community. Thirdly, though Maharaja Ranjit Singh did not belong to the Jat caste, yet as a shrewd ruler he could understand the position of the Jats within the Sikh community and this led him to create a powerful Jat aristocracy. Not only that, he recruited Jats into the army on a preferential basis, particularly those Jats who belonged to the central Punjab districts of Amritsar and Lahore. The British continued the same policy with the exception that they did not confine the recruitment to central Punjab. At the time of the annexation of Punjab by the British in 1849 the Jats had already acquired the status of an upper caste' (Judge, 2001).

The egalitarianism of the Sikhism and of the Jats reinforced each other. Besides, the Jat patriarchal norms also penetrated the new society emerging in Punjab.

## III

While Punjab ethnography was part of colonial ethnography, it had some distinctive features. Colonial ethnography has not been monolithic; there are diversities within it, and this is best brought out in the case of Punjab ethnography. Denzil Ibbetson later participated in the discussions held in 1885 on the format to be drawn up for the ethnographic survey that focussed on caste. But he had started earlier with an ethnographic format of his own in which he collected ethnographic information about the communities of Punjab in 1881 census. In fact Punjab pioneered the intensive phase of colonial ethnography which started with the census of 1881. Ibbetson looked at the census of 1881 not only as a means of collecting information on selected subjects but as a 'sketch of salient features of native societies in the Punjab'. He had a larger view of the census. As he said,

'A census report is not light reading and men take it up not to read it through, but to obtain from it information on some definite point. It is therefore more important that it should be complete than that it should be brief and so long as its arrangement directs the students at once to the place where he will find what he wants without compelling him to wade through irrelevant matter the fuller the information which he there finds on the subjects, the more valuable will the report to him. I have therefore omitted nothing relevant that seems to me to be interesting or useful simply because it occupied space' (Ibbetson, Introduction).

Thus was census ethnography born which furnished for the first time information on a community, its internal structure and variation. Punjab had thus an ethnography that was distinct from the ethnography of other parts of the country. The census report was published in 1883. A separate volume under the title *Punjab Ethnography* containing information about religions, languages, races, castes and tribes was issued in 1883. In 1916 another volume containing the ethnological information was published under the title *Punjab Castes.*

H.A. Rose built upon the foundation laid by Ibbetson. He also avoided using physiometry but provided a little more of the ethnographic materials along the lines laid down by Ibbetson, as the Ethnographic Survey of India 1901-1908 was extended to the Punjab. The material generated by the survey was presented in the format of the Ethnographic Survey. However, Punjab material was not entirely based on an ethnographic survey like in other provinces. In fact H.A. Rose's book titled *Glossary of the Tribes and Castes of Punjab and North-West Frontier Province* continued to be based primarily on the census report of 1883 by late Sir Denzil Ibbetson and the census report of the Punjab of 1892 by Sr. Edward Maclagan. The Punjab chapter of colonial ethnography appears to be a little different from similar volumes for other provinces.

The methodology adopted by Ibbetson and others in other provinces was almost similar. They relied on the evidence furnished by 'gentlemen' informants, and put their testimony through repeated checks. Yet the conceptual framework of Ibbetson's ethnography was not only pioneering but also refreshing in contrast to later ethnographers. First, as mentioned above, although compiled under the rubric of race, tribe and caste, it was singularly free from the discussion of race. The exploration of race was considered by ethnographers like Risley and Crooke as one of the modes for understanding Indian social organization. Secondly, Ibbetson looked at the communities *in situ* as they were in terms of their occupation, status, access to resources and relationships of power. He not only studied the internal structure of the communities but also its variations. He did not go by the text only but also by the reality of relationships. Ibbetson is credited with a dynamic view of communities in Punjab which was historically placed in a situation of fluidity and rapid change. The caste was neither perpetual nor immutable. In his studies Ibbetson emphasised, as mentioned above, their linkages with the space, occupational mobility, heterogeneity, the dignity of the people, their zeal for life, etc.

Ethnographers earlier described all communities as tribes. The distinction between tribe and caste did not fully emerge until the census of 1901. Though Ibbetson was aware of all pervasiveness of caste structures and caste values, he tried to make a distinction between caste and tribe. Occupation was the primary basis of castes, reinforced by status and caste rules. A tribe was bound by the notions of 'common origin, common habitat, common customs and modes of thought'. A tribe, particularly a clan was strongly linked with territory. He applied the structure or category of caste to identify the social organization among the Brahman, Hindu non-agricultural, mercantile castes of the Khatris, Aroras and Banias, who were held together by rules of endogamy, notions of purity and pollution, etc. The concept of tribe was applied by Ibbetson to agricultural castes based on the notion of common descent and to Muslim communities such as Baloch and Pathan and to pastoral and other groups on the periphery. However Ibbetson also describes tribal divisions within the priestly and mercantile castes, among artisans and 'menial' castes and among women. It is obvious that the situation was fluid. Today there are few who share his view, though they agree with Ibbetson's view on the dynamism of the caste and of the social situation and the change noted by him in meanings of such groups such as Jats, Rajputs not only historically but also ethnically. The ethnographic profile of India that emerges under the People of India project which is closer to the ethnography of Ibbetson has community rather than tribe and caste as its focus which shares a lot of traits, to larger or lesser extent, and the tribe is a community relatively isolated, distant and backward, less complex and stratified, more cohesive and egalitarian.

The other concerns of colonial ethnography could be briefly be discussed. The colonial ethnographers and administrators like Ibbetson romanticized the Jats in the well known words—'the most important of the Punjab peoples . . . the peculiar and most prominent product of the plains of the five rivers . . . the husbandman, the peasant, and the prayer for revenue *par-excellence* of the Province' (Ibbetson, quoted in Rose's *Glossary*, Vol. II, p. 366)—just as Tod idealized the Rajputs to the neglect of other components of the same community or other communities, and ignored the other perceptions. The Jats particularly Jat Sikhs have proved themselves worthy of these observations, but the ethnographic scenario is much too complex, and there is an inexorable movement towards equality and pluralism. There are few takers of the stereotypes of communities in colonial and non-colonial literature.

Another finding of colonial ethnography was about the model of Rajputization which was ubiquitous among most of the communities of Punjab, particularly the low placed ones who considered themselves descendants of Rajputs but had lost their status through the process of degradation that occurred in phases. Punjab had a large Rajput population particularly in the hills. The Dalits now do not invoke this model and instead stress their identity *in situ* which reflects self respect and self confidence. The colonial ethnographers also devoted considerable space to exploring the linkages of the Khatris with the Kshatriyas and the transformation of the warriors into traders and businessmen, which has been reported from Gujarat and Rajasthan. The etymological derivative of Khatri from Kshatriya is indisputable as is the pre-eminent position of the Khatri in Punjab society. But today such transformation appears to be problematic. There is a difference in the ethos of warriors and of traders. The Khatris also had some land which suggests a peasant origin. There was a section with martial surnames. The Khatris also occupied important positions as generals, administrators, political and social leaders. Thus the Khatri seem to have a complex origin. Similarly, the linkages of Rajputs and Jats Ahir and Gujjar were stressed by ethnographers. This notion contained the seeds of an organization, the Ajgar (Ahir, Jat, Gujjar and Rajput) which was sought to be built up by political leaders. The difference between the Jats and Rajputs and others were cultural rather than biological, and unity efforts broke down on the issue of sororate, *karewa* and remarriage.

The colonial administrators had a soft corner for the agricultural castes which formed the bedrock of rural society and economy and were sensitive to their exploitation by Hindu moneylenders. Therefore Punjab pioneered the legislation, the Punjab Alienation of Land Act of 1900 which debarred the traditional non-agricultural castes from buying land belonging to the agricultural tribes.

All ethnographic accounts are unanimous in reporting that conversion to Islam did not make any difference to the caste status of the believers or the social customs including rules of marriage and inheritance, apart from a little beard and shaved upper chin that appeared on the face of the new converts, a change in names and a rudimentary knowledge and practice of the new religion. Similarly, conversion to the Sikhism did not mean even more a break with the past. But all this changed as the colonial period closed. The identities of the Hindu/Muslim/Sikh were well consolidated under the influence of colonial policy of promoting orthodoxification and under the influence of various religious movements among the three communities which led to each distancing itself from the other. Fundamentalism emerged, articulated by religious organizations, from the latter half of the nineteenth century, Anjuman among the Muslims, Arya Samaj among the Hindus and Singh Sabha among the Sikhs. Each first reacted against the Christian missionaries and employed the missionaries' mode of polemics and their vocabulary in denouncing them and then turned upon one another on the home ground. They also promoted social reforms. The Arya Samaj movement (1871) among the Hindus promoted education both among men and women, advocated widow remarriage, 'restored' the ritual rites to the women who were permitted to participate in *yajnya*, tried to uplift some of the lowest of the low groups such as Dom by giving them a new name (Mahasya), and bringing them the benefits of education. The life cycle ceremonies were organized around the *yajnya* and made simple and inexpensive. The Singh Sabha movement (1872) that followed tried to establish the Sikh as a separate community, denounce the Brahmans for their betrayal of Sikh Gurus, abjure the Brahmanical practices, promote education and develop Punjabi literature. There were sharp differences among the three main communities in the matter of language and script. The Muslims adopted Urdu in Perso-Arabic script, the Sikhs favoured Punjabi in Gurumukhi script and the Hindus were for Hindi in Devanagari script. Almost a hundred years of scramble for a share in the power structure, search for roots in the course of identity formation, fear and mistrust, distanced the three major religious communities from one another on the eve of the independence. The riots and migrations following partition did the rest in alienating communities. It is said that the Punjabi middle class that emerged in the colonial period was more communal than secular and that few educated persons in the Punjab identified themselves as Punjabis and with Punjabiyat, and both the regional identity and Indian nationalism were casualities for the time being. However such evidence as we have now from literature and historical writings suggests that these larger identities survived and even became stronger at many levels, individual, familial, political, cultural, etc.

If Rose and Ibbetson were to visit Punjab today, they would find the ethnographic scenario hugely changed. The picturesque Punjab hills are out. There are no scheduled tribes in Punjab, but some of the 'tribal' traits that Rose and Ibbetson identified in terms of the spirit of the people, their *joi de vivre* or their *esprit de core* and the strongly rooted clans particularly among Jats, etc., still survive. Both Ibbetson and Rose would be delighted to see the prosperity in the regions which were backward at the time of partition, brought about as result of the sheer hard work of the immigrants. They would have also noticed continuity in terms of identity, change and resilience in many aspects of the ethnographic scenario.

After partition most of the communities who came from Pakistan were settled as far as practicable in the areas similar to the areas they migrated from under a well conceived rehabilitation plan.

There is now a large floating population of agricultural labour and other workers from other states estimated at 1.5 million. We have however not studied them because they do not form a community permanently settled in rural areas of Punjab and they are not enfranchised. Most of the Muslim communities have moved out of Punjab though there is still a sizeable population at Malerkotla. The Muslim population in Punjab has gone up in the last census.

The Sikhs have emerged as a dominant community forming 62 per cent of the population communities, most of them concentrated in the rural areas of Punjab. The Hindus come next, in terms of population, mostly distributed in cities. Before partition the Sikhs had been in a majority only in the tahsil of Taran Taran. In colonial Punjab, for example, Sikhs constituted only around 12 per cent of the total population, the Muslims were 51 per cent of the population and the Hindus accounted for the remaining 36 per cent. The proportion of Sikh population in Maharaja Ranjit Singh's 'Sikh Kingdom' of the Punjab was reportedly even less, 10 per cent of the total population.

The post-colonial period saw consolidation of identities in Punjab. Excellent studies have appeared on the rise of identities particularly Sikh identity. The phases and stages through which it has evolved are known, from a welter of identities into a homogeneous religious community. The landmarks highlighted were the Gurudwara Act in 1925 which identified the Sikhs and recognized the *amritdhari* as a dominant element, formation of Akali party (1920) as the political arm of the Panth movement of Punjabi Sabha and the formation of Punjab. The Sikh Jat emerged as the dominant element in politics, administration and professions. The Namdharis and Nirankaris have been declared non-Sikhs. In fact the homogenization or consolidation of all communities, religious or ethnic, in the situation of crises and struggles is a major feature of Punjab situation, as elsewhere.

## IV

While no physiometric measurment was taken as part of colonial ethnography in Punjab, as elsewhere under the influence of the theory of race, as mentioned above, the Punjab ethnographers keenly observed the morphological features and facial complexion of the populations and speculated a great deal about their affinities and origins. Thus we were told that Jats and Rajputs represented in the two waves of immigration of the Indo-Scythian and Aryans respectively. Others were of the opinion that the Jats, Rajputs, Gujars were the same people. Ibbetson identified the Doms with the indigenous people, described in the Vedas as short, black, and snub nosed. Today we have moved away from such discussions and describe the two categories of populations of the old Punjab, the higher and the lower generally in terms of the Caucasoid and the Australoid. Even within these morphological types and between them there is a range of variations, making generalization difficult.

According to the All India Physiometric Survey undertaken by the Anthropological Survey of India, the populations of Punjab are above medium to tall in stature, have long head, narrow to broad nose and face. There are other dimensions. Dermatoglyphic studies indicate preponderance of loops (47.50-59.30 per cent) over whorls (33.30-43.80 per cent). The frequency of arches varies from 2.43 per cent to 7.40 per cent. Incidence of colour blindness ranges from 2.04 per cent to 9.60 per cent and G6PD from 2.06 per cent to 8.14 per cent. B blood group gene (10.70-58.99 per cent) generally preponderates A. The frequency of M gene varies from 51.00-71.57 per cent. R1 haplotype ranges from 47.20-66.38 per cent. On the other hand r haplotype is below 33 per cent (16.41-33.50 per cent). Biochemical variants have been extensively studied both in Scheduled Castes and caste population, viz, Hp1 (16.00-24.30 per cent), Pa (25.00-43.00 per cent), Pb (57.00), AK1 (87.10-92.30 per cent), PGDA (97.20 per cent), and ADH (81.50-90.60 per cent). Transferrin T6B (0.00-1.39 per cent) and T6D (0.00-1.04 per cent) have been reported from the populations of Punjab.

Punjabi identity is primarily defined by language. Though the ancestry of Punjabi language is traced to the twelfth century, the two streams of the writings of Muslim Sufis and the Sikh Gurus in the fifteenth century mark the definitive beginning of Punjabi language and literature. However, Persian and later Urdu was the official language of the province till independence. The notification of Urdu as the official language led to popular support for Punjabi. The printing press was introduced. The Christan missionaries developed Punjabi prose. The Singh Sabha writers from the later half of the nineteenth century and others contributed enormously to the development of the Punjabi literature. The Singh Sabha demanded the recognition of Punjabi written in Gurumukhi script as the official language. Punjabi written in Gurumukhi script became the official language after independence in Punjab and in neighbouring states with Punjabi populations.

According to 1981 census, Punjabi is spoken by the largest number of persons (14,146,581) followed by Hindi (2,549,098 ), Urdu (34,189) and Dogri (24,155). The Gorkhali/Napali and Lahnda/Multani are spoken by 4,350 and 934 persons respectively. Punjabi is spoken by 92.14 per cent people of whom 73.38 per cent are in rural areas and 26.62 per cent in urban areas. Hindi comes second spoken by 7.20 per cent people, out of whom 68 per cent live in urban areas. It is interesting to note the number of Punjabi speakers went up by 34 per cent in 1971-81, as Hindus returned Punjabi as their mother tongue, but it dropped to 19 per cent during 1981-91, mainly because of the disturbed conditions. In all, seventeen languages are spoken in the state, according to the POI. Punjabi is spoken by the largest number of communities (57). Hindi and Urdu languages are spoken by 22 and 9 communities respectively. Of the 18 communities who are linguistically heterogeneous, 14 communities belong to Punjabi and Hindi languages. Pasto is an Indo-Iranian language, Bauria and Sansi are unclassified languages and all other languages belong to the Indo-Aryan sub family.

Hindi speakers are bilingual in Punjabi (875,346), Urdu (65,553 ) and Sanskrit (8,844). Punjabi speakers are bilingual in Hindi (3,402,862) and Urdu (191,270). Urdu speakers are bilingual in Punjabi (7,387) and Hindi (2,048). Other linguistic minorities are bilingual in Hindi and Punjabi languages.

The post-Gupta Siddhamatrika script or early Nagari developed into the Sharada script in Kashmir and Punjab from the eighth century onward. A variant of Sharada script called Landa used by Kashmiri Brahmans was developed by the second Sikh Guru, Angad Dev into the Gurumukhi script in the sixteenth century. This became another identity marker of Sikhism. The holy *Guru Granth Sahib* was written in this script, which was later advocated by Sikh reformers as the script for Punjabi. At present Gurumukhi, Devanagari and Perso-Arabic scripts are commonly in use. Punjabi written in Gurumukhi is the official language.

## V

Sikhism was born in Punjab which had its own cluster of communities called *jat* or *zat quom, biradari*, etc., for a community or a part of it. *Quom* could be used for ethnic/regional identity. Punjab shared with other parts of north-west India, the presence of the warrior caste of Rajput who were mainly in the hills, ritual performing Brahmans and a substantial community of Baniyas from outside. However Punjab with its trade routes and flourishing trade, inspite of political turmoil had its own communities of traders and business men, shopkeepers and merchants, its Khatris and Aroras who enjoyed high status. The Khatri was a dominant community in the central districts of old Punjab and had a sizeable presence in Rawalpindi and Hazara now in Pakistan, and in the Punjab hills. The Aroras were dominant in the south-western part of the old Punjab. They were also agriculturalists, moneylenders and were even engaged in weaving clothes and baskets. Baniyas were active in east Punjab. The Rajputs and Brahmans were prominent in the hills, though they were also distributed the plains. The Muslim Jat was predominant in the western parts of old Punjab. The Sikh and Hindu Jats were present in fairely large numbers in central and eastern parts.

The census of India 1881, showed the social composition of Sikh who drawn mostly from Jats, artisans, Chuhras, Brahmans, Rajputs in the plains, etc. Over thc colonial censuses, one could also see the decline in the population of Hindu-Jats who accepted Sikhism. In the 1931 census, the percentage of Jats fell to 60 per cent while Khatri, Arora remained at 2.25 per cent and 3.43 per cent and the artisans formed 11 per cent of the population (Tarkhan 5.87 per cent, Jheer 1.31 per cent, Lohar 1.05 per cent, Sunar 0.79 per cent, Chimba 1.14 per cent, Nai 1.05 per cent). The lowest castes described as menial castes who converted to Sikhism were Chamar (4.8 per cent) and Chuhra (2.29 per cent). Thus the agriculture castes formed about 66 per cent, trading and business class about 6 per cent, artisans 11 per cent, and menials about 7 per cent of the Sikh population. The population of the Khatris and the Aroras among the Sikhs gradually went down.

Inter caste equation within the Sikh Panth changed. The Sikh Gurus belonged to the Khatri caste which was prominent in the beginning. The Khatri membership of the Panth declined during the period 1911-31. The Jat emerged as the dominant group within the panth from the seventeenth-eighteenth centuries onward. The Aroras were relatively a late arrival. The artisans particularly Tarkhans (carpenter) followed the Jat landlords into Sikh religion. Later they took the name Ramgarhia after their leader Jassa Singh Ramgarhia captured the Amritsar Fort named Ramgarh. The Sikh Tarkhans now include a few members of other artisan castes like Lohar, Raj and Nai. The Dalits consists of Mazhabi Sikhs (Chuhra/sweeper) and Ramdasia (Chamars/ leather workers). There is a smaller group called Ranghreta, a group of Chuhras who had brought the severed head of Guru Tegh Bahadur to his son for cremation; they are now identified with Mazhabis. The conversion of these lower castes to Sikhism as to Hinduism under the Arya Samaj movement was a feature of the social reform process at work in the latter half of the nineteenth century. They were also coming into their own, with a new name Ad-Dharmi; and an agenda for social reform in the second and third decades of the twentith century.

According to the 1891 census, the Muslim, Hindu and Sikh respectively formed 41, 51, and 7 per cent of the Punjab population. The major communities of the old Punjab and their approximate population according to 1931 census in terms of their strength were as follows: Jat (60,70,032), Rajput (23,51,650), Jat Sikh (15,31,676), Brahman (10,58,598), Gujjar (6,96,442), Arain/Araeen/Rain (5,12,956), Rajput Muslim (4,57,252), and Agarwal/Vaish Agarwal (2,14,294). The 1981 census has the following population for major Scheduled Castes: Majhabi (13,66,843), Balmiki (12,21,145), Ad-Dharmi (6,80,132) and Chamar Groups (12,21,145).

The Scheduled Castes in Punjab form the largest proportion of the population in any state. Of the total 95 communities studied under POI project, 33 communities are the Scheduled Castes. The Scheduled Castes in the state include Adi-Dharmi/Ad-Dharmi, Balmiki/Valmiki, Bangali, Barar, Batwal, Bawria/Bawari/Bawariya, Bazigar, Chamar, Regar/Raigar, Darai/Darain, Dhanak/Dhanuk, Dhogri/Dogri/Dom/ Dum/Domb, Gandhila, Kabir Panthi, Koli, Majhabi, Megh and others. At one time they were the only source of labour. Today, they are mobile, confident and assertive.

As mentioned earlier there are no Scheduled Tribes in Punjab. The minorities include Muslims, Jains, Buddhists, Christians, etc. The communities which are engaged in specialized services include

Acharaj. Gujjar is the only community which may be described as a pastoral nomad.

An interesting feature again is the extension of some occupation groups, typical of the north-west region into Punjab such as Sikligar, Gagra, Singikat, Dhea, Bawria, Gandhila, and Sirkiband, etc. Punjab has a number of small communities pursuing interesting vocations.

Of the communities we have studied, the larger groups are formed by *peasants*, Jats particularly Arain, Kamboj; *artisans* such as: Dhobi, Julaha, Kabir Panthi, Kumhar, Lohar, Nalband, Ramgarhia, Chamar, etc.; *agricultural labour*: Chamar, Chuhra, etc.; *cultural workers/ entertainers*: Madari, Perna, Bazigars, Mirasi, Bharai, Gagra, etc.; *traders*, *businessmen* and *moneylenders*: Khatri, Bania, Ahluwalia, Sood, Saini, Sunar, Rajput, Bania/Baniya, Arora, Khatri, Bhatia, Jain. etc.

Some of the communities of Punjab who identify themselves as indigenous ones are Ad-Dharmi, Arain/Araeen/Rain, Jat Sikh, Mazhabi/Majhabi, Rajput Jat, Khatri, Arora and Bhatia. The immigrant communities include Ahir, Banjara, Gaddi and Gorkha Nepali, fishing community in the state is Jheewar/Jhinwar.

Of the total 95 communities studied in Punjab, 45 communities (45.3 per cent) live in rural areas and only 6 communities (6.3 per cent) live in urban settings. About 41 communities (43.3 per cent) have been living in rural/urban settings.

The communities are either identified regionally or locally or nationally. Historical/ethnographic accounts are available for about 50 communities. Family geneologies are maintained at Hardwar, Kurukshetra and other places by family priests and updated on every suitable occasion.

For obvious reasons, such as partition a majority of the communities (56) have reported to their present habitat, which has been recorded in oral tradition or otherwise.

The communities experience extreme cold in winter and scorching heat in summer, extremes of temperature, and two monsoons. Most of the communities (86) live in the plains and a few in hilly terrain (10) and some in semi arid regions (11). Punjab is perceived as generally a low humidity region (86) with medium rainfall (78).

The ethnographic world of Punjab described above was reflected in Punjabi literature 1750-1850 (Johal, 2000).

Identity, *inter-alia* is reflected in structure of personal names, particularly surnames which are derived from ecology, settlement or village, family and religion. Most of the *gots* are derived from villages

(Khanna, Moga, Badal, etc.). Punjab vocabulary is rich in surnames associated with plants, animals, etc. Few regions of India have been as influenced as Punjab by religious and political movements in determining personal names. Arya Samaj gave Vedic names to its adherents, and Punjab has some of the most Sanskritized names in the country for both men and women. Sikh names are derived from the great Gurus and Sikh shrines (Guru Charan, Guru Sharan, Guru Darshan, Harbhajan, Harpreet, Swaran, Harminder). The suffix Singh is used for all irrespective of castes demonstrating equality and also martial organization but history tells us that it took sometime for the suffix Singh to be widely adopted and that Rai continued to be the suffix for some time. The women were enjoined to use Kaur as a suffix. The Singh Sabha insisted on the use of the name of the village of birth as a surname. Punjab thus offers the largest example of names of villages being used as a suffix. However there are secular names too, derived from professions particularly the army (Karnail, Jarnail etc.). Both male and female names have the same names avoiding the feminine gender, such as Prem.

## VI

We have used an excellent study of a Sikh village, Dalake (I.P. Singh, 1959), as bench mark to show the range of change that occurred between this study in 1959 and the POI project (1985-95).

Punjab food basket consists of rice and wheat followed by maize and barley. Of pulses *gram*, *masoor*, *moong*, *urad*, and *moth*, in that order are the favourite. Of mediums of cooking, *desi* ghee, vanaspati, mustard, groundnut and sunflower are popular. Peas and beans are consumed at the level as elsewhere, but the consumption of roots and tubers is much lower than the national average. The study of the Sikh village suggests that the daily food of an average villager consists of buttermilk and one green vegetable or pulses. 'Tea is very common and is drunk at least twice a day; but this tea contains plenty of milk. The quantity of food eaten is also large. An average villager eats *chapatis*, made often from about half a *seer* of wheat or maize flour, and drinks half a litre of tea at one time. During the summer he drinks at least three liters of buttermilk in one day. Bets are laid on the number of *chapatis*, meat, or sweets eaten, or sugar cane juice or milk drunk' (Singh, 1959).

Neither fruit nor vegetable was part of the traditional menu in rural Punjab. Now though Punjab is rich in food, in terms of calories, a recent study suggests lack of adequate nutrition due to low intake of fruits, green vegetables, etc. According to the POI data, there has been a general increase in the consumption of vegetables and fruits, and members in 72.94 per cent of the communities take vegetables in moderate quantity and those in only 5.88 per cent of the communities in high quantity. While consumption of milk is lower than the national average that of milk products is the highest. While intake of cereals is at the same level as elsewhere, intake of pulses has fallen. The intake of food has increased faster than intake of vegetables and fruits. The Punjabis prefer *roti* to rice despite their being rice producers and consumers of recent origin. In day to day parlance *roti* is a synonym for meals.

Sikhism forbids smoking and use of *kath*/catechu. This explains the low incidence of smoking *bidi*, indigenous cheroot/pipe and tobacco, taking loose tobacco and even betel and snuff. The *pan* belt of India does not extend to the north-western region and *pan* chewing is on a smaller scale. However, smoking cigarette is slightly higher than the national average apparently among the non-Sikh population and urban classes.

Drinking is prohibited by Sikh religion. As the Sikh village study says, most of the wine drunk in the village is country made, usually distilled by the Mazhabis from *gur* 'brown sugar'. Wine is not drunk alone, but in groups which usually consist of relatives and friends and exclude persons belonging to a hostile group or enemies. Foreign liquor was tasted by only a few in 1959. Today Punjab's prosperity is reflected in the consumption of alcohol, which is highest in the country netting the collection of the highest excise. Most of these drinks are purchased from market. Punjab reports the largest incidence of drinking occasionally by men (82.11 per cent against the national average of 53.27 per cent) purchased from open market (81.05 per cent against the national average of 66.49 per cent). Drinking, occasional or regular by women is lowest in the country.

Impact of Vaishnava traditions explains the strong presence of vegetarianism among Jats, religious sects both Hindu and Sikh, and some Brahman and Baniya groups. Sikhism prescribed non-vegeterianism or consumption of meat by *jhatka*; however, social reform groups among Sikhs such as Namdhari, Nirankari, Radhaswami are vegetarians. The number of women vegetarian in Punjabi communities is almost three times the national average, while that of women non-vegetarian is only slightly less (68.42 per cent against the national average of 72.25 per cent). Women's access to food and drink is restricted. Consumption of beef (cow and ox) is the lowest while that of pork is above the national average.

In food habits there has thus been a marked change from vegetarianism to non-vegetarianism as brought out in our data. Members in as many as 25 communities (29.41 per cent) report change of food habits from vegetarian to non-vegetarian particularly among Jats, Banias and other traditionally vegetarian communities: members of the younger generation are turning to non-vegetarianism. The change from non-vegetarian to vegetarian is reported at the same level as from vegetarian to non-vegetarian among members of the same communities (28.2 per cent).

Like other cultural regions in India Punjab is distinguished by its culture. Historically it was the only region where dress particularly headdress or *pagri* was ordained as a symbol of identity. The scholars now tell us that *pagri* emerged as the symbol of the Khalsa Sikhs, much later in Sikh history (MacLeod, *The Turban: Symbol of Sikh Identity*, 2001). But the tradition of wearing turban was an older one. There were different colours of turban associated with different regions and even different peoples. Members of a political party once preferred to wear a black turban which has now given way to dark brown. There were distinct styles of wearing a turban, one like a peak projected like a beak (*chonch*), the other *turra* like the peacock (*turla*), and the third white *pagri* worn by Namadhari (Kooka) 'with the bottom edge drawn horizontally across the forehead' (MacLeod) supposed to be oldest one. The traditional wear for women consisting of the *ghaghra, chadar/ghunghat* (veil) has now given way to *salwar-kameej* and the sight of women going round in veil or following men keeping some distance is not common. There is now a better understanding of *burqa* (veil) which is also seen protection against harsher aspects of ecology such as dust and heat.

## VII

Colonial ethnography highlighted heterogeneity in terms of divisions, endogamous or exogamous, and hierarchy. Punjab still has an extraordinary range of heterogeneity in terms of divisions such as exogamous units called *al, got, gotra, mukh*, etc. Large communities in Punjab such as Khatri (164), Kamboj (84), Teli (64), Bhatia (84), Sud (52), Jheewar (110), Bania, Sud, Kurmi, etc., are clusters of a large number of *gots* or exogamous divisions ranging from 52-300. The Khatris were stratified along the traditional divisions *char–barah–*

*bavanjah* or 4–12–52 convention, hierarchcally placed and hypergamously related. The *gots* to which the Sikh Gurus belonged such as Bedi, Sondhi, Trehan, Bhalla are placed higher than others. Today, stratification and hierarchy among the Khatri and other groups have weakend and almost disappeared in cities. The Jats hold on to the notions of egalitarianism, clan exogamy and patriarchy. The Jat *gots*, about 300 (in and outside Punjab) are all placed equally, in spite of light hearted attempts made by Gill at oneupmanship and the claims of the 'aristocratic' *gots* like Sidhu, Sandhu, Dhillon. The other communities with a large number of clan include traders and artisan groups. At one time the carpenters (Tarkhan) and iron-smith (Lohar) were considered inter-changable in their roles or performed each other's roles. Later they separated and the Sikligar who made weapons and Nalbandh who made horse shoe for transport joined this group. The Sikh Tarkhan unlike Hindu Tarkhan thus expanded to include many groups.

Our data also suggest that social divisions exist in 86 communities (90.53 per cent against the national average of 81.51 per cent) mostly in terms of exogamous divisions (*got*, etc.). Moiety exists in one community, Sansi/Sansuja. The role of these divisions is to indicate status and descent.

Social division exists with hierarchies in 22 commnities (23.16 per cent against the national average of 22.57 per cent).

Punjab reports less of differentiation at social level (17.89 per cent against the national average of 48.39 per cent) due to the impact of Sikhism and more of differentiation at economic, occupational, educational and territorial levels due to rapid pace of growth. This also shows that disparities caused by the green revolution are deepening and manifesting themselves.

Differentiation among the Sikh has been studied by scholars who perceive them in term of the identity-markers, particularly the most important and visible among them, being the hair and how it is kept. There are (i) the *sahajdharis* who believe in Guru Nanak, but are not baptised and do not follow the code including the identity markers prescribed by Guru Gobind Singh, (ii) the *keshdharis* who have various styles: some trim their beard, but keep unshorn hair; some trim their hair and beard but wear a turban, and so on, 'a baffling variety' (Judge, 2001), (iii) the *amritdhari* who are the followers of Guru Gobind Singh, baptised, and keep long unshorn hair, adopt the title 'Singh', (iv) the *monas* are Sikhs without hair and cut their hair. The *amritdhari* have emerged as the dominant group. The *sahajdhari* have a larger proportion of the Khatri, Aroras and Ahluwalias; they also are dominant in Sikh sects and are considered closer to the Hindu matrix. The *sahajdhari* who played a glorious role in Sikh history, are now marginalized and constitute about 10 per cent of the Sikh population.

A Sardar, now a common term of address for all Sikhs denotes in fact the upper crust of Sikh society. The Sikh darbar conferred the title Sardar on high ranking persons, generals and officials. In the Sikh village, Daleke the people belonging to various castes professing Sikhism have been divided broadly into two groups: the *sardars* (the upper castes) and the *mazhabis* (the scavengers). The first group includes Jats, Kamboj, Tarkhan, Kumhars, Sunars, and Nais, who visit each other's houses, interdine, and attend marriage functions and other festive occasions, and go to the fairs together and celebrate most of the festivals commonally. These caste groups can be identified, however, in the same manner as in a Hindu village. The higher group of *sardars* is further subdivided into agriculturists and non-agriculturists, the latter including traders and artisans. The agriculturist group considers itself higher than the non-agriculturists (I.P. Singh, 1959).

Endogamy is widely returned as the norm. Community endogamy is the rule at the most of the communities (100 per cent) at the normative level. Inter community marriage has taken place among members of some communities (23.16 per cent). Child marriage is reported in some communities (6.32 per cent) followed by *gaona* (3.16 per cent). Adult marriage is favoured by the majority (93.68 per cent). Monogamy is the norm (92.63 per cent). However sororal polygyny is practiced (5.26 per cent) and so also non-sororal polygyny (13.68 per cent). Franternal polyandry is practiced in one community, Jat (1.05 per cent) and polygynandry in one community, Gujjar (1.05 per cent).

Endogamy at clan (6.32 per cent) and *gotra* (11.58 per cent) levels is reportedly higher than the national average. This type of endogamy is generally prohibited because it amounts to incest. But it was reported on a small scale in situations where population was small. Colonial ethnography reported it and Punjab still posts higher incidence of clan or *gotra* endogamy for almost the same reason.

There were restrictions on marriages contracted between the communities of different regions in the past. The people of Doaba used to take brides from Malwa in the past but there was no reciprocity from Malwa. However, presently the people of Malwa, Doaba and Majha have started inter zonal marriages more frequently.

Of the northern states Punjab shows the highest incidence of village exogamy (67.37 per cent), which is next only to *got* exogamy (80 per cent). The first among many factors was due to the fact that the village was founded by one lineage the members of which considered the daughter of any one as the daughter of the lineage. Other communities who came in later continued with this practice.

Similarly, the incidence of consanguinity (parallel cousin) in Punjab is higher than the national average among the Muslim communities (11). The incidence of cross cousin is small (FSD 10.58 per cent; MBD 5.26 per cent) but significant. Punjab reports a higher number of cross-cousin marriages outside the Jat groups. This was explained by our informants in the following way. The Sikhs and Hindu had a smaller population in the north-western parts of India before partition, so this practice was allowed particularly among non-Jats. This practice existed on a small scale for the reasons given and for keeping property particularly land together. This practice continued among refugees after partition. It is reported among sections of the Aroras, Bhatia and Khatris under the POI.

Colonial ethnography reported hypergamy across castes such as the Khatri/Arora, Jat and others, across segments among large communities such as the Khatri. Our data suggests that hypergamy of either kind does not seem to prevail as much because all groups and all hypergamous units are trying to be equal to one another, and only two communities including Jat report hypergamy (2.11 per cent against national average of 4.44 per cent) and none reports hypogamy. These two communities account for instances of hypergamy continuing across Jats and lower groups. The practice of hypergamy among Sikh Jats had its roots in the practice of female infanticide which kept the proportion of women low, a situation which was met in two ways, namely, polyandry and purchase of women from outside. The Jats accepted the women from lower castes, but did not give their daughters to them. The children from such unions were adopted into the community and were accepted as equals in status and property rights. It is therefore said that though the Sikh religion could not create an egalitarian community, yet the structure of the caste underwent a change with such resilience in traditional practices. (Judge, 2001). This was however more sociological than religious.

In the past there also existed territorial hypergamy. As mentioned above, there were no marriages contracted between the people of Doaba and Malwa in the past. The people of Doaba used to take the brides from the Malwa region the past but not vice-a-versa. However, with the break down of isolation the people of Malwa, Doaba and Majha have presently started inter regional marriages more frequently.

Our project did not return any incidence of polyandry. So strong have been the impact of education and modernity, the pull of a nuclear family and the norms of monogamy that very few admit even the existence of any form of polyandry. However, the qualitative data shows the sporadic existence of polyandry. Hershman defines a polyandrous marriage as a relationship 'where a number of men and a single woman have a stable sexual and economic relationship and occupy a single joint household' (p. 177). He also proceeds to give a table showing the incidence of polyandry in a village (pp. 182-3) and concludes as follows:

'Polyandry is a recognized state of affairs in Punjabi Society and it is basically condoned. The Punjabis themselves advance economic arguments to explain why polyandrous relationships should occur, but these explanations fail to explain why most non-monogamous relationships whether marital or adulterous, are with close kin and especially within the joint family. I would suggest that a better version of the "keeping the land together" argument is that of "keeping agnates together". It is marriage which divides the brothers and if they marry communally and have common heirs they may remain friends and workmates throughout their lives' (Hershman, p.187).

Many other forms of marriage have been reported in ethnography, past and present. Colonial ethnography mentioned three forms of marriage, i.e. *punn*, without price; *takka* for a bride price and *vatta*, by exchange involving a reciprocal *betrothal.* The People of India project report seven forms of marriage, the most important being marriage by negotiation (92.63 per cent) and by mitual consent (26.32 per cent). Marriage by exchange is low (5.26 per cent) in Punjab, there is only one community reporting marriage by purchase which was rampant in the past.

Bride price in cash is paid by members in communities (10.53 per cent) which is little higher than the national average and in kind in only 2 communities which is much below the national average. The transition from bride price to dowry is negligible (3.16 per cent against national average of 20.69 per cent) showing its connection with hypergamy. Dowry in kind (60 per cent against national average of 14.07 per cent) and dowry in cash and in kind (30.53 per cent) have emerged as the major mode of payment at marriage. This supports the point to be made later that dowry in kind and in cash is being treated as the equivalent of the girls' share in property.

Punjab reports the highest permissibility of traditional forms of marriage, sororate and levirate among 86 communities (90.53 per cent) though in practice it was limited at the places of our study (7.87 per cent for both).

Increase in age at marriage is widely reported. Remarriage of both widow and widower is permitted on a larger scale than the national average. In fact remarriage of widow (98.95 per cent against national average of 81.36 per cent) is slightly higher than widower remarriage (97.89 per cent against the national average of 96.29 per cent). This *inter alia* is due to advocacy of widow remarriage among the higher classes from the latter half of the ninteenth century. Similarly, divorce is widely permitted (97.89 per cent against the national average of 81.86 per cent) on grounds of adultery, barreness, maladjustment, all in higher degree than the national average.

Punjab reports a larger incidence of avoidance and a higher incidence of joking relationship. There is also higher incidence of conflict within the family over property and check on freedom and challenge to authority.

The word *sala* is mildly abusive all over north India, it is even an endearing term at places. But it is a term of severe opprobrium in Punjab. It is said that a ruler would not marry off a sister because he would not like to be called a *sala*. This is attributed to the dubious role or the role of a *sala* in the marriage of his sister particularly in rituals such as *bidai* when the sister leaves the parental household, performed in token of transfer of control over the sister to her husband.

Of marriage symbols, vermilion is the symbol most widely used by women in 25 communities, followed by *bangle* (81.6 per cent); *bindi* continues to be popular (60.5 per cent) followed by toe-ring, ear ring, etc. *Tali* from the south is a new entrant (10.5 per cent).

Both Sikhism and Arya Samaj made life cycle ceremonies simple and inexpensive. Many ceremonies have been curtailed. Punjab reports the lowest incidence of puberty rites predelivery rituals, sacred thread (*janeu*), *mundan* for female. Notion of pollution following birth and death persists. The Hindus celebrate *mundan* for boys and *annaprashan* (the first feeding of cereals). Marriage is performed at the bride's house and consummation of marriage takes place at bridegroom's house. Our data confirms that rituals have been drastically curtailed (67.37 per cent of communities) they are less elaborate, and less expensive, but post ritual ceremonies like feasts, etc., are more expensive. Sanatani rituals continue to be more elaborate, time cousuming and expensive.

The rule of residence is patriocal (94.74 per cent). The members of the communities live in nuclear family (74.74 per cent) along side vertically extended family (73.68 per cent). Though the incidence of nuclear family is rising, extended families are strongly entrenched and functional in business, economy and family affairs.

Male equigeniture is the rule (91.58 per cent). Such is the impact of patriliny that womens right was not even spoken of in the course of field study. Succession as head of the family goes to the eldest son (98.95 per cent).

The dead are cremated in most of the communities (86.32 per cent) and only some are buried (18.95 per cent). Disposal of bones in water is widely reported (84.21 per cent). Punjab is known for its unique custom of ritual mourning called *siapa* performed by a group of breast beating professional mourners. It has been immortalized in the film *Rudali*, located in Rajasthan which tells the story of a woman Rudali, a mourner, amidst the haunting melodies from the Brahmaputra valley, and ends up with the lamentations of the lone woman—not a group—who breaks down under stress.

*Varna* order is widely recognized. Nine of them recognize themselves as Brahmans including 1 Muslim and 2 Sikh groups; 62 as Kshatriyas including 1 Muslim and 14 Sikh groups; 9 as Vaishyas including 1 Muslim and 3 Sikh groups: and 36 as Shudras including 1 Christan and 15 Sikh groups. The Kshatriya Sikh groups have matrimonial relations with the former Rajput chiefs.

We generated information on the three-fold stratification of Punjab communities in terms of the high, the middle and the low, which reveals the following picture: 40 per cent of the communities have high self perception, 30.58 per cent, of them have the middle level perception, and 28.23 per cent of them have low self perception. This reflects upward social mobility of the largest number of communities of Punjab following improvement in economic conditions. The Kamboj are not only now perceive their linkages stretching back in time but also spread over a large part of the country and even South Asia. Other communities with high self perception are Saini, Arain, Arora and Sood. However an interesting feature of the perceptions in Punjab is that others' perceptions do not match self perceptions. In fact others' perceptions are mostly low (54.74 per cent), middle level (32.63 per cent), both higher than the national average and high (11.58 per cent).

We have presented data on sharing of traits by communities. With the Sikh traditions of *sangat* and *pangat* Punjab reports higher incidence of inter community marriages, putative friendship, acceptance and exchange of water and food than the national average. However sharing of cremation or the burial ground is on the low side and cases of discrimination against Dalits have been reported when they have been denied access or allowed to have a cremation ground of their own. Punjab also reports higher incidence of participation in festivals and roles of various communities in festivals, and a higher rise of professional classes and leadership at village level. Interestingly Punjab continues to lead in defence services with representation of members from the largest number of communities (51 communities), 45.9 per cent against national level average of 28.37 per cent.

A majority of communities profess Hinduism (71), followed by Sikhism (38) and Islam (13). According to POI data of the total 95 communities studied in Punjab, 74.7 per cent are Hindus, 40.0 per cent Sikhs, 13.7 per cent Muslims, 2.1 per cent Christians, 2.1 per cent Jains and 1.1 per cent Buddhists. According to 1991 census of the total population of Punjab 62.95 per cent are Sikhs, 34.46 per cent are Hindus, 1.18 per cent Muslims, 1.11 per cent Christians, 0.12 per cent Buddhists, 0.10 per cent Jains and 0.01 per cent follow other religions.

An interesting feature of the Punjab communities is the division of some of them into Hindu–Sikh and Hindu–Muslim and Muslim–Sikh religious segments. The first include Arora, Krora, Khatri, Ahluwalia, Bhatia, Jat, Ramgarhia, Saini, etc. The examples of the second are Sunar, Kamboh, etc.; there are Muslim and Sikh among Nalband and Pasi; Muslim and Hindu among Pasi and Kabir Panthi. The segments continue to maintain close relationships. The segments of the communities belonging to both Sikh and Hindu religion have *roti* and *beti* relationship (inter dining and inter marriage). Those segments following Sikh, Hindu and Muslim religions share elements of material culture, dress, food, house type, folklore, language and dialects spoken in the regions of Punjab.

Sanatan Brahmanism is widely reported to be relatively weak in Punjab. This is attributed to the advent of Islam and rise of Sikhism, conversion of a large number of Hindus including high castes like Rajputs, almost enbloc, and the anti-Brahmanical orientation of Singh Sabha. Finally Arya Samaj movement created its base among the Jats, Khatris and Untouchables. The Jats did not like to be degraded as Shudras in the Brahmanical order and took to Arya Samaj; it is said that the Jats made Arya Samaj and Arya Samaj made the Jats. The same could be said about the relationship of Jat Sikhs and Sikhism. The movement gave them a sense of self respect, and history by linking them with the Vedas and promoted education. Similarily, Arya Samaj worked among the artisans and the Doms called Mahasya, who were marginalized in the Brahmanical order. The Sanatan form of Brahmanism did lose ground.

Our data suggest the constriction of folk Hinduism as evident in the lesser number of deities at family, clan and at village levels because of the small population of the Hindus and their concentration in cities in sharp contrast to the family or *pir* affiliation which is flourishing. The Hindus continue to worship their deities. *Varna* order exists. The sacred specialists are more from the communities other than one's own, i.e. from Brahmans and other groups. The Sikhs have no role for Brahmns, no priesthood of their own, and the *granthis* could be from any community. The Brahman communities are small (4.70 per cent). The Brahmans may not be as visible in Punjab as they are elsewhere but they are doing well.

Sikhism being a monotheistic religion it frowns upon ancestor worship, visit to *dargahs*, worship of folk deities and belief in folk cults. Our data shows that they survive albeit on a small scale. People have reported ancestors worship (76.3 per cent), worship of deities (26.5 per cent) clan deities (7.6 per cent) village deities (26.3 per cent) and deities of wider pantheon (34.2 per cent). In fact in the countryside worship of folk deties such as Guga, the Naga deity, a protector of crops and who also cures snake bite is widely reported. In Gurdaspur district women go around during the month of *Shravan*, dancing and singing which is probably a remnant of Nag worship. Similarily the cults of Mata Rani and Sanji during Navratra/Dussehra are also popular. Visits to shrines, offering of *chadar* at *dargah* of saints are still common.

Punjab is a repository of rich and varied folk traditions, translated into literatures, and represented in folk dances and songs. Punjab has been a centre of classical music amdist vibrant folk traditions. The holy *Granth Sahib* is set to *ragas* and the *ragis* keep up this tradition. The Patiala *gharana* of Hindustani music was one of the many patronized by the princely states. In recent years Punjabi Pop music is the rage. The folk dances exemplified by the vigorous *bhangra* are performed by men. The women have their exclusive *giddha*, a slow moving, little known dance form coming to the limelight. In the traditional forms men and women do not dance together, and this is at a level lower than elsewhere. They dance separately at a level higher than elsewhere.

Punjab reports a higher mix of economic social and religious elements in festivals. Thirty-one festivals are celebrated, as reported from a Sikh village, fifteen of them jointly by Hindus and Sikhs which include the festivals marked by change of season that determins agriculture operations such as Baisakhi (festival of harvesting known as Baisakhi is the most important festival), Savani, Lohri and Basant. Other festivals commonly observed by Hindu and Sikh are Holy, Diwali, Dussehra, Rakhi, Navratra (in honour of mother Goddess Durga) and *Shraddh* (homage to ancestors). The last two were banned by the Sikh Gurus but are still reportedly observed by Sikhs in the village with modification. Saints are worshipped irrespective of their faith. One Muslim *pir* has been transformed into a Sikh *pir*. The snake is worshipped in the form of snake god (Guga Navami). There are six festivals specific to Sikh religious history. Role of the Brahmans in Sikh religion has ended. The Sikh–Hindu participation (*bhaichara*) in festivals continues.

## VIII

Occupations of communities are generally related to ecology and resource endowment, such as land (31), forest (9), water (6). The largest number of communities are engaged in agriculture (28), cattle breeding and animal husbandary (17), fishing (13), followed by a small number in hunting gathering (2). Punjab has a large number of non-pastoral nomads (12), unskilled labour are reported from 61 communities and members of unorganized services from 26 communities. There is a larger concentration of artisan communities (31) and a large coverage in business trade and industry (36) and in organized services (57).

The 1931 census reported a larger representation of Sikh Khatris and Aroras than the Jats, in services and professions, trade and business. Occupational diversification has grown with economic development. The larger communities report occupational diversification on a larger scale from traditional occupations and their modernization to new professions and organized services. The smaller communities have taken up labour as subsidiary occupations. Punjabi artisans have modernized the traditional technology and become very mobile.

In the traditional Punjabi society the Khatris, Aroras, Bhatias, Banias, Ahluwalias, Sood, Saini, Sunar, Rajputs are primarily engaged in business. The Jat Sikhs are the major land-holding agricultural community, while the Kamboj are direct, intensive cultivators and the Arain are horticulturalists.

Punjab has a number of small communities engaged in miscellaneous traditional occupations. The Bahrupia, Bhatra, Mirasi, Nath, etc., are entertainers and cultural workers. The Gujjar are in animal husbandry. Jheewar supply water. The Sapela and Bangali are snake charmers, Barar make weavers. Batwal act as chowkidars, Bauria are rope makers, Bazigars are acrobats, Bharbhuja fry grains, Bharai are drum beaters, Dheas make winnowing fans. There are folk medicine men: Gagra use leeches to extract blood to cure, and Singhikat use horn to extract blood from the infected parts of the body. The artisans specific to Punjab and the north-west are Megh (leather workers), Nalband who make horse shoe, Ramgarhia Tarkhan are carpenters, Sikligarh polish the arms such as swords, Penja are cotton scutcher, The Sansi who once begged during daytime and committed theft at night are now well settled. The small communities are moving away from their traditional occupation to secondry occupations as agricultural and industrial labour. They are rickshaw puller, hawkers, etc. Still low in caste hierarchy the Ad-dharmi, Chamar, Khatik, Mochi, who work in leather have diversified into weaving which occupies a higher place in social hierarchy, defence services and other Govt. jobs. The lowest of the low, the Balmiki, Bhangi or Chuhra work as *safaiwala*, agricultural labour, contract labour or *sanji*. The non-pastoral nomads include itinerant groups like Sansi, Bawaria, Dhea, Gandhilas, Bazigars, Sikligars, Sirkibands who have started living a settled life.

In the Sikh village the caste system continues with some changes. The priest has no caste. The Mazhabi has a separate well and lives and sits separately. The Nais do not cut hair or shape beard but continue to act as messengers and match makers. The Chhimba traditional washerman now work as tailors. The Mehras are still water carriers except that they collect water from water pumps installed at some houses. Kumhars, the potters besides their occupation of making and selling pottery have also learnt the craft of weaving. Tarkhans, the traditional carpenters are very mobile. The Jats continue to command respect as founders, peasant proprietors of the village, working with landless labour (*sepis* or *kamin*). The Kamboj are direct cultivators, working with their hand, and practicing intensive agriculture (I.P. Singh, 1959).

Punjab has a very strong tradition of *biradari* panchayat or traditional caste council which exists among 59 communities (62.11 per cent) along side the statutory panchayat (87 per cent) and village council (18 per cent). These bodies undertake welfare measures. Elections to traditional bodies are by voice vote. The caste panchayats exercise social control and hand down punishment in cases of rape, adultery, theft, etc., impose fine in cash and may order social boycott, among members of the caste.

## IX

Punjab is the foremost state in terms of per capta income (Rs. 4,935) with literacy of 67 per cent female literacy of 62 per cent. It has the smallest number of population living below poverty line (*India Reducing Poverty, Accelerating Development, A World Bank Country Study*, Oxford, 2000). According to an earlier study, the per capita income in Punjab is the highest amongst all states. The growth rate of Punjab economy was higher than that of the overall Indian economy. This was made possible with the effective implementation of lard consolidation and infrastructural development in the early phases, the green and white revolutions, industrial development and urbanization. Its percentage share of urban population was 29.5 per cent in 1991 and has gone upto 33.95 per cent in 2001 and it ranks fifth among the major Indian states. The development of only small scale industry was encouraged till the 1990s (Sethi, Raj Mohani, 'Is Punjab a Developed State or It is a Contradiction in terms' 2001). We are further told,

'Within this policy framewrok, the decade of the fifties saw the emergence of cycle parts and hosiery industries and that of the 60's the resource based industries such as those of improved agricultural implements, while the decade of the 70's saw a shift towards the production of export oriented items such as food products, bicycles, hosiery goods, hand tools, leather products and sports goods. The small scale agro-based industry which is labour intensive both a big boost because of the transfer of resources from the agrarian to the industrial economy. Its per capita net state domestic product in the small scale industrial sector touched the third position at the all India level, and by the end of the 70's the state was making a significant contribution in earning the much needed foreign exchange' (Bhalla cited in Sethi 2001).

The Ramgarhias played a vital role the development of small sector industries.

The decades of the 1980s and 1990s witnessed the slowing down of the momentum generated by the green revolution. The green and industrial revolutions reached a plateau. The average cost of production per hectare of land rose considerably as a result of increased labour and irrigation costs accompanied by over mechanization. Mechanization of agriculture has resulted in unemployment by drastically cutting down the number of days of employment for an average farm hand. The existing need for farm labour being met by the use of migrant labour, the local educated youth who comprise 80 per cent of the rural unemployed do not consider farming as a useful enterprise and look for jobs in the non-farm sector. The decline in productivity levels was due to decline in the number of operational holdings, a rise in 'reverse tenancy' as a result of leasing out land by the small and medium farmers. About 20 per cent of the total cultivating households joined the ranks of agricultural labour and the number of education unemployed swelled. The net state domestic product has come down to 2.89 in 1995-6 from 5.19 in 1989-90, and the per capita income during the same period fell from 3.43 per cent to 2.28 per cent (Sethi, 2001). Punjab lags far behind the industrially developed states such as Gujarat and Maharashtra even in the small scale industrial sector. Those living below poverty line constitute 11 per cent of the population.

The POI project was undertaken (1985-90) when Punjab economy had reached a plateau. Even so one could see the positive impact of infrastructural development. As a progressive state, Punjab reports a positive perception of various development programmes by members of its communities. Development process on the whole is generally favourably perceived. The boys and girls are encouraged to take up education. People are favouring modern medical facilities. Roads and railways have reached out to almost all parts of the state. The female literary rate in Punjab according to 1991 census is 50.4 per cent which is higher than the all-India literacy level of the females, i.e. 39.3 per cent. Birth rate of 23.5 per cent and infant mortality of 51 per cent, are on the high side but lower than infant mortality at the all India level of 79 per 1,000 births. In Punjab 82.1 per cent communities prefer education for boys and 67.4 per cent for girls. Religion wise break up shows that 81.7 per cent Hindus, 84.6 per cent Muslims, 84.2 per cent Sikhs, cent per cent Christians and cent per cent Jains prefer education for boys. Similarly 66.2 per cent Hindus, 76.9 per cent Muslims, 71.9 per cent Sikhs and cent per cent Christians prefer education for girls.

Family welfare is accepted by members in 76.8 per cent communities. Religion wise break up shows that 78.9 per cent Hindus, 69.2 per cent Muslims, 78.9 per cent Sikhs and cent per cent Jains accept the family welfare programmes. The modern methods of family welfare programmes are adopted by members in 44 communities (46.3 per cent). Sterilization for men is reported among 10 (10.5 per cent) communities against, strangely, sterilization for women among 10 (10.5 per cent) communities, the same number the general preference is for three children.

Employment through IRDP programme has benefited a small number of communities, 8 (8.4 per cent) and only 3 communities (3.2 per cent) are covered by the programmes launched by voluntary organizations. Saving is favoured and dependence on moneylenders is less. Communication networks and schools exist close by. Television is watched by members among 47 communities (49.5 per cent), and the cinema is visited by members among 56 communities (58.9 per cent).

The white and green revolutions of Punjab have been followed by the greening of environment. Planting of trees on a large scale in the countryside is a welcome relief for the kind of mono cropping that was practiced in the earlier stages. Punjab has led the country in the use of organic manure, *gobar* gas plan and locally grown biomass. According to the POI data, in matter of fuel resources Punjab more than in another states is using *gobar* gas, cow-dung cake and coal. The 1991 census data on Housing and Amenities supplements POI data by highlighting Punjab use of cowdung cake, wood, bio-gas and in addition cooking gas. Use of coal has declined. Obviously the use of biomass and locally grown wood are the important inputs. This has an important implication for environment and gender relations.

Under the POI twenty-three communities have reported child labour. They include Scheduled Castes (11) and others (12). According to 1981 census the population of child labour in Punjab is small (2,16,939) which has declined further since. They are employed in all sorts of jobs ranging from domestic help to running shops and *dhaba*.

Scholars have noted the role of non-economic factors such as cultural mores and value systems which are important indicators of societal development.

'One major fallout of the green revolution in Punjab is that the rise in incomes has ushered in a culture of conspicuous consumption and emphasizes on material aspects of culture than on the non-material aspects. State is now trying to cope with another problem that of rural suicides. The major reasons for these suicides are growing inadequateness, impoverisation and a fall in the real incomes of the medium and small farmers households during the 90's. Traditional support structures such as the joint family, "Biradari", Village Panchayats and other humanitarian social organizations have become more or less redundant in the modern context while their place has been usurped by a heightened sense of individualism' (Sethi, 2001).

As mentioned above Punjab has the largest share of the Scheduled Castes living in it, that is, 28.31 per cent of the total population of the state. They control, only 0.40 per cent of the total land holding of the state. They have however benefited from green revolution and various reform movements. Occupational diversification following the growth of economy has helped the scheduled castes to move away from their traditional occupations. We are further told,

'Resultantly, majority of them still suffer from poverty, have low levels of education, and are engaged in agricultural labour and other occupations that have a low prestige in society. Most of them are also victims of crime and its incidence in increasing every year. In recent years, the scheduled castes have been mobilized by the politicians who consider them as safe vote banks. This development has increased conflicts between the scheduled castes and the higher castes. However, one positive factor in this whole development is that the intercaste conflicts have not yet assumed a communitarian color' (Jodhka cited in Sethi, 2001).

Sikhism's message of equality is accepted at cognitive level. In the study of Sikh village that social equality is a major element of Sikhism and a day to day experience has been brought out clearly. It is not only historically that the Sikh Gurus advocated the equality of castes. Even now, the villagers of Dalake point to this as one of the superior qualities of their faith (I.P. Singh, 1959). There were sincere efforts to bring together the large mass of the oppressed people and the downtrodden, improve their status and empower them. Sikh religion has undermined the practice of untouchability but not ended it. However, traces of inequality and untouchability remain. As matter stands today while the caste system has weakened, it has not disappeared, the Ramgarhia, Majhabi, and Ramdasia remain distinct components of the Panth and atrocities and discriminatory practices committed against the Dalits continue to be reported.

## X

The concept of Nirankar is gender neutral. The votaries of Nirankar have been activists. Guru Nanak was outraged to see the sufferings of the women of all groups Hindu, Muslim, Bhatt and Thakur, their humiliation in the hands of conquering armies who stripped them of their honour and carried them off. One of probably the first gender sensitive statements has come from Guru Nanak 'From woman is man born, inside her he is conceived . . . from woman originate new generations. . . . Why revile her of whom are born great ones of the earth?' (*Adi Granth*). Bhai Gurudas was forthright on gender equality. 'Women, was not only not inferior to man but also has equal status and responsibility before god' (*Adi Granth*). However, these principles seldom matched the patriarchal practices. The gender issues in Punjab have been a subject of critical investigation and contemporary concern. In this frontier region ravaged by invaders, while on the one hand the situation of instability strengthened patriarchal authority and control, on the other hand it also etched the image of women as a symbol of honour identified with control over female sexuality (which explains honour killing) an object of plunder and rape, a piece of property, clad in *purdah*.

Studies in gender relations during the colonial period (Anshu Malhotra, 2002) suggest that patriarchal norms were reinforced in the higher social order both of the Sikhs and the Hindus. However, differences between the lower castes and the higher caste groups in observing castes and social codes remained. Widow remarriage, bride price, higher work participation by women showed that the lower caste groups had and still have a greater understanding and resilience in dealing with matters involving female sexuality. Widow remarriage was never a problem. Female infanticide did not exist as the girl was never considered a liability or a symbol of honour. Killing and gifting or selling of daughters were interrelated problems for the higher order called '*beti mar*', who also treated widows badly. Later in the nineteenth century, Arya Samaj advocated widow remarriage. Even *niyoga*, i.e. congress with the widow which was rarely in vogue was sought to be retrieved from the Dharmashastras for the same purpose, but it caused such embarrassment all a around that it was not pursued.

As mentioned earlier, both Sikhism and Arya Samaj promoted women's education and restored the religious role of women. The partition is said to have liberated the Punjabi middle class women from traditional restrictions by encouraging them to take up education and enter professions and achieve a measure of social mobility. The study of the Sikh village (Singh, 1959) shows that while women controlled household affairs and decided matters within the household, they had no role in outside matters, no representation in institutions. The POI data shows that the situation has changed. Though their role in decision-making outside the household is small, their participation in politics is growing and they are exercising greater social control. Those who are educated and live in the city are employed as teachers, clerks, nurses, administraters, doctors, etc. The *purdah* which was common among the women of all communities is presently confined to the lower order women only. The status of women is still generally perceived as low (82.11 per cent against the national average of 72.19 per cent) except in some sections.

Our data also shows a decline in the role of women in fetching water, collecting fuel and fodder, following development of infra-structure including supply of drinking water and plantation of trees. There has been a decline in women's participation in economic and agriculural activities, animal husbandry and fishing following mechanization of agricultral operations and the enhanced role of men in them. As a result women's contribution to income and their control over expenditure has diclined, they have been confined to only household jobs (71.58 per cent against the national average of 21.61 per cent). There has also been a corresponding eroson of their roles in social functions, rituals and religious sphere.

On the whole, on the issue of gender equality, it is said that 'the last five decades of development in the state show a definite anti-female bias which has led to a systematic deprivation of its women folk' (Sethi, 2001). The crucial question is about women's right in property. Our data suggest that dowry in kind is paid by members in 57 communities (60 per cent against the national average of 14.07 per cent). Dowry, mentioned above is being increasingly seen as representing the equivalent of women's right in landed or ancestral property. There is also a suggestion that Sikhs should have their own code which should recognize the practice of keeping land within the family among the agnates and suitably compensate daughters/sisters.

There is a long history of gender discrimination and gender violence in Punjab and some parts of north-west India which has been described in terms of passage from female infanticide to female foeticide. This practice was attributed to the mindset of the sections of the higher castes including Sikhs and Hindus who came to be known as *betimar*, as mentioned earlier. The colonial ethnography is full of graphic, gruesome details of female infanticide, which was masked in the sweet but misleading code word, *dudh nahana* (bathing in milk). In 1881, Deputy Commissioner of Hoshiarpur in the Punjab, reported on the subject as follows:

'Forty years ago probably many hundreds of female children were annually buried in this district immediately after birth. When several female children were born in succession, the destruction of the last born was carried out with the following observance—a piece of gur (molasses) was placed in the mouth of the child, a skein of cotton was laid on her breast and the following incantation recited two or three times: 'eat *gur*, spin your thread ! We don't want you, but a brother instead'. The infants were usually put into *gharras* or waterpots and buried into the ground illustrating the subject of the small proportional number of females' (cited in Risley, *The People of India*, 1915).

The colonial ethnographers and administrators attributed female infanticide to social reasons,

'But there is not the slightest doubt that the life of a girl is less valued and worse cared for than that of a boy, chiefly indeed, among the hypergamous classes who cannot find husbands for them, the higher castes of the eastern Punjab who will not hell their daughters, and the Hindus who spend much money on their marriage and account it shameful to leave them unmarried; but also in a less degree and as a relic of the old fighting days, and perhaps from the contagion of Hindu ideas, *among all other classes of the Punjab people without distinction of race, religion, or locality*' (italics mine) . . . One can only say that ignorance and an unconscious ill-treatment of females at all ages may result from the low estimation in which savage and backward races hold women. Of all the data obtained the most significant is the mortality among female infants in years of famine' (cited in Risley, *The People of India*, 1915).

Risley reported a more gruesome case of child murder by brother, 'More recondite methods were also sometimes adopted. A Panjabi friend of mine, a member of a tribe which followed the custom of hypergamy, with whom I was discussing the subject of female infanticide, told me that when he was eight years old he was summoned to his mother's beside to sanction and assist at the murder of a newborn girl. His father being away from home, he was called upon to exercise the patria potestas as the eldest male member of the household then present. The child was given him to hold, and the midwife poured over her head tow large jars of water, chilled almost to freezing by being put out on the roof during a December night. Her face instantly turned black and she died in the arms of her terrified brother. All the girls that were born met with a similar fate. The mother complied reluctantly with the barbarous usage of the family, but the horror of the thing was with her through life, and when she was dying her remorse conjured up a ghastly vision of the spirits of her murdered children, standing at her bedside armed with iron hooks and crying vindictively to the soul still lingering in her body; 'Come out, come out that we may tear you in pieces'. This, however, happened nearly fifty years ago, and my friend assures me that in his tribe at any rate systematic infanticide has disappeared under the influence of popular education, and that twenty girls may now be seen where in his boyhood hardly one could be found' (Risley, *The People of India*, 1915).

The incidence of female infanticide did decline as a result of reform movements and spread of education, but other discriminatory practices have continued during the post-colonial period. This is evident from declining sex ratio. According to the POI data there has been some improvement in the status of women in some communities. Status of women is perceived as equal in 14 communities which is higher than the national average. This may be attributed to the work done social reformers in the field of female education, women's employment, women's role in maintaining family which is as ubiquitous as elsewhere in the country. A role in political sphere is emerging. But a more urgent and holistic strategy is needed to stem the rapidly deteoriating sex ratio in Punjab which is a cause for concern. The sharply declining population of girl child in 0 to 6 years age group as revealed by the census 2001 has been attributed to female foeticide practiced at a large number of clinics which have been mushroomed over the state in flagarant violation of the law prohibiting it. The release of the data by the census 2001 has led to a public uproar. However, the whole question is linked with the old mindset in the patriarchal order which refuses to recognize women's right in property and provide an opportunity for equal development. This mindset is slowly changing.

## XI

Punjabi diaspora has been a subject of much interest. It has been said that there are more Punjabis living out of the land of their birth within the country and outside. The Gypsies called Romas are considered closer to the Jat, Sikh, Punjabi, Hindu, Rajput complex with its focal point in the earstwhile Punjab plains and adjourning areas and Uttar Pradesh (Bhalla, 1992). Under the POI project we have studied the Assamese Sikhs which were once closely integrated with Vaishnava *namghar* tradition, Dakhini Sikh, and Banjara Sikh in the south. There were also Sindhi Sikhs, who believe in Guru Nanak. Other communities of Punjab who migrated to urban centres in other parts in the country included the Khatri, artisans and Mazhabi. After independence a significant part of the Sikh population was settled outside Punjab in the tarai region of U.P., etc., and the Punjabi and Sikhs settled in all parts of the country. Everywhere Punjabiyat denote new work ethic, a new culture, cuisine and *dhaba*, culture (*salwar-kameej*), kirana shops, technology and transport revolution, a robust common sense and a capacity to laugh at oneself !

Before we conclude, there are two aspects that need to be emphasised. First Punjab has been one of the most dynamic regions in India's history and its people have been one of the most mobile, pragmatic and progressive. Much of this can be explained by the rise of Sikhism in Punjab and its tenets of dignity of labour, equality, brotherhood. The symbolism of baptism into the Khalsa, the pure—and the equal—had a profound impact. The Gurus' message of equality reverberated through history and was picked up by activists and poets like Subramania Bharati. Four hundred years on, Subramania Bharati's long poem in Tamil 'The Saga of Guru Gobind' invokes the spirit of the Khalsa in the words of the Guru as follows:

*Dear disciples, from this moment ! In thought, deed and life ! You are all one caste !*

*Wipe away divisions, divisions kill ! The Aryans divide us ! Into a thousand castes !*

*Let dividers divide and die! You Khalsas belong to one caste ! The caste of the brave warrior ! Sworn to practice, protect and uphold ! Righteousness, God, Truth and Freedom ! A caste sworn to destroy tyranny and injustice ! A republican caste based on fraternal friendship! An immortal caste, aware of timeless life and known no fear of death.* (Translated from V.N. Narayanan, '*A* "Khalsa" for all times', *The Hindustan Times*, Sunday, 11 April 1999.)

Secondly, syncretism is under attack (Khalsa, 2001) everywhere as the unidimentional processes of identity formation, homogenization, religious and political consolidation, and exclusiveness muster strong. History is being rewritten and the texts reinterpreted to suit one or the other view point. In a multiethnic and plural society, roots and linkages are to be considered objectively. The Punjabi ethos and traditions particularly in terms of Punjabiyat should continue to be developed, recreated, and carried forward. Throughout our project we saw living examples of *bhaichara*, comraderie and goodwill amidst violence and mayhem which could be ascribed to many factors including the message of the masters—the respect for the sacred and tolerance is a vibrant reality in the countryside—and its translation and transmission through a culture that developed in the land of the five rivers.

We undertook this project in Punjab in collaboration with local scholars and university departments of anthropology under the most difficult circumstances. It is to the credit of our scholars, particularly the coordinator and the local scholars, the local administration and local informants that we continued to work in spite of the difficulties. It was again with difficulty that we could organize the seminar on People of India, Punjab and Chandigarh with the support of the Department of Human Biology, Punjabi University, Patiala even when the campus was disturbed. The book is appearing at a time when Punjab has regained its peace. The celebrations of the three hundred years of the founding of the Khalsa and the two hundredth anniversary of the establishment of the Sikh kingdom by Maharaja Ranjit Singh highlighted not only the identity of the Sikh but also the universal ideals of social equality, pluralism and tolerance. The elections have restored the democractic process and the results of the recent elections are widely regarded as reflecting people's current preference for development over identity.

K.S. Singh

# ACKNOWLEDGEMENTS

We express our sincere thanks to all the informants, who extended their full cooperation. We thank the Chief Secretary, Government of Punjab and other officers for cooperation with our investigators. Thanks are particularly due to Shri Ajit Singh Sandhu, Deputy Director, Census Operations, Punjab, for valuable suggestions at the time of the collection of field data and about location of various Scheduled Castes. We are indebted to Prof. J.C. Sharma and Dr. R.S. Balgir of the Department of Anthropology, Punjab University, Chandigarh; Dr. K. Gopala Iyer, Dr. K.C. Kayastha, Shri Virinder Singh, Rakesh Kumar Sharma, Ku. Kiran Jain, all of the Department of Sociology, Punjab University, Chandigarh; Prof. I.J.S. Bansal, Dr. A.S. Bhanwar and Dr. D.K. Kansal, of the Department of Human Biology, Panjabi University, Patiala; Prof. P.S. Jammu, Department of Sociology, Panjabi University, Patiala; Dr. (Mrs.) Sharda Sidhu, Department of Biology, Guru Nanak Dev University, Amritsar. Our thanks are also due to the Vice-Chancellor and the head of Human Biology Department, Panjabi University, Patiala for collaborating with the Anthropological Survey of India in organizing the workshop on People of India: Punjab and Chandigarh, at Patiala from 21 to 23 August 1989. We thank Shri Janmeja Singh Johal and Shri Surinderjit Singh for the photographs on Punjab.

The General Editor acknowledges the outstanding contributions made to the understanding of history, religion, society and ethnography of Punjab by W.H. McLeod, J.S. Grewal and N. Gerald Barrier, J.P.S. Uberoi, Harjot Oberoi among many others. The three noted scholars, Rajmohani Sethi, Paramjit Judge and Surinder Jodhka made excellent presentations on contemporary Punjab ethnography at the seminar on Punjab ethnography held on the occasion Golden Jubilee of the Indian Sociological Association at Amritsar in December 2001. The General Editor also thanks the distinguished anthropologist Prof. I.P. Singh and the former Chief Secretary of Punjab, Sri S.S. Dhanoa for discussions.

ACKNOWLEDGEMENTS

We express our sincere thanks to all the informants, who extended their full cooperation. We thank the Chief Secretary, Government of Punjab and other officers for cooperation with our investigators. Thanks are particularly due to Shri Ajit Singh Sandhu, Deputy Director, Census Operations, Punjab, for valuable suggestions at the time of the collection of field data and about location of various Scheduled Castes. We are indebted to Prof. J.C. Sharma and Dr. R.S. Balgir of the Department of Anthropology, Punjab University, Chandigarh; Dr. K. Gopal Iyer, Dr. K.C. Rayastha, Shri Virinder Singh, Rakesh Kumar Sharma, Ku. Kiran Jain, all of the Department of Sociology, Punjab University, Chandigarh; Prof. I.J.S. Bansal, Dr. A.S. Bhanwar and Dr. D.K. Kansal of the Department of Human Biology, Punjabi University, Patiala; Prof. P.S. Jammu, Department of Sociology, Punjabi University, Patiala; Dr. (Mrs.) Sharda Sidhu, Department of Biology, Guru Nanak Dev University, Amritsar. Our thanks are also due to the Vice Chancellor and the head of Human Biology Department, Punjabi University, Patiala for collaborating with the Anthropological Survey of India in organizing the workshop on People of India: Punjab and Chandigarh, at Patiala from 21 to 23 August 1993. We thank Shri Harmeja Singh Johal and Shri Surinderjit Singh for the photographs on Punjab.

The General Editor acknowledges the outstanding contributions made to the understanding of history, religion, society and ethnography of Punjab by W.H. McLeod, J.S. Grewal and N. Gerald Barrier, J.P.S. Uberoi, Harjot Oberoi among many others. The three noted scholars, Rajmohan Sethi, Paramjit Judge and Surinder Jodhka made excellent presentations on contemporary Punjab ethnography at the seminar on Punjab ethnography held on the occasion Golden Jubilee of the Indian Sociological Association at Amritsar in December 2001. The General Editor also thanks the distinguished anthropologist Prof. I.P. Singh and the former Chief Secretary of Punjab, Shri S.S. Dhanoa for discussions.

# INTRODUCTION

Punjab, earlier known as Sapta Sindhu, has been traditionally a land of peasantry who believe in hard work. Punjab is no longer the land of the five rivers, but its identity defined by culture and history remains inact.

Punjab state is situated in the north-west of the Indian Union approximately between $29^0$ 33' and $32^0$ 32' N latitude and $73^0$ 54' and $76^0$ 56' E longitude. It is bounded by Jammu & Kashmir in the north, by Himachal Pradesh on the east and on the south by Haryana. Punjab is one of the smallest states covering an area of 50,372 sq. km forming 1.6 per cent of the total area of the country. Physiographically the state may be divided into three parts: (i) The Sivalik hills in the north-east with an elevation of 300 to 1,000 metres; (ii) the narrow undulating foothill zone dissected by closely spaced torrents (*choes*), several of which terminate in the plain below without joining any stream; (iii) the flat alluvial plains of sub-mountain tract which is narrow and constitutes the small strips of the territory stretching between the Himalaya and the Indo-Gangetic plains into which the spurs of the Himalaya run. The upper portion of the districts of Gurdaspur, Hoshiarpur and Ropar lie in this region. The flat alluvial plains form the largest natural region of the state comprizing the eight remaining districts Amritsar, Kapurthala, Jalandhar, Ludhiana, Patiala, Sangrur, Bhatinda and Ferozepur. The three snow-fed perennial rivers the Satluj, Beas and Ravi flowing through the state, and the 95 tributaries of the Indus river serve as the most important source of irrigation. The sub-mountain region has forests and hilly soils which are slightly acidic and rich in humus. The soil in the districts of Ferozepur and Bhatinda is sandy and arid. Alluvial soils covers the remaining districts of the state.

The climate of Punjab ranges from bracing cold in winter to scorching heat in summer. Extremes of temperature and the two monsoons produce a variety of seasons and constantly changing landscape.

Punjab has traditionally been divided into three culture zones: (i) Malwa, (ii) Majha and (iii) Doaba. The communities of the present Punjab see themselves as belonging to one of the three regions. For instance, the Sikhs inhabiting the areas south of the Satluj river are called Malwa Sikhs (Ludhiana district is in Malwa area); between the

Satluj and Beas rivers there are Doaba Sikhs and those inhabiting, north and north-west of the Beas, Majha Sikhs. Of the three, the Majha Sikhs consider themselves superior since they feel that they observe the religious tenets more closely than the other two communities. The Majha Sikhs also believe that they possess greater physical vigour than the Sikhs of the Doaba and Malwa areas. However, there does not appear to be great cultural difference among the Sikhs of these areas (Izmirlian, 1979: 26).

Punjab has served as a cradle of Indian civilization and as a melting pot of innumerable ethnic entities. Its antiquity goes deep into the past. The banks of the Indus nurtured advanced and fairly organized rural communities using implements of copper and bronze around 2500 B.C. The sculptures, pottery, jewellery, fabrics, seals embossed with human and animal figures and architecture demonstrate that the people of the Indus valley had attained a high degree of civilization. Cities flourished between 2500 B.C. to 1500 B.C., and were presumably destroyed by the Aryans. The Aryans were followed by the Parthian hordes under Darius (521-485 B.C.), who conquered northern Punjab. Around the fourth century B.C., Greek references mention that Punjab, was a land inhabited by warlike *gana*—Malava, Kahudraka, Madra, Ushinara, Gandhara, Kaikey, Bharata, and Yaudhey. The term *mall* (champion) comes from Malava, and *yoddha* (warrior) is connected with the Yaudhey clan. The Hindustani word *pahalwan* (wrestler) is derived from Pahlava, who migrated from Iran to Punjab and got miscegenated with the local population in course of time. Thereafter, Greek armies led by Alexander crossed the Indus and advanced as far as the Beas. Punjab, at that time, was mostly tribal. Though rich in human and animal life, it always remained disunited and indulged in constant internal conflicts. It was Chandragupta Maurya, who effected political unification of Punjab and led the people of Punjab in revolt against remnants of the Greek rule. The people of Greek origin left behind by Alexander were thus divested of their political power by the rising Mauryas. Bactrians were followed by the Scythian tribes and the Mongoloid Huns. The Huns were subdued and expelled by the Vardhanas, but Harshvardhan's empire soon disintegrated.

After the Aryans from Central Asia, came the Iranian, Tibetan, Kamboj, Pahlava, Hun, Pathan and Mongol who subsequently settled down as part of the Punjabi community. When Subaktagin and later his son Mehmood of Ghazni tried to cross the borders of Punjab, they were resisted by the Sahi rulers of the Punjab.

Muslim invaders started pouring into the Punjab. Mahmud Ghazni came in A.D. 1001, closely followed by the Afghans, Gori, Tughlak, Suri and Lodhi. The Afghans were followed by Taimur and his descendant Babar, who defeated Ibrahim Lodhi at Panipat in A.D. 1526. Humayun, who succeeded Babar lost and recovered his kingdom by defeating Sikandar Suri at Sirhind. The Mughals were now firmly seated on the throne for the next one and a half centuries till their power saw a decline after the death of Aurangzeb in 1707.

During the reigns of Akbar, Jahangir and Shahjahan, Lahore, the capital of the Punjab, witnessed its heyday, as it was equidistant between Delhi and Kashmir and between Agra and Kabul. Akbar's successors often moved from Delhi to Kashmir via Lahore, Bhimbar and Pir Panjal in order to escape the heat of the northern plains during the summer.

Various religious faiths flourished in the Punjab. Hinduism, Buddhism, Islam and Sikhism have left a long lasting impression. The Aryans introduced Vedic religions based on *veda* (knowledge) and *sruti* (hearing). They are also said to have introduced caste system. Under this social system, the Brahmans were given the highest place in social hierarchy to be followed by Kshatriyas, Vaishyas and Shudras. Thus Brahmanical Hinduism came into being wherein the autochthones were denied all social privileges and pushed out of the centre-stage. Some of them were declared as Untouchables and were assigned 'polluting' jobs. However, an important aspect of Hinduism was its philosophy of the Vedas and the commentaries written about them that gave spiritual sustenance. The Upanishads and the epics which followed determined the ethical code of behaviour of the Hindu masses.

Bhakti movement in India started as a reaction to the rigid Brahmanical order. The liberal Hindu reformers endeavoured for a better adaptability of Hinduism by a larger section of the Hindu society. Efforts were made to throw temples open to all classes irrespective of the caste hierarchy. The earlier proponents were Shankaracharya, Ramanuj, Namdev, Jaidev and Ramanand. They stressed oneness of God, who was the Ultimate Truth. The best way to serve God was by absolute submission to his will. The way to approach Him was through *tapasya* (mediation) and chanting of *mantras* (hymns), under the guidance of a *guru* (spiritual preceptor). The fifteenth and sixteenth centuries saw a swift spread of the Bhakti movement throughout India. Chaitanya Mahaprabhu in Bengal, Gyaneshwar, Namdev and Tukaram in Maharashtra, Mira Bai in Rajasthan, Kabir, Surdas and

Tulsidas in Uttar Pradesh and Guru Nanak Dev in the Punjab were the leading poponents of their day.

The most important event which took place in the medievel Punjab was the emergence of Guru Nanak Dev, a contemporary of Babar. The faith Sikhism, he preached, was a synthesis of Hinduism and Islam, but more than that Guru Nanak Dev was a reformer *par excellance.* He protested many aspects of the predominant Hindu society and the arrogant and aggressive behaviour of the ruling Muslim society. Guru Nanak Dev would think of himself as neither Hindu nor Muslim, but as an enlightened member of humanity proclaiming without fear the oneness of all mankind. This humanistic approach to the solution of all the prevalent social ills led Guru Nanak to forge and develop altogether a new system of human values that stressed the oneness of man; that men of all beliefs and religions are brothers born of the same source and created by the Supreme Creator. Guru Nanak visualized a Utopia. He merged the concept of a welfare state with religion, raised his voice against caste discrimination and disagreed with the Muslims, who thought that the non-believers were inferior infidels. The caste hierarchy in Hindu society and the superior (conformist) and inferior (nonconformist) dichotomy as imposed by the Muslim rulers were repugnant to him. Thus, Guru Nanak Dev is the most important landmark in the history of the recent religions in the history of world religions.

Guru Nanak Dev, the chief propounder of Bhakti movement in Punjab, was the founder of Sikhism. He preached the theory of *samsarg*—of birth, death and rebirth in a cyclic manner. God is the cause of all creations and sets this world and the life within in motion. Human beings being oblivious of death indulge in pleasure, but the virtuous ones abstain from indulging in worldly pleasures; they seek and find Truth. To him God was a spiritual concept—if God is the ultimate Truth, to speak untruth is to be ungodly. Guru Nanak Dev established the institution of 'Guru'. Without a *guru*, he stressed, no one can attain *moksha* (salvation). The Guru guides his followers to the path of Truth. He disciplines them as a rogue elephant is disciplined from running amok; he applies the *jyan anjan* (salve of knowledge) to a follower's eyes enabling him to see the Truth (God); He is the divine ferryman, who takes them across the *bhav sagar* (ocean of life). He insisted on the separation of God and Guru; Guru is to be consulted, respected and cherished, but not to be worshipped. He is a teacher, but no incarnation of God. Asceticism, penance or torturing one's body as a step towards enlightenment were anathema to him.

'Be in the world but not wordly', he said. Human birth, he explained, is a priceless gift, an opportunity that God offers to humans to escape the cycle of birth, death and birth. The aim of life is yoga, the union with God.

Guru Nanak Dev was followed by Guru Angad, Guru Amar Das, Guru Ram Das, Guru Arjan Dev, Guru Tegh Bahadur and Guru Gobind Singh. Each of the succeeding Gurus added his own reflections, ideologies and thoughts in *Shri Guru Granth Sahib* the Holy Sikh scripture, which was compiled by the fifth Guru, Shri Guru Arjan Dev. The sacred scripture contains hymns composed by Hindu and Muslim saints as well as the contributions of the Gurus.

The tenth Guru, Guru Gobind Singh laid the foundation of the Khalsa (the pure) on 1 April 1699 at Anandpur Sahib and gave Sikhs their identity, and a family name, Singh (lion). Anandpur Sahib is also known as the Keshgarh Sahib because it was here that the Sikhs were told by Guru Gobind Singh to keep their *kesh* (hair), alongwith the other four identification markers.

Maharaja Ranjit Singh (A.D. 1780 to 1839) extended his kingdom from Satluj to Khyber Pass and from Kashmir to Sind. The kingdom of Maharaja Ranjit Singh was annexed by the British. In the colonial period the landlords of Punjab benefited from the canal system introduced by the British. The Sikhs were among Punjab's biggest landholders. The Sikhs, a martial race were also recruited in the British army. However, the Sikhs had to suffer a lot during the partition of the Punjab in 1947. Their high spirits and hard work have enabled the Sikhs of the Punjab to once again establish themselves and became prosperous.

The state of Punjab was reorganized on 1 November 1966. The twelve districts of the state are Gurdaspur, Amritsar, Ferozepur, Ludhiana, Jalandhar, Kapurthala, Hoshiarpur, Rupnagar, Patiala, Sangrur, Bhatinda, and Faridkot with a total area of 50,372 sq. km. The total population of the state is 1,67,88, 915 individuals, which inhabit 12,342 villages and 134 towns. The sex ratio is 884 and 865 for the rural and urban areas with 27.68 per cent and 72.32 per cent population respectively. The Scheduled Castes constitute 26.87 per cent of the total population of the state. There is no Scheduled Tribe. The literacy rate is 41.28 per cent. The women (33.70 per cent) are less educated than men (35.21 per cent). Literacy is higher in the urban areas (57.14 per cent) than the rural areas (35.21 per cent). The men are primarily engaged either in agriculture (19.66 per cent), agricultural labour (11.72 per cent) or household industry

(1.33 per cent). Majority of the population of Punjab follow Sikhism (60.75 per cent); there are adherents of Hinduism (36.93 per cent), while the followers of Christianity, Islam and Jainism are in a minority with a population of about one per cent each (*Census of India*, 1981).

Punjabi communities offer an interesting religious profile. The number of communities professing Hinduism are thirty-eight, Islam nine, Sikhism seven, Buddhism, Jainism, Christianity one each. Thirty-four communities follow both Hinduism and Sikhism; two communities named the Suniars and the Kamboj follow Hinduism, Sikhism and Islam; one community has members of both Jainism and Hinduism and another community follows both Hinduism and Buddhism.

Seventeen languages are spoken in Punjab: Bagri, Banjari, Bauria, Dogri, Haryanvi, Hindi, Hindustani, Marwari, Multani, Nepali, Odki, Pahari, Pasto, Punjabi, Rajasthani, Sansi and Urdu. The Sikhs speak in Punjabi and prefer to use Gurmukhi script. The Hindus in Punjab speak in Punjabi, but write in Devanagari or Perso-Arabic script. In the cities English is spoken among the elite sections and the use of Roman script is common.

The Sikhs can be recognized by their *kesh* covered with a turban, a *kirpan* (dagger) and *kara* (iron-bangle). A section of the Hindus may be recognized by a *tilak* (mark on their forehead) and round turban. Traditional dresses have now been replaced by Western apparel. *Salwar*, *kameez* and *dupatta* is the common dress of the Punjabi women. Hindu women apply *sindur* (vermilion) in the hair parting.

*Dal-roti* is the staple food of the people of Punjab. The food habits of the rural and urban people are different. Those who live in the villages and attend to manual work from morning till evening, specially the peasants, take rich food with plenty of milk, milk products and clarified butter. *Sarson da sag* and *makki di roti* is a favourite both in the rural and urban areas during the winter months. *Lassi*, tea, mango shake, fruits juices are a common drink. Mutton and chicken are taken occasionally. The intake of alcoholic drinks specially on festive occasions is common.

Wheat is the staple food. The meals in the rural areas consist of *roti* (leavened wheat cakes) eaten with dal (pulses), *makhan* (butter), *achar* (pickles) and *lassi* (whipped curd).

Maize is eaten in the form of cakes, popcorn, or roasted stubs. Pulses eaten by the people are *masoor* (lentils), *moth*, *moong* (green gram) and *urad*. The puddings eaten are *kheer*, *sewain*, *karah* or *halwa* or *khand* (sugar mixed with clarified butter). Milk is usually served after dinner. Conventional north Indian sweets *jalebi, laddoo, barfi, imirti, khilan* are distributed and eaten during festivel occasions. *Gur* is distributed among the neighbours and kin to mark events such as the birth of a male child, purchasing a buffalo, a child going to school for the first time or the foundation laying ceremony of a house.

Khushwant Singh makes the following observations about the Sikh food: 'Sikh peasants eat the healthiest of food. Although they are not vegetarian by conviction, few can afford to eat meat except on special occasions such as wedding. The Sikh staple diet is wheat, buffalo milk and milk products. They are great ones in eating curds and drinking buttermilk. During the winter months, mashed mustard plants in the form of spinach capped with the liberal blobs of butter supplement the corn cakes. This diet is the chief reason for the Sikhs' excellent physique and virility. It explains the Sikh's prodigious stamina, his dominance in the Indian world of sports of his fighing qualities. An English dietician carried out an interesting experiment with albino rates. He fed groups with the food of different Indian communities. At the end of eighty days the rats eating the Sikh diet weighed more than the rats eating the diet of any other community, Pathan, Rajputs, Maratha and Gurkha' (ibid., 89).

During the last few decades tea has become the most important beverage. It is prepared with brown sugar and is taken in the morning, at noon and in the evening. Besides tea, coffee too has become a favourite drink of the elite. In summer people drink aerated water, syrups and *shikanjbee, jal jeera* and *kanji.* Gram flour (*besan*) is mostly used for preparing *pakora* and curry. In recent years people have started taking chillies in large quantities. Cooking medium is generally vegetable and mustard oil. Clarified butter (*ghee*) is generally used by the well-to-do persons. Mutton is consumed on special occasions. Alcohol is consumed by men in large quantities especially during Baisakhi, Diwali, and Lohri. Smoking is common among non-Sikhs. 'Peeo te jeeo' (drink and live) is the current philosophy (Gill, 1973: 115).

The concept of *siana* (elderly person) is prevalent in interior villages of Punjab. The decision of the *siana* is accepted by both the parties. The village *panchayat* also settles the disputes within its jurisdiction. Otherwise, the individual can approach the court of law which is considered a costly affair by the lower castes of a village. In the cities, there are *panchayats* of the various communities which settle their disputes. Denotified tribes such as Sansi, Gandhila, Kutchband, Bauria, Bangala, Dhea, Sirkiband, Sikligar, Singikat, and

Bazigars have their own traditional caste *panchayats* and they settle their own disputes, impose cash fines or excommunicate individuals for violating the norms of the society, but they do not approach the court of law.

Social division in Punjab has been aptly delineated by Singh (1967), Leaf (1972), and Hershman (1981). Unlike the usual contour of caste system in other parts of the cow-belt in India, where Brahmans enjoy a prominent and predominant position irrespective of their numerical strength, it is the Jat in Punjab who occupy the role of *jajman* (patron) and stand at the centre of a complex economic and ritual relationship. There are relatively few villages in Punjab, where other castes such as Brahman or Carpenters are the landowners and perform the function of village *jajman.* Thus the Jat constitute the Sardar (upper castes) groups. This group also includes some of the artisan castes such as Kamboh, Tarkhan, Sunar, Chimba and Nai. The Sardar can be subdivided into agriculturists and traders. The former being agriculturists, they consider themselves superior to other castes. Their claim is strengthened by the fact that they are the masters of the land and some of them even belong to the ex-ruling families. Ownership of land is definitely a major criterion for determining the status in Sikh villages as most of its adherents are agriculturists, who at one time were warriors and conquered large tracts of land.

Traders in Punjab are considered lower than the agriculturists. The Khatris will not rank higher than the Jat not because of their birth but since they earned their living by trade they will be considered lower in status. But if a Khatri family possesses a large tract of land, its members will be regarded as of equal status. One of the reasons attributed for not giving a higher rank to Brahmans was their occupational diversification from priesthood to trade. Kamboh too were treated inferior to Jat for similar reasons. Next to agriculturist castes come the artisan castes, viz., Tarkhan (carpenters) and Kumhar (potters), who are said to occupy a higher status because of their better economic position. Nai (barber), Sunar (goldsmith) and Chimba (tailors) occupy, almost the same status in the village society. Sansi and Chamar are considered lower in hierarchy than the Mazhabi (Sikh). Those Chuhras, who have embraced Christianity occupy the same status as that of Mazhabi Sikh. Some of them have become barbers to make a living and raise ther social status.

The above scheme of social stratification in Punjab is somewhat practically different from the traditional Hindu caste model which necessitates factors like birth, pollution, occupational specialization and commensality as the determinants of caste identity. The Sikh do not believe in any one of the above listed factors. The factors playing an important role in social stratification in Punjab are territory, agricultural lands, numerical dominance, profession, occupational diversification and mobility. The Chuhras occupy the lowest position. The Mazhabis, i.e. the Sikh Chuhras are however, avoided in terms of spatial differentiaiton.

*Ghar* (household) is a domestic and commensal unit that owns property jointly. *Al* or *sake* are the close agnates who constitute a minimal lineage, occupy households and own fields adjacent to one another. They often share rights in a common irrigation well. Sometimes there is a joint shrine to a common ancestor of the lineage. Agnates of minimal lineage are reversionary co-parceners in each other's property. The members also have abiding obligation in mutual participation in *rites de passage*, such as, mourning rites and ritual solidarity at wedding, etc. Flow of ritual presentations is maintained at a greater rate within a minimal lineage than outside it. *Patti* or *biradari* are major lineage members which occupy the same residential ward of a village. Their fields tend to be clustered together and they may share a common village well and members of service castes. They are reversionary co-parceners in the case of there being no closer collateral agnatic lineage. As regards ritual role of *patti/ biradari* members, they form a broad *rite de passage* group within which there reciprocal obligation, e.g. every household must send a man on the wedding party of a man of the group. *Got* are localized clans or maximal lineages, who occupy a single village and its land. Agnates have the first right of refusal on land before it can be alienated from clan ownership. They exhibit broad limits of ritual group. In case of death in one major lineage, men and women of other major lineages go to mourn and offer condolences jointly as a group. They also maintain a common temple.

The Punjabi family and kinship has been intensivly and exhaustively studied by Leaf (1972), Das (1976), Izmirlian (1979) and Hersh-man (1981). Murray J. Leaf (1972) considers the system of concepts that defines relationship among the people on the basis of their place in a system of putative kinship groups and kinship relations makes up the 'conscious sociological current'. Kinship as a 'conscious sociological model' permits people, acting as individuals, to agree on a set of enduring relationships that appear to underlie their actions and give their actions a dependable moral basis. Leaf employs the mode of analysis to describe the Sikh kinship system as system of definitions that is also a system of information. He furnishes the basic pattern of definitions of the Punjabi terminology, the complete set of categories for any person's kinship relations. Leaf disagreed with Krober's view, who saw terminologies as system of concepts that were linguistic and yet existed 'in a rigid biological framework' divorced from the institutions of society. To Leaf, concepts are embedded in a mnemonic framework, phonological and conceivable as rituals are to religious concepts. The general concepts of the terminology are identical to those of institutions—they are embodied in institutional rules and rituals, just as they are in the phonology . . . terminologies but genealogical interrelationships of individuals into an institutional framework of concepts, the indefinite number of possible groupings of domains . . . are reduced to a well established and widely promulgated derivative models. The more prominent of such derivative models in the kinship system are models of households groups, the *parivar* (family), of individual life cycles for men and women, of the *patti*, or the *got* (clan) and of the *jat* or *biradari* (castes). Each such domain is connected logically with a particular concept of 'property' (*jaidad*) in Punjab. The term *jaidad* connotes 'ancestral property' conditioned by rule of inheritance or ownership pertaining to dis-position of property of people who die. The rule is that all sons inherit equal shares in property of the father; they acquire these rights from birth, and that the rights of sons pre-empt the rights of brothers. None of them can sell his share of property without the permission of the others, and in the event of sale by one party the other can exercise their right of pre-emption forcing the buyer to sell back to them at the price he has paid. Sons can even pre-empt a sale by father to his own brother. If one of the sons or the father were to die, his share would be divided equally among the remaining co-owners and if one of the two were to die, the survivor would become the owner of the whole original unit. This rule of inheritance does not apply to 'self-acquired' property.

Harry Izmirlian (1979) while studying structure and strategy in Sikh society, finds Punjabi family patrilineal. Rules of marriage are endogamous with respect to caste and exogamous with respect to the village in which one is born and the clan to which one belongs. The women move away from their natal village to the village of their husbands after the wedding ceremony. A newly married couple most frequently live in the house of the groom's parents, forming a joint family (ibid. 107). Marriage outside the caste is very rare. Polygynous relations are rare among the Punjabi. However, polyandrous relations are more frequently found (ibid. 107). A number of brothers will often share the sexual privilage of one wife. Most villagers presume that this is the case when there is but one married son among a number of brothers. (This presumption appears to be justified, for in taking genealogies, a number of persons were not certain as to which of two brothers was their biological father.) (Ibid. 108.)

Hershman (1981) also confirms polyandry in Punjab and states, 'in the area where I worked I came across numerous instances of a woman being married to one brother, usually the eldest, but being shared by those brothers younger than him. Sexual access to the wife of the eldest brother reduced, in some cases, the likelihood of other brothers marrying. In many instances I know of, it was a permanent arrangement and none of the other brothers would marry . . . it seemed to be a practice associated with less well-to-do families owning under ten acres of land. It was said that it was associated with the need to keep small land holdings undivided as, if there was only one woman, and there was an arrangement among the brothers themselves to hold her in common, it was unlikely that during their life time the land would be divided . . . women then were regarded as the possession of the family, and in rural areas where the family lived jointly, the wife was known as adi-karwali (half-wife) for all his younger unmarried brothers.'

It is important to consider, why it is generally only the Jat and tanner castes of Punjab who adopt the strategem of polyandrous marriage in order to overcome economic difficulties. High castes generally consider polyandry to be an abominable institution and they associate its practice with the Jats and with low castes. Whereas the Brahmans, for example consider it essential that a woman be a virgin at marriage and do not practice widow remarriage, this is not the case among the tanners and the Jats. The Jats, as owners of land have always stood in a position of power in relation to the landless tanner and agricultural labourers and have generally exploited sexually both married and unmarried tanner women (Pettigrew, 1978: 44).

Hypergamy has also been reported by Hershman, who observes that 'Tanners . . . in some cases sell their daughters to Jats, who cannot obtain wives in the normal way. Such occurances are, however, comparatively rare' (ibid.). Both the Jats and tanners are reported to practise widow remarriage. The Jats, who are meat eaters and do not maintain the same ideals of caste purity, as for example, the Hindu Brahmans, regularly practice widow remarriage and widow inheritance. There is a formalized ceremony of secondary marriage 'which is performed by the Sikh priest within the Sikh temple. This is called *kareva* or *chadar paona* (literally "to place a cloth"). In this ceremony the groom marries a widow simply by placing a cloth over her head.'

Harry Izmirlian (1979: 107-8) is also of the view that widow remarriage is standard practice and often takes the form of levirate. Widow remarriage is explained by Sikh as a reaction to the scarcity of women in Punjab and an intentional deviation from Hinduism.

Veena Das (1976) is more interested in dealing with interpersonal relationships within the families and *biradari* context and as a direct product of biological forces of procreation and copulation.

'The two fundamental facts of biology with which kinship morality has to reckon, the Punjabis say, are the facts of procreation and copulaton. The Punjabi theory of procreation is that the woman provides the field and man provides the seed. . . . The quality of the offspring is determined by the quality of seed. Nonetheless, the field should be able to bear the seed. If the seed is very powerful it will "burn the field" Hence it is important that the qualities of the genitor and geniterix are evently matched. The man's role in procreation ends with the depositing of seed and this is seen as *gharbadhana*, the gift of conception, given by the man to woman' (ibid.).

She further says, 'The mutual love of the mother and the child is considered "pre-social" in that it comes spontaneously and flows from natural, unlearned behaviour. People often say that a wife is replaceable since the woman is as good as another for the purposes of procreation, but that mother is irreplaceable. As a proof of this they often quote the fact that when in pain a person always calls his mother ('haay maan') but never his father or his wife. Thus, they argue, when all one's defences are down as in sickness, and all the masks of of social obligation have been laid aside, one turns for comfort to the mother.'

The typical patterns of interaction between a husband and a wife in this phase of their life have been described in considerable detail (Karve, 1958; Madan, 1975).

Fairs and festivals in Punjab are celebrated with gusto. Lohari, Basant Panchmi, Shivratri, Hola Mohala, Holi, Baisakhi, Rakhi, Dussehra and Diwali deserve a special mention. The Kartarpur Baisakhi fair and the Baba Sodal fair of Jalandhar attract thousands of people. The Shahidi Mela of Sardar Bhagat Singh at the village Khatkar Kalan in tahsil Nawashahr too attract a large gathering on 23 March every year. Kila Raipur witnesses one of the biggest sport events in the rural areas of Punjab. Among the important Muslim festivals are Id-ul-Fitr and Id-ul-Zuha. The Christians celebrate New Year's Day, Good Friday, Easter and Christmas. Guruparabs are celebrated with great solemnity by the Sikhs. Big diwans are held on the birthdays of Guru Nanak Dev and Guru Gobind Singh and the martyrdom days of Guru Arjan Dev and Guru Tegh Bahadur. The Pargat Din of Guru Ravi Das is celebrated in the month of February with great enthusiasm.

Punjab is thus a state with a rich cultural heritage and has, over the years, emerged as an excellent industrial and trade centre in the country besides being known as the granary of India. Not only is the per capita income of the state more than double of the national average, but it also offers a better quality of life.

It has been a matter of curious examination that in spite of all the trouble and turmoil in Punjab for the last decade, the agricultural and industrial production has maintained its tempo. The history of Punjab, a mixture of difficult times defying odds, surviving defeats and repeated conquest by aliens has bequeathed to its people a unique psyche of self-respect, hard work, optimism, capacity to take risks and perseverance against odds. It has helped to generate an ideal temperament to build entrepreneurship and instict of survival.

Independence in 1947 had its negative repercussion on Punjab. The state was partitioned with the agriculturally more prosperous areas going to Pakistan. Over four million people migrated to Punjab from West Pakistan and the once prosperous state of Punjab was reduced to a state deficit in food grains. The second partition, that is, division of Haryana and Himachal Pradesh, deprived it of its skeletal industrial base around Delhi as well as the tourist attractions of Himachal. From a deficit situation at the time of partition, the state achieved a position where it now contributed 60 per cent of the national food reserves although its area is less than 2 per cent of the country. Today, it has a vast network of canals and over 80 per cent land of the total cultivable area, making it the most irrigated state of India. The wheat and rice yield are also the highest in the country owing to enterprise of the people and these back-up services.

Punjab has made its transition from a purely agricultural economy to one of the country's cognizable industrial power and that too without any major state or central investment in industry. Punjab has shown that it is entrepreneurship that creates sustainable economic growth. Today Punjab has the largest per million number of self-employed entrepreneurs in the country. This industrial and agricultural growth has been coupled with infrastructural growth along with an undoubtedly good network of roads with well developed transport system. These factors together have given a fillip to improvement in the quality of life of the general populace. Education is well spread and there exists a network of higher education including medical, engineering and technical institutions. The growth and prosperity, visible in the life of both urban and rural population, have attracted a large number of migratory population here in search of livelihood.

Precisely what sustains Punjab against odds: historic or economic? It is the typically Punjabi ethos of unsatiated thirst of growth even in adversity.

Industry in Punjab has been affected to a great extent during the last twelve years due to terrorism. Large numbers of industrialists migrated from the state to safer places. Industries involving textiles, machine tools, woollen shawls, paper, and rice suffered heavily due to this exodus. The people of Punjab stood united in adverse times and by extending all help to the new government, they have been able to heal the wounds of the state for the first time during the last ten years. The perspirations the Punjabis coupled with the dogged determination and sincerity of the new government has brought the much wanted tranquility to the state and the business, trade and industry have once again started flourishing.

As one enters Punjab from Haryana and moves towards Rajpura on Sher Shah Suri Marg, one is greeted with several units making cycles, vanaspati, yarn, cables, biscuits and other food articles. Sarhind has almost merged with Mandi Gobindgrah, the steel town of the north with 125 rerolling mills which too has further joined the country's biggest food grains market. This area produces sewing machines, diesel engines and steel and has a vast network of steel mills churning out goods worth Rs. 1,000 crore annually. Ludhiana, the home of small and middle range machines, blankets and food products alone produces goods worth Rs. 1,700 crore and is the real beehive of Punjab. The industrial belt extending from Ludhiana to Jalandhar produces quality agricultural implements, textiles, sugar, steel, sports goods, machinary and hand tools. Amritsar is the home of carpets, machinary, textiles and engineering goods.

In short, Punjab's journey from bloodshed to peace and from peace to prosperity has been remarkable. This could happen only due to unstinted courage and whole hearted cooperation of the peace-loving people of Punjab. The state government with strong will, determination, and clear vision has brought about a miraculous transformation in the security environment of the state in about a year, thus ensuring spirit of self-confidence, hope and faith in the future, bright prospects for trade and industry, opportunity for investors, strong infrastructure and productive work-force for growth and progress, stable political and economic environment and uplift of all sections of society.

Sir Denzil Ibbetson was the first to publish the monumental ethnographic account of the people of Punjab entitled *Punjab Castes* (*Races, Caste and Tribes*) (1916). This is the earliest scientific and literary research exercise for administrative purposes. It was based on the *Census of Punjab, 1881* and published in 1883. Sir Denzil Ibbetson, later published *Punjab Ethnography* in 1883 including the information related to the religions, languages, races, castes and tribes of the people of Punjab. Since the first publications of ethnographic account of the people of Punjab by Ibbetson, the territorial boundaries and the census population figures for each community have undergone a change, but the information related to etymology, legends of origin and migration of each community of the state of Punjab is still relevant under the contemporary situations.

The second monumental ethnographic contribution is in the form of compiled work published in three volumes by H.A. Rose (1919). It is based on the *Census Report of Punjab*, 1883 by Sir Denzil Ibbetson and *Census Report of Punjab*, 1892 by Sir Edward Maclagan. This compiled work by Rose (1919) was entitled *Glossary of the Tribes and Castes of the Punjab and North-West Frontier Province.* No major ethnographic study has been undertaken in the state of Punjab after Ibbetson (1916) and Rose (1919) before the People of India project.

Out of ninty-five communities studied under the People of India project Malwa accounts for fifty-three communities, Majha nine and Doaba eight. Twenty-two communities are distributed in the three zones: Malwa–Doaba thirteen, Majha–Malwa six and Majha–Doaba three. Eighty-six communities have been studied in urban areas and nine in various villages. Out of ninety-five communities studied in Punjab under 'People of India' project, there are thirty-four communities belonging to Scheduled Castes, and thirty-four communities belonging to 'Other Backward Classes' according to the state list and twenty-seven communities do not enjoy any constitutional status.

# ACHARAJ

According to popular belief, after the battle of Mahabharata ended, Dronacharya collected the children of the Brahmans and Kshatriyas. He assigned them duties to perform fifteen rituals, such as birth, marriage, etc. The most intelligent of these disciples was trained to perform death rituals and was named Acharya, 'the learned'. He was also called Maha Brahman, the great *pandit*, the one who exercises impure or inauspicious functions. With the passage of time, 'Acharya' became 'Acharaj' or 'Achraj', which is resented by the members of community. They feel that the term 'Acharya' is more dignified. The Acharaj are also called Gujarati Brahman, as some of them migrated from Gujarat to Punjab. All the Acharaj are Hindu and are distributed in all the districts of Punjab, both in urban and rural areas. Their exact population is not known but according to Ibbetson's report, they numbered 1,476 in Gurdaspur district and between one hundred and two hundred in other districts towards the close of the nineteenth century.

Punjabi language is most commonly used by them both at home and in dealing with others. They use both Gurmukhi and Devanagari scripts. The educated generation also uses English. Earlier there were special identification markers for the male members of the community in the forms of *sikha* (lock of hairs), *janeu* (sacred thread) and *tilak* (mark on the forehead).

They eat both vegetarian and non-vegetarian food though earlier they were strictly vegetarian and also avoided taking onion and garlic. Wheat, pulses, seasonal vegetables, rice and maize form their regular diet. Locally available fruits like banana, mango, grapes, papaya, guava, peaches and apple are consumed. The most commonly consumed pulses are *urad* (black gram) *moong* (green gram) and *chana* (bengal gram). Cooking media are vegetable *ghee*, oil and *desi ghee* (clarified butter). Non-vegetarians among them eat mutton, chicken, fish and egg. Milk and milk products are consumed adequately. Tea, coffee and buttermilk are also used in plenty. Alcoholic drinks were avoided earlier. However, for the new generation drinking alcoholic beverages has become a symbol of prosperity and prestige. In some Acharaj families, on occasions such as birth of a male child, betrothal, marriage, or such happy social occasions, drinks are freely served and consumed. Those who are engaged in priestly profession or who perform death rituals, however, do not drink. These priests are strict vegetarians and avoid even onion and garlic. Liquor and sweets are avoided on Tuesdays and during mourning period. Their women avoid meat and liquor. In recent times, there has been noticeable increase in the consumption of meat, eggs and fish in this community; liquor intake has also increased.

The Acharaj seems to be a composite group without any subcaste but *gots* exist among them. Some of these major *gots* are Bhardwaj, Gautam, Attri, Vashist, Vishwamitar, Asil, Badar, Parasar and Sandal. No hierarchy exists among these *gots*; differentiation within the community, however, exists on economic, occupational, and educational levels. The Acharaj are aware of, and recognize, their place in the *varna* system as Brahman. They consider themselves at par with other Brahmans, but other Brahmans consider the Acharaj as socially inferior to them.

The Acharaj are endogamous at community level. Marriage takes place with some relations, e.g. with a maternal uncle, brother-in-law's sister, father's sister's son. Consanguinous marriages are thus allowed in the case of the Acharaj. Age at marriage is around seventeen to eighteen years for both boys and girls. In the past, marriages were solemnized even at the age of six to eight years. Monogamy is the rule. Marriage symbols for women are *bindi*, *sindur*, *mangal sutra*, red dress and also finger ring, toe ring, ear- and noserings. These symbols are commonly used by the newly wed, while others use these on social occasions.

The concept of *kanyadan* (giving away of daughter) exists among the Acharaj. Dowry is paid by them in cash and kind voluntarily; any demand regarding dowry is socially resented. Rule of residence after marriage is patrilocal. Divorce is permissible on the grounds of adultery and moral turpitude. Either husband or wife can ask for divorce with the approval of community elders. Remarriage is permitted in case of young widows and divorcees. The widowed and divorced males can remarry freely. A young widow may be remarried to her deceased husband's younger brother and this practice is called *chadar paona*. Intercommunity marriages are now permissible with the other castes like the Khatri. Nuclear families are on the increase among the Acharaj.

Interpersonal relations of respect, love and feeling of fear of elders is observed in an Acharaj family. Avoidance relationships are observed between a man and his daughter-in-law, a woman and her husband's elder brother. Joking relationship exists between a man and his wife's sister, younger brother and elder brother's wife. Conflicts often crop up on account of property dispute, challenge to the authority of elders, check on freedom of youngers, etc. Male equigeniture is the rule of inheritance among the Acharaj. These days the daughters also can claim their share. Succession is by the eldest son. Women do household work, collect fuel and potable water. They also participate in social, ritual and religious affairs of the family but are politically inactive except for casting votes at the time of elections. All the important decisions of a family are taken by the male members. However, the opinion of the ladies on matters like negotiating marriage of a son or a daughter may be obtained. Post-delivery pollution period is observed for one-and-a-quarter months. The naming ceremony is observed and *mundan* is performed in cases of male children only. *Mundan* ceremony is performed at one, three or five years of age. The childhood ritual of first feeding of cereals, *gurti*, is also reported.

The main marriage rituals are performed at the bride's residence and the feast is hosted by the bride's parents. The marriage ceremony is solemnized by performing *pheras* (circumambulation) around the sacred fire amidst chanting of the Vedic *mantras*. Consummation of marriage is at the bride-groom's residence. The dead are cremated and the bones are immersed in the holy Ganga at Hardwar. Death rites, in the form of annual *shradh*, are performed. Observance of pollution period after death continues for seventeen days. Life-cycle rituals are being curtailed nowadays as they have become more expensive.

Priestly work is now performed by very few among the Acharaj. They are mainly employed in the white-collar jobs as teachers, bank officials and army officers. Agriculture is the source of livelihood for a few. The very poor among them even work as labourers, cows and buffaloes are also reared by some. Milk is sold to private purchasers and also supplied to milkmen's co-operatives.

The Acharaj worship Lord Rama and Krishna as their major deities. Sacred shrines and centres of piligrimage for them are Hardwar, Vaishnodevi, Amarnath, Jwalaji, etc. Services of other Brahmans are availed of by them for performing birth, marriage rites, etc. Their major festivals are Dussehra, Diwali, Holi, Lohri, Janmashtami and Sakrant. These festivals are of socio-economic and religious significance.

The Acharaj traditionally accept water and food from and exchange the same with all other local Hindu communities except the Scheduled

Castes. They also participate in the rituals and social functions of their neighbours and share wells and other water sources, crematoria, religious shrines, with other local communities like the Jat, Brahman, and Kshatriya and participate in traditional festivals and festivities with them. Their attitude towards developmental programmes is favourable and impact on the community is perceptible. Both males and females are highly educated. The attitude of the community towards family planning is very positive. The community is fully aware of the advantages of a small family. Modern methods of family planning including sterilization are used by them. Facilities for drinking water are available to them in the form of handpumps, tube wells and water taps. They are adequately enjoying the fruits of developmental programmes.

RAKESH KUMAR

# AD-DHARMI

The Ad-Dharmis are a Scheduled Caste and skin tanning is their primary occupation. During 1935-6, Ad-Dharmi Mandal started a movement for their right to own a house and to vote.Though this caste has originated from the Chamar community, under the influence of the movement launched by the Ad-Dharmi Mandal, they call themselves Ad-Dharmi.

According to *Census of India* (1981), the total population of the Ad-Dharmi in the state of Punjab is 6,80,132, which includes 3,61,514 males and 3,18,618 females. The Ad-Dharmis are distributed in the districts of Jalandhar Hoshiarpur, Kapurthala, Patiala and Bhatinda. They speak Punjabi language and use Devanagari and Gurmukhi scripts.

Most of the males wear shirt and *pyjama* or *dhoti* and turban. Females wear *salwar* and *kameez* with *dupatta*.

Ad-Dharmis eat non-vegetarian food. Wheat is their staple food; *chapati* prepared from the flour of wheat and maize is eaten. *Makki di roti* (maize flour *roti*) and *sarson da sag* (mustard leaves preparation) are relished by them during the winter season. *Moong*, gram, *urad*, *masur*, *moth* are some of the pulses eaten by them. They cook food in groundnut oil. Pure *ghee* is also used for smearing the *chapaties* or for preparing *tarka* (gravy). Milk and milk products such as curd, tea and mango-shake are consumed in large quantity. Alcoholic drinks are consumed. Seasonal fruits such as mango, banana, orange are their favourites.

The Ad-Dharmi are an endogamous community and are divided into several exogamous *gots* such as Bangur, Badan, Birdi, Bal, Banga, Bains, Bhardwaj, Bhargu, Chakhu, Chokhria, Chandar, Chumar, Chopra, Duggal, Dharbhanga, Jassal, Kauldhar, Kaith, Kalsi, Mahi, Hohe, Pod, Rai, Ratu, Sandhu, Soniara, Sund, Suman, Sidhu, Shergill and Thind. They recognize *varna* system and fall under the Shudra *varna*. Though they consider themselves to be of equal status with their neighbours, these neighbours accord them an inferior status.

Before independence of India, child marriage was practised among the Ad-Dharmis. At present the age for marriage for boys is twenty years and girls get married at around eighteen years of age. Marriages are negotiated by the parents with the help of a *bicholia* (mediator).

A person is not supposed to marry within his or her father's, mother's, paternal and maternal grandmother's *gots*. The *kurmai* (betrothal) is solemnized with payment of one rupee to the would-be groom by his would-be in-laws. This sum is known as *shagun*. Those who can afford to also gift clothes to the boy and his close relatives. Form of marriage is monogamy and the symbol of marriage is *sindur* or vermilion in the hair parting. Dowry in the form of gifts is offered to the girl at the time of marriage. The girl after marriage stays with her parents-in-law.

On the wedding day, the groom, accompanied by his people, the *barat*, arrives at the bride's town or village and stays at a *barat ghar* for taking rest. Then he moves in a procession towards the *pandal* where the actual marriage ceremony has to be performed. The bride's people decorate the *pandal* according to their means. The arrival of the *barat* at the gate of the *pandal* is followed by a ceremony known as the *milni* (ritual welcome). Relatives of the boy and the girl are introduced to each other on this occasion and exchange garlands, etc. This ceremony is followed by the ceremony of *lavan phere* (circumambulation), whereby marriage is solemnized. Relatives of the boy occupy one side of the *pandal*, while those of the girl sit opposite them. After the ceremony of *lavan phere* is over, the parents and relatives of the groom and the bride bless and wish the newly married couple. The groom's people take their lunch and leave for their place along with the newly weds by the evening. Earlier, the groom's people used to stay at the bride's place for three days. Now the whole marriage ceremony is over on the same day. Consummation of marriage is at the groom's place on the next day. In the past, marriage and *muklawa* (consummation of marriage) used to take place on different occasions, sometimes after a gap of four to five years.

At present marriage alliances are preferably arranged between families of same status. Divorce is permitted among the Ad-Dharmi. The various reasons for divorce can be barrenness, impotency, lack of male issue, adultery, etc. Compensation for divorce has to be given by the spouse who seeks divorce. Husband and wife both have equal right to seek divorce. Responsibility for children is decided in the case of divorce by mutual understanding or some times according to the orders of the court of law. Remarriage of divorcees is allowed though divorce is discouraged. Marriage symbols are strictly adhered to by the Ad-Dharmi women. Dowry is prevalent among those families who can afford it.

Extended type of family is common. However, nuclear families are also coming up at the cost of the extended ones. Those who are well-educated and are in the services prefer a nuclear family. In Ad-Dharmi families, avoidance relationship exists between a man and his mother-in-law; a woman and her father-in-law; a man and his younger brother's wife, while joking relationships is maintained between a woman and her husband's younger brother; a man and his wife's sister; and between the co-brothers. Major reasons of conflict and confrontation in the families may be property, challenge to the authority of elders and quarrel over the children. On most of the occasions minor differences or misunderstandings are solved through mutual discussions. If the problem is more serious and it becomes difficult to arrive at a compromise, help of the elders of neighbouring communities can also be sought. All the sons of an Ad-Dharmi family share the property of their father equally. The eldest son is entitled for succession.

Presently, women of the Ad-Dharmi are aware of their role for a better family life. Apart from the household activities, women also help the male members of their family in many other ways. They, however, do not play a role directly in the economic activities, social functions or rituals. But indirectly, by extending their hand of cooperation women do help in increasing the family income.

Birth of a child takes place at the natal home of the mother. However, subsequent births take place at her in-laws' house. Some precautions are taken during the late phase of the pregnancy. The birth of a first child is always welcomed and is a matter of rejoicing if it is a male child. Mango leaves are tied to the front door at the birth of male child. A pollution period is observed for forty days. The ceremony known as *chhati* (a ritual on the completion of six months) is also observed on the occasion of birth of a male child. On this occasion, after the religious ceremony, a feast known as *roti*, is offered to close relatives and members of the community. The elders bless the child for a long life. The newborn child is named either by family members or by the *pandit*.

Marriage ceremony takes place at bride's residence. In the past, specially before Independence, the marriage party used to stay for two nights. But at present, all ceremonies are completed on the day of the *lavan phere*. The *barat* or marriage party, returns along with the bride in the evening. Reception is arranged in honour of the newly wedded couple. All the close relatives and members join in on this occasion and give their blessings and good wishes to the couple. Consummation of marriage takes place on the same or on the subsequent night. There is a ceremony in which all the articles presented to the girl in the form of gifts are displayed. This is known as *daj dikhana*. At her in-laws' house, the newly married girl prepares sweet rice or *roti*. This ceremony reflects that she has been accepted by the family.

In case a member of the Ad-Dharmi dies at an old age, he is given due respect. The dead is taken to the pyre in a procession known as *janaja*. Brass band is also arranged to play music. Pollution caused by death is observed for sixteen days, after which a religious ceremony for purification is performed. The adult is cremated whereas in the case of a child the dead body is buried. The bones, called *phul*, are immersed at Hardwar. A feast for members of the community is also arranged. Ancestor worship among the Ad-Dharmi was prevalent in the pre-Independence period. Members of the community used to observe the *shradh* (ancestor worship) ceremony. These days this ritual of ancestor worship is not observed regularly. Among the Ad-Dharmi, some rituals related to birth, marriage and death are still observed with the same spirit as in the past. However, some of the rituals are being avoided and some are becoming of shorter duration.

Most of the male members work for tanneries or shoe manufacturing factories, or as labourers. They prepare shoes known as *jutti* (footwear). This is used by most of the Punjabi people.

Ad-Dharmis have their own *panchayat* known as *Khan-di-panchayat*. The *panchayat* take decisions on the basis of facts related to a specific charge. The main punishment is to compensate the loss, reprimand or begging of pardon by the person found guilty by the *panchayat*. The *gram panchayat* attends to the major problems of the village, related to all the communities, and it is an elected body. However, the *panchayat* of thc Ad-Dharmi is elected unanimously.

Ad-Dharmis are the followers of Guru Ravidas. For this reason they are also known as Ravidasia. They have *gurdwaras* and *dharamshalas* in every village as well as their own temples of Shri Guru Ravidas. They believe both in Hinduism and Sikhism. The *sadharan path* or *akhand path* ceremony is performed on birth, marriage and death ceremonies. The major festival of the Ad-Dharmi is the birthday of Guru Ravidas, which is celebrated as Pragat-Diwas. The Ad-Dharmis celebrate Holi, Diwali, Dussehra and Lohri festivals. In villages, the walls of the Ad-Dharmi houses, which are *kachcha*, are decorated with paintings having various motifs. Floors are also painted sometimes. These people share folk songs and folk music with their neighbours.

Better educational facilities existing at present have resulted in better job opportunities among the Ad-Dharmis. However, places where they are engaged in hide work are full of nauseating smell. This has resulted in the comparative isolation of this community from other communities of their neighbourhood. Educated persons of these localities may have a different attitude, but both the Scheduled Castes and the other castes do not maintain close relations with them. The Ad-Dharmis have their own tubewells or wells for the supply of drinking water. Restrictions for exchange of food between the Ad-Dharmi and other Hindu castes can be realized after close observation. Patron-client relations with other communities are always cordial.

Members of the community hold white-collar jobs as teachers, administrators, businessmen and are in defence services. Political leadership has emerged at the village and state levels among them. Formal education has been favourably accepted by both boys and girls and some of them have continued their studies upto the post-graduate level. The community has been benefitted by various modern medicare schemes and family welfare schemes.

Drinking water is available within the locality and most of the families have their own water resources. However, they are well covered by the public distribution system and have ration cards for getting various articles at cheaper rates. Banking facilities for saving and investment are available to the Ad-Dharmis. Though most of the individuals are engaged in leatherwork, those who are educated have got regular jobs either in the state government or central government offices located in Punjab or outside. Wood, cow-dung and sawdust are used by them as fuel. A large number of people of this community have migrated to Western countries in search of better employment opportunities there.

SWARAN SINGH

# AHERI

The term Thori, Aheri, Heri and Naik appear to be synonymous. Rose (1919) has pointed out that the Thori and the Aheri refer to the same caste. They used to carry merchandise on pack animals. Rose also stated that the Thori seem to have connections with the Banjara. Tod (1960) observed that the headmen of both Thori and Banjara are called Naik. The Aheri are considered true hunters. However, 'Naik' was a term of honour and 'Thori' a term of contempt. Even today the different groups mentioned above consider themselves to be of common origin. They, however, claim to be the descendants of Rajput and that their ancestors were in the army of Rajput kings. Because of their bravery and heroic deeds they were called Naik. Accordingly, they claim that they are migrants to Punjab from Rajasthan. The migration, according to them, took place during the days of Maharana Pratap. The Mughals had let loose a reign of terror on them, and in order to save their honour they had to migrate to Punjab.

Today their population in Punjab is concentrated in districts of Patiala, Bhatinda, Ferozepur and Faridkot. They are found in small numbers in other districts also. According to the 1921 census, the Aheri in Punjab numbered 16,756 and the Thori were 13,435. They speak Rajasthani dialect with their family members and kinsmen but with others they speak Punjabi language. They use both Gurmukhi and Devanagari scripts. In the past their men wore *dhoti* and women *ghagra* (skirt) and *karia* (silver bangles worn on the ankles). They are fighting for the Scheduled Tribe status by using the common rubric of 'Naik' for all the people known as Aheri, Heri and Thori. The basis for this claim lies in their assertion that they are occupationally akin to the Banjara. It may incidentally be mentioned that the Banjara in the states of Gujarat, Maharashtra, Karnataka and Andhra Pradesh are called Naik. They were declared 'criminal tribes' by the British, though the accounts of Rose suggest that they were not involved in criminal activities.

The different synonyms are indicative of different subgroupings among this community. There is a layer of social differentiation among them. The Naik consider themselves as most superior in the social status as compared to others. The Heri or Aheri consider the Thori to be inferior in status. These subgroups are generally exogamous. They marry among themselves except with the Thori, whose past occupation seems to be associated with carcass. These groups are hesitant in contracting marital ties with the Thori, though the observation of these restrictions are now gradually becoming weak. All these groups have common *gots*. Some of their important *gots* are: Bhata, Chahurwal, Charan, Chandalia, Dekhta, Dahinwal, Dharoria, Dharuheria, Ganchand, Ghaman, Gogal, Gotala, Hajipuria, Jhindia, Junbal, Mahta, Mewal, Panwal, Rathor, Sagaria, Sailingia, Samelwal, Sandlas, Sarsut and Sendhi.

They observe *got* exogamy; monogamy is the rule. Marriage symbols for the ladies are *bindi* (dot on forehead), *chura* (red bangles) and red coloured dress. Wearing of ring on finger, ears and nose is also common. During social occasions these symbols are more strictly observed. The ritual of *kanyadan* exists and dowry is not a compulsion; it is again a function of the income differential. Divorce is permitted in case a spouse is involved in extra marital and objectionable conduct. The settlement of divorce cases is undertaken in the *biradari panchayat* (community council). Widow remarriage is permissible. A young widow may be married to her deceased husband's younger brother and this practice is locally called as *chadar paona*.

The nuclear family type is common, though there are extended families also. The established interpersonal relations of respect, love and fear of elders exist in the family. Avoidance relationship is observed between the father-in-law and daughter-in-law, a woman and her husband's elder brother. In fact a lady is expected to avoid all elderly males of her in-laws' village. Joking relationship is observed between a girl and her sister's husband; a boy and his elder brother's wife. Conflict and confrontation crop up in a family on account of property disputes, challenge to the authority of elders and marital disputes. Male equigeniture is the rule of inheritance and the eldest son succeeds the authority of father.

Women of this community carry out household chores and collect fuel, in addition to taking part in wage-earning activities. They also participate in social, ritual and religious affairs of the family, but have limited role in the mechanism of social control. Decisions are taken by the male members of the family. Then opinion of women on matters like negotiating marriage of a son or a daughter may be obtained. Majority of them do not contribute to family income. Post-delivery pollution called *sootak* is observed for one and a quarter month. The *mundan* is performed by the Thori at the age of one, three, four or five years. The first-feeding of cereals is observed in the form of a ceremony known as *gurti*.

The main marriage rituals are performed at the bride's residence. Once a match is decided, the ceremony of *rokiya* (provisional engagement) is performed in which the girl's parents give some sweets and a small amount of cash to the boy and his parents and other family members. This is followed by *sagai* (formal betrothal) where again some cash and sweets are given to the boy and his close relatives by the girl's parents. On the marriage day, the *barat* (boys relatives, friends, neighbours and other invitees) goes in a procession to the bride's residence. The *barat* is received by the girl's side and *milni* (ceremonial reception of *barat*) takes place. Then, members of the *barat* are entertained with food. Proper marriage ceremony is performed by the community priest, known as *dadaji* or *purohit*, amidst the chanting of Vedic *mantras* in front of the sacred fire. They take seven *pheras* around the fire. The *barat* then returns to the groom's place where consummation of marriage takes place.

The dead are cremated. On the fourth day, the bones are collected from the cremation ground for immersion. They observe mourning for twelve days. On the twelfth day *rasam pagri*, or *uthala*, takes place where relatives of the bereaved family and friends join in praying for the deceased. After this the family attends to the normal duties.

The members of the community are primarily employed as labourers in agriculture and brick kilns. Those living in the towns are mostly casual labourers or rickshaw pullers. In Bahadurgarh village, near Punjabi University, Patiala, they are working as industrial labourers. Most of them are landless. Their women also work as agricultural labourers in wheat harvesting, paddy transplantation and paddy harvesting. Child labour is also high among them. Very few of them are in white-collar government jobs. Generally their children are illiterate. In the village Daru Kuttan in Patiala district, four boys were found to be matriculates, but they were unemployed.

Earlier, they had the traditional *biradari panchayat*, which was quite effective in settling small disputes. This institution is becoming weak now, though it is still operating in most of the villages. Aheris observe restriction in eating and drinking with the local Scheduled Castes. They worship Rupnath once a year by going to Rajasthan. On this occasion they sacrifice a goat and distribute its meat among their community members. This takes place on the tenth of Magh (around 23 January) every year. They observe most of the local Hindu festivals. These days, their songs, folklores and art-forms have become part of Punjabi culture. They share wells and other water sources, cremation ground and religious shrines with other communities.

Their attitude towards development programmes is one of apathy and ambivalence. All of them live below poverty line. Only a few of those who are very poor, have acquired yellow cards for taking loans in order to start their own business or to purchase cows or buffaloes. Electricity is available in only 50 per cent of their houses. Their fuel sources are wood and cow-dung cakes. A few of them had taken loans for buying rickshaws, *rebris* (carts), setting up tea stalls, etc. They are one of the poorest sections of the Punjabi society.

K. Gopala Iyer
Rakesh Kumar

# AHIR

The term 'Gwala' stands for a Hindu cowherd and shepherd, generally an Ahir. Ibbeston (1916) observes: 'The Ahirs are properly a pastoral caste, their name being derived from the Sanskrit *abhira*, or milkman.' The Ahir, or Gwala, in Punjab migrated from Uttar Pradesh, both during the British period and after Independence. The early migrants are settled in Jalandhar and Ferozepur cantonments and the later migrants are settled in the cities of Jalandhar, Ludhiana and Ferozepur. A large number of them are also seasonal migrants to Punjab as agricultural and industrial workers. Within the homes they still speak in Hindi but with outsiders they fluently converse in Punjabi, particularly the early migrants who have settled here for generations. The male dress includes *kurta* (shirt), *chadra*, *dhoti* and *pagri* (turban). The female wear *salwar*, *kameez* and *dupatta* (long scarf) and a few also wear *sari*.

*Dal* and *roti*, or *chapati*, is their customary food. The main cereals consumed by them are wheat, and maize; commonly used pulses are *moth*, *moong*, *masur* and *urad*. They take seasonal vegetables. Milk, butter, curd, tea and *lassi* are taken in sufficient quantity. Groundnut or mustard oil is used as cooking media. They take alcoholic drinks specially on the occasion of birth of a male child or marriage ceremony in the family. Changes in food habits include increase in the use of vegetables, alcoholic drinks and non-vegetarian food. They smoke *bidi*, cigarettes and a few chew *paan*. The early migrants have less contact with their original homes in Uttar Pradesh; they have developed close relationship with their castemen in Ferozepur and Ambala Cantonments as also with their kindred in Jagadhari and Yamunanagar. Those who have migrated after Independence have strong ties with their caste and kin in their state of origin. The term 'Gwala' or 'Ahir' nowadays is held as derogatory and 'Yadav' is considered to be a more appropriate term. However, the Punjab government has included only the term 'Gwala' in the list of Backward Classes. Hence, for the purpose of availing educational and other facilities they enlist themselves as 'Gwalas'.

According to Ibbetson (1916: 202), 'The Ahirs of the North-West Province have three great sections, the Nandbans of the central *doab*, Jadubans of upper *doab* and the Mathra country and the Gwaliar and the Gwalbans of the lower *doab* at Banaras.'

Among the early migrants, there are three subgroups known as Yadav, Gaderia and Kathuar. They relate themselves with the Nandbansi, Jadubansi, and Gualbansi respectively. Gwala is the occupational term common for all the three. Yadav subgroups consider themselves of superior social status to Kathura and Gaderia (also known as Pal). Each group is strictly endogamous. Further, their marital relationship is confined within their groups in the cantonment and city areas of Ferozepur, Ambala, Ludhiana and Jagadhari. Their caste brethren in Uttar Pradesh consider them to be of lower social status. The post-Independence migrants have maintained close links with their village of origin and their marital relations are preferably made in U.P. only. The Ahirs consider themselves to be of high social status but the members of the high caste groups consider them to be of low status. They are endogamous and observe *got* and village exogamy.

Marriages are arranged by negotiation. The symbols of marriage are vermilion in the hair parting, bangles, ear, nose and finger rings. Dowry is paid by the girl's parents at the time of marriage and the amount varies with the economic condition of the family. Child marriage has been replaced by adult marriage and the age at marriage varies between thirteen years and twenty-five years for both the boys and the girls, the boy being generally three to four years older than the girl. They are patrilocal. Divorce and remarriage is allowed. Reasons for divorce may be adultery, barrenness, maladjustment, cruelty or insanity. Compensation, status of children are decided depending upon the merits of the case and age of the children.

Family types among them are both nuclear and joint. Avoidance relationship is observed by a woman with her father-in-law and husband's elder brother. Joking relationship is maintained between elder brother's wife and husband's younger brother; *jeeja* (sister's husband) and *sali* (wife's sister). Points of conflict in a family may be property, check on the freedom of children and such other issues. Sons equally inherit their father's property, while the eldest son succeeds father's authority. Changes in family include increase in the number of nuclear families. Women carry out household chores with status lower than that of males. Women take part in agriculture, animal husbandry, and social functions. Pre-delivery restrictions are observed, as well as postnatal restrictions for forty days. Naming ceremony is observed in the form of a *chhati* on the eve of the first birthday of the child. Marriage rituals are performed at the bride's residence. A feast for the marriage party and close relatives is offered by the girl's parents. A marriage is solemnized by performing seven *pheras* or circumambulation.

Ahirs cremate their dead and the bones of the dead are immersed in water at Hardwar in the Ganga. They observe ancestor worship. Changes in life cycle rituals include curtailment of rituals. They believe in Hindu religion, and worship all Hindu gods and goddesses and celebrate Holi, Diwali, Dussehra and Lohri festivals. The sacred specialist serving them is from other communities who performs birth, marriage and death rites. Festivals are of socio-economic and religious significance to them. During spare time women engage themselves in knitting. They have some folklores and folk-tales.

The main source of livelihood for the early migrants was trade in milk. They kept herds of milch animals and sold milk to the cantonments. They were given sufficient space to keep large herds of milch animals and also cultivable land to grow fodder and agricultural crops. For the last two decades the cantonments have been expanding and the lands given to them are being taken back at a fast pace. This crisis of space is felt more at Jalandhar Cantonment. As a result, their traditional occupation is shrinking day by day. It is now being reduced to supplementary sources of subsistence. The incidence of illiteracy is still high among them. Among the younger generations one can find acquisition of some education, which has enabled them to switch over to services and other petty jobs. In Jalandhar Cantonment they are demanding allocation of alternate plots of land from the local administration to sustain their livelihood on milch animals.

The early migrants in Ferozepur are more backward, illiterate and less diverse in terms of occupation as compared to their counterparts in Jalandhar Contonment. The post-Independence migrants are engaged in service and other occupations and not dependent on milch animals. Since the mid-1960s one can also notice another stream of migrants among them who are coming as migrant labourers to work both in agriculture and industries in Punjab. Their migration is seasonal in character and they have no contacts with the earlier migrants. They have formed one association, known as Uttar Pradesh Kalyan Parishad, which has within its fold their caste men who are engaged in service. They have also included in this association other castes from U.P. who work in the state of Punjab.

They maintain good relationship with other Punjabi communities. The older generation is still conservative in matters relating to the caste system but the younger generation has a more liberal outwork.

Dowry is not yet a problem among them. According to Ibbetson (1916: 202), 'They are almost all Hindus and are said to trace their origin from Mathra. They are industrious, patient and orderly, and though they are ill spoken of in the proverbs of the countryside, yet that is probably only because the Jat is jealous of them as being even better cultivators than him.'

They follow Hindu Vedic rituals in marriage and other functions. Brahmans are invited for both social and religious functions. Divorce is considered a social stigma. Women have lower status and do not have a prominent role in decision-making. They celebrate male child's birth but not that of a female child. Funeral rites are observed on the eighteenth day and the ashes are immersed at Hardwar. The women on delivering children are not allowed to enter the kitchen for forty days after delivery.

Those who have migrated to Punjab after Independence have been able to knit themselves into a kind of common association. Those who migrated earlier do not have a formal organization but have developed informal ties with their brethren in Jalandhar, Ferozepur, Ludhiana, etc. The impact of development programmes on this community is marginal. There are a couple of prosperous households among them particularly in Jalandhar who have considerable amount of movable and immovable assets. The bulk of this community both at Jalandhar and Ferozepur belongs to lower middle class.

K. Gopala Iyer

# AHLUWALIA

The Ahluwalia community is also known as Walia, a shorter form of Ahluwalia. The term Ahluwalia has been derived from the name of village Ahlu situated near Lahore. It was founded by Sada Singh or Sadhu Singh (Conran and Craik, 1940: 495). The famous Sikh general, Jassa Singh Ahluwalia, was a descendant of Sada Singh. He founded the Kapurthala state of Punjab. All Ahluwalias trace their descents from this state and the Ahlu village. According to Rose the term *kalal* is derived from the word *kulal* or a potter. He further distinguished between Karal and Kalal. As noted by him Karals claimed Rajput ancestry and derived their name from Karauli in Rajasthan. He distinguished the Karals and Kulals on basis of *gots* and pointed out that Kalals were also Hindus, but embraced Sikhism more frequently (Rose, 1919: 438-9). Ibbetson pointed out that Kalal were also called Kalwar and Nebs, the latter name being conjoined to Nabha and Patiala. More important than this is the distinction drawn by Ibbetson between Muslim Kalal called Kak Kezai and Sikh Kalal called Ahluwalia. According to him both of them had abandoned their traditional profession, and were engaged in vegetable trade, etc. (Ibbetson, 1916: 325). The gradual transformation of Kalals into Kak Kezai has been noted in the Gazetteer of Gurdaspur district. The Kak Kezai traced their origin among Pathans. The Ahluwalia put the name of their community as Ahluwalia or their *gots* Pal, Jaspal, etc., after their first names.

The town of Kapurthala is said to have been founded by Rana Kapur, a Rajput immigrant from Jaisalmer, through whom the Ahluwalias claim a connection with the ruling Rajput house of Jaisalmer. The Ahluwalias even now claim their Rajput origins. However, at present the Ahluwalias derive their identity from Jassa Singh Ahluwalia, the founder of Kapurthala state.

The Ahluwalias are widely distributed in Punjab and outside. However, the main concentration of the community is in the districts of Kapurthala, Amritsar and Patiala. Generally, Ahluwalias are settled in urban areas. This is due to their greater involvement in business and commerce. Few Ahluwalias have taken up agriculture as their primary occupation. Outside Punjab, Ahluwalias are spread out as far as Mumbai and Calcutta. Although most Ahluwalias trace their origin to places near Kapurthala, few of them are migrants from districts of Rawalpindi and Sialkot in West Punjab (now in Pakistan). Even within India, movement of the community in urban areas was well pronounced. Many of them left the rural areas only two or three generations earlier.

This community has both Sikhs and Hindus among them. They were baptized by Sardar Jassa Singh Ahluwalia. The Hindus are generally Arya Samaji. Ahluwalias generally use Ahluwalia or Walia, as their name, but also use their *gots* as surnames. Both Hindu and Sikh Ahluwalia intermarry with each other.

Food habits of the Ahluwalias are mixed. They are generally non-vegetarians. Wheat is the main cereal consumed by Ahluwalias though there is a marginal intake of rice as well as maize. These people take all available pulses. In the past, fruits such as *ber* and *amrood* (guava), which were traditionally grown in the area, were eaten but now all available fruits are consumed. Milk is taken by the community. Some members of the community consume liquor. All types of available cooking oils are used. The community claims to consume the best food and feels proud of its excellence in cuisine.

Ahluwalias have *gots* as divisions. Main *gots* of Ahluwalias are Maunik, Jaspal, Jaiswal, Malik, Hoon, Pal, Judge, Sand, Sikand, Lal, Raikhy. Rose had distinguished Karals having fifty-two clans or *gots*, which included Tulsi and Pital in Kapurthala, from those of Karol. Kalal had Bhagar, Bhamral, Bhandari, Bharwathia, Bhukai, Bimbat, Hatyar, Jaj, Janwathia, Ladhathia, Mammak, Paintal and Pal. Now, except for Pal and Jaj, the latter probably represents the present-day Judge, no other *gots* of Ahluwalia and Kalal are common (Rose, 1919: 438-9). The two *gots* of Karal, noted by Rose, are not there among the Ahluwalias. Further, except for Rekhi, even sections of Ahluwalia like Tulsi, Mali, Phul, Sad, and Segal are no more present among Ahluwalia.

Marriage ceremony takes place by *anand karaj* or Vedic rites. Marriage is solemnized by performing *pheras* by the bride and the groom around *Guru Granth Sahib*, or holy fire. The age at marriage has increased in recent years. These days a bride's age is generally twenty; it is around twenty-five years in the case of the groom. Marriages are generally arranged through a *vichola* (mediator). Arranged inter-caste marriages are generally with the Khatri. The Ahluwalias assign much importance to the display of economic status at the time of marriage.

Monogamy is the rule in the community. There is no known practice of marriage by *chadar andazi* (widow remarriage). However, these days widow remarriage is being encouraged. Ahluwalias claim that compulsory or forced dowry system does not exist in the community. Although divorce is accepted, it is generally not much approved. The community encourages women to take up jobs. Few of them claim that women of the community are becoming increasingly Westernized. In spite of this there is an acknowledged domination of males, although females are not completely ignored.

The community shows great flexibility in their birth and death ritual practices. *Namkaran* ceremony for the new-born child is performed by taking a *vak* from *Guru Granth Sahib* or by Vedic rites.

The dead are cremated, while infants are buried. *Bhog* ceremony takes place on the seventh, tenth, or thirteenth day. Remains of the dead are immersed at Kiratpur or Hardwar. A ceremony known as *vada karana* is performed when a very old member of the community passes away. It is marked by celebration and feast for the community and the neighbourhood. The eldest son lights the funeral pyre. They are not very strict about observing death rituals like *shradh*. It is optional and varies from family to family. Women are allowed to accompany the dead body to the cremation ground.

Ahluwalia families are increasingly becoming nuclear. However, the tradition of joint family has not completely withered away. Traditional joking relationship between *jeeja* and *sali* and between *dewar* and *bhabi* still continues. The Ahluwalias share the folk-songs, fairs and festivals with their neighbouring communities. However, these days they celebrate 'Jassa Singh Ahluwalia day' in the month of May every year.

The community has well-organized Ahluwalia *sabhas* (community associations) in all cities of north-west India. The main function of these *sabhas* is to promote solidarity among the members of the community. The *sabhas* celebrate 'Jassa Singh Ahluwalia day', marked by the gathering of the community members and cultural functions. Ahluwalia Sabha brings out a monthly magazine of the community known as *Ahluwalia Patrika*, which mainly carries matrimonial information.

The community is well exposed to modern developments and ideas. Ahluwalias are generally well educated which is true of both men and women. They are favourably inclined to family planning and avail of all modern amenities.

The Ahluwalias have shifted their attention to business of all types. This is in addition to their inclination to serve in armed forces since the days of Jassa Singh Ahluwalia, who is identified as a great warrior as well as agriculturist. They have many renowned personalities among them with many retired and serving generals in the Indian army. There are some famous industrialists, hoteliers, political leaders and cine artistes in the community. In addition, there are a number of lawyers, bank and government officers including IAS officers among them.

The community distinguishes itself from the Jat and others. In their self-perception they do not consider themselves lower than any other community, including Jat, who consider themselves as the highest in the area. This perception is based upon their identification as warriors and agriculturists and also due to the attainment of high educational and economic status today. Some of them even claim to be of higher status than the Jat, because Jats are only agriculturists, while the Ahluwalias are men of agriculture as well as commerce. Rose has described them as a 'class of very varying status' (Rose, 1919: 438-9). According to Ibbetson, they were engaged in the trade of shoes, vegetables, in which many men of 'good caste object to deal'. Further, Ibbetson has noted that the community had risen in social esteem when it abandoned its traditional occupation of distillation and adopted the new name of Ahluwalia (Ibbetson, 1916: 325). However, he noted that these people are known for their enterprise, energy, and obstinacy.

VIRINDER SINGH
K. GOPALA IYER

# ARAIN

The Arain or Rain is a caste of gardeners. The term *bagban*, Persian equivalent of the Hindi word *mali*, means a gardener and is commonly used for the Arain. The Arains are considered to be good cultivators and industrious people.

According to Ibbetson (1916: 194), 'They are almost without exception Musalmans and would appear to be a true Punjab tribe, to have come from the neighbourhood of Multan and to have some affinity with the Kamboh.' Ibbetson further observed, of the Arains of Jalandhar that they are commonly believed to be descended from Kambohs. The Jalandhar Arains have traced their origin from the direction of Hissar. The Jalandhar Arains themselves say they are descended from Rai Chajju of Ujjain, who held the whole of the Sirsa district in Jagir, while the Karnal Arains also trace their origin from Sirsa. On the whole it would appear probable that the Arains originally came from the lower Indus and spread up the five rivers of the Punjab; and that at an early stage in their history a section of them moved up the Ghaggar, perhaps then a permanent river flowing into the Indus, and there gained for themselves a position of some importance. As the Ghaggar dried up and the neighbouring country became more arid they moved into the Yamuna districts and Cis-Satluj tract generally and perhaps spread along the fort of the bitts across the line of movement of their brethren who were moving up the valleys of the larger rivers. Their alleged connection with the Malis is probably based only upon common occupation; but there does seem some reason to think that they may perhaps be akin to the Kamboh, though the difference must be more than one of religion only, as many of the Kambohs are Musalman. According to Rose (1919: 15), 'the nucleus of their caste was probably a body of Hindu Sainis or Kamboh cultivators, who were converted to Islam at an early period. Thus in Jalandhar the Arains say they came from Sirsa, Rasia and Delhi and claim descent from Rai Jaj (grandson of Lau, founder of Lahore) who ruled Sirsa: that they were converted in the twelfth century and migrated to Jalandhar Doab about 300 years ago. But the Bhuttas claim descent from Raja Bhuta, fifth in descent from Raja Karn and say they were forcibly converted to Islam even earlier—by Mahmud of Ghazni—and driven from Uch.'

Most of the members of the Arain community have migrated during Partition to Pakistan. In Punjab the Arains have large concentrations at Malerkotla, Ludhiana and Rahira. The Arains speak Urdu and Punjabi among themselves as well as with members of other communities. They use the Arabic script but some of them who are well educated can write the Roman script also, apart from Devanagari. The males wear shirt, *dhoti* or *lungi*, cap or *pagri*, whereas the females wear *salwar*, *kameez* and *dupatta*.

*Dal* and *roti* is their staple food. During winter, *makki di roti* and *sarson da sag* is also common. However, as they grow vegetables, the consumption of vegetables, both during summer and winter season, is also moderate. They take eggs and meat. The use of rice is more common during festivals and marriage ceremonies. Gram, *moth*, *masur*, *urad* and peas are some of the pulses of their daily use. Mustard and groundnut oil are used as cooking medium. Apart from this *desi ghee* is also used for smearing the *roti*. Tea is taken in the morning and in the afternoon. *Lassi* is preferred with lunch or when available. The Arain do not consume alcoholic drinks. Fruits such as mangoes, oranges and bananas are taken by them seasonally. Among them there is an increase in consumption of vegetables. This may primarily be attributed to the considerable increase in the price of meat. There is slight increase in the use of fruits. However, they prefer *roti* to rice.

Some of the common clans of the Arain community, according to Ibbetson (1916: 196-7), are Multani, Ghalar, Munda, Hansi Bahman, Bheudu, Goher, Balgoria, Galru, Malani, Nain, Chandor, Dhange, Bhatti, Bhuta, Janjun, Dhudhi, Bami Ghalan, Wahand, Qutbshahi, Jatali, and Chechar. Self-perception of the Arain is high. They are aware of the *varna* system but do not recognize their place in it. Though Ibbetson (1916: 196-7) has mentioned twenty-three clans of the Arain, they themselves have denied any such differentiation. As they grow vegetables and for this purpose night soil is generally used as fertilizer, the Brahman, Rajput and even the agricultural communities consider them to be of low status. This observation gathers support from the similiar observation by Ibbetson (1916: 188).

The Arains marry within their own community. According to them they are allowed to marry any person except those who are the offspring of the same mother (*dudh da rista*). Sometimes they avoid marrying their mother's sister's daughter and their father's sister's daughter. Sororate (junior) and levirate (junior) is also permitted. The Arains used to marry off their daughters between ten to fifteen years of age. This was followed by the ceremony of *muklawa* (consummation of marriage), after attainment of adulthood by the spouses. However, at present they marry their children when they attain adulthood, and a marriage is consummated after two days from the marriage ceremony. Marriage is arranged by negotiation either directly or with the help of a *vichola*. Form of marriage is generally monogamy. However the Arain males can go for polygyny also. The married girls wear glass bangles, necklace, earring and nose-ring. The sum of *mehar* is decided by the would-be brides's parents, and the amount varies. The amount of *mehar* may range from thirty-two rupees to one lakh rupees. The girl after the marriage stays with her husband's family.

Divorce among the Arain is allowed with social and religious approval. It is generally discouraged and elders try to settle the matter by negotiations between the spouses. Divorce may result due to maladjustment, barrenness and lack of male child. Compensation is to be given to the wife's parents. The wife can never ask for divorce in this community. A mother of three or four children is usually not pressurized for divorce. However, under very special circumstances, if the divorce is sanctioned, the father keeps the grown-up children with him, while minors are left with the mother till they are grown up and can decide for themselves. Widow and widower remarriage is permitted, if they are of marriageable age. Similar is also true for the male and female divorcees. Earlier, exogamy was observed by this community at the *gotra* level. At present, they avoid the incestuous categories and mother's sister's daughter and father's sister's daughter.

Most of the Arain families are extended, which include the parents, their married sons and unmarried daughters. However, if the sons after their marriage do not get on well with their parents, they may start living separately with their wives and children. Such nuclear families are on the increase.

In an Arain family avoidance relationship is observed between mother-in-law and son-in-law; daughter-in-law and father-in-law; younger brother's wife and husband's elder brother. There are joking relationships among the sister- in-law (*bhabi*) and brother-in-law (*dewar*), between sisters-in-law, i.e. *deorani* and *jathani*; between the co-brothers-in-law, i.e. *sadus*. The various reasons of conflicts and contradiction in a family of the Arain may be related to property, distribution of work, petty issues related to the problems of children, etc.

Only males inherit the property of their father equally, whereas the eldest son succeeds the authority. Nuclear families are slightly on the increase, however extended ones are still prevalent in large numbers.

Among those, who are engaged in growing vegetables or in agriculture, the women also extend a helping hand in agricultural operations and at the same time also look after domestic animals. Among the very poor families, the women and small girls help in the collection of fuel. Most of them have their own source of drinking water or it is available to them within a short distance. Women are considered to be of lower status than men.

Most of the times, for the first delivery, the would-be mother is sent to her parent's house. Certain postnatal restrictions on mother are imposed for forty days. The head of the newborn child is shaved within a period of forty days and if financial condition of the child's parents allows, a function is arranged. Circumcision is performed on the male children when they are around seven to ten years of age. A feast is also arranged for the members of the community. After attainment of puberty, girls start wearing *burqa* (veil), when they go outdoors.

Marriages are arranged by negotiation and marriage rituals are performed at the bride's house. The marriage ceremony is called *nikah* and is performed according to the Islamic tenets. A feast is hosted by the bride's parents for the community members. It is called '*roti*' . The groom's people are served food first, then the relatives of the bride. The bride then goes to her in-laws' and returns to her parents' house alongwith the husband on the next day. This is called *phera pana.* On the next day, she returns to her husband's house. Consummation of marriage is at the bridegroom's residence.

The Arains bury their dead with the head facing the western direction. On the third day, they invite the members of the community and offer prayers. On the tenth or twentieth day, *roti* to the poor, and the clothes to the *faqirs* are offered. The rituals observed by them are becoming more expensive and, as a result, these are gradually being curtailed.

Most of the Arains are engaged in agriculture or as gardeners and hence they depend on land. Land is owned by the individuals and the Arain either work on their own land or as daily labourers or sharecroppers. Most of those who own land have very small plots for agriculture or gardening.

The primary occupation of the Arain community is gardening (*bagbani*). In the past they were also engaged in agriculture. Now, the number of agriculturists among them is not large. Some of the Arains are wage labourers, or are engaged in white-washing houses, welding or soldering, and nickel plating utensils (*bhande kalai karna*), plying bullock carts for carrying load. Some of them engage themselves as *sanji*, or sharecropper, on annual basis. They may get some money as advance also, which is adjusted at the time of harvesting, depending upon the production of the crop. Some landless Arains work either as industrial or agricultural labourers. The children of poor families work to earn wages. Some of these children work as agricultural labourers or in the tea stalls or for the industries. These child labourers are paid in cash.

The Arain have their traditional caste council at an all-India level, which is known as Jamaat-e-Arian and has its head office at Lucknow. The members of the caste council are elected by voice vote. Also, they have *mohalla chaudharies*, the local level leaders, who deal with the local problems. These problems may be related to marriage, engagement, divorce, remarriage, property disputes, etc. Earlier the traditional caste council used to ex-communicate an individual for violation of the decisions of the council. But, at present there is no such punishment.

The community professes Islam. They offer their Friday prayers at the local mosques and also offer prayers at the tomb of Baba Haider Sheikh. The sacred specialist at the mosque may or may not be from the Arain community. He performs various duties related to worship (*namaz*), and other rites associated with birth, circumcision, marriage and death. Id is the main festival. They also join other Muslim communities during Muharram and take out *tazias*.

The women and unmarried girls engage themselves in embroidery in their leisure hours. On the occasions of birth and marriage, the women sing songs. The young boys dance *bhangra* and girls even perform folk-dance on such occasions as a marriage.

The Arains join other Muslim communities on the occasions of birth, marriage and death. It may be mentioned here that they invite persons from other religious groups on occasions such as marriage and exchange greetings with them at Id. No restriction on the part of the Arain on acceptance of water and food from members of other communities belonging to their own religion as well as others has been reported. They share wells and other sources of water with the neighbouring communities and burial grounds with other Muslim groups.

The Arain traditionally join Kamboh, Rajput, Gujjar, Kumhar, Teli and other Muslim communities in celebrating festivals. On occasions of birth, marriage and death these communities extend financial assistance on mutual basis.

Both boys and girls attend the Islamia High School at Malerkotla or at other places. But the girls drop out earlier than the boys. Very few boys join college for higher studies. The primary reason for dropping out is their economic condition. The Wakf Board awards scholarships to meritorious students so that they can continue higher studies. But the number of such scholarships is not large.

They get medical treatment from government hopitals and on certain occasions they also approach the private medical practitioners. The Arain are aware of the family welfare schemes. However, those who adopt family planning methods are few. Generally, women get operated at the nearby government hospitals. The average family has more than three children. They used to get drinking water from wells, but as the water table has now gone lower than 65 feet, they now get water for drinking purposes from handpumps.

They use electricity for domestic purposes. Those, who are not engaged in agriculture but have small-scale industry, use electric power for running their industry. Cow-dung, wood and sometimes cooking coal are used as fuel sources. Apart from natural manure, they also use organic manures and insecticides, but their use is very low. The mothers get immunized before delivery and the children get vaccinated from government hospitals. Those who are economically weaker have been provided with yellow cards to get loans from the banks.

SWARAN SINGH

# ARORA

This business community of Punjab is considered to be somewhat lower but of equal mercantile energy to the Khatri and are called Ror, Rora, or Arora. In the north-western and south-western Punjab, the Arora were commonly known as Kirar, which was considered to be derogatory (Ibbetson, 1916). According to Sir George Campbell (Rose, 1919), the Arora are considered Khatri ethnologically and genetically. Pandit Radha Shastri (1912) maintains that the Arora are Chandrabansi Khatri, descendants of Arjuna. This view is supported by a mythical belief prevalent among the Arora that like the Khatri, they were dispersed by Paras Ram. When persecuted they concealed their caste identity and called themselves as *aur*, meaning 'other', which became Auro or Arora. In addition to this folk etymological explanation of the term Arora, there is another tradition among those Aroras who have migrated from West Pakistan. According to them, they were driven by Paras Ram towards Multan near which they found Arorkot. There are various mythical accounts of the community about its own origin

In the *treta* age there appeared an incarnation of Vishnu, named Paras Ram, to put an end to the tyranny of Raja Sahasar Bahu and to free the Brahmans from the oppression of the Khatris. Paras Ram made twenty-one expeditions against the Khatris, dispersed and ruined them. A number of the Khatris, who on being questioned by Paras Ram did not disclose their caste and said they were *aur* or others, were not molested, but were ordered to migrate to Sind. Hence the name Arora.

Sutji has also written in the *Lhu Suter Puran* or *Origin of the World*, that during his twenty-first expedition against the Khatris, Paras Ram, met a person who, with the members of his family and relatives, was going well armed to the field of battle. Paras Ram found these people defending their own lives and not taking an offensive role. On being questioned by Paras Ram, they said that they were Khatri, and it was not proper for them to attack a Brahman. Paras Ram then said they were *arat*—a Sanskrit word meaning 'devoid of anger'. The term Arora is thus a corruption of the word *arat*. Paras Ram blessed them and allowed them to depart. They went to Sind, founded a city and called it Arorkot (Diwan Jamait Rai, 1913).

Like Khatris, Aroras also form an important segment of the business community in Punjab. In pre-Partition India, their business activity was centred in the north-west countries. Later on, they all shifted to India and became a part of the growing mainstream of life. In this country they have mostly settled along the Grand Trunk Road.

Their mother tongue is Punjabi and they normally use the dialect of that part of Punjab, where they had lived before Partition. They used to speak the local dialect of their native place in inter-personal com-munication. For keeping their accounts they used Landa script and for academic purposes made use of Urdu, Persian and English.

The Aroras are thrifty and industrious, capable of bearing any amount of hardship and privation. The proverb 'when an Arora girds up his loins he makes it two miles to Lahore', seems far from truth. The trade of the country outside the larger alien settlements, is almost entirely in their hands. After Independence, the Aroras have become one of the most industrious community. These people are now leading in professions and services and many are top intellectuals of independent India. They are settled all over the country today.

A few bio-anthropological studies have been conducted on the Aroras. B and O blood groups are more frequent among them. Frequency of secretres (84.72 per cent) outweighs that of non-secretors. All the individuals have been found to belong to Rh +ve type. High incidence of non-tasters (55.55 per cent) has been found among them. A careful study of mean menarcheal age of Arora population indicates that the age among Arora females ranges from 13.74 years to 14.09 years (Biswas, 1967; Ghosh and Kumar, 1973; Ahuja, 1976 and Sharma, 1982). Arora females experienced highest average total pregnancies than other populations of Punjab during their total reproductive life span (Ahuja, 1976).

Keeping in view the frequency of the type and nature of normal eating and drinking patterns, Aroras can be termed as vegetarian and non-drinkers, who occasionally, specially during festivals and cere-monies, consume meat and alcoholic drinks. Their staple food comprises wheat, rice, *dal*, vegetables and milk. Traditionally there was a pattern of two meals a day, but now they are shifting to three meals a day. The guest is treated especially with a sweet dish before meals, wine and non-vegetarian preparations. Now the food habits of the Arora have become region specific, as they are settled all over India, specially in the northern parts. Milk is an important part of their daily diet.

The Aroras, like Khatris, are divided into four territorial groups (Parkash Tandon, 1961). These are: Uttaradis (Northern), Dakhana

(Southern), Dahra (Western) and Sindhi. Following is the available account about the beginning and significance of these divisions among the Aroras of Punjab.

In the year 195 Vikrami (A.D. 138) during the reign of Maharaja Sal Jati, the successor of Raja Sal Wahan, the Aroras of Bhai Pahu Mall Wale living at Multan excommunicated a Khatri, named Bhola Dhawan for his misconduct. Bhola had two nephews, his sister's sons, Dewa Mall and Sewa Mall, Malhotra Khatris by caste. They adhered to their maternal uncle, so they also were excommunicated. Other Khatris also took sides and there was a split between the Aroras and the Khatris. At this time Aroras of Arorkot were an important and wealthy community. Having heard of the dissensions among the Aroras and Khatris of Multan, the Arorkotwalas tried to settle the dispute but failed. They called a meeting of all the Aroras by sending a written invitation at Arorkot on the banks of Indus. The conference was held on the day of Vijaya Dashami in the year 200 Vikrami (October A.D. 143). Four hundred *panches* were among 43,200 Aroras who attended this meeting. Twelve castes of Bhats, twelve castes of artisans, barbers and others were also present. The president Gosain Sidh Bhoj and other Brahmans sat on the east, the Arorbans arranged themselves on the north, south and west. The president divided them into 408 sections giving them names after leaders or after their characteristics or after their occupation, e.g. Mahujas after Mana tail; Manak after Manak tail; Chanwala—those who sold rice.

Having divided them into *al* or sections, Gosain Sidh began to lay down rules for their ceremonies which led to hot discussions. Some wished to introduce reforms, while there were others who kept neutral. No decisions could be arrived at. The meeting was adjourned till the following day. The president asked them to sit in the following order the next day: to the north (*Uttar*) those who wished to maintain old customs; to the south (*Dakhan*) those who wished to introduce reforms; to the west (*Pachham*) those who did not want to any side and remain as neutral. The people, therefore, sat in the above order. The president divided them into three groups: Uttradis—'northerners', Dakhanas—'southerners' and Dahras. It was decided that each group should intermarry within its own subcastes (Diwan Jamait Rai, 1913).

Dakhanas and Dahra intermarry in some parts but not in others. Utradis appears to be endogamous. After examining the various theories regarding the origin of Aroras, Pandit Radha Shastri (1912) maintains that the Aroras are Chandrabansi Khatris, descendants of Arjuna. Though the Aroras belong to the upper echelons of Hindu social system, it has been observed they are not very rigid about the traditional bonds of the caste system. Intercaste and widow remarriage were very common among them even before Independence. Though the original territorial distinction among Aroras is still maintained in a few places, these groups have ceased to be endogamous. There are several cases of intermarriage between the Sonar (goldsmith) and the Arora. As regards the limits of consanguinity, they observe the normal practice of restrictions as are recognized by Punjabi Hindus; but there are slight local modifications. In some places four generations of the mother's side and seven generations of the father's side are not considered for selecting a bride. Marriages in the same family are preferred. The Punjabi Aroras will not allow their girls to marry outside the community, but they have considerably widened their own field in taking wives from other groups.

The girls were usually married earlier between twelve and eighteen years of age, their husbands being older by two to five years. But now with the spread of education the age of marriage has become twenty-plus for both girls and boys. Marriage by exchange is common in Punjabi Aroras. It is termed *matter*, *badli* (exchange), *kano wati* (exchange of sides) or *amna samna* (opposite each other). They have a set of elaborate wedding ceremonies, but the form of marriage remained *pun sat*, i.e. the free gift of a girl in marriage to a suitable man. The girl after marriage ceremonies goes to live with her husband when the couple is given a send-off along with gifts in the form of *daj* (dowry).

Remarriage of widows is common amongst the Arora. The deceased husband's brother has the first claim to marry the widow provided he has no wife living. In fact the widow is free to choose her second husband with the advice and consent of her parents. A period of five to twelve months must generally elapse after the death of the first husband before the second marriage takes place. In most parts the ceremony is very simple and is called *chadar* or *pata paona*. Divorced ladies have also been remarried. Aroras have married casteless Marwari women. There have been instances of their keeping Muslim wives. Among the Aroras monogamy is the social norm. In some cases of childlessness, or to adjust the deceased brother's wife, a second wife is taken.

Aroras being a business community, joint family system has remained most suitable. After marriage a man does not immediately set up a home of his own. He brings his wife to his mother, under whose absolute control, she must remain for a time.

In such a joint family system, behaviour norms are decided by the elder male members with the help of their spouses under the guidance of the eldest couple. These norms are executed under the supervision of the eldest lady of the house with the cooperation of all the members. The behaviour norms are strictly applied to children so that they learn how to behave. Boys and girls are treated with different norms in the joint family. The boys were taught to assume authority, command and responsibility; the girls were considered *praya dhan* 'other's wealth' to be kept faithfully. She is loved and in some families the young unmarried girl is considered a *devi* 'a goddess' and she is regarded that way.

The relationship between mother-in-law and daughter-in-law is a mixture of love-hate-regard type. Now the joint family system is breaking up. Earlier, inheritance in the family used to flow through the male members. But, now the female members of the family have got equal right as far as the inheritance of property is concerned. But this right is seldom exercised.

Life-cycle rituals and ceremonies among the Arora commence with the onset of pregnancy. These are first performed in the second, third or fourth month of pregnancy. The next phase of antenatal rituals starts with the beginning of the seventh month. These rituals are mostly observed during the first pregnancy. The birth of a male child is celebrated by holding feasts and giving gifts to various people in the village and among the relatives. The newborn is breast-fed after ritual washing of the mother's breast. The mother and the newborn child are put to confinement for forty days. This is called *chilla*. The mother takes her first bath on the fifth or seventh or thirteenth day. After this, she is allowed to leave the bed but not the house. After the fortieth day, the mother and the child visit sacred places such as temples. All these practices are followed strictly in case of a male child only. The child is named on the sixth day by an elderly woman or man of the family. The ceremony is called *chhati*. On this day *puja* is performed by the priest. The newborn child is ritually given a *chola*, a dress made from an old cloth on the sixth or seventh day.

To arrange a match for marriage, parents of the boy approach the girl's family. A priest or a *mirasi* is sent to the girl's family after verbal consent of both sides. He consults the horoscopes of the boy and the girl and tries to look for a possible correlation in planets. He, in the presence of family and *biradari* (community) members of the girl's family, is given some sweets and a coconut as a *shagun* (blessing) to be delivered to the boy's side. In the boy's house, the priest, in the presence of family and *biradari* members, presents the same *shagun* to the boy. The assembly offers *wadhai* (congratulations) to the parents and the betrothal is announced. Sweets are distributed and some gifts and offerings are made to the priest. In some families this ceremony is performed in the presence of the girl's father. Both the sides consult Brahman priests for a suitable date of *lagan* (the hour of marriage ceremony), who, in return, are given some *dakhana* (fee).

The bridegroom is given a ceremonial bath, a turban decorated with *sehra* and *kalgi* is tied around his head and he is given a *goti*, a piece of coloured wood and a sword. The *junj* or marriage procession then starts for the house of the bride.

Certain ceremonies are performed at the bride's house before arrival of the *junj*. On entering the bride's house, the bridegroom is given a seat and a glass of milk. Both groom and bride bathe and put on new clothes and ornaments. They are then conducted to the *vedi* or marriage booth. The Brahman conducts the seven *pheras* and the bride's father performs the *kanyadan*. The *junj* is treated with feasts during their stay at the bride's house. The girl is given *daj*. Then the bride is taken to her new house. Some ceremonies are conducted at the boy's house after he brings the bride for the first time. Unless the spouses are minor, consummation takes place the same night.

Death rituals start immediately after the death of an individual and continue throughout the life of coming generations. In some cases the young ones of both sexes are buried and not cremated. A child's corpse is bathed, wrapped in a shroud, carried to the *masaan* (cremation ground) and buried. When an adult is about to die he is placed on the ground with his head to the north. Ganga water is poured into his mouth and a *jot* (lamp) is placed close to his head. A plate containing some grain, sugar-candy and some money is placed in contact with his hand. This is called *jam-ji-thali* and is given to the Brahman.

The corpse is wrapped in a cotton shroud after a bath. The hair of a married woman is washed and plaited and red thread inserted in it. Vermilion is applied to her hair and *surma* is put in her eyes. She is made up as a young bride. The corpse is taken to the *masaan* by the *kandhi*. The eldest son of the deceased performs all the rituals connected with cremation. On the fourth day, *chautha*, the principal mourners go to the *masaan* to collect the bones (*phul chugna*). These are immersed in the Ganga. The mourning lasts ten days. On the tenth day a rite, *kriya* is performed. The sons of the deceased are given *pagries* (turbans) by their relatives and *biradari* as a mark of responsibility. The Brahmin is given on this day a bedsheet, bedding, cooking pots and clothes in the name of the deceased. After that the annual *shradh* is performed.

Traditionally, Aroras had most of their business activities in the north-western part of pre-Partition India. The extent of their trade had varied from a street hawker to an international trader. Now, after Independence, they have no caste-specific economic activity. Still they are famous as traders. Arora can be found active in almost all walks of life from administration to business and industry.

In the past, they used to have a *panchayat* or *mahajan* (community council) consisting of some knowledgeable men. The office-bearers of the *panchayat* then were the president or *mukhi*, his deputy, the *chaudhary* and a paid servant, the *tahlwa*. The offices of *mukhi* and *chaudhary* were hereditary. The eldest son ordinarily succeeded his father to the office of the head of family. The number of *panch* (members) varied from place to place. Where the number of families was small, the head of a rich family was recognized as a *panch*; in a larger area only men of influence and affluence served as members. Each local *panchayat* was self-contained and acted independently, but in dealing with serious breaches of social norms, the elders and *panchayats* of other areas were consulted.

If Hinduism is considered to be a way of life, the Aroras can be described as Hindus. They have been influenced by the reformist movements, active in their region. The foremost impact upon them had been of the Sikh reformist cum religious movement of Guru Nanak Devji. Under the influence of this movement, there has developed a division of Hindu and Sikh Aroras. Still we can find members of both religions in the same family. At the folk level both the Hindu and Sikh Aroras in general observe the traditional Hindu rituals and ceremonies though among the Sikh Arora the enthusiasm is lacking. The development of new socio-religious organizations like the Nirankari, Radhaswami, Advait, Sant Mandals have affected and influenced the Aroras, like other communities of the region. Though some of them are followers of certain sects, in practice they seldom are sectarian. They read Sikh scriptures, and go to *mandir* and *gurdwara*.

There is no community-specific art and culture of the Punjabi Arora. Still, ladies are often well-versed in preparing pickles and such delicacies. They are famous for their *papad*-making and needlework. Their needlework, specially *phulkari* (threadwork in flower-making) and *bag* (thread work depicting garden) has become known all over India. This work is done on *dupattas*, the piece of cloth ladies cover their heads with, *chadran* or bed sheets and chair, sofa or table covers. Menfolk dance at special occasions with coloured sticks in their hands forming a circle. This is called *daka* or *tipari*.

Aroras have experienced the general impact of development programmes like any other neighbouring community. The Punjabi Arora have shown a definite rise in literacy and education, better health and medical care, drinking water and employment facilities after Independence.

SHARDA SIDHU

# BAHURUPIA

In Sanskrit, *bahu* is 'many' and *rup* mean 'form', hence Bahurupia denotes an actor. The Bahurupia visited people in the guises of a pedlar, milkman, or somebody else, and asked for rewards when they passed undetected (Ibbetson, 1916: 236). Now these people have taken up settled agriculture as their primary occupation. It has also been observed by Ibbetson that in some districts a family or a colony of Bahurupia had obtained land and settled down on it and became a caste from a loose occupational group.

The oral tradition of this community is quite obscure and written records are lacking. These people were looked down upon by the upper caste in this area. They, however, want to forget their past. The octogenarians among them hold very strong views on the derogatory reference to them. Now they have a tendency of linking their past with the Rajput origin and point out that their subcastes are similar to those of Rajputs. These subcastes are identified as Rathore, Pawar and Chauhan. They also identify the Rajput *gots* in their caste. For example, they mention that in the Rathore subcaste among them the specific *gots* are Gagrana, Bhanana, Ramane, Sakhane, etc. Among the Pawar subcastes the specific *gots* are Shant, Majhraut, Karnaut, etc.

Rose (1919: 34) states that in the Sialkot district, the Bahurupias claim connection with the rajas of Chittaur and say that they accompanied Akbar in an expedition against the Pathans after which they settled down to cultivation on the banks of the Chenab. Rose also mentions the four Rajput endogamous clans among them as Rathore, Chauhan, Pawar and Sapawat. However, this does not necessarily make them Rajput. One educated Bahurupia contacted the Rajput caste association of Punjab but they (the Rajput) did not consider the Bahurupias as part of them. There has been no marital relationship of this community with the Rajput within the living memory. Further, a scrutiny of the writings on Rajputs could not establish their connection with this caste. The educated Bahurupia was of the opinion that his elders were keen to erase the stigma associated with this community by claiming their Rajput origin. He states that his intensive efforts and search to trace the identity of this community have led him to conclude that neither the written record nor the social practice stand testimony to their Rajput origin.

The octogenarians of this community also give another plea of their higher status origin. Invariably the Bahurupias are Sikhs and the account of Rose (1919: 34) also points out that even a century back the Bahurupias were Sikh. These old person traced their association with Guru Gobind Singh's militant tradition. They establish their identity with the heroic *khalsa* tradition and claim that they are Sikh Rajput. They also pointed out that there are some Bahurupia families, whose members fought for Ranjit Singh's army in Jamraud fort. They take pride in associating themselves with the militant Sikh tradition and their distinct placement as 'warriors' . They also claim that they did not succumb to the Mughal tyranny.

The description of the community by Rose indicates that they were located in the districts of Gurdaspur, Sialkot, Gujarat, Hoshiarpur, Jalandhar, Gujranwala, etc. Today, they can be located in the villages of Kaleejpur (Gurdaspur district), Bhalowal Kulian (Hoshiarpur district), Jagjitpur (near Phagwara), Pilkhani (near Rajpura) and in a few villages of Patiala and Ludhiana districts.

They communicate in local Punjabi dialect and the script used is Gurmukhi. They have mixed food habits. There are both vegetarians and non-vegetarians among them. Wheat, rice, pulses and seasonal vegetables are their staple food. Locally available fruits such as, banana, mango, grape, papaya, guava and apple are consumed by this community intermittently. Cooking medium is vegetable oil. Non-vegetarian diet includes mutton, chicken, fish and eggs. They also consume milk and milk products. Alcoholic drinks are occasionally used during festivals, marriage occasion, etc. These drinks are mainly purchased from the market. They have increased their meat and liquor consumption. They consider themselves superior to the Scheduled Castes but below castes such as Jat, Brahman, etc.

These people are endogamous and their age at marriage ranges from eighteen to twenty years for both boys and girls. Child marriage was practised before Independence. Parents' consent is necessary for marriage. They follow Sikh rituals for performing marriage. Role of mediator also assumes importance in the settlement of marriage. Invariably marriages are solemnized and legitimized by *gurdwara* priests. Monogamy is the rule. The wearing of ring in finger, ear and nose by the ladies as marriage symbol is common. During social occasions these are more strictly observed. Performance of *kanyadan* exists and dowry is given both in cash and kind. Divorce is permissible on grounds of extra marital relations and objectionable conduct. Settlement of divorce cases is undertaken by an informal *panchayat* (caste council). Widow remarriage is permissible. A young widow may be married to her deceased husband's younger brother and this practice is locally called as *chadar paona.*

The extended and nuclear family types are prevalent among the Bahurupia. Respect, love and fear of elders exist in the family. Avoidance relationship is observed between father-in-law and daughter-in-law, while joking relationship is seen between wife's sister and sister's husband; husband's younger brother and elder brother's wife. Conflict and confrontation crops up in a family on account of property disputes, challenge to the authority of elders and marital disputes.

Male equigeniture is the rule of inheritance and all sons equally inherit their father's property. Daughters claim no share and leave that to their brothers. Succession is by the eldest son. There is a decline in extended families and rise in nuclear families.

Women help their menfolk in agricultural operations and various related activities. They participate in animal husbandry and collection of fuel and also partake in social, ritual and religious affairs of the family, but have limited role in the mechanism of social control. All the decisions are taken by the male members of the family. The opinion of women on such matters as negotiating the marriage of a son or a daughter may be obtained. But on all major issues the final decision is taken by the male members. Women do contribute to family income in the form of paddy transplantation, threshing, etc. They earn wages from these.

Post-delivery pollution called *sootak* is observed for one and quarter month. The main marriage rituals are performed at the bride's residence. After a match for marriage is made, a ceremony called *rokiya* is performed in which the girl's parents give some cash to the boy's parents and other family members (e.g. bridegroom's sister, elder brother's wife). This is followed by *sagai* (engagement) before actual marriage, where again cash, sweets, clothes are given to the boy and his close relatives by the girl's parents. On the marriage day, the *barat* (marriage procession consisting of boys relatives, friends, neighbours and other invitees) goes to the bride's residence. The proper marriage ceremony is performed by a *gurdwara* priest around the *Guru Granth Sahib* amongst chanting of hymns by a *granthi*. The *barat* then returns to the groom's place. Consummation of marriage takes place at the groom's residence.

Among the Bahurupia, the dead are cremated and the bones are im-mersed in the holy Ganga at Hardwar and also in Satluj at Kiratpur

Sahib in Roop Nagar district. On the fourth day, the bones are collected from the cremation ground for immersion in water. This is called *phul chugna* (collection of bones). On the seventeenth day, *rasam pagri* takes place, where relatives, members of the community and friends pray for the departed soul. After this, the family attends to the normal duties. The life-cycle rituals are becoming more expensive.

The Bahurupias were often tenants to the dominant Rajput landlords of the area. They also worked as agricultural labourers. Besides, they also made baskets. Rope-making (locally known as *van watna*, mat-weaving and preparation of rope nets was also a part of their traditional occupation, as could be noticed from the description about them by Rose (1919: 34). They continue with these occupations even today. The Bahurupias have also started entering into other occupations as army personnel, school teachers, policemen, clerks, etc. One of the Bahurupias interviewed, who is a school teacher, has imparted medical and engineering education to his sons and daughters. His younger son is a captain in the army. It shows gradual social and occupational mobility taking place in this community.

Earlier, they had their caste *panchayat*. Nowadays either the disputes are referred to statutory village *panchayat* at village level or to the law courts for settlement. The traditional method of solving any dispute through the elders in the family still continues. The major festivals of the Bahurupia are Lohri, Diwali, Dussehra, Holi and Baisakhi. They visit the sacred Sikh shrines at Amritsar and Anandpur Sahib and also visit Vaishno Devi, Jawalaji and Chintpurni. Oral traditions in the form of folk songs, folklore and folk tales are shared with other communities of the region.

They share water resources, cremation ground and religious shrines with other local communities and take part in festivals with them. They serve some local landowners belonging to Rajput and other communities as tenants. Political leadership has emerged at village *panchayat* level.

The Bahurupias' attitude towards development programme is positive and the impact on the community is perceptible. The boys are taking advantage of formal education, not so the girls. Most of the Bahurupias are illiterate.

Facilities of drinking water are available in the form of handpumps. Only few well-off Bahurupia families own television sets. Some of the Bahurupia families have electricity in their houses. The fuel source is cow-dung cakes. Medical teams and social welfare staff often visit their villages for necessary help and check-ups. The facility of fair price shops is available and sugar and kerosene oil are supplied at controlled price. Banking facilities are available and they avail of loans for animal husbandry, rope-making machines and establishing shops.

RAKESH KUMAR

# BAIRAGI

The Bairagi, who are also known as Baregi, which according to Ibbetson (1916: 227) 'is more correctly spelled Vairagi, signifies any one devoid of passion'. But the word is usually applied in the Punjab to a regular order of Vaishnava devotees said to have been founded by Sir Anand, the twelfth disciple of Ramanand. They are divided into several sections, among which may be mentioned the Ramanandi who worship Ram Chandra, the Radhabalabhi, who specially worship Radha the wife of Krishna, the Ramanandi whose chief object of reverence is Salij Ram, and the Ramanuji who adore Mahadeo; though the last two would appear to be Saiva rather than Vaishnava. They for the most part collect in monasteries and are an exceedingly respectable class of *faqirs*, but many of the wandering mendicants also call themselves Bairagis. Their distinct mark is a string of brown crinkled beads.

The cult of Rama and Krishna is called the Bairagis, who trace their origin from Ramanuja. This cult rose to power in north India during the time of Ramanand. The Bairagis have four orders: Ramanandi, Vishnu Swami, Nimanandi and Madhvachari. The Ramanandis are the devotees of Ram Chandra, and Ayodhya is sacred to them. *Trisul* is their insignia which is marked on their foreheads. The Nimanandis are the followers of Krishna and celebrate his birthday. *Bhagawad Gita* is sacred scripture to them. They visit Vrindaban, Mathura and Dwarka as their sacred places (Rose, 1919: 35).

Rose (1919: 37) reports that the Bairagis of one *sampradai* do not marry the members of another *sampradai* and their own *dwara*. The Bairagis do not avoid taking food from another Bairagi, but those who belong to the highest order such as the Brahman Bairagis will take food from Brahman Bairagis only. The Bairagis avoid non-vegetarian food and alcoholic drinks but some of them do take them.

They are vegetarian, use groundnut oil or pure *ghee* as cooking medium. They take milk and milk products. Though alcoholic drinks are prohibited, a few take these on special occasions. Fruits are taken seasonally. No change has taken place in their food habit in recent years. Acording to Rose (1919: 37), 'the connection of the earliest form of Sikhism with the Bairagi doctrine is obscure, but it is clear that it was a close one. The Kalladhari, the ancestor of the Bedi family of Una, was also the predecessor of the Brahman Kalladhari *mahants* of Dharamsal in Una *tahsil*, who are Bairagis, as well as followers of Guru Nanak, whence they are called Vaishnav-Nanak-Panthi.'

Rose (1919: 36), states that the Bairagis can be easily identified as they keep long hair called *jata* and wear coarse loincloths. They generally suffix 'das' to their name. The five rules of the Bairagis are as follows:

their foreheads are marked with *chandan*,
he must wear a rosary of *tulsi*,
he must repeat some *mantra* of Krishna,
he must visit Dwarka,
he must worship Krishna.

Some of these *mahants* are powerful and economically well-off. Some of these Bairagis are also good scholars in the field of Sanskrit.

They are divided into two *gots* Nimanadi and Sukhnandi, and have fifty-two *dwaras*. Marriage between the Kaheri Kanthi and Duhri Kanthi is allowed. They are considered by others to be of high status, while their own perception is also high. Though they are aware of the *varna* system, they do not recognize thier place in the same. It is an endogamous community and exogamy is practised at village and *got* level. Marriages are arranged, when the boys and girls are between twenty to twenty-five years of age, with the help of a *vichola*. The *mangani* (engagement) ceremony is performed with a payment of one rupee by the girl's father to the boy. The marriage is solemnized according to the Hindu tradition of seven *pheras*, which are performed in the morning. *Sindur* and bangles are the symbols of marriage. Dowry, depending upon the financial condition of the girl's parents, is also offered, which includes clothes, utensils, bedding, one bed, *sindur* and make-up box. No ornaments are given in dowry. They are patrilocal. Owing to barrenness or maladjustment, divorce is allowed, though very rarely. Remarriage is also permitted.

There are nuclear and joint families. Property, check on the freedom of youngsters or challenge to the authority of elders may cause conflicts in a family. All the sons equally share the property of their father. It may so happen that the father may give his property to one son only depending upon his wish. The eldest son succeeds the authority of the father. Women have role in agricultural operations, animal husbandry, social functions and rituals. However, the status of women is low. They attend to various household jobs. Postnatal restrictions on a mother are observed and at the same time post-delivery pollution period is observed. *Mundan* ceremony is observed. Thread wearing, that is *janeu* ceremony is observed at the time of marriage. Marriage rituals are observed at the residence of the bridegroom. The bride's parents also offer *roti* (feast) to the groom's people. Marriage is consummated at the groom's residence.

The Bairagis cremate their dead and observe pollution period. After fourteen days of death, prayers are offered and a feast for the members of the community is also arranged. The bones of the dead are immersed in the Ganga at Hardwar. They also worship their ancestors.

The Bairagis are scattered all over the state of Punjab. Those Bairagis who had a normal family life are called *gribastis*. According to *Census of India* (1911: 447), the population of the Bairagis (*gribastis*) was 13,994 individuals including 8,935 males and 5,059 females, who lived as beggars, while 23,985 Bairagis lead a normal married life (*gribasti*) and belonged to the Sanatan Dharma sect and their population was 37,979 individuals which included 22,529 males and 15,450 females.

Bairagis belong to the Hindu religion, but there are a few, who have become Sikh also. The sacred specialist is from their own community. Lohri, Diwali and Dussehra are celebrated by this community. These festivals are of economic, social and religious significance for them. Change of religion has taken place. Crafts such as weaving and embroidery and oral traditions of folk song, folk tale and folklore are reported. They participate in folk dance on special occasions also.

The Jat, Khatri and Rajput traditionally exchange and accept water and food from them. They participate in the festivals and festivities. There are a few in defence services. Political leadership has emerged from this community at village level. Formal education is favoured by them for both boys and girls. They however study upto secondary and primary levels respectively. These children often drop out due to economic or social reasons. The Bairagis take advantage of modern medicare and family planning methods. Drinking water is available to them from wells or handpumps. Most of them are self-employed either in agriculture or animal husbandry. They use electricity, wood or cow-dung cakes for fuel. Irrigation, organic manure, chemical ferilizers, insecticides, midday meal scheme and immunization of children are also availed of. They have ration cards and get sugar and kerosene oil from fair price shops. A few poor families have yellow cards to get loan from the banks. Though the attitude towards saving is favourable. They also depend for loan on moneylenders.

SWARAN SINGH

# BALMIKI

The Balmikis are known as Chuhra and Bhangi in the rural and urban areas respectively. As they are the followers of Bhagwan Valmiki, so they are termed as the Balmikis. Rose (1919: 41), states that there are many synonyms of the Chuhras. The Chamar is perhaps a Chuhra by origin but they work in leather and hence been put in the same category of Chuhra-Chamar like the Mochi-Julaha. As the sweeper he is called Khak-rob or Mehtar; as a worker in leather he is termed Dhed, as a weaver, Megh, or Jallad, i.e. as an executioner. As a tanner the Chuhra is called Khatik and as a breeder of swine the Chuhra is called a Hali. If they change their religion, they are called *Mazhabi* if they become Sikh, and Musali if they embrace Islam.

Ibbetson (1916) included them alongwith the Dhanak and Khatik. According to him, socially they are the lowest of the low; lower perhaps than the nomadic Sansi and the nomadic Nat. According to *Census of India* (1981), they are a Scheduled Caste with total population of 5,32,628 individuals in Punjab, which includes 2,82,877 males and 2,49,751 females, and have their maximum concentration in the districts of Jalandhar, followed by Patiala, Kapurthala and Firozepur, while the districts of Gurdaspur, Amritsar and Bhatinda have comparatively fewer population. Their distribution is very much scattered. A minimum of one family in each village of Punjab may be a better expression of their distribution.

In the towns, they live in separate colonies, but in rural areas they have their houses on the outskirt of the village. In the past, most of the people of this community had *kachcha* (unbaked bricks) houses but owing to better employment opportunities and their hard work, some families now have *pukka* houses; at least the walls of many houses are of burnt bricks. Hygenic conditions of these houses are comparatively better.

They speak Punjabi and Hindi languages. Use of Punjabi among the Chuhra is more frequent in rural areas. Most of the individuals of this community are illiterate. However, those who are educated, use Gurmukhi and Devanagari scripts. Their common dress is shirt, *pyjama*, trousers or *lungi* among the men and *salwar*, *kameez*, *dupatta* or *sari*, blouse, petticoat among women.

Rose (1911: 190), described the food habits of the Chuhras which have undergone a change as they have to bear various pressures of different kinds in the various areas. In this regard the Chuhras were considered superior to the Sansi, who eat jackals and inferior to the Musali who have stopped eating the flesh of animals which died a natural death. Similarly Ibbetson (1914), also mentioned that they keep animals such as pigs and fowls, which is still true.

The food habits of the Balmikis have undergone a tremendous change. They take mutton and pork. Their staple food is *dal* and *roti*. In villages, they collect *dal* or any other vegetable prepared for lunch and *chaptatis* or *rotis* from each house where they serve. The whole family takes this food collected from different households. This practice is no longer prevalent in the towns. Groundnut and mustard oils are mostly used as cooking media. Tea and *lassi* are frequently used. Those who work as agricultural labourers, get *missi roti* prepared from the flour of wheat or maize mixed with gram flour which they take with pickled lemon, chillies or mango with *lassi* or tea as drink. It is considered very nutritious for those engaged in hard labour. Among seasonal fruits, these people have a preferance for mango.

Ibbetson (1914) states that there are several *gots* of the Chuhras and they are scattered all over the state. Most of these *gots* have been claimed to be either of Rajput or Jat origin, i.e. Bohat, Sarwan, Bhatti, Pail-powar, Lute, Jhae, Tengre claim to be of Rajput origin. Gill *got* is of Jat origin.

Most of the Chuhra at the villages level have embraced Sikhism and no longer continue their traditional occupation of removing night soil; they are now known as Mazhabi and occupy a higher position than the Chuhra, who are still continuing their job of scavenging and sweeping houses and streets. The Bhangi in the towns still carry on their traditional occupation and occupy the lowest position in the social hierarchy. In villages people usually defecate in the open, and they do not need anybody for removal of night soil, unless somebody is sick or the females are strictly secluded. The Balmikis are endogamous and divided into different exagamous *gots*. Some of their *gots* are as follows: Gill, Nahar, Sahotra, Bhatti, Sabarwal, Atwal, Khosla, Bali, Chauhan, Kalyan, Thaper, Malhotra, Mattu, Bains, Hans, Tank, Khandyare, Batra, Teji, Mann, Sindhu, Sondhi, Moong and Bagan.

Chuhra, Bhangi or Balmiki come under the Shudra category of the four-fold classification of Hindu caste hierarchy. They perceive themselves of subordinate status and the same view is held about them by the neighbouring communities. Child marriage, which was in practice in the pre-Independance days, is very rare these days.

When the boys and girls attain adulthood their parents start searching for a suitable match for their children. Age at marriage among the boys and girls is around twenty-five years and eighteen years respectively. Marriages are mostly arranged through negotiation. In a Balmiki marriage dowry is paid, the amount of which depends on the financial conditions of the bride's parents. These people are patrilocal. Divorce and remarriage is permitted. Reasons for divorce can be incompatability, lack of male child or barrenness. Marriage symbols include, *chura* (bangles), pink clothes, *bindi*, *sindur*. Ladies of this community have been noted to use the marriage symbols regularly. Husband and wife have equal rights to ask for divorce. However, the incidence of divorce is very rare. The impact of education and better communication have resulted in increase of age at marriage and better economic conditions have resulted in more dowry.

Nuclear family has been reported to be common in the cities, where most of the individuals, both males and females work in the municipal committees as *safaiwalas* (scavengers). However, at the village level, joint families are still common. Sometimes the newly married couples prefer to stay separately resulting in the formation of nuclear families. At present the new generation does not show as much respect to their elders as their elders did in the past. However, affection between the elders and young of the family is still prevalent in many families. Daughters-in-law maintain distance from their fathers-in-law. The custom of *purdah*, i.e. *ghoonghat* (veil) is still prevalent in the villages. The newly married girls even in cities, use *ghoonghat* in the presence of the elders including father-in-law and husband's elder brother. Avoidance relationship is also observed between the mother-in-law and her son-in-law. Joking relationship is maintained between *dewar* and *bharjai*, i.e. husband's younger brother and brother's wife; *nanad* and *bharjai*, i.e. husband's sister and brother's wife; *jeeja* and *sali*, i.e. sister's husband and wife's sister.

The main points of conflict and contradiction in a family are mostly confined to the disputes between the children. Conflict over property is rare among these people, who generally own little or no property. Sometimes, if the freedom of the younger members of the family is restrained, it may also be a cause of conflict. In most of the cases, it is resolved through compromise with the help of elders. Property, if any, is inherited equally by all the children. If the property is not enough for all the children, the sisters may give away their share to the brothers. The eldest son succeeds the father.

Individuals move from villages to cities in search of jobs and some of them settle down in the cities along with their families. This has resulted in the increase of nuclear families at the cost of joint families. Women of this community take part in the household activities, besides working as *safaiwalas* in the government or municipal offices, or in the households and enjoy equal status with their menfolk. The women work in the agricultural fields as casual labourers.

Delivery of the first child takes place at the parents' house of the would-be mother, but there is no such practice for the birth of subsequent children. Postnatal restrictions are observed for forty days. However, some women start going back to normal routine work even after five days of the birth. A ceremony, known as *bahar badhana*, is performed after thirteen days of birth, when mother of the new-born is allowed to come out of seclusion. The naming ceremony is also performed which is known as *jewa*, the future of the child is also deciphered on this occasion.

The Balmikis prefer to marry after attaining adulthood. Child marriage, which was common in the past, specially before Independance, is no more in practice. Marriage is arranged by negotiation with the help of a *vichola*, who arranges the modalities in connection with the marriage. A ceremony, known as *thaka*, is performed before marriage, when a token sum, known as *sagan* (betrothal offering), which may be one rupee and twenty-five paise, or according to the wish of the parents of the girl, is made to the boy and his close relatives. The ceromony of *rokna* is performed after about fifteen days or one month of *thaka*. Three days before the marriage, the ceremony of *batna* is performed. The boy and girl are not allowed to go out during these three days. The main purpose of this confinement is to avoid any accident at the eleventh hour. *Kangana* is tied to the wrist of the boy and girl. This is done by the brother-in-law, i.e. *jeeja*. The bridegroom, his friends and relatives go in procession to the bride's place accompanied by a band with the bridegroom on horseback. Dance specially *bhangra* is performed by the young boys. After the marriage procession arrives at the *barat ghar*, the ceremony of *milni* is performed. The relatives of both sides are introduced to each other. The marriage party is served with breakfast and dinner. The main ceremony, that is *phera*, is performed during 4 a.m. to 7 a.m. Seven such *pheras* are performed. After marriage, the bride goes to stay at the residence of her in-laws.

The Balmikis cremate their dead. Pollution period is observed for thirteen days. The relatives and members of the community are offered feast known as *roti* after the pollution period is over. The dead body, in case of a very old person, is taken out in the form of *babban*, i.e. it is decorated and a band party leads the procession. They immerse the mortal remains of the deceased in the Ganga at Hardwar.

Various rituals from birth till death require a lot of money. On each ceremony or function, the members of the community are offered a feast. Apart from this, there are various rituals which also involve some expenditure. It has been noted that various rituals and functions have become shorter and at the same time expensive.

The Balmiki are considered lowest of the low in the Hindu caste system. Their primary occupation is that of a scavenger. Males and females both do this job. In the cities, the males are employed in the municipality offices as *safaiwalas*, while the females are engaged in the job of removal of night soil also. However in villages they do not touch the night soil, but mainly work as scavenger to remove the cow-dung and prepare cow-dung cakes. This is known as *goha-kuda*. In return they get wheat or maize seasonally according to the number of animals. The males are good labourers and work in the agricultural fields either on yearly or daily wage basis. They also rear pigs and fowls, work as messengers and carry the news of death, marriage, birth from house to house. They get free *roti* with or without *dal* or *sabji* (vegetables) from the houses, where they work. Agriculture labourers get breakfast, lunch, and dinner free. The requirement of cloth is fulfilled by the seasonal purchase from the nearby market on cash or credit. The Balmiki are mostly landless people. However, government has distributed free residential plots among them in villages. A scheme for giving them non-repayable money for construction of houses is also under implementation. Many families have been benefitted by this scheme.

In Ludhiana, most of them work at the municipal corporation and have their union known as Safai Majdoor Federation. There are district-level Balmiki *sabhas* or associations for all the districts of the state. The function of this *sabha* is to attend to all the problems related to their community. There is also a Punjab Pradesh Balmiki Sabha. At the village level, most of the inter and intra-family conflicts are resolved by elderly persons whose verdicts are acceptable to both the parties. Sometimes their problems are also placed before the village *panchayat*. However, various *mohallas* or localities have their own *sabhas* which attend to various matters including small family problems, divorce, remarriage, disputes related to common walls, areas, etc. Most of the conflicts are resolved by discussions. The guilty persons are sometimes warned or asked to pay the penalty.

The Balmiki belong to the Hindu religion. Their main religious place is Ram Tirath at Amritsar. The main festivals are held on the occasion of Kartik Purnima, Kankhal, at Hardwar, Balmiki Ashram, Kurukshetra and Ghati Mahal, Ludhiana. Pargat Din (birthday) of Bhagwan Balmiki, which falls in the month of October every year is also their main festival.

Most of the Balmikis have mud houses. They decorate the walls of their houses attractively, specially during Dussehra. The girls arrange *sangi* and decorate it on the front wall of the house. They worship it during Dussehra for ten days and on the tenth day, they immerse it in the village pond. This tradition is still being maintained both in cities and in villages.

They accept water, *kachcha* and *pukka* food and *sidha* from members of all other communities. However the members of the other communities have some reservations in accepting water and food from them. It may be pointed out that those who are well educated have entirely different response. They have their own source of drinking water. But no such restrictions, as reported in the past regarding the use of wells, tube wells, schools, roads, *panchayat ghar*, religious places, are observed. However, they have their separate cremation ground. They maintain cultivator-labour relationship with other communities at village level. Owing to the job reservation policy of the government and better educational opportunities for them, they are presently holding white-collar jobs in the administration. There are some doctors among them.

Both boys and girls are being encouraged to attend schools and colleges. Some of them also study upto the university level. The number of drop-outs is also significant. There is no restriction on the girls to go to colleges. But sometimes, as they have to support their families, they find it difficult to continue higher education. When they approach the government dispensaries or hospitals, they get free consultation. Apart from this, they make full use of modern family planning methods. Most of the couples prefer three children. In cities, most of the houses have been provided with water through taps. However, in villages, some of them have their own handpumps installed with government loan. Public distribution system is being availed of by them. The government has given yellow cards to help procure cash aids. There is provision for loans, for their own business, from the nationalized banks. They depend on moneylenders and shopkeepers for loan under very special situations. The government has opened various vocational training centres to impart training to the members of various Scheduled Caste communities so that they may earn their livelihood. Reservation policy has helped them to have regular government jobs. Besides, they take loans to establish piggeries. They listen to radio programmes and some families have television sets also. Wood, cow-dung cakes and coal is the main source of fuel used by these people.

SWARAN SINGH

# BANGALI

The Bangali, Sapera, Sapela, Sipado or Jogi are a community of nomadic people, whose main occupation is to play *bin* (gourd pipe) and snake charming. According to Ibbetson (1974) 'In the Punjab . . . none of these people have been returned in our census tables as Bangali by caste, and they are sometimes said to be a Sansi clan and as the word Bangali seems to be applied in some districts to all Kanjars and in others to all *sipados* or snake charmers . . . , that in the Delhi division Bangalis have been included with Sansi. . . . The Bangalis have very probably been included with *jogis* in the returns. There are a vagrant tribe of immigrants from Bangal. They keep dogs and donkeys and exhibit snakes, and have a dialect of their own. . . The name is also applied generally to Muslim jugglers.'

Bangalis have been listed as a Scheduled Caste. According to the *Census of India* (1981), the total population of Bangali in the state of Punjab is 1,600 individuals (846 males and 754 females). They have their maximum concentration in the district of Jalandhar followed by Gurdaspur. They sleep on floor and live in *jhopris* (hutments). It has been reported, when Maharana Pratap was defeated and took shelter in the jungles, these people were his followers and took a vow not to live in *pukka* houses and to sleep on the floor till they regained their lost glory. As they could not win and regain their empire, instead of going back to Rajasthan, they lived in the jungles. They keep donkeys to carry their luggage as they move from place to place in search of food.

As these people lived in forests earlier, they ate what they could hunt or collect and used dogs for hunting. In the thick forest they learnt the art of handling snakes of different types including the cobra. Often these people are seen passing through the streets playing *bin* (gourd pipe) and carrying snakes in their baskets. At present the government is making an attempt to provide them with *pukka* houses. However, in spite of the sincere efforts of the government, some of the elders refuse to live in *pukka* houses. Most of their habitats are on the outskirts of villages. It is said that they take meat of tortoise and jackal and do not feel cold even during the coldest nights of the winter season.

Most of them are illiterate but through their association with the villagers and city-people some have learnt Punjabi language. When they speak with members of their own community, they use a different dialect. Their males wear Rajasthani type of turban, jacket, *dhoti*, shirt, *mundra* (earring), and *mala*. They wear brick-colour clothes when they move out on *phere* (rounds). Their ladies wear *salwar*, *kameez* and *dupatta*.

Wheat is their staple food. Pulses, which are taken often are *moth*, lentil and gram. Consumption of vegetables is less as compared with pulses. Vegetable *ghee* is used as cooking medium. They take alcoholic drinks on special occasions such as marriage. Tea with molasses or sugar is taken frequently. Fruits such as mangoes are taken seasonally. They also take *bhang* on special occasions. There is not much change in their food habits.

Some of their *gots* are Mehra, Chohan, Kira, Aag, and Potry. Marriage between closely related individuals is not allowed. At the time of marriage various *gots* are checked and compared. They practise *got* exogamy. However under very rare cases marriage within the same *got* is permitted.

Their self-perception is low as they take meat of dead animals. At the same time, other communities consider them inferior. They do recognize *varna* system and place themselves in the Shudra category. The Bangali, Dhea and Gandhila intermarry, though all the three communities have different occupation such as snake charming, making winnowing fans and keeping donkeys respectively. It may also be observed that their first preference is community endogamy. The age at marriage for the boys and girls is from eighteen to nineteen years. The parents negotiate a match for marriage. Child marriage which was in practice before Independence has now been replaced by adult marriage. Monogamy is the form of marriage. There are no symbols of marriage for women. However, they may use *sindur* sometimes. At the time of marriage the parents of the girl are supposed to give a dowry to the boy which consists of *padmnag* (king cobra), *sapda manka* (a button-like object which, when applied at the spot of snakebite, can extract the poison), *gidar singi* (jackal husk), *jholi* (side bag to carry articles including snake basket, etc.) and *saral* (python).

After marriage the wife stays with her husband's family. They make their own *tapari* (huts) and keep all the articles of their daily use there. Divorce is permitted among the community. The *panchayat* (community council) decides about the divorce. However, an attempt is always made for an agreement known as *rajinama*. *Panchayat* is constituted of ten to twenty members. The guilty is fined and the amount of fine ranges from one hundred to two hundred rupees. The reason for divorce may be either incompatibility, barrenness, adultery, impotency or insanity. In the case of divorce, compensation is paid to the wife. Husband and wife have equal right to seek divorce. If the divorced couple have small children, they remain with their mother and when grown up they sometimes stay at their father's house. Remarriage of widow and widower is allowed. Marriage rules have not undergone much change.

The Bangali lives in small groups of ten to thirteen families and move in search of food from place to place. The space in a hut is sufficient to accommodate a small family. The newly married couple may have their own hut to live in. The group move as a whole from one place to another. Husband, wife and their unmarried children live together and prepare their food together. Some amount of distance is maintained between a woman and her father-in-law, a man and his mother-in- law, and sister-in-law and elder brother-in-law. Joking relationship is observed between a woman and her younger brother-in-law, a man and his sister-in-law and between co-brothers. The main points of conflict in a family may be petty issues related to fighting of the children or sharing a common space or handpump. On most of the occasions the matter is settled by the women by mutual discussion. The elders very rarely interfere in their affairs. The eldest son enjoys the right of succession; sons and daughters have equal rights in inheriting their father's property, if any. The main function of the women of this community is to look after their households. They are considered to be equal to the males. These women visit neighbouring villages to beg for *atta*. They also graze the goats and asses.

Post-delivery restrictions on mothers have been reported for forty days. On the third day of the birth of a child, the ritual known as *chowke charana* is observed, when the mother and the child are taken outdoor for the first time. *Sehra* is tied to the front door of the hut. *Sehra* is a string made of leaves specially of mango or *jamun*. No naming ceremony is observed. Often it is left to the census takers, *chowkidar* or sometimes the school teacher for giving a suitable name to their child. Marriage rituals are performed at the bride's residence, the major one being seven *pheras* around the four poles erected for the purpose. After completion of marriage ceremony, close relatives and other invitees are entertained with a feast. Consummation of marriage is at groom's residence.

They cremate the dead whose remains are later immersed in water. A funeral feast known as *roti* is hosted for the members of the community any day between thirteen to forty days after death and arrangement is made according to the financial condition of the family. At the time of cremation the head of the dead body is kept in the south and feet in the north direction. Various life cycle rituals have been curtailed as these have become more expensive.

The economy of the Bangali is based on the forest, from where they catch snakes, collect various medicinal plants and herbs. Males of this community are engaged in snake charming and selling indigenous medicines which they prepare from the roots and branches of various wild plants. They treat dental caries, piles and various skin diseases such as leucoderma. They leave their *dera* or huts in the early hours of the day and visit villages and towns to display their snakes, specially the cobra. The Bangali males are expert *bin* players. The females move from house to house in villages or towns to beg. The males sometimes work as daily labourers known as *dihadi jota.* On most occasions the payment of wage is received in cash; however, payment is also received in kind, specially during the harvesting of wheat crop.

The three communities, namely, Bangali, Dhea and Gandila have one *panchayat.* In case of disputes related to divorce, marriage, murder, etc., the members of the *panchayat* or *sabha* discuss the matter and arrive at a decision, which has to be honoured, otherwise the persons who violate the directives of the *panchayat* are outcast. Other offences, which are the subject matter of deliberation of the *panchayat*, include adultery, rape, elopement, and theft. They worship Guru Gorakh Nath and Gugapir at Chapar (district Sangrur) besides snakes. The main functions of their priests are worship, religious teaching, performing birth, marriage and death rites. Festivals have socio-economic and religious significance. There are also some family and community deities which are worshipped. They accept water and food from the members of high castes. However, the latter maintain distance and do not accept food and water from them.

These people move from place to place and generally settle down near the grain market of a town. The Punjab government is arranging for their settlement. Traditionally, they live in huts, but recently a grant of two thousand rupees was being given to them for construction of *pukka* houses. This grant has been recently raised to five thousand rupees. This is non refundable grant. In Dugri, one of their settlements, there are eight *pukka* houses and sixteen huts. The government has also arranged for one handpump, while they have four handpumps of their own. They have their own cremation ground. But the religious shrine at Chapar is being shared by them with members of other communities. As they are still in a nomadic state, they do not take significant part in the traditional festivals and festivities and do not have modern inter-community linkages.

In spite of sincere attempts by the state government for their settlement at Dugri (near Ludhiana town), they have not yet started sending their wards to the nearby school. They do not consult doctors at the time of illness as they are well-versed in indigenous health practices. They prepare medicines from the roots and tubers of different plants for treatment of different diseases. They not only treat themselves, but also extend their treatment to other communities. Handpumps are the main source of drinking water for them. They may deploy themselves as daily labourers. Cow-dung and firewood are the main sources of fuel. Whatever they earn, they keep a fraction of it for their further use. They help each other at the time of economic crisis.

SWARAN SINGH

# BANIA (AGGARWAL)

The Bania call themselves Aggarwal and comprise a subsection of Vaishya division of Manu's four-fold *varna* classification (Lakshmanna, 1973). Some preferred to affix their names to titles such as Gupta, Dalmia, Modi, Singhania, Sriram and Bajaj. The people of other communities refer to them by titles such as 'Bania', 'Sahukar', 'Lala', 'Seth' or 'Kirar' and view them as moneyed people as they have originally been the bankers and moneylenders to other communities, particularly the agricultural classes. Bania is a term derived from *vanik*, meaning a trader, as the community has been traditionally engaged mainly in trade and commerce. The origin of the Bania community of Punjab may be traced back to Maharaja Agarsen of Agarsen state, who organized a component of the Vaish community into eighteen *gots*. The *Mahabharata* and Buddhist and Jain literature, are the chief sources of information about them. The Agarsen state comprised Fatehpur, Sikar, Jhunjhunu, Nawalagarh, a portion of Rajasthan in west; Mahendragarh, Hissar (now in Haryana) in the south; Punjab in the north and the territory upto Agra in the east. Agroha which is in ruins now and forms a part of Hissar district was its capital. Until two or three decades before Independence, majority of them lived in the villages of undivided Punjab. They carried on flourishing business there and exercised complete economic domination over the majority of other communities. Although vast majority of them restrict themselves to the *mandis* and business centres in cities and towns of Punjab and some nearby states like Rajasthan, Uttar Pradesh and Delhi, quite a few migrated to far off places and are today found in varying numbers in almost every state of India especially Madhya Pradesh, Maharashtra, Orissa, Assam and West Bengal.

They speak Punjabi language. Although there may be some regional variation in the dialects of the language spoken at home in case of some sections of the community which migrated to different parts of India, their mother tongue invariably remains Punjabi. The traditional dress of the Bania males consists of a *dhoti*, *kurta* and cap. But most of the educated men today wear the Western dress, while the middle-class people generally wear *kurta* and *pyjama*. The women wear *jamper* and *salwar*. However, *saree* has also become quite popular among the Bania women today. Their population according to the census reports of 1881 was 3,64,355 (Ibbetson, 1916) while that estimated in 1973 is about one crore (Gupta, 1973).

Only few bioanthropological studies have been conducted on them. The males weigh 54.5 kg on an average with a height of 168.7 cm. Similarly average weight and height among Bania females measure 52.6 kg and 150.9 cm respectively. Dermatoglythric traits show average frequencies of whorls, loops and arches as 39, 56 and 5 per cent respectively among the male, whereas among female frequencies are 31.7, 55.8 and 12.5 respectively. Serological investigations (Gupta, 1972) revealed a high percentage of A phenotype (42.2 per cent) among (33.3 per cent) women while in men B genotype is higher (33.3 per cent) than A phenotype. Similarly Rh (D) is preponderant (above 90 per cent) blood group among this community.

They are strictly vegetarian. It has been only a few decades since a few urban males have started taking eggs and sometimes meat. The staple food of the community is *chapati* made of wheat flour. Their routine diet consists of curd and *chapati* with a glass of milk or *lassi* at breakfast, *chapati* and a vegetable at lunch, *dal-roti* at dinner and another glass of milk before going to bed. Sometimes rice replaces half of the *chapatis* at lunch and dinner. Most commonly used pulse is *mungi dal.* All types of seasonal vegetables and fruits are consumed by the community. The cooking medium is vegetable oil, while the affluent ones have been using *desi ghee* for cooking. The use of garlic and onions is also restricted only to a few families. Traditionally majority of elderly males used to smoke loose tobacco in *hookah* which is fast disappearing; a few males have taken to cigarette smoking.

It is sometimes said that the Bania is not a true caste, but merely an occupational term equivalent to 'shopkeepers', and that the great divisions of Banias—the Aggarwal (most numerous, more than 93 per cent), Oswal (1.5 per cent), Mahesri (1.5 per cent) and Saralia (3 per cent), and unspecified (1 per cent), really occupy the position of castes (Ibbetson, 1916). This is in the sense true as the above sub-divisions do not intermarry, and possibly represent stocks of different origin and if caste is used in the same sense as tribe, these sections are separate communities. But if one considers the *varna* classification, all the Banias have Vaishya descent, which is extremely wider classification dividing all Hindus only into four divisions made up of numerous endogamous groups or sub-castes in this sense.

They are divided into the *gots* of Garg, Goyal, Bansal, Singhal (Singal or Singla), Mittal, Jindal (Jittal), Kansal, Mansal, Mangla, Tayal, Tingal,

Bindal, Dheran, Eren (Aeran), Kuffal, Mudgil (Modgil), Kuchlas and Gond or Gharan (referred to as half *got*). The Aggarwals are an endogāmous group but are exogamous at the *got* level. Consanguinity is strictly prohibited. Since Garg and Goyal *got* are abundant (it is said that Garg and Goyal are one half and the rest make up the other half), so intra-*got* marriages in these cases, and otherwise, are not resented by the community, especially keeping in view the new values in the choice of a spouse.

Girls' age generally ranges from nineteen to twenty-four years, while boys' range from twenty to twenty-seven years at the time of marriage. Earlier barbers, or *pandits*, acted as go-between in arranging marriages, a function ideally suited to their profession because each one of them had *jajmani* dealings with a number of families and were also connected by networks between themselves. Traditionally, the marriage ceremonies are divided into four major parts—*rokna*, *god bharna*, *lagan* and *byah*. In *rokna* the bride's side finalises the matrimonial alliance by giving a symbolic cash gift of one rupee, fifty-one or one hundred and one rupees to the boy. *God bharna* is the reverse of *rokna* ceremony in which groom's family brings gifts such as a *lehnga* and a *choli* besides some gold ornaments for the bride. In *lagan*, the priest reads the names of the individuals getting married, their respective relatives, then the time and date is fixed for actual *byah* (marriage). Finally actual *byah* takes place. On this day, the *barat* is taken by the groom's people to the bride's house for the proper marriage ceremony which is a gala occasion.

The custom of paying dowry an Aggarwal Bania marriage is an important aspect. The dowry consists of gold ornaments, cash and household articles such as television, refrigerator, sofa sets, dinning table, double bed and scooter or car, etc. A wide variation occurs in the value of dowry provided by the girl's parents depending upon the economic status of the boy's family and education level of the boy, and may range from five thousand rupees in the case of a very poor family to two lakh rupees, or even more, in the case of a rich boy or an IAS officer or a doctor. The residence after marriage of a girl is her in-laws' house. There is no provision for divorce and therefore, it is not allowed. In the event of death of wife, the widower may remarry; preference goes to marrying the wife's younger sister, if possible.

Joint family system is the most prevalent form of family and a large number of relatives share a common household, the eldest male being its *karta* or the man in command. However, a considerable number of them live in separate houses, mainly due to their different places of work. Majority of the rituals are to be performed by the female folk in the family.

Interpersonal relations in a family form a good network. A son's birth, especially of the first one, is an occasion for great rejoicing in the family. After the death of father, sons take on their father's status by assuming his social and ritual duties as well as his property. Inter-family relations are very cordial. In case of disputes, *bari* (supreme) caste *panchayat* settles issues. Use of violence to settle disputes is completely prohibited.

Traditionally, women did not have the right over the ancestral property; they were given secondary status compared with their male counterparts in all walks of life. They participate in all the social, ritual and religious activities of the family but do not have any control over money or family assets except some personal ornaments. Women are exceptionally devoted to their husbands and take great pains to ensure their happiness and comfort. The males consult their wives before taking any policy decision in all walks of life. Although the final decision lies with the husbands, they give great consideration to the suggestions made by their wives. Women carry on domestic chores, such as cooking, cleaning utensils and the house and looking after the children.

Most Bania women move to their natal home for deliveries, especially of the first child, either during the seventh month or the ninth month of pregnancy. Six days after the birth of a son, a ceremony, called *chhati-pujan* (sixth day worship) is performed. Another ceremony takes place after forty days of birth following *jalwa pujan* (end of confinement of mother) before the mother takes up household duties. The naming ceremony is performed by a *pandit*; the baby is held in the father's lap and the mother sits beside him. A name is chosen by elders, preferably beginning with a particular alphabet best suited to the child according to his horoscope. *Mundan* ceremony is performed on the first, second or fifth birthday in case of a boy child only. This involves a ritual shaving of the boy's head by *jajmani* barber and a *puja* is performed by a *pandit*. Appropriately, the boy wears a turban and clothes presented by his *mama* (mother's brother). Most families have an ancestral place (reckoned in the male line) at which the *mundan* ceremony is performed—a particular temple or well in a village. For the girl, the corresponding ceremony is ear-piercing.

The death ceremony is called *aparakriya* or *kriyakaram*. The dead is given a bath and carried on the *arthi* (where the dead body is decorated and placed on a wooden ladder) by his sons, relatives and close friends on shoulders to the *sive* (crematorium) where the dead is cremated in a pyre lit by the eldest son. Next morning, the remaining ashes are collected and carried to the Ganga preferably at Hardwar where the death is recorded by a *khandani purohit* (family priest). On the death of father, all the sons used to shave their heads and their beards and moustache but now this is done only by the eldest son. Normal life is suspended during the period of mourning. The men do not shave nor do they go to work. The fourth day of mourning is *uthavani*, when all those connected in social life with the deceased come and sit in silence in the memory of the deceased for about half an hour. A ritual on the seventeenth day marks the beginning of normal life and a new status to the eldest male member in the family. The *pandit* performs a ceremony during which turbans are worn by the sons who had shaved their heads. The turbans are presented to them by their *mama*. The *pandits* are fed, given clothes and utensils.

The main economic resource of the community is trade and business. This involves purchase of goods, at a lower price and their sale at the highest possible price in order to make profit. They trade in all items except leather goods. The community lays stress on the accumulation of wealth through savings. Only a very few of them work as servants to the big business houses and they receive payment in cash. Recently, quite a considerable number of the community individuals have taken to other intellectual professions. Consequently, there are some doctors, engineers, teachers, scientists and philosophers in the community.

Traditionally, they had an effective and powerful organization for social control. At the apex, there was the Vaishya Bisa Aggarwal or Bania Bari Panchayat, followed by the local level *panchayats* and finally, the individual households. Any individual who, by his actions, brought down the status of the community had to be strictly dealt with. The *panchayat* had authority in intercaste matters, in matters that concerned all caste men in general. The *panchayat* was backed by both religious and political authority. A person punished by the caste *panchayat* could not share the *hookah* with his caste men. The next stage in the sanctions was *hookah-pani* stopped. These decisions were reversible. The decisions of the *panchayat* were binding on everyone. The *panchayats* were powerful and could fine, reprimand individuals as well as set in motion a social boycott or excommunication which would even alienate members of one's own household, except a person's wife and minor children. An important activity of the *bari panchayat* included giving of sewing machines to poor women and getting poor girls of the community married by collecting funds from the rich. However, business affairs of the community were completely out of its purview. Today, the *panchayat* has lost its teeth. It can pass resolutions, but cannot enforce them. Now, its strength is confined to persuasion only. People can openly flout *panchayat* laws and only moral pressure can be brought upon some to conform. The *hookah* has completely disappeared from the scene and has been replaced by cigarettes. *Panchayat* meetings have been reduced to about once in two or three months. In the past twenty years *bari panchayat* has passed many resolutions for social reforms including prohibition of polygyny, permission for remarriage of young widows, ban on dowry display and stopping the playing of English-style music at marriages. But violation of these is common occurrence.

The Aggarwal Banias consider Brahmans their religious *gurus*. They accept them as priests in temples, go-between in marriages and leaders in prescribing and conducting rituals. *Tirth yatra* (journey to sacred centres) is a holy tradition. Kashi (Varanasi) is the most celebrated holy place and they consider it as a city of *moksha* (salvation). They visit Hardwar with their families for a dip in the Ganga and would not normally miss such religious fairs as Kumbh *mela*, solar eclipse and Ardha Kumbh *mela* at Kurukshetra and the annual gathering at Garhmukteshwar in Uttar Pradesh. Those who succeed in completing the pilgrimage of the four religious centres, *dhams*, namely Badrinath, Rameshwaram, Jagannath and Dwarkapuri, regard themselves as extremely fortunate. They celebrate their festivals according to the lunar calendar; festivals such as Janamashtami or Krishna Jyanti, Ganesh Chaturthi, the Ramanavami and Navaratri or Dussehra. Diwali is one of the most important religious festivals when every house is beautifully decorated with lights symbolizing the reception of Rama, Lakshman and Sita on their return from *banvas* (exile). Now, these religious ceremonies have been reduced to one tenth or so and are observed with less enthusiasm.

They have not specialized in any plastic or graphic art or craft. Their oral traditions are religious songs such as *bhajans*, *aartis* and songs sung by the ladies, mostly during marriage ceremonies. The musical instrument used with these songs is *dholak*. The *bhajans* are group recitals in temples and religious ceremonies at home. The majority of marriage ceremonies are accomplished by reciting *dohas*—small poems taunting the boy being married and his relatives by his female in-laws especially the sisters-in-law causing laughter among the ladies.

Aggarwal Banias keep social relations with majority of the neighbouring communities except the Scheduled Castes. They are closely associated to Brahmans and barbers by a system of *jajmani*. The washermen and scavengers are paid for services rendered by them. Making payments in cash and kind both to the *pandits* for performing religious and matrimonial rituals were considered a great '*punh*' resulting in salvation. They consider themselves equal to all other Vaishya communities such as Marwari, Saralias, Maheshwari, Oswal, Jaiswal, Poswal and Khandelwal. The community shares its religious shrines, cremation ground with other Hindu communities. They are linked to agricultural communities by way of their moneylending activity and by acting as commission agents and stockists of farm produce. The farmers approach the Banias (*sahukars*) for loans at the time of major household expenditures such as marriage, purchase of land, or cattle.

The children of this community go for formal education. A large number of male children go to colleges and universities. The parents prefer to train their sons to become doctors, engineers, professors, gazetted and administrative officers. They make best use of modern medicare system and have a favourable attitude towards family planning. However only a few have undergone sterilization after three to four children. Their water sources are handpumps or municipal tube wells. Some of the members of the community have established large and small scale industries and many have built residential accommodation availing of government loans. Majority of the Banias are getting their ration through public distribution system. The community is known for its regular savings from the income. The savings are further invested for multiplying it through lending on heavy rate of interest, to farmers or by purchasing gold for emergency securities.

An important observation concerning the community is that a Bania Aggarwal businessman can be depended upon to stand by the transactions struck with him even orally, inspite of any adverse price fluctuations. His anxiety to promote and safeguard his business is, however, often mistaken for selfishness or greed. He has strong family bonds and takes meticulous care to cater to the needs and requirements of every member of his family. A serious drawback of the community is that it is disunited, torn asunder by rivalries and jealousies. The community is very economical in routine family expenditure, but the lavish expenditure incurred on marriages and for building an ornate house is considered prestigious by the entire community. A popular saying goes: *Baniya ki kamai, byah aur makan ne khai* (Bania's earnings are consumed by marriage and house).

D.K. KANSAL

# BARAR

The Barar, Burar and Berar are recognized as Scheduled Castes in Punjab. They are an occupational group engaged in making *kanghi* (comb), which are used by the weavers. According to Rose (1919: 64-5) 'the Barar is a low caste given to begging and roguery. In Jalandhar the Barars make *chhaj* (winnowing fans), *chhaura* (baskets and sieves) of reed. They also hunt with dogs. . . . "The Barars believe in Lal Beg. . . . Some of the castes are vagrant and form a link between the Sansi and Chuhras." This no longer seems to be true.'

According to *Census of India* (1911: 448), 'the total population of the Barar is 6,119 which includes 3,300 males and 2,819 females. The Barars (Dhai), who are chiefly Hindus, are distributed in the Ambala, Karnal, Kangra, Hoshiarpur, Jalandhar, Lahore, Amritsar, and Gurdaspur districts and the states of Nahan, Simla and Patiala. They are basket-makers and bamboo workers and belong to the low castes of the hills'. The Barars of Banga (district Hoshiarpur) migrated from the district of Kangra (Himachal Pradesh) about one hundred and fifty years ago or six generations back. The main reason of migration by the Barar community from Himachal Pradesh to the plains areas of Punjab was lack of business prospects in the hilly areas due to modernization of textile industry and the shifting from handlooms to powerlooms; and the business prospects of the Barar community started declining day by day.

The total population of the Barar in Punjab, according to *Census of India* (1981) is 4,761 individuals, which includes 2,562 males and 2,199 females. Hoshiarpur district has the maximum concentration with 574 individuals. In this district their concetration is found at Singriwal, Baria and Saila Khurd. In the district of Jalandhar they are found at Adampur and Nawanshahr (Kalam Road).

They speak Pahari and Punjabi. Most of the individuals interviewed were illiterate, hence they were not in a position to specify the script used. The Pahari dialect is used while communicating with the individuals of its own community and Punjabi language for communicating with others. The men wear shirt, *dhoti* or *pyjama*, while their women wear *salwar*, *kameez* and *dupatta*.

Rice is their staple food. They also take wheat and maize or whatever cereal is available. When they get an opportunity they take non-vegetarian food. There is no restriction on the women for taking non-vegetarian food. The cooking medium is mustard or groundnut oil. Men take alcoholic drinks occasionally, specially on the birth of a male child or during a marriage ceremony.

The Barars are endogamous and have the following *gots*: Kalsi, Heer, Chandle, Cheemar, Ghai, Chular, Doom and Dadama. They are aware of the *varna* system, recognize it, and place themselves under the Shudra category. In Banga where the Barars were contacted, the members of other communities consider them to be of low status.

The marriage between the individuals of the same *got* is not allowed. Age at marriage is eighteen years for girls and twenty years for boys. In pre-Independence times there used to be child marriage but now it is no longer in practice. Marriage is arranged by the parents of the boy and the girl by negtiotion. The form of marriage is monogamy. The girls after marriage put vermilion in the hair parting. They also use bangles, *bindi* and ear and nose ring. The dowry includes a cot, *peti* (big wooden or a steel trunk), few gold ornaments, utensils and clothes for the girl and the boy, and close relatives of the boy. After marriage, the girl comes and stays with parents of her husband. Among the Barars, desertion, separation, divorce and remarriage are not allowed.

Joint family has been found to be the most common among Barars. Such a family includes parents, married brothers and their children and unmarried sisters. Avoidance relationship is maintained between a man and his mother-in-law, a woman and her father-in-law and elder brother-in-law. Joking relationships is observed by a man with his wife's sister, with his elder brother's wife, and with his co-brothers. Differences over small issues sometimes lead to heated exchange between the ladies, which are resolved by mutual discussions. These small issues include the flow of water from the bathroom or kitchen, direction of smoke emanated from the kitchen, quarrel between the children, etc.

The Barars have small *kachcha* houses. Sons and daughters have equal share in the inherited property of their parents, but the girls prefer to maintain good relations with their brothers after the death of their father and for the sake of this, they forego whatever is due to them from the property of their father. Eldest son is entitled for succession.

The main functions of women in the family apart from bringing up children, is to attend to various household activities, which include col-lection of fuel, bringing drinking water from nearby taps or handpumps, and cooking food. The girls before marriage help their mothers in various household activities and thus get training for doing similar jobs after their marriage in their in-laws' house.

Pre-delivery restrictions are observed only during the last stage of pregnancy. Postnatal restrictions on the mother are observed for forty days. But as the Barar are an economically poor community, it is not possible for women to confine themselves for such a long period. When they find it convenient and feel fit the mother of the newborn starts attending to the light jobs in the household, but abstains from doing heavy work. The midwife (*dai*) ties a black thread with copper coins and beads or *taragadi* around the waist of a male child. The midwife gets clothes, grain and some money as *dan* (gift). They also offer feast known as *roti* to the members of the community. Drinks are also served on this occasion. The *mundan* or tonsure ceremony can be performed at any stage.

The boy and the girl are engaged through negotiation by their parents and the ceremony of *kurmai* (engagement) is performed with payment of one rupee to the boy by the girl's father. After a period of about two years the marriage is arranged. Marriage rituals are performed in a *mandap* at the bride's residence. The performance of seven *pheras* solemnizes the marriage ceremony, and it is generally performed in the early hours of the day. The feast known as *roti* is offered to the guests and the members of the Barar community. The consummation of marriage is at the bridegroom's residence. The death ceremony is observed after sixteen days of cremation. A ceremony known as *kujia bharna* (to fill small earthen pots with water) is also performed. There are sixteen *kujias* (including *darbio* and *duna*). This period is con-sidered as a pollution period. The life-cycle rituals among the Barar are being curtailed because these are becoming more expensive.

The primary occupation of the Barar continues to be making combs for weavers. The raw material, the reed, is collected from tall grass that grow on river banks or on the sides of roads. They are economically very poor. There is very little demand of the *kanghis* made by them. This has compelled many of them to work as agricultural labourers.

The Barars have their own caste *panchayat*. The *pradhan* of the caste *panchayat* is always nominated. He should be an intelligent person. The caste *panchayat*, apart from *pradhan* includes four or five members. The main function of the caste *panchayat* is to have social control over the community. Punishment is not considered to be good thing among the Barar. Instead, the loss is to be compensated. Social boycott is also one of the punishments. The guilty is sometimes asked to stay in a well as a form of punishment. Cash fines are very rare.

The Barars worship Baba Balak Nath and other gods and goddesses. They are followers of Hindu religion, though they visit Sikh shrines also. They celebrate the birthday of Maharishi Balmiki. According to Ibbetson (1919), 'He is not a scavenger by occupation, though he is said to worship Lal Beg, the Chura deity.' The main festivals celebrated by them are Diwali, Dussehra, Holi and also the Guruparab. Sacred specialists serving them are from other communities and their role is to worship, perform birth rites, marriage ceremonies and death rites.

Their festivals are of social and religious significance for them. Some of the families have embraced Sikhism.

The Barars accept water, *kachcha*, *pukka* and *sidha* food from other communities. However, the high caste communities do not accept food and water from them. They have their own water sources and do not share the same with other communities. Similarly, cremation ground is not shared. They have free access to the various religious places. They participate in the traditional festivals and festivities and maintain certain patron-client relations with other communities. The Barars have few teachers and some persons engaged in government services. Education is favoured for both boys and girls but they drop out from schools due to economic reasons. There are primary health centres wherefrom they get medical treatment when needed. Attitude towards family planning is favourable; and they prefer to have three children. Couples sometimes use modern methods of family planning. Handpump is the source of drinking water for them, and these are situated within the locality. Some of the families have radio. Most families cannot afford electric connections, but few enjoy this facility. Main source of fuel is firewood, cow-dung or sawdust. Immunization programmes for infants are available. Government has given them the facility of yellow cards.

SWARAN SINGH

# BATWAL

The Batwals trace their origin from a place called Batmalu, in Srinagar. The same place is know as Batbal in Jammu, and thus the Batwal came to be known after this place. The term Batbal, was modified later on to Batwal in the lower ranges and in the plains of Punjab. The Batwals are also termed Batware. They used to act as village watchmen. As the term 'boundary' is rendered as *bat*, it is believed by some that the community derived its name from the occupation of 'safeguarding the boundary'. According to Ibbetson (1916: 332) 'the Barawala and Batwala terms are used to express the same thing, the former being more commonly used in the lower hills and the later in the mountain range of Kangra'. This observation is valid even today. However, his observation that Lahbar or Balahar of the plains correspond very closely to Barwala and Batwal and denote the village watchman or messenger is not valid now. As messengers, the Batwal used to assemble people for *begar* (forced labour) and they were also called Kirawak or Kirauk (ibid.). However, at present the term Haukara is used instead of Kirawak or Kirauk. The Batwals are also referred to as Barwal. Ibbetson was of the view that this latter term has been derived from Baharwalas, meaning outsiders. However, in view of the fact that not only the Batwal, but also other Scheduled Caste groups, dwelt in the outskirts of villages, Ibbeston's view does not sound logical. The Batwal are Hindu by religion. Those who lived in villages, dominated by the Muslim community, embraced Islam and were termed as Barwal. This has also been specified by Ibbetson (ibid). It may further be mentiond that the Batwal are agriculturists whereas the Barwal are weavers.

The Batwals believe that when Alexander, the Greek king, attacked Bharatpur (in Rajasthan), the Batwals, along with other communities, fled into the jungles and dispersed in all directions. They settled down, wherever they found a suitable place. A group of them went to Jammu, another went to Sialkot, Layalpur and further west; still another group went in eastern and southern directions. The Batwal adopted the language and customs of the local inhabitants.

The Batwals have been listed as one of the Scheduled Castes and according to *Census of India* (1981), the population of the Batwals in Punjab is 9,367 individuals, which includes 4,989 males and 4,378 females. Gurdaspur district has maximum concentration followed by Hoshiarpur district.

The Batwals speak Punjabi language among themselves as well as with members of other communites. They can also speak Hindi. Those who are literate use Gurmukhi script.

The usual dress of the Batwals consists of *salwar*, *kameez* and *dupatta* (long scarf) for women, while men wear *kurta*, *dhoti*, *pyjama* or trousers. The dress and ornaments worn by the Batwal community have changed. In the past, men used to wear *lancha* or *chadra*, with a border, *kameez* and *pagri*. The use of such clothes has become occasional now. The dress of the women was *kurti* (shirt), *ghagri* (skirt) and *chunni* or *dupatta*. The *kurti* was decorated with silver *alies* (bigger than the size of a silver coin). Use of silver ornaments, such as *tabitari*, *dauni* (for forehead), *hamail* (necklace), *dhada* (ornament for upper arm) *band* (ornament for forearm), no more exists. *Nath*, *borth* (ornament for the nose) and *railan*, *dhage* either of silver or *pashmina*, *dandia* and *cheelkan* (ear ornaments) are no more used by women.

*Dal* and *roti* form their staple food. Followers of the Arya Samaj abstain from non-vegetarian food and alcoholic drinks. *Sarson da sag* and *makki di roti* are relished in winter. Pulses used by the Batwal are gram, *urad*, *moong*, *masur*, *moth*, while the vegetables include cauliflower, brinjal, ladies' finger, beans, *laoki*, *tinda*, *ghia*, *petha*. Mango, banana and oranges are furits generally eaten by them. *Lassi* (buttermilk) and tea are the non-alcoholic drinks used very frequently.

In the past *missi* or *nimki* (*roti* made of a mixture of wheat and gram flour) alongwith *lassi* was their favourite diet. *Karhi* (curry) was prepared from rice broth. Plants of *maina* (like *methi*) were preserved after drying and its *bhurji* was used, when there was scarcity of food. The crop of *cheena*, *batkangan*, *suank*, *mandal*, *chari*, *makai*, *jon*, *masar* and *kangani* were grown in the *maru* land (without irrigation facilities). During marriage parties *bure-di-khand* (sugar in powder form) and *ghee* were their favourite dishes.

Rice eating was occasional and it was taken during birth, marriage or death ceremonies only. Use of vegetables has increased as compared with pulses. Chewing of betel leaves or consuming tobacco products is restricted to the Hindu Batwals only.

The Batwal are divided into thirteen different *gots*, whose names have been mostly derived from names of places. Basae is a *got* and this name has been derived from the river Bias, meaning those who settled on the banks of river Bias; Chariya, i.e those who were the inhabitants of Simla; Thage derived their name after Tagore; Kainth trace their origin from Kaithal in Haryana; Lakhotra is from Lakhimpur (Uttar Pradesh); Loria, from Lahore (in Pakistan); Mandee are those who belong to the area of Mand (jungle); Mottan is from Mottan in Srinagar, at the grave of Mottan Sahib, where people offer their prayers. Nakhotra derived its name from Nagpur; Nandan because Krishna was brought up at Nand Nagri (in Uttar Pradesh), so those who came from Anand Nagri were called Nandan; Sajotra trace their origin from Sajjanpur (Shahjahanpur) in Uttar Pradesh; Sargotra are named after a place Sara which is situated in Uttar Pradesh or those who were engaged in Sarwad, or Sarkanda, for making Sirkia or Sapar; and Targotra are those who marry avoiding three *gotras* and hence they are so called.

In the past there was differentiation at occupational and religious levels also. The Hindus who were agriculturists were called Batwal, whereas the Muslims were weavers and called Barwal. As the Barwal are now in Pakistan, in the Indian part of Punjab there is no such differentiation. The Batwal consider themselves to be of high status after coming under the influence of the Arya Samaj or other sects like Namdhari, Radhaswami, Nirankari or Nihang. The other 'high' caste communities consider the Batwals inferior to them. However, the Batwals definitely occupy a superior status than the Chamars and Chuhra castes.

The Batwals marry within their own community, but marriage between the same *got* is not allowed. The Batwal also observe village exogamy. They sometimes go for hypogamy. The age at marriage for boys is twenty to twenty-two years, whereas for girls it is eighteen to twenty. The Batwal arrange marriage by negotiation with the help of a *vichola*. Married girls use *sindur* in the hair parting, *bindi*, earring, glass bangles as the symbols of their marriage. Dowry which varies according to the financial condition of the girl's parents, is paid at the time of marriage in the form of furniture, gold ornaments; *tyor* (*salwar*, *kameez* and *dupatta*) to the closely related ladies of the boy's family and *pagri* to the male relations. Five or eleven rupees are also offered along with the *tyor*, or the turban. *Wari* (clothes and ornaments) is also offered to the girl by the boy's parents before marriage. Those who are not economically solvent, reduce the number of the items given in dowry or *wari*. After marriage, the married girls stay at the residence of their husbands. Divorce with judicial approval is permitted. However, incidents of divorce are very few among the Batwal. After the Batwals became Arya Samajis, remarriage of the divorcees has been allowed. Remarriage of the widow is called *bathana*; it is termed *chadar paona* in case she marries the younger brother of her deceased husband. Widower remarriage is permitted. He may marry the younger sister of his deceased wife.

There is no change in the marriage rules, but change in age at marriage is observed. Child marriage is no more practised. In the past, the age of marriage was ten to twelve years, and after a gap of two to three years, the ceremony of *muklawa* (consummation of marriage) was followed. Presently the ceremony of marriage takes place when boys and girls attain adulthood and after a gap of two days the *muklawa* follows. In the past, basic qualification of the boy for marriage was his physical fitness and that of the girl was her interest in household activites. However, at present the parents of the girls search for a boy, who is either in the services or has his own independent source of income. Use of *sindur* has been initiated after the Batwal became Arya Samajis, while use of ornaments has been reduced to the minimum. The furniture consisting of a *palang* (cot), *pidi* (small stool) and *charkha* (spinning wheel) have been replaced by a double bed and sofa set. The bridegroom's father was offered a *raija* of *khadi* of five yards at the time of the reception of *barat*. This has been replaced by a *khes* (cotton blanket), turban or blanket. Earlier the views of the boy or the girl were never taken into consideration, while taking decision about their marriage. There was a proverb that he, or she can even be married to a *munj da majura* (toy) meaning thereby that the decision of the parents was always honoured by their children as far as their marriage was concerned. However, nowadays the parents of the boy/girl discuss the matter with their children and have their views before getting them married. Dissolution of marriage was allowed earlier with social approval. But at present the Batwals approach the court of law and obtain judicial approval for the divorce.

The Batwals have extended and nuclear families. In these families avoidance and joking relations are observed. Avoidance relationships are maintained between the father-in-law and daughter-in-law, husband's elder brother and younger brother's wife, mother-in-law and son-in- law. Joking relationship is observed between *dewar* and *bhabi*, *nanad* and *bharjai*, *sadu* (co-brothers), *jeeja* and *sali*. Various points of conflict and confrontation in a Batwal family may be petty issues related to either the children or the ladies, e.g. an article of daily use is not lent to one by the other; some member of the family is not behaving properly with a lady in the absence of her husband;

the relative or guest of one member of the family does not offer sweets or money to the children of the other members of the family; one member of a family is not having a high opinion about the relatives of the other members of the family. The children may exchange blows while playing which may also be a reason of tension between the elder members of the family; the children do not listen to the advice of the elders and do not agree to their point of view or when freedom of the youngsters is checked. All the sons inherit the property of their father equally. If there is no son, the daughters get equal share of the property of their father. The eldest son gets succession. The nuclear families are on the increase and the joint families are decreasing.

Among the Batwals, the status of women is considered lower than that of their men. Their primary duty is to attend to the household routine. Some of the women may engage themselves as maidservants or they may knit sweaters in order to assist in supporting their families. In the villages women may also work in agricultural fields and look after the domestic animals. Women participate in various rituals of their own community associated with birth, marriage and death.

Among the Arya Samaji Batwals, when the woman becomes pregnant, the ritual of *gharbadhan* is observed. After the birth of a child, post-delivery restrictions, for a period of forty days are observed. After forty days the ritual of *chowki charhana* or *jat karan sanskar* is performed. The Batwal also perform *namkaran* ceremony. When the child is about two to three years of age or he starts speaking, the ceremony of *mundan* is peformed. On the occasion of *mundan*, the *hawan* (oblation fire) is also performed. The ritual of *kan widhna* (piercing of earlobe) and *nak widhna* (piercing of the nose) is performed among the girls, when they are around ten to twelve years of age.

The Batwals marry within their own community but they do not marry within the same *got*. The ceremony of *mangani* (engagement) is performed before the marriage. The ritual of *sagan* is performed by the parents of the girl when, the would-be groom is presented one rupee and an engement ring, or a watch. The boy's parents also offer *sagan* to the girl in the form of an engagement ring, sweets and *tyor*. This is termed *chunni charhana*. Among the Batwal, marriage ceremony is performed in the morning. It consists of seven *pheras* around the sacred fire according to Vedic traditions or according to the tradition of *anand karaj*. Marriage rituals are performed at the bride's residence. Feast is offered to the groom's people by the girl's parents. Consummation of marriage is at the residence of the bridegroom.

The Batwals cremate their dead which is called *dag dena*, with the head towards the north and feet towards the south. For the peace of the soul of the dead, *hawan* and *sadharan-path* is performed among the Hindu and Sikh Batwals respectively. A feast, which is termed as *roti*, is also offered to the members of the community if some elderly person dies. The Batwals immerse the bones of their dead in the Ganga at Hardwar, which is called *phul-paona*. They also perform *shradh* ceremony.

Among the Batwals, the various rituals associated with the life cycle are being curtailed, as these have become expensive. In the past, when there was no ceremony of *pheras*, any elderly person could recite, *aka bakka, deo narateo dhaka* by taking *atta da pedda* (wheat flour balls) in his hand, and it was considered completion of the marriage ceremony. In the past, groom's people used to stay for two nights and marriage ceremony was performed during night. Nowadays, the groom's people arrive in the morning. The marriage ceremony is performed before midday, and they return in the evening. The Batwals used to bury their dead about a hundred years back.

The Batwals were *chowkidars* or messengers, who also supplied *coolies* for *begar*. The British allotted *ahata* (land) to some of the Batwals and they started cultivating land. Those who were not given land started doing work as *sangi* (contract labourers). Some of the villages where the Batwals have land in Punjab are: Bhadurpur, Bhaore, Chaute Miani, Azadpur, Habowal, Kakowal, Machiawara, Nuraeawal, Sarhind, Walipur, etc. In cities, the Batwals engage themselves as rickshaw-pullers, industrial labourers, casual labourers, masons, blacksmiths, *rehriwala* (mule cart owner). Some of them also manufacture bicycle saddles, blades and machines for the table and ceiling fans. The Batwals have direct link with the local market. They work as *sangi* in the villages of Batala *tahsil* of Gurdaspur district. As the population of the Batwals has increased, it is not possible for all of them to either own or work on agricultural land. This has resulted in the access of casual or industrial labour. Children below fifteen years of age who do not attend school, work in various factories as labourers. The mode of payment is cash.

The Batwals had their traditional *panchayat* about fifty years ago. Such *panchayats* were delegated with the powers of ex-communicating an individual or punishing him by imposing a fine as deemed fit depending upon the enormity of the crime. But now, the

Batwals approach the court of law to settle their disputes. The village *panchayats* now look after the welfare of all the communities.

The Batwal is a Hindu or Sikh by religion. Some Batwals embraced Islam in the pre-Independence years. They mostly live in areas which now are part of Pakistan. The sacred specialist among the Batwals is either from their own community or from other community. All rituals related to birth, childhood, marriage and death are performed by sacred specialists.

The Batwals have come under the influence of the Arya Samaj movement launched by Swami Dayanand. They have stopped taking non-vegetarian food and alcoholic drinks. A section of the Batwals has also come under the influence of various sects such as Sacha-Sauda at Sarsi in Haryana, Namdhari at Jeevan Nagar and Bhaini Sahib, Radhaswami at Biasa, Nirankari at Delhi and Punjab and Nihangs at Gurdaspur. All these sects also preach against taking non-vegetarian food and alcoholic drinks.

Wall and floor painting, *sanji* (Durga worship during Dussehra festival) and *gurdas* (where the newly wedded couple worship) are some of the examples of the art among the Batwals. The women do embroidery on cloth and weave *daris* (druggets) at village level. Ladies, at marriage ceremonies join men in singing songs and perform *giddha*, the traditional folk-dance. The men perform *bhangra* dance on the occasion of marriage.

Untouchability was observed with the Batwal in the past. However, after the Batwal came under the influence of Arya Samaj, or Sacha-Sauda, Namdhari, Radhaswami, Nirankari, Nihang sects, the social status of the Batwal has elevated. The Batwals share with the members of other communities the source of water, roads, schools, religious places and can take part in the traditional festivals with them. They have separate cremation ground. At the villages, cultivator and labourer relationship is maintained by the Batwals with others.

The Batwals are employed as teachers and are also in defence services, but their number is too small. The boys and girls belonging to the Batwal community attend schools. But they do not continue their studies after fifth or eighth class due to their poor economic conditions; the girls sometimes drop out to help their mothers in the household work. They get medical facilities from local civil hospitals. They get the facility of immunization of child and mother. They are aware of various family planning methods and several of them have adopted the use of contraceptives. The source of drinking water is water taps in the cities and handpumps in the villages. Most of the

Batwals are employed as cultivators, share-croppers, agriculture and industrial labour, rickshaw pullers and porters. Various extension and voluntary agencies supply them information of different nature. They have electric connections and use electricity for domestic purposes and their small-scale industries. Wood and cow-dung are the fuel resource. Those who are engaged in agriculture in villages use chemical fertilizers, organic manure and insecticides. Tube wells are used for irrigation purpose. The Batwals have been supplied with ration cards to get sugar and kerosene oil at subsidised rates. They have the custom of helping the members of their community by contributing an amount which has to be returned to the contributor, when there will be a function related to marriage or death. This is called *neota-bhaji.*

SWARAN SINGH

# BAURIA

The Bauria, also termed as Bawaria, are a Scheduled Caste. According to *Census of India* (1981), their total population was 62,624 individuals, comprising 32,986 males and 29,638 females. They are found mainly in the districts of Ferozepur followed by Bhatinda, Ludhiana and Sangrur. The word *baur* means net, while the meaning of *bawar* is noose. The Baurias are a hunting people who consider themselves Rajput. They migrated to Punjab from Chittorgarh (Rajasthan).

Ibbetson (1916: 276), reports that there are three sections of the Baurias such as the Bidawati of Bikaner, Kalkarmalia, who are found in Ferozepur, and Kaparia who have a high concentration in Delhi. The Bidawati consider themselves to be superior to the rest. All these three sections do not intermarry. Out of these the Kalkarmalia still engage themselves in hunting. The Kaparia are nomadic, while the Bidawati lead a settled life.

A story regarding their origin and migration states that during a battle between the Mughals and Rajputs, the latter were bringing back to life all their dead soldiers by sprinkling water of a magical *bauli* (stair well) on them. The Mughals came to know about the secret and sent a spy, a Rajput, to contaminate the water with cow's blood. The spy was later caught and designated *bhitya* (polluted). This person was the ancestor to Baurias.

The Baurias say they are also known as Bhatti from *bhitya*. Similar observations were also made by Rose (1919: 73). Reportedly, the Rajput had stopped interdining with them. They were forced to leave the fort and go to the jungles. In the jungles, they started taking fruits and hunting wild animals. The net to trap the wild animals is known as *baur* hence they are called Bauria. According to *Census of India* (1911: 449), *banwar* or *wanwar* means 'a rope net made for catching pig. The term Bauwaria is still used indiscriminately in the central and western Punjab for Mahtam, Labana, and even Baloch hunters who net pigs.' They make baskets called *tokra*, and prepare *van* of *munj* (rope). According to Rose (1919: 76) 'the Baurias are strict Hindus, refusing to eat anything even *ghee*, which has been touched by a Mohammedan, though they will drink water from a *bhishti's* skin, but not that kept in his house. Baurias will only eat meat procured by themselves or killed by *jhatka*. Pork they eschew, but not the flesh of wild pig. The *nilgai* is regarded as a cow and never eaten, nor is the flesh of a he buffalo save by the Baurias of Shekhawati in Jaipur. As they are no longer permitted to possess swords, they slaughter with the *chhuri*. The Bawarias dialect is called Ghirhar and sometimes as Pashtu.

They speak Punjabi language with the members of other communities but, within their own community they speak Bauria language. The Sikh men wear turban and the women's dress is *salwar*, *kameez* and *dupatta*. Wheat is their staple food, taken with vegetables and pulses. Rice is taken only occasionally. Alcoholic drinks are taken on special occasions; such as birth of a male child and marriage ceremony. *Makai di roti* and *sarson da sag* is enjoyed specially during the winter season. Tea, *lassi* and milk are consumed, though fruits are taken occasionally. The Hindu Bauria smoke *bidi*.

According to Rose (1919:74), 'in Gurgaon and tracts round that District the Baurias are divided into numerous groups. Of these the most important, locally is the Jarulawala or Laturia, so called because its members wear long hair, like Sikhs. This group is endogamous and includes 14 *gots:* 1. Badgujar, 2. Chauhan, 3. Pauwar, 4. Rathaur, 5. Agotia, 6. Baghotia, 7. Berara, 8. Chaond, 9. Dabria, 10. Gangwal, 11. Jagotia, 12. Kotia, 13. Katoria, 14. Mewatia. These 14 are strictly exogamous.'

They have twelve divisions at subgroup level. It is sometimes said that as they have *bara* (twelve) divisions, they are called Bauria. Eight out of the twelve subgroups of the Baurias are as follows: 1. Nithawat, 2. Righawat, 3. Dauawat, 4. Sunawat, 5. Chaplawat, 6. Mutawat, 7. Sadawat, and 8. Milawat. The informants have not endorsed the three sections noted by Ibbeston, namely Bidawati, Jangli and Kaparia. Solanki, Chohan, Pamar, Sungre, Dhaudal are some of their common *gots*. They marry among themselves but not within their own *gots*. When the boys and girls are eighteen to twenty years of age, their parents arrange their marriage. But the boy and girl should be of the same age. Earlier the parents of the boy and the girl used to share expenditure of marriage equally, but now it has been replaced by the dowry, which is given depending upon the financial condition of the girl's parents. They consider themselves as superior in social hierarchy in comparison to the members of other Scheduled Caste communities.

Divorce is permitted by their *panchayat*. Remarriage is also allowed. In case of divorce the expenditure of marriage is to be returned to the girl's parents. Families are mostly joint, but nuclear families also exist. The property is the main issue of conflict in a family. Sons inherit their father's property equally and the eldest son gets the succession. Women, apart from household jobs, help their husbands in agricultural operations, collection of wood, etc. However neither do they have decision-making powers, nor can they control family expenditure. Women have lower status than men. At the birth of a male child, they celebrate first Lohri and distribute *gur* (jaggery). Some post-delivery restrictions are observed by the mother. Earlier, the groom, his friends and relatives used to arrive by *rath* (bullock cart), and the duration of their stay was for three days. There were seven *pheras* earlier for solemnizing marrige; now the groom and his people stay overnight. The seven *pheras* have been replaced by the four *lavan pheras* (*anand karaj*). They cremate their dead. The *akhand path* (recitation of *Guru Granth Sahib*) ends the mourning period which varies between ten and thirteen days depending upon the age of deceased. Earlier it was after sixteen days of death.

According to Rose (1919: 77), the various customs of the Bauria are as follows: 'The child's name is chosen by a Brahman. On the fifth day after birth the mother takes a *lota* full of water on her head to the nearest well, a Brahmani and Nain, with other women, accompanying her and singing songs. She takes with her *bhanjor* (moistened grain) of gram or *bajra* and after worshipping the well throws some of the *bhanjor*, with a little water out of her *lota* and a *matka* brought by the Brahmani and Nain into the well. The rest of the *bhanjor* is distributed among the children. The mother is deemed purified on the tenth day.'

About marriage Rose (1919) states that 'girl's father intimates the date fixed for her wedding by sending a *saha-chitthi* written in Sanskrit and on the day fixed the wedding party goes to the girl's house. The bridegroom wears the *sehra* and his forehead is smeared with *haldi*. The Bauria bride wears a necklace made of horse hair on which are threaded gold and silver beads. This is called *sohag sutra* and it is worn till the husband's death, when it is burnt with his corpse. On the third day after a funeral, boiled rice is distributed among young girls. On the third day following, the ashes are collected; rice is laid on seven *pipal* leaves and placed at the foot of the tree, certain persons are told to watch from a distance. If a crow eats the rice, it is a good omen; but bad if dog devours it. The period of mourning lasts twelve days.'

The Baurias cultivate the land on *theka* (contract) and make payment to the owner of the land after selling their produce. Their *panchayat* consists of intelligent and elderly persons. They also have their district *panchayat*, which resolves marriage disputes and property matters and punishes the guilty by imposing fine, which ranges from five hundred to one thousand rupees. Earlier, they used to socially boycott the person committing offences. Earlier, they were followers of Hinduism. Rose (1911: 73) states that the Baurias used to worship their ancestors and certain other deities. Ram Deo, supposed to be an incarnation of Krishna is specially worshipped by Panwat sect of the Baurias. The Baurias also used to worship Kali and Lalta Masani and a section of the Baurias pay their devotion to Nar Singh. Presently they have changed their religion to Sikhism. Hanuman, Gosain was their god, they used to offer him rice and *kadahi* (feast) on the occasion of Holi after the arrival of the new crop. They celebrate Diwali, Lohri, Guruparab and Dussehra.

They invite members of other communities on marriage, death and birth ceremonies. They exchange and accept water and food with the members of other communities and maintain cultivator-tenant relationship. They have their own *dharamshala* (common religious place).

Though the condition for availing education and health facilities are favoured, most of the boys are under-matriculate. They avail of the medical facilities as and when needed. Handpumps are the main source of drinking water. Wood, cow-dung and dried plants of maize and cotton are used as fuel. Motor pumps are used for irrigation. Ration cards supplied to them are used to get sugar and kerosene oil. Yellow cards have been issued to the economically weaker families for getting loans from banks.

SWARAN SINGH

# BAZIGAR

The Bazigar have been recognized as a scheduled caste. Their population according to *Census of India* (1981), is 1,20,250 which consists of 62,488 males and 57,762 females. They are found in all the districts; the districts of Patiala, followed by Ferozepur, Sangrur, Bhatinda, Gurdaspur, have the highest concentration. According to the *Census of India* (1911), 'the Bazigars, who are mostly Hindus are scattered all over the province. They are a Gipsy tribe of vagrant habits, who wander about practising acrobatic feats. They are also known as Badi and are akin to the Nats.' Rose (1919: 79) has observed that 'the Bazigar is usually a Muhammadan, the Nat, a Hindu. Among the Bazigar both sexes perform, but among Nats only the males. Some say the Bazigar is a tumbler and the Nat a rope-dancer, others that the former is a juggler and also an acrobat, the latter an acrobat only. In the Eastern Punjab the Bazigar is termed Badi.'

Ibbetson (1919) further states that Bazigar is a Persian word meaning 'he who does *bazi*' or any sort of game or play, but it is applied only to jugglers and acrobats. Presently some of the Baziagar have migrated from Rajasthan but they speak Punjabi language. The males wear a turban, *dhoti* and *kurta*, while their female's dress is *kurti*, *salwar*, and *chunni*. They are non-vegetarian, but take mutton only. Gram, *moong*, *moth* and *masur* are pulses generally used by them. Wheat is their staple cereal whereas rice is taken occasionally. Groundnut and mustard oil are used for cooking. *Lassi*, tea and *bhang* (*thandai*) are some of their non-alcoholic drinks. Alcoholic drinks are taken on special occasions such as marriage and birth of a male child. Fruits are consummed seasonally.

They have five subgroups, Jogi, Badtia, Mushal, Dharamsot and Namsot, and their *gots* are—Jogi: Ropana, Hari, Bukan, Chanan, Bala, Koklia, Rama and Badru; Badtia: Tatu, Phatu, Rama, Mali, Botha, Buda; Mushal: Khetia, Kamalu, Mathria, Ghogria and Abchana; Dharamsot: Ramdana, Baludede, Dudede and Bhattidede. Namsot have no *gots*.

The Jogi, Badtia, Mushal and Dharamsot marry outside their sub-groups, while the Namsot can marry only among themselves. It is an endogamous community. When the boys and girls attain the age between fourteen years and eighteen, their parents arrange their marriage by negotiation with the help of a *vichola*. The form of marriage is monogamy. Sikh Bazigars marry according to the Sikh rites of four *lavan pheras (anand karaj)*. The bride price, ranging from sixteen to thirty-two rupees, is given to the bride's parents. Their rule of residence is patrilocal. Divorce and remarriage among the Bazigars are allowed with permission from the caste *panchayat*. In case of divorce, compensation has to be paid to the aggrieved spouse. The divorce, known as *talaq*, is sanctioned for reasons such as adultery or a spouse being deaf or mute. Remarriage known as *karewa* is permitted. Specific symbol of marriage among the Bazigar is the *haldi ka tika*, a turmeric paste dot on the forehead of a married girl. Type of family is joint family but nuclear families are also coming up.

Check on the freedom of youngsters and challenge to the authority of elders are the reasons of conflict and confrontation. Sons inherit the property of their father equally; the eldest son gets succesion. Women attend to household activities, including collection of wood, fetching water from the handpump and rearing domestic animals. They are of lower status in comparison to males and have no say in decision-making or in the mechanism of social control. Post-delivery re-strictions are observed for forty days and *namkaran* is done by the *dai* (midwife).

The dead are cremated and pollution period is observed for twelve or thirteen days for old men and women respectively.

Their primary occupation of these people used to be performing acrobatics. Generally, there were twelve villages allotted to a family of Bazigar and the show of *bazi* was held annually in one of these villages. In other words, the *bazi* show was held after twelve years in each village. Where the *bazi* was to be held, the members of the village were informed sufficiently in advance, and contribution, ranging from five to ten rupees, was collected from each household. This contribution was possible in kind also, in the form of wheat or maize. The major items of a *bazi* show, in addition to different items of acrobatics were *chhal* (high jump), primarily of three types: *suli di chhal*, *khatdi* and *manja tapni*. Apart from this, they also engaged themselves in business and animal husbandry. They have their own traditional *panchayat* and its *lambardar* or leader, is elected by voice vote. He takes all the decisions, related to the disputed matters after hearing both the parties. The main quality of the *lambardar* is the ability to speak fluently and there is a proverb for: *mukh bhaya, rag aya*. A sum of two hundred rupees and a bed, known as *manja* is provided to the members of the *panchayat* by the plantiff; this money is used for providing refreshment, specially drinks to the *panchayat* and it continues until an agreement is arrived at. The form of punishment includes both fine and social boycott. They have now embraced Sikhism, but earlier they used to worship *Pirkhana*. They worship *Guru Granth Sahib* and visit *gurdwaras*. They celebrate Holi, Diwali, Dussehra and Lohri along with members of other communities. On the occasion of a *bazi* they beat the drums, known as *dhol*.

There is no restriction on them for visiting religious places, schools and in sharing sources of water and roads with the members of other communities. However, they have their own cremation ground. They used to have patron-client relationship and accept and exchange food with the Jat Sikhs, and not with members of other high caste communities of their village.

Only a few among them are educated, the community lacks the modern intercommunity linkages. Most of the couples do not use modern family planning methods. Handpumps are their source of drinking water. They have radios, transistors but no television sets. Members of this community have ration cards to get the essential items at subsidized rates. Attitude of the Bazigars towards saving is positive.

SWARAN SINGH

# BHANJRA

The term *bhanjra* has been derived from *bhajna*, meaning to run away. It is said that during the rule of Emperor Aurangzeb, the Bhanjra preferred to flee to the jungles instead of converting themselves to Islam. They were Hindu and Hindi was their mother tongue. As they moved on in order to avoid conversion to Islam, they were termed by others as Bhanjra. In the jungles they started preparing *duna*, or leaf-cups, from the leaves of *dhak* tree. This profession is still continued. Apart from this, they also prepare *chik* or blinds, from bamboo. They were Khatris and engaged in bamboo work, hence, they were also known as 'Bans-pad Khatris'. At Tandaurmud, they became followers of Arya Samaj and therefore were called Mahasha. They are known as Doom in the hilly areas. It has been informed that the Doom, Mahasha and Bhanjra were one and the same. They marry among themselves. However, the Batwal Mahasha are separate from the above-mentioned communities. According to Rose (1919) 'The Bhanjra, a synonym for Dumna in the lower hills of Hoshiarpur and Gurdaspur, make sieves, winnowing fans and other articles of grass and bamboo. Like the Sansi, Sarial and Daoli, the Bhanjra may be regarded as an occupational group of the Dumnas, with whom they intermarry'.

The Bhanjra are a Scheduled Caste and according to *Census of India* (1981), total concentration of Bhanjra community in Punjab is 3,557 individuals, with 1,862 males and 1,695 females. They have maximum concentration in the district of Hoshiarpur.

They speak Hindi while communicating with the members of their own community. Their children learn Punjabi in schools. The Bhanjra men wear *dhoti* with shirt and turban, while their women wear *salwar*, *kameez* and *dupatta* and during winter, they also wear a shawl.

The Bhanjras are vegetarian but they take eggs and chicken also, though rarely. Wheat is their staple food. Pulses such as *moong*, *masur*, *moth*, gram and *urad* are taken very frequently. *Lassi* is their favourite drink. Among sweets, *laddoos* are served by them on special occasions such as birth, marriage ceremony and the feast at the time of death ceremony. Mustard and groundnut oil are used in cooking. Those who can afford use *desi ghee* for cooking purpose. Consumption of alcoholic drinks is negligible. Fruits are taken occasionally. It has been observed that these people have started consuming more non-vegetarian food than earlier.

The Bhanjras are endogamous and are divided into different exogamous *gots*. The following *gots* were reported: Baloch (Dhanot), Mashalu, Khadyal (Bajata), Playal, Salor, Khatyar, Mangroor, Chandle, Bhati, Tarwar, Bhabnaor, Chanoria, Hajoria and Chaghya.

They are aware of the *varna* system and recognize their place as Shudras and consider themselves as of low status. Other communities consider them as of low status but not as low as the Bhangi or Chuhras.

Child marriage which was prevalent in the pre-Independence times among these people has been replaced by adult marriage. Age at marriage among the boys and girls of the community ranges from twenty-one to thirty years. Often, a boy and a girl meet at some social occasion, approve each other and inform their parents about their choice. Then the girl's people, accompanied by a *vichola*, visit the boy's house to propose the match and offer a token gift, *shagun*, of two rupees. *Roti* is also offered to the boy. The girl's father and her close relatives first offer *shagun* to the boy. The girl also gets her *shagun* from her would-be in-laws; this consists of *chunni*, *laddoo* and two to five rupees. The girl may come to her in-laws' house with five to seven small utensils and without any ornament. The form of marriage is monogamy. The women use vermilion in the hair parting, ear-ring and bangles as marriage symbols. A married girl stays with her husband at his parent's house. Divorce and remarriage among the Bhanjra are not permitted.

The expenditure on dowry is on the increase and those who can afford spend more for this purpose which was not the case in the past. Extended type of family is most common among the Bhanjra. The parents, their married sons and unmarried children stay together and eat together. The elders look after the younger members of the family and treat them with love and affection. The young members of the family take care of their elders in old age. Avoidance relations is observed by the daughter-in-law with her father-in-law and mother-in-law with her son-in-law. A woman also avoids her husband's elder brothers. On the other hand, joking relations are observed between the *dewar* and *bhabi*; *deorani* and *jathani*; and between the *sadus*. In a joint family, members maintain cordial relations with each other and though there is love and joking relation, occasions of conflict and confrontation also occur; the main reason is the distribution of property. Sometimes the youngsters may not listen to the advice of the elders. The children may also quarrel among themselves causing rift and tension.

Usually the male children inherit the parental property. In case there is no male child, girls are entitled to inherit property. Sometimes females get half share of the property left by their parents. The eldest son is entitled to the succession of his father. Nuclear families are on the increase as a result of break up of joint families.

Women are considered low in status as compared to men. Decision-making is the domain of the head of family. Women look after the husband and the children and attend to household activities. They may also help in making *dunas* of leaves, which are used as bowls. They contribute to the family income indirectly by collecting wood, bamboo and *dhak* leaves.

The delivery of the first child is always preferred at the would-be mother's parent's house. Her mother gives necessary instructions regarding the restrictions at various stages of pregnancy. Travelling during the last stage of pregnancy is avoided. Post-delivery confinement for a period of forty days is observed. *Mirasi* and *jhiri* tie the *sehra* (which consists of mango leaves tied to a string) on the front door after the birth of a male child in family. According to the convenience, *roti* (feast) is offered to close relatives and members of the community. The *mundan* ceremony of male child is also arranged on this occasion.

When the boys and girls attain adulthood, their parents negotiate matches for their marriage. A marriage is solemnized by the performance of seven *pheras*, generally performed in the early hours of the day, at the bride's house. A feast, or *roti* is offered to eleven members of the community and to close relatives. If a relative comes to know of such a ceremony, they do not wait for a formal invitation to attend it. This indicates the solidarity among the members of the community. A day before the departure of the *barat* the bridegroom's parents also host a feast for their close relatives and members of the community. Consummation of marriage is at the bridegroom's house. Women of the community pay visits to see the bride and offer her *shagun*.

When someone in the community dies at old age, the dead body is decorated and taken to the cremation ground in a procession called *janaja*. The dead are cremated and mourning period lasts for sixteen days, after which the ceremonies known as *jarbia*, *kujia* and *duna bharna* are performed. Though some of the rituals have been curtailed, yet those which are performed are getting more extravagant.

Forest is the main resource of the Bhanjras though the forests in Punjab are controlled by the government. They collect leaves of the *dhak* tree to make the *dunas*. They also prepare *chiks* (blinds) from the bamboo or reed. The leaves of *dhak* trees are used for making the *dunas* only, as the animals do not eat these leaves. They get the reeds from grass which grows on the banks of the nearby rivers. Most of them are landless. They have their own houses to live in and most of these are *pukka* houses.

In addition to the primary occupation of preparing *dunas* and *chiks*, they also engage themselves in white-washing the houses and other such jobs. They maintain a direct link with the market and the local market.

The Bhanjras have their own traditional caste *panchayat*, known as Bhanjra Biradari Sabha. The *pradhan* of the *sabha* is nominated. He has to be a learned and honest person, who can analyse a situation and give his verdict without any fear or favour. The main function of the traditional *panchayat* is social control, while the statutory *panchayat* implements the development and welfare programmes. To achieve its target, the traditional caste *panchayat* may ex-communicate persons found at fault, particularly in matters related to marriage. However, there is no provision of imposing cash fine among the Bhanjras.

The Bhanjra profess Hinduism and worship Baba Balak Nath, Chintpurni Devi in addition to the *Gurus*, *Pirs* and *Paigambers*. The sacred specialists serving them are from other communities, who worship, perform birth, marriage and death rites. Diwali, Holi and Dussehra are the major festivals of the Bhanjra. These festivals are of religious and social significance. At Mukerian, they visit a pious man, Mahant Baba Balandu and hoist a flag in his honour. During the festival of Dussehra, maidens decorate the walls of their houses with paintings. The Bhanjra have their own folk-songs which women and girls sing on festive occasions such as marriage.

They accept water, *sidha*, *kachcha*, and *pukka* food from all the neighbouring communities whereas other communities accept water and food from those Bhanjra who are economically better off and keep themselves clean. The Bhanjra share well and tap water with other communities but have separate cremation ground. The religious shrines of the area are shared by them with others. They invite the members of other communities to their social functions and visit them on similar occasions.

Formal education is favoured by these people for both boys and girls. However, most of the boys and girls are not in a position to continue their studies beyond the eighth class. There is only one matriculate at Ludhiana (Killa Mahala). The main reason for dropping out of school among the boys and girls is poverty. Instead of continuing their studies, the parents insist on their children to take up their traditional occupation.

Attitude of Bhanjras towards modern medicare system is positive. They visit privately-run dispensaries, in addition to government health clinics. Their attitude towards the family welfare schemes has changed recently, as compared with the past when they preferred large families. The reason for the change is that they feel it difficult to manage a big family. Now they prefer to have two to three children per couple.

The Bhanjras generally draw drinking water from handpumps. In municipal areas, they are supplied water through taps. As most of the members of the Bhanjras are illiterate, it is difficult for them to get jobs in the government departments, except as labourers. Most of them are self-employed in their own traditional occupation. Some families have radios and they keep themselves informed about the various developments around them.

The houses of the Bhanjras have electric connections. Wood is the major source of fuel for them apart from cooking coal. They sometimes use kerosene oil as a substitute. The midday meal scheme was in operation in the government schools few years ago. Facilities of immunization of the mother and infant are availed of by the members of the community. The Bhanjra have ration cards to procure essential items such as sugar, pulses, cereals, kerosene oil and stationery articles at low rates. The government of Punjab has distributed yellow cards for the economically weaker Bhanjra families. Individuals having yellow cards can have non-refundable loans from the banks.

SWARAN SINGH

# BHARAI

The Bharai according to Ibbetson (1916: 229), derives its name from Sakhi Sarwar, who one day said to Bukan Jat '*tujhe piri di*' (the saint's mouth has fallen on thee), hence the name Pirhai. There is another account according to which the Sakhi Sayyid was invited to a feast by an Afghan chief who offered his daughter's hand in marriage. The saint accepted the offer. The *Mirasi* was last to attend the marriage and he declined to accept the gift of the saint which included a small piece of blue cloth, on provocation from the Jats and Pathans. The same piece of cloth was offered to Shaikh Buddha, who was a Jat and advised to tie it around his head and beat a drum. 'You and your' descendants have come under our protection, *panah* and you shall be called a *panahi*, said the saint.

The term Bharai itself is usually derived from *chauki bharna*, 'to keep a vigil' in which are sung praises of the Sakhi. But another and less simple account says that owing to his marriage Sayyid Ahmad incurred the enmity of the Jats and Pathans of Shahkot and left that place for Afghanistan, accompanied by Bibi Bai Rana Mian and his younger brother. Twenty-five miles from Dera Ghazi Khan they halted. No water was to be found, so the Sayyid mounted his mare Kale Kakki and at every step she took water came up. His pursuers, however were close at hand and when they approached Sakhi they slayed and buried him at the place, where he fell. The spot is known as Nigaha and still abounds in springs. Years later, Isa, a merchant of Bokhara and a devotee of Sakhi Sarwar was voyaging in the Indian ocean when a storm arose. Isa invoked the Saint's aid and saved the ship. On landing, he journeyed to Multan where he learnt that the Saint had been killed. On reaching Nigaha he found no traces of his tomb, but no fire could be kindled on that spot and in the morning as they loaded the camels their legs broke. Sakhi Sarwar descended from the hill on his mare, holding a spear in his hand and warned the merchant that he had desecrated his tomb and must rebuild it.

He was then to bring a blind man, a leper and an eunuch from Bokhara and entrust its supervision to them. One day when the blind man stumbled near the tomb he saved himself by clutching at some *kahi* grass where upon his sight was restored; his descendants are still known as Kahi. The eunuch was also cured and his descendants are called Shaikh. The leper too recovered, and his descendants, the

Kalang, are still found in Nigaha. To commemorate their cures all three beat the drum, and Sakhi Sarwar appeared to them saying, 'He who is my follower will ever beat the drum and will remain *barahi* (big) "sound"; nor will he ever lack anything.' Hence the pilgrims to Nigaha became known as Bharais. However, at Malerkotla they have migrated from a village Himtana which is at a distance of about 5 km. They are also engaged in agriculture. Thier ancestor was Gabara Jat. Hence they are also known as Jat Bharai. Their *gots* are the same as those of the Jats.

They speak Punjabi and Urdu with the members of their family and outdsiders. Gurmukhi, Perso-Arabic or Roman scripts are used. Bharai insignia according to Rose (1919: 86) 'are drum (*dhol*) beaten with a curiously shaped stick, like a start crook; a wallet (*khallar*) hung round the neck by a string'. Males wear shirt, *lungi*, pants and *pagri*, the females wear *salwar*, *kameez* and *dupatta*. Married women use *burqa* (veil), while moving out of their houses.

Rose (1919: 86) writing about their food habits mentioned that 'at many places the Bharais eat only goat's flesh, and that leprosy would afflict him who ate any other kind of flesh. But this restriction is certainly not universal. Beef is avoided, because it is said the Bharais have many Hindu votaries.' *Dal-roti* is their staple food. They eat eggs, fish, mutton occasionally, in addition to the locally available vegetables. Rice is served on special occasions such as marriage ceremony, death and circumcision. Groundnut oil and pure *ghee* are used as cooking medium. Milk, milk products, tea and *lassi* are taken frequently. Fruits are consumed, when available. They chew *paan* and smoke cigarettes.

According to Rose (1911: 86), 'strictly speaking the Bharais do not form a caste, but an occupational group or spiritual brotherhood which comprises men of many castes, Dogar, Habri, Rawat, Dum, Rajput, Mochi, Gujar, Tarkhan and last but not the least Jat. . . . Thus Jats Bharai may only marry a Jat woman . . . in Kapurthala it is said that being Mohammedans, marriage within the *got* is permitted and that Rajput Bharai may take wives from Jat Bharais. There appears indeed to be no absolute or even general rule, but the tendency apparently is for the Bharais recruited from any one caste to form a separate caste of Bharais, marrying only in that caste, e.g. in Ludhiana the Jat Bharai only marries a Bharai Jatni and the *gots* avoided are the same as among the Jats. The Jat Bharais are numerous. . . . The Jat Bharais have several *gots*. Dhillon, Deol, Grewal, Man, Randhawa, Jham, Karki and Badecha.'

Presently, they are divided into *gots* such as Gill, Dhariwal, Deol,

Chatha Chema. These *gots* were used to regulate marriage alliances about twenty years ago. But at present it has lost its value. They consider themselves as belonging to high status, but do not recognize, the *varna* system. They are endogamous and marry among themselves except those who are their real brothers or sisters. Adult marriage is performed between eighteen and twenty years of age. Marriage is arranged by negotiation with the help of a *vichola*. They can keep more than one wife. *Mehar* is promised at the time of marriage and minimum amount of *mehar* can be thirty-two rupees (silver) and six *annas*.

Rule of residence is patrilocal. According to the religious sacrament, *talaq* is allowed in case of maladjustment; divorce compensation is given to the wife; either party can divorce and children stay either with mother or with father. Remarriage is permitted. They have nuclear and joint families and members observe avoidance and joking relationship. Property, check on the freedom of youngsters or challenge to the authority of elders may cause conflicts in the family. All sons equally inherit their father's property while the eldest son gets succession. Status of women is low. They attend to the various household activities, work in agricultural fields, look after domestic animals, bring potable water, attend to various social functions related to birth, marriage and death ceremonies.

Pre-delivery restrictions are observed. Pollution period is observed if it is the first delivery. Postnatal restrictions on mother are observed for forty days. Circumcision is performed among males when they are five to six years of age. *Aqiqa* ceremony is also performed. Their girls on attaining adulthood, start wearing *burqa*. The *nikah* or marriage ceremony is performed according to Islamic tradition at the bride's residence. They observe a death pollution period. After three days of death, prayers are offered by a *maulavi* from the Holy Quran. They bury the dead with head towards western direction. Most of the Bharai are engaged in agriculture while some of them are still continuing their traditional occupation of beating drums on the occasion of marriage and death. This has now been replaced by the band parties that play all types of musical instruments.

Some have petty business or are engaged as labourers. The *chaudhary* of the *mohalla* attends to matters related to divorce, remarriage and marriage disputes. There used to be impose cash fines to the guilty about ten to fifteen years back and the guilty had to offer a feast to the community as fine. In villages they have statutory *panchayats* to look after the welfare of all the communities of the village. According to *Census of India* (1911: 449), 'the total population of the Bharais is 58,400 individuals, which includes 32,166 males and 26,234 females. The Bharais (Bharain) are met with almost all over the province. They are mostly Musalmans'. The *maulvi* can be from any community, who leads the *namaz* on birth, marriage and death ceremonies. They play musical instruments of all types and also sing songs on special occasions such as marriage. In villages they use drums.

They accept and exchange food and water from all Muslim communities. They have the same burial place (*qabristan*) as the other Muslim communities. They participate in traditional festivals and festivities. They have patron-client relationship. There are a few in administration, in defence services or as teachers. Political leadership has emerged at the village level only.

Formal education is favoured for both boys and girls. They study upto secondary level, some of the boys even join colleges, one has done his post-graduation. Attitude towards traditional and modern medicare is positive and they make use of both. Similarly, they use various family planning methods. Drinking water facilities are available and they have handpumps for this purpose. In the cities, they make use if media and communication facilities. They get various types of information through the extension agencies or political parties. They use electricity. Firewood, cow-dung cakes and coal are used as fuel resources. They have ration cards to get sugar, kerosene oil and rapeseed oil at subsidized rates.

SWARAN SINGH

# BHARBHUNJA

The Bharbhunjas are also known as Mehra. They are the traditional grain roaster, drawing membership from the larger Jhinwar group. They are distributed throughout the state. They speak Punjabi both within the kin groups and use both Gurmukhi and Devanagari scripts. Elderly males wear *dhoti* and *kurta* while younger ones wear trousers and shirts, women wear *salwar* and *kameez.*

They take both vegetarian and non-vegetarian food. *Roti* with *dal* and *sabzi* form their staple diet. Locally available pulses and vegetables are consumed. Cereals consumed are wheat, maize and rice. Egg eaters among them are considered non-vegetarian. Some of them occasionally take mutton and chicken. *Ghee,* mustard oil and other refined vegetable oil are used for cooking. Tea is the most favoured non-alcoholic drink. They consume roots and tubers such as onion, potato, ginger, sweet potato, carrot and radish. Men drink occasionally. Milk and milk products are consumed. Smoking is prevalent among the Hindu Bharbhunja who smoke *bidi,* cigarette and *hookah.*

They are further divided into a number of clans called *gots* such as Behal, Samala, Dehn, Sinhotra, Lendichuk, Memotra which regulate marriage alliance and determine descent and ancestry. They consider themselves of middle social status though others consider them of low social status. The community perceives itself as Kashyap Rajput.

In marriage, community endogamy is the rule and exogamy is practised at clan and village levels. Earlier they used to leave four *gots* while choosing a mate, that is of self, mother's, paternal grandmother's and maternal grandmother's. But now only two *gots* are left, i.e. of self and of mother's. Marriages are negotiated when the boy and the girl attain adulthood and are around twenty years of age. Monogamy is the rule, *kanyadan* exists and dowry is given in both cash and kind. Marriage symbols are vermilion and *bindi* and rule of residence is patrilocal. Traditionally divorce is not allowed. Widow remarriage has sanction. It has been observed that there is an increase in age at marriage, marriage symbols not being observed strictly, incidences of divorce are showing a rising trend and a more liberal attitude towards remarriage is developing.

Both nuclear and extended family types have been reported. Traditional interpersonal relations of love, respect, fear, avoidance and joking are seen as in other neighbouring communities. The young members of the family get love, affection and care while elders command respect and authority. Avoidance relationship is observed between daughter-in-law and father-in-law, husband's elder brother and younger brother's wife. Joking relationship is observed between husband's younger brother and elder brother's wife, sister's husband and wife's younger brothers and sisters and between grand-parents and grandchildren. Interpersonal relations of conflict and confrontation are also seen in the families on account of property, check on the freedom of youngsters and challenge to the authority of elders. The rule of inheritance is male equigeniture and succession goes to the eldest son. Inter-family linkages are cordial. Changes observed in the institution of family are rise in the formation of nuclear families, progressive decline of extended family system and lack of cohesion among kins and family members.

Women's role is basically confined to household activities and in animal husbandry, collection of fuel, bringing potable water and in religious and ritual affairs. In addition, they also help in the traditional occupation of the community and take up jobs as maidservants. They contribute to family income but have a low status.

Pre-delivery restrictions are observed. Post-delivery pollution is observed for one-and-a-quarter months in case of a boy and thirteen days for a girl. This is called *sootak.* Birth of a male child is celebrated by distributing sweets. Later after the *sootak* is over, *chowke charhna* ritual is performed. Naming and *mundan* ceremonies are informal. *Mundan* is performed in the first, third or fifth year. Marriage rituals are performed at the bride's house. Some of the rituals are performed at the groom's residence. The marriage rituals include *rok, mangni, shagun, barat, pheras* and *doli.* Actual marriage is performed by *pheras* around the sacred fire among the Hindu Bharbhunja and around *Guru Granth Sahib* among the Sikh Bharbhunja. Consummation of marriage is at the groom's residence. The dead are cremated and bones immersed in water. Post-death pollution period is observed for eleven days in case of women and thirteen days in case of males. The bones, called *phul,* are collected on the *chautha* and are immersed in the holy Ganga. The *kriya/uthala* or *rasam pagri,* takes place as the last ritual on the eleventh or thirteenth day. Life-cycle rituals are becoming shorter and more expensive.

The Bharbunjas are a non-agricultural community, traditionally engaged in grain-roasting and preparation of sweets. A few have taken to petty shopkeeping and are plying rickshaw or *tonga.* Many males work as cooks and run *dhaba* or tea-shop. Some have taken to business and animal husbandry. The raw material required for the Bharbhunja traders is purchased in the market and transactions are made in cash. Some children of this community work to earn. There are persons among the Bharbhunja who reportedly practise black magic, behave as if they are in trance and make a living out of this. Women of this community earn through working as maid-servants and as midwives

Those staying in rural areas are governed by the statutory *panchayat* which is composed of persons from different communities and have a defined role in planning and implementing developmental activities. The elders usually solve the routine family or caste disputes. The aggrieved party is free to appeal to the law enforcing officials. Those living in urban areas are governed by the local civil and judicial laws.

They follow both Hinduism and Sikhism and attend or visit the respective fairs, festivals and shrines. Lohri, Holi, Diwali, Dussehra, Baisakhi and Guruparabs are the common festivals. Punjabi folk songs, folklore and folk tales form the oral traditions of the community. Services of a Brahman priest or *granthi* are required for performing birth, marriage and death rites.

They traditionally accept from and exchange water and food with Jhinwar but not with Chuhra, Chamar, Dheha, Dhobi, Nai and Muslim. They share cremation ground, religious shrines and water sources with other communities.

In formal education Bharbhunja boys are able to take up studies upto school level but drop out subsequently due to lack of economic resources as they have to earn and support their families. Girls also drop out owing to poverty. Their attitude is positive towards both indigenous and modern medicare. They visit local dispensaries, government hospitals and private doctors for various ailments. They have a positive attitude towards modern methods of family planning. The facility of supply of drinking water is availed of and so is electricity. Wood, cow-dung cakes and kerosene oil are used as fuel. Those who stay in urban areas use liquified petroleum gas (L.P.G.) as fuel. The facilities of ration shop and banks are availed of by the community. Their attitude towards saving is positive.

A.K. BHATIA

# BHATIA

The Bhatia claim to be the descendants of Lord Krishna and had ruled Jaisalmer in Rajasthan before migrating to Punjab, Sindh, Gujarat, Bombay and Frontier districts of Dera Ismail Khan, Bannu and Multan in A.D. 1152 during the second invasion of Muhammad Gauri. Small territorial groupings also exist among them like Multani, Banu, Sialkoti, Frontier Bhatia, etc., depending on the name of the territory from where they have migrated into the present day Punjab.

According to one legend Raja Jai Singh who was a direct descendant of Lord Krishna, and a ruler of Mathura had three sons namely Vijay Raj, Abhiraj and Vijaypal. During an attack on Madhpuri, Raja Jai Singh was killed and Vijaypal took over the throne. He did not treat his other two brothers well. Vijay Raj and Abhiraj left the palace and distributed all their wealth to the poor and needy and became followers of Mother Goddess Amba. After spending twelve months in worshiping Goddess Amba, the two brothers felt that the Goddess was not happy with them, and so they decided to sacrifice their lives by immolating themselves by plunging into a *bhatti* (oven). At this, they were blessed by the Goddess and ordained that Abhiraj should go to Jaisalmer and Vijaypal to Kuchh and Sindh. Abhiraj established his rule in Jaisalmer and his descendants were first known as Bhatti and were later called Bhatia. Vijay Raj attacked Kuchh and established his rule there. His descendants are known as Jarjate.

In A.D. 1151, Muhammad Gauri attacked Jaisalmer with an army of twenty thousand soldiers, but was pushed back by the Bhatia soldiers who inflicted a death toll of five thousand soldiers on Muhammad Gauri. In A.D. 1152, he again attacked Jaisalmer but this time the Bhatia ruler was defeated in the war. On the day of *Ekadashi* of *Phagun* in A.D. 1152, about two thousand Bhatia soldiers left Jaisalmer for Punjab, Sindh, Gujarat, Bombay and Frontier areas, where they settled and flourished subsequently in trade and industry. Many consider them to be Khatri only.

They are distributed mostly in the urban areas of Punjab, Haryana, Delhi, Gujarat and some areas of western Uttar Pradesh and Himachal Pradesh. They speak Punjabi within the family and with kin groups and Punjabi, Hindi, English and Urdu in their contacts with others. The scripts used by them are Devanagari, Gurmukhi, Roman and Arabic.

At present both vegetarian and non-vegetarian food habits prevail among them. During pre-Partition time, very few of them used to take meat and eggs. But at present, non-vegetarianism is equally prevalent. People of older generation do not take garlic and *masoor dal.* Their staple food is wheat, rice, pulses, and locally available vegetables. Maize also constitutes an important place in the diet. Pulses consumed are *urad, moong,* gram and *moth.* Earlier the cooking medium was only *desi ghee,* but now it has been replaced by *vanaspati ghee,* refined oil and mustard oil. Non-alcoholic drinks such as tea, *lassi,* milk and milk products are taken regularly.

Though alcoholic drinks were a taboo earlier, and a person or a family taking alcoholic drinks was treated as outcaste, these days the men take the drinks in varying frequency, particularly on joyous occasions. Liquor is purchased from the market. Locally available fruits are consumed very frequently. Among changes in food habits, there is an increase in the intake of meat, eggs, alcoholic drinks and in the consumption of rice. Spicy food and sweets are not taken during mourning periods but on joyous occasions. Many avoid the intake of onions, eggs and meat on Tuesdays and during Navratras. The first day of every month of the Hindu calendar, called Sakrant is also equally pious. Amritdhari Sikhs avoid liquor and meat throughout their lives. On Baisakhi day, *halwa* (pudding) mixed with first wheat and grams of the season is traditionally eaten. People going on journeys to holy places do not take non-vegetarian food and liquor. Smoking habits are seen among the Hindu Bhatias.

As already mentioned, the community is divided into different territorial groups such as Bhatia of Banu, Multani Bhatia, Jhangi Bhatia, Frontier Bhatia, Sialkoti, Wazirabadi, Pishori, etc., depending on the territory to which they belonged before migrating to the present-day Punjab after Partition.

They are divided into eighty-four sub-sections called *nukhs.* The names of these clans are based on the *mukhias* (leaders) who lead the migratory groups at the time of their migration from Jaisalmer. These eighty-four sub-sections, called *nukhs,* are divided into two broad groups: Group I, Bari, includes Babla Dhagga, Anda, Balaha, Jawa, Soni, Gandhi, Chichra, Chakab, Kandal, Ghanghal, Kore. The first three constitute the *dhai ghar* (two-and-a-half houses) whereas Balaha and Jawa forms the *char ghar* (four houses). All of these together are of *bara ghar* (twelve houses) status. The *dhai ghar,* traditionally, will not give their daughters to any other group but they may take daughters from *char ghar.* A breach of this rule would lead to degradation and hence the same section may be both *dhai ghar* and *char ghar.* Group II is Bunjahi which comprises the remaining sections such as Baila, Chotak, Dholia and Naida. There is also a lower group called Gand who are the offsprings of Bhatia married to widowed Arora women.

Two of the clans, Sachdeva and Gulati, separated from the Bhatias and joined the Arora community. The chief function of these subdivisions is to regulate marriage alliance and indicate descent and ancestory. There are changes in some of the clan names due to spelling and pronounciation variation only. Normally, the community name is itself used as surname but in a few cases, such as Gandhi and Soni, clan names one used as surnames. They have a high self-perception for their being of Rajput origin. They are Bhatti Rajputs, and according to Ibbetson (1916), their Rajput ancestory is beyond any doubt. They are known as true and strict Hindus who used to strictly abstain from meat, liquor, and tobacco. They consider themselves at par with other communities of Rajput and Kshatriya origin. They are aware of and recognize the *varna* system. They perceive themselves to be next only to Brahmans in terms of *varna* hierarchy. They also consider themselves superior to Khatri, Arora, Jat and Bania of Punjab.

They are endogamous and practise clan and village exogamy. Consanguineous marriages are strictly prohibited. Earlier, child marriage was in practice and age at marriage for boys was fifteen to sixteen years and for girls it was about ten years. At present, the age at marriage ranges from twenty to twenty-five years for both boys and girls. Marriages are negotiated whereas earlier exchange marriage (*vatta-satta*) used to be practised. Monogamy is the form of marriage. Symbol of marriage is vermilion, gold bangles, *bindi* and ring, but are not followed strictly. Use of *mehndi* is prohibited. The practice of *kanyadan* exists. Dowry is in kind and cash. The rule of residence after marriage is patrilocal.

Divorce may take place due to maladjustment, barresness, lack of male issue, chronic illness or insanity. Either male or female can divorce and it is with judicial approval. In case of divorce, marriage expenditure is to be returned. Children are a liability of either father or mother. Widow remarriage is not permissible, but widower and divorcee remarriage may take place. Traditionally, widows were treated like untouchables and they were not allowed to touch any food or take part in any social functions. Widower remarriage though allowed is not celebrated. It has to be a very simple affair. There will be no ritual of *ghori-charhna*. The widow will, however, continue to stay in her deceased husband's house. Among changes in marriage related matters, there is an increase in age at marriage and incidence of divorce; there is liberalization in observance of rules regarding divorce and re-marriage.

Both nuclear and extended family types exist. Interpersonal relations of respect, love, fear, avoidance, obligations, joking and even confrontation exist in the family. Elders, both male and female, command respect in the family. Avoidance relationship exists between *nuh* (daughter-in-law) and *sauhra* (father-in-law), *jeth* (husband's elder brother) and younger brother's wife. Not only *jeth* and *sauhra*, but also other elder adult males are avoided. Even elder male members of the *biradari* (brotherhood) and village folk are avoided. The women used to practise *purdah*. Joking relationship exists between *jeeja-sali*, *dewar-bhabi*, and grandparents and grandchildren, particularly maternal ones. Conflict and confrontation arise due to property disputes, challenge to the authority of elders, check on the freedom of youngsters, disrespect to traditional norms and due to work-load in the joint families. All males have equal right in the property as per rules of inheritance. Succession goes to the eldest son. There is a trend of change showing an increase in the formation of nuclear families and decline of the joint family system. There is also change in inheritance rules; daughters also have equal legal right in the property, but in practice, daughters do not claim legal share in the property, and in case any one does, it leads to strained relationship between brothers and sisters.

Earlier, women used to observe *purdah* and were confined only to house-hold chores, but they did have a role in rituals and religious affairs. At present, with the women of the community becoming more educated and enlightened and having started contributing to family income by taking up various jobs and professions, their role and status in the family have changed remarkably. Besides rituals and religious participation, they also fully partake in social and political activities. Equal rights and adult franchise endowed on women have changed their outlook towards family and society.

Pre-delivery ritual, *reetan*, is observed during the seventh month of preganancy. In this, a *puja* is performed and parents of the expactant mother bring clothes, sweets and some cash for the family. Pre-delivery and post-natal restrictions are observed. The post-delivery pollution called *sootak* is observed for thirteen days. During this period, mother and the new born are confined to a solitary room. On the thirteenth day, the mother takes a ritual bath, performs *puja* and cooks something sweet, that is *sooji-ka-halwa*, in the kitchen to be served to family members and neighbours. Thereafter, the post-delivery pollution is terminated. The naming ceremony of the new-born is also observed on the thirteenth day. *Mundan* ceremony among the Hindu Bhatias, is observed either in the first, third or fifth year in case of a male child. In some territorial groups of the Bhatia, *mundan* ceremony is performed stealthily.

Marriage rituals are performed at the bride's residence. Among the Hindu Bhatias, marriage rituals consist of four or seven *lavan phere* around the sacred fire. The Sikh Bhatias, have four *lavan phere* around *Guru Granth Sahib* which is called *anand karaj.* Before the marriage ceremony, *barat* consisting of relatives, friends and neighbours is feasted by the bride's parents. It is preceeded by *shagun*, *milani*, and *jaimala* ceremony. The traditional Punjabi custom of *rok*, *thaka* and *chunni charhana* is observed. The consummation of marriage is at the groom's residence.

The dead are cremated and their bones are immersed in water. Children dying at young age are buried. After the death, pollution period of thirteen days is observed in the family. On the fourth day called *chautha*, the *rakh* are immersed in running water; on the tenth day, called *dasvin*, the bones are taken for immersion in the Ganga at Hardwar. From the fourth to the thirteenth day, *puja*, *havan* or *paath* is performed daily. The one performing the last rites will not eat onion, garlic and non-vegetarian food for ten days. He will sleep only on the ground. On thirteenth day, the *rasam pagari*, *kirya* or *uthala* takes place. Thereafter, the family starts attending to routine duties. On the seventeenth day, *satarwin* is performed when seventeen Brahmans are fed and given some money. For a full year, no festival or festivity is observed in the family. Annual *sharadh* are performed. The change in the life-cycle rituals is that these have been curtailed.

The Bhatias are a non-agricultural community, with very few owners of agricultural land and are by and large, engaged in trade, industry and business. Many are self-employed and are also in government and private service. The community has enterpreneurs, scholars, creative artists, teachers, administrators, scientists, engineers, bureaucrats, doctors and defence personnel.

There used to be traditional *biradari* system at village, district and regional levels, which used to look after the interests of the community and intra-community problems pertaining to domestic feuds, property and marriage disputes. These *biradaries* were headed by some members whose membership was not permanent and were nominated by voice vote. They used to recommend social boycott of families found to be offenders, and no one would they take a bride from these families nor would allow any one to give brides to these families. In modern times, the efficiency and existence of such *biradari panchayats* is not recognized, though older members of the community still continue to respect the *biradari* wherever it exists. In any case, such *biradaries* never had any statutory powers. The traditional method of solving any dispute by the intervention of the elders in the family still persists in the community. However, if any dispute remains unresolved, the aggrieved party is free to approach the court of law for justice.

The Bhatias profess two main religions, that is Hinduism and Sikhism. Some also follow Arya Samaj, Nirankari and Radhaswami sects. The deities of wider pantheon order are worshipped by Hindu Bhatias. They have special reverence for Lord Krishna, from whom the community traces its descent. The traditional sacred centres, shrines and pilgrimages of Hindu religion are visited by Hindu Bhatias, and the *gurdwaras* and shrines sacred to Sikhs are worshipped by Sikh Bhatias. The services of a Brahman or a *granthi* (Sikh priest) are used for worshipping and for performing birth, marriage and death rites. The major fairs and festivals are Lohri, Baisakhi, Dussehra, Diwali, Holi and Janamashtami and various Guruparabs. These festivals are of socio-religious significance. The pattern of change is exhibited in terms of many Bhatias having changed over to Sikhism and Arya Samaj sect. But the pre-change customs and practices are still common to many Bhatias.

The heroic tales of Hindu gods and goddesses and of Sikh Gurus are narrated in the community. In dance, the traditional *bhangra* and *giddha* dance are performed during joyous occasions, festivals and festivities. The traditional musical instruments are *dhol*, *dholki* and *daphali*.

The traditional intercommunity linkages are with the Brahman for ritual purposes and with all other non-Scheduled Caste communities for social and occupational purposes. They do not accept or exchange water and food with Shudras, Scheduled Castes, Muslims and those dealing in leather. However, with other communities, free commensal relations are observed. They will neither take brides from other community nor would they give brides to other communities. They have access to wells and water sources, roads, schools, temples and cremation grounds with other communities except with Scheduled

Castes, Muslims and Chamars. In modern intercommunity linkages they are more liberal, and marital relationship with Brahman, Khatri, and Arora communities are seen. Being in trade and industry and also in white-collar jobs, in defence, in engineering and medical profession, as administrators and scientists, as creative artists and bureaucrats, political workers and leaders, they have linkages with other local communities. Many have settled outside India in different professions thus further widening modern intercommunity linkage.

The literacy rate was not very high particularly for the girls and they used to drop out mostly from primary education as that used to be considered enough for them. The girls were also not sent outside the village schools for higher classes and were married at an early age. But the boys and menfolk, were usually literate. At present, however, there are equal opportunities for boys and girls to achieve academic excellence. The girls and boys normally study upto graduate/post-graduate level and are even going in for professional degrees.

Both indigenous and modern medicare are availed of. Their attitude towards family planning is favourable, with couples prefering one to three children. The community being mostly confined to urban areas, facilities of drinking water are readily available. Those who are self-employed are engaged in industry, trade, transport and contractorship. Electricity is available to the community. Fuel sources used to be firewood and cow-dung cakes, earlier, but now it has been replaced by coal, kerosene oil and L.P.G. Public distribution system is used only for sugar and kerosene oil, that too by a limited number of people in the community.

A.K. BHATIA

# BHATRA

The Bhatras are described as the traditional pedlar, fortune-teller, astrologer, religious-singer and pedigree-teller. They are also known as Bhat, Charan, Darpi, Ramiya, Jyotshi, Digpal, Rana, Rathore, Rau or Swali but Bhatra is the most common term used for them. According to one view, the Bhatra word appears to be a diminutive of the Sanskrit *bhatta* meaning a bard or a singer. In Kashmiri, Bhat means a learned person. They claim Brahmanical origin and according to one account (Ibbetson, 1916), they are the descendents of one Madhomal—a Brahman *rishi* (saint) who was a singer and poet. He once loved and wedded a dancing girl by the name of Kam Kundala. From this marriage, descended the Bhatra or as they were also known, Madhwas—from Madho Mal. This tradition is said to be preserved in the *Mahabharata* and *Singhasan-Batisi.* According to one legend, Madho was born and died in Sri Lanka. During the reign of Babar, Guru Nanak visited the island and made a disciple of Changa Bhatra, a descendant of Madho. A Sikh temple known as Dera Baba was built in Sri Lanka to the Guru's memory at the Madhwa's original home. Numerous persons became followers, many of whom were converted to Sikhism and followed Guru Nanak back to India. They initially did not settle in Punjab but were found chiefly along the banks of Ganga selling cheap ornaments and so-called Vedic medicines. Later on, they migrated to Hoshiarpur and Sialkot (now in Pakistan) and then spread throughout the state.

They are distributed throughout the state, mainly in the big cities and towns of Punjab. They speak Punjabi at home and with kin groups as also with others but occasionally shifting over to Hindi at times. The script used is both Devanagari and Gurmukhi. Normal Punjabi dress is worn by both men and women. Men wear typical white turban.

In food habits, they used to be pure vegetarian but now a few have started occasionally taking non-vegetarian diet and eggs. Their staple food is wheat, rice and pulses. They consume locally available vegetables, fruits and pulses in varying degrees. Food is cooked in *ghee*, groundnut or mustard oil. Roots and tubers in the form of vegetables are eaten. Alcoholic drinks were prohibited earlier but the new generation occasionally takes alcoholic drinks especially on the occasions of festivals and festivities in the family, such as marriage or birth of a male child. Consumption of milk and milk products is high. They take tea, *lassi*, sweets prepared from milk and also curd in varying quantity. Use of sweets increases on joyous occasions in the family or during various festivals. Intake of fruit, pulses, milk and other food items varies depending on the economic condition of the family.

The Bhatras have various *gots* but no hierarchy exists among them. The main function of these *gots* is to regulate marriage alliance and to indicate descent and ancestry. According to one account, there are twenty-two *gots* in the Bhatra community. Some of them are: Bhains, Bhatti, Bhotiwal, Digwa, Gami, Gojra, Kag, Kasba, Lande, Lar, Lohi, Rathore and Rod. They are aware of the *varna* system and used to recognize their place as Brahman-Bhat Brahman. Their claim of Brahmanical origin is supported by the fact that earlier they used to wear *janeu* and apply *tilak* (mark on the forehead) which has subsequently been abandoned due to their conversion to Sikhism. Self-perception of the community is high as they believe to be equal to Brahmans and thus being superior to the Kshatriya and the Vaish. Other local communities consider them to be of low status on account of their occupations of seeking alms, fortune-telling, and astrology.

In marriage, they practise endogamy at the community level and exogamy at *got* level. Marriage within the same *got* or that of the mother and grandmother is not allowed. Marriage within blood-relations is considered as incest. The age at marriage is eighteen years for the girl and twenty-one years for the boy. Child marriage was practised earlier but now marriages are solemnized when the boy and the girl have attained adulthood. Marriages are negotiated by the elders, whereas relatives help in finding a suitable match for the boy and the girl. Monogamy is followed strictly. The marriage symbols are vermilion, bangles, *bindi* and finger-ring.

The concept of *kanyadan* exists and dowry, given in cash and kind, consists of clothes, household articles and jewellery or gold. After marriage, the bride stays with her in-laws. Divorce is normally not allowed. Even in extreme cases of maladjustment, barrenness and sickness, the institution of marriage is respected in its true tradition. A man or a woman becoming a widow at a very early age, may be allowed to remarry. Widower remarriage with wife's younger sister may be allowed if both the families find it convenient and agree for the same. Changes such as increase in age at marriage, liberalization of rules for remarriage and not observing marriage symbols strictly, are taking place with the passage of time.

Both the nuclear and joint family types exist in Bhatra. Traditional interpersonal relations of respect, love, avoidance, joking and obligations are observed in the family. The elders are feared and respected, while the young members of the family receive love and affection. Avoidance relationships exists between father-in-law and daughter-in-law, younger brother's wife and husband's elder brother, and between ladies and elder male community members. Joking relationship is observed between elder brother's wife and husband's younger brother, wife's younger sister and sister's husband, grand-parents and grandchildren and wife's brother and sister's husband. Conflict and confrontation arise in dealings related to property matters, check on freedom of youngsters and challenge to the authority of elders. In a joint family, the division of work is the most common point of conflict. Only male members of the family have a share in property. Daughters are not allowed a share in the property as per the tradition though according to the prevailing law, daughters can claim their share in the property but such claim normally leads to strained relations. Succession goes to the eldest son. Inter-family linkages are very strong in the community. There has been a rise in the formation of nuclear families resulting in decline of extended family system.

Women have traditionally low status in the community. They are confined to household jobs only. Some may add to family income by stitching clothes and knitting at home. They do have a role in social functions, religious and ritual activities and mechanism of social control. Owing to adult franchise, women have a limited role in political sphere. But no social, religious, ritual and festivity is complete without the active participation of the womenfolk in a family. Their opinion is normally sought, especially of elderly women, for settling a marriage, purchase of a house or property and items of family utility.

Pre-delivery rituals are observed in the seventh month and are called *ritan*. On this occasion, *panjiri* (a sweet preparation of flour) is sent by the would-be mother's parents and is distributed in the family and neighbourhood. Antenatal restrictions are also imposed on the woman who is not allowed strenuous household works. Post-delivery pollution is observed for forty-one days and is called *sootak*. The naming ceremony is observed when the child is one-and-a-quarter months old. The naming ceremony becomes a special occasion if it is a male child especially in cases of financially sound families.

Marriage rituals are performed partially at bridegroom's residence and partially at the bride's place. The marriage ceremony consists of four *pheras* around the sacred *Guru Granth Sahib* and is performed by a *granthi* among the Sikh Bhatra. A feast is given by the parents of the bride. Consummation of marriage is at groom's residence.

Dead bodies are cremated and bones are immersed in water. Pollution period is observed for thirteen days. The dead are remembered every year and *akhand path* (non-stop recital of *Guru Granth Sahib*) is arranged in memory of the deceased relatives and friends. The life cycle rituals are being curtailed.

Some Bhatras are traditional alms-seekers, going from door to door and market to market and asking for money and *atta* (flour). They collect alms in the form of *atta* and cash on Tuesdays in the name of Mangal Devta and on Saturday in the name of Shani Devta. On Saturdays they ask for coins and mustard oil. They tell about Shani and Mangal being annoyed and suggesting a way out and thus earning money. Since they are also traditional astrologers and fortune-tellers, they are found on the roadside with a parrot or a cow asking for money for telling people ways and means to overcome their problems or foretelling their future. They sell cheap ornaments for women and sing on various religious occasions, and as such are engaged as *gurdwara granthi, sevadars* (religious attendants) in *langars* (community kitchen) and as Nihangs. They are also reputed to sell herbs and so-called Vedic medicines. In earlier times, the gullible patients were made to sign a bond for fifty rupees or more as fee, if they recovered from illness. They also indulge in face-reading and selling rings, stones and other talisman for warding off trouble or protection against an evil eye or an evil soul.

Some of the educated younger members have taken up jobs in the organized sectors. The Bhatras are a landless community. Children below fifteen years are also engaged in collecting alms on Tuesdays and Saturdays. They also pierce children's noses and ears for rings and get their service charges.

The community has one main *panchayat* at Ludhiana which controls and looks after the affairs of the community and plans and implements schemes for their upliftment. Besides, there are also *mohalla panchayat* (area councils) where there is a concentration of families belonging to the Bhatra community. It normally has four office-bearers called *pradhan, chhota pradhan, chogduar* and *khajanchi*. They are normally elected by a voice vote and are learned, active and enlightened members. After Independence, they are governed by statutory bodies such as municipal committee and civic corporation, which plan and implement welfare schemes for all the inhabitants of the area, irrespective of caste and creed. Those living in rural areas are controlled and governed by the statutory village *panchayats* which have heterogenous composition. They are thus governed by the prevalent local laws.

The Bhatra follow Sikh religion. They revere all the ten Gurus and follow their teachings. The sacred shrines and centres for pilgrimage are the same as for other Sikhs. The sacred specialist is the *gurdwara granthi*, who may be either from the same community or from other sikh community. The role of a *granthi* is to worship, impart religious teachings and perform birth, marriage and death rites. They observe and celebrate Holi, Diwali and Baisakhi besides all the Guruparabs. Some of the festivals and festivities are a mixture of rituals from both Hinduism and Sikhism such as worshipping the planets Mangal and Shani. They participate and celebrate various festivals with great fervour; for those engaged in their traditional occupation, these are occasions for more earnings. At the time of solar or lunar eclipse, they receive special offerings to ward off the fear of its impact on an individual's life and health.

The community shares folk songs, folklore and folk tales with other local Punjabi communities. Folk songs are sung at marriages, birth of a child and other happy occasions. Both men and women participate in dance on such occasions. *Bhangra* or *giddha* is the traditional dance performed then.

They traditionally accept and exchange water and food with other local communities of trading, agricultural and industrial class but not with Chuhra, Chamar, and other Scheduled Castes. They accept *sukka atta* (dry flour), oil and dry food from Chuhra and Chamar but not cooked food. They prefer to marry within their own community. Putative kinship of a *dharam bhai* may exist on an individual basis in the immediate neighbourhood with other communities. They share water sources with other communities, in case the same is not available in the house of the individual family. They also share cremation ground with other local communities, visit the same religious shrines and participate in the local festivals and festivities. They have a specific role on such occasions by giving religious sermons.

The community has educated members, who hold white-collar jobs and are entrepreneurs and in business. Being traditional singers of religious hymns, the community has creative artistes who are good radio and TV singers.

In their attitude towards development programmes, the community shows a positive trend. Literacy and education are favoured for boys and partially favoured for girls. Both the boys and the girls are provided with an opportunity to study, though it is more encouraging for the boys. Many are reported to have received graduate and post-graduate level formal education. Some have even undergone training courses in the various polytechnics.

In health and medical care, both indigenous and modern medicare are used. They visit government hospitals, dispensaries and also private doctors when they require medical treatment. They are fully aware of the advantages of small family, though choice for the number of children vary from individual to individual and family to family. Some of them use modern methods of family planning.

Drinking water is available to individual families from pipelines or handpumps. Dissemination of information is through extension agencies, political parties and voluntary religious and social organizations. Electricity is available in every house. Kerosene oil, firewood, coal, dung cakes and even L.P.G. which is used by some well-off families are used as fuel. The facilities of ration through fair price shops are availed of. Their attitude towards saving is favourable.

A.K. BHATIA

# BRAHMAN

Ibbeston (1916: 218-321), states that 'the Brahman caste or class is divided into ten great sections, all based upon geographical distribution, which differ in customs and standing and do not intermarry. They again are divided into two groups each containing five sections as follows:

A. The five Dravidas (south of Vindhyas)
The Maharashtra (of the Maharashtra)
The Tailanga or Andhra (of the Telugu)
The Dravida (of the Tamil or Dravida)
The Karnataka (of the Carnatic)
The Gurjara of Gujarati (of Gujarat in Sindh)

B. The five Gaurs (north of the Vindhyas)
The Gaur (of Gaur, probably not Bengal)
The Saraswat or Sarsur (of Punjab, beyond the Saraswati)
The Kanya Kubja (of Kanauj)
The Maithila (of the Mithila country)
The Utkala (of Orissa)

Ibbetson (1916) further mentions that, 'the Punjab Brahmans belong, for most part, to the Gaur in the Jamna and south-eastern hills, and to the Sarsut in the remainder of the province. . . . It may be said that the line drawn north-east and south-west through Simla and Patiala roughly divides the Gaur from the Sarsut.' Different sections of the Brahmans are defined by Ibbetson as follows:

The Gaur Brahman: There has been much dispute about the position of the Gaur from which this section is named. Their traditional place of origin is Haryana and their present home is the portion of the North-West Province lying west of Aligarh and Mathura, and the part of Punjab defined above; and they are separated from Bengal by other sections of the castes. . . . The Gaur Brahmans are far more strict in all caste observances than the Sarsut Brahmans, from whose hands they will not eat bread, and upon whom they look down.

The Sarsut Brahman is the Brahman of the Punjab proper and takes his name from the Saraswati which lies near the eastern boundary. He is certainly much less rigid in his observance of caste rule, eating and smoking with most of the stricter Hindu castes such as Baniyas, Khatris, Suds, and Kayasths.

The Gujarati and Dakaut Brahmans: These men are scattered in small numbers all over the province. The Gujarati Brahmans probably belong to the Gurjara section already mentioned. The Dakaut or Dakotra Brahman are fortune-tellers and astrologers and came from northern Rajputana. They belong to Panj Gaur group of which they are sometimes in Rajputana, which is their home, considered as separate section.

The Pushkarna Brahmans take their name from the sacred lake of Pushkar or Pokhar near Ajmer. One section of them is said to have been originally Beldars or Ods who were raised to the Brahmanical rank as a reward for excavating the tank. They still worship the pick-axe. They are the hereditary Brahmans of the Rajputana Bhatias, and are more strict in caste matters than the Sarsut.

The Maha Brahman or Acharj: This is the Brahman who performs the funeral ceremonies. After the cremation he is seated on the dead man's bedstead and the son lifts him up bedstead and all, and make obeisance to him. He then receives the bedsteads and all the wearing apparel of the dead man. He is considered so impure that in many villages he is not allowed to come inside the gate.

The Muhial, Moyal or Mial Brahmans: There is a sub section of the Sarsut section, who are said to be so named from the seven *muhins* or clans of which they consist. They are almost confined to the sub-mountain salt range tract. They say that some of their ancestors rose to high position under the Mughals; since then they have abandoned all performance of priestly functions, or claim to sacredotal character, and cultivate land, but especially take service in the army as clerk. Another story derives their name from a place called Mava, now deserted.

The Dharukra Brahman are Gaur Brahmans of the Delhi territory, who have taken to widow-marriage, and with whom other Brahmans will not intermarry. They are much the same as the Dase or Doghla Brahmans.

Chamarwa and Gurra Brahmans: These are the Brahmans who minister to the Chamars, Aheris and other outcastes. They are not recognized as Brahmans by the other classes; and though they wear the sacred thread it is possible that their claim to Brahman origin is unfounded. Yet on the whole it seems most probable that they are true Brahmans by descent, but have fallen from their high position. They are often called Chamarwa Sadhs.

The Brahmans of Punjab are mainly Sarsut but one can also find the Pushkarnas, Muhials, Bhojki, Dakochi, etc., among them. The Pushkarna are relatively lesser in number. The Muhial Brahmans are described by Rose as secular Brahmans who derive their name from Muhin; a sum of money is given by them at weddings to Bhats and Jajaks. The Sarsut is the major group among Brahmans of Punjab. They serve various Hindu castes including the Scheduled Castes. Hence the status of Brahmans was determined by the status of the caste which they serve. The first in the hierarchy of Brahmans are the Shuktas. The second subcaste group are the Brahman from the Khatri, the third group are the Arora Brahman, the fourth are the Jat Brahman and the fifth subgroup are the Brahman of inferior castes, who are called Chamarwa.

They are, however, widely distributed throughout Punjab. The Brahman empirically studied are the Muhials in the village Talabpur Pandori of Gurdaspur district. It has three hundred Brahman households. They migrated from Pakistan (from Shakargarh) after Partition. According to them, the major subgroups among the Brahman are Saraswat, Gaur, Muhial, Bhardwaj, Sangotra, Acharya, etc. The male dress comprises shirt, *dhoti* or pant, with a sandalwood paste *tilak* on their forehead, some of them keep *choti* (tuft of hair) on their head. Some wear *kharawan* (footwear made of wood). The female dress is *salwar, kameez* and *dupatta*. Their food habits are similar to those of local Punjabis. *Dal-roti* is their staple food and cereals include wheat, maize and rice; pulses eaten are gram, *moth, urad, moong*, peas and beans. Cooking medium is mustard oil, groundnut oil, and a few, who can afford it, use *desi ghee* also. Consumption of alcoholic drinks is generally avoided. Tea and *lassi* are the beverages enjoyed by the community. They take fruits occasionally. The older generation among them are vegetarian, but the younger generation have taken to non-vegetarian diet. Changes in food habits include the increase in the use of vegetables, onion and garlic and non-vegetarian food, such as eggs and mutton.

There are various subcaste categories among the Brahman in Punjab and some of them have been specified earlier. Each subcaste has its own *gots*. For example, there are eighty-four *gots* among Pushkarnas, seventeen *gots* among Astri (a sub-caste among Sarsut), twelve *gots* among Barajati, twenty *gots* among Halbaha (subcaste among Sarsut) and so on. The Brahman in Punjab observe subcaste endogamy and *got* exogamy. The superior subcaste among them observe four *got* exogamy. The status of Brahmans in Punjab is generally lower as compared to their counterparts in southern and eastern India, including

U.P. The status distinction on subcaste lines is still observed among them.

There are seven *gots* among Muhial who were subjected to empirical study. They are Datta, Mohan, Bali, Vaid, Chhibar, Latu and Bhanwal who observe subcaste endogamy and *gots* exogamy. Marriage rules are in consonance with the Hindu Vedic rituals. Consent of boys is generally taken before settling a marriage; girl's consent is not considered important. The mediator plays an important role in settling matches for marriage. Though child marriage was prevalent in the past, now the age at marriage for girls ranges from eighteen to twenty-five years and that for boys from twenty-two to thrity years. Dowry is practised among them. The *barat* party includes forty to forty-five persons. When marriage is initially agreed between boys and girls, a small function called *roka* is performed which is followed by *thaka* when sweets are distributed and ornaments are presented and the final is *shagun* before marriage. At *shagun* a fridge, television set, sweets and money may be gifted. Divorce is prohibited among the Brahmans.

Of late, the impact of Radhaswami faction is being felt. The birth of a male child is celebrated but not of a female. On the eleventh day after death, some rites are performed and a gift is extended to the Acharya Brahman. At the end of the first year of death, *shradh* ceremony is observed and at the end of the fourth year *chavarkhi* is observed; on this occasion, the family priest is fed.

All the Brahmans in this village have land. Nearly 50 per cent have ten to twenty acres of land, three to four families have more than twenty acres and the rest, less than ten acres. There are six tractors possessed by the community and twenty tubewells and ten threshers. Such a situation, however does not exist as far as other Brahmans of the states are concerned. Nearly 60 per cent of their adults are employed in various services. The *sarpanch* of the *panchayat* is from their own village. They have a caste association at Gurdaspur where they meet once in a year. This association also provides utensils during festivals, marriage and other occasions and also extends help to the widows in the form of private education, skills, etc., to them. The Muhial Brahman have also their association at an all-India level, but other Brahman communities are weak in terms of social solidarity.

They observe restriction on eating and drinking with the low castes. There is good cooperation between Brahmans, Scheduled Castes and Sikhs in this village. Their males are well-educated and the females are also educated though instances of higher education among the girls are comparatively few. They are paid in cash in lieu of their services rendered at the time of various birth, marriage of death rites. Modern inter community linkages are either in teaching, administration, business or defence services. Family planning methods are popular among them. Three or four children in a family are preferred. For medical facilities they approach either the health centres or private practitioners. Some of them also practise Ayurvedic treatment and render help to other individuals in villages. Source of water is handpumps. Those who live in cities utilize piped water facility. Most of them work as priests, health practitioners, businessmen or in agriculture. They take advantage of media and communication facilities. They use electricity, and those who are engaged in agriculture have tube wells, use chemical, and organic fertilizers, insecticides. Im-munization facilities to mother and child are available. They have ration card facilities.

K. Gopala Iyer

# CHAMAR

The term 'Chamar' is derived from the Sanskrit word *charmakar* (worker in hides). Hence the Chamars are tanners and leather workers. Those of them, who have embraced Sikh religion are called Ramdasia after Guru Ramdas. In the Malwa and Doaba regions there are a large population of the Chamars who have been converted to Sikhism and they do not work in leather and have instead taken to handloom or pitloom and as a result have occupied a higher social status than the workers in leather. The Sikh Chamars are also called Ramdasia because it was their Guru Ramdas, who first took them into the folds of Sikhism. The Hindu Chamars are also called Ravidasi as they follow the teachings of Bhagat Ravidas. The other synonyms of the Chamars are the Jatia, Golia or Raigar. The Jatia Chamar have their concentration in the area bordering the state of Rajasthan and they work mostly in camel hides. The Raigars generally have the lowest position among the Chamars. The Chamars, according to one story related by Rose (1911: 148): took its origin traditionally from the two brothers Chanu and Banu. The story tells of Chanu who removed the carcase of a cow with his own hands and as a result he was made an outcaste by his fellow castemen and sebsequently took to leather work. Another version of the story is that the Gat told his brother Mat not to remove the carcase and later on disassociated himself for doing so. The Chamars are considered to be the descendants of the Mat. There are five subcastes, who do not intermarry. Chandor took their origin from Benares may be due to Bhagat Kabir, Raidasi or Ravidasi are the followers of Bhagat Ravidas, Jatia have high concentration in the areas neighbouring Haryana. Chamar are found in Ludhiana and Jalandhar, and Golia, who are further divided into (i) Buna, being those Sikh Chamars, who have taken to weaving; (ii) and the Chamars in Patiala district who are further divided into Bagri Chamars, who have migrated from Bagar (Rajasthan) and the Desi Chamars are those, who make *jutti* (footwear).

They have been recognized as Scheduled Caste and according to *Census of India* (1981), their total population is 12,21,145 (6,60,835 males and 5,60,310 females) whereas, in 1911 it was 1,128,704 individuals. They have their maximum concentration in the districts of Ludhiana, Sangrur, Patiala and Bhatinda. In the villages their wards are known as *vehras.* They speak Punjabi language and those who are literates use Gurmukhi, Devanagari and Roman scripts both with the members of their community and other communities. However, the Ramdasi, who are weavers (Julahas) live separately from the Chamar. The Sikhs wear turban. Men wear shirt and pants or *pyjama*. Women wear *salwar*, *kameez* and *dupatta*. Wheat is their staple food. Rice is taken occasionally. They take pulses such as gram, *urad*, *moong*, *masur* and *moth*. Their cooking medium is groundnut oil and mustard oil. They take tea and *lassi.* Alcoholic drinks are taken occasionally. Curd and butter are also used. Consumption of fruits is very low.

The Ramdasi, Ravidasi, Jatia and Raigar do not intermarry. They have exogamous *gots* such as Sidhu, Kauldhar, Kataria, Kalra, Chauhan, Bhatti, Badhan, Bains, Batoi, Ghameri, Hir, Jal, Kathana, Mahri, Phundwal and Sindhu and their function is to regulate marriage alliances. They recognize their status as Shudras. Marriage is arranged by negotiation by the parents of the boy and the girl, when they attain adulthood around eighteen to twenty years of age with the help of the *vichola.* Women use vermilion. Dowry is offered in kind. The rule of residence after marriage is patrilocal, divorce and remarriage are permitted, when husband and wife fail to adjust with each other. Barrenness and impotency are other reasons for divorce. They have joint families in which there may be conflict and confrontation between members of the family relating to matters of property, interests of children and contribution towards the family income. The sons inherit property of their father equally. Women attend to the household activities and children and in villages they keep domestic animals, collect cow-dung and firewood and cut grass. They also work in the fields as labourers. They have a low status. The ceremony of *namkaran* is performed. The marriage ceremony is according to traditions of seven or four *lavan pheres.*

The Chamars are engaged in leather work; they also supply agricultural labour as they are hard workers; they also work as *sanjis* (contract labourers). They remove the dead cows and buffaloes from the houses of the Jat Sikhs and remove their skin and tan them. In the interior villages of the state there are still patron-client relationships and they get a fixed amount of grains after every harvest. A scetion of the Chamars also prepare *khes*, *khadi* cloth on their handlooms.

Some work as labourers either on daily wages or on annual contract (*sanjh*), while the others work in skin and hide, few work as government servants. They have their own *panchayat*, an elderly person known as *siana* (village elder) is elected as *lambardar*. Matters relating to marriage disputes and divorce are settled by the *panchayat* and a fine ranging from five hundred to one thousand rupees is imposed depending upon the nature of offence. According to *Census of India* (1911: 450) the total population of Chamars is 11,28,704 individuals which comprises 6,13,671 males and 5,15,033 females.

The Hindu and Sikh Chamars are found in all the districts of the state. The Chamar community is one of the oldest community and even has its mention as charmkar (leather workers), one of the degraded Shudras in the *Manusmriti*. The Chamar community due to its occupation was subjected to all humiliations in the past.

The Ramdasi worship Hindu gods and gurus including Guru Ravidas, and the *Guru Granth Sahib*. A change of religion has been noticed. In the villages, where they have *kachcha* houses, the front doors and the interior walls are decorated with floral designs.

Untouchability as practised in the past is still prevalent to some extent and some members of other communities still avoid taking water and food from them. They have separate *dharamshala*, sources of water and cremation ground. But generally there are no restrictions for sharing places of worship. The patron-client and cultivator-labourer relationships still exist. They have thrown up a few teachers, doctors and administrators.

Formal education for boys and girls both is favoured. The boys study up to matriculation and a few also join colleges, but not the girls. Handpumps are the source of drinking water. Most of the individuals work as agricultural or industrial labourers, apart from their own traditional occupation. They listen to radio more frequently than they watch television. Cow-dung, dried maize plants, groundnut plants are used as fuel. Facilities for immunization are available.

SWARAN SINGH

# CHANG

Ibbetson's account (1916: 199) states that the Chang people are known as Ghrith in Kangra, as Bahti in the eastern and Chang in the western portion of the lower ranges but were considered identical. Ibbetson also quotes Barnes to indicate that Chang is only another name for the Ghrith. About their origin, Ghirth legends say that the Almighty was eating and felt thirsty but had no water. He placed a lamp of *ghee* on the ground and called out 'come Ghrith', and a Ghrith, the progenitor of the race was 'produced and was sent to get water in a *lota* (water jar)'. This is supposed to date back to the birth of Krishna. The progenitor served Krishna and afterwards the Brahman by order of Krishna. Wakefield (1893: 10) points out that no original home of their is known outside the Kangra district. He, of course, mentions that there are Ghrith in the Doab who are known there by the names of Chang or Bahti. It is, however, difficult to know how these names arose. During the course of field interviews it was found that the people of this community in Pathankot *tahsil* called themselves Chang and as Bahti, in Hoshiarpur district and they agreed that all the three names are identical. None of their prominent community leaders could explain how the three names came about. One of the octogenarians, a well-informed person of the community, reflected that as the Ghrith expanded themselves beyond Kangra district the extended community beyond the limit of Kangra was termed Bahti (said to be derived from Hindi term *brihat* meaning 'expansion'). The term 'Chang' seems to denote the backward and hilly areas which they inhabit. However, it is difficult to substantiate this. It transpired during the course of the interview that the Muslim invasions made them migrate from Himachal to Gurdaspur, Amritsar, and Hoshiarpur districts.

According to the 1931 census their population was 1.25 lakh. They were distributed over Kangra, Amritsar, Gurdaspur (Pathankot *tahsil*) and Hoshiarpur districts. Those in Hoshiarpur, Gurdaspur, and Amritsar districts speak Punjabi at home and with outsiders, whereas in Kangra district they speak Dogri or Pahari languages. They use Devanagari and Gurmukhi scripts. Ibbetson (1981: 200) observes that they are said to be of Rajput origin, but there is no reliable information on the subject. He quotes Barnes (1850: 199) to indicate that they belong to the Shudra division of Hindus.

They are basically non-vegetarian. According to the *Kangra District Gazetteer*, they drink wine and eat pork, clovenfooted animals such as sheep, goats, deer, jungle fowl and all kinds of fish. Consumption of non-vegetarian food is quite common among them even today and is particularly relished by the younger generation. Those who are followers of Radhaswami sect are strict vegetarian and also avoid taking onion and garlic. Wheat, maize, rice, pulses and seasoned vegetables are part of their regular diet. Locally available fruits like mango, banana, grape, papaya, guava, peaches and apple are consumed. Cooking medium is vegetable *ghee*, oil and *desi ghee*. Milk and milk products are also consumed moderately. Tea intake has increased during last three decades. Earlier, alcoholic drinks were less frequent but now it has become a fashion and symbol of status. On happy occasions such as birth of a male child or marriage alcoholic drinks are freely served and consumed. Those following the Radhaswami sect or are baptized as Sikh avoid liquor and use of tobacco. Earlier *hookah* was common but now *bidi* and cigarettes is preferred.

All the three synonyms of Ghrith, Bahti, and Chang are equal in status. There have been several attempts since the 1930's to have a single caste term to signify their identity, but without success. The younger generations are keen to know their distinct identity which is posing a problem to their elders. However, the low status attached to them by the dominant castes has been one of the great irritants among this community. The community leaders had its first *sabha* in 1914 in Simla. Its office was later shifted to Lahore. In 1930, the *sabha* was named Kshatriya Ghrith, Bahti, Chang Maha Sabha and it was registered in this name. One of their major activist was Rai Sahib Chaudhary Gian Singh who was made president of the association in 1930. In 1927, the British government rewarded him with the title of Rai Sahib, after which he vigorously aroused the consciousness of his castemen by travelling from village to village. His major stress was to awaken the community to use education as a vehicle for social mobility. He also got the status of backward caste for his community immediately after Independence. He was even successful in getting his community men recruited in the police, army, the services and medical profession and also in important positions in the Army, Navy and Airforce, in white-collar jobs and in the legal professions.

The differentiation of this community can be noticed today along territorial, economic, occupational, religious and social lines. One of the major irritants has been that after the creation of Himachal Pradesh as a separate state, the Ghrith have not been given the status of

Backward Caste in that state which their brethren enjoy in Punjab particularly in respect of educational facilities. According to the *Kangra District Gazetteer* (1893: 23) there are a great many *firkas* such as Sial, Panjla, Thirku, Sakre, Panyan, Thimbu, Hangaria, Jalorich, Barol, Panyaria, Kathe, Chakotra, Bhut, Balaru Banjara, etc. Ibbetson (1916: 200) states that their subdivisions are Kandal, Bhardwaj, Pathari, Chhabru, Reru, Badial, Chhora, Battu, etc. Chhabru were found only in Hoshiarpur and Chhora and Battu only in Kangra. The others were in both districts. But they have a large number of divisions. A great part of these are named after villages and others after trade and occupation. Few are possibly totemistic in origin.

The nomenclature of these sects are as follows (a) name of animals or plants: Dhare, Ghara, Khunla, Gidar, Gadohari and Garuri, etc.; (b) name of occupations or nicknames: Surangiala, Nande, Mormar, Jukhnu, Paniari, Masand, Lokria, Ghora, Hariala, Saini, Hutla, Khaugar, Lahu, Topa, Kumhar, Naul and Pathrala, etc.; (c) name of colour: Kala, Kahra, Nila; (d) Khera, Banyanu, Dadda, Khunla, Ladharia, Ghurl, Khajura and Khatta.

The *Kangra District Gazetteer* (1893: 10) records that the well-known castes with whom the Ghrith will eat, drink and smoke are the Nai and Jhinwar. From Kalals downward they abstain from such interaction. Rajputs and certain Brahman will eat *pukka* food but not rice or *dal* with Ghriths. They will also drink with them but not smoke. The castes such as Rajputs, Brahman, Kshatriya will not smoke with them. They have a strong sense of pride of their being cultivators since the past and hence consider their status as equal to other agricultural castes. They however, consider the Jat to be superior to themselves and agricultural castes like Labanas, Sainis, Kamboj, etc., as equal. They invariably consider the Scheduled Castes including Mahashas and Aryas as inferior to themselves and observe food and eating restrictions with them. But, they freely interdine with other agricultural and other castes.

The *Kangra District Gazetteer* (1893: 4-6) discusses in details the traditional marriage procedure among the Ghrith. A Ghrith must marry a Ghrith; he must not marry a descendant of any of his paternal ancestors nor of his maternal grandfathers. They strictly observed subcaste and *got* exogamy. In the past this community practised polygamy. Girls were married under twelve years and elders choice for mates was decisive. A mediator or *rubaru*, goes to the parents of the girl and announces the proposal to them. If they accept, a day is arranged for the ceremony of betrothal (*nata*).

On this day the mediator conducts the boy's father or other guardians [. . . .] to the girl's house. He takes with him butter, *dahi* (yoghurt), grain, *gur* and clothes for the girl, and two rupees two paise in cash (and jewels, only if rich enough), and if a price for the girl has been agreed upon they take that too. These are placed in a wicker basket near a pitcher of water and an oil lamp is kept ready for the occasion. They are made to sit on a square mat made of sugar cane stalks. The boy's party bows with joined hands to the lamp and water vessel, dips his fingers into the *gur* and *ghee* and puts it in the mouth. Then both the boy's party and girl's sit down together for the first time. The go-between takes the money and the clothes to the girl who is with the women in another room, gives the money to her alongwith the clothes. Then the *rubaru* comes back and receiving the girl's price from the boy's father, gives it to the girl's father. The boy's father gives a token amount to the girl's party, the barber, the *purohit* and the *nai*. The boy's party stays till night, when the girl's family entertains them with a meal. After the meal, the girl's mother calls in other women of the village, for singing songs; they are paid money by the boy's father. From this time until marriage, boy's father sends once a year rice or maize, cream, *gur* and clothes for the girl.

On the marriage day, the boy is shaved, washed with *batna* to make him clean and dressed in a *kwah* (red *cholu*) and a red *pagri*, red *pyjamas* and *sehra* (tasselled head-dress). *Mehndi* is smeared on his hand to make his fingers red and he is carried in a *palki* to the girl's house. There, a *nain* (female barber) spreads a cloth on which the girl's father and the boy sit. The girl's father then gives to the boy's father's *nain* a little *bakhshish*, and the boy's father does the same to the other *nain*. The girl's party then takes the boy into the house. Later the girl's *purohit* reads the Vedic *mantras* to the couple, who later go into the *sahn* and drive four poles, previously adorned, into the ground and place others joining their tops. The boy and girl then sit underneath and *mantras* are read. Then they walk four times round the poles with ends of their clothes tied together. The marriage ceremony is now complete, the parties are given a feast at the bride's house. Then behind the *purdah*, the bride's head is anointed with *chaunk*. The bridegroom, either on the same or the next day, takes the bride to his father's house if it is near enough. Here the bride and bridegroom are made to sit before a lighted lamp and a *ghara* of water to which they bow with folded hands. They are then given *ghee* and *gur* to eat after which the bridegroom changes his wedding dress. The bridegroom takes the bride to his mother after which the bride, the *nain*, the midwife and those who had carried the gifts (given by the bride's parents) and also the *kahars* are feasted. The next day they take the bride to her parental home. If she is not of age, she sleeps with her mother-in- law. If she has attained puberty, she sleeps in a separate room with her husband. Then two or three months later the bridegroom takes her to his father-in-law's house and brings her back to his father's house again where she remains until her parents send for her. The marriage customs and rituals today are broadly the same except for minor changes.

The Chang are endogamous practising village, *got*, and subcaste exogamy. However, the Ghrith, Chang, and Bahti intermarried freely in the past and continue to do so even today (Ibbetson, 1916: 199). Monogamy is the rule. Child marriage was practised in the past, when marriages were soleminized at as early an age as six to eight years. Seventeen to eighteen is the minimum age at marriage for both boys and girls. Marriage symbols are *bindi*, *sindur* and finger, toe, ear and nose rings. The concept of *kanyadan* exists and dowry is given in cash and kind, but any demand regarding dowry is socially resented; rule of residence after marriage is patrilocal. Divorce is normally not allowed, but it is permissible with compensation only on ground of adultery and moral turpitude. Divorce can be initiated both by husband and wife and effected with the approval of community elders. Children after divorce become liability of the father. Remarriage is permitted in case of young widows and divorcees.

Widows and divorced males remarry freely and as per requirement. The young widow may be remarried to her deceased husband's younger brother and this practice is called *chadar paona*. Some of the salient changes in marriage practices are perceptible. Now, along with the parents' choice of mates, consent of boys and girls are also taken. Though marriages are strictly endogamous, yet marriages with upper castes such as Jats, Khatris, etc., are encouraged. Intermarriage between Hindu and Sikh Changs takes place freely. There were large numbers of Sikhs among Changs in the village Malikpur who married with the Hindu Changs, Bahtis and Ghriths. In such a situation marriage practices are invariably based on Sikh rituals that is *anand karaj*. Instances of marriages based on Vedic rituals amongst such families are also found. Another noticeable change is that *barat* is now restricted to fifty people instead to over one hundred in the past, and the marriage ceremony including the feast is a one-day affair and not three days as in the past.

Joint families are more common in villages, whereas nuclear ones are common in cities. The established interpersonal relations of respect, love and fear of elders exist in the family. Avoidance relationship is observed between father-in-law and daughter-in-law, husband's elder brother and his wife and all the family, village and community male and female elders. Joking relationship is seen between wife's sister and sister's husband, husband's younger brother and his wife. Conflict erupts particularly on account of property disputes. Inter-generational conflict is also noticed. Male equigeniture is the rule of inheritance and all sons equally inherit their father's property. Now daughters are also entitled for their share of property. Succession is by the eldest son.

Status of a woman is also reflected through the attitude exhibited towards widow remarrige. According to the *Kangra District Gazetteer* (1893), the widows in this community may remarry and that they should marry the husband's younger or elder brother, if anyone of them is alive. If these do not exist she must marry the next of kin among the collaterals and in case this also is not possible she must marry a Ghrith with no distinction of *got.* Remarriage of a widow is not to take place within a year of her husband's death though now this rule is relaxed. Permissibility of widow remarriage is a liberating influence on the otherwise oppressive practices among the Hindu upper castes which made a young widow suffer lifelong. Divorce is permitted but not against the will of the wife. It is locally called *chhodni.* This community follows the Hindu law of inheritance as stated earlier and therefore all inherit according to the rule of *chindewand.* Participation of women in activities such as agricultural operations and animal husbandry is prevalent today as in the past. The women take part in social, ritual and religious affairs but not in political activity except casting their vote. However, their opinion is sought at the time of the marriage negotiations.

Post-delivery pollution period is observed for one-and-a-quarter months. Naming ceremony is observed, *mundan* ceremony takes place when the child is one, three or five years of age. First feeding of cereals, called *gurti,* as practised in the past continues even today.

The dead are cremated and bones are collected and immersed in the holy Ganga at Hardwar. Ancestor worship in the form of annual *shradh* is reported. Pollution after death is observed in the family from eleven to seventeen days and ends usually in the form of a feast hosted by the family to the relatives, community members and villagers.

The Chang were mainly cultivators. The *Kangra District Gazetteer*

(1893: 9) mentions that the Ghrith were primarily engaged in agriculture. Some of them were owner-cultivators, but large numbers were tenants and also agricultural labourers. Few of them were also engaged as masons, brass workers, *halwais*, etc. However, agriculture was the characteristic occupation of this caste and is still considered to be the most honourable one. Even today, agriculture is the most important occupation in the villages which was noticed in Malikpur and Adampur villages; the villagers take special pride in calling themselves cultivators. In the past their economic status as tenants-at-will kept them in a subordinate position to the dominant Rajput landlords in Kangra district and Jat landlords in the districts of Gurdaspur and Hoshiarpur. They had to struggle against their domination and exploitation both in the courts and through mobilizaion. Their low economic status was also responsible for their low social status and is as a result of the sustained struggle that a majority among them are landowners today. The villages of Sarna, Faridanagar, Malikpur, Jamalpur, Burjua, etc., are mainly populated by the Chang, and in these villages, they are primarily cultivators. In the village of Adamwal in Hoshiarpur district, 75 per cent of them were landowners and 25 per cent landless. The main crops grown by the cultivators are paddy, wheat, maize, *jowar*, *urad* (*mah dal*), etc. Some of them have also leased their land to supplement their income. It is both on share cropping basis and fixed rent. In the share-cropping system the expenditure on fertilizer, water, and seed are shared equally between the landowner and the share cropper. The produce is shared equally but the labour cost has to be entirely borne by the share cropper. The fixed rent varies from one thousand to two thousand rupees per acre in the year. Other expenditure has to be fully borne by the tenants.

The traditional caste *panchayat* existed in this community in the past primarily as mechanism of social control. It had a role in awarding punishment in the form of social boycott or imposing fines for crimes and offences like dispute over land and water, sexual crimes, violation of traditional norms, etc. Now the statutory village *panchayat* takes care of these matters and if not settled, these are also taken to the court of law. However, as earlier stated, their caste organization has taken a new dimension since the early twentieth century and ever since it is no more confined to the traditional village issues. Now it is taking up such issues which it considers vital for the existence and growth of the community as a whole. The caste identity is intimately tied with the community's future aspirations. It was for this purpose that they formed their caste association in 1930 and have continued uninterrupted since then. Its leaders have been able to get Backward Class status for their community. Part of this struggle still continues in terms of getting the Backward Class status for the Ghrith in Kangra district in Himachal Pardesh. Today they have formed their community organization at tahsil, district and state level. They have their community association in cities such as Hoshiarpur, Chandigarh, Delhi, etc. Both their local *sabha* and the Maha Sabha meet regularly or at least once in a year. On the one hand while they have been able to consolidate, it has also led to the development of fissures among them. One such manifestation is the publication of their monthly magazines separately from Kangra, Chandigarh, and Delhi. Each one of these magazines not only gives vent to their own subcommunity problems but also leads to acrimony and charges against each other. At Hoshiarpur, they have also con-structed one Bhawan. These tendencies point to the widening chasm between their caste brethren in Himachal (particularly in Kangra district) and Punjab.

The *Kangra District Gazetteer* (1893) mentions that this community was primarily Hindu. It mentions their celebrated temple at Kangra, which is known as Bhagwati Temple and also mentions that for them the Gurus of the Sikhs and Golden Temple at Amritsar are also important for visit and worship. It also notes that there is no particular preference to either of the temples. They also worship Shiva who is also known as Jakhs. This deity is worshipped in the form of a stone generally placed among bushes and is supposed to be common among all Hindus owning cattle. The milch cattle are devoted to particular Jakhs and offerings are made for them to their particular Jakhs, when the cattle bear calves. This practice is declining now. In the past there was *nag* or snake worship which was considered very important for every family. This worship used to be the first thing in the morning for everyone and was performed by pouring little water over the stones (*Kangra District Gazetteer*, 1893: 30). The special yearly worship of the *nag* is undertaken on the fifth of the month of *Sawan* (Nag Panchmi). The daily worship of snakes is no more in practice, but the yearly worship is still performed. This community also has the concept of 'Sidh'. The 'Sidhs' are shrines and most important one is Dewat Sidh, whose chief shrine is in the Hamirpur district of Himachal Pradesh. This is not only confined to this community, but also among other local communities. When the crops ripened the shrine of the nearest Sidh was visited on Sunday. This practice is on the decline now. Sidhs were supposed to be special protectors of boys (*Kangra District Gazetteer*, 1893: 30). The Ghrith also used to venerate the tombs of celebrated Muslim saints, which is no more found in practice.

The twentieth century has seen quite important changes in the religious affiliation and religious belief systems of this community. The first impact was that of Arya Samaj among them. It had its attraction for this community particularly because Arya Samaj movement believed in widow remarriage. Some of them have emerged as active Arya Samaj preachers. Impact of Sikh religion is also visible, especially in the village of Malikpur, in Pathankot tahsil, the Sikhs constituted 50 per cent population of this community. In the village Adampur, one Bahti was *gurdwara* priest. Of late, the Radhaswami sect and its belief system has become quite popular among them because of the extreme simplicity of this faith and the very popular and effective communication system, which they have been able to develop with the masses. The common festivals observed by this commuity are Diwali, Holi, Lohri, Baisakhi, etc.

This community is known to have been superstitious and believing in evil spirits. There was the belief that very occasionally a man becomes possessed which is manifested by contortions and that the evil spirits could be exorcized by the charms of a Brahman or the *mahant* of Saloh temple. This practice is less common nowadays. Similarly, before starting an agricultural operation, services of a Brahman were required for finding the propitious day. Similarly, before sowing, a Brahman was consulted as to which particular grain would be most suitable to sow first. There was also a custom to sacrifice a goat in the first field in the village, on the spot where crop ripens. These superstitions are on the decline now.

Political leadership has emerged at state level and one ex-finance minister of Punjab belongs to Chang community. The Changs' attitude towards development programme is positive and the impact on the community is perceptible. Formal education facilities are availed of by both boys and girls. The boys study upto high school and some have even received college education. Some are doctors, teachers, engineers, advocates, and bank employees. Girls study upto high school level and many have received college education. Some girls are teacher, nurses, doctors and in clerical jobs in various offices. In respect of health and medical care, both modern and indigenous medicare are favoured and available. A government dispensary is available in the village. Their attitude towards family planning is very positive as the community is fully aware of the advantages of a small family. Couples indicate preference for one to three children. Modern methods of family planning, including sterilization, are used by the Changs. Facilities of drinking water are available in the form of handpump, tube well and pipe-water. They avail of the opportunities under the rural employment programmes. Modern agricultural machinery in the form of tractors and threshers are also used.

RAKESH KUMAR
K. GOPALA IYER

# CHHIMBE

The Chimbe, Chhimbe, Chimba, Cheembe, Chimpa and Chhipi are the synonyms of the community, which is commonly known as *darzi* (tailor), all over of Punjab, on account of their traditional occupation of stitching clothes. Those who are engaged in the traditional occupation are respectfully addressed as 'Masterji'. The community has two broad subgroups based on religion, i.e. Hindu Chimbe and Sikh Chimbe, majority of them subscribe to Sikhism. Besides this religious dichotomy, the community has many clans namely: Brah, Dhami, Jassal, Kareer, Kainth, Madahar, Purba, Rekhso, Sappal, Sarao, Battu, Sirio, Tank, Mukar, Garcha and Rohilla.

According to Rose (1919) one Bamdeo lived at Pind Lapur in Maharashtra. One night, he entertained Krishna and Udhoji, but as the latter was a leper, the villagers objected to his presence nearby. Udhoji concealed himself in a *sipi* (oyster shell) and when Bamdeo went to wash clothes, he found the shell and placed it in the sun. It produced the child, Namdeo, who was fostered by Bamdeo's wife. Namdeo taught his son Tank and daughter's son, Rohilla, the art of dyeing, printing and washing of clothes. They are believed to be the descendants of Baba Nam Dev who was born before the birth of Guru Nanak Devji and was a great worshipper of Lord Krishna, and after going around in different parts of India, he came over to Punjab and settled in the village Kuman in district Gurdaspur, where he stayed for about fourteen years.

The descendants of Baba Nam Dev took to stiching, washing, dyeing and printing clothes. The washing of clothes was subsequently left by this community to confine itself to the profession of tailoring, dying and printing of clothes only. The profession of washing clothes was taken up by the Dhobis who are believed to be, at one time, part of the Chimbe community. They are distributed in all the districts of Punjab, both in urban and rural areas, though more numerous in urban areas, on account of occupational advantage.

Punjabi is most commonly used both at home and in dealing with others. Chhimbes use Gurmukhi or Devanagari script but the older generation use Perso-Arbic script. The educated generation also use English to communicate with others.

They take both vegetarian and non-vegetarian food but some are strictly vegetarian, like those following the Radhaswami sect. Wheat, pulses and seasonal vegetables are generally consumed, rice and maize are also eaten. Locally available fruits such as banana, mango, grapes, papaya, guava, peach and apple are eaten occasionally. Pulses frequently consumed are *urad, moong* and gram, cooking medium is vegetable *ghee* and oil. The non-vegetarians eat mutton, chicken, fish and eggs. Milk and milk products, tea, coffee and butter milk are also consumed in plenty. Alcoholic drinks used to be taboo earlier, but on account of Westernization they now consume these drinks on occasions such as birth of a child (especially male), betrothal, marriage or on any happy occasion.

Those following the Namdhari sect or those Sikhs who have undergone the *amrit chhakna* (baptism) ceremony, do not drink and are strictly vegetarian, avoiding even eggs. Liquor and sweets are avoided during mouring periods. On Tuesdays, many do not take liquor or meat. Their women avoid wearing *kanch* (glass) bracelets and application of *henna*. In terms of change in food habits, there is a tremendous increase in the intake of meat, eggs and fish, liquor intake has also increased since Independence.

The community has evolved into four main social divisions based on religion; Hindu, Sikh, Namdhari, Radhaswami, though majority of them subscribe to Sikh religion. The main function of the subgroups, clans and *gots* is to regulate marriage alliances and indicate descent and ancestry. Use of clan name as surname is becoming more prevalent now, though earlier it was not so. Some differentiation has also arisen in terms of the occupation pursued, as those who have left their traditional occupation of tailoring tend to interact more with the folk of their own kind.

According to Ibbetson (1916), the Hindu Chhimbe are divided into two subcastes, i.e. Tank and Rohilla which may not intermarry, but may eat and smoke together. The Tank claim to be higher in status than the Rohilla. Self-perception of the community is of medium level *vis-a-vis* other communities in the local social hierarchy. Being an important occupational group and providing services of immense utility, other communities have a good perception of the community. However, they are considered socially inferior to Khatri, Bhatia, Arora, Bania, Brahman and Jats, as they will neither take their daughters nor would they give their daughters in marriage to the Chimbe. Socially, they are at par with groups like Ramgarhias.

The community is endogamous, practising clan and *got* exogamy. Village exogamy is also practised. Exchange marriage called *batta-*

*satta* used to be practised earlier. Hypergamy and hypogamy are prevalent. Sororate and levirate forms of marriage are also observed. Age at marriage is about twenty years for boys and about seventeen years for girls. Marriage is negotiated by the parents or by other elders of both the families. Monogamy is the rule, symbols of marriage in the form of vermilion, bangles and *bindi* are found but are not strictly followed. Dowry is given by the girl's parents in the form of clothes, jewellary and household articles. Sometimes cash is given. The amount of dowry in the form of cash and kind depends on the economic status of the girl's parents. After marriage, newly-weds either stay with the parents or may live in a separate house.

Divorce was not permitted earlier and was looked down upon, now it may take place due to maladjustment, chronic illness, barrenness or due to absence of a male issue. Usually, it is the husband, who initiates divorce, but now women, particularly those who are educated, may also be initiator of divorce proceedings. Normally, the boy's side would return all the dowry received by them including at times, even the marriage expenditure incurred by the bride's side. If the divorce is given by the girl, the dowry and other gifts received by the husband in marriage are not returned. No rule is followed regarding giving compensation to the divorced party. The liability of the children is usually fixed by the elders of both the sides. Widow remarriage is not permissible, though marriage of the male and female divorcee may be allowed. There is a perceptible change in terms of increase in age at marriage, change in rule of residence, divorce, and liberalization of rules for remarriage.

Both nuclear and extended types of family exist in the community. Interpersonal relationship of love, fear, avoidance, obligation, joking, conflict and confrontation are seen in the families. Avoidance relationship is found between daughter-in-law and father-in-law; between younger brother's wife and husband's elder brother. Joking relationship exists between sister's husband and wife's sister; husband's younger brother and elder brother's wife; and between maternal grandparents and daughter's children. Children respect the elders in the family. Conflicts arise due to disrespectful behaviour towards elders or challenge to the authority of elders check on freedom of youngsters.

The community is patrilineal with right to inheritance being equal to all the male children. With the death of the father, the eldest son takes over as head of the household. Inter-family linkages are very strong between the brother-in-law (*dewar*) and sister-in-law (*bhabhi*).

Changes in family are indicated by the increase in the formation of nuclear families, decline of joint family system and change in the inheritance rules as now daughters also have equal right in property as per the law of the land. Women have a high status in society. They help the menfolk in their traditional occupation, in taking decisions regarding the family affairs, setting and acquiring of new property and in social and religious functions and rituals.

Antenatal restrictions on the mother are imposed in the form of less workload in the household. A pregnant woman avoids going to offer condolence to another family where a death has occurred except to those who are closely related. Post-delivery observation of pollution period is practised for thirteen days, when the mother would be confined to a room and will not partake in the household chores. Elderly male relations will not enter the room in which the mother is confined. This period is called *sootak*. After the prescribed period, she will take a bath, perform some *puja* and take up the routine of the family work. Normally, some close relatives join on this occasion and a small feast is arranged. The woman's parents will join in, in the occasion with some gifts in the form of clothes, toys and cash. The newborn child wears clothes on this occasion which are presented by the woman's parents.

Naming ceremony is observed and name may be given to the neonate by some elder persons in the family or by a priest. A feast is also arranged on this occasion. Among the Hindus, *mundan* ceremony is performed at the age of plus two years in case of a male child only. The ceremony is preceded by a *puja* and after the *mundan*, a feast is given. The maternal grandparents will bring gifts in the form of clothes and cash.

After a marriage alliance has been negotiated and agreed upon by both the parents, the girl's parents present some cash to the boy and to the boy's parents and other family members. This is called the *rok*. This is followed by the *sagai* where again cash, sweets, fruit and some clothes are given to the boy and his close relatives by the girls parents. An auspicious day is fixed for the proper marriage ceremony. A day before the actual marriage or at times in the morning of the marriage day, *shagun* is brought by the girl's side to the bridegroom's place consisting of eleven or twenty-one packets of sweets and some fruit. A *thali* (big plate) containing dry fruits such as almonds, dry coconut, *kujas* (sugar cups) and cash varying from one hundred and one to one thousand one hundred rupees is given to the boy. Some cash is given to the boy's parents, sisters, brother-in-laws, grandparents, uncles and aunts, and varies in amount from rupees eleven to rupees five hundred and one; between the *sagai* and *shagun*, a ceremony called *chunni charhana* is performed by the boy's side at the girl's place. The boy's parents give a *chunni* (a head cover) or a *sari* to the girl which she wears at that time.

On the marriage day a *barat* consisting of the boy's relatives, friends, neighbours and other invitees goes to the bride's residence. The *barat* is received by the girl's side and *milni* takes place. Then the *barat* is given a feast. The proper marriage ceremony is performed by the temple priest amidst the chanting of the Vedic *mantras* around the sacred fire or around the *Guru Granth Sahib* amidst chanting of hymns by the *gurdwara* priest. It consists of seven or four *pheras*. The *barat* then returns to the groom's place. The consummation of marriage is at the groom's residence.

The dead are cremated. On the fourth day after death, *phul chugna* is performed, that is, the bones are brought from the cremation ground for immersion in water. The Hindus do it at Hardwar while Sikhs prefer to do it at Kiratpur Sahib in Ropar district of Punjab. A period of thirteen days is observed as the pollution period. On the thirteenth day, *rasam pagri* or *uthala* takes place, where relatives, members of the community and friends join to pray for the deceased soul. After this, the family attends to the normal duties.

The primary occupation of the community is tailoring, draping, dyeing and printing of clothes. Though tailoring, being a lucrative pursuit, has been taken over by many other communities including the high castes, yet the Chhimbe, by and large, have confined themselves to this occupation. Some members, who have received education, have also entered into other trades, government and private jobs. In urban areas, payments are made in cash. However, in rural areas, sometimes payment is done both in cash and kind. Since Independence, tailoring has become a very paying business and the community has become prosperous. The latest boom in readymade garments and changing fashion trends have brought considerable status and prosperity to those who are still engaged in this traditional occupation.

In earlier times, there used to be *biradari* system at different local levels looking after the affairs and resolving disputes in the community. A few elders and respectable members used to preside over to deliberate over the cases of dispute. Mostly the disputes were sorted out amicably by the *biradari*. Those not obeying the dictate of the *biradari* were socially boycotted. Nowadays, either the disputes are referred to the statutory *gram panchayats* at village level or to the local courts for settlements. The traditional way of solving any dispute through the elders in the family still continues.

The community worships Baba Nam Dev besides the traditional deities of Hindu religion and the Sikh Gurus especially Guru Ram Rai. The *samadhi* of Baba Nam Dev at village Kuman, district Gurdaspur in Punjab is the most sacred shrine for the community. Being strong devouts and followers of Sikhism, the Sikh Chimbe also visit the other shrines sacred to Sikhs. For Hindus, Hardwar is the most sacred centre for pilgrimage. Their major festivals are Lohri, Dewali, Dussehra, Janamashtami and Holi. On the Lohri festival, a fair is held at Kuman village for three days. Here, Baba Nam Dev stayed for fourteen years; other communities also participate in the fair. About 3 km from this *samadhi* is a *gurdwara* associated with Baba Nam Dev.

The traditional art of cloth printing of this community, which has been adopted by some other communities also as mode of subsistence is losing significance.

Folk tales of Baba Nam Dev exist in the community. One of these goes: 'Once a cow belonging to the king died. He called Baba Nam Dev and asked him to breathe life into the cow. Baba Nam Dev said he was only an ordinary man and how could he perform this miracle. The king got annoyed and ordered that the Baba be thrown from the hilltop. But he survived the fall and was thrown on a deadly anthill. Lord Krishna appeared and told Babaji that he could turn this earth upside down and tear it apart if Babaji so desired. But Baba Nam Dev, being a pious soul, requested Lord Krishna that the king's cow should be made alive. The cow thus became alive. Another tale follows: 'Once Baba Nam Dev was going to eat his food consisting of *roti* and *dal*. A dog came and ran away with the *roti*. The Baba ran after the dog to retrieve his *roti*. But he found that it was not a dog but Lord Krishna himself.'

The Chhimbe have social and occupational linkages with practically all the local communities, such as the Bania, Khatri, Arora, Jat and Brahman as they extend services in clading them. In terms of occupation, some restrictions were imposed earlier on tailoring clothes of the lower castes. In social terms, the community joins in moments of joy and sorrow with all other communities. Intercommunity marriage relationship exists with other backward communities like Ramgarhia, Saini, Sunar and even Jat. They take the services of a Brahman and a *granthi* for various rituals. They participate freely in socio-political and religious activities and functions at the local, district and state levels. In association with other local communities, they contribute to the political environs of the state.

Literacy rate which was generally low in pre-Partition times is increasing due to the recognition of the importance of education for both boys and girls. They have not only become literate, but are also receiving higher education because of accessibility to schools and colleges in Punjab.

The Chhimbe are in no way lagging behind in enjoying the fruits of the developmental programme launched by the government. Having good facilities of radio, television, newspaper, rail and road connection, the impact of the communication on this community is visible. Banking, other savings and investment opportunities are being utilized fully by this community.

A.K. BHATIA

# CHRISTIANS

The Christians in Punjab, also know as *Isai*, have a number of denominations such as Salvation Army, Catholics, adherents of the Church of North India, Baptist, Fernicuster, Methodist, etc. A large number of members of this community use Massey, with their names. There are differences among scholars about the origins of Christianity in the state. According to one view, there was no Christianity in north India prior to the nineteenth century (Webster, 1976: 3-4). Others, maintain that Saint Thomas, the founder of Christianity in India, came to this area in the first century A.D. After he had completed his work in this area, he went to south India. The Western tradition maintains that St. Thomas reached India, following the then well-known trade routes sometimes in the middle of the first century of the Christian era. He preached the Gospel in Parthia and India and converted many, including members of royal families. He suffered martyrdom in India, and was buried here (A.M. Mundanan, 1982). Saint Thomas preached in the Punjab; but he could not establish a permanent church. History of Christianity can be dated from 1834, when John C. Lowrie established at Ludhiana the first mission station at the Ludhiana (later Punjab) Mission of the Presbyterian Church of U.S.A. The next mission was the Church Missionary Society, which was set up at Amritsar in 1851. Roman Catholics started their work in Punjab in 1888. Various groups of American Methodists, the Salvation Army, New Zealand Presbyterians, Seventh Day Adventists and Penticostals followed them.

In the days of Maharaja Ranjit Singh, no Christian preachers were allowed in his territory. However, he invited Dr. Lowrie of Ludhiana to Lahore and asked him to set up school for English education. To test the closed door policy of Ranjit Singh on religion, a preacher Golaknath was sent to Phillaur. He was arrested and sent back with a warning not to return. After sometime Rev. John S. Woodside was invited to set up an American Presbyterian Mission at Kapurthala. It was temporarily closed in 1865. Later, Prince Harnam Singh of Kapurthala family became Christian and made a claim to the throne. However, he held high offices in the Church and the state in British India. His daughter Raj Kumari Amrit Kaur, also held high offices in India and the World Health Organization (Loehline, 1973: 183-5). The Christian missionaries also suffered during this period. Two

Christian followers of Sant Hakim Singh of Raipur (near Ludhiana) were poisoned: one died, the other became the famous Sadhu Sunder Singh (Loehlin, 1973: 185-9).

The primary aim of missionary activity is Punjab was evangelism. It was carried out by preaching the gospel in towns and villages. Many schools, colleges, clinics, hospitals, asylums and orphanages were established. They undertook relief work in times of famine, epidemics and earthquakes. As a result the Christian community in the Punjab increased from 3,823 in 1881 to 49,301 in 1947. This process was accompanied by the development of Western education in Ludhiana and Jalandhar, where many Mission schools were set up. The outstanding institutions included the Baring High School (now Baring Union Christian College) in Batala, Alexandra High School, Amritsar, United Christian Schools, Suranasi near Jalandhar, Christian Medical College at Ludhiana and N.D. Victor Model School at Moga. These schools provided leadership not only for the Church but also for Brahmo Samaj, Arya Samaj, Singh Sabhas, Chief Khalsa Diwan. Anjuman-i-Himayat-i-Islam, and Muhammadan Educational Conference (Webster, 1976: 140).

Thus a large number of Meghs, Chamars, and Chuhras got converted to Christianity, which led to an increase in the size of the Christian community and also changed its character. This trend of conversion to Christianity was opposed by All-India Suddhi Sabha. The rise of Adi-Dharam movement also reasserted the traditional religion of the Punjab outcastes and checked the trend towards conversion (Webster, 1982: 140-1).

The Christians of the Punjab had an 'ambiguous' position with the Indian nationalist movement. They preferred security under the 'autocratic regime' to the uncertainties of democracy. However, Raja Harnam Singh, S.K. Rudra, C.F. Andrews, Raj Kumari Amrit Kaur, and S.K. Dutta were committed nationalists. Even the nationalist movement leading to transfer of power from foreign to Indian pastors and lawmen was very significant. It led to the formation of 'a Native Church for the Natives of India in 1877 and Ludhiana Mission, to transfer power from foreign mission organizations to the Indian Church bodies'. The struggle was successful by 1957 (Webster, 1976: 141).

The Christians faced a crisis in the wake of partition of the Punjab. They had to show their identity as Christians by marking their houses and clothes with the cross or by recitation of the Lords Prayer, Ten Commandments and Apostles Creed. Many Christian agencies provided relief on both sides of the border. In its long-term effects the partition split the educated Christian elite into two. There was scarcity of personnel to man church, ecclesiastical, educational and medical institutions. Moreover, the community faced an entirely new situation, when it was computed as a minority in a democratic government, with no autocratic government to support it. Effective translations of the Bible were made by American Presbyterians into the languages spoken in Punjab and North-West Frontier Province. William Carey had translated the New Testament into Punjabi. Dr. John Newton had improved this translation. Levi Janvier and John Newton were the co-authors of Punjabi grammar. An Urdu weekly, *Nur Afshan* (The Light), published from Ludhiana was a contribution to religious journalism, by American Baptists (Pathak 1967: 40-50). Many American Protestant missions were founded in the Punjab.

The community in the state these days perceives its distribution at national and international levels. It has not migrated to its present place but has been growing in number at the present places of settlement in the state. Originally, it came in existence by conversions from other communities.

The number of Roman Catholics had doubled between 1901 and 1911. In 1921, the total Christian population was 3,46,259. In 1941 the population of the community increased to 4,86,038. They are fairly spread out, but are found chiefly in Gurdaspur, Amritsar and Ferozepur districts. The community in the state speaks Punjabi language within the family and kinship, which is written in Gurmukhi script, the older generation uses Arabic script also. With other communities the Punjabi, Hindi, Urdu or English language is used with the respective script.

The members of the community takes all types of locally available food. Both men and women of the community occasionally take non-vegetarian food. Consumption of vegetables is moderate, fruits are occasionally consumed. Wheat, rice *jowar, bajra* and maize are the most commonly used cereals, and pulses taken include gram, *tur, urad, moong,* peas beans, *masur* and *moth*. Cooking medium includes *vanaspati* (most commonly used), animal fat, mustard and sunflower oil. Men occasionally take alcoholic drinks which is procured from market, but until recently it used to be home-made as well. Milk and milk products also form part of diet. The members of the community smokes *bidis* and cigarettes.

The community has many denominations and is also differentiated at economic and occupational levels. A predominant section is employed as agricultural labourers, others work as rickshaw-pullers, *baledar* and a few are employed in railways and defence establishments, in hospitals as nurses and medical technicians and now even as constables in the police and Border Security Force besides various other jobs. The community is also territorially differentiated and has different levels of education. The social differentiation helps to indicate status and regulates marriage alliances. There is a tendency to get matrimonial alliances with better-educated persons, with non-agricultural occupations. There has been no change in the surnames, class names or titles. Some members suffix Massey to their names. A few consider themselves of medium status. Though the community does not recognize *varna* system, it is conscious of its low status. In spite of this consciousness the caste is not pronounced in the community because most original converts are from lower castes in the state. It is generally recognized that the conversions have provided better status to them. And this is one reason why there has been no reconversions back to Hinduism under the post-Independence reservation policy which provided benefits to the Scheduled Castes.

Marriages are contracted at the community level and also generally at the denomination level, yet inter-denomination marriages are acceptable. They practice exogamy at village level. These marriages are contracted by negotiations or even by mutual consent. Consent of the boy and girl is generally asked for. Ring ceremony is performed at the time of marriage. The Baptist do not have even the ring ceremony. The bride wears a white dress with a veil at the time of marriage. Rules of residence after marriage continues to be patrilocal. Divorce with judicial approval for various reasons is permissible by both parties. Compensation and custody of the children is decided by the court. Marriage of widows and divorced women is permissible, and is performed with full ceremony. The community lives in nuclear families in urban areas and in vertically extended families in rural areas. Avoidance and joking relationship have been influenced by local culture. Joking between *sali* and *jeeja* and *dewar* and *bhabi* continue. Although women are legally entitled to inherit parental property, prevalent practice is of male equigeniture; succession rules also favour the eldest son. There has been a rise in the number of nuclear families. Women have generally low status as compared with men. However, they enjoy better status than in other commuities. In rural areas, they have role in animal husbandary and agricultural operations. They have accepted the profession of nursing and are also school teachers. The Roman Catholic church allows women to become nuns.

The community observes only a few rituals. Some post-delivery rituals are observed for an unspecified number of days. Naming ceremony is held but there are no strict rules about it. Baptism may accompany the event of naming. Baptism is performed in various ways. Marriage rituals are performed at the church and both the sides arrange a feast at their respective places. In case of inter-denomination marriage, the rites are performed at the bride's church. There is a practice to register the marriage at the church. The dead are buried. The burial ground is jointly shared by different denominations of the community. There is no ancestor worship though there is a practice to remember the dead by placing flowers on the grave, on the death anniversaries.

Land is the main source of income for the community even though land is owned by other communities. This community itself is engaged mainly in agricultural labour. Only 5 per cent of these people in Batala tahsil of Gurdaspur district own small patches of agricultural land whereas 80 per cent of them are engaged as agricultural labour. Others work as labour and skilled worker in hospitals and cantonments. There are only a few included in the Punjab Civil Service personnel. Some work in hospitals as nurses and medical technicians, and a few are teachers in private schools. Child labour exist particularly in the agricultural operations. The agricultural labour from the community is being replaced by the labour from Bihar and so they have shifted their operation as labour to the towns in mechanical outfits or work in grain markets. In Gurdaspur area 50 per cent of the *panches* belong to this community. There are more than ten *sarpanches* in Ferozpure district. A nominated body of the community at the state level also exists. It is known as the Punjab Christain Sabha with head office at Batala. The Sabha fights for the rights of the community. To maintain record and preserve peace and discipline, pastorate committees exist.

The community has various denominations united by common reverence for the Bible which is the holy book for all. There are variations in the practices of various denominations. In Gurdaspur district, the Salvation Army has maximum followers in the rural areas. The Church of North India has the most following in urban areas. The Church owns some agricultural land in Gurdaspur and Amritsar districts. Owing to encroachment the land holdings of the church have declined of late. A few saints, such as Saint Xavier and Saint Thomas are held in great esteem among the Roman Catholics and various medical and educational institutions are named after them. Festivals such as Diwali, Lohri, etc., are celebrated. Christmas is celebrated with gaiety. Other communities also participate and greet this community on this day. A midnight mass is held in churches at all places. However, all communities hold separate masses. The well-known Chuhra-Chamar conversion movement of the early decades of this century was the most vigorous part of this movement. Pre-change practices have been modified and even forgotten altogether. These days, a few members of the community have reported as Scheduled Castes to enjoy the benefits of reservation policy. The community sings the folk songs sung by other communities.

The community has free exchange with other communities and exchanges all types of *jal* or *chal*, *kachcha*, *sidha* and *pukka* food with other communities. A few intercommunity marriages have been reported. It shares water resources with other communities but has its own burial grounds or cemeteries. It has its own church buildings at various places and participates in the traditional fairs and festivals. The Christians have good relations with cultivators as agricultural labourers in rural areas. There has been increase in the recruitment number of this community in the police and the Border Security Force. A few have been promoted to Punjab Civil Service from minorities quota. It has well established leadership at *panchayat* level.

The community has experienced a variable impact of various developmental activities. Its attitude to education is very favourable for both boys and girls and it has many educational institutions. A few boys get education upto graduation, and occasionally upto university level. They drop out due to economic reasons or the need to support their family. A few girls also study upto graduation level but they often have to drop out because of poverty. The attitude of the community to modern medicare is positive. Both the sexes have accepted modern methods of family planning, and couples prefer one or two children. Members of the community are both employed as well as self-employed. Coal and firewood and cow-dung cakes are the most commonly used fuels. It has availed of the benefits of fair price/ration shops. Its attitudes to savings is positive.

VIRINDER SINGH

# DAOLI

The Daoli community is located in the hills near the banks of rivers in Punjab. Their place of habitation is near the rivers, is also linked with their traditional occupation of refining gold from the sands of the rivers. According to Rose (1919: 317), the community in the low hills of Una *tahsil* was known as Daoli and in the higher hills of Kangra was called Sansoi. This has been confirmed by Ibbetson (1916: 317). Rose had also pointed out that Daoli correspond to the Khir of plains, who were gold workers. The traditional profession of gold-working by Daolis had been completely abandoned in Punjab, a long time back. Even Ibbetson (1916: 317) had noted that Daolis were operating water-mills as well. At present this is the main profession of the Daolis of Punjab along with fishing in the rivers. In spite of these changes in the profession, the community is identified with gold-working to the extent that it is known as Soni also; a term derived from Punjabi word *sona* (gold), and *soni* is someone who works with gold. These days the community is more popularly known as ghapatia (operator of water-mill) a term derived from their present occupation. Even Daolis themselves seem to have accepted the new name.

The community claims Rajput descent. According to a few elders of the community, they migrated to the present place of habitation after the war of the Rajputs led by Rana Partap with Akbar. In this war the Rajputs were defeated and a large number of them were massacred by the Mughal army. Others, fled the field and vowed to win back their kingdom. The word trick has a vernacular parallel *dao* in Punjabi and Hindi languages. Hence those who fled the field were known as Daoli that is those who used tricks, or *dao.* Since they had fled the field, this is perceived by the community as the factor responsible for their low status. Daolis are unable to give any account of adaptation of the occupation of extracting gold. However, they point out that this profession of refining gold was followed by them since the times of their great grandfathers. Some Sikh members of the community feel proud of the fact that the tenth Guru, Guru Gobind Singh, referred to the community in his great literary work, *Chandi Di War.*

Their population is concentrated on the banks of rivers in Punjab. Daolis live in the following villages near river Satluj in district Ropar:

Manikpur, Govindpur, Lodhipur, Khameda, Nahana Das Gakian, Khanpur, Zandvadi, Mangli, Dabgoda, Kalitre, Daroli and Berhampur villages.

The Daolis have a unique pattern of settlement in villages. Their houses are separated from the main village setlement, by a distance of a few hundred metres. This is necessitated by the need of having their settlements near water courses adjacent to the rivers. Daoli settlements are usually on common land or *shamlat* land and are cut off from all the main villages. Besides these settlements are not continuous but are fragmented into a chain of cluster of houses. Inhabitants of these clusters are called *toli* (a gang or group of people). So, Daoli settlement in a village can have many *tolis*. However, Daolis of all villages do not live in *tolis*. Probably the operation of many water-mills necessitated their settlement in *tolis*, at different places at the banks of water streams. They speak the local dialects of the Punjabi language.

The habitations of Daolis near the river have also influenced their eating habits and fish forms an important part of their diet. Almost all Daolis are non-vegetarian. They take all types of food and consume liquor as well. In spite of their claims to the contrary, it is reported that they consume *desi* liquor also. Among cereals, wheat is most commonly used, in addition to maize and occasional use of rice. Depending upon the economic position, fruits also find a place in the diet of Daolis. Generally *vanaspati ghee* and mustard oil are used as cooking medium.

Marriage ceremony takes place according to the Vedic rites or by Sikh ceremony of *anand karaj*. Marriages are arranged by the exclusion of *gots* of both parents of the bride and the groom. The community has the following *gots*—Bhatti, Tarabe, Chauhan, Chandala, Khokhar, Chaigod, Bhagaskia, Langlorco, Phalarda, Rakhe, Taglait, Tanoode, Mandoni, Kathadoo and Bhagnovia. Some Daolis call these *gots* as *als* (family or lineage). However, the condition of the exclusion of *gots* is satisfied. There is no restriction on marriage between Sikh and Hindu Daolis.

A Daoli marriage is settled through a *vichola*. The *vichola* is generally an elderly member of the community, known to both the families. Earlier, marriage was peformed at the age of twelve to eighteen years; and now age at marriage between eighteen and twenty years is more acceptable. There is no compulsory dowry system; it is left to the choice of the parents of the bride. Although the marriage ceremony takes place according to Vedic or Sikh rites, yet the community follows some unique customs and practices. When the groom returns to his house after the marriage, accompanied by his bride, the couple worship *talwar* (sword) and *pipal* tree. The worship of *pipal* by the Daolis is common with other communities of the region. However, the practice of sword worship is specific to their community.

A ceremony called *vaheda*, is performed to celebrate the birth of a child. As a token of happiness sweets are distributed among members of the community. After the birth of the child, the mother is not allowed to enter the kitchen for at least thirteen days. A ceremony of *bahar badhana* (showing the newborn to strangers) is performed after five or ten days. Till that time the child is confined to the house.

Death ceremony of old Daolis is called *sohala* (praise for the dead) and is observed after sixteen days. It is a happy occasion and is marked by distribution of sweets. The death of the younger people is called *pad* and takes place ten days after the death. Daolis also follow the annual ceremony of *shradh*. A priest leads all these ceremonies.

Status of women among Daolis is not very high. Only sons inherit property from their parents and daughters are not allowed to share this property. However, the community allows divorce by the women both by *panchayat* as well as by the court. Even widow remarriage is allowed. However, the remarriage does not take place with full Vedic rites or *anand karaj*. It is known as *badhana*. Women are allowed to work outside their homes as many Daoli women work as agricultural labourers. Only a few of them observe the tradition of *purdah* but they are not allowed to talk to outsiders. Only the birth of male child is celebrated.

Over the years economic position of the Daolis has deteriorated. They had to abandon their traditional occupation of extracting gold from sand found in the river beds. Some Daolis point out that the construction of Bhakhra reservoir is the main reason for this. However, it appears that the Daolis had abandoned their profession long before the construction of Bhakhra complex. Main reason of their abandoning the traditional occupation was the introduction of new technological innovations, which rendered the primitive technique, used by Daolis, economically unviable. However, the Bhakhra factor is otherwise also very important in the economic life of the Daolis. The uncertain flow of water from this reservoir has adversely affected their occupation of running water-mills and fishing. This either leads to floods which submerge the *gharats* or the flow of water is too meagre to operate them on, which has ruined their occupation. In addition to this even fishing becomes impossible because of uncertain flow of water. Daolis also point out other reasons for their declining economc position; the water-mills are not able to economically compete with the electrically operated flour mills. Consequently, the *gharats* have declined in importance and people do not favour them. As a result they have to take the grains from the houses situated at long distances and deliver the flour at the doors of the people. The position of fishing industry is not different. The Punjab government has auctioned the fishing rights to big contractors, and as a result the Daolis have to sell their fish to these contractors at very low rates. This has led to decline in the income from this source also. Now the Daolis have to supplement their income from other sources such as agricultural labour in the nearby fields.

The community is also facing harassment from some of the dominant landowners of the locality, through whose territory water flows to the point where Daolis operate their *gharats*. They are forced to pay to these landowners. They want continuous and assured supply of water through channels and also to end the pollution of water by the fertilizer factory. In addition, they want end to the illegal payment to the local landlords for the use of water, which is their right. The community points out that operation of the *gharat* involves the cooperation of the whole family, including women and children and is a major source of their livelihood.

The community follows mixed religious practices. They worship Hindu deities and follow the teachings of Sikh Gurus as well. This was also noted by Ibbetson who has pointed out that none of the Daolis was Muslim (Ibbetson, 1916: 317). Among the Hindu deities, Baba Balak Nath is most commonly worshipped. A Daoli family can have both Sikh as well as Hindu members. Even when it is not so, intermarriage between Hindu and Sikh Daoli families is very common. Both Sikh and Hindu rituals are practised at the time of marriage as suited to the occasion, even though the Daoli settlement of Lodhipur is exclusively a Sikh settlement. In general, the number of Sikhs in Daoli community has increased over the years.

The community has little awareness of various development facilities existing for their upliftment. Some Daolis have acquired yellow cards and have availed of the loans. Some of them have purchased buffaloes with these loans. Others have acquired a *thela* (cart). Daolis have accepted the family welfare programmes. However, no hygienic supply of drinking water is available. They continue to use water from the nearby wells.

Some Daolis have access to educational facilities. Many of them have got education upto fifth class and few of them upto tenth class. Children of Daolis studying beyond fifth class get a stipend of rupees five per month. Owing to the acquisition of education some Daolis have been able to enter into military service. A few of them are employed in the Punjab State Electricity Board. There is one Daoli who is a food inspector and another is a builder in the railways. The community claims to have a doctor in their community. They have been benefitted by the various development programmes.

The community is fighting for its recognition as a Scheduled Caste. Now that there is a consciousness on this issue, they have formed a union, known as Sharatia Sabha, which has been agitating for the recognition of the community as a Scheduled Caste.

VIRINDER SINGH

# DARAIN

Ibbetson has included Darain (Dren) within the broader rubric of 'Mallah'. Under this category he included Mohana, Taru and Darain. The Dren and Taru, according to Ibbetson (1916: 308) carry travellers across the rapid mountain torrents on inflated hides. The term 'Darian' is derived from the word *dariya* meaning 'river' and since their occupation was associated with river, the caste was termed as Darain. According to informants in the villages of Darkuan in Sartee and Phangota in Dhar Block (district Gurdaspur), their old generations carried timber from one place to the other along the river which covered considerable distance. The forest contractors had to carry their timber through the rivers Beas and Ravi to different points. One such point was Madhopur, 10 km away from Pathankot. The task of Darains was to ensure the smooth floating of timber from the point of origin to the destination. The mouth of the river was narrow towards the hill and wider towards the plain. The Darains had also to clear the flow of timber from the narrow ends where possibility of obstruction was higher. At the point of destination they had to collect all the timber at river bank and tie it into big bundles.

The Darain have migrated to Dhar Block from Chamba district. They had migrated here during the time of their great grandfathers. Presently Darains are located in three *panchayats* of Dhar Block, namely, Darkuan Panchayat (40 households), Sartee Panchayat (10 households) and Phangota Panchayat (7 households). They are also located in other nearby villages of Chamba district namely, Panohta, Khairi, Magir-Gatti, Kandla and Mazra. According to *Census of India* (1981), the total population of the Darain is 156 individuals, which has 83 males and 73 females.

Their work is carried on for nine months in a year before the onset of the rainy season and has now declined due to improvement in the transportation system. They speak Pahari language mixed with Punjabi which they themselves call *kachra boli*. They use both Gurmukhi and Devanagari scripts. Punjabi langauge is taught in local schools. For all practical purposes the linguistic affinity of the people of this area is closer to those of the neighbouring Chamba district. They are enlisted in the Scheduled Caste category.

Their staple diet consists of wheat, rice, maize and the pulses used are *mah* (*urad*), *kulth* and gram. There is no restriction on eating fish and meat. Fish is available in the nearby river Ravi. Milk is a scarce commodity for them as very few of them have milch animals. Owing to poverty they cannot purchase fruits and vegetables.

Some of the groupings or major social divisions among them consist of Rana, Jarial, Lande, Chauhan, etc. Every subgrouping has equal status. They are poor and hence homogeneous economically. Their homogeneity is reflected in the social, religious and political spheres also. Major territorial divisions among them are the Darain of Dhar Block and the neighbouring Chamba district on the one hand and those of Kangra on the other. They consider themselves equal in status to that of the Megh which are also in the Scheduled Caste category.

In marital relationship, they follow caste endogamy but *got* exogamy. Marriages have, however, taken place within the village which does not violate the *got* exogamy. Most of the marital alliances take place in the village of Chamba district. Child marriages were taking place until four decades earlier. Their marriages are conducted according to Vedic rituals. However, of the usual seven *pheras* around the fire, four are conducted at the girl's place at the time of marriage and three *pheras* are conducted at the bridegroom's place. They consult the Brahmans for *lagan* for an auspicious date. The custom of dowry is practised and items include, bed, cot, chairs, ornaments, etc. Divorce is less frequent. Widow remarriage exists in the form of younger brother marrying the widow of his elder brother, which is called *chadar tanaza*. Symbols of marriage are similar to those of other Hindus. Divorce is neither encouraged nor prevented. The person who initiates divorce has to pay compensation. Immediately after the marriage, the couple establishes a separate family. Even married girls have the right to inherit property. The women work as agricultural labour.

The birth of a male child is regarded as auspicious and sweets such as *batasha* (sugar candy) are distributed five days after the birth. On the completion of one year of the male child, close relatives are invited. *Mundan* ceremony is celebrated within the family and it is not necessary to go to any important religious place on this occasion.

The dead are cremated and ashes are immersed in the river Ravi which is at a stones throw from the village. Until the tenth day they neither sleep on the cot nor change clothes. On the thirteenth day, they invite close relatives and perform funeral rites at the end of each month until the sixth month after death. On the completion of one year, the *shradh* or *barkhi* (anniversary) is observed. At the end of the fourth year again *shradh* ceremony has to be performed.

The traditional occupation of timber carrying on river water has been almost extinct for over a decade. Most of them are reduced to the status of landless labourer. Every household is invariably a tenant having taken on lease 2 to 5 acres of land. Most of them have their own plough and bullocks. It is interesting to note that many of them have been tenants to the same landlords for over twenty years. They have to pay a fixed amount of one hundred and sixty kilograms of grains per acre as rent. Over and above that they have to bear 100 per cent expenses. They also work as daily wage labourers in road construction and at the Thein Dam.

The Darain have their caste association in Kangra town. However, the Darain of Dhar Block and neighbouring villages of Chamba district are not part of this association. This lends credence to the fact that the Darain of Punjab are an isolated lot from their main stock, which is concentrated in the district of Kangra. It is also surprising that they do not enter into marital relationship with the Darains of Kangra district. In Chamba and in Dhar Block also, they are not closely knit into a caste association. Most of them are Hindu. Only two members of one family have adopted Sikh religion. They have constructed a small temple in the village to propitiate the souls of their ancestors to whom they pay their respect on important social occasions such as a marriage. They also worship Khwaja Pir. Every year they sacrifice a goat during the month of *Sawan* which falls towards the middle of July, which is *beejna*. They believe that if the goat shivers just before the sacrifice then Khwaja Pir is happy. So far, within their memory there has been no such occasion when Khwaja Pir was unhappy. After the sacrifice the meat is served to the community. For this, five to ten rupees are collected from each household and even the Rajput and Brahmans are invited on this occassion. This worship is necessary to satisfy the water-god.

The Welfare Department has constructed a common meeting place for the Schedule Caste known as *dharamshala*. The Megh, Batwal and Darain collectively use this facility. Six persons among them have taken loans for sericulture obtaining a subsidy of two thousand rupees. There is only one matriculate among them. Eighty per cent of them have yellow card facility. They send their children to school as there is one primary school in the village. They are aware of the family welfare schemes. They prefer three to four children. They take advantage of the various medicare facilities.

RAKESH KUMAR

# DHANAK

Dhanak is a Scheduled Caste and its numerical strength is 46,298 individuals, comprising 24,751 males and 21,358 females (*Census of India*, 1981). According to *Census of India* (1911: 453), 'the total population of Dhanak is 83,256 which includes 44,220 males and 39,036 females. The Dhanaks are mostly Hindus and are found in the Delhi division (except Simla), Ferozepur districts, Loharu, Dujana, Pataudi and Phulkian states. They are scavangers and weavers. The difference betwen a Dhanak and a Chuhra is that the former while doing general scavenging will not remove night soil.' Ibbetson (1916) observes that the Dhanaks are converted from hunters of the jungles into scanvengers and weavers. The name Dhanak has been derived from *dhanushaka* (bowman). In Punjab they do not engage thmselves as hunters, but as sweepers. However, Rose (1919: 35) states that the 'Dhanak, a caste essentially of Hindustan and not of the Punjab proper, are confined to the South-East of the province.' The Chuhra are said to look down on them, but they are apparently of equal status as neither will eat the leftovers of the other.

The women, young boys, and girls sweep grains (*dhan*) from the roads, as the bags containing wheat are transported from the railway wagons to godowns. The word Dhanak appears to have been derived from *dhan* (food grains) primarily due to the reason that most of them are engaged in collecting the grain, clean it, fill it in the bags and load and unload it at the *mandis* (grain markets), storage and railway stations. They work on commission, daily wages or contract basis. Apart from this, some of the Dhanaks also engage themselves as weavers. One of the reasons for their being called Dhanak is that they are followers of Dhanakmuni. The ancestors of the Dhanak were also working on handlooms as weavers. There is a temple of Dhanakmuni each at Rohtak and Amritsar. The Dhanak take out a procession in the memory of Dhanakmuni on the eve of full moon in the month of May every year. They speak Hindi and Haryanvi within their community and Punjabi with others. Most of the individuals are still illiterate. The males wear *pagri*, *dhoti*, *kameez* and a jacket. However, the females use *kameez* and *salwar* with *dupatta*. They take *dal* and *roti* as their staple food and when they can afford it they take non-vegetarian food which includes mutton, chicken, eggs and pork. They do not take alcoholic drinks regularly. Rice is used on special occasions. Mustard oil or groundnut oil is used as medium of cooking.

Dhanaks are an endogamous community, divided into different *gots.* Some of the common *gots* of the Dhanak are Barania, Noorgrain, Indora, Khannagbal, Khatak, Soraba, Mania, Bagria. They are endogamous and marry leaving the *gots* of their father, mother and grandmother. Marriage is arranged by negotiations, with the help of a *vichola.* Village exogamy is also observed. After the engagement marriage takes place, when the boy and the girl are betwenen eighteen to twenty years old. The bride is always younger than the groom. The marriage is performed according to the tradition of seven *pheras.* A feast is given to the members of the community by the parents of both the boy and the girl.

Divorce and remarriage are allowed under special circumstances. The joint family system is still prevalent and the usual distance is maintained by the younger members of the family from their elders. Vermilion and glass bangles are used as symbols of marriage. Dowry is in existence depending on the financial condition of the parents of the girl. After marriage the girl goes to stay with her husband. Maladjustment, cruelty, failure to bear a male child, barrenness and adultery are the main reasons for divorce. The traditional *panchayat* decides about the divorce and its compensation is given to the aggrieved party. Sons inherit equally the property of their father. The eldest son gets succession. Women contribute towards the family income and have low social status. Apart from this, women attend to all the houshold routine work, collection of firewood, bringing of water, besides performing various rituals. After birth, post-delivery restrictions are observed for forty days.

The Dhanak cremate their dead and the bones of the dead are disposed of in the Ganges. They have a traditional registered caste *panchayat* called, Dhanak Biradari Sudhar Sabha at Chandigarh. It has a *pradhan*, secretary, treasurer and some members. Most of the cases of dispute are settled by the *panchayat.* On most of the occasions they come to a consensus which is called *rajinama* (compromise). The *panchayat* listens to the problems of the contending parties and delivers its judgement. They are the followers of Hinduism and worship Goddess Kali, Vaishno Devi, Hanuman and Lord Vishnu. Shivratri, Diwali and Dussehra are their main festivals. They have their own traditional songs, folk tales and folklore.

Though there are no restrictions on accepting and exchanging food and water among the Dhanak and other communities in the cities, at the village level these restrictions are still observed. They have separate cremation ground but the same religious shrine for worhsip. Patron-client relationship does exist. Most of them work as labourers as they are illiterate. Modern inter-community linkages are lacking among them.

Though conditions for education (for males and females), health and medical care and family welfare are favourable, they do not make use of the facilities. Drinking water is available. They listen to radio. Extension agencies, political parties and voluntary agencies disseminate information of various types. Some of the houses have electric connections. Cow-dung cakes and wood are used as fuel sources. They have ration cards to draw various essential items. They have devloped the habit to save a portion of their earning for their future requirements.

SWARAN SINGH

# DHEA

The Dhea, Dhaya or Deha is a Scheduled Caste of Punjab. According to *Census of India* (1981), the total population of Dhea community in the state of Punjab is 4,783 individuals, with 2,455 males and 2,328 females. The Dheas are concentrated at a number of places. Some of these places are: Phillaur (250 families), Kartarpur, Manohar Nagar, Ludhiana (350 families), Phagwara (300 families), Banga (15 families), Nawasahar Doaba (25 families), Garh Shanker (15 families), Saila (15 families), Biasa (40-50 families), Jalandhar (Buta Mandi), Mahalpur (Nakodar), Hoshiarpur (20 families), Kachche Quarter, Barowal (Amritsar), Jallabad, Khemkaran, Patti, Bhiki Gurdaspur, Batala, Mahalpur, Bilga, Kalanaur, Barnala, Moga, Abohar, Bathinda, Bhadaor, Jagraon, Kotkapura, Halvara, Raikot, Mandi Ahmedgarh, Malerkotla (Haider Sheikh, near Chamar Majri), Dhuri (10-15 families), Sangrur (300-400 families). Dheas are an occupational community primarily engaged in making winnowing fans and toys from reed and waste paper. They sell these items in different villages. The males sell winnowing fans, while the females sell toys. They are also known as Shaj-ghare, which means those who prepare *shaj* (winnowing fan). They have migrated to their present habitat from Rajputana and claim themselves to be of Rajput descent. After the defeat of their kings they moved into the jungles and adapted themselves to taking all sorts of food found in the jungles in order to survive.

At present they take meat of tortoise, *billa* (wild cat), *gidar* (jackal), *goh* (big lizard), *seh* (porcupine), *neola* (mongoose). They live in the huts prepared from grass and reed. The old persons still prefer to sleep on the floor in their huts. They do not appreciate the government's policy of providing them with *pukka* houses due to obvious reasons. They still do not take food in utensils. It has been noticed that all these restrictions, which they are following are due to their taking an oath, that until they do not get their past glory back and their kingdom, they will not live in *pukka* houses, sleep on cots and take food in metallic utensils. However, some of the families have changed and they live in *pukka* houses and use utensils for taking food. Most of the individuals are illiterate, but they speak Punjabi with the members of their own community and others. The men wear *lungi*, *kurta*, *pagri*, and their ears are also pierced, while the dress of their women is *salwar*, *kameez* and *dupatta*. They wear *jutti*.

Wheat and maize form their staple food. Pulses and vegetables are used rarely. Mustard and groundnut oils are used as cooking medium. Men take alcoholic drinks at the time of birth of a male child, marriage ceremony or when a meeting of the traditional *panchayat* is held. Apart from this, they take *lassi* and tea. A change in their food habits is being observed at present. They have now started taking more pulses and vegetables. They smoke *bidi*.

The Dheas are divided into different *gots*. Some of their common *gots* are Kalyana, Sarbar, Jhuni (Sandhu), Thual, Pandare, Channal, Lahoria, Sohote, Dharor and Khusar, etc. The *got* is not always the criterion for their marriage. They can marry among their own *gots*. The Dheas consider themselves of low status, but higher than that of the Balmiki, whereas members of other communities also consider them as of low status. They are aware of the *varna* system and recognize their place in it as Shudra.

Boys and girls get married, when the age of the girl is eighteen to twenty years and of the boy's is twenty to twenty-five years. Earlier, child marriage was in practice, when the boys and girls used to get married around five to seven years of age. Marriage is arranged by negotiation between the parents. Monogamy is the usual form of marriage and a Brahman solemnizes it. There are seven *pheras*, which are conducted with recitation of *mantras*. Dowry is in kind and consists of four items, namely *manja* (cot), *pidi* (stool), utensils and ornaments. However, no cash is given as a dowry.

After marriage the girl stays with her husband. The newly married women use vermilion, glass bangles, earring as symbols of marriage. They are patrilocal, after marriage they stay with their parents and later have a separate hut nearby. Divorce is permitted with the sanction of the traditional caste *panchayat*. A fine which ranges from three hundred to two thousand rupees is also imposed on the boy or girl depending upon the enormity of the fault. The main reasons for divorce are maladjustment, cruelty, insanity, barrenness. Divorce compensation is given to the aggrieved party. Widow remarrige, known as *chadar pratha* is allowed.

Families of the Dhea live together. They have their separate *kulis* (huts). The husband and wife live together in a hut along with their young children. Usual mode of avoidance and joking relationship is observed in a family and a distance is maintained by the daughter-in-law from her father-in-law. The brother-in-law has the joking relationship with his sister-in-law.

All male children inherit equally the property of their father if it exists and the eldest son gets succession. Some changes in the family have been observed. They were nomadic earlier, and most of them are still nomadic. However, owing to the financial assistance rendered by the government, a section of them have started settled living. Some of them also have *pukka* houses with electricity but the more orthodox among them, especially those who belong to the older generation, still prefer to live in huts. They live in joint families.

Women have a role to play in the household activities, bringing drinking water and collecting wood for fuel. They have a low status though they contribute to the family income. Various rituals at birth are observed among the Dhea. Pre-delivery restrictions are observed specially during the first pregnancy. Post-delivery restrictions on the mother are also imposed. The midwife does the *namkaran* of the child and she gets rupees five for the same. In the presence of the *panchayat*, which consists of ten members, the *shagun* is given; the ceremony of *mangana* is performed with presenting one rupee and twenty-five paise and *ladoos* and *patasa* are offered. The boy gets *pag* (turban) and the girl is given clothes which include *salwar*, *kameez* and *dupatta*. The marriage rituals are performed at the bride's residence where a feast (*roti*) is given for the close relatives one day before the actual date of marriage. After the seven *pheras* another feast is arranged for the *barat* and other close relatives by the bride's parents. Consummation of marriage takes place at the bridegroom's residence.

They cremate their dead and the bones of the dead are immersed in water. On death a function is held after twelve to thirteen days, if the person dies at an old age. *Pag*, and clothes are presented to the relatives who come to mourn the death of an elderly person. They also get *atta*, sugar and money. Changes in the life-cycle rituals include reduction in the number of days of post-delivery restriction period on the mother and the pollution period. The rituals have been curtailed.

The primary occupation of the Dhea community is to make *chaj*. They also collect bones and work with leather. Apart from this they also engage themselves as hawkers and sell bedcovers and blankets. The mode of payment is both in kind and in cash. They travel on foot and visit different villages in order to sell their products. The winnowing fans are purchased mostly by the farmers in the village. In villages they get maize or wheat in exchange for their products. The women sell toys of reed and wastepaper.

The Dheas have their own traditional *panchayat*. Their *panchayat* at Ludhiana is known as Ludhiana Dhea Panchayat and its *lambardar* is elected by voice vote. The main criterion for selection of the *lambardar* is that he should be alert, expert, and vocal. The *panchayat* decides about matters related to marriage alliances, elopement, theft, etc. It imposes punishment in the form of fine and social boycott; small matters are settled within the family. In case the local *panchayat* fails to arrive at a settlement acceptable to both the parties, the *lambardars* of other areas are invited who together settle the disputes; the collective decision of the *lambardars* is binding on both the parties. They also impose fines depending upon the nature of offence. The person who summons the *panchayat* pays for the expenditure related to drinks and food till the *panchayat* arrives at a final decision.

They are followers of Maharishi Balmiki and, therefore, are also referred to as Balmiki Dhea. Apart from this they worship Lalan Bala, Goddess Kali, Baba Balak Nath, and all the Hindu gods and goddesses. The community at Ludhiana has its own place of worship which is represented by seven *devis*, Baba Balak Nath and Maharishi Balmiki who are worshipped on different days of the week. On Sunday, Baba Balak Nath, on Thursday Baba Balmiki and on Tuesday the goddesses are worshipped. Diwali and Lohri festivals are celebrated by them. They also visit other Hindu temples. The *pujari*, who performs the rites associated with birth marriage and death is not from their own community. They also celebrate Holi, Dussehra and Bhagwan Balmiki Pargat Diwas, as their festivals. Most of these festivals are of social and religious significance for them. They have their oral traditions. At the time of marriage they sing their folk-songs. They use drums and *dholkis* as musical instruments at the time of marriage.

The Dheas accept food and water from all the communities. As they use animal intestines in preparing winnowing fans and take all sorts of foods, which is not considered clean, the members of other communities, such as Brahman, Jat, Khatri, Bania, Teli, and Lohar do not accept water and food from them. They have their own source of drinking water, cremation ground and religious shrine. But there are no restrictions on them to use the handpumps of other communities and to visit other religious shrines.

Municipal corporation supplies them drinking water. Most of them are self-employed either in their own traditional occupation of making winnowing fans and toys or work as daily labourers or hawkers.

They listen to the radio. They have electricity where they are settled and have *pukka* houses, but those who live in the *kulis* do not have electric connection. Cow-dung, coal and wood are used as fuel. When they live near the cities and have settled life, a few of their children have very recently started attending the free primary schools. Those who have ration cards get sugar and *ghee* only. They depend upon the moneylenders for loan at the time of need.

SWARAN SINGH

# DHOBI

The Dhobi derive their name from the word *dhona* which means 'to wash'. Since time immemorial they are engaged in the profession of washing and ironing clothes and claim to have migrated from Kanauj area. They are distributed throughout the state. They use Punjabi within the kin group and with others. Menfolk of the community invariably wear small gold earrings called *murkian*. Elderly men wear *kameez* and *pyjama* while the young ones wear trousers and shirt. Women wear *salwar* and *kameez*. Presently, they are trying to gain the status of Scheduled Caste. They take non-vegetarian food occasionally whereas *roti* with *dal* and *sabzi* forms their staple diet. Locally available pulses and vegetables are consumed. Wheat, maize and rice are the cereals consumed by them. Egg eaters are considered non-vegetarians. Some of them take mutton, chicken and fish. Women are generally vegetarians. *Ghee*, mustard oil and other refined oils form the cooking medium. Tea is the most favoured non-alcoholic drink with the members of all age groups. They consume roots and tubers in the form of onion, potatoes, ginger, radish, and carrot. Milk and milk products are consumed in varying quantities. They smoke *bidi*, cigarettes and *hookah*.

The community is divided into a number of *gots* such as Chuhan, Punwar, Tunwar, and Rajoria. These regulate marriage alliance and indicate descent and ancestory. They are considered just above the Scheduled Castes and are deemed as clean Shudra. In the community, endogamy is the rule and exogamy is practised at clan and village level. Earlier they used to leave four *gots* for fixing the marriage like that of self, mother's and grandmother's (both paternal and maternal). But now only the *got* of self and mother's are avoided. Marriages are negotiated when boys and girls attain adulthood and are around twenty years of age. Monogamy is the rule. *Kanyadan* exists and dowry is given in both cash and kind consisting of household articles and jewellery. *Bindi*, bangles and *sindur* form the marriage symbols. The newly weds, strictly observe the marriage symbols especially during family gatherings, fairs and festivals. The rule of residence after marriage is patrilocal. Divorce is traditionally not permitted. Widow/widower and divorcee remarriage is also not permitted. Regarding changes in marriage customs, there is an increase in age at marriage, marriage symbols are not observed strictly. Increase in the incidence of divorce and liberal attitude towards remarriage has been observed in recent years. Women's role is mainly confined to the household chores and looking after the family. They also attend and take part in ritual and religious affairs. Womenfolk of the community also help in the traditional occupation of washing and ironing the clothes. Women contribute to family income, but have a low status as they do not have decision-making powers or control on family expenditure.

Pre-delivery restrictions are imposed. Post-delivery pollution period is observed for thirteen or forty days. It is known as *sootak*. The birth of the male child is celebrated by distributing sweets. After *sootak* period, *chowke charhna* ritual is performed. Naming and *mundan* ceremonies are informal. *Mundan* is generally performed in the first, third or fifth year of the child. Marriage rituals are performed at the bride's residence and a feast is given for the bride's parents. Marriage rituals include *rok*, *mangni*, *shagun*, *barat*, *phere* and *doli*. The actual marriage is performed by *phere* round the sacred fire and the rituals are presided over by a Brahman priest. Consummation of marriage is at the groom's residence. The dead are cremated and bones immersed in flowing water. Post-death pollution is observed for eleven days for women and thirteen days for men. The bones called *phul* are collected on the fourth day and are immersed in the holy Ganga. *Kirya*, *uthala* or *rasam pagri* takes place as the last ritual on the eleventh or the thirteenth day. The life-cycle rituals are becoming shorter.

Both nuclear and extended family types exist. The traditional inter-personal relations of love, fear, respect avoidance and conflict are seen, as in other local communities. The young members of the family get love, affection and care, while elders command respect and authority. Avoidance relationship is observed between daughter-in-law and father-in-law, husband's elder brother and younger brother's wife. Limited joking relationship is found between husband's younger brother and elder brother's wife, sister's husband and wife's younger brothers and sisters, and grandparents and grand-children. Inter-personal relations of conflict and confrontations are also seen in the family on account of property, check on the freedom of youngsters and challenge to the authority of elders. The rule of residence is male equigeniture and succession is by the eldest son. Inter-family linkages are cordial. In recent years, there is rise in the formation of nuclear families, progressive decline of extended family system and poor interpersonal relationship in the families.

They are an occupational community engaged in washing and ironing of clothes. Some have also taken to other occupations such as dry-cleaning, shopkeeping, hosiery and plying rickshaw and auto-rickshaw. Transactions are made in cash. Child labour exists to augment the income of the family. They have a Dhobi Sabha to look after their occupational needs and to sort out other social needs at the community level.

The elders in the family usually sort out the routine family or inter-family disputes in the community. Ad hoc *biradari* consisting of few elders and enlightened members of the community may also be formed for solving community or inter-family disputes. If not satisfied, the aggrieved party is free to approach the court of law. Those living in urban areas are governed by the local civil and judiciary bodies. Those living in rural areas are governed by the statutory *panchayat* which is heterogeneous. They have defined role in planning and implementing developmental activities.

They subscribe to Hindu religion and Hindu way of life. Lohri, Holi, Diwali, Dussehra, Baisakhi, Janamashtami and Shivratri are the common festivals of the community. Services of a Brahman priest are availed of for performing birth, marriage and death rites and for religious teaching. Women know knitting and embroidery. They share Punjabi folk songs, folk tales and folklores with other local communities.

The Dhobis do not accept and exchange food and water with Scheduled Castes and Muslim communities. They accept water and food from other communities but do not exchange with them. 'Higher' castes do not accept water and food from their hands, traditionally. However, this rigidity is losing ground particularly in the urban areas. They share cremation ground, religious shrines and water sources with other communities of the state. They traditionally do not extend their services to the Scheduled Castes. Both boys and girls drop out of school due to economic reasons, poverty and lack of interest in studies. The attitude is positive for family planning as modern methods of family planning including sterilization for men are accepted. They use both indigenous and modern medicare. They visit local government dis-pensaries, hospitals and private practitioners according to their needs. Drinking water and electricity are available in the locality. They listen to radio, watch television and visit the cinema for entertainment. They are availing of the benefits under Rural Employment Guarantee Schemes. Coal, wood, kerosene oil or even liquified petroleum gas (L.P.G.) is used as fuel.

A.K. Bhatia

# DHOGRI

The Dhogri were originally residing in Dalhousie which was a part of Chamba state during the British rule. They were also found in the Kangra district. Their population in 1881 was 1,412 in Kangra district and 302 in Chamba state (Rose, 1919: 239; Ibbetson, 1916: 313). Even now their major population is concentrated in the districts of Chamba and Kangra with a spill over in the Dhar block of Gurdaspur district.

The name of this community is derived from their traditional occupation of burning charcoal and iron smelting. The view of this community seems to confirm the interpretation of Ibbetson (ibid. 313). It depicts that the name is derived from *dhonkni*, *dhangri* or *dhonkri* (bellows) which has taken the form of Dhogri in actual use. One of the respondent reflected that his own ancestors were in the village Doda Sarain in Jammu (Kistwar). The district of Gurdaspur also borders with the Kathua district of Jammu & Kashmir, the natural division being the river Ravi. His great grandfather was a *thanedar* (police station incharge), who was originally belonging to the Rajput caste (their subcaste being Rana). He married a Dhograni (a woman from Dhogri caste) and so he was made an outcaste but was accepted as a part of the Dhogri caste. It may here be mentioned that Rane is a distinct exogamous group among the Dhogris. The language spoken by them is a mixture of Dogri and Punjabi. They use Gurmukhi and Devanagari scripts.

Their constitutional status is that of a Scheduled Caste. Total population of the Dhogri in the Punjab state is 265 individuals which comprises 146 men and 119 women (*Census of India*, 1981).

Their staple food is rice, wheat and maize along withpulses such as *chana, kulthi* and *arhar*. They occasionally consume non-vegetarian food. They consume chicken once in a while, as they domesticate the local variety. Consumption of indigenous alcohol is common.

They could identify only two major subgroups among them, viz., Rane and Dagwal which are exogamous. The two *gots* were identified as Attari and Bhardwaj which are also exogamous.

They equate themselves with the Lohars and Tarkhans and have strong afinity with them. But they consider the local Scheduled Castes such as the Megh, the Batwal, the Chamar, etc., to be of lower status than themselves. They also recognize the castes like the Rajput and Brahmans as of higher status than themselves. Economically they are homogeneous and invariably of very low economic status.

They follow Hindu marriage practices. The practice of child marriage is no longer common, though it was a practice in the past. Monogamy is the usual form of marriage. Parental choice weighs in the decision of acquiring mates. Generally, marriage takes place within their own caste, but they also prefer marriage partners with the Lohars (blacksmith) and Tarkhans (carpenters). Their marriage with the Lohars and Tarkhans appears to be the recent trend. Similarly, their marriage with Lohars and Tarkhans of Himachal Pradesh is also of relatively recent origin and the incidence is fairly low. The territorial linkages of marital relationship seem to be confined to a limited area. They practise Vedic rituals. The Brahman priests are invited to perform marriage ceremonies in which the couple take seven *pheras* around the sacred fire according to Vedic practice. Though, they state that they observe subcaste exogamy both from the father's and mother's side as also similar *got* exogamy, but this appears to be a distinct possibility in view of their limited population as also lack of active marital interaction between their caste men.

Symbols of marriage are similar to other Hindu castes such as wearing of red bangles, vermilion mark on the forehead, etc. The practice of dowry exists not by compulsion but by voluntary desire. The voluntarism has invariably brought into effect the observance of dowry according to the financial capacity. Dowry is paid mostly in kind which includes utensils, bed, watch, etc., clothes for the bridegroom and the bride and also ornaments for the bride. Patrilocal residence is the rule.

Divorce is not encouraged, but when it becomes inevitable, it is accompanied with economic sanctions equivalent to marriage expenses. This is true in case of divorce initiated from either side. Widow remarrige is allowed. A common practice is marriage between younger brother and the wife of the deceased elder brother which is termed in local parlance as *chingrada*. On this occasion, the full marital procedure is not adopted but close relations are invited along with the *sarpanch* of the village to legitimize the new relationship.

After marriage there is the tendency to establish an independent family by the married couple which indicates the nuclear family as the predominant structural feature. The rules of inheritance are governed by Hindu law of inheritance. The brother and unmarried sisters also have equal right to land. The eldest son becomes the head of the family after the death of the father. The women also participate in working as labour. They also bring fodder and take care of the livestock. The authority of males is invariably reflected in major decisions. Preferential treatment is given to the male child as compared to the female ones.

Birth of a male child is accompanied with the distribution of sweets particularly *batasha* but the birth of female child is devoid of ceremony. The *mundan* ceremony of the male child takes place any time between the first and the fifth year and is celebrated by inviting close relatives. Death rites are similar to those of other Hindus. The dead body is cremated. The first ten days after the death are considered impure and polluting. Clothes are not to be changed during the first ten days and non-vegetarian diet is also prohibited. On the tenth day, purification ceremony is held. On the thirteenth day, funeral rites are performed. The ashes are immersed at Hardwar.

Traditional occupation of this community was manufacturing charcoal by burning wood. The procedure was to dump big logs of wood in the ditch and ignite them for a week to ten days for the preparation of charcoal. It was done for the contractors and their labour charges were fixed per sack of charcoal. This was the principal occupation of this community until twenty-five years back. They used to undertake this activity in Himachal Pradesh as also in the neighbouring tracts of Jammu and Kashmir. This activity kept bulk of this community absorbed for nearly six months in as much as their women were also engaged in selling charcoal. It was one of the primary means of subsistence.

Some of them were also engaged as blacksmiths in some villages. The account of Rose (ibid 239) shows that they were also engaged as tenants to the landlords which was governed by semibonded relationship. The transition to new economic activities has been seen during last twenty-five years. Some of them have accepted the vocation of blacksmithy and carpentry. For repairing plough they receive remuneration in terms of food grain. The families in Hara had taken to the occupation of blacksmithy after their settlement in village Hara for over fifty years. The family continues primarily with the occupation of Lohar (blacksmith) even today. For example, in the village of Hara Khokhiyal the two Dhogri families (both are brothers) work for the landlords consisting of sixty-two ploughs. For each plough they get a remuneration of 24 kg of grain every six months which is in the form of wheat, paddy, maize, etc. They have to make and repair all instruments associated with plough. Each family gets roughly 7 quintals of grain at the end of six months. All Dhogri families in an around Hara village work as blacksmiths and carpenters. This renders greater legitimacy for their incorporation within the rubric of Lohar-Tarkhan. This would also expand their base in terms of larger choices for marital alliences. Most of them are landless and are subservient to their Rajput landlords. So the patron-client relationship has endured and has not so far been threatened with eviction. Their loyalty and submission also entitles them to the grant of *ex gratia* in terms of fodder and fuel. In the village of Kotari two to three families of Dhogris have acquired some piece of cultivable land. A few of them are gradually transforming themselves as agriculturists. Most of them still cling to the occupation of preparing charcoal (which sustains them for four months in a year) and for the rest part of the year, they work as wage labourers in road construction work. The formation of corporations both in Himachal Pradesh and Jammu & Kashmir has considerably hit their traditional occupation particularly during the last ten years. The bulk of Dhogris in Dalhousie still seem to be dependent on the traditional economic activities for half the year, but there is a gradual depletion. Their children get free education and supply of free books.

The ancestors of Dhogris are located at Dalhousie, where these families go to propitiate and worship once in four to five years on important social occasions. They also sacrifice goat to satisfy their ancestors.

RAKESH KUMAR

# DHOSALI

The name of the community is derived form *dusa*, which means the small piece of straw with which leaves are pinned together to make plates and cups. The community was identified more by its occupation than other practices. According to Baden Powell (1872: 306) Dhosali were: 'A class of people who make *duna* [little cups] and *pattal* [plates] out of leaves, in which Hindus eat food or carry sweetmeats from the shops. They fasten the leaves together with strips of book or sheath toli gathered from stalls of 'munj' and even work patterns on leaves with thin strips of the same. They originally were hill people, but some few are found in Lahore, Amritsar, and elsewhere.'

The community has a very thin population in Punjab. Only few families have been left with much changed practices it has been absorbed in the mainstream. Ibbetson (1916: 336-7), and Rose (1919: 247) had identified their main settlements in Hoshiarpur district. This feature of geographical distribution of the Dhosali community continues to be substantially correct even now. The concentration of Dhosalis is even now in parts of Kangra district in Himachal Pradesh, which were part of Hoshiarpur district in the United Punjab. The few families of the community which were left in Punjab, were confined to the sub-hilly areas of Hoshiarpur district. At present some families have been uprooted and dispersed over large areas. *Census of India* (1891: 2) shows that the population of the community in the then undivided Punjab was 2,524; out of this 2,576 were Hindus, 15 Sikhs and 33 Muslims.

The Dhosalis speaks a dialect of Punjabi language, which is influenced by Pahari language. The Badla and Rampur Haler, the villages to which Dhosalis of Punjab belong, are located on the foothills, adjacent to the Kangra district of Himachal Pradesh, which is an indication of the influence of culture of Himachal Pradesh. The community in the Punjab uses typical Punjabi dress. Women wear same ornaments as other Punjabis. It takes both vegetarian as well as non-vegetarian diet, which includes eggs, fish, and meat. Wheat is the most commonly used cereal. Maize and rice are also taken. Commonly available fruits are taken depending upon the economic conditions. Mustard oil and *vanaspati ghee* are most commonly used for cooking.

In Punjab, the members of the Dhosali community are no more engaged in their traditional occupation. This occupation has been taken over by other communities, such as the Ghumars.

According to Ibbetson (1916: 336-7), and Rose (1919: 247), the marriage of Dhosalis was solemnized within the caste itself. The practice seems to have changed among Dhosalis of Punjab. Some members of the community are married to Brahmans and Khatris. Whenever marriage is performed four *gots* are excluded. These are the *gots* of parents of the groom and the bride. Some of their *gots* are Kundal, Bhardwaj and Pathania. Marriage ceremony is solemnized with seven *pheras*. The Brahmans perform this ceremony; marriages are arranged by the parents; engagement ceremony generally precedes the marriage.

The ceremonies at the time of birth and death are similar to those of other local communities. These ceremonies are performed according to the Hindu rites. Some Dhosalis also prepare *janam patris* or horoscopes, of the newborn children. The mother of the of newborn child is not allowed to do domestic work for a few days. *Namkaran* is performed by a priest. Some Dhosalis also practice the custom of *mundan*. The dead are cremated. However, if a young child dies the practice is to bury him. A ceremony is held after thirteen days of death, and is known as *pagdi*. But number of days may be twelve or even fourteen.

The status of women is low. These days divorce is allowed. There is no reported case of widow remarriage or the remarriage of a divorced woman, in the community. Women are not allowed to have a share in parental properties. However, it is not considered bad if a woman goes to work outside her home.

Religious practices of the Dhosalis are diverse. Although Dhosalis generally practise Hindusim, their religious practices are not uniform and consistent. Some of the informants in the course of this study were the followers of Baba Balak Nath (related to Shiva, a Hindu god and is worshipped by all communities. An annual fair is organized at the shrine, a day after Janamashtami). The community has some members who believe in Sanatan Dharma and Arya Samaj. The Dhosalis worship other gods and goddesses. Only a few Dhosalis believe in *tantra* or magic.

The Dhosalis are well exposed to new ideas and developmental process. Some of their children are able to get education upto matriculation, or more. A few of them have entered into government services as drivers and accountants, some have joined military service.

The attitude of Dhosalis to family planning is good as they have accepted the family planning programmes. Dhosali households have been able to benefit from electricity supply and sometimes also water supply. A few of them are holders of yellow cards and have secured loans, which have been used for various purposes to support their new occupations. Despite this change in the occuption, the economic position of Dhosalis is not good. The community is not able to recollect any Dhosali having ever been in an influential political position. There has never been any reported member of village *panchayat* or Member of Legislative Assembly.

Of late Dhosalis of Punjab have acquired a better social status as now they mix freely with other castes including the Brahmans and Khatris. Recently the Dhosalis have started considering themselves as equal to Rajputs. They at least trace their origins to the Rajputs. These claims are based upon their system of *gots* which is common with Rajputs to some extent. They were treated as 'low caste of superior standing' (Ibbestson, 1916: 336-7). However, Rose had pointed out that Khatris practised untouchability towards them (Rose, 1919: 247). The present study has revealed that the Dhosalis were never considered untouchables or outcastes. The village *sarpanch* and other informants from Brahman, Khatri and other castes have pointed out that their status was equal to that of Chimbas (a caste which work as tailors) of the village. The simple fact that the Dhosali supplied cups and *pattals* for marriage ceremonies ruled out existence of untouchability, as this did not involve any unclean work.

VIRINDER SINGH

# DOOM

The Doom, Dom, Dumna or Mahara are recognized as a Scheduled Caste in the state of Punjab. The Dom or Dumna can either be executioner (Jallad) or a corpse-burner and in the Hoshiarpur district; he is also referred as Dumna. Dum in the areas bordering on the state of Himachal Pradesh work in bamboo, and are sometimes called Dum-Mirasis, who play *tabla, sarangi.* The Dums are also termed as Mirasis and have patron-client relationship with the lower castes, such as the Dhanaks, Julahas, Bhangis, Chamars, Jhiwars (Rose, 1919: 249).

According to their story, the origin of the Dooms is as follows: Guru Vashisht informed Raja Gurukul that he intended to perform a *yajna* on Tuesday. Raja Gurukul asked the specific reasons why the *yajna* was to be performed on that particular day and not on any other day. Raja Gurukul became anxious as Indra was to perform the *yajna* on the same day. Vashisht left in anger. When Vishwamitra asked Raja Gurukul why he was worried, he told Vishwamitra that Guru Vashisht had left and hence *yajna* could not be performed. Vishwamitra told the Raja to accept him as his *guru.* When the *yajna* started, a mother who had one hundred sons was invited and asked to bless the host. But Vishwamitra was told that he could not perform the *yajna.* The Raja told him that he could not stop him from doing so because he was arranging for a *yajna.* The children told the Raja that he would have only one son in his future generations. Later on Vishwamitra told the Raja to tell the sons to move out of the city. The Raja accused Vishwamitra of cheating the people. At this, Vishwamitra cursed the Raja to become a 'Dom'. Hence the name of Doom came into existence, which means, 'who graze the animal'.

The Doom rank below the Chuhras. In Ludhiana they are different from and lower than the Mirasi. The Dumna, called Domra and even Dum is the Chuhra of the hills proper and is also found in large numbers in the sub-mountain areas of Kangra, Hoshiarpur and Gurdaspur. Like the Chuhra of the plains he is something more than a scavenger; but whereas the Chuhra works in grass, the Dumna adds to this occupation the trade of working in bamboo, a material not available to the Chuhra. He makes sieves, winnowing fans, matting, grass ropes and string and generally all the vessels, baskets, screens, furniture and other articles which are ordinarily made of bamboo.

When he confines himself to this sort of work and gives up scavenging, he appears to be called Bhanjra, at any rate in the lower hills and occasionally Sarial. Their clans are Kalotra, Manglu, Pargat, Drahe and Lalotra. According to *Census of India* (1981), the total concentration of the Dooms in the state of Punjab is 1,24,924 individuals, which include 66,301 males and 58,623 females. They are the followers of Guru Nabha Bhagat. There is a temple at Jammu in the name of Nabha Bhagat. In Jammu the Dooms have a large concentration. They have migrated to Punjab after 1947. At Ludhiana the Dooms have their concentration at Slem Tapri, Ghantaghar (Clock Tower), Jawahar Camp, Simlapuri, Tajpur Road, Mukatpura Muhalla and Islam Ganj.

They speak both Punjabi and Hindi. The men wear *kurta*, *pyjama* or *dhoti*, turban, while the dress of their women consists of *salwar*, *kameez* and *dupatta*. *Jutti* is the footwear for both the males and females. Wheat is their staple food, while their ordinary food is *dal* and *roti*. They prefer pulses to vegetables. When they can afford it, they take eggs, fish and pork. Alcoholic drinks are taken on special occasions. Tea and *lassi* are also taken frequently. The cooking medium is mustard oil which is being replaced by groundnut oil. The consumption of fruits is very rare.

The Dooms have different *gots* for the purpose of regulating their marriages. Some of their *gots* are Kanths, Kalotra, Majhotra, Bhadotra, Sambal and Jallandhrea. As they do menial jobs, they do not consider themselves to be of high status and similarly, members of other communities also perceive them as of low status. However, as some of them have become Arya Samaji and also wear the sacred thread, they feel they have become Aryas or Mahashas, though, in spite of their conversion, they are still considered to be unclean. Dooms marry among themselves and marriage with in the same *gots* is not allowed. In the past they used to marry outside the *got* of their mother, father, mother's sister and father's sister. However, now they marry outside the *got* of their mother, grandmother and father. They marry when the boy and girl attain the age of eighteen to twenty years. Services of a *vichola* were utilized earlier, but now, parents of the boy and girl negotiate and finalize the marriage of their children. Marriage is performed according to the Hindu or Sikh traditions.

The symbols of marriage are *sindur* in the hair parting and wearing of *tikka* and *chura*. Dowry is permitted in the form of clothes, furniture, utensils, ornaments depending upon the financial condition of the girl's parents. Divorce is not permitted among the Dooms. However, remarriage which is termed as *karewa*, is permitted. A typical family is a joint family and includes parents and their married and unmarried children. Sons inherit the property equally. The eldest son gets succession. The Dooms maintain very good inter-family linkages.

At the time of birth of a child, post-delivery restrictions on the mother are observed for forty days; this is called *silla*. They tie a *sehra* (leaves of mango tree) as a *sagan* on the front door. A feast is also arranged for the members of the community. Before marriage, *mangani* (the ceremony of engagment) takes place. The girl's parents offer *thuthi*, one *rumal*, one rupee and one *bhayli* (*gur*). The ritual of *thaka* or *rokni* is also performed by offering five to ten rupees to the boy. As *shagun*, clothes, sweets, fruits and a sum of eleven to fifty-one rupees are offered to the parents of the boy. Marriage is arranged in consultation with the girl's father who is given about one week's time. In most of the cases the marriage and *muklawa* takes place in quick succession, though sometimes there is also a gap of about one to two months. The consummation of marriage is at the groom's residence.

When a person dies at an old age, there is a custom to throw *phulia*, *batasha* and small coins, when the dead body is taken out in procession to the crematorium. The ceremony for purification and peace of the soul of the dead person is observed either on the tenth or seventeenth day. The feast known as *roti* is offered to the members of the community. The Dooms, were also not allowed entry to the religious places. They became Arya Samaji and got an opportunity for development. Most of them in Punjab are engaged as labourers, some of them pull carts and rickshaws. In the villages they work as daily labourers or go to the cities as labourers and return to their villages in the evening. Some of them also engage themselves in animal husbandry.

Harijan Mahashya Sudhar Sabha of Ludhiana and Islamganj look into the various local issues, while the Akhil Bhartiya Mahashya Maha Sabha (Akhawa), Dinanagar, looks into the matters of common interest at an all-India level. Various issues related to marriage, petty issues, household affairs and police cases, if any, are looked after by the local Sabha. Earlier they used to excommunicate an individual and stop his *hookah pani*, but now no such punishments are imposed.

They worship the Hindu deities. A few, who became Sikhs follow the tenets of Sikhism. For those who have become Arya Samaji, there are no restrictions in exchanging food and water, but not with those who have not become Arya Samaji, the people of higher social status still do not exchange water and food with them. Boys and girls have started attending schools recently. There is a government dispensary which enables them to make use of modern medicare when required. They have water taps as source of drinking water. Most of the persons are self-employed. They have electricity. Coal, dung cakes and wood are used as fuel. They have ration cards. The aged have yellow cards for taking loans from banks.

SWARAN SINGH

# GADDI

The Gaddi are invariably associated with the people living in the districts of Chamba and Kangra of Himachal Pradesh. This area is also known as Bharmaur region, and according to popular belief this place is the 'abode' (the term *gaddi* means seat or throne) of Lord Shiva. Every year on the eve of Janamashtami devotees throng here to have a dip in the holy water of the Mani-Mahesh. They appear to have been driven to the forest of the Dhauladhar Range from the plains due to the persecution during the Mughal rule. This is substantiated from the accounts of Barnes and Lyall (1850), Guha (1935), Shashi (1977), etc. Their main traditional occupations have been sheep-breeding which is also indicative of the term *gaddi.* They are thus primarily an occupational group (Shashi, 1977) and with the passage of time, the occupational group has become coterminus with the community.

During the winter season the Gaddi migrate, along with their flock of sheep, to Punjab for grazing particularly to Pathankot area in Gurdaspur district and return to Bharmaur region by the month of March. They are not permanent residents of Punjab. However, they are enlisted as Scheduled Tribe in the district of Chamba but not in Kangra district. Their dialect is 'Pahari' which they also refer to as 'Gaddi bhasha'. Its variant in Chamba district is known as Chameali and Bhallali, whereas the dialect spoken in Kangra district is known as Kangri. This dialect is an admixture of Sanskrit, Hindi, Punjabi and Urdu. They also speak Hindi with Pahari accent.

They have their distinct dress pattern; men wear a high-peaked cap with flaps which can also cover the ears in severe cold. Their costume consists of a woollen *chola* stretched from neck to knees. Some of them also wear turban; women are dressed in a *kurti* (shirt) and *pyjama* during summer season, in winter they cover themselves with an overcoat called *luanchari.* They also cover their body with a woollen shawl and woollen *chadru* (bedsheet). Those in service has given up their traditional dress. They do not observe restriction on eating non-vegetarian food which includes meat of sheep, goat and fish. Wheat and pulses are their staple diet. They take vegetables two to three times a week. On social and festive occasions, they prepare special food such as *krah-puri*, sweets made of maize, *rajmah-chawal* and *kheer* (rice cooked with milk and sugar). They also sacrifice sheep or goat during certain festivals and also prepare a special dish from their meat. Apple is their favourite seasonal fruit. Their festive occasions become more lively with the use of their favourite home-brewed drink called *sur*. Their women do not take alcoholic drinks at all, though smoking is not forbidden. The males among them are fond of tobacco. Of late, they have also started consuming liquor sold in the market.

They are divided into upper castes (Brahman and Rajput) and lower castes (consisting of Sippis, Riharas and Hallis). These castes are hierarchically arranged. They observe caste endogamy and do not interdine with members of lower castes. Even among the lower castes the Sippis do not accept water and cooked food from the Riharas. All the caste members accept uncooked food from each other. Restrictions are also observed in sharing *hookah*. Caste restrictions in eating and drinking are observed by the Brahman and Rajput with castes such as the Sippi and Rehara.

Their marriages generally take place outside the village. They maintain caste endogamy, i.e. a Rajput Gaddi marries within the Rajput caste and so on. The boys get married at the age of fifteen to twenty-five years and girls between fifteen and twenty. Marriage is decided by elders. Bride-price does not exist but due to the poor economic condition marriages by exchange or services are not uncommon. Dowry is in the incipient form which consists of a small number of utensils and elementary items of furniture depending upon the financial status. The most prevalent form of marriage is known locally as *dan pun* marriage. This type of marriage is considered superior to all other kinds of marriages. The families of bride and bridegroom exchange gifts.

The second most popular form of marriage is known as *batta satta* (marriage by exchange). In this form of marriage brothers and sisters between the two families are exchanged. Polygamy is also common for which the main motivating factor is death of the spouse, desertion and absence of children. One could also notice few cases of marriages by registration taking place recently. Boy's parents send a mediator to negotiate with the girl's parents and in case it is agreeable, a *purohit* is consulted for fixing the date of betrothal ceremony and the date of marriage called *lakhnotri*. At the wedding ceremony Ganapati *puja* is performed. The bridegroom wears the apparel of a *jogi* (saint) with a *dhoti* and *mundras* (earrings); a satchel is slung over his shoulder, a black woollen rope tied around his wrist and he carries a bow and an arrow. A *mrigshala* (deer skin) covers his back. He wears a sacred thread and carries a stick of *timbu* along with him.

The priest performs the sacred thread ceremony after which the bridegroom takes the sacred bath. He also shoots arrows. The boy is then made to sit on a sheepskin. Few drops of oil are poured on his head by close relatives which is followed by a bath. This custom is known as *tel sand* ceremony. At the time of departure of the marriage party of one hundred to one hundred and fifty persons to the bride's place, the boy puts on red clothes and *sehra*. On arrival at the bride's village at the fixed time for *lagan*, the bride is brought to the marriage *mandap* under *bedi* for full Hindu rites to be observed. There is a mixture of both nuclear and joint families. The Gaddi follow patrilocal rule of descent and patrilocal rule of residence. Father (after him the next elder male member) acts as the head of the family. Property is distributed equally among the male children. In case of more than one wife, property is equally distributed between the wives. Daughters have no right to property. Birth of the male child is celebrated. Divorce is permitted with the consent of *biradari* but the husband is to return the dowry to his wife. In case of wife taking initiative in divorce, her new partner has to compensate. The children remain with the divorced father. Widow remarriage is also permissible.

They believe in magic or *jadoo-tuna*. There are *chellas* of the magician, who are believed to speak on behalf of the deity. Their words are obeyed as a command from God or spirits associated with causing sickness, death of the family members and animals, etc. They also believe in the devil and wear *tawiz* to avoid the evil spirits. The *chellas* play an important role in the religious and social life of Gaddis. They are believed to be endowed with power to forecast, communicate with spirits and ensure health and wealth. This community is mainly Shaivaites. They have deep faith in the gods and goddesses such as Durga, Rama, Krishna and other *pahari* deities such as Kilong, Ajaipal, etc. The share of these gods are ensured before the harvested crops are taken home. They perform a number of ceremonies and animal sacrifice (goat and sheep) to please the gods. *Sur* is offered to the deities as sacred drink to pacify the anger of the gods. They also undertake *katha*, *navala* and *shanti path*. They believe that Shiva's blessings can remove ailments, misfortune and natural calamities. Contact with women during the menstruation period is considered polluting and so she is not allowed to enter the kitchen from two to four days. Impurity due to childbirth is considered highly polluting. Women are not permitted to enter the kitchen from twenty-one to twenty-five days after childbirth. Only after the performance of *guntrala* ceremony (mixture of cow urine thrown on all the clothes in the house), they are allowed to cook. Death pollution rites are observed for ten to fifteen days. During this period no function is celebrated.

Traditional occupation of the Gaddis was rearing sheep. During the winter they would move down the hills. Gradually there is a transformation among them from nomadic to settled life. Many of them have switched over to the new occupations of government services. Now they are settling down in agriculture and are also working as labourers. Only a few of them are now dependent on rearing sheep, their traditional occupation. This transformation was perceived more among their community in Kangra district in view of the reservation facilities provided to the Scheduled Tribes. Their women are active and assist men in economic pursuit. They participate in agricultural operations, livestock care, collecting fuel and also in weaving and spinning. Their non-school-going children also contribute to the family income. Exchange of labour is practised both in agriculture and sheep-rearing. Hiring of labour has emerged as a new phenomenon.

They sell their raw material to private parties from whom they contract loans. Government agencies have not been able to make much impact in the rearing of sheep involving a number of activities such as grazing, taking care of animals and shearing them, spinning and weaving of wool, etc. The Sippi caste is treated as experts in cutting wool. Spinning is done invariably by female family members. Weaving is a common operation for both males and females. Hiring of labour for weaving is in an incipient stage. Taking care of sheep and goats is usually the function of males. They are forced to move along with their sheep in search of fodder, especially in the winter season, to places such as Bhungal, Una, Lahaul, Jammu, Mandi, Kulu, Sirmaur, Sundernagar, Hamirpur, Manikaran, Sarka Ghat, Nagrota, Nurpur, Dhauladhar range, Chakki and the neighbouring areas of Punjab. They form themselves into groups while moving from one place to another; these groups consist of their relatives and *biradari* people. Preparation of food is usually a shaved task.

Women are generally left behind under the care of joint family. Whenever they accompany the group they assist in cooking food. The long absence of the male adversely affects the upbringing of the children as a result of which there is now an urge for settled life.

Majority of them have small agricultural holdings. Cultivation is carried on in small and scattered plots. The main crops grown are wheat, rice, barley, mustard and pulses. Incidence of leasing in and out is very low. Majority had *kachcha* houses. Their poor economic conditions compels them to exchange labour for hiring plough animals. Nearly half of them are below poverty line. The average family size varies from six to eight individuals.

Every community has its separate *jal-chal.* The Brahman and Rajput do not take *pukka* food from the Sippi, Halli and Badi. The Rajput and Brahman are closely interrelated. Acharyas come at death ceremony and are provided with *dakshina.* Every community has its *purohit.* They have *biradari* and *panchayat adalat* to decide various issues. *Hookah-pani bandh* is preliminary punishment which is considered a social boycott or isolation. The *biradari* takes decision on moving sheep and goats to a new pasture. It also settles divorce compensation and commends the culprit to take oath at one of the sacred places such as Mani-Mahesh. A statutory *panchayat* or *adalat* is proposed. Of late, there has been a tendency among this community for leading a settled life and so the incidence of seasonal migration at community level is getting minimised. The government has also settled quite a sizeable chunk among them on the land acquired as surplus land under the land ceiling law.

Illiteracy is very high among the Gaddi. Boys and girls have educational facilities and students are eligible for scholarships in Scheduled Tribe areas. However, girls do not continue their studies beyond middle standard. In the villages they sell wool, shawls and other finished goods to the private parties because they can get loans from them.

K. Gopala Iyer
Rakesh Kumar

# GADERIA

The Gaderias are also termed as Gadderia, Gaddaria or Gadaria. According to *Census of India* (1911: 455), 'the Gaddarias were chiefly Hindus returned, mostly in the Gurgaon, Delhi, Karnal, Ambala, Lahore districts and the Kalsia, Nahan and Patiala states. They had taken largely to blanket weaving. The total population of Gadderia was 21,946 individuals, which included 12,393 males and 9,553 females. According to Rose (1919: 255), the Gadaria is the shepherd and goatherd and confined to the Jumna zone in the Punjab, the Gadaria, even in that part of the province, almost ceased to be distinctively a shepherd, as the cultivating classes themselves often pasture their own flocks, and has become rather a blanket weaver being indeed as often called Kambalia as Gadaria.'

The Gaderia trace their origin from a Sanskrit word *gadd* which means *bhed* (sheep). They are shepherd, and goatherds and have recently migrated to Punjab. The migration is also recalled in the oral tradition of the community. They speak Hindi and Punjabi languages with the members of their community and outsiders. The men wear shirt, trousers and white *dhoti* and their women wear *salwar/kameez* and *dupatta*. They take eggs, mutton and chicken. Consumption of vegetables is moderate. *Dal* and *roti* is their staple food. Groundnut oil is used as cooking medium. They take milk and milk products, tea, and *lassi*. A few may take alcoholic drinks on special occasions. They smoke *bidi* and cigarrette.

They are divided into *gots*, some of these being Phul, Hiranbal, Kakante, Chadail, Toor, Sirambal, etc. These *gots* are used to regulate their marriage alliances. They consider themselves of Rajput origin, but the members of high castes consider them of low status. They are aware of the *varna* system but do not recognize their place in it. It is an endogamous community, but practice exogamy at the *got* and village levels. They do not marry between the *gots* of mother, father, maternal grandmother and grandfather.

Marriage is arranged by negotiations, when the boy is around twenty to twenty-two years of age and the girl is between eighteen to twenty years old. Monogamy is the form of marriage. Symbols of marriage for the bride are *sindur,* bangles, *bindi*, finger-ring and nose-ring. Dowry in kind is allowed, which includes cloth, ornaments, beddings, watch, cycle and *peti* (big trunk), depending upon the financial condition of the girl's parents. They are patrilocal. Divorce for reasions of maladjustment, and cruelty is allowed. Compensation is given to the wife. Both husband and wife can seek divorce either from court or *panchayat*. Children can stay either with their mother or father. Remarriage is allowed. When a widow marries her deceased husband's younger brother, it is called *chadar paoni*. Widower remarriage is called *karewa* and the widow's as *bathaona*.

Nuclear and joint family types are both prevalent. Property and confrontation between the father and the sons, between brothers and check on the freedom of youngsters in the family may lead to conflicts in the family. All the sons get equal share in their father's property. The eldest son gets the right of succession. Nuclear families are on increase at the cost of joint families.

Women occupy a lower status than that of men. They attend to various household activities and in addition they also look after the domestic animals, work in agricultural fields, collect fuel and bring water for drinking purposes. Postnatal restrictions for a mother are observed for forty days which is called *shila*. *Chowke charhana* ceremony is performed after the completion of birth pollution.

The marriage ceremony is performed according to the traditions of seven *pheras* around the sacred fire at the bride's residence. Feast is offered by the bride's parents to the marriage party. Consummation of marriage is at the groom's residence. They cremate the dead (*dag dena*) and the bones are immersed in the Ganga at Hardwar. They also worship their ancestors, in ceremony known as *shradh*.

They are engaged in their traditional occupation of grazing sheeps and goats in addition to settled agriculture and as labourers. The number of agricultural and casual labourers is increasing. The mode of payment is by cash. Three to four villages together form a *panchayat* to settle disputes. The concept of *siana* (village elder) is there who attends to the problems of the Gaderia. They also approach the court of law to settle the marriage and divorce cases. They profess Hinduism and worship Hindu gods and goddesses, celebrate Hindu festivals and festivities. The *pujari* (sacred specialist) comes from other communities who attends to the rites of birth, marriage and death. Festivals are of socio-economic and religious significance. There are wall and floor paintings in the houses. Ladies during their spare time attend to embroidery (*kasida*) or weave *daris*. On the occasions of marriage boys and girls dance and sing folk songs.

All the communities of the village invite them on special occasions and they also invite them and take water and food with them. There was untouchability in the past, but it is not prevalent now. They share wells, roads, schools, places of worship and take part in various festivals and festivities with other communities. They have separate cremation ground. A few community members are in defence services.

The boys and girls study upto secondary level. Dropout in school is due to economic reasons. Attitude towards modern medicare and family planning is favourable. They prefer three children and use methods of family welfare other than sterlization. Some of them listen to radio. Dissemination of information is through political parties. They use electricity. Dung cakes, *tanda* (dried maize plants), *chitya* (dried cotten plants) are used as fuel. Tube wells, organic manure, chemical fertilizers, insecticides and immunization of mother and child and ration card facilities are available. Attitude towards saving is positive. They help each other with contribution on special occasions such as marriage and death, but in addition to that they take loans from the moneylenders also.

SWARAN SINGH

# GAGRA

The Gagra or Gagri or Gogri and Jokharu, a very small community, are nomadic and engage themselves in catching, keeping and applying leeches. Some of them, also prepare *sirkis* or mats from grass and reed.

The Gagras are also called Jonkawale. Their traditional occupation is to catch and apply leeches. The word *jonk* (leech) has given rise to its synonym Jonkawala. The number of individuals of this community is decreasing as they do not identify themselves as Gagra but with other nomadic communities of the state. They have migrated from their ancestral place of Gagomal in 1955 due to flood. According to *Census of India* (1981), their total concentration in the state is 413 individuals, consisting of 244 males and 169 females only.

They speak Punjabi. Men wear shirt, *dhoti* and *pagri*; the women wear *salwar*, *kameez* and *dupatta*. They have been recognized as a Scheduled Caste. Their food habits have undergone a change. They were nomadic and used to hunt in the jungles in the past, and take the meat of such animals as *kachoo* (tortoise), *billa* (wild cat) and *saha* (hare) and so on. But now, as the jungles are no more in existence and the animals for hunting are not available, they take *dal-roti* as their staple food. They eat eggs and consumption of vegetables is moderate. Alcoholic drinks and fruits are taken occasionally. Consumption of milk products is very rare. They smoke *bidi*.

They are divided into different *gots*, which regulate their marriage alliances. Some of their *gots* are: Chohan, Mattoo, Gharu, Khokhar, Momoy. They consider themselves of low status and other communities also have the same opinion about them. They are aware of the *varna* system and recognize their status as Shudra. They are an endogamous community but observe exogamy at *got* level. They exclude the *got* of mother's sister and father's sister.

Ibbetson (1916: 279) states that they are for the most part Musalmans who marry by *nikah*. However, presently the marriages among Sikh Gagra are solemnized according to the tradition of *anand karaj*. The marriage is arranged by negotiations with the help of a *vichola*. If the parents of the boy and girl agree for the marriage of their children, even the brother, mother's brother or sister's husband can be a mediator. Bangles of glass and *bindi* are the symbols of marriage and monogamy is the form of marriage. Dowry is permitted in kind but it is not a very common practice. They are patrilocal. Divorce due to maladjustment is allowed. Both husband and wife are entitled for divorce. In case of a divorce, children can stay either with their mother or father. Remarriage of widow, widower, male and female divorcee is also allowed.

Families are both nuclear and joint. The avoidance and joking relationships are observed between the members of the family. Challenge to the authority of the elders or check on freedom of young members of the family may cause conflict. Males inherit the property of their father equally and the eldest son gets succession. The status of women is low. They attend to various household activities and also bring potable water. The woman neither contribute to the family income nor control its expenditure. Post-delivery pollution and restrictions are observed. Before marriage there is a ceremony of *mangani*. *Shagun* is given by the girl's parents to the boy in the form of one rupee and twenty-five paise, eleven or twenty-one rupees, a *pagri*, *gur* and *chhuhara*, while the girl is presented with clothes by the parents of the boy on this occasion. Marriage ceremony takes place at the residence of the bride. Bride's parents also offer feast to the marriage party. They invite the girl on the second day of marriage and send her back to her in-law's house after seven days. Consummation of marriage is at the bridegroom's residence. They bury their dead and observe pollution.

They are engaged in their primary occupation of catching and applying leeches and *singhis*; a few of them also work as sweepers in the municipality. They also ply rickshaw and work as casual labourers.

They have their own traditional *panchayat* headed by a *nambardar*. The *panchayat* has one nominated member each from different *gots*. Statutory *panchayats* have existed since Independence. The traditional *panchayat* settles matters related to divorce and marriage disputes and its decision is final and is obligatory to both the parties. The *panchayat* can impose fines ranging from one thousand rupees to one thousand two hundred rupees. Non-compliance of a decision results in the ex-communication of the offender who is not allowed the use of utensils for drinking water. No one among them approaches the police or a court of law to settle disputes. Worship is performed according to the Hindu, Sikh and Christian traditions. Many of them had embraced Christianity. They also worship Baba Balmiki. They celebrate all the festivals which are of social and religious significance. Though there is a change of religion yet the former practices survive. Women sing Punjabi folk-songs on the occasions of marriage.

The Gagras accept from, and exchange food and water with other communities, namely the Chuhra and other people living in their locality, with whom they have their daily interaction. Untouchability as practised in the past has not been reported. They have separate cremation ground. They share the traditional festivals and festivities. They lack modern inter-community linkages.

Formal education, though partly favourable for boys, is not favoured for girls. Boys study upto primary level but the girls do not study. They visit primary health centre for the modern medicare. Usually couples have on an average, three children. They get information through political parties. Wood is their main fuel source. They have ration cards to get sugar and kerosene oil. They depend on moneylenders for loan, if the money for social functions as collected with mutual help, is not sufficient.

SWARAN SINGH

# GANDHILA

The Gandhila is small nomadic community who are under a vow to be barefooted and bareheaded and it is their occupation to keep donkeys and also engage in their trade.

According to *Census of India* (1981), the total population of the Gandhila in the state of Punjab is 1,869 individuals, with 1000 males and 869 females. The Gandhilas mostly live in Jalandhar and Patiala. According to a story related by their *pradhan*, at one stage the Gandhila were called Chouhan. There was a fight between Sambal Singh and Ajit Mal on one side and Babar on the other. Sambal Singh and Ajit Mal were the rulers of Delhi and were defeated by the Mughal king Babar. The Rajputs took an oath not to sleep on the bed or eat in the golden or silver utensils, till they had their kingdom restored. They went into the jungles where, in order to satisfy their hunger they had to eat all sorts of food. In the jungles, they met Bangalas who used to hunt animals for food. The Bangalas told them that they were deserters but had horses and guns and advised them to keep donkeys instead of horses. So they caught a few donkeys and started living with the Bangalas. In the meantime, the Mughals sent their forces to capture the defeated Rajput kings. On enquiry they told the Mughal forces that they are *gadhewalas*, i.e. who keep donkeys. Hence they were known as Gadhela or Gandhilas. Later, when the British came to India, they came to know that the people living in the huts were good fighters and might not allow them to settle down and as a result, the British declared them as Criminal Tribes, imposed Criminal Act and put them behind the bars. This Act was withdrawn in 1952, and they were declared as denotified.

They speak in their own language within their community and call this language Pasto. But with other communities they speak Punjabi language. Men wear a *lungi*, *kurta* and *pyjama* while the women wear *salwar*, *kameez* and *dupatta*. They eat the food which consists of *roti*, *dal* and vegetables. Alcoholic drinks are used occasionally and on festivals or marriage ceremonies. Consumption of fruits is also occasional. They smoke *bidi*.

The Gandhila have different *gots*. Some of their *gots* are: Billa, Sadhiana, Kale, Nakorea, Dangroo. They do not marry among their own *got*. If it is not possible to get a mate outside their own *got*, they marry among their own *got.* They intermarry with the Dhea and Bangala. Village endogamy is permitted. Marriage is arranged by negotiation. Earlier child marriage was in practice, but has been replaced by adult marriage. The boy's relatives first approach the parents of the girl with the proposal of marriage. Betrothal or *mangani* is thus fixed. *Shagun*, which ranges from one hundred to three hundred rupees is offered at the time of *mangani* and one hundred fifty to three hundred and fifty rupees or sometimes five hundred and twenty-five rupees at the time of marriage.

Marriage is solemnized by seven *pheras.* A feast is offered to the members of the community. After marriage the newly married couple may have their own hut, but live together with other members of their community. Divorce and remarriage is also permitted among the Gandhila by their *panchayat.* Cruelty, maladjustment, adultery may be some of the reasons of divorce. Compensation is given to the aggrieved party. Both husband and wife have right for divorce. Remarriage of widow, widower, sororate and levirate are also permitted among the Gandhila.

A daughter-in-law maintains avoidance from her father-in-law; avoidance relationships are also maintained between the mother-in-law and son-in-law, sister-in-law and brother-in-law. Joking relationship exists between sister-in-law and brother-in-law. Points of conflict may be the sharing of common source of water, common place for playing of children, marriage disputes, etc. Sons inherit the property of their father equally and the eldest son gets succession.

The primary role of the women is to attend to the various household jobs which includes bringing up of the children, cooking food, and bringing drinking water. They have a lower status than men among the Gandhila.

Post-delivery restrictions for a period of forty days are observed. They name their children according to their wish. Earlier the names of the Gandhila were after Muslim names, but now the names are like other Hindus. Marriage ceremony takes place at the bride's parent's house. Consummation of marriage is at the bridegroom's house.

The Gandhila cremate their dead and also observe pollution period. In case the person dies at an old age, a ceremony is held between twelveth and sixteenth day for purification, and peace of the soul of the dead person. A feast is given to the members of the community. The rituals at present have been curtailed.

Begging is an old occupation of the Gandhila. They also make toys from reed or paper. They also engage themselves as hawkers and sell bedsheets and cloth and are in the trade of dealing in donkeys.

The Gandhilas have their own traditional *panchayat*. All the members of the community follow their *pradhan*. The duty of the *pradhan* is to take a decision in consultation with the members of its community. The *pradhan* or *sarpanch* is elected by voice vote. The main quality of the *pradhan* is that he should be in a position to take a decision according to the time and situation. The *pradhan* is elected for his whole lifetime.

They never approach the court of law. If anybody approaches the police or a court, he or she is fined. They have tough social laws; if anybody abuses his wife he can also be fined. In case of a quarrel, they settle the dispute themselves. The punishment is based strictly on the magnitude of the fault. The cash fine ranges from twenty-five to one hundred rupees in case of divorce. The boy is fined twice as much as the expenditure incurred on his marriage by the parents of his wife. If the girl's parents refuse to send the girl, all the expenditure incurred by the boy's parents is to be returned to them. If the police takes into custody any member of the Gandhila community, he has to pay the fine and can be excommunicated. Any person dealing with him is also excommunicated. If such a person pays the fine and asks pardon from the community, he is taken back into the community.

They worship all the Hindu goddesses such as Chintpurni Devi, Jawala Devi, Kali Devi, Naina Devi, Vaishno Devi, Kangrawali Devi and Mansa Devi. On the eve of Diwali, they worship their dead. They light a lamp in the honour of Baba Sabal Singh. The main *puja* is held on Diwali. The *puja* is performed with a bottle of liquor, chicken and sweets. Dussehra and Lohri are the other main festivals.

The Gandhilas exchange water and food with the communities who live in the neighbouring huts. They share place of worship with them and participate in traditional festivals and festivities. Formal education is partly favourable for both boys and girls, but many of them do not go to schools, and those who go study upto primary level only. They have their own traditional medicare, and the attitude towards the modern medicare is not favourable. Attitude towards the family welfare programme is favourable and they prefer to have three children only. They use tap water for drinking purpose. Mostly they are self-employed. They listen to the radio. Some of them use electricity. They use firewood and cow-dung as fuel. They have ration cards to get sugar, rice, *atta*, etc., from the fair price shops. They have recently developed a habit of saving money.

SWARAN SINGH

# GHUMIAR (MUSLIM)

According to *Census of India* (1911: 464) Kumhars lived almost everywhere, and were potters and brick-burners. They were described as indispensable to the agriculture, where they supplied earthen pots for the well gear. Total population of Kumhars was 5,50,450 individuals, comprising 2,29,738 males and 2,50,712 females. Rose (1919: 562), states that Kumhar, Ghumiar, Ghumar, Khubar, Kubhar, Khuhar, Kubar, or as he is more often called in the Punjab, Ghumiar, is the potter, and brick-burner of the country.

They supply earthen vessels, which are of daily household use by the various communities both in the rural and the urban areas. They supply earthen lamps on the eve of Diwali, or new vessels, when the new harvest arrives in each village household, with which they still have a patron-client relationship. They also keep donkeys and supply manure, bricks, carry soil or dust. They also carry the food grains to the nearest market on cash payment. Owing to their association with the donkey, the Ghumiars are considered to be of a lower status than the Lohars, who work with iron and the Chamars who work in leather.

The male dress is shirt, *lungi*, *safa* (turban), while the females wear *salwar, kameez* and *dupatta*. The Muslim women use *burqa* (veil). They are distributed in all the villages with at least one family in each village. They eat wheat, maize, vegetables and pulses such as gram, *urad, moong*. Groundnut oil is used as a cooking medium. They take milk and milk products; fruits are taken occasionally. They smoke *bidi* and cigarette and chew *paan*.

There is differentiation at occupational levels. One of their two groups works as potters and is called Chakbians while the other group keeps donkeys and is also engaged as potters and is called Prajapatis. These two groups do not intermarry. They are considered of low social status. They have few *gots* such as Sokhal, Kadain, Chound and Taggar. Though they are aware of the *varna* system, they do not recognize their place in it. They marry within their own community and practise consanguinity at parallel and cross cousin levels. Marriage is arranged when the boys and girls are around eighteen to twenty-five years of age. Dowry is allowed and rule of residence is patrilocal. Divorce and remarriage are allowed according to the Islamic tradition. Among the changes in marriage rules there is an increase in age at marriage.

Family is either joint or nuclear. All the sons inherit the property of their father equally, the eldest son gets the right of succession. Among changes in the family set-up is increase in the number of nuclear families and decrease in the joint families. Women have low status. They attend to the various household jobs. They observe post-delivery pollution period and restrictions. Circumcision is performed in boys around five to nine years of age. The marriage rituals are performed at the residence of the bride according to the Islamic tradition of *nikah*. They bury their dead. Rituals have been curtailed.

As potters they make various types of earthen vessels by baking them in the kiln called *awa*. They transport various items either on donkeys or on *reda* (mule cart) and also engage themselves as unskilled labourers. Child labour exists. Mode of payment is both by cash and kind.

Rose (1919: 568-9), mentions that the Kumhar have a somewhat elaborate system of caste government. Thus in the south eastern districts, the Kumhars have *chauntras* at each large town or city, e.g. at Delhi and to this place all disputes, unless tried on the spot, are brought for trial before a *panchayat*. Each *chauntra* has its *chaudhury* whose office is not usually hereditary and he presides over the *panchayat*. The Multani Kumhars of Malerkotla have only a loose system of referring disputes, especially those relating to marriage, to arbitration by the elders of the subcaste. But the Desi subcaste in this state has an ancient system of administration. The *chaudhury*, who lives at Basi in Patiala holds a *sanad* bestowed on him by some ruler, which confers him authority to decide disputes within the caste. This *sanad* descends from father to son. At a wedding, the *chaudhury* gets one rupee and a *pagri* which is presented to him personally or sent to him through a Mirasi. Presently, at Malerkotla they do not have their traditional *panchayat* but at Sherpur they have one. Depending upon the nature of a crime, the *panchayat* imposes cash fines or excommunicate the individual.

The Kumhars have two territorial groups—Desi and Multani in Malerkotla, and Nabha. The Desi women wear a *pahan* (gown) over the trousers, which hang from the neck, while the Multani women wear a petticoat. In Gurdaspur the division is into Punjabi and Kashmiri.

Id-ul-Fitr and Id-ul-Zuha are their main festivals. The festivals are of social, economic and religious significance. Wall painting and pottery are their art and craft. Oral traditions are shared with other Punjabi communities. They accept and exchange water and food with all Muslim communities. Brahman, Jat, Bania, Rajput and other such castes do not accept water and food from them. They share places of worship, burial ground, festivals and festivities with other communities belonging to their religion. In the villages patron-client relationship exists.

Formal education is favoured for both boys and girls, but they cannot afford to study beyond primary level. The maximum is upto eighth class due to poverty. They make use of modern medicare and family welfare programme. Handpump is used for drinking water. They avail themselves of the facilities of electricity, media and communication. They use wood and dung cakes as a fuel resource. Subsidized ration facilities are available to them. They do not depend on moneylenders for loan.

SWARAN SINGH

# GORKHAS

The Gorkha or Gurkha are also known as Nepali at some places in the state. It has a number of subgroups—Gurungs, Magars, Newars, Denwars, Bhotiyas, Khas, Limbus, etc. Members of the community use Bahadur with their names, e.g. Dal Bhadur, Nar Bhadur, etc. Different meanings of the term Gurkha have been suggested. According to one view it means *gau-raksha* or keeper of cows (Crooke, 1896: 468). An alternative view links the origin of this term with the history of the name of the place. In this view the district Gurkha in Nepal was named after a holy man Guraknath. He lived in a cave at that place and becuase of the settlement of his devotees, a new village sprang up. It was named Gurkha, and later developed into a town. Gradually the district around this town was also named after this town. Guru Guraknath is still revered by the members of this community. In the armed forces the battlecry of Gurkhas is '*Guru Guraknath ki Jai*' (Victory to Guru Guraknath) (Bonerjee, 1975: 98).

According to W. Crooke the name was applied to 'an aggregate of various races, who inhabit the numerous valleys interspersed through the mountains of Nepal'. He relied on the *Imperial Gazetteer* to note that in physiognomy, Gurkha resembled the Tartar and the Chinese and had no resemblance to Hindus in their features, religions or manners. In the eastern parts the aboriginal tribes still remained, in the west all inhabitants claim desecent from Hindus, and consisted of the Brahmans and Kshatriyas with various subdivisions such as Magars, Gurungs, Newars, Dhenwars, Bhotiyas, Bharnas and Jariyas (Crooke, 1896: 468).

Bonerjee (1898) has provided some account of history and ethnography of the community. The Central Division of Nepal contains the original district of Gurkha. According to him: 'The Raja of this tract conquered whole of Nepal. The chief inhabitants of Gurkha were mainly the Mongol races of Magars and Gurungs; and mixed Arya-Mongol races were known as the Khas and Thakur. There are some other races—partly aboriginal Indian—residing in Gurkha; but the term Gurkha is applied to all inhabitants of the district of Gurkha no matter how diverse may have been their ethnic origin. The terms Gurkha and Gurkhasli are, therefore, geographical and not ethnic; that is, they do not connote any one tribe or race, but are equally applied to distinct tribes by virtue of a common habitat in the locality known as Gurkha. The other tribes and races of Nepal, which are not connected with the district of Gurkha, are not Gurkhali at all.' The principality of Gurkha, has no recorded history before the fifteenth century A.D. However, in recent historic period, streams of Mongolian immigration took place giving rise to Magar and Gurung population. And in a later period the Aryan immigration from south resulted in mixed Aryan and Mongol races of Thakurs and Khas. These mixed races even converted Magars and Gurungs to modified Hinduism. They also acquired political and religious domination over them.

The community recalls its origin in Nepal. It started migrating to the present place about a hundred years back, and this migration is still continuing. Some of them have permanently settled in the place. Others generally go back to Nepal temporarily and came back after some time. According to estimates its population in few towns of Punjab amounts to two hundred in Ferozepur city, five hundred in Ludhiana, two hundred in Moga and one hundred in Zira. They speak Nepali language at home and with its kin group, which is written in Devanagari script. However, during conversation with other communties they use Hindi and occasionally Punjabi as well. They can be distinguished by their Mongoloid features, which are otherwise absent in Punjab's population. Both men and women of the community are non-vegetarian. Fruit consumption is occasional and vegetable consumption is moderate. They take both wheat and rice, but consumption of rice is more than that of *roti.* Only gram and pea are taken as pulses. Cooking medium includes *vanaspati,* animal fats, groundnut and mustard oil. Men take alcoholic drinks regularly.

The community has divisions at caste and subcaste levels. At the place of field research the community mostly bolonged to the Thapa subcaste. There were few Gurungs, Sarki and Kaimis as well. Gurkhas have the following castes or subcastes—Thapa, Gurung, Ghatri, Damai, Kami, Sarki and Sunar. However, the last three were considered inferior because of their endogamous practices. In 1911 the following castes were noted in the state: Abohara, Dama, Charti, Gurung, Khas, Khawas, Magar, Nagar Koti, Pun, Pana. Burathoke, Ghole, Ghirat, Karke, Limbe, Rae, Rawat, Rohi, Sarke (*Census of India,* 1911: 456).

According to Bonerjee Khas, Thakurs, Magars, Sunuwars, Newars, Murmis, Kirantis, and Limbus were the principal tribes inhabiting Nepal. The Khas had resulted from the fusion of two racial elements—Mongol and Aryan. A large mixed population had originated from the marriages of Brahmans and Rajputs with Magars and Gurungs.

The word Khas, is derived from *khasnu*. *Khasnu* means 'to fall', the race resulting from illegitimate connections. However, the term Khas also included the pure descendants of Brahmans and Rajputs, called Bukharias. It also included pure descendants of Magar and Gurung tribes. Owing to the different meanings of the term Khas, they now called themselves Chettris. However, the Khas were acknowledged as a dominant people in Nepal. They were slighter and less sturdy; but more warlike than Gurung and Magar. They spoke Khas-Khura, Hindi mixed with Mongol dialect. Captain Vansittart had mentioned nineteen tribes of Khas (Bonerjee, 1977: 105-7): Adhinari, Baniya, Basniet, Bandmari, Bisht, Bohra, Bukha, Burathoki, Ghagrti, Karki, Khadka, Khatris, Konwar, Manjhi, Hanat, Rana, Roka, Thapa and Rawat.

The Thakurs like the Khas are of mixed Aryan and Mongol blood. They have status next to Brahmans, and the reigning family of Nepal. They have eighteen sections, of which Sahi is considered the best. Gurungs are pure Mongol. They have little or no Aryan blood. Their Hinduism is influenced by their original faith. They are least Brahmanical, and have recently reclaimed Lamaism. They are divided into two groups—Charjat and Solajat. The Charjat were divided into four classes—Ghallea, Lamchania, Lama and Ghotani. The Solajat are divided in eighty-six classes. They are stronger, and more muscular than others. Magars are also of pure Mongol blood. However, they are more Brahmanical in their customs and beliefs. The mixed Khas is more the result of mixing of blood with Magars than with Gurungs. They are divided into six classes—Aliea, Thapa, Puh, Gharti, Rana and Burathoki. Except Gharti, all are of pure Mongol blood. Ghartis have a large strain of Aryan blood. On the other hand, Ranas have the highest social status. Sunuwars, are ethnologically closely aligned with Magars and Gurungs, with whom their traditions and physique resemble to a large extent.

They have three sections, viz., Jetha, Malla and Khacha. The Jethas have ten subclasses: Dus Thare are mainly Buddhists; and Mallas have twelve subclasses. They are Hindu in belief. Sunars are also called Sunapars and Mukhias. But, they are not recruited into the army. Newaris are of Mongolian origin, with mixed Aryan blood. They have Mongoloid features. However, some of them have etymology in their language. They follow Lamaism but Hinduism has also influenced them. They are engaged in agriculture, handicrafts and trade, and are not enlisted in Gurkha regiments. The Murmis are of pure Mongol origin and migrated from Bhutan. They are also known as Lama, Tamang, Saiying and Ishang. They are Buddhist and Lamaic in practices but are looked down upon by other Nepalis because they indulge in manual work and take beef. They have two subdivisions—pure Murmis are called Barath Amang, and mixed Murmis are called Atharajat. The former are considered of higher social status.

The term Kirantie is applied to closely allied three tribes, the Limbus or Yakthumeas, the Khambus and Yakas. Their original religion was Lamaism, but now believe in Hinduism. They indulge in hunting and trading. The Limbus are also called Tasang and trace their origin from ten brothers who lived in Kashi. They are also of mixed blood, but with predominant Mongol blood. They have soldierly qualities and are recruited by Gurkha regiments. The Rais are similar to Limbus. It is a title granted by the Gurkhas to the Khambus and Yakkas (Bonerjee, 1975: 91-118). Differentiation with hierarchy exists among the Gurkhas.

The Thapas are considered the best caste or class. As pointed out earlier the endogamous castes or the classes like Kami, Sarki and Sonar are considered superior. The community is also differentiated at economic, religious, occupational and educational levels. It has members working as *chowkidars* (watchmen), employees in the State Electricity Board and other such organizations and even as waiters. They have both educated as well as illiterate members in their ranks. They mainly believe in Hinduism; but some of them are followers of Buddhism. This differentiation serves the purpose of regulation of marriage alliance, exercise of social control and indication of social status. There has been no change in surnames, clan names or titles. Their self-perception is very high, others consider them of medium status. The community is aware of *varna* system and also recognizes it. Depending upon caste or class, they identify themselves as Kshatriya or Brahman. They do not have clear-cut rules. Some classes or castes as pointed out above are endogamous. However, others are exogamous. They practise village exogamy, but few marriages have been within the locality itself. There is a practice of hypergamy as well. As Thapas are considered the highest in the community, other castes or classes seek to marry girls in their families.

However, the Thapas do not marry with lower castes. They practise adult marriage which takes place by negotiation; a few cases of marriage by elopement also exist. The marriages among them tend to be monogamous though a few cases of polyandry do exist. Usual Hindu symbols of marriage such as vermilion, bangles, *bindi*, finger-

and toe-rings, nose-pin and *mangalsutra* are used. Practice of *kanyadan* exists, and dowry is given in kind. After marriage, patrilocal rules of residence prevail. Divorce is possible for either party, but with judicial approval. The community allows divorce in case of impotency, barreness and lack of male issue. Compensation in case of judicial divorce shall be in favour of the aggrieved party, and custody of children is also to be decided by the court. Remarriage of both male and female divorcees, widows and widowers is allowed by the community. There has been change in the rules of marriage as these have been liberalized. Age of marriage has also increased and marriage symbols are not observed strictly.

The community generally lives in nuclear families but some families are vertically extended as well. Avoidance relationship exists between father-in-law and daughter-in-law; mother-in-law and son-in-law. Disputes in family arise because of property matters or due to challenge to the authority of elders. Rules of inheritance favour male equigeniture. Sons from all marriages shall get the share of property. Succession rules are not clear, but the community claims that these favour the eldest son. There has been decline of extended family system and number of nuclear families has risen. Women are considered equal to men. They have decision-making powers, participate in economic activities, contribute to family income and also control family expenditure. Mostly, women of the community work as domestic servants; or they do household jobs. They have a role in social functions, religious rituals and mechanism of social control.

Post-delivery observation of pollution is reported. But the community is not clear about the length of period of pollution. Birth of both boys and girls is celebrated. Naming ceremony takes place after eleven days. It is solemnized by a *pandit*. In this community no *dai* or midwife is called at the time of birth, only family members do the job.

Marriage rituals are performed at the bride's place. No compulsory dowry is asked for. *Barat* goes early in the morning to the girl's house where the marriage is solemnized by seven *pheras*, according to Vedic rites. A feast is arranged by both sides at the time of marriage. The bridegroom wears white dress and the bride dons a red *saree* at the time of marriage. Consummation of marriage is at the groom's residence.

Pollution period is observed at the time of death. The dead are either cremated or buried. According to the community, the lower castes bury their dead. Under the influence of Tibetian customs, the Buddhist Gorkha bury their dead. The bones are immersed in water. Ancestor worship in the form of *shradh* is also practised by a few. Rituals are now curtailed and are being made less elaborate.

The community is completely landless in the state. During British times they mainly served in Gurkha regiments. Although government service has continued to a large extent, the nature of employment has undergone a change. Now the community is employed in Punjab State Electricity Board as linemen and *chowkidars* in various government institutions. The latter type of employment is also there in private undertakings. They also work as unskilled labourers in houses or hostels. Child labour exists in the form of minor workers at restaurants. Payment of wages is in cash. Gurkha *sabhas* exist in various towns. These are elected by voice vote. These *sabhas* also exist in Jalalabad, Ludhiana, Ferozepur, Gurdaspur, and various other towns. The com-munity is also aware of the existence of Akhil Bharatiya Gorkha Samaj Samiti based in Calcutta; the local *sabhas* were formed at its initiative. The community mainly believes in Hindu religion. However, there are followers of Buddhism also. Durga is the deity of a wider pantheon which is worshipped. There is Durga *puja* for three days at the time of Dussehra from Shatami day onwards. Buddhist members hold Lord Buddha in great reverence. The followers of Buddhism from Jalalabad visit Dharamshala, the seat of the Dalai Lama on a regular basis. The *pandits* perform worship, impart religious teaching and perform birth, marraige, and death rites, and they belong to other community. Festivals are of social and religious significance. Hindus observe Durga Puja on Dussehra days and Buddhists celebrate Buddha Jayanti. The community joins others in celebration of local festivals such as Baisakhi, Basant and Lohri, but does not celebrate Diwali or Holi. It has its oral tradition, and both males and females sing folk songs.

In the state of Punjab the community has free and open interaction with other communities. It exchanges all types of *jal*, *chal*, *kachcha*, *sidha*, *pukka* food with other communities. A few intercommunity remarriages, have also been reported. They share water resources, cremation ground, religious places, and festivals with other communities. They are conscious of their voting rights; and they cast their vote in elections.

The community has benefitted from the developmental programmes in the state. Education is favoured for both boys and girls. The new generation is able to get education up to graduation level. But generally, boys drop out because they have to earn to support the family, and girls because there is no school nearby. The community makes full use of modern medicare. Both men and women have accepted modern techniques of family welfare. There is no special preferance for sterilization on the basis of sex and couples prefer one or two children. The Gurkhas have utilized facilities of water and electricity amply; they get drinking water from handpumps or public water works system. They use firewood, coal and kerosene oil as fuel. They have access to post and telegraph offices. Information dissemination takes place by political parties or government extension agencies. Their attitude to savings is favourable. A few members have acquired yellow cards and have applied for loans in banks.

VIRINDER SINGH

# GOSAIN

The Gosain is a Shiva order corresponding in many ways with the Bairagis among Vaishnavas. They are also called Bawa and Girname. They migrated to Punjab from Pakistan after Independence. They speak Punjabi and Hindi languages and use Gurmukhi or Devanagari scripts, while communicating with the members of their own community or outsiders. The older people, when going out for begging, wear *bana* which includes a saffron coloured shirt, a *dhoti*, and a necklace of beads. They are pure vegetarian. *Dal* and *roti* is their staple food. Those who have taken *gurumantra* do not take alcoholic drinks. However, they take alcoholic drinks on special occasions, as they are also the followers of Bhairav. Groundnut oil is used as a cooking medium. They take milk and milk products, smoke bidi or loose tobacoo. Fruits are consumed seasonally.

The Gosains are sometimes recruited by adopting *chelas*, from pure castes who may be willing to dedicate their sons to them, but in practice marriage is the rule. Those who marry are known as *gharbari* and form an endogamous group. Sons do not succeed unless adopted as *chelas*. Widows are entitled to maintenance. The secular Gosains do retain the *choti* and wear a *pagri* dyed in red ochre.

The religious or *matdhari* Gosains form their own fraternities, and though they do not marry reportedly keep women. They are divided into different *akharas* each under a *mohant*, who has supreme control over all its property. The mohant designates his successor. But if the mohant dies without naming his successor, the fraternity of the Gosains meet and elects a new mohant. After, the installation of the mohant the late mohant's property is distributed by him as he feels like. The Gosain is buried, in a *samadhi*, and he is supposed to be re-united with God after death. Initiation consists of the cutting of the choti, the head is then shaved and *gurumantra* is read. At the time of initiation every Gosain is given a name by his guru which ends in gir, puri, tirath, arram, asan or nath. The Gosain also have *gots* and they are further divided into (1) *matdhari* (whose dwelling hut, is inside the village and who may engage in all worldly pursuits, but not marry), (2) *asandhari* (whose house is on the outskirts of the village) or (3) *abdhut* (who wander about begging. Gosains are generally clad in garments dyed with *geru* (a dye).

The Gosains are divided into separate gotras namely Jogde, Jayde, Pawar, Sidhu, Chohan, Chahal, Atwal, Tank, Sarsut (Sarsur), Suniara. These gotras regulate the marriage alliances. They are aware of varna system. They consider themselves as of high status, but the members of the other communities have a mixed feeling about them. They are endogamous at community level, but observe exogamy at *gotra* level. Marriage is arranged by negotiation with the help of a *vichola* (mediator), when their boys and girls are around eighteen to twenty years of age. The ceremony of *mangani* (engagement) is performed by offering one rupee in *thuthi* (earthen cup) to the boy. Similarly, the girl is also offered *shagun* and cloth on this occasion. The marriage is fixed by consulting the Pandit (priest). Marriage is performed either according to the Hindu tradition of seven pheras or *anand karaj* (four lavan-phera) of Sikh traditions. Monogamy is the rule. *Sindur* (vermilion) and bangles are the symbols of marriage. Depending upon the financial condition of the girl's parents, dowry in kind is offered which includes cloth, furniture and big trunk (*petti*). After marriage the girl stays with her husband. In case of mal-adjustment, divorce is allowed with the judicial approval. Compensation is given to the aggrieved party. However, both the husband and wife can divorce. The children as per decision can stay either with the mother or with the father. Remarriage of widow, widower, male and female divorcee, is permitted. Both nuclear and joint families are common. Avoidance relationship and joking relationship are observed between the different members of the family. Property and challenge to the authority of elders cause conflicts and confrontations in a family. Sons inherit the property of their father equally, while the eldest son gets the succession as the head of the family. Women have a low status and they attend to house-hold activities. Post-natal restrictions are observed for five to seven days. Post-delivery pollution is also observed. *Mundan* (shaving of head hair) ceremony is performed either at the temple of Baba Balak Nath, Chintpurni or at the temple of Mata.

Marriage rituals are performed at the bride's residence. *Roti* (feast) is given by bride's parents to the marriage party. Nuptial ceremony is performed at groom's residence. They cremate their dead. *Samadhi* is offered to those, who have taken *gurumantra*. Bones of the dead are disposed off in the Ganga at Hardwar. *Shradh* ceremony is also observed.

The Gosains are engaged either in begging; they also work as casual labourers, or as rickshaw-pullers, carpenters, etc. Child labour has been reported. The children work in factories or in hotels. They have their own traditional *panchayat*, the members of *panchayat* are elected by voice vote. The *panchayat* settles all their local disputes related to marriage and divorce.

As most of them belong to Hinduism, they celebrate all the festivals of Hindus including Shivratri and Janamashtami. The sacred specialists are from other communities, who attend to various rites associated with birth, marriage and death. The festivals are of socio-economic and religious significance for them. They engage themselves in weaving or embroidery.

They invite and visit the members of various communities such as Balmiki, Jat, Mahajan, Brahman, Megh or others. They exchange food and water with them and use the same cremating ground. Festivals and festivities are celebrated equally by them alongwith the other communities.

Formal education is favoured for both boys and girls. They do not study beyond primary level due to poor economic conditions. The boys are to earn and support their parents. They visit nearby hospitals for treatment. They use family planning methods other than sterilization and prefer three children. Drinking water is available in the locality. Handpump is used to supply drinking water. They are self-employed. They avail of the media and communication facilities. They use electricity, fuel wood, cow-dung cakes or kerosene oil. They get kerosene oil, sugar and *atta* on ration cards. Attitude towards saving is favourable. At the time of need they extend financial help to each other.

SWARAN SINGH

# GUJJAR (HINDU)

The term 'Gujjar' is the spoken form of the Sanskrit word *gurjara*, the original name of the tract of land in western India where Gujjars had a very powerful and extensive kingdom called Gurjaradesa during the medieval age (Munshi, 1954). There are numerous views prevalent about the origin of Gujjar. Cunningham (1924) places them among the Scythian tribes who conquered Kabul about 100 B.C. and marched into India. They established themselves in Kashmir and north-western India where such places as Gujranwala and Gujrat (now both in Pakistan) are a testimony to their early settlements. By the middle of the fifth century they had built a Gujjar kingdom. Smith (1924) traces their origin to the White-Huns who, in about A.D. 465 poured into India as nomadic hordes. Ibbetson (1916) says they came after Huns, became Hindus and eventually founded the kingdom of Rajasthan. He suggests that Gujjar, Jat and perhaps Ahir are of one ethnic stock who entered India at different times and settled in different places.

A more likely origin of Gujjars appears to be through intermixture between early Indo-Aryans and later tribal immigrants possibly Scythians and Huns. This theory is supported by considerable linguistic affinity of the Gujjar language with the Indo-Aryan (Indo-Iranian) languages together with certain socio-religious practices and *got* (clan) names which are common among Gujjars, Jats and Rajputs. Bingley (1978) states that west of Indus and the Ravi, the Jats and Gujjars became Muslims and being a conquered people of no political importance were looked down upon by the Pathans, Mughals and Muslims of Rajput descent, who seized their land and drove them to seek a living as nomads, wandering with their herds over the grazing grounds of the great western plains of Punjab. Today Muslim Gujjars are mostly confined to the states of Jammu & Kashmir and Himachal Pradesh and lead a pastoral and semi-nomadic life whereas Hindu Gujjars are found in Punjab, Haryana, Delhi, western Uttar Pradesh, Gujarat, Rajasthan, and Madhya Pradesh and are essentially agriculturists and pastoralists. Both these Gujjar groups today live in complete social and geographical isolation.

In Punjab they are mostly settled in Ropar and Hoshiarpur districts. However, sporadic settlements also exist in Gurdaspur, Jalandhar, Ludhiana and Patiala districts. In Ropar district their villages are situated in the foothills of Shivaliks and the adjoining plains where earlier they used to graze their cattle as nomadic people. Their language is a part of the Indo-Iranian group of languages. They speak a Gujari dialect mixed with Punjabi. They have no script of their own but are now learning Hindi and Gurmukhi scripts. Men wear *dhoti* or *lungi* or sometimes a narrow *pyjama* and a *kurta* and jacket with long sleeves. During winters they wear a waistcoat or woollen coat reaching the knee called *angrakha* and use quilt or *razai*, shawl or *chadar* over their shoulders. They also wear heavy turbans, generally white, and keep beards and moustache. Women wear long shirts and *salwars* with *dupatta* or head cover. They also wear finger rings, earrings, necklaces of gold or silver.

They are mostly vegetarian and are fond of milk and buttermilk. Principal meals are taken twice a day. They consume wheat, gram, *jowar*, rice and maize in various forms, that is, *chapati*, *khichari*, *dalia* and porridge. Pulses and jaggery are common constituents of their diet. Leafy greens and other seasonal vegetables are also eaten but not in sufficient quantity. They also take *bhang*, opium, chew and smoke tobacco. Alcoholic drinks which are purchased from the market are now on the increase. Those who have migrated out of the villages have also taken to non-vegetarian diet. Fruits and honey are rarely eaten. Free fats are also rare in their diet.

They are divided into a large number of exogamous clans or *gots*. In Majarian village itself as many as seventeen *gots* have been identified; these are: Gorsi, Kals, Mundan, Maisi, Charh, Saradne, Gauharia, Kheppar, Poswal, Kasne, Pumble, Jinnar, Wanne, Chauhan, Chechi, Gandawal and Dehdars. Quite a sizeable population of Gujjars have got converted to Sikhism and follow Sikh religion and practices, although they continue to worship Hindu deities which are worshiped by Hindu Gujjars. They recognize the Hindu *varna* system and its hierarchy, that is Brahman, Kshatriya, Vaish and Shudra. They consider themselves as part of the Kshatriyas. Hindu Gujjars share the same village and the village well with Brahmans, Jats and Khatris. The Scheduled Castes live in a separate village usually on the outskirts of the Gujjar village, although they work for the Gujjars as farm labour for which they are paid in cash and kind.

Fraternal polyandry was the most predominant societal profile until recently, but now monogamy is gaining ground especially among those who have migrated to urban areas. Marriage by exchange (generally brother, sister), locally called *batta* is a rule. This is based on the dictum 'take my sister and give your sister'. Owing to lack of sufficient number of marriageable sisters in a family, many males remain unmarried. Fraternal polyandry is the only answer to the problem. Generally the eldest brother marries and the other brothers share the woman. After the death of the elder brother, the next in age becomes the legal husband after performing the *karewa* (levirate) ceremony. In case the second brother is married then any of the brothers irrespective of age gets an opportunity to marry the widow. Consequently there is at times a wide gap of age between married partners. A *karewa* marriage generally takes place at least one year after widowhood. It is performed by throwing a red *chadar* over the head of the woman and putting *chura* or bangles on her arms in the presence of the members of his community. The children of the *karewa* marriage have equal rights in the family with the other children from regular marriage. Polygynous marriages among Hindu Gujjars are not altogether unknown. Some times in addition to one's own wife, one may marry the widow of one's brother or one may have more than one wife. Marriages and other social ceremonies of Hindu Gujjars resemble those of the surrounding Hindu populations broadly and are performed according to Hindu rites. Marriages at younger ages are arranged by the parents while at older ages these are arranged by mutual consent of the partners concerned. Dowry in kind is given or taken according to circumstances and one's capacity.

They are a patriarchal, patrilocal and patrilineal society, residence after marriage, inheritance of property and succession are therefore governed according to rules of those institutions. All the sons get equal share in the father's property. Daughters are given their share in the form of dowry at the time of their marriage. Adopted sons or stepsons have equal right in father's or stepfather's property along with real sons.

Divorce among Hindu Gujjars is almost unknown. However, the village *panchayat* may allow divorce on grounds of unchastity or under special circumstances. A woman may leave her husband and start living with another man along with her children. No money is exchanged in such cases. Both nuclear as well as joint and extended families (married brothers and their children or parents and their married children) are prevalent among the Hindu Gujjars. The domicile size of the family varies from three to ten or even more living under the same roof and catered through the same kitchen. Women enjoy respect and a high social status. They assist menfolk in agriculture and tending the cattle, bring wood and fuel from the jungle, draw water, spin, weave and bring up children. Recently they have started managing the village shop in the absence of menfolk. They also manage the household, repair and plaster the floor and walls of the house.

Birth of a son in the family is celebrated with gaiety. The village deity is worshipped by lighting a lamp and offering food and milk. More affluent families throw a feast in the community.

*Mundan* ceremony is done on a male child at the age of three or four years. The head hair is shaved off at the shrine of the family goddess which is usually situated far away from the village. Some even perform this ceremony at holy places such as Hardwar, Kangra Devi or Naina Devi temples. Offerings of sweets and other eatables are made to the deity. The priest and the barber are also offered money and sweets.

The dead are cremated at the village cremation grounds situated on the banks of a rivulet near by. Son or nephew lights the pyre after the body is given a bath and offering of wheat flour balls. On the third day, the members of the family collect the ashes and consign them to the river. Those who can afford take them to Hardwar or other holy places to be consigned to the holy rivers and perform *pind-daan* and other ceremonies under the guidance of local priests. The one who lights the pyre and the sons get their heads shaved the lead an austere life for thirteen days. Thirteenth day marks the end of the mourning period which is followed by feeding a Brahman and offering him clothes and other necessities of life, who in turn prays for peace and salvation of the departed soul. Infants and younger children after death are given burial in the fields or on the river banks without any elaborate ceremony.

A man without a son can adopt a male heir as his son. The son adopted is generally his brother's son or a male cousin in the line of male descendants. The ceremony is called *god-lena* which is celebrated in the community with feast and formal declaration of the adoption. The adopted son enjoys the same rights even after the birth of a son to the adopter.

Gujjars are settled agriculturists and pastoralists. The land holdings per household varies from 5 to 50 *bighas* depending upon the size of the household. Each household has four to ten or more buffaloes. A few have cows and goats in addition to buffaloes. Agricultural produce is usually consumed in the household or kept in reserve for the lean period. Only surplus is marketed. Buffalo milk is the main source of income which is disposed off in markets of the nearby towns. As they are located close to the city of Chandigarh, they enjoy better marketing facilities for their agricultural produce as well as milk at remunerative prices. Besides, Chandigarh and other towns of Punjab have also provided them easy employment ever since the Hindu Gujjars have been declared a backward community. Major avenues of their employment are police and armed forces, though some of them also find employment in the government offices as peons. A few educated ones have also joined white-collar jobs in banks and other offices as clerks. In Majarian village itself atleast one or two members of each household are working outside the village thus augmenting the family income. Only rarely will a Gujjar be found to be working as a labourer. Shopkeeping was unknown among the Gujjars till recently. Nowadays a few progressive Gujjars have opened groceries.

All interpersonal disputes arising out of socio-economic activities were settled by a council of elders drawn from households on the basis of general consensus, and its verdict was final and binding on the parties concerned. However, in the post-Independence era, like in other villages, Gujjars also have their *gram panchayat* consisting of a *sarpanch* and five or more *panches*, depending upon the size of the population or number of households under the village, which are elected every five years. Most of the disputes are now resolved by the *gram panchayat.*

The religion of the Punjab Gujjars is essentially Hinduism although they are ignorant of the details of the Puranic mythology. They speak of God as Ishwar or Parmeshwar or a supreme being who guides their destiny. The village deity or 'Nagar-Khera', also called *Pir*, plays an important role in the lives of Gujjars. Its temple in the form of a small structure with or without a triangular saffron coloured flag is situated under or near a *pipal* tree on the fringe of the village. Gujjars visit the Nagar-Khera to pay their obeisance every Sunday and other religious occasions. At marriage or on the birth of a son in the family, the village deity is worshipped by lighting a lamp and offering eatables. The first milk of buffalo or cow, or the first yield from farm is offered to the deity first before it is consumed in the family or sent out for selling. Gujjars also worship other gods and goddesses such as Sitala Devi, Durga, Shiva, Brahma, Vishnu, Rama, Krishna, Hanuman, etc. They also worship the sun as Surya Narayan. Cows and snakes are also venerated. They also worship plants and trees such as *tulsi*, *pipal*, banian, *amla*, etc. Rivers like the Ganga and the Yamuna are considered sacred and visit holy places such as Kashi, Hardwar, Badrinath and Kedarnath are visited. Those who have taken to Sikhism worship Sikh Gurus besides Hindu *devis* and *devatas* and visit temples and *gurdwaras* alike. They celebrate almost all the Hindu fairs and festivals such as Holi, Diwali, Ram Naumi, Basant Panchami,

Baisakhi, Amavas, Nag Panchami, Dussehra, Navratras, Janamashtami, Rakshabandhan, Anant Chaudash, etc. Art and craft are not much in evidence except occasional wall paintings of animal and floral designs or colour-washing of their houses. Handicrafts are also conspicuously absent. Folk-songs and dances are also not much in evidence except on marriage or other such social occasions. Musical instruments are also absent except an occasional *dholak* or a membrane drum.

They are considered inferior to the Jats, the Rajputs and the Sainis who are their immediate neighbours, in social standing but they eat and smoke together. Intermarriages, however, do not take place. With economic emancipation things have changed, Gujjars have become as enterprising as their neighbours and engage themselves in more productive activities. They not only live in greater harmony with other caste groups in the village but also are as hospitable to outsiders as the Jat. Their relationship with Scheduled Castes is that of master and servant. Scheduled Castes who work for them as farm labourer or scavanger of dead cattle for which they are paid in both cash and kind.

They are taking advantage of the developmental programmes though not of the same order as the other caste groups specially the Jats. Gujjars now well recognize the importance of education. Both boys and girls go to primary school which is usually situated in the village or near the village. Boys may continue their education upto high school or may even go to college such as the ones of the Majari village. Gujjars are fully aware of the employment opportunities that the government programmes such as the IRDP offer them. Of late, they have taken up jobs in banks and government offices as peons and *chowkidars* in nearby towns.

Gujjars are aware of family planning programmes but many of them have large families. They, however, take advantage of government hospitals in the nearby towns for medical treatment and antenatal and postnatal care for mother and child. They get seeds, chemical fertilizers and agricultural implements on subsidized rates. They are also aware of government sponsored public distribution system and take advantage of buying things of daily use such as kerosene oil, salt, sugar and cloth at cheaper rates. They are also aware of banking and post-office saving facilities and loans offered by various agencies for the purpose of agricultural implements including tractors and threshers or boring a tube well or purchasing more milch cattle.

J.C. Sharma
R.S. Balgir

# GUJJAR (MUSLIM)

The Gujjars had Tomars or Tunwar as one of their ruling class, who descended from Raja Jaula. Parihar claimed descent from Toramana, the king of White Huns. The other divisions of the Gujjars such as Solankis, Parmars, Chauhans are of Rajput origin. The Gujjars trace their origin as far back as the sixth century A.D., when the invasion of the Central Asiatic people such as Huns and Gujjars took place and they settled down specially in Rajasthan and Punjab states. Around A.D. 840 the Gujjars raided north India and had their capital at Kanauj under Bhoja I (Rose, 1919: 310).

The state of Gujarat derived its origin from the town of Gujrat, the site where the ancient city Udanagari stood at one time. According to one tradition Raja Bachanpal, who came from Gangetic Doab laid its foundation. Subsequently, it was Ali Khan, a Gujar who restored the city. According to another version Gujrat town was restored by Rani Gujran wife of Badr Sain in A.D. 118. Shankara Varma of Kashmir invaded Gujardesa in A.D. 883. Raja of Thanesar, Prabhakara Vardnana in the sixth century also attacked the Hun settlement in Punjab in order to firmly establish the Gurjara race in Gujarat.

About the Gujjar in Punjab, Rose commented (1919: 307), thus 'They essentially belong to the lower ranges and sub-mountain tracts; and though they have spread down the Jumna in considerable numbers, they are almost confined to the riverine low lands.'

The Gujjars have a high concentration in the hilly regions and the sub-mountain tracts. The true Gujjar herds-men in all these areas have a common language, they are pastoral and nomadic, who take their herds up during the summer seasons and descend into the valley during the winter seasons. Most of them are Muslims, the conversion perhaps took place during the times of Aurangzeb. The Jalandhar Gujjars date their conversion from the time of Aurangzeb, a very probable date. The Ferozepur Gujjars say that they came from Daranagar in the south of India, that they moved to Rania in Sirsa, and again to Ferozepur via Kasur. The Muslim Gujjars of all the eastern half of the province retained more of their Hindu customs than do the majority of their converted neighbours. Their women, for instance, wear petticoats instead of drawers and red instead of blue. In Jalandhar the Gujjar shoe is usually of a peculiar make, the upper leather covering little of the foot.

Rose (1919: 310) suggested 'that Jats and Gujars were all of one ethnic stock, and there was a close communion between them. It is however possible that the Jats were the camel graziers and perhaps husbandmen, the Gujars the cow-herds of the hills, and the Ahirs the cow-herds of the plains.'

The Gujjars perceive their identity at regional level. They speak Punjabi and Urdu languages and use Perso-Arabic or Gurmukhi scripts. Bio-anthropological information for the Muslim Gujjars is on serogenetic markers (Balgir and Sharma, 1988). They take cereals such as wheat and maize; *urad, moong* and *moth* as pulses besides vegetables. Groundnut oil is used as a cooking medium. They take mutton and chicken occasionally. They take milk and milk products. Fruits are taken seasonally. They smoke *bidi* and cigarettes.

The Gujjars are endogamous at the community level and practise consanguinity. Marriage, according to the Islamic rite of *nikah* is arranged by parents of boy and girl, when they attain adulthood. Polygyny is also allowed. Those who can afford give dowry and *mehar* is also announced. They are patrilocal. *Talaq* or divorce and remarriage is allowed. Among changes in marriage rules is increase in the age at marriage. Family type is vertically extended or is nuclear. Avoidance, joking relationship and conflicts in a family exist. Sons get equal share in their father's property, while the eldest son gets succession. Among changes in the family include increase in nuclear families and decrease in the extended ones. Women have low status. Apart from their household duties, they look after the *dangars* (buffaloes). Birth of the first male child is celebrated. Postnatal restrictions and pollution period is observed, circumcision of boys is performed between five to nine years of age. Marriage takes place at the bride's residence, where a feast is given by the girl's parents. Consummation of marriage is on the next day of marriage at bridegroom's residence. They bury their dead and prayers are offered on the third day. Various life-cycle rituals have been curtailed because of the ever rising costs.

By occupation the Gujjars are pastoral. They were once settled agriculturists but as they incurred great losses in agriculture, they disposed of their agricultural land. They keep buffaloes whose milk is transported to Saharanpur, Ambala, Khanna, Chandigarh, Amritsar and Hoshiarpur. Something like a regular *siapa* (breast beating) is observed on the death of a buffalo, the women mourning for it almost as if for a human being. A similar custom is noted, in which the women may often be seen with veiled faces weeping over the death of a milch buffalo. Their traditional *panchayat* is called *Gujjaran di panchayat.* Those who live in the villages have their interests are protected by the village *panchayat. Maulavi* performs various rites associated with birth, marriage and death. Id is their main festival. They offer special *namaz* in the mosques on Friday. The oral traditions of the Punjab are also associated with them, such as folk songs and folk dance.

They accept and exchange water and food from all the Muslim communities. They share the burial ground and place of worship with other Muslims. Patron-client relationship exists in the village.

Attitude towards formal education is positive but as the boys and girls have to look after the buffaloes, they cannot find time to attend schools and to their studies. They study mostly upto primary level. A few however have qualified upto graduation and post-graduation levels recently. They take facilities of modern medicare and family welfare schemes. Drinking water is obtained by handpumps. They take advantage of media, communication and electricity facilities. Dung cakes and firewood are used as fuel sources. Immunization facilities are availed. They get sugar, kerosene oil at subsidized rates from fair price shops. Their attitude towards saving is positive.

SWARAN SINGH

# JAIN

The Jain claim that Lord Parsavnatha and Lord Mahavira were mere Prophets of Jain religion and the real founder of Jainism was Lord Rshabha, the first Tirthankara. Lord Parsavnatha is regarded as the twenty-third Tirthankara and Lord Mahavira was the twenty-fourth Tirthankara of Jainism (Sangave, 1959: 374, 375).

It may be mentioned that in Jain ethics, utmost importance is given to *ahimsa* (non-violence). *Ahimsa* may be considered as the essence of Jain religion. The rules of conduct in Jainism are based on the foundation of *ahimsa.* The Jain ethic places an elaborate role of conduct both for layman and ascetic. It divides the vows into two categories, i.e. *anuvrata* (small vows) and *mahavrata* (great vows). The householder has to practise the small vows with minimum injury to others. They are divided into two main sects namely Digambaras and Svetambaras. Digambaras are divided into three subsects, namely Bispanthi, Terapanthi, and Taranpanthi. Svetambaras are further divided into three subsects, namely Pujera, Bistola or Sthankvasi and Terapanthi. It may be stated here that Svetambaras outnumber Digambaras.

They are distributed throughout the country. Their total population in India according to the 1981 census is 32,06,038 individuals. They are more concentrated in the states of Maharashtra, Rajasthan, Gujarat, Madhya Pradesh and Uttar Pradesh. Their total population in Punjab according to the *Census of India* (1981) is 27,049 individuals. According to the 1971 census their total population in Punjab was 12,113 individuals which shows that their population has more than doubled within a decade. This may be attributed to the impact of industrialization and urbanization of some districts of Punjab specially Ludhiana, Amritsar and Jalandhar and these places attracted them in small numbers from the other states. Distribution of Jains in urban areas is 93.5 per cent and in rural areas is 6.5 per cent. Their concentration is higher in districts such as Ludhiana (7,892), Sangrur (3,507), Amritsar (2,455), Jalandhar (2,440), Hoshiarpur (2,099) followed by districts of Patiala, Bhatinda and Rupnagar.

In Punjab among the Jain sects, the two well-known communities are Osavalas (Oswals) and Agarvalas (Agarwals). Osavalas are known as Bhavara Jains in Punjab and Agarvalas are Bania (Banias). The name Osavala is derived from the town of Osiya or Osiyanagar in Marwar. According to the traditional legend of their origin, the king of Osiyanagar had no son and got one son through the blessings of a Jain ascetic. The people then drove the ascetic from the town, feeling that the king would become a Jain, but Osadevi the guardian goddess of the place, told the ascetic to convert the king by miracle. So she took a small piece of cotton and passed it along the back of the saint. It immediately became a snake and bit Jayachanda, the son of the king. All effort to save his life was in vain and he died. As his corpse was about to be burnt the ascetic sent one of his disciples and stopped the cremation. Then the king came with the body of his son and stood with his hands folded before the saint. The saint ordered that the dead body be taken back to the place where the prince had been bitten and that the prince was to lie down beside it as before. At night the snake returned and removed the poison from the body of the prince with the result the prince was restored to life. Then the king with all his court and people, adopted the Jain religion and those who were thus converted were known as Osavalas. Osavalas practise the principle of non-violence and the principles which are laid down for laymen and laywomen. The adoption of the principle of non-violence, non-possession, *brahmacharya*, and *satya*, entitles them as Bhavaras.

Agarvalas have migrated to Punjab from Agra. It is believed that Agarvalas are the decendents of King Agrasena (Aggarsain) of Champavati in north India. He had eighteen sons who were married to eighteen daughters of a Naga king. When Agrasena died his eighteen sons established a town Agroha in Punjab and they were called Agarvalas from that time after their father.

The religious scripture of Jains are written in Hindi, Sanskrit and Prakrit languages. They speak Punjabi language and use Devanagari script with the members of their own community and family. However with outsiders they speak in either Punjabi, Hindi or English depending upon the language of the person concerned. The old men wear *dhoti* and *kurta*; shirt and trousers. The women wear *saree* and sometimes wear Punjabi suits including *salwar*, *kameez* and *dupatta*. There is no religious restriction among Jains with regard to wearing of particular clothes. But the monks among the different sects have different markers of identification. Digambara monks are naked and nuns wear white and yellow clothes, whereas Svetambara monks wear white clothes and cover their mouth with white cloths. They wear the ornaments which are commonly used by the people of the state. The Jain community has a flag which is of white colour and it is covered with the sign of *swastik*. The three dots above the *swastik* stand for three jewels; true insight, right knowledge and proper conduct. These three provide the means to escape from the cycle of bondage represented by *swastika*. Finally at the very top there is a small crescent with a dot mounted upon it; the uppermost portion of universe, with the liberated soul resting just within its edge. As a Jain enters the temple, he typically wears only three simple pieces of clothing and carries a plate filled with flowers, fruits, uncooked rice and incense. Having approached the main shrine, the layman sits on a mat and using rice grains forms a *swastik* on a plate or wooden plank. By forming these symbols prior to actual worship of Tirthankara one shows that his *puja* (worship) has its ultimate purpose in the attainment of *moksha* (Jain, 1979: 200).

The Jains are very particular regarding their food and drinks. Since their ethical code is based on the main principle of *ahimsa*, its thorough applicability is in the matters of food and drink also. The householders are expected not to make use of flesh, wine and honey. They do not take non-vegetarian food. They have also to abstain from eating *kandamules* (underground stems and roots) such as potatoes, onion, garlic, raddish, turnip, carrot, beetroot, which are believed to contain small insects. The prescribed food consists of pulses and vegetables such as ladies' fingers and *ghiya* (gourd). Further it is necessary for them to take their meals during daytime because *himsa* is inevitable when food is prepared or taken in the absence of sunlight. Therefore, they have to avoid taking food at night. Those who cannot follow it all the time, at least do it during the *chaturmas* (four months of rainy season) when there is a large growth of small insects. Nowadays changes are taking place with regard to food habits. Women are pure vegetarian. They do not take food at night. Younger men do not observe the restrictions with regard to *kandmula* and night eating. Milk and fruits are consumed widely in large quantity. Alcoholic drinks and all kinds of intoxicants are prohibited. But alcoholic drinks are taken by men only outside the home on special occasions. A few men take non-vegetarian food on special occasions. Smoking is common among males only. There is no punishment or excommunication for those Jains who make use of prohibited items food and alcoholic drinks.

Generally, it is believed that there are eighty-four subcastes in the Jain community. However, in Punjab, the most commonly found are Agarvalas, Osavalas, Khandelvalas, Budholas, Jaisavalas and

Paravadas (Sangave, 1959: 127). *Gots* which are found among Osavalas in Punjab are Dull, Ducard, Linga, Gothi and Coher. In the beginning there were eighteen *gots* of Osavala, but these were further divided into 498 *gots*. The different *gots* of Srimali caste are Gaidya and Kathariya.

Osavala Jains consider themselves superior to Agarvalas, but Agarvalas perceive themselves superior to Osavala. In comparison to other castes in Punjab, Osavalas and Agarvalas occupy the topmost position, followed by Khandelvalas. The social ranking in terms of caste hierarchy is accounted both in terms of Jain ethic and economic position. In reality, interdining is not completely prohibited. The notion of purity and pollution is not so strong among Svetambaras as it is in Digambaras. Among Svetambaras, the recruitment of monk from Scheduled Castes are allowed but Digambara monks are initiated from higher castes only. According to Digambaras, Scheduled Castes cannot become ascetics of high order and are not entitled to *moksha* and they are not allowed to worship the idols in Jain temple. Other communities in Punjab, perceive Jains as pure vegetarian economically wealthy, and religious-minded.

The girls are married around eighteen years and the age at marriage for boys is twenty years. Monogamy is the form of marriage. Importance is given to consent in marriage. The symbols of marriage are similar to those of Hindus. Dowry is practised among Agarvalas both in cash and kind. Among Osvalas dowry is given in kind, though there is no compulsion of giving dowry by bride's parents. Among Jains marriages are performed during the day only. After marriage the girl goes to her husband's house. Divorce rate is very low. But divorce is permitted on certain conditions. Both husband and wife can take divorce. The rules regarding divorce are governed by local customs. Widow remarriage does find expression in religious scriptures. Among Agarvalas, widow remarriage is permitted but Osavalas are conservative regarding widow remarriage.

Joint family system is prominent. The joint family is the secret of success of their business. An empirical study conducted by Sood (1985) on business families in Ludhiana shows the dominance of joint family. The cause for emergence of nuclear family may be attributed to the process of urbanization and industralization. As a result of this, the individuals who migrated to urban areas set up nuclear family. Avoidance relationships are observed among Agarvalas between daughter-in-law and father-in-law, sister-in-law and elder brother-in-law. Pattern of avoidance relationship is similar among Svetambaras and Digambaras. However, avoidance relationship are not practised by Osavala Jains. Joking relationship takes place between sister-in-law and brother-in-law as also between grandparents and grandchildren in Agarvalas. Among Osavalas jokes between daughters-in-law are common. All the sons get equal share in their father's property. The daughter's share of property is spent on her marriage. Conflict and confrontation does not take place in property matter but youngers now challenge the authority of elders.

Religious scriptures have granted high status to women. The religious independence given to Jain women had its repercussions in the social fields also. Equality of opportunity accorded to women in the religious sphere was manifest in several social spheres of action. In Punjab, the women do not contribute to family income but they control family expenditure. Women do only household jobs. Women play an important role in social functions, rituals and religious matters. It is believed that women are more devoted to religion than men. Women have a place in mechanism of social control.

There are ceremonies prescribed by religion to be performed at appropriate time and hence they are known as *sanskaras* or sacraments. The Digambaras and Svetambaras, prescribe different ceremonies. Digambaras have to pass through fifty-three ceremonies as mentioned in their sacred book *Adipurana.* Five of these are related to the predelivery rituals. Six of them are to be performed in the first year of child, another five at the pre-adolescent and adolescent period. Five of the rituals relate to laymen's duties as householder, and the other eleven rituals relate to the ascetic stage of life usually after fulfilling the duties of householder, and finally there are twenty-one rituals which relate to the status of the individual after death (Sangave, 1959: 249-63). Altogether these fifty-three ceremonies indicate the direction of progress for a laymen to the state of *moksha* (final liberation).

According to Svetambaras, a layman has to pass through sixteen ceremonies as prescribed in their sacred book, *Acharadinakara.* Two of the ceremonies are related to pre-delivery rituals, four rituals relate to the birth and associated ceremony until the sixth day. One ritual relates to the purification ceremony of the mother (who is consider impure because of delivery), another six rituals relate to the various ceremonies at different points of child's life until he becomes an adult. The fourteen rituals relate to the marriage ceremonies. The fifteen rituals ensures happiness in the world and a good place in the next birth and the final ritual relate to the death ceremony. Osavala Jains usually observe specifically two predelivery rituals. Marriage rituals are performed at the bride's residence and feast is given by the bride's parents in marriage. The dead are cremated among both Osvalas and Agarvalas. Jain ascetics are cremated by their followers. The bones of an ascetic are preserved in *samadhi.* Ancestor worship continues in the form of *shradh* ceremony. This is more similarities among Agarvalas than Osvalas. On the whole there is the tendency of curtailing the details of ritual and only the basic minimum rituals are observed. The decline in the elaborate ritual observation could be attributed to weakening hold of caste system among Jains and also because they predominantly live in urban areas where strict observance of rituals is generally not adhered to.

Study on occupational mobility among Jain showed that 45 per cent of the respondents are businessmen, 12 per cent are in professional jobs and administrative service, 41 per cent in clerical jobs and petty business, and 2 per cent do manual jobs.

Traditional caste *panchayat* does not exist nowadays. But the sects' organizations perform only religious functions such as maintanence of temples, and making necessary arrangements for the celebration of religious festivals.

In Punjab, Digambaras temples are in small number but Svetambaras Sthanks or Pasara are numerous. Jain monks are initiated from other communities also. They perform religious functions, namely, worship and teaching. Svetambaras monks also encourage people to open schools, colleges and dispensaries, etc. At Malerkotla, various social institutions are run by the Jains. Jains have a large number of festivals of their own which have social and religious importance. The names of their various festivals are Parybavshana, Srvtapanchami, Mahavir Jayanti, Akshayya Triya. They also celebrate some of the Hindu festivals such as Holi, Diwali, Dussehra, Raksha Bandhan and Navratra.

The religious life of the Jains is changing fast. The individuals' visit to Jain temple, or Svetambara monks is decreasing day by day. The Jains who observe the laymen rules are in small number. This change in religious life may be attributed to process of urbanization and industralization, rationalization which has affected each aspect of our life.

Among Jains purity and avoidance of pollution was practised. Now the Jains attend death and religious ceremonies of other communities as well. However, the Digambara Jains do not visit Hindu temples. But Svetambaras Jains are more liberal in their outlook than Digambara Jains. Jains of both sects exchange *pukka* food and water with other communities. Economic relations with other communities are good. Community has entrepreneurs, scholars, creative artists, teachers, engineers and doctors. Jains are found in all professions and they hold important positions in various departments of central and state governments.

Educational programme is favoured for both the boys and girls. The girls study up to graduation level and then they discontinue their studies due to social reasons. The boys generally study upto graduation. Community's attitude toward traditional and modern medicine is positive. They make full use of both modern and traditional medicare. A couple prefers two to three children and practise family planning methods. Drinking water sources are tube wells, tap water, and handpump. Apart from Jain monks, who avoid the use of various modern amenities such as radios, television and electricity, people in general use electricity, listen to radios, watch television and visit the cinema. Fuel resources are kerosene oil and *gobar* gas. The attitude of the community toward saving is positive.

KIRAN JAIN

# JAT (HINDU)

Some early ethnographic writings had argued that the Jats were the descendants of Indo-Scythian groups which invaded India during the period between 200 B.C. and A.D. 600 and settled here. Scholars and others who do not subscribe to this, argue that the linguistic, religious and anthropometric characteristics of Jats and Scythians are different. It has even been contended that they are from the Indo-Aryan stock. Some of these controversies were noted by Crooke (1896: 25) as well as James Tod (1896: 291).

Bonerjee (1898) expressed similar views: Juts who were of Scythian origins, migrated to the Indian subcontinent much later then the Aryans; and subdued the tract earlier occupied by the Rajputs. He claims that King Kanishka and Lord Buddha were of Jat or Scythian origins. In early Christian era, parts of Punjab had a flourishing Jat kingdom, which collapsed to the Aryan influence and Muslim invaders. Jats were fairly distributed over large tracts of land under the pressures of fresh migrations (Bonerjee, 1975: 131). Risley had challenged the theory about the Scythian origins of Jats. He had even questioned the assumption that Jats have something to do with the people once called Getae by Herodotus. In Fugen's view, within certain limitations Jats and Rajputs were originally one race; but instead of the Rajputs remaining stationary and the Jats falling in social scale, it is the Rajput who has risen, while the Jat has remained stationary or risen only slightly, Jats, like Sivgotri, claim descent form the '*jata*' of god Shiva. W. Crooke was of the opinion, whatever the position, earlier, in times contemporary to him the two formed the common stock. The division was more social than ethnic. It was noted by Ibbetson and *Punjab Census Report* (Rose, 1919: 361) that the line separating Jats, Rajputs and certain other castes was almost impossible of definition. Rose (1919: 357, 361) has noted some events in history, where Jats were involved.

According to Crooke (1896: 29), 'In physique the Jats are generally of fair height, but below the average of Rajputs or other castes. Their chest measurement and weight are in fair proportion to their height; the extremities, especially the lower, are often disproportionate to their normal length. Proportionately speaking the women are of very strong physique, exceeding men in this respect. The prevailing complexion is fair and colour of the eyes and the hair is dark, fine and straight; beard and moustache scanty, and the former not usually worn. The crania are of tolerably fair size and shape, often elongated, altogether a lower type than the Brahman skull.'

They are said to possess courage and fidelity, are industrious and persevering in their habits, and are of an agile and muscular frame.

The census data about selective districts of Punjab from 1881 to 1931 shows that Hindu Jat population had progressively declined in Punjab. It was due to the influence of Sikhism. Hindu Jat population in the state declined from 14,45,374 in 1881 to 9,92,308 in 1931 by about half a million. Sikh Jat population increased by over a million in the same period from 12,22,673 in 1881, to 21,33,152 in 1931 (*Census of India*, 1931). In 1931, the total Hindu Jat population of undivided Punjab was 9,92,309, out of which 5,47,531 were males and 4,44,958 females. Out of the total, 7,72,546 resided in British territory and 6,40,101 resided in princely states. Total Jat population was 60,39,130 (*Census of India*, 1931). In earlier censuses the Hindu Jat population was 14,45,374 in 1881, 16,79,177 in 1891, 1,539,574 in 1901, 10,00,085 in 1911, 10,46,396 in 1921 and 9,92,309 in 1931.

They speak Bagdi dialect at home and with kin groups. However, they use Punjabi, in their communication with other communities. The women of this community wear *borla* as a mark of *suhagan*. The women of the community are vegetarian and men are occasional non-vegetarian. Consumption of vegetables is moderate and of fruit is occasional. Men take alcoholic drinks. Wheat, maize and barley are the commonly used cereals. Rice is also used. Pulses taken include gram, *urad, moong*, peas and beans, *masur* and *moth*. The commonly used cooking medium includes *desi ghee*, groundnut and mustard oils and *vanaspati*. They have changed from vegetarian to non-vegetarian diet and prefer *roti* to rice. Consumption of vegetables and fruit has increased.

Social divisions exist at various levels. Bingley (1904: 29-30) has noted that Jats were separated by the Jamuna river into two sections, which were further divided into Deswali or Hele and Pahchhade or Dhe. The Deswali were the original Jats who had territorial divisions. Deswali derived from the plains or country and Bagri derived from Bagar or upland in Bikaner. The former claimed to be superior to the latter. In addition to this there was a division on the basis of Shiv *gotra* and Kashib *gotra*. The former claimed to be *asli* and descendants of Shiva (Rose, 1919: 375). However, Crooke (1896: 28) has provided a different account of these divisions. According to him Man, Heb and Bhular considered themselves *asli* because they had descended from '*jata*' of Lord Shiva; but derived their Rajput ancestry. But in the south-east a different division prevailed between Shivgotri claiming descendant from Shiva and Karibgotri claiming Rajput connections.

The census of 1891 had noted many subcastes of the community. Some of these were—Ahlawat, Aulak, Bhainiwal, Bains, Bajwa, Bal, Bhangu, Phullar, Bhutta Bhuttar, Buta, Chahil, Chatta, Chhadar, Chima, China, Dagar, Dalal, Dehia, Deo, Deswal; Dhankar, Dhariwal, Dhillon, Dhindsa, Dhotar, Gandhi, Ghatwal, Ghuman, Gill, Golia, Goraia, Harral, Her, Hinjara, Ithwal, Jakhar, Kahlon, Kang; Langah, Langrial, Lodike; Mahil, Man, Mangat, Marral, Hinmol; Pannun, Pawania, Phogat, Randhawa, Rathi, Sait, Sharawat, Sangwan; Srarah, Sarai, Sidhu, Sandhu; Sipra, Sohal, Sumar; Tahim, Tarar, Varaich, Vrik. Out of these Ahlawat, Dagar, Dalal, Deswal, Chatwal, Harral, Langah, Iodike, Iangrial, Mrabal, Phogat, Pathi, Sangwan, were not reported in the Ferozepur district, the present place of field research.

However, the present survey has been able to record a few of these *gots*. They included the following *gots*: Nain, Bahadu, Saharan, Ginja, Kadawasara, Ladhowaal, Rinwan, Sihar, Jakhar, Kaajal, Punia, Phambo, Jaani, Jeani, Jhuria, Kaarela, Bijrania, Kaali Panan, Jhajadia, Duddi, Neol, Potaliya, Dahyaya, Bagad, Godara, Bhedkut Jaat or Bishnoi. Some villages are dominated by a particular *got*, e.g. village Kerian is dominated by Bijornia *got*, and Khanpur village is dominated by Dhaka *got*. Substantial numbers of this community in this area have Jhunja and Bhadoo *got*.

A large number follow Sanatan Dharma; but some follow Arya Samaj. The community can be differentiated at educational level between illiterate and literate members. It has members belonging to various economic sections. Mostly the community engages in agriculture, sometimes in horticulture, but it has members in the services as well. These differentiations help to regulate marriage alliances and indicate social status. They recognize the *varna* system and have a very high self-perception, which is also acknowledged by other communities. They claim their place equivalent to Kshatriyas. Marriages are mostly endogamous at community level. The communitiy is divided into exogamous clans called *got*. The rules of marriage used to be that a person could not marry a person belonging to the *got* of his father, mother's father, maternal grandmothers' father or paternal grandmothers' father. This is called four *got* rule. In modern times this rule, which effectively prevented marriage among close kins even thrice removed, has been relaxed.

Another rule of marriage is that two families, even when they fulfil all other conditions, shall not be joined by marriage, if they live in the same village or if their villages have a common boundary. This is called *sim-simna bhaichara* (behaving like brothers because the boundaries meet). Because of these restrictions, Jats have a very widely dispersed kin (Karve, 1964: 972). Moreover, no marriage can be contracted in any of the *gots* within the village. They are called brothers (Sharma, 1973: 86). Some changes have been noted in the observance of *got* avoidance in marriage. These days the *got* of mother's father is not taken into consideration (Lewis, 1958: 86). However, the *got* membership still remains ascriptive; and all children belong to father's *got*. The *got* affiliation remains unaffacted by marriage. Children shall take the *got* of their father and married women receive the *got* of the husband. There is no hierarchy of *gots* among Jats, and therefore no practice of hypergamy is followed.

*Got* is considered the largest consanguineal kinship group among the Jats. No *gotra* is confined to one village, but it is widely distributed in several villages. It is a 'segmentry unilineal group' and in a village it is represented by *khandan*, which is composed of many *kunbas* and the *kunba* is constituted of many families (Sharma, 1978: 89). Among Jats the *got* is synonymous with clan (Pradhana, 1966). It is a 'non-localised, exogamous, patrilineal clan' (Sharma, 1973: 84). There are some cases of hypergamy. The Jats shall not marry their girls with the members of other communities, but can take wives from other communities. Earlier there was a practice of marriage of the younger brother of the deceased, with his wife. However, this is not accepted these days as marriages are now performed at adulthood, and are monogamous. These are settled by negotiations by the parents. The opinion of the bride and groom is seldom asked.

The usual Hindus marriage symbol such as vermilion, bangles, *chura*, *mangalsutra*, *bindi*, finger ring or earrings and nose stud are used. Women wear silken red dress and males wear *kesri* (saffron) turban at the time of marriage. The bride wears headgear or *borla*, at the time of marriage, and continues to wear it as long as her husband is alive. It is common with the Bagri culture of this area. The dress of the bride has changed from *ghagra* to *salwar* and *kameez*. There is a tradition of *kanyadan*. Practice of dowry in kind also continues in the community, but it is not demanded. According to the informants only few disputes arise because of dowry.

Rules of residence after marriage continue to be patrilocal. Divorce is accepted by the community by social approval as well as by judicial means. It is generally becuase of impotency or barrenness. However, in the latter case bigamy occurs with the approval of the first wife. On divorce, compensation can be given to any party, but it is not demanded. The custody of a child is mutually decided. Either party can ask for divorce. Remarriage of divorced women or widower is not allowed with full ceremony. There has been increase in the age of marriage. The community continues to live in vertically extended and even horizontally extended families though the tendency for nuclear families is very strong. Avoidance relationship exists between *saas* and *jawai*; *sasur* and *bahu*; and also between *jeth* and *bhabi*. There exists joking relationship between the *sali* and *jeeja*; and between *dewar* and *bhabi*. Disputes in the families are linked with property matters or with the challenge to the authority of elders. Male equigeniture is the rule of inheritance although daughter are legally entitled to inherit the paternal property. It is customary to deny them their share.

Women do the household work and have a role in social functions, rituals and mechanism of social control. They do not visit the cremation ground. They engage themselves in animal husbandry and agricultural operation only when there is harvesting season of cotton crop. Some members of the community have pointed out that a few women of poor families also participate in agricultural operation as wage labourers. But it was denied by others. In earlier days, it was a general practice for the women to go to their parent's house for the birth of the first child which is not done these days. On the child's coming to the father's house a ceremony of *shooshak* and *sir dhawan*, takes place when the mother is provided with clothes by her parents and parents-in-law. Post-delivery pollution period is observed for a few days. Naming ceremony is done by the *pandit*, or priest, after five, seven or nine days of birth. However, the performance this ceremony by the family itself is also accepted. *Mundan* ceremony of male child is performed at home six months after the birth.

Marriage, in some cases, is preceded by *sagai* which is performed by putting a *tikka* on the forehead of the groom. The *barat* visits the residence of the bride, where marriage rituals are performed by Vedic rites, but *shlokas* (religious verses) from *Ramayana* are also recited. At the time of entry of *barat*, the mother of the bride welcomes the groom who carries a stick of *beri* tree, and strikes it on one spot on the door of the house. The ceremony is known as *tarun sahela*. The relatives of bride and groom serve food before marriage, which is called *banora*. Before leaving the canopy, or *mandap*, where the marriage ceremony is to be performed, the groom cuts the string with an iron rod. It is known as *van bethana*. The consummation of marriage is at the groom's place.

After a death in the family, pollution is observed for twelve days. Then a ceremony, known as *bahranwa,* is observed. *Pagdi* ceremony also takes place on that day. If an old man dies, sweets are distributed. The eldest son lights the pyre. The remains of the dead are immersed in the Ganga at Hardwar. The rituals are being curtailed.

The agricultural land is the main source of the Jats' livelihood, and it is controlled by individual proprietors, or by the family. They are mainly a land-owning community. A few also work as labourers during crop season. Traditionally, the community was engaged mainly in settled agriculture and also in animal husbandary. Both these occupations still continue. The main crops are cotton and wheat. A few more villages have also started cultivation of paddy. These days they are also engaged in horticulture and grow citrus fruits, and grapes. Abohar and Fazilka areas of Ferozepur districts are the richest horticultural tract in Punjab. Those who are in services are very well placed. The agricultural produce is sold in Abohar and Fazilka markets. Those with small landholdings also work on the land of others. Child labour is prevalent in the harvesting season of cotton.

The statutory village *panchayats* exist, which though heterogeneous in composition are, in many villages, dominated by this community. They have usual powers of punishment and rewards, but generally act in case of water disputes. In earlier days there was a system of *nyat,* by the traditional caste council, where the defaulting members were affected social sanction and one of the ways was to ask him to carry a *jutti.* This practice has been discontinued after Independence. The community believes in various sects of Hinduism. It mainly believes in Sanatan Dharma whereas some are Arya Samajis. Of late a few have also started believing in Radhaswami sect. They, however, worship Hanuman, Krishna, and Shiva. The community has a special reverence, as part of Bagdi culture for a festival at Salasar in Churu district of Rajasthan, which is held on *Pooranmashi* (full moon day) of Usaj month. The Bagdis of all places assemble there for three-four days. The sacred specialists belong to the community of Brahmans which performs birth, death, and marriage rites. They also conduct worship and impart religious teachings. The festivals of the community are of economic, social and religious significance. They celebrate Janamashtami, Shivratri, Dussehra, and Diwali. They also participate in Lohri and Baisakhi festivals. A few have started going to

Radhaswami Satsang, but without renouncing their earlier faith. They have an oral tradition. Both sexes sing songs of Bagdi culture. The Bhat keep the genealogy of the families.

The community has very free interaction with other communities. They exchange all types of *jal/chal*, *kachcha*, *pukka* and *sidha* food with other communities. No untouchability is practised against the lower castes in this area. Some in the community are of the view that it exists but is restricted only in older generations. However, in the region, the community considers itself as the superior most. A few cases of intercommunity marriages have been reported, but it is not a general practice. The community believes in various sects of Hinduism and has matrimonial relations without inhibitions with these sects. They share crematoria, water resources, religious shrines and festivals with other communities. Cultivator-labour relationships exist. The wages to the agricultural labourers are paid in cash. They have good relations with labourers as cultivators.

Some recent writings have also reflected on the status of the community. In the opinion of Singh (1988: 3-5), justice, action and truth are the basic ingredients of Jat character. These facts reveal that a Jat's life is full of action, courage and adventure as he works in the way which he deems to be just and true. This requires instant decision, bold action to march forward and the possession of a well-built body. Such has also been the views of Sarkar who says that 'the Jat is more honest, more industrious, more sturdy and no less than the races of our frontier mountains'. He also points out the views of Qanungo who has said, 'Jat is a Jat after all, whether he be a Hindu, Sikh or Muslim, he tenaciously clings to his trial name as a proud heritage, and with it the tradition of kinship'. The Jats also abhor rigidity, religious hypocrisy and orthodoxy. The Aryan characteristics of his love for unionism was noted by Panini who described it as 'Jat/Jhat Sanghat—Jat/Jhat is one who believes in unionism or confederacies.' In the modern profession there is only a marginal participation of the community. They have some as personnel in defence forces and border security force. In the village under study few persons are employed in railways and also as *patwari* in the village. There is one DSP of the state police, one is *tahsildar* and a few MBBS doctors are also from this community. It has many *panches* and *sarpanches* at village level. It had one MLA and one MP and a union cabinet minister.

Education has been partly favoured for both boys and girls. Boys get education upto matriculation, and only a few upto college level. This is because of the need of agricultural operations. There is less education for girls, owing to social reasons. The community has a positive attitude to modern medicine. It has also accepted the modern techniques of family welfare. The couples favour one or two children. A few villages have primary health centres. Drinking water is available from handpumps. The community also uses electricity. It is self-employed in agricultural, animal husbandary, horticulture and transport sectors. The people have access to radio facilities, a few rich houses have television sets. Dissemination of information is through voluntary agencies, political parties and extension services. They use firewood, cow-dung cakes, coal, kerosene oil and *gobar* gas as fuels. They have an inconsistent attitude to savings, but a section of them have a positive attitude. They have access to food/ration through fair price shops as well. As an agricultural community it avails of irrigation facilities mainly from the canal or rainfall. There are few tube wells.They use organic manure, chemical fertilizers, insecticides, tractors, even harvesting combines in the agricultural operations.

VIRINDER SINGH

# JAT (SIKH)

The Jat-Sikh of Punjab call themselves 'Sardar' or 'Jat-Sikh', while the other people usually refer to them by the synonyms 'Jat-Jamindar' and 'Jat-Sardar'. The community constitutes the dominant rural folk of Punjab. However, no reference about the present Jat-Sikh exists in *Jati-Puran*, but the reference to their predecessors does exist therein. The origin of Jat-Sikh community is very recent and the historical record can be traced back only to some four hundred years. During the Guruship of the fifth Sikh Guru Arjan Devji (1581 to 1606) and afterwards, a large number of the Majha Jats embraced Sikhism and subsequently restricted marrying within this subgroup of Jats known as Jat-Sikhs. This gave rise to a new community in Punjab. The basic characters of the Jats, i.e. physical toughness, bravery, courage, loyalty, self-respect and equality have not only been preserved but further enhanced in the Jat-Sikhs of Punjab. A Persian-English dictionary defines *gut/guta* (Jat) as 'great' or 'grand'.

The Jat-Sikh of Punjab are generally tall, strongly built, smart, handsome, unsophisticated and self-willed (Dwivedi, 1970). However, the community does not keep the racial purity and is endogamous within the community and exogamous at the medium (regional level). However, quite a few are also distributed in nearby states such as Haryana, Himachal Pradesh, Rajasthan, western U.P., and the cities of Delhi and Chandigarh.

They speak in Punjabi language. The traditional dress of a rural male Jat-Sikh is *kurta*, *parna* and a turban and that of a female it is *salwar*, *kameez*, and *dupatta*. But many of the urban, educted people wear Western dress.

The majority of the males of the community are non-vegetarian; while majoritiy of the females cook non-vegetarian food, they prefer to remain vegetarian. Chicken, mutton and eggs are the main non-vegetarian diet components of the community. The staple diet of the community is wheat flour, buffalo milk and its products. Wheat flour is supplemented by maize, gram and sometimes *bajra* flour. The traditional diet consists of curd and *chapati* with a glass of *lassi* or milk at breakfast; *chapati* and vegetables at lunch; *dal-roti* or meat and *chapati* at dinner supplemented by an additional glass of milk just before going to sleep at night. Occasionally rice replaces some of the *chapati* content, say once a week at lunch or dinner. The community consumes sufficient vegetables, salads, and pulses. All varieties of pulses are used, but the most frequently used pulses are *moong, masur, urad* and *moth*. During winter months *sarson da sag* and *makki di roti* are commonly relished food of the community. All types of seasonal fruits and vegetables are consumed in abundance. Their traditional cooking medium is groundnut oil or mustard oil, with the exception of a few rich families, who use clarified butter or *desi ghee* for cooking. More recently, refined vegetable oil is becoming more popular cooking medium among the urban and more educated families. *Desi ghee* is commonly used as a taste enhancer in majority of the houses. Drinking of alcohol is quite common among the males of the community particularly on festive occasions. There is a trend of change in food habits as there is increased use of pulses replacing meat consumption; vegetables and fruit consumption is also on the increase.

The community believes in social equality and does not recognize *varna* system. However, classification of the society into subcastes and *gots* does exist. The community has numerous clans, namely: Aulak, Bains, Bal, Bajwa, Bhuller, Brar, Chahal, Chathah, Cheema, Dhariwal, Dhillon, Dhindsas, Gandhi, Ghuman, Grewal, Her, Kang, Mahal, Mangat, Mann, Odi, Pannu, Punia, Randhawa, Sahi, Sidhu, Sandhu, Sohal, Varaich, Virk. Some of their gots are Antal, Atwal, Attri, Aulakh, Babbar, Bajad, Ballan, Vains, Bassi, Bath, Belari, Bhambu, Bhangu, Bhinder, Bhatti, Bhoparai, Budhwar, Bura (Boora), Chatha, Cheema, Chhina, Chimi, Dogar, Dahima, Dahiya, Dhall, Dangi, Darad, Dasval, Deol (Deval), Dhami (Dhama), Dhaliwal, Dhanda, Dhanoya, Dharan, Ddhindval, Dosanjh, Gaur, Gauraya, Ghangas, Ghuman, Godha, Godra, Guliya, Gumar, Gondal, Gussar, Johl (Jauhl), Jatrana, Johiya, Jaun, Kajla, Kak, Kakkar, Kallan, Kahlon, Kang, Katariya, Khar, Khokhar, Kler, Klular, Kundu, Lalli, Lamba, Lathwal, Lohan, Lohariya, Machhar, Madhan, Mahil, Malik, Malli (Mall), Mann Mangat, Mand, Mande, Minhas, Mirdha, Mitha, Maur, Mund, Nalwa, Nain, Narmal, Nassir, Nahra, Nuniya, Ohlan, Ojala, Odhran, Payal, Panghal, Panesar, Pannu, Panyag, Pawar, Parasmal, Phulka, Piru, Potaliya, Puniya (Pauniya, Punia), Rai , Rana, Rangha, Rathi, Rathol, Rathor, Randhawa, Rawat, Riar, Rose (Raj), Ruhit, Sahota, Sahraut (Sahravat), Samra, Sangha, Sangwan, Sandhu, Saran, Saroha, Saranh, Sekhon, Shahi, Shergill, Sibia, Sihmor, Sidhu, Sikarwar, Sohi, Solanki, Syal, Thakkhar, Tanwar, Thind, Tiwana, Tur, Tusar, Tumar, Utar, Virk, Warraich (Wairaish), Watdhan, etc. There is some differentiation based on social, economic and occupational basis.

The Jats marry within their own community and thus form an

endogamous group which is exogamous at the *got* level. However some males, who are unable to get a wife among Jats marry women from any other community, usually of a lower caste. Junior sororate, and junior or senior levirate are allowed. Generally, marriage takes place at adulthood. Since 1940, mariages in the community are taking place by mutual consent, and the bride's family now gives her some dowry. Form of mariage is monogamous and girl's age at marriage nowadays ranges usually between eighteen to twenty-three years while that of a boy from twenty to twenty-six years. A girl crossing the age of twenty-four usually becomes a source of great worry to her parents, while the delay in a boy's marriage does not cause the same level of anxiety. Post-marital residence is patrilocal; remarriage of both widow and widower are allowed. The main changes in the pattern of marriage system are increase in age at marriage and bride-price giving way to dowry.

The main marriage ceremony, known as *anand karaj*, takes place at the bride's residence. *Anand karaj,* 'the ceremony of bliss' is a general way of Sikh marriages common to other Sikh communities. The bridegroom leaves his home on horseback accompanied by his friends and relations (*barat* or *junj*) and arrives at the bride's house in a procession with music band. They are received by the male relations of the bride and entertained with dinner. In arranged marriages, this is often the first time the bridal pair see each other (Singh, 1972). In the early hours of the dawn, professional singers, called *ragis* sing hymns prescribed for *asa di war* (morning worship). After these hymns, the bridal pair is asked to come and sit in front of the *Guru Granth Sahib.*

A Sikh priest reads the hymns from the *Guru Granth Sahib* at the marriage ceremony. The *ragis* follow this by singing hymns. Now, the bridegroom steps in holding one end of a piece of cloth, while the bride holds the other end and follows him. The brothers and close male relatives of the bride help her round the *Guru Granth Sahib* behind her groom. These circumambulations round the *Guru Granth Sahib* are repeated four times and the couple are pronounced husband and wife. A few hours after this ceremony, the bride leaves her parental home (*doli*) with her husband. In the past when marriages took place at a very young age, the marriage ceremony served as betrothal only and the bride returned to her parents to live with them until she attained puberty. The marriage would be consummated after she left her home for the second time (*muklawa*) to live with her husband.

Traditionally, the community has been living in extended families.

Golden Temple

Folk song singer (late) Sh. Lal Chand Jumla Jat

Musical instrument Nigoja player

Panj Piaras:
leading a religious
procession

Dhadhi Jatha

Bus driver

Julaha

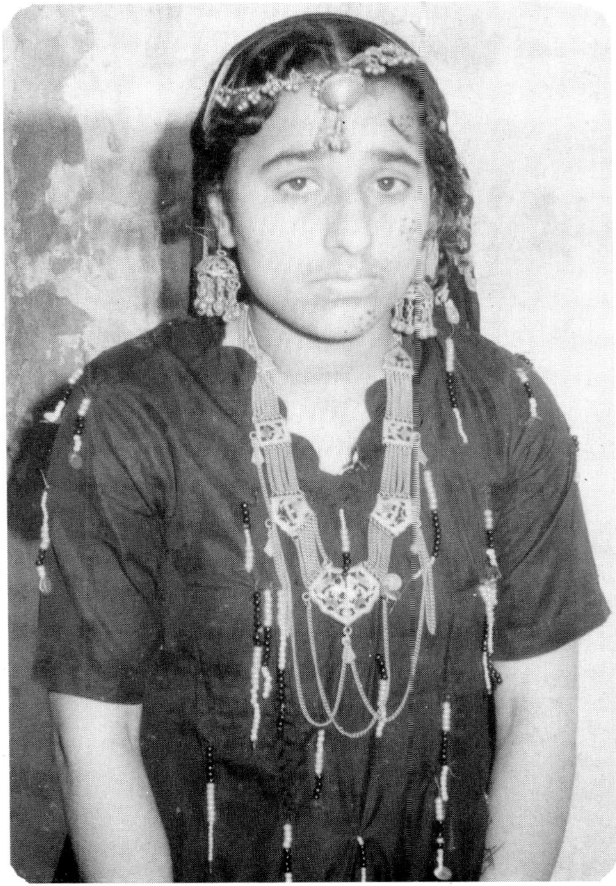

Gaddria Lohar Woman

Ghumiar

Woman preparing her food

Sugar cane juice

Ladies in festive mood

Baba Sheikh Farid

Gosain

Fish and duck farming

Recently, a considerable number of them have started living in nuclear families, mainly due to their leaving homes on entering into professions other than agriculture. Authority in a family is distributed in three spheres: economic, ritual and moral. As long as the father remains a successful earning hand, he is generally not overruled in economic matters. Majority of the community's economic needs are fulfilled by getting credit from the *artya*. The seniormost male (who may be non-earning) member of the joint family is responsible for social and moral control of the household and is to ensure that the moral code is followed properly. The ritual sphere usually lies with the female elders. Interpersonal relations in a family form a good network. A son's birth, especially of the first one, is an occasion for great rejoicing and jubiliation in the family. The main cause of conflict among the members of a joint family is disputes over property especially land. The rules of inheritance are male equigeniture, succession by the eldest son.

Women in the community have been given inferior position without right over the ancestral property. However, they have significant role to play in all the social, ritual and religious activities of the family, yet they are usually not allowed to influence any political, economic or any other major decision taken by their male counterparts in the family. In other words, women have lower status than men. Women usually do only household jobs and in addition they have responsibility of taking mid-day meals for their men working in the agricultural fields. These are purchased, and even sold during days of distress, at the instance of men. All household chores such as cooking, cleaning the house, milking the cattle, looking after children are done by women. Inspite of their constitutional and legal right over the ancestral property, only very few women claim their share from their brothers.

Life-cycle rituals include birth, child-naming, *gundana*, *pahul* (baptism) marriage and death. Although there are no recognized ceremonies connected with the birth of a child, yet some people of the community believe in reciting the first five verses of the morning prayer in the ears of a newborn baby. Majority of the rural people prefer to have deliveries at home with the help of a *dai* and only a few urban, educated people chose to have deliveries in hospitals. The *Guru Granth Sahib* is opened at random and the child is given a name beginning with the first letter of the first word on the top of the page. All male names of Jat Sikhs end with 'Singh' and all female names with 'Kaur'.

Traditionally, when a child's hair is plaited for the first time the community celebrates this occasion in a great ceremonial and festive manner. The ritual connected with this ceremony is the same as performed by Guru Gobind Singh at the first baptism in A.D. 1699. The baptism is performed at a congregation. *Amrit* is prepared by mixing sugar in water and stirring it with a *khanda* (double-edged dagger) along with the recitation of selected passages of the scriptures including Guru Gobind Singh's composition, the *Japji Sahib*. A palmful of *amrit* is splashed on the child's face with the words '*Sri Wahe Guru Ji Ka Khalsa, Sri Wahe Guru Ji Ki Fateh*.' The *pahul* not only imposes all the obligations of the faith, it also confers rights. Thereafter a person has access to the holiest of the shrines, that is, the Akal Takht in the Golden Temple at Amritsar, where the sacred relics of the Sikh Gurus are placed. He, or she, has now the right to enter into matrimony (Singh, 1972).

The dead are cremated and the death is mourned by sitting around the deceased and reciting prayers. Wailing, crying and breast-beating which is very common in northern Indian communities, is prohibited among the Jat-Sikhs. Before being taken for cremation, the corpse is bathed and dressed in the emblems of the faith. The funeral pyre is lit by the son or the nearest male relative. Ashes are thrown into the rivers, preferably in the Beas at Kiratpur Sahib. Celebration of death anniversaries at *shradhs* are forbidden. It is customary to remove all furniture and sit and sleep on the floor. On the last day of mourning, *bhog* ceremony is held when friends and relatives assemble to participate in the singing of hymns and recitation of *Guru Granth Sahib*. If the occasion is the death of the head of the household, his eldest son is officially recognized as the new head by having a turban tied on his head in front of the assembled gathering.

The community celebrates all the Hindu festivals of Punjab. The members wear yellow clothes on Basant Panchami, or the Spring festival, sprinkle coloured water on Holi, assemble at the Baisakhi fair and light lamps at Diwali. However, the religious part of each festival takes place in the *gurdwara* instead of the Hindu temple. In addition to these, the community has a few other exclusively Sikh festivals. Of these, six are important, these are the birthdays (Guruparabs) of Guru Nanak Dev and Guru Gobind Singh, the martyrdoms of the fifth Guru, Guru Arjan Dev, and the ninth Guru, Guru Tegh Bahadur and the two sons of Guru Gobind Singh , the day of the founding of the Khalsa and Hola Mohalla is chiefly celebrated at Anandpur Sahib soon after Holi. The usual form of each of these festivals is to take out the *Guru Granth Sahib* in procession through the city. The holy scripture is placed on top of a flower-bedecked van. On either side two men carry the Sikh ensigns (*Nishan Sahib*). Five men representing the first five converts, march in front of the van witih drawn swords. The women walk behind the van whereas the men group themselves into parties of singers and go in front. Another prominent feature of these celebrations is the mass feeding of devotees at the *Guru ka langar* (the kitchen of the Guru).

The main economic resource of the community is agriculture. The vast majority are peasants living in scattered villages and hamlets and are reasonably prosperous and have good, comfortable homes with courtyards where their cattle are tethered. Families continue to live jointly until the land is divided. The community holds the major area of agricultural land of Punjab. The land is controlled by the families by proprietorship and often divided into parts equal to the number of sons after the death of their parents. The agricultural produce is mainly sold by their specified middle-men (*artyas*) in the nearby towns on whom the community men have great faith. Presently, the percentage of literacy amongst the community has increased considerably with the result that a large number has also taken to white-collar occupations to become engineers, doctors, scientists, teachers, artists, lawyers, etc. The Jats have also excelled as soldiers and a sizeable number earn their living from army, navy and air force services. Traditionally, only males have been engaged in earning a livelihood. Big farmers in the community hire a large number of agricultural labour and the employees are usually paid in the form of some cash and a part of the agricultural produce at the time of harvest.

The social control in the community is well in the hands of the village *panchayat*. Even in villages where the community people are not represented in majority in the village *panchayat*, the *panchayat's* verdict is fully respected by the community and majority of the problems are attempted to be settled at the *panchayat* level. However, with recent awareness of judicial courts in the nearby towns nowadays, a large number of social and family disputes are referred to the courts. Formal *panchayats* existed even after Partition of the country. However, the main role of the *panchayat* has been reduced to mainly general village welfare activities. Keeping in view their inability to implement punishments, the *panchayats* presently avoid declaring any punishments. The oral traditions are folk-songs generally common with other communities of Punjab. In addition there are songs for sister's pride in her brother, for daughter's love for her mother; *bolis* and *tappas*.

The intercommunity relations are very cordial. The Jat-Sikhs sing and dance together with other local communities of Punjab. Their crematorium is common with other communities. They share the festivals, happy and sorrowful occasions of a majority of the surrounding communities. Similarly, they invite others on their functions and attend the functions of other communties to strengthen friendly ties and drink and dine with the other community people. The landlord-cultivator, the patron-client relationships are extremely strong and continue with the same people for years together. They invite and attend the marriage ceremonies of other communities with a great sense of participation and responsibility. The community is more closely associated with Banias or trading community of the nearby towns and has close ties with them as their middlemen and advisers not only for selling their harvest but also for their main purchases from that town and from other cities for articles not available locally. Other communities visit their *gurdwaras* and they visit the Hindu religious places quite frequently and particiate in common socio-religious festivals and festivities. They look upon all other communities as equals and consider themselves not less than any of the highest community.

The community has extensively benefitted from the developmental programmes launched by the government. Both boys and girls get formal school education and a few also attain higher education. A large number of modern agricultural equipments have recently replaced the old traditional way of sowing and reaping the harvest. Consequently, the agricultural production per hectare of land has increased manyfold. They gladly accept the modern agricultural methods.

Attitude to both indigenous and modern medicare is favourable and majority of the community people now avail of the hospital facilities available locally or in nearby towns and cities. Drinking water is obtained from tube wells and handpumps. Even tap water is now also available in most of the villages and is made full use of by the community. About 50 per cent of the people have a favourable attitude towards family planning. Recently, there is seen a changing trend and more and more people are adopting the temporary family planning techniques and couples prefer usually three children.

They listen to the radio, watch television and visit cinema houses, too. Roads and electricity have been provided to their villages and almost every household has electricity connection. Fuel resources of the community are extremely variable depending upon the economic status of the family and range from cow-dung cakes, firewood, sawdust, coal, kerosene oil, *gobar* gas to L.P.G. Although many irrigation sources such as canals, rivers and seasonal rains are available, yet the use of tube wells is most frequent by this agricultural community. A considerable number of people make use of Integrated Child Developmental Services and utilize mother-infant care and immunization facilities. Similarly, the community avails of the facility of food distribution through fair price shops. The use of organic manure, chemical fertilizers and insecticides is very common.

D.K. KANSAL

# JHANGAM

The Jhangam, are also commonly known as Talliawale, Babaji and Shiv Bhagat. The community is distributed throughout north India and its male members are easily recognized by the typical turban with peacock feathers, *morepankh* spreading from the top of it; ropes of black thread tied around their shoulder and waist and a *talli* or a bell in their hand and singing songs in praise of Lord Shiva and begging for alms from door to door. The *morepankh* or *kalgi* represents the holy Ganga and the black ropes respresent *nag devta*—the attire of Lord Shiva. They are followers of Lord Shiva and believe themselves to be his descendants. They believe that they were produced by Shiva from his thigh. There reference exists in *Jati-Puran* and *Shiv-Puran.* They all originally hail from present-day Haryana, chiefly from the districts of Karnal, Sonepat, Kurukshetra and Jind. Now, they are distributed throughout Punjab, mainly living in cities, towns and urban areas. They keep shifting from one place to another changing their *deras.* They speak Hindi and Punjabi within the family and kin groups and Punjabi dialect with others. Those who can read and write use the Gurmukhi and Devanagari scripts. Male members of the community wear a special kind of easily distinguishable dress, while womenfolk do not have any community-specific dress.

The community claims to be strictly vegetarian with both men and women abstaining from egg, meat and wine. Onion and garlic is allowed. Locally available seasonal vegetables and pulses of all kinds such as gram, *urad*, *moong*, peas, and beans are eaten by the community. The staple food is *dal-roti* or *dal-chawal.* The food is cooked in *ghee* or groundnut or mustard oil. Smoking is allowed among adult male members. They smoke *bidi*, cigarette or even loose tobacco in a *hookah*. Non-alcoholic beverages, especially tea is very frequently taken. Milk and milk products are used depending on the purchasing power.

Subgroups exist in the Jhangam in the form of various *gots.* Their function is to regulate marriage alliance and indicate descent and ancestry. They all use the name of their community as surname. The community considers itself Shiv-Rohit recognizing its place in the *varna* system as Brahman.

The Jhangam is an endogamous community practising *got* exogamy though marriage within the same village is allowed, while negotiating marriage within the blood relations is strictly prohibited. Marriages are strictly within the community itself. In earlier times child marriage was allowed, but now it does not take place anymore. Adult marriage is allowed, when the boy has attained the age of twenty years and a girl is of eighteen years. Marriages are negotiated by the elders. Monogamy is the rule. Marriage symbols are in the form of bangles, *bindi*, finger, toe and earrings or nose-ring and nose stud. Younger married women observe the marriage symbol more carefully but women of older age do not observe the symbol strictly. Widows, however, do not wear clothes of bright colours. Dowry system is prevalent and consists of household articles, clothes, jewellery, utensils or even cash at times. *Kanyadan* exists. Rule of residence after marriage is patrilocal. Divorce is permissible under extreme situations of maladjustment. It is allowed after social approval given by the *panchayat*, a five-member committee. Divorce compensation may be given to the wife and the children are kept either with the mother or the father depending on the age of children. Widow or widower remarriage is not allowed. Male divorcee remarriage is permissible. In changes observed in the institution of marriage, there is an increase in age at marriage, increase in the incidence of divorce and liberalization of rules for remarriage.

Both nuclear and extended family types exist in the Jhangam. Traditional interpersonal relations of respect, love, fear, avoidance, obligation, joking and conflict are observed in each family. Elders command respect in the family, while youngsters in the family are loved. Avoidance relationship is observed between daughter-in-law and father-in-law and husband's elder brother and younger brother's wife. Avoidance relationship is also observed by women with other family and community elders. Normally, *purdah* is observed in these cases. Joking relationship is seen between sister's husband and wife's sister; husband's younger brother and elder brother's wife as also between grandparents with grandchildren. Younger members in the family have an obligation towards family elders to look after them for their needs, health and demands. Conflicts and confrontation arise in the family due to check on the freedom of youngsters and challenge to the authority of elders. In a joint family, there is a traditional conflict between *sas* (husband's mother) and *bahu* (son's wife). Conflicts and confrontations also arise due to work divisions between the ladies and taking sides when children pick up quarrels. Inheritance is by male equigeniture and succession is by eldest son. Owing to legal provisions daughters also have a share now in the parental belongings, but if daughters demand the same, it leads to souring of relationship between brothers and sisters. Inter-family relationship is very strong in the community. Changes in the institution of family includes the rise in formation of nuclear families and decline of extended family system.

Women are confined to the household jobs such as cooking, washing clothes, looking after the children and maintaining a house. They also collect fuel and bring potable water. They have a role in ritual and religious matters as no ritual and religious ceremony is considered complete without womenfolk in it. In various social functions in the family such as marriage, birth and death, women have an effective role to play. They have an appropriate place in the mechanism of social control. Women have otherwise low status in the family *vis-a-vis* menfolk. The position of very old women in the family is different as their opinion is taken for various domestic activities. On account of women having a voting right, they indirectly contribute to the political activities and political system.

Rituals are observed on the occasion of birth, childhood, marriage and death. Antenatal rituals are normally not observed though pre-delivery restrictions exist on mother in the from of work activities. She may not be allowed strenuous household jobs. In some cases, however, pre-delivery ritual in the form of *ritan* is observed whereby the pregnant woman is given some clothes and other gifts by her parents in the seventh month of pregnancy. Post-delivery pollution period is observed for seven days during which child and the mother are confined to a solitary room. After seven days, the mother and the child are given a ritual bath; she performs *puja* and wears new clothes. Thereafter she is deemed to be purified. Naming ceremony as such is not performed and name of a child is decided on the basis of the positioin of stars and planets. In childhood rituals, *mundan* ceremony is performed in case of male children only. *Mundan* is performed on the day of first Shivratri and is called *chuttia katana*. The ceremony is performed by the paternal uncle, i.e. *chacha* or *tau* or by an old lady of the family.

In marriage, initial rituals such as *sehra* or *ghori* are performed at the bridegroom's residence. Thereafter, the marriage party proceeds with pomp and show to the bride's residence, where they are entertained with a feast. Marriage rituals are performed at the bride's residence around the sacred fire. Consummation of marriage is at the groom's residence. The dead are cremated and the bones are immersed in water. The post-death pollution period is observed for thirteen days. After the thirteenth day, the community members and relatives assemble and pray for the departed soul. Normal work is started thereafter. In changes in life-cycle rituals, the rituals are reported to be curtailed and becoming more expensive.

Religious begging by the male members of the community is the main occupation and source of income of the community. They go from door to door asking for *atta* or cash, singing in praise of Lord Shiva, '*Bhola Nath Bhandar Bharenge*'—Lord Shiva will bring prosperity. Earlier it was confined to Monday only , but nowadays they can be seen throughout the week. Dressed in their typical attire, they collect whatever is offered to them. The localities are divided among Jhangams who beg. They also keep shifting from one *dera* to another and from one city to another. On the eve of Shivratri they move around in groups and collect money and food for the Shivratri *bhandara*. On this occasion, they even make collections from shops and market places. With the influence of education, some have taken to miscelleneous jobs in private and government services, thus discarding the traditional occupation. Some have also taken to self-employment in animal husbandry, and in general merchandise. There is not much change in the occupational and economic activities of the community after Independence, but for few cases of employment in government and private services and in miscellaneous self-employment.

The mechanism of social control in the community is through the *panchayat* which consists of five nominated members, who are enlightened, learned or senior in age. They look after the routine family or inter-family disputes especially pertaining to marriage or disrespect to established traditional norms and behaviour of the community. The post-Independence statutory *panchayat*, wherever it exists, plans and implement welfare and developmental schemes. After Independence the role and influence of traditional *jati panchayat* is decreasing as by and large the community is covered by the established laws of the land. The Jhangam follows Hinduism especially revering and following Lord Shiva. They also worship deities of wider pantheon order. They respect and visit traditional Hindu shrines and places of pilgrimages. Diwali, Dussehra and Holi are celebrated with great joy and religious fervour. Shivratri is, however, the major festival that they celebrate. The sacred specialists come from their own community. They perform birth, marriage and death rites. The festivals are celebrated as they are of socio-economic and socio-religious significance.

Oral traditions are shared with other communities, though folk songs, folk tales and folklore in reverence and praise of Lord Shiva exist. They use a small *talli* as a supporting musical instrument at the time of worship and *puja*.

Traditional intercommunity linkages exist at ritual, social and occupational levels. As 'Shiv *purohit*' they perform rituals in the houses of various local communities. In occupation also, they visit the houses for offerings of all the communities except the Scheduled Castes. Barring those communities which were earlier treated as untouchables, they accept/exchange water, *kachcha, pukka* and *sidha* food. They share water sources and crematorium with other communities and visit the same religious shrines as other communities. They participate in the traditional festivals and festivities of other Hindu communities. They render ritual services to other communities.

The literacy rate in the Jhangam community is low. Boys attain graduate degree at times, but it is not favoured for the girls. They drop out of school after primary level being unable to study further due to social reasons. Giving higher education to girls is not favoured. In health and medical care, modern medicines are favoured. For treatment, they visit government dispensaries, health centres and hospitals beside getting treatment from private doctors. In family planning, some are convinced of the small family norms. Those who opt for family planning go in for modern methods of family planning including sterilization. Number of children preferred in the family varies, though three children norm appears to be minimum. In the hope of getting a son, some opt for bigger sized family.

The facilities of clean drinking water are available in the localities, in the form of piped water, handpumps and tube wells. They listen to radio, occasionally visit the cinema and get an opportunity to watch television also. The dissemination of information is through extension agencies, political parties and voluntary social organizations. Electricity is available. They use fuel such as firewood, cow-dung cakes and kerosene oil. The mother-infant immunization is availed of. Ration and banking facilities are available in the localities inhabited by them.

A.K. BHATIA

# JHINWAR

The Jhinwar or Jhinur are also known as Mehre. In Patiala, Bhatinda, Sangrur, Faridkot, Ferozpur and Ropar districts of Punjab, they are called Jhinwars and are mostly Sikh, whereas in Ludhiana, Jalandhar, Amritsar and Hoshiarpur districts they are known as Mehre and are mostly Hindu. These days, they prefer to call themselves Kashyap Rajput and are included in the list of backward communities by this name. Machiare or Mallah are the other names by which they are also known. There are different names by which Jhinwars are known throughout India. In Uttar Pradesh, they are known as Nishad and Kahar, in Jammu & Kashmir, they are known as Pench and in coastal areas, as Mallah.

Their history of origin and migration is obscure. They are believed to be descendants of one Kashyap Rishi who lived during the time of Lord Ram. They believe that in the remote past they were concentrated in central India from where they spread to all over the country. When Guru Gobind Singh, the tenth Sikh Guru, founded the Khalsa Panth, one of the *panj piaras* (the loved five) who offered their lives to the Guru, was a Jhinwar by the name of Himmata, who later came to be known as Baba Himmat Singhji.

They are distributed in the urban and rural areas of Punjab in varying numbers. They speak Punjabi, Hindi and Urdu and some of the educated can also speak English. They eat both vegetarian and non-vegetarian food with wheat, rice and pulses as staple grains. All types of locally available seasonal fruits such as mango, banana, orange, watermelon and papaya, are eaten by them. Vegetables and pulses are consumed by them in varying amount. Because of the white revolution in Punjab, milk and milk products are readily available both in urban and rural areas and are taken by them frequently.

Consumption of alcoholic drinks was prohibited earlier but nowadays no such restriction is observed. Alcoholic drinks are consumed mostly on festivals, marriages and birth of male child. Tea and coffee are also consumed frequently. Smoking is prohibited for young ones and women. Offering a *hookah* is part of their welcome gesture in the rural areas.

Being devotees of Goddess Durga, consumption of onion, garlic, eggs, meat and liquor is prohibited among them during Navratra.

These restrictions are also observed on Tuesdays and during mourning periods. A woman, during menstruation is also not expected to consume these things. She is not even allowed to enter the family kitchen or touch any cooked food to be eaten by other family members. Change in food habits is evident from the fact that more and more people are eating non-vegetarian food, and use of alcohol has also increased.

The Jhinwars appear to be remarkably a composite caste, comprising several subgroups, whose names have been derived from the occupations they pursue or have pursued earlier. In Punjab two divisions can be seen among them on the basis of the religion they subscribe to, i.e. a decade or so ago, even the distinction on the religious basis was not pronounced, but it is becoming so, because of various socio-political reasons.

The Jhinwars are divided into 110 clans:

| | | | | |
|---|---|---|---|---|
| Jhoje | Rangru | Bhathiara | Jaspat | Lunj |
| Titriye | Malra | Bhockak | Jhansal | Galna |
| Lambsar | Ruhal | Tonk(Tank) | Bhagre | Bole |
| Tawna | Rattre | Udeyan | Sunsoy | Sua |
| Lalne | Bhatifour | Gadre | Gaghial | Baldi |
| Subhjauge | Bhat | Talah | Saugne | Bhalti |
| Bagal | Sandhu | Bartri | Bargote | Gunghal |
| Barni | Dhibri | Chundgund | Bihal | Fauiti |
| Barain | Babial | Sandal | Bharani | Papial |
| Mausor | Narausi | Jhagre | Makh | Moole |
| Khubhjange | Kushal | Kaushal | Rachpuria | Chibar |
| Dube | Puar | Bachpuria | Sanghe | Bharat |
| Rura | Dari | Gade | Jaswal | Dari |
| Tinder | Palhiara | Dabler | Allar | Kalyan |
| Kangar | Sauge | Tak | Kanoje | Tor |
| Khas | Bhinde | Baljotra | Chot | Khutan |
| Sanotra | Dhochauk | Warki | Bhuubal | Dhongi |
| Rahalu | Makh | Daragiri | Chot | Tatre |
| Neele | Daragari | Bamotra | Padan | Rahelu |
| Panne | Kerere | Mubimar | Choodgoond | Bharath |
| Mangle | Manota | Naag | Bhasule | Kainth |
| Kang | Tunge | Lalacu | Mamotra | Tamna |

The main function of these clans is to regulate marriages and indicate descent. There is an increase in the incidence of using clan names as surnames, particularly those which resemble the high caste clans.

Self-perception of the community is high as they claim Rajput origin but other local communities of Punjab such as Khatri, Brahman, Arora, Jat, Bania, etc., treat them only as clean Shudras. They have started using the surname of Dogra to indicate Rajput descent. The community practises clan and village exogamy. Monogamy is the rule. A boy has to attain the age of twenty years and a girl eighteen years before their marriage proposal can be initiated. Some elderly person from the girl's side approaches the boy's parents and a marriage proposal is considered taking in view economic conditions and social status of the families. In earlier times, a boy was not allowed to see his prospective bride. Only the women of his family were allowed to meet the girl. Nowadays no such restriction is imposed. Dowry system is prevalent and consists of household articles, clothes, jewellery and some cash.

Rule of residence after marriage is patrilocal. Traditionally, the community did not practise divorce. Even when a woman is unable to bear a child, or was struck with some incurable disease, divorce was not allowed because such a situation was taken as the will of Devi Mata. Widow remarriage was also discouraged. The symbols of marriage are *sindur*, *bindi*, and lac bangles.

Nowadays, couples are getting divorced on grounds of adultery, mal-adjustment, and if there is no male child. It takes place with social or judicial approval. In case of divorce suit being initiated by the husband, the marriage expenditure incurred by his wife's natal family has to be returned by him, if divorce is granted. But if it is initiated by the wife, no such compensation has to be paid. Children are the liability of either husband or wife.

Both nuclear and extended family types are noticed in the community. The traditional interpersonal relations of respect, avoidance and joking are observed in a family. The male elders avoid entering the place where daughters or *bahu* are sitting. The *bahu* will use *purdah* while meeting her *sasur*, *jeth* or the elder male relatives of the husband. Joking relationships are prevalent between *jeeja* and *sali*, *mama* and *bhanja*, *naani* and *dhota*. The society is patrilineal with the right of inheriting property being equal for all the sons. Daughters are not given any share in the property.

All the major decisions are normally taken by the male members. But the womenfolk contribute substantially to the economy of the family. Beside attending to various household chores, such as cooking, washing, sweeping, etc., they also help the menfolk in attending to the various traditional occupations. They would take up the job of utensil cleaning or of a cook or even work as a midwife to earn money for the family. As part of the changing trends, the *purdah* system is becoming less prevalent. Owing to legal provisions, the daughters can also ask for a share in the ancestral property, if they so desire.

After a child has been delivered, the mother is not allowed to take part in any household activity for thirteen days. After that she takes a bath, performs *puja* and is allowed to take up normal household duties. A feast is normally arranged after the birth of a male child, when the members of the community, neighbours and village elders are invited. Sweets, *puri-halwa,* or even a lunch, depending on the economic condition of the family, are served. Sometimes even liquor is also served as part of the feasting. However, no such feast is arranged to celebrate birth of a female child in the family.

After a marriage alliance has been negotiated, an appropriate auspicious date agreeable to both the families is fixed. On the fixed date, a group of people consisting of the members of the groom's family, their relatives, neighbours and friends, proceed to the bride's place where they are received by the bride's father and other relatives. The groom's father embraces the bride's father and receives from him some cash or some gift. This is known as *milni* ceremony. The *milni* also takes place between the elder brothers and the maternal uncles of both the bride and the groom. The groom's people are then treated with a feast. Among the Hindu Jhinwar, the marriage ceremony is conducted by a Brahman and takes place at night. The boy and the girl perform seven *pheras* around the *vedi* (sacred fire) amidst chanting of *mantras.* Among the Sikh Jhinwar the ceremony is performed by a *granthi* and the couple takes four *pheras* around *Guru Granth Sahib.* The marriage ceremony of Sikh Jhinwars takes place in daytime.

Dead bodies are cremated according to the typical Hindu and Sikh rites. The eldest son performs the last rites. Children dying at young age are buried. The mourning period is for thirteen days. On the thirteenth day, a rite known as *rasam pagri* is performed, when a *puja* takes place and members of the family, relatives, neighbours pray for the departed soul and well-being of the family. The family, thereafter, attends to routine duties.

The Jhinwars are regarded as water-carriers and many of their occupations are connected with water such as cooking, fishing, boatmanship, well-sinking and cultivation of *singhara* or waternuts. They are also now described as village serviles working in agricultural fields, supplying baskets, mats and fishing nets, bringing water to other men, working in the fields, to the houses where women are secluded and at weddings and feasting and other similar occasions.

Earlier, they also worked as butchers, fishermen, palanquin bearers and parchers of grains. In urban areas, their women work in other families, whereas the men have become the owners of, or cooks at, the wayside *dhabas* and restaurants. They also take up miscellaneous occupations such as masonry, rickshaw pullers, welders and construction labourers. *Jajmani* system was prevalent few years ago where they used to extend their services to the *jajmans* round the year and used to get some agricultural produce in return. Now this system is on decline as every service is rendered in lieu of cash.

The community has a registered *sabha* or *biradari* at the state level which has ten members. There are also smaller district and local units at village level, which function under the supervision of the state *sabha*. Composition of such units varies and mostly includes the elders and some educated or enlightened members of the community. The function of these units is to sort out routine problems arising within the community related to matrimonial or property disputes. These councils used to punish offenders in the form of social boycott or by imposing fine. But nowadays these bodies mostly act as mediator. Any one not agreeing to the decision awarded by the *biradari* or the *panches* is free to go to court of law. But in such cases, the *biradari* will normally give testimony in the court against the wrong-doers.

The Sikh Jhinwars profess Sikhism and worship *Guru Granth Sahib* and the ten Gurus. The sacred places visited by them are the famous *gurdwaras* at Amritsar, Anandpur Sahib, Patna Sahib, Nankana Sahib (now in Pakistan) and Paonta Sahib (in Himachal Pradesh.)

The Hindu Jhinwars are staunch devotees of the goddess Durga and other Hindu deities. Their sacred places include Hardwar and Vaishno Devi (in Jammu). The Jhinwar have a sacred shrine at Chiri near Jammu, where there are temples of different subgroups.

Services of a Brahman or a *gurdwara granthi* are availed of on different occasions. The major festivals of these people are Diwali, Dussehra, Holi, Lohri and Baisakhi. During the post-Independence years, some non-Sikh Jhinwars had embraced Sikhism and among Hindus some have become followers of the Arya Samaj. They have traditional folk songs and folk tales in praise of the Goddess Durga.

The Jhinwars interact with other local communities on festivals and festivities. Their traditional association with water confers such purity on them that they can enter any Hindu kitchen, even a Brahman's *chauka*. On marriage and other occasions where food has to be prepared for a large number of people, they are engaged in cooking and serving the food.

Economically, they interact with all the major communities of Punjab, be it Brahman, Khatri, Bania or any one of the agricultural communities by doing miscellaneous services such as cooking food, running *dhabas*, providing agricultural labour. In the sphere of politics, they keep close association with other backward communities. As members of various political parties, they take active part in the political system.

Religiously, being staunch devotees of the goddess Durga, they partake in the *puja* and ceremonies along with other communities. Being proud of having contributed in the advent and spread of *khalsa panth*, they also visit *gurdwaras* and take part in *langars*.

Their literacy rate is quite low and it was particularly so before India attained independence. Now they are sending their children to schools and some have also received higher education. They fully utilize the health services provided by the government dispensaries and hospitals. As the traditional water-carriers, they are aware of the advantages of drinking clean water and personal hygiene. The Punjab government has provided electricity to all the villages in the state including those inhabited by Jhinwar. They are also utilizing communication amenities by using radio sets and, in urban areas, many of them have television sets.

The rapid industrialization and modernization of Punjab has resulted in their taking advantage of various employment opportunities coming in their way. They have taken up jobs in government agencies and factories. The self-employment schemes and the bank loans offered by the nationalized banks are being used by them to improve their economic conditions.

A.K. BHATIA

# KABIRPANTHI

The followers of Bhagat Kabir, who was the disciple of Ramanand are called Kabirpanthis. Bhagat Kabir was born at Banaras and he was adopted by a Muslim Julaha. According to a story, Kabir desired to be a disciple of Ramanand but he refused him as he was a Muslim. One day Kabir lay down on the stairs by which Ramanand went to bathe in the Ganges. The moment Ramanand touched Kabir with his foot he said 'Ram Bolo' which Kabir took as his *gurumantra*. After initial reluctance Ramanand took Kabir as his disciple. As far as the origin is concerned, the Julahas and the Chamars have the same origin. The difference lies in their occupation. The Julahas do not work in leather and they are considered as equals both by those who belong to either Hinduism or Islam and they are artisans. Rose (1919: 413) states that traditionally there were two divisions of the Julahas namely the Deswal and the Telis. The Muslim Julahas observe the Islamic, customs and festivals. The Hindu Julahas are termed as the Kabirpanthis and the Ramdasia respectively, who are engaged in the weaving instead of shoe-making. Rose further states:

'The Ramdasis are the followers of Ram Das, the Chamar who was a *chela* of Lakhmir. Having abandoned his calling as a shoe-maker, he took up weaving and followed the teaching of the *Granth*. The Ramdasi do not eat, smoke or intermarry with the Chamar. . . . Some of their *gots* are: Bhangar, Barah, Berwal, Sokri, Chohan, Saroe, Samjar, Senhmar, Mati and Goru.'

The Kabirpanthi have been recognized as a Scheduled Caste. According to the *Census of India* (1981), their total population is 56,888 individuals, which includes 30,535 males and 26,353 females. They are weavers by profession and use either *khadi* (handloom) or *kumbal* (pitloom) for weaving. We find Koli-Julahas, Chamar-Julahas, Mochi-Julahas, Ramdasi-Julahas and so forth. 'It is probable that after a few generations these men drop the prefix which denotes their low origin and become Julahas pure and simple' (Ibbetson, 1919: 302).

They speak Punjabi language and use Gurmukhi script. The males wear *kameez*, *pyjama* and turban, while their female wear *salwar*, *kameez* and *dupatta*. The males who are educated and working in the government offices wear trousers, shirts and put on suits during winter. Those who are Radhaswamis are vegetarian. They may take egg, onion, garlic, *masur dal* but not alcoholic drinks. It may be mentioned here that those who are non-vegetarian take chicken and mutton only. Wheat is their staple food, rice is taken occasionally. *Makki di roti* and *sarson da sag* are relished especially during the winter season. *Dal* such as *moong, masur, moth, urad* and gram are taken either for lunch or dinner. Consumption of vegetables has increased recently. Mustard and groundnut oils are the cooking media. Tea, *lassi* and curd are consumed in sufficient quantity. Alcoholic drinks are taken by the males especially to celebrate birth of a male child or during marriage ceremonies. Those who follow Sikhism do not smoke.

The Julahas are endogamous and are divided into different exogamous *gots*. Some of the *gots* are Kore, Sampla, Bungar, Mahimi, Mahto, Khokhar, Nigha, Chuan, Bhatia, Sandhu, Kaler, Siman, Sian, Karda, Sidhu and Mall. Marriages are arranged when the boys and girls attain adulthood. There are no specific symbols of marriage among the married women. However, some of the girls use *sindur* in the hair parting, glass bangles, earring, nose-ring during marriage ceremony. Dowry in kind is given at the time of marriage, according to the financial condition of the girl's parents. The rule of residence among them is patrilocal. Divorce is permitted under very special circumstances, if both husband and wife are not in a position to make adjustments with each other. Barreness or desire to have a male child are other reasons to seek divorce. Compensation known as *kharcha* is to be given to the aggrieved party. Both the husband and wife have equal rights to ask for divorce. Children of a divorced couple are looked after by the mother till they attain adulthood. Later on if the children like, they may return to their father. In most of the cases children prefer to stay with their mother. Remarriage is also allowed.

The families are mostly joint families though there is an increase at present in the number of nuclear families. The sons inherit equal shares of the property of their father. The eldest son gets succession. The women attend to the household chores, look after the domestic animals, help in the various processes of weaving. However, they have low status, and do not control the family purse. The midwife names the child in consultation with elderly ladies of the family. Marriage rituals are performed at the bride's residence. The parents of the boy and the girl negotiate a match for marriage with the help of a *vichola*, or matchmaker. Engagement ceremony, known as *mangani*, takes place when some gifts, known as *shagun* is given to the boy. *Roti* is served to the groom's party by the girl's parents. Consummation of marriage is at the bridegroom's house. They cremate their dead and the bones are immersed in the Ganga. They have their own *panchayat*, which looks into various disputes related to marriage, engagement, etc. However, it is not as powerful at present as it was in the past. The Sikhs among them worship *Guru Granth Sahib*, while the Hindus visit temples to offer their prayers. The sacred specialists serving them are from other communities.

They have interdining relationship with the Ramdasi Sikhs. They accept food from different castes except the Chamar and Balmiki. There are no restrictions in sharing water source, and place of worship with other communities. The community has teachers, administrators, individuals in white-collar jobs and persons in defence services.

Their outlook towards formal education, modern medicare and family planning programmes is positive. There are few boys and girls who have been educated upto graduate level. They make use of health services offered by the government hospitals. Handpumps are the source of drinking water for them. They listen to radio, visit cinema and a few families have television sets. Firewood and cow-dung cakes are the fuel resources used. Their attitude towards saving is positive.

SWARAN SINGH

# KAMBOH/KAMBOJ

The educated persons among the Kamboj of Punjab and Haryana prefer to call themselves Kamboj. The term is spelt differently as Kamboj (Nehru, 1961: 110), Kamboja, Kambhoja (Majumdar, 1966: 904), Kamoh (Middletone, 1923: 344) and Koombho (Forbes, 1973: 271), Kambos (Ibbetson, 1916). The etymology of the word currently suggests that they are related to the places and people such as Kanbi (Pocock, 1972: 60), Kunbi (Sherring, 1974: 99), Kabui, Kamta, Kamti (Chib, 1982: 102), Kabui (Habib, 1982: 8A), Kama or Kaman, Khambri, Khambayat, Cambay (Habib, 1982: 14A); Kambodge, Kambodia, Kampuchea, and most probably Kambe, Kamo, Kamu, Kambo (Murdock, 1959), Khampa and Kamaon. It may also be noted that almost all the people referred to above belong to the lower stratum of dominant agricultural castes of their respective regions. For example the Kanbis of Gujarat are related to Patels as Kamboj of Punjab are related to Jats, and Kamas of Andhra Pradesh are related to the Reddies. The position of these communities has to be understood with reference to their history, which most probably they have in common, and a very brief account of this is in order.

Though references to the Kambojas, and the areas they ruled, are available in several works on ancient history, yet no authentic history theirs is available. Dardi (1979), Kamboj (1980) and Thind (1973), have tried to reconstruct it, but their ethnic bias decreases its utility and reliability. However, from the references given by these authors (particularly Dardi) collected from other sources, it may be concluded that the Kambojas, ancestors of the Kambos, migrated from Badakhshan area in Pamir mountains, now in southern Russia, at least three thousand years back. Buddha Prakash (1964: 154), Vidyalankar, Stein, trans. Kalhan (1900: 136), Nehru (1967: 210), Sircar (1963: 251, 57), Smith, Faucher, G.C. Gokhale, Bimla Charn Law and several others came to the conclusion that the Kambojas had their principalities in north-western India, i.e. in Jammu & Kashmir, Afghanistan, Kabul and Kandahar. A *rishi*, Kamboj Opmaneu, is mentioned in the *Rig Veda*. Arthur Anthony MacDonell and R.C. Majumdar take them as an Aryan group, and several authors trace their relationships with Afghans and Iranians. In the *Ramayana* of Balmiki by Bhagwan Dass Gautam, the horses of the Kambojas are compared to those of Lord Indra, and

Sugriva urges Shatbal to search for Sitạ in the land of the Kambojas.

In the *Mahabharata* they are referred to as the people in white clothes who came for a sacred bath at Kurukshetra. Two of their princes, Sudakshana and Chandra Verma (of Dhote *got*) participated in the battle on the side of the Kurus, along with one *akshuhni* army of Kambojas, Yavanas and Shakas. The latter two were commanded by the former. It is stated that the Kamboja, warriors, after bathing, recited some hymns, or *mantras* and wearing white clothes moved to fight the Pandavas. Ultimately Arjuna killed Sudakshana and Dhruystdhumna killed Chandra Verma. In this epic there is also mention of Karan and Duryodhana conquering Kambojdesh; and the Kambojas presented to Yudhisthira deer skins, three hundred camels, and hundreds of maidservants, elephants and ponies. Kambojas are also stated to have conquered Mathura.

B.C. Law, K.P. Jayaswal, and Romila Thapar (1977: 58) mention Kamboj Mahajanapad among sixteen states to the north-west of Ghandhar during Buddhist times. Romila Thapar noted that Kambojas changed from monarchy to republic during 600-321 B.C. Before 530 B.C. King Cyrus of Persia crossed Hindu Kush and received tribute from the Kambojas. According to Rapson (1968: 105) Ỳasaka in *Nirukta*, a text of 500 B.C., tells us that the speech of the Kambojas differed in certain respects from the ordinary indigenous speach of north-western India.

The Kambojas were subjugated by the Mauryas, who took them into their army and also dispersed them in different parts of India. V.A. Smith notes that Ashoka sent monks to propagate Buddhism among people such as Kambojas, who inhabited territories situated on the boundaries of his empire, and who perhaps, used to pay tribute to him. One branch of these people went to Gujarat, where they are reported to have their capital at Dwarka. The preponderance of Kanbis in this area, and the name of Cape of Cambay (Khambat), besides historical references and oral traditions bear testimony to this. Besides, the fact that some *gots* of the Marathas, e.g. Chandi, Dhote, are found among the Kambos of Punjab confirm the ethnic affinity among these people. Others were pushed towards east and dispersed in eastern Uttar Pradesh and Bengal, where they are known as Kunbis; Andhra, where they are known as Kammas and in the Himalayas, where they are called Khampas. Towards the beginning of the Christian era, many had lost the old glory and it is during these times that the Kambojas were included among the twelve Kshatriya tribes who had fallen as *mlechhas*.

It is from Utkal that the overseas migration of the Kambojas started, which dates back to first century A.D. and they went to that land, which would be known as Kambodia/Combodia. Detailed account of the formation of their state, and the continuation of their rule till Prince Norodom Sihanouk is available. Thapar (ibid, 179) noted sea trade between the Pallavas and the Kambojas of Kambodia during A.D. 500. Majumdar (1966: 224) mentions that the Burmese king on one occasion seized a princess sent by the Ceylonese king to the king of Kambodia in twelfth century A.D. Majumdar (ibid.: 24) holds that in the Pala Kingdom the rulers belonged to Kamboja family, and notes (ibid.: 736) the decline of Kamboja empire around A.D. 1001. Not all the Kambos, however, migrated and many remained in this region as Majumdar observes that the Abdal *got* of the Kamboj paid tribute to the Khalifa during A.D. 813-33, but their principality fell and they became Muslims. General Shahbaz Khan, a Kamboj, was a *mansabdar* and incharge of a contingent of five thousand soldiers during the reign of Akbar and he first served in Assam and then in Gujarat. Beside him, several other nobles belonged to this community.

Sultanpur Lodhi remained the headquarters of Guru Nanak, and as a major chunk of the Kamboj population lived in this area, Kambos were among those people who became Sikh at an early stage. Bhai Mani Singh, Bhai Diala, Bhai Sati Dass, S. Sukha Singh, Akali Phula Singh are some of the important Sikhs who hailed from this community.

According to Ibbetson (1916: 139), in 1881 the Kambos constituted 6 per cent of the population of Punjab, 12 per cent of them living in princely states, and 4 per cent in British territory. However, their actual population was higher, because many of them reported themselves as Kamboj. Clubbing these two categories together Maclegan (1892: 343) totalled their number at 1,98,725 in 1921; 1,46,687 returning them as Kamboh and 52,038 as Kamboj. According to 1931 census their population figure stood at 2,39,355.

According oral traditions, the Kamboj came to Punjab from Mathura, and it is considered probably that the Mughal rulers settled them in this region to increase agricultural output as they are still known among the best of intensive farmers. However, the possibility of their having been here since antiquity cannot be ruled out. An analysis of their habitation pattern shows that they lived along the rivers, where settled agriculture was easy. Starting from the west, their main concentration towards the middle of the nineteenth century, was along the Ravi, particularly in Kasur and Chuhnian *tahsils* of Lahore district and in the Montgomery district along the Satluj. Another major concentration of them was at the confluence of the Satluj and Beas in Kapurthala and Jalandhar districts, from where it continues along the Satluj and the Beas upto Fazilka. Again, starting from the area adjacent to Chandigarh along the Ghaggar beyond Sirsa district, one finds Kamboj villages. Similarly another concentration of them lies along the Markanda in Ambala, Kurukshetra, Karnal, Muzaffarnagar and Saharanpur districts along the Jamuna.

During the last decades of the nineteenth and the first quarter of the twentieth century they moved to Sheikhupura, Layalpur and Montgomery districts, now in Pakistan. During the 1930s, they purchased land in Ganganagar district, now in Rajasthan, as a canal was being dug there for irrigation. After Partition, of India, Hindu Kamboj from Montgomery settled in Fazilka and Abohar *tahsils* of Ferozepur district and then migrated further to Sirsa and Fatehabad areas of Hissar. Sikh Kamboj who migrated from Pakistan settled in Ferozepur and Zira *tahsils* of Ferozepur district, Amritsar, Kapurthala, Jalandhar and Patiala, from where they further moved towards Karnal, Kurukshtera, Saharanpur and Tarai areas of Uttar Pradesh.

Among the Kamboj most of the Sikhs take almost all non-vegetarian food items. Mainly Hindus are vegetarian. Wheat, pulses and vegetables, are the staple food for all. None avoids garlic or onion. All prefer *desi ghee*, i.e. home-made clarified butter, but vegetable oil is also being used. Alcoholic drinks are consumed more by Sikh Kamboj. The Hindus and Muslims use tobacco. Change in food habits is characterized by the increasing use of vegetables, fruits, meat, eggs and alcohol.

The Kamboj of this region are divided into two sections or subcastes, which are by and large endogamous. These sections are the aggregates of fifty-two and eighty-four *gots* called *bawun* and *chaurasi gotia* respectively. The latter are sometimes called Kalmi (pen wielders) Kamboj also, because many among them took to trade, commerce and clerical jobs, and thus developed cultural differentiation, as the former were predominantly agriculturists.

In addition, the community is divided into different religious groups. Many of them are Muslims, most of whom live in Pakistan, but majority of Muslims living at Malerkotla are Kamboj. The Hindu Kamboj of Punjab live in cities such as Patiala and Amritsar, but most of those who migrated from Montgomery live in Ferozepur, Jalalabad, Fazilka and Abohar *tahsils* Sikh Kamboj are concentrated mostly in Sultanpur Lodhi, Kapurthala, Nakodar, Nurmahal, Patiala, Rajpura, Zira, Jandiala Guru and Amritsar *tahsils*. The Sikh Kamboj form over

3 per cent of the Sikhs in Punjab, and a few of them, follow Namdhari and Nirankari sects.

These divisions into subcastes, religious and occupational categories mostly regulate marriage alliances while inter-subcaste marriages have started taking place, interreligion marriages are rare, particularly between Muslim and non-Muslim Kamboj. On the whole, religious divisions seem to have gone a long way in cutting across caste affiliations among the Kamboj of Punjab. Besides, both of these types of divisions influence the political orientations of the people.

Rose (1919: 524) lists the *bawan gots* among them as: Abdal, Ajaipal, Angyare, Bhandari, Barrar, Ban, Baneyak/Wanyayak, Pathane, Banuri, Batti, Begi, Chatrath, Chandi, Dhote, Dhanju, Dasre, Gallon, Hande, Josan/Joshan, Jammu/Jamon, Joie, Jaure, Jahani, Jaj/Judge, Jatmal, Jhand, Karse, Kaure, Khindhi/Khitte, Lore, Lal, Mutti/Matte, Mehrok, Mahesi, Momi/Mome, Nagpal, Nandan/Nandhe, Naru, Nagre, Pandhu, Pathan, Rattanpal, Rao, Sandhe, Shahi, Surme, Sahige, Samme, Soie, Sarkure, Thind, Totie, Takhe, Tarni/Turne. Here the number has gone higher than fifty-two because of the difference in the list of various writers.

Rose names only six of the eighty-four *gots*, but other authors have given an exhaustiive list of these after considerable verification. Some of these are: Aglawe, Angotre, Ambre, Sarkure, Soni, Soi, Solehre, Soki, Sanik, Sandhere, Suhage, Senapti, Harse, Kalre, Kosle, Kukar, Kalas, Khokhar, Khinde, Gainde, Gagre, Gugan, Gandi/Gandhi, Gose, Gaure, Gilawe, Giele, Gadre, Ghasite, Chivere, Chauphal, Chichare, Chamre, Chirye, Chimre/Chimne, Chine, Chachot, Chanane, Jangle, Jaman, Jham, Jhand, Thathe, Dolyan, Dehte, Dode, Dange, Dare, Dhill, Taprie, Tagal, Topchi, Thegre, Dutane, Dehele, Daral, Dhawre, Nepal, Nuri, Nibber, Nagamber, Nohrie, Pandhe, Phokni, Bargote, Bagyan, Behar, Bahman, Bastaux, Bahram, Basra, Basi, Banjal, Badban, Bangare, Mande, Makker/Makaure, Machhlie, Mall, Mumsarang/Sarange, Maile, Multani, Latumbe, Late, Lehange, Langhere, Lande.

The community carries memories of its Kshatriya past, which is supported by the commonness of some of their *gots* with the Kshatriya and Rajputs. At the same time there seems to be an agreement on their placement among the Vaishyas in the contemporary world, which is organized on the basis of occupation and ownership of wealth.

With a few exceptions the community observes the rule of religious, caste and subcaste endogamy. As the demarcation between subcastes is not clear to most people, caste becomes a more effective endogamous group, but inter-religion marriages do take place among the Hindu and Sikh Kamboj. Both village and *got* exogamy is observed by the Hindu and Sikh Kamboj.

In the case of marriage taking place before reaching adulthood, the *gauna*, or *muklawa* ceremony would take place in the third, fifth or seventh (odd) year after marriage.

Marriages among all the Kamboj are contracted by mutual negotiations among the near kinsmen. A Kamboj marriage has generally been monogamous, but in exceptional cases (among rich people, or in case a couple does not have a child, or a male child) polygyny has taken place.

Dowry is given by the well-to-do families only. Groom's people offer *vari* (clothes and ornaments) to the girl, while the bride's family offers the groom *daj* (clothes, ornaments, utensils and furniture, etc.).

The Kamboj rule of residence is patrilocal, and in the modern urban setting, neolocal families are being established. Divorce is very rare as kinship pressures are quite strong. However, in case of extreme maladjustment or adultery it is possible. Both men and women may seek divorce. If a man seeks it, he may have to pay the dowry back in case the divorce takes place within a short period from marriage. If a woman seeks it, she may have to leave her dowry. The children generally live with their father. Both widowers and widows can remarry, so can a divorced man and a woman.

Significant changes are taking place in the system of marriage among the Kamboj. Age at marriage has been rising and instead of there being a time gap, engagement and marriage now tend to take placc in quick succession. *Punn* (without exchange) form of marriage has become a rule. As far as the rules regarding exchange of gifts is concerned, the emphasis on ornaments (*gehne*) for the girls is yielding fast to more gifts (*daj*) for the boy's side. Strict adherence to patrilocal rule of residence is giving in, and among the educated persons, number of neolocal families is increasing.

The predominant form is joint family, but in urban areas nuclear family type is emerging. Relationship between father-in-law and daughter-in-law, a man and his younger brother's wife are marked by avoidance; while those between a man and his elder brother's wife and wife's sister may be described as joking relationships.

The main causes of family conflict are property, woman and land. Conflict between daughter-in-law and mother-in-law is usual and leads to the break-up of families. Among brothers, land is the general cause of conflict. With the acquisition of education, technological and political know-how by the younger generation the intergenerational conflict is increasing and the elderly people are losing importance.

The property is inherited along the male line, in which all the sons get equal share. Daughters are given dowry, protection and gifts on different lifecycle ceremonies. Laws about the equal distribution of family property among all the male and female descendants have not yet got a following as it is only rarely that the daughters lay claim to parental property, and if they do, it leads to straining of relations with their brothers. Generally, the girls give up their share in favour of their brothers.

Women's role in various activities differs slightly in different areas. Except in the Majha area, and among the people migrating from there to the colonies in west Punjab, now in Pakistan, where they worked only within the house, women did participate in agricultural operations, tended animals, in addition to fetching water, collecting fuel and doing other household chores. Nowhere is there notable restriction on women's participation in social ceremonies and religious functions, except in case of Muslim women. They seldom participate in politics at higher level, but in household affairs they play a significant role. By and large men control boys and women control girls. The status of Kamboj women is however lower than that of men, but their role in family management is more than men's.

In some cases an *akhand path* (non-stop recital of *Guru Granth Sahib*) performed after the birth of a male child, or before a marriage takes place. After such a *path*, relatives are given a feast and clothes. The mother of a new-born is given purificatory bath after thirteen days in some cases. She shuns heavy work before delivery.

Marriage rites vary from one religious group to another. Sikh Kamboj take four rounds of the *Granth Sahib*, whereas Hindus make seven *pheras* around the fire lit on a *vedi*, or a raised platform, while the Brahman priest recites *shlokas*. In all the cases the groom's people attending the marriage are treated with a feast by the bride's father.

The Hindu and Sikh Kamboj cremate their dead. Sikhs immerse the remains in a stream in Kiratpur, near Anandpur Sahib. Mourning terminates on any convenient day before the seventeenth day. In the case of Sikhs it concludes with *bhog* of *saptahik path*, after recital of the *Guru Granth Sahib* for seven days.

The Kamboj along with the Sainis and Arains are known for intensive cultivation and for orchards and growing vegetables. Their settlements are spread around rivers, streams, canals, or in areas where water can be drawn through tube wells. They tend to have settlements excusively of their own, but now after Partition multicaste villages have come up. Though there are some big Kambo landlords, on an average, one Kambo has less land than an average Jat, and many, particularly in princely states, have been tenants.

The Kamboj, as an agriculturist community, are engaged in production of vegetables, fruits or cereals specifically for commercial purposes, along with animal husbandry. They took to trade and commerce and other professional occupations long back and there are many who called them Khatri, a trading caste. Children do help their parents in agriculture, but by and large they are not wage-earning child labourers. Generally they are governed by the laws made by the state, but the traditional *panchayats* have not totally withered away, minor problems are still solved by the *panchayats.* They have the reputation of being a peace-loving community and incidences of crime among them are very rare.

Most of the Kamboj of Punjab are Sikh. They constitute a little over 3 per cent of the Sikh society, and are dispersed throughout the state.

They carry oral traditions, have rich accounts on them in history books and have written some books on their own history. In earlier times the Kambos were known for their white horses. They had been publishing *Kamboj Samachar* from Jalandhar. *Jai Kamboj* is now being published from Chandigrah. They sing folk songs which they share with other communities inhabiting the region to which they belong. At present it is difficult to associate any music with the Kamboj, but Bishan Singh Kamboj (1980: 336) from etymological evidence concludes that *rag* Kamboji and *ragnis* Khambhati and Kamboda are the contributions of this community.

Traditionally, this community has been placed in the middle rung of society having commensal relations with all the castes except the artisans and Scheduled Castes. Brahmans have been serving them food and accepting all sorts of food from them. They visit the same shrines the high castes visit. They have also been patronizing the serving castes as their *jajmans.*

Now the community is fast amalgamating into the newly developing modern socio-economic set-up. They took to trade, commerce and other urban occupations long back and many of their *got* names are common with Khatris and Aroras, the two urban communities of Punjab. Several industrialists and businessmen hail from this community. Now there are over twenty teachers in the universities, about fifty college teachers and hundreds of school teachers in Punjab.

There are a few poets and writers among them, more than a thousand in white-collar jobs, over fifty are doctors, engineers, army officers and gazetted officers. It has a good number of political leaders at village block and district levels and few members at the state legislative assembly. Two political leaders from this community, have held the charge of the state's cabinet minister more than once. This community is well integrated in the economic, political, social and administrative system of the country.

They make use of all systems of medicines and are not averse to family welfare programmes. They fetch their drinking water from tubewells or handpumps and try to make use of different development schemes. In the use of mass media and communication such as radio, televison, cinema, railways and electricity, they do not lag behind other agricultural communities. They make use of canals and tube wells for irrigation and as good agriculturists, they use all sorts of nutrients, insecticides and machinery. Being frugal by nature they make good use of banks.

P.S. JAMMU

# KAMBOH/KAMBOJ (MUSLIM)

The Kamboh (Muslim) is one of the finest cultivator communities in the state. They are hard working, but they do not engage themselves as gardeners like the Arains. They have perhaps migrated from the west and have high concentration in Kapurthala, Patiala, Jalandhar. They trace their origin from Persia or Garh Gajni. The Kamboh and the Arains are stated to be closely related. Earlier the distinction was at religious levels. The Arains were mostly Hindus. Now the Kamboh may either be a Muslim, Hindu or a Sikh and the Arains are Muslims. The Arains grow vegetable like the Muslims. But the Kambohs also engage themselves in agriculture; business and trade, private and government services. There are two divisions of the Kambohs, i.e. Qalmis and Khakis. The Qalmi Kambohs engage themselves in literary activities while the Khaki Kambohs deploy themselves in agriculture. The Kambohs are also termed as Kambojs.

According to Rose (1911: 444), the popular accounts of the origin of the name Kamboh are (1) a powerful Raja of the solar race whose capital was at Ajudhia, marched to Derat and having killed Parmar, its Raja, took possession of his kingdom. He founded Warangar and his son established another town, which he named Dejapur and the cities of Lambani and Gajni. The latter was his capital, and lay near the city of Kamboh the peninsular south of Gujarat. At the Solono festival, when he was performing a religious rite, he was attacked by an enemy who had conspired with his *purohit*; his city was plundered and its people massacred. Of those who escaped some fled to Samana along the Ghaggar, passing by Jaipur and Sirhind, on their way, thence spread over the country between the Jamuna and the Satluj and after wandering through the country watered by the Satluj and Beas scattered over the whole of Punjab. They are called Kamboh because they came from Gajni near Kamboh. Others assert that the name is a corruption of *Kam Budh* (man of little intellect) because they did not take up arms on the Solono day, but preferred to die. (2) Raja Sodakush, a Kamboh of the solar race and descendant of the God Chander Burman sided with the Kauravas in their fight with the Pandavas. He perished with nearly all his men in the battlefield and those who escaped settled in Nabha and came to be called Kambji whence Kamboh. (3) Kamboh is said to be compounded of *Kai* and

*Anboh* and they are said to be descended from Kai dynasty of Persia to which the emperors Kai Kans, Kai Khusro, Kai Kubad, Kai-Lehreshab and Darius all belonged. When they migrated to Punjab, they came to be called Kai-ambohs or Kambohs. (4) Hazrat Abdulla, son of Zuber was sent with a large army to conquer Persia, where he settled and built many huts on the bank of the river. The Persians could not understand their tongue (Arabic) so they became Kam-go, or taciturn.

The first account is the one favoured by the Kambohs themselves but the fact remains that Solono festival is not observed by them, because they regard it as inauspicious. They do not observe the Solono or tie the *rakhri*; at the *pheras* their *purohits* proclaim Garh Gajni or Ghaggar Bas as their original home; their *gots* correspond with those of the Brahmans and Kshatriya; they perform the *parojan* or *bandhan* ceremony; they worship weapons at Dussehra and wear them at weddings; they cut the *jand* tree and sacrifice a he-goat at a marriage (Rose, 1919: 444).

The Kamboh (Muslims) are concentrated in different parts of Punjab including Sanam, Jalandhar, Ferozepur, Malerkotla, Amritsar, Kapurthala areas. They have eighty-four *gots* and the names of all these eighty-four *gots* are specified in *Tahreek-e-Kamboj*. The Kamboh are also called Kamboj. It has now been reported that the Kamboh are Khatri and since the times of Lord Buddha, they were engaged in varied occupations. Mostly they engage themselves in agriculture. The Hindu, Muslim and the Sikh Kambohs have common *gots*. The Kambohs were having their estates in Multan since the epic of *Mahabharata*. It was the Kamboh community, who fought against the Mughals, with the result they lost their kingdom. After the defeat, the king of Multan, Wali Sahib, was imprisoned and he embraced Islam. Some of the Kambohs later on also embraced Islam. This account is based on their current self-perception.

The Kambohs Muslims have two groups: (i) *bawan-gota*, i.e. fifty-two *gots*, (ii) *chaurasi-gota*, i.e. eighty-four *gots*. It is said that when Garh Gajni was destroyed, a Chaurasi Kamboh took refuge with a bard named Kammachi and so the ancestor of the *bawan-gota* severed all connections with him. The Kamboh first settled in Lalachi, in Patiala, where they founded thirty-two villages. The Lalachi Kambohs claim to be *bawan-gotas*. A section of these Kambohs embraced Islam only under Jahangir and hence the mass of the *bawan-gotas* became Muslims, while the bulk of eighty-four *gotas* remained Hindus. The two most important centres of the *bawan-gotas* are Sanaur and Sunam in Patiala. The 'fifty-two' are in their own estimation superior to the 'eighty-four-*gotas*'. The latter are found in the Banur, Dhuri Taluqs of Patiala, in Malerkotla, Nabha and Amritisar.

The members of the Kamboh community speak Punjabi and Urdu with the members of their own family and their own community. With others who speak in Hindi, Punjabi or Urdu, they speak in the language of that individual. They write in the Perso-Arabic script. Males wear shirt and *lungi* and cap or turban, while their females wear *salwar*, *kameez* and *dupatta* and *burqa*, when they have to move out of their house. The Kambohs claim the status of religious and linguistic minority in the state of Punjab.

They take *roti* as their staple food, with pulses such as *moong*, *moth*, *urad*, *gram* and *masur*. There is no restriction for them to take eggs, mutton and chicken, onion or garlic. Vegetables which they grow in sufficiently large quantity are also consumed by them. *Sarson da sag* and *makki di roti* are eaten during the winter months. Those who can afford, use *desi ghee* which is prepared from butter for making *tarka* and smearing the *roti*. Groundnut and mustard oil is used as cooking medium. Alcoholic drinks are not taken even on special occasions of marriage or birth of a child. However, tea with plenty of milk is taken frequently. *Lassi* is very commonly used among the Kambohs. Consumption of fruits is very limited. However, during the season, mangoes and bananas are commonly used by them.

As mentioned at the outset, the Kamboh community is divided into eighty-four *gots* the main function of which is to regulate marriage alliances. Common *gots* being Sianae, Rattanman, Sondh, Sindh, Kore and Jore. The Kambohs considers themselves high and other communities also hold them in high esteem.

Kambohs also belong to Hindu and Sikh religion, apart from the majority adhering to Muslim religion. But the Muslim Kambohs marry among the members of their own religion and community.

When boys and girls are about eighteen-twenty years of age, they get married. Marriage is arranged by negotiations with the help of a *vichola* and earlier, they used to get married by exchange (*batta-satta)*, which is no more in practice today.

Monogamy is the common form of marriage among the Kamboh Muslims, though polygamy is permitted in their religion. Earring and glass bangles are used by married ladies. The father of the girl, depending upon his financial position, announces the amount of *mehar* in the presence of a *maulavi* called *alam* and two witnesses. The amount of *mehar* may vary from rupees thirty-two to any higher amount. Dowry in kind consists of clothes to the girl, bed, a *peti* (big trunk), utensils, *razais* and ornaments of gold.

After marriage, the married girl lives with her husband in his parental house. Divorce is allowed under very special circumstances. The traditional *panchayat* of the community decides all such cases. They fine an individual, who leaves his wife with her parents. And at the same time, if the parents of the girl do not allow their daughter to go to her in-laws' house they are pressurized to let their daughter to go to her husband. At the same time, if the married girl of four children is forced to stay with her parents, a fine which ranges from two to four thousand rupees is imposed on the husband and has to be paid in cash by him and is also forced to take along with him. For such matters they do not have to approach the *panchayat* again. Sororate and levirate remarriages with the sanction of the traditional *panchayat* are also allowed. There is an increase in age at marriage. Divorce is now not encouraged and the incidence of divorce is on decline.

Vertically extended type of family is more prevalent among the Kamboh Muslims. Avoidance relationship is maintained between mother-in-law and son-in-law, daughter-in-law and father-in-law, sister-in-law and brother-in-law; joking relationship is observed between the sister-in-law and brother-in-law. Conflicts in joint family are sometimes related to property, distribution of work for male members and sharing of income. However, it is for the head of the family to resolve all these issues by mutual discussion and sometimes he has to impose his orders. The sons inherit the property of their father equally, and in the absence of sons, the daughters share the same. At the same time, the eldest son gets succession. No major changes in the in-heritance rules and succession rules are observed. There is increase in the number of nuclear families and decrease in joint families.

The primary role of women is to look after their families and to attend to various household activities. In those families, whose income from the agriculture is sufficient, the women do not work in the fields, but they look after the domestic animals. Sometimes situation may so demand that women may have to help their husbands in the field as well as look after the cattle. There is no direct role in economic activities but indirectly the women do their bit by helping their husbands in the fields and saving expenses by providing extra labour in the field. Women play a constructive role in the rituals performed on birth, marriage and death. Inspite of all their contributions, women have a considerably low status.

When a woman becomes pregnant, it is an occasion of celebration in the family. During the first pregnancy, the mother-in-law and the mother give advice and put necessary restrictions on her movements. Post-delivery restrictions for one month and one week are also observed by the mother. Now this period has been reduced considerably. Post-delivery pollution period is also observed after which the birth of a male child is celebrated, and the head of the neonate is shaved within forty days. According to the financial position, silver is also given to the newly born boy on this occasion in the form of a chain or ornament. When the boys are around six-seven years of age, the ceremony of circumcision is performed when close relatives are invited. Sweet rice is served on this occasion.

Child marriage among the Kamboh Muslim community was in vogue about fifty years back. Engagement ceremony, known as *mangani*, is performed with the help of a *vichola* who communicates with both the parties. Depending upon the financial condition of the girl's parents, the ceremony of *mangani* is performed. *Mangani* is performed with *sawa rupaiya*, i.e. one rupee and twenty-five paise, to ten rupees. These coins are of silver. A gold ring is presented to the boy and bangles to the girl along with an appropriate *shagun*. The ceremony is termed *churiyan charhana*. The marriage party used to stay for two days earlier but at present the marriage party arrives in the morning and all the rituals of marriage are completed on the same day. Marriage rituals are performed at the residence of the bride and the ceremony called *nikah* is performed in the presence of two witnesses and a *maulavi*. The father of the girl agrees and the witnesses take expressed consent of the girl. This follows a feast for the marriage party, called *roti*. All the ornaments, garments, furniture, etc., are handed over to the girl in the presence of the *panchayat*. Consummation of marriage is at the bridegroom's residence.

The Kamboh Muslims are buried after death. A bath is given to the dead body which is then put into a *qabar*, dug in the north-south direction with the face towards the west. On the third day of death, all the members of the community gather at the house and recite verses from the Holy Quran.

The Kamboh depend upon land which is controlled by the individuals. They have small pieces of land for agriculture. Those who have sufficient land for cultivation are few in number. They are settled agriculturists and grow wheat and seasonal vegetables. Apart from this they engage themselves as agricultural labourers. The link with the market exists directly and the local market is fully regulated.

With the increase of population the number of those engaging themselves as casual and agricultural labourers is increasing. On holidays, children help their parents in the fields. Sometimes, a child has to drop out from school to help in the field. Agricultural produce is sold in the nearby market and payment is made in cash. They have their own traditional *panchayat* called Kamboh Panchayat which is elected by voice vote. Any elderly person, who can look after the interest of the community and can give a balanced decision on the basis of facts is nominated as the *pradhan* of the community. who is assisted by three-four members. The caste *panchayat* and formal *panchayats* are two different organizations. The *panchayat* of the Kamboh resolves disputes of its own castes. If a married girl is forced to stay with her parents or girl's parents do not allow their daughter to go to her husband's house, the caste *panchayat* looks into such matters. If a married woman who is a mother of three or four children is forced to stay with her parents, under these circumstances the caste *panchayat* has a role to play too. In the first instance, the *panchayat* tries to pressurize the guilty to correct himself. The incidence of excommunication (*hookah pani band karna*) was frequent in the past, but now it is being replaced by a fine. Apart from the cases related to marriage disputes and divorce, the *panchayat* also decides matters related to property disputes and theft.

They are the followers of Islam and Quran Sharif is their holy scripture. They offer their prayers in the *masjid* and also visit the *samadhi* of Baba Hayder Sheikh at Malerkotla on festivals. They follow all the festivals associated with Islam. They also observe Muharram, the mourning event for the Muslims. The members of Sikh and Hindu religion also join them on their festivals, and they in return exchange greetings on the eve of the Hindu and Sikh festivals. The sacred specialist may or may not be from the Kamboh community, and his function is to worship, to give religious teaching, perform marriage and birth ceremonies and death rites.

Folk songs of Punjab, which are very much common among other communities, are also sung by them. The men and women both participate in such songs or dance separately. *Dholak* or *dhol* is the instrument used on such occasions. The Kamboh exchange and accept food and water with all the Muslim communities at Malerkotla. Sometimes, such relations are also extended to other communities belonging to both Hindu and Sikh religions. They have separate burial grounds. They exchange greetings on Diwali and Id with members of other communities.

Very few among them are educated and are in the services. The community has some members who are working as teachers and as clerks in defence services. They have their own school, Kamboh High School as well as a Government College. But very few reach the college level. Most of them pass primary school and after that assist their parents in their traditional occupation of agriculture. The main reason for dropping out from schools is economic. Among the girls the number of drop-outs is still higher. When any individual becomes seriously ill, they approach the medical attendant for medicare. Though there is a government hospital yet they do not visit the same until a very serious case of illness.

They prefer to have around four or even more children. Most of the families have their own source of water, that is, the handpump. Being an agriculturist community, the Kamboh Muslims are mostly self-employed. They have either their own land for cultivation or work on others land for this purpose.

Various extension agencies and political parties impart various types of information that may help them to boost their agricultural production.

They get electric supply for domestic purpose and for various agricultural processes such as to run the water pump sets, threshers, etc. Cow-dung, wood and coal are used as fuel. Some of the families have water-pump sets which run on diesel engine while the others use electric motors to run their tube wells. They use both organic and chemical fertilizers and insecticides. Immunization facilities for children are availed of.

They have been given ration cards to get sugar and kerosene oil at subsidized rates. The economically poor individuals of the community have been provided with yellow cards to get loans from the natioinalized banks. Apart from this, they save some money for their future requirements. The members of their own community help each other during difficult times and contribute on the occasions of marriage and other social occasions.

SWARAN SINGH

# KAYASTHA

The name of the Kayastha is derived from either of the two Sanskrit words *kayesamsthita*, 'staying at home', or *kayastha*, i.e. 'situated in the body' (or sprung from Brahma). The community has been described as the writer class of India (Crooke, 1896: 679) and was called 'the functional or occupational type of caste' by Risley (1969: 76). In the *Encyclopaedia India* (1981: 595), the term Kayastha has been referred to as 'the most prominent term to indicate a fixed class or caste of professional writers; it first occurs in the *Visnudharmasutra* in connection with king's office and his appointed clerks preparing a document to be signed by the superintendent and stamped with the king's seal'.

Next, it is found in the *Yajnavalkya Smriti*. It was a group or class of people, who chose to enter the ministerial service of the state and came from different *varnas* and castes. In the course of time such people developed into a community and ultimately into a caste. Kane (1939: 740-2) also pointed out that the word *kayastha* did not occur in ancient *Dharamasutras* of Gautama, Apastamba, Baudhayana or Vasistha or *Manusmriti*. According to him *Visnudharmasutra* refers to *Rajasaksikas Lekhya*, which was a document written by the Kayastha appointed by the king and attested by the superintendent of that office. In the opinion of Kane, Kayastha was an officer and not the caste. Mijaksara had described Kayasthas as accountants and scribes, who were favourites of the king. Apararka explained that they were incharge of collection of the taxes. In these writings Kayasthas have been mentioned as officials and not a caste. It was Usanas, who referred to them as one of forty castes. Usanas pointed out that the first letters of *kaak* (crow), *yama* and *sthapati* (carpenter) were taken to form the word Kasyastha, which signified the embodiment of greed, cruelty, and paring.

In *Vedavyasasmriti*, the community is referred to as a subdivision of the Shudras. In these two *smritis* the Kayasthas formed a caste. In *Machhakatika* and *Mudrarakshasa* the community has been referred to as the *Lekhakar* (writer) and persons, who matter little respectively (cf. Kane, 1938-9). Kane concludes that in the first century of the Christian era, Kayastha was a mere scribe, although in some areas it formed a caste also. Lekhaka was not always a Kayastha. In *Harscarita*, the Lekhaka has been mentioned as Karanika. In the inscriptions of fifth and sixth centuries A.D., Kayastha was hardly ever mentioned. The earliest inscription in which it was referred was of Sivagana in Malawa, dated A.D. 738-9. In the opinion of Buhler (cf. Kane, 1938-9: 742), the word 'lajuka', in the fourth pillar edict of Ashoka, was the name of a writer class, which was later called Divara or Kayastha. Kane thus concludes that a Kayastha was originally an official entrusted with state or public writing work, that he generally abused his office and got rich thereby, that the office was held sometimes at least even by Brahamans and that in some territories it might have been held by separate caste. There are analogous instances of this kind. In Bengal there is a caste of Vaidyas, while there is no such caste in the Deccan, where Vaidyas (physicians) are found among several castes including the Brahamans.

In the *Affairs of the East India Company* (1812, rpt. 1984, Vol. I: 195), the prosperity of the community was noted. The account says: 'Dinagepour, called also the *havillee* of the *circar* of Penjerah, and sometimes classed with Edarckpoor, under the head of Aurangabad, was conferred by Joffer Khan, like all other great Zamindaris, towards the latter end of his government, in the first instance, on a very intelligent landholder of the caste of Koyt or writer, named Ramnahat, originally from upper Hindustan. This man was supposed to have acquired great wealth by the discovery of buried treasure, in digging tanks for the improvement of agriculture, and had therefore repeated applications from the *nazim* for pecuniary aids, under the real or feigned distress of the state. The truth may be that by amelioration and good management, in rendering productive the extensive wastes within the circle of his jurisdication, or secret enlargement of his frontiers on all sides, particularly towards Cooch Beyher, he might have realized the moral of the fable, in obtaining riches through necessary operations of husbandry, conducted with intelligence, industry and good fortune. But however, this may have been, by personal dress, and anticipating the wants or desire of the sovereign representatives, in paying large douceurs over and above his current revenue, he enjoyed the annual special privilege of administering internally his own district, without being subject like other zamindars, to either *hustahood* investigations, or the immediate control of a Mussalman aumildar.'

This account attests to the success and intelligence of the community. It also refers to the ownership of land by the community. So during British times the community had started owning land as well. This fact was also noted in the *Imperial Gazetteer of India* (Vol. XVII: 163, Vol. XII: 33-78; Vol. II: 183; Vol. V: 77). According to these accounts it was a landowning community in districts of Mandala, Etah, Fatehpur, Varanasi and Agra. It was also noted that in the Central Provinces it was a major landowning class along with Brahmans, Rajputs and Banias (*Imperial Gazetteer of India*, Vol. X: 25). These records also noted that they were a better educated community (ibid., Vol. X: 96-140, Vol. XI: 107), which in search of employment migrated to various places. It was one of the most numerous castes in the districts of Backergunge; Calcutta, Nadia, Faridpur, Gaya, Jessore, Khulina, Mandala, Midanapur, Pabna, Twenty-four Parganas.

Even Baines (1976: 38-9) had noted that principal supply of minister to Mughul regime and to the then British government was from this community. In Gujarat it was introduced from upper Ganga region by the Mughal viceroys. However, in the Deccan the well entrenched Brahmans did not leave room for this community. Still, an offshoot of this community called Prabhu settled in Bombay. The British merchants found them very useful and for sometimes the term *prabhu* and clerk were synonymous. Baines noted during his times that the main settlement of the community was in lower Bengal. And this section of the community did not intermarry with their caste fellows in Bihar. The property of this community as writer class increased in British times.

The community gradually settled in other princely states and also at the places of substantial British settlement, like Ambala. Ibbetson (1916: 263) had noted that it was a writer's class in this state, but it was not indigenous to this place. In his opinion it was found only in the administrative and commercial centres of the state. He also noted that in hilly areas of the state, the term Kayasth was used for an occupation; and was applied to members of the mixed caste formed by the intermarriage of Brahmans and Kayastha. The caste could be Mahajan; and their occupation could be Kayasth. Ibbetson (ibid.) had also noted the observation of Baines that Kayasths of hills, who were entitled to wear *janeu*, were different from Kayasthas of the plains, who were considered Shudras, and were not entitled to wear *janeu*.

Rose (1919: 436-7) had also broadly agreed with the observation of Ibbetson. He maintained that in hills the community was an accountant class, and in plains a well-known writer class. He did not mention the distinction based upon *janeu*. According to him, the Kayasthas had sprung from the body of Brahma, who had by virtue of his ascetic powers given birth to a son called Chitra Gupta. He bade this son to serve Yama Raja and make the people fulfil their *karma.* His descendants were called Kayasths or Kayakasthan or 'the one who resides in the body'.

The community can be identified at national level. But its main areas of settlement have been in Uttar Pradesh, Bihar, and West Bengal. From these areas it has migrated to various places, and got employment in various princely states. In Punjab also, the first settlements started in Jind state, and then it spread to various other places. This migration is recalled in the oral tradition. In this state, they are settled in all urban areas, as a service community.

The community uses Kayastha as surname. This is a practice unique in this area. In other states, only the name of the subcaste is used. They speak, Punjabi, Hindi and Pahari languages with its kin group. In conversation with others they often use Urdu and English. Written communication is in Gurmukhi, Devanagari, Perso-Arabic and Roman scripts. In earlier times, in British India, the community spoke Awadhi and Bhojpuri at their place of settlement (*Imperial Gazetteer of India*, Vol. X: 140; Vol. XXII: 87). At that time the normal language used by the community for correspondence was Persian (Balbour, Vol. V, 1976: 527).

In 1881, the population of the community in the state was 13,420 (*Census of India*, 1881: 321). It showed a slight increase to 13,598 in 1891, and again showed a small decline to 13,272 in 1901. In 1901 there were 797 females per thousand male population of this community (*Census of India*, 1901: Vol. 17, 347, 354). In 1901, the total population of the community was 21,49,331 (*Census of India*, 1901). In 1911, the total population of the community in the state was 13,374. Out of this 7,477 were males and 5,897 were females. Only 42 were Sikhs, and 71 were Muslims. Remaining members were Hindus. British territory accounted for 11,610 population; and native states 1,764 (*Census of India*, 1911: 262-3). In 1911, the total population of the community in India was 21,78,300 (*Census of India*, 1911: 202).

Both men and women of the community are regular non-vegetarian. It uses wheat, rice and maize as staple food and uses more rice than *roti*, but the consumption of the latter is increasing. It takes all locally used pulses, which include gram, *urad*, *moong*, *masur*, *moth* and peas. This is in marked contrast to the food habits of the community in other areas of the country, where special preference is shown for *urad.* The cooking medium consists of *vanaspati*, animal fats, groundnut, sunflower and mustard oils. Both men and women take alcoholic drinks purchased from the market. Consumption of fruit is occasional. There has been an increase in the use of pulses, vegetables and fruit. The use of non-vegetarian food has increased considerably over the years.

Some biological traits of the community were noted in early ethnographic records. The Kayasthas of Bengal along with the Brahamans and Muslims of that area; showed 'probably a blend of Dravidian and Mongoloid elements, with a strain of Indo-Aryan blood in the higher groups. The head is broad; complexion is dark; hair on the face is usually plentiful; stature is medium; nose is medium, with a tendency to broad' (*Imperial Gazetteer of India*: 294). The Mongolo-Dravidian features of the Kayasthas of Bengal were also noted by other ethnographic records. According to these records their head type was 'brachy-cephlic'; and nasal index was 70.4 (*Census of India*, 1901: 497-500).

Social divisions exist in the community at subgroup and *got* level. The community has twelve *gots*. The origin of *got* has been narrated by Rose (1919: 437). According to him, Chitragupta had two wives. From the first wife who was daughter of Manu, he got four sons—Mathur, Bhatnagar, Saksena and Srivastava. And from Sansaraman who was a *rishi's* daughter, he had eight sons—Nigam, Avshat, Gaur, Karam, Balmik, Vanaya, Kulsarsat and Suraj Dhaj. The groups of the community are named after these twelve sons. During the times of Rose not all twelve groups were represented in Punjab. In Jind only four, Mathur, Bhatnagar, Saksena and Srivastava, were found. At places, all mixed together but at places the Saksena and Srivastava did not smoke together from the same *hookah* or ate *kachchi roti*. He noted there were about eighty-four *als* of the community, and in Jind they had a Kashyap *got*. These days, subgroups which are endogamous exist in the community. However, members of the community in the state mostly belong to the four subcastes Mathur, Bhatnagar, Saksena and Srivastava. There is differentiation with hierarchy, e.g. Mathurs consider themselves as superior-most. But it does not affect marriage relations, since all subgroups are endogamous. However, even subgroup exogamy is being practised. It is also differentiated at occupational levels.

They are mainly employed in private or government services, but a large number have entered professions such as law, medicine, etc. A few are there in business as well. Although educational level of the community is generally good, yet its members have acquired variable education. Similarly, at economic level also they are relatively a well-to-do communitiy. The differentiation acts as a means of social control and indicate status. There have been no changes in surname, clan names and titles in the recent past. But the community seems to have differentiated from its places of origins, by the practice of Kayastha, Mahajan, etc., as surnames.

In its self-perception, the community considers itself of high level, but other communities consider it of medium status. It has some ambiguity in its placing in the *varna* system. A larger number of its members assert Kshatriya origin. Others maintain that it was a fifth *varna* created by Brahma to keep account of other four *varnas*. There has been much controversy as to the status of the community. In Punjab, these days it claims to be of reasonably high status. This relates to their better educational status. They are conscious of their status and believe in caste status. Others place themselves as equal to Vaishyas. The latter position is accepted by other communities, which consider it of medium status. In the earlier times the community was identified with Vaishyas, whose claims for identification with ancient Kshatriyas were not admitted. It was even claimed that at least in Bengal, Kayasthas and Shudras were aligned; but the former had higher status than the latter, but it was not unusual for the lower group to rise to a higher group in course of time (Gait, 1971: 236-7). This shows a lower placing of the community in the *varna* system, at least in parts of India, during British times.

The controversy relating to the placing of the community in the *varna* system has also been noted by Risley (1967: 92, 117). It refers to *Skanda Purana*, which recounts the episode of Parsuram raid upon Kshatriyas, the object of which was to show that the community is by birth Kshatriya, of full blood. However, owing to the observance of the ceremonies of Shudras, it was called *vratya* or incomplete Kshatriyas. Risely even referred to a judgement of the high court of Calcutta and that too by a Kayastha judge, that tried to establish that the community was Shudra, because their funeral usage was akin to that of Shudras. However, this controversy relates to the Kayasthas of Bengal. The community in Punjab has always enjoyed better status. Ibbetson had included them among miscellaneous castes along with Bisnois, Chahzangs and Kanchans. In his opinion only Kayasthas were true caste among them (1916: 259, 263).

The community practises a marriage system, which is endogamous at community level. However, in the past, intercommunity marriages had taken place. But preference was given to endogamy at the community level. Those practising exogamy at the community level, very frequently called by the surnames of the concurrence of community. Within the community, preference is given to subcaste endogamy. However, even subcaste exogamy is reported. This is in marked contrast to the community in Uttar Pradesh and Bihar, where subcaste endogamy is strictly followed. The floating population as well as the recent migrants from other areas do not intermarry with the local community. Moreover, the community with mixed blood is avoided by pure Kayasthas for settlement of marriages. Marriages are generally exogamous at village level. There is an unsubstantiated claim of exogamy at the level. These days there is no practice of hypergamy or hypogamy. In earlier times there was fear of ex-communicatioin in case somebody married a woman of low status.

Marriages are performed at adulthood and are settled by negotiations. Preference is shown to those cases, in which a family can arrange a decent marriage. The system of monogamy is the rule. The offspring of union with lower caste women (which is no longer in practice) were called *shagirdpesha*. They formed a regular caste and divided into endogamous groups, with reference to the caste of the male parent. This practice was shared with other higher castes. But *shagirdpesha* of one caste did not marry with that of another (Risley, 1969: 83-4).

All Hindu symbols of marriage are used by the community. These include vermilion, bangles, *mangalsutra*, *bindi*, finger, toe and earrings and nose stud. Generally, the bride wears a red attire at the time of marriage. The rituals of *kanyadan* exists. Dowry system is extensively practised, and it is generally given in cash. After marriage, rules of residence are partilocal. The community allows divorce by law. Compensation is provided to the aggrieved party and responsibility of the children can be given to either parents. The remarriage of male and female divorcees, widows and widowers is allowed. But in case of female divorcees or widows, full marriage ceremony is not observed. There has been a change in the rules of mariage, which have become liberal.

These days the community lives in nuclear families. However, there are few cases of vertically extended families also, and this is declining very fast. Joking relationshps exist in the families between *dewar* and *bhabi* and between *sali* and *jeeja*. Avoidence relationships exist between *sasur* and *bahu*; and between *saas* and *jawai*. These relationships show the influence of local culture. The disputes arise in the community due to matters linked to the property, and in few cases also due to the challenge to the authority of elders.

Inheritance is by male equigeniture and succession rules favour the eldest son. Women of the community have low status as compared to men. The women contribute to the family income and control family expenditure. They have role in social functions, rituals, religious sphere and mechanisms of social control. Post-delivery pollution and restrictions are observed for a variable number of days. The community observes the naming ceremony for both male and female children. *Mundan* ceremony is performed in case of male children. Marriage rituals are observed at the bride's place; and consummation of marriage takes place at the groom's place. A feast is arranged by both the parties of marriage at their respective places. The dead are cremated, and bones are immersed in the Ganga at Hardwar. The community observes pollution for thirteen days after death; after this the rituals of *pehrwan* is observed.

They have been traditionally a community employed in services. These days they are employed in government depatments as well as private establishments at various levels. They have many members in administrative services, teaching, etc. They are also well represented in medical and legal professions. It has a direct access to daily and fully regulated market on cash basis.

Kayasthas believe in various sects of Hinduism. But the main following is of Sanatan Dharma. There are also believers in Arya Samaj among them. The community worships the deity Chitragupta on all ceremonial occasions. This is because the community traces its descent from it . The families keep a photograph of the deity at their home. It was reported in the earlier records (Crooke: 679-80) that the com-munity had variable religious practices in Bengal and Bihar. In Bengal it believed in both Saktis and Vaisnavism; and in Bihar it had believed in Kabirpanth and Nanakpanth. This variability is also reflected in this state, as has been noted earlier. The community also practises the ceremony of *dawat puja* when the child starts going to the school. The sacred specialistis of the community are from the other community, i.e. Brahman. They conduct worship and impart religious teachings and also lead birth, marriage and death rites. The community observes all local festivals such as Diwali, Dussehra, Janamashtami, Ramnavami, Lohri, Basant, etc. These are of economic, social and religious importance. The Kayastha community has no traditional arts or crafts of its own but has an oral tradition, and the local folk songs are sung by both men and women. Folk tales and folk songs also exist.

It exchanges *jal* or *chal, kachcha, pukka, sidha* food with other communities. There are some cases of intercommunity marriages. They share water sources and festivals with other communities. They also share religious places, and cremation ground with other communities.

The Kayasthas have scholars, teachers, administrators, engineers and doctors in its ranks. The members of the community commonly hold white-collar jobs and are represented in defence services also. In this state, a few local political activists are there. One of them was a member of the District Congress Committee at Amritsar.

The community has benefited from the developmental activities. Education has been good for the boys and girls, who get education up to post-graduation. Boys drop out only because of lack of good performance, and girls drop out in some cases due to social reasons. Their attitude to modern medicare and modern techniques of family welfare is extremely positive. Couples prefer one or two children. They make full use of water and electricity supply system. The dissemination of information is through extension agencies, political parties and voluntary agencies. They use coal, kerosene oil, solar energy and L.P.G. gas as fuels. They have availed of the benefits of public distribution system and their attitude to savings is positive.

VIRINDER SINGH
K.C. KAYASTHA

# KHATIK

The Khatiks are good tanners and dyers of goatskin. According to a legend about their origin, Brahma assigned to them a goat's skin, bark of a tree, lac, so the Khatiks graze cattle, dye the skins of goat and tan hides with bark and lac. The Khatiks are recognized as a Scheduled Caste and according to the *Census of India*, 1981, their total population is 8,932 individuals, with 4,636 males and 4,296 females.

The Khatiks have migrated from Uttar Pradesh and those who are Hindus keep pigs, while the Musalman Khatiks are tanners and work in leather of cow and buffalo hides. Those who are Hindus speak Hindi, and Punjabi language and use Devanagari script while the Muslims speak Urdu and Punjabi and use Perso-Arabic script. The males wear shirt, *dhoti* or *lungi*, while their females wear *salwar*, *kameez* and *dupatta*. Wheat is their staple food; pulses are taken in large quantity, they also take mutton, eggs, milk and curd and smoke *bidi*.

Rose (1919: 500), states that the Khatiks are sometimes confused with the Charmrang, but the latter tans buffaloes and ox hides with lime and does not dye leather, so he ranks below the Khatik who tans and dyes only sheep and goat skins, using salt and juice of the *madar* (*Calotrois procera*) but no lime. On the other hand, the Khatiks are certainly below the Chamars because they will even act as a butcher. About the relationship of Pasi and Khatik. Rose (1916: 704) observed that 'a Pasi is closely allied to the Khatik'.

They also marry among their close relatives except those, with whom they are related by blood. The boys and girls get married between twenty to twenty-four years of age. The marriages are arranged by negotiation by the parents with the help of a *vichola*. Polygyny is allowed among the Muslim Khatiks. Vermilion is a symbol of marriage among Khatik women. Dowry is reported but it consists of five utensils only. Among Muslims the *mehar* is given. The boys and girls, after their marriage stay with their parents. Divorce and remarriage is allowed. The families are joint, vertically extended. The sons inherit the property of their father equally. The eldest son gets succession.

The women do not enjoy a high status. They look after the various household activities. Pre-delivery restrictions and post-delivery observance of pollution is reported. Postnatal restrictions on mother are also observed. Among Muslims, circumcision is performed in males. Marriage rituals are performed at the bride's residence and the marriage party, on most of occasions, returns after the marriage ceremony on the same day. The marriage is performed according to the respective religious traditions of the Khatik. The feast is given to the marriage party by the parents of the bride.

The Hindu Khatiks cremate, whereas the Muslim Khatik bury their dead. The Hindus immerse the bones in water. They have their traditional *panchayat*. They nominate a *chaudhary* to settle various disputes related to marriage, engagement, property and other petty issues. It may be mentioned here that they do not approach the court of law for settlement of their disputes. Among the Khatiks of Malerkotla, the Nawab had formed the *mohalla panchayats*, but these are no more in existence. Now, the *chaudhary* of the *mohalla* listens to various problems and arranges for an agreement between the contending parties.

As they work in tanneries and piggeries, which is not considered a clean job, the members of the high castes maintain distance and refrain from accepting food and water from them though they accept food and water from other communities. They share road and places of worship at present with the members of other communities. They have a separate cremation or burial ground.

The conditions for education and family welfare are favourable. They get medicines from hospitals. Handpumps are the source of drinking water. They use electricity. Cow-dung cakes and wood are their fuel source. Immunization programme is availed of by them. They have ration card and yellow card facility.

SWARAN SINGH

# KHATRI

The Khatri form a major part of the business community in Punjab. 'Khatri' is presented as the Punjabi version of *kshatriya*, a name given to a warrior. But Fick says 'Kshatriya corresponds to the Vedic *rajanya* and is applied to the successors of the conquering families under whose leadership the Aryan stocks had secured their new settlements in the Gangetic lands' (Tandon, 1961). The Kshatriya then were not by any means of one and the same race. They represented the political power and embodied the idea of a community which stood above the caste (Rose, 1919). Quite apart from resemblance of the names Kshatriya and Khatri, the position of Kshatriya in ancient times finds very close parallels in relation to modern Hindu castes in Punjab.

The transformation from Kshatriya to Khatri has been explained by a folk-tale (Rose, 1919) which runs as follows: Parsuram, the Brahman and the sixth incarnation of Vishnu exterminated the Kshatriya in twenty-one attacks, and not content with slaughtering the men he destroyed even the infants in the womb. So the Kshatriya women fled to Sarsut Brahmans of Kurukshetra on the Saraswati and when Parsuram demanded their surrender the Brahmans declared them as their daughters. Parsuram in his wrath made them eat *kachcha bhojan* from their hands as a test of the relationship and only when they did so, did he spare the community. So their children were called Khatris instead of Chhatris. Rose (1919) found some historicial legends which say clearly that the Khatri caste is made up of three elements that is solar, lunar and the Agni-Kula. Of these, some families became Brahmans and others remained Kshatriya. The Khatri caste occupies a different position among the business communities of Punjab. It is considered that they have a superior physique and energy. A Khatri is not merely a shopkeeper. He is considered to be belonging to one of the martial races of India.

The Khatris used to control the whole trade of Punjab and most part of Afghanistan in pre-Independence India. Even in villages, these people helped in keeping the accounts, and did the banking business in addition to sale and purchase of grain. They were considered humble dealers, shopkeepers and moneylenders by the local population. They were certainly a well-established community even before the Partition of India. They speak Punjabi and use Gurmukhi,

Devanagari, Roman and Perso-Arabic scripts. They are both vegetarian and non-vegetarian. Milk forms a part of morning and bedtime drink. Alcoholic drinks are served mostly on special occasions.

They are divided into four subcastes and each subcaste is termed with the number of houses or *ghars.* According to hierarchical order, first comes the Bahris, the group of twelve Khatri houses, followed by another fifty-two houses thus called Bunjahis and then the Sarin and Khokhran Khatris. Bahris are divided into senior: Kapur, Khanna, Malhotra or Mehra, Kakar and junior: Chopra, Talwar, Saihgal, Dhawan, Wadhaun, Tannan, Bohra or Wohra, Mahindhru. Bunjahi name is derived from *bawanja* (fifty-two) section. These are divided into subgroups: Khokhran (group of eight section), Bunjahi-Khas or Kalan (group of twelve sections), Barha or elder Bunjahi (group of forty sections), Chhota or younger Bunjahi (group of one hundred). Sarin comprise a large number of sections and is divided into two subgroups: Barha (twelve sections) and Chhota (one hundred and eight sections). The general principle of hierarchy underlying the Khatri organization is that higher the circle within which a daughter may be given in marriage, the more exalted is the social position of the family in its own group. The *got* names of Khatris are believed to have been derived from various titles of military characters, for example, Bhalla is derived from *bhall* (a spear), Bhasin from *bhas* (brilliana) and *karach* (armour).

While selecting a mate for a boy or a girl, four *gots,* namely those of father, mother, father's mother, mother's mother are avoided. The age at marriage depends on the status of the family. Child marriage remained common traditionally. In the old days though the girls were married at an early age yet the *muklawa* (consummation) took place when they reached puberty.

The marriage is arranged by the parents. Boy or girl can marry by mutual consent arranged by the parents. Monogamy is the rule. There is the tradition of joint family system. The eldest male member usually bears all the social and family responsibilities after the death of his father. All inheritance goes to the sons.

Traditionally the news of pregnancy of the daughter-in-law was sent ceremoniously to her parents through a *raja* (barber). The girl, normally, was sent to her parent's house for the delivery of her first child. It was a traditional practice to deliver at her parent's home. The whole work was completed with the help of a midwife. The mother of the newborn is confined for a period of forty days. The *janeu* wearing ceremony is performed at the age of eight years. The *biradari* and relatives get together, and under the guidance of a Brahman they make the child wear the *janeu*. In some cases, the boy's head is shaved on this occasion.

The marriage ceremonies begin with *shagun*. This is arranged by a *vichola*, usually a relative or a barber. The first ceremony after the *shagun* is *bhocha* or betrothal. Invitation for marriage is sent to all the relatives through the *raja*. At night, women and girls gather in the courtyard and sing traditional songs called *suhag de geet*. There is a series of ceremonies which are performed during the last two days including the *gona*, *mayan*, *shanti path*, *choora* and the wedding proper. At the boy's house also invitation is sent to all relatives and *biradari* members for the *shehra bandi* and *milni* ceremony. With the spread of education and social change, the marriage ceremonies have become more general and less caste-specific.

Next to birth and marriage, death is another significant point in the social life of individuals. The elders instruct the family members to lay the dying person on the floor. This ceremony is called *thalle* or *bhunje lahona*. The dead body is given a ceremonial bath before taking it for cremation. The *pandit* appoints the son, brother, father or husband of the dead to perform the last rites. There is a set of practices comprising *phul chugna*, *chautha*, *daswan* and *kriya* after the cremation. *Rasam pagri* is the last ceremony.

General trade is their main occupation. All the Sikh Gurus were Khatri. There is evidence that Maharaja Ranjit Singh's chief functionaries were also Khatris. Even under Muslim rulers in the northern-western India they rose to high administrative posts. Traditionally they form the business communities in rural and urban Punjab; they keep the accounts, act as moneylenders and trade in the sale and purchase of agricultural products.

Khatri *biradari* is loose and undefined but in times of need it becomes a closely-knit group and is led by the elders of the group. In the same families, followers of both Hindu and Sikh religions can be found, so much so that if one brother follows the traditional Hindu religion, the other one may be the follower of Sikh religion. As a result of this common religious and historical background, inter-marriages between Hindu and Sikh Khatri can be found. They observe weekly fasts, monthly *masia* (new moon) and *punia* (full moon), biannual *navrata* and annual Lohri, Basant Panchami, Baisakhi, Dussehra, Diwali and *shradhs*.

As a business community they come into contact with other sections of the society. Other professional castes which came into contact with the Khatris at various social functions are Bhands, Rasdharis (clowns and jokers), Bazigars (acrobats), Saperas (snake charmers), Madaris (jugglers and Bahurupia), etc. They have been extensively benefited by the various developmental programmes, including education, family welfare, communication and banking facilities.

SHARDA SIDHU

# KORI/KOLI

Rose (1919: 553), reports that the residents of Kullu and the Rajas of Kullu were called Koli Rajas who had their origin from the Kanets. The Kolis of the hills could be identified in the same category as the Dagi and the Sippi. The third category of the Koli were those who were engaged in weaving. The Koli of the hills and the plains are the same. The Dagis are also an offshoot of the Kolis. They got their name from dragging the dead cattle (dangars) and they took to removing the carcasses of cattle. They are called the Dagi-Kolis. The Kolis rank above the Chamars. The Kolis from whom the Kanets traditionally drink water are called the Sucha Kolis. At one stage the Kanets occupied the Shimla hills; there were numerous deaths of cattle and the Chamars were not available to remove such a large number of dead animals. There was a practice that nobody would take his meals till the dead animal were removed from their houses. Some Kanet families removed the dead animals but they were excommunicated as they were polluted and were thence termed as Kolis.

The Kolis and Kanets share their *gots*. They have Sandilya and Kashyap *gots*. They have the same social standing as the Jhinwars. According to another story the Kanet father had two sons from his two wives and divided his property between them. There was an agreement that whosoever would plough the field first would get the first share. The younger brother went to plough the field earlier and the elder brother in revenge killed the bullock, with the result he was made an outcaste. He had two sons, one was very good and the other was guilty of skinning and eating the dead oxen. The Kolis descended from the first one and the Dagolis from the second one.

*The Census of India* (1911: 464), states that 'Koris are Hindus with the exception of 25 Sikhs and 28 Muhammadans. They are found chiefly in the cantonments. It is really a subcaste of Purbia Chamars. They seldom work in leather but confine themselves to weaving and general labour.'

The Kori or Koli is a Scheduled Caste community of Punjab. According to *Census of India* (1981), the total population of the Koli or Kori caste is 5,652 individuals with 3,591 males and 2,061 females. They are found in all the districts of Punjab, but their concentration is least in the districts of Hoshiarpur and Sangrur. The Kori and Koli are engaged in the trade and occupation of hides and weaving. The Kori are the immigrants from Uttar Pradesh especially the districts of Pratapgarh, Gonda and Bahraich, while the Koli are confined to the hill ranges of Himachal Pradesh. Presently they do not work in hides but weaving remains their traditional occupation.

They have adapted the culture of Punjab in respect of the language, dress and food habits. They speak in Punjabi and Hindi languages. The males wear *kameez*, *kurta* and *dhoti* or pant, whereas the females wear *salwar*, *kameez* and *dupatta*. Most of them are vegetarian but some take mutton and eggs occasionally. Wheat is their staple food and pulses such as gram, *moong*, *masur* and *moth* are taken more frequently than vegetables, Vegetable oil is used as a cooking medium. Those who can afford take pure *ghee* also. The birth of a male child and marriage ceremonies are the occasions when alcoholic drinks are consumed by the males. Consumption of fruits is occasional. They also smoke.

They marry among themselves. They have Kashyap *got*. Marriage between close relaltives is not allowed. It is arranged when the boy and girl attains adulthood, i.e. between eighteen and twenty years of age. The married girls use vermilion, glass bangles, earring as symbol of marriage. Divorce and remarriage with the sanction of the caste *panchayat* is permitted. Joint families are still common though nuclear families are on increase. The male children inherit equally the property of the father, and the daughters get the same only in case there is no male child. The eldest son succeeds to the authority. The primary role of the women is to attend to the household duties.

Pre-delivery rituals and post-delivery pollution and postnatal restrictions on the mother are observed. There is no specific name giving ceremony but the midwife or any elderly lady may help in selecting the name for the newborn child.

When the boys and girls attain adulthood, their parents start looking for a suitable match for them, with the help of a *vichola*, who may also happen be one of their relatives. If both the sides agree, the ritual of *rokana* followed by *magana* is performed. The *shagun*, in the form of one rupee and a cloth, for the boy and his parents is offered on this occasion. The boy and his close relatives visit the girl's house to perform the ceremony of *chunni charhana*. The *shagun* is also offered to the girl on this occasion.

The Brahman performs the marriage ceremony. The feast known as *roti* is offered to the marriage party by the girl's parents. The parents of the girl offer gifts at the time of marriage known as *daj* or *dahej* which includes clothes for the boy, his parents and close relatives, utensils and some furniture. Consummation of marriage is at the bridegroom's house.

They cremate their dead. The pollution period is observed which varies from eight to thirteen days. The bones of the dead are immersed in the Ganga at Hardwar. Ancestor worship is also observed. Weaving, vegetable selling, government services, working as unskilled labourer in agriculture and industrial establishments are some of the occupations of the Kolis or Koris.

The Kori have their own traditional caste *panchayat* which is called Kori Panchayat Sabha, at Serai Bhagwan Das, Putlighar, Amritsar. It has its *pradhan*, secretary and treasurer. They are affiliated to the Uttar Pradesh Sanjut Kori Mahasabha. The local and petty issues are taken care of by the local *panchayat*, whereas the main body looks after their main policy issues. The members of the *panchayat* are elected by voice vote. The *panchayat* tries to arrive at an agreement which is binding on both the parties. One of their main problems is that they have been staying in the Bhagwan Das Serai (inn) since 1919 and all the tenants want that they should be given the right of ownership.

They are Hindus and worship Hindu gods and goddesses. The sacred specialist who perform the birth, marriage and death rites, are not from their community. They are from other higher communities. The community has its own oral traditions such as folk song, folklore and folk tales. The Kori exchange food with other communities. The food is mainly exchanged with the communities equal or below them. They have their own cremation ground, but source of water is shared with other communities living in the *serai.*

Very few individuals are well-educated. Some are in white-collar jobs and also in the administration. The impact of education and family welfare programmes has been well-received. Boys and girls study upto matriculation. The boys sometimes join colleges. There is a primary health centre to provide treatment to the needy individuals. Electricity and water are also available to them. Coal, kerosene oil and firewood are used as fuel. Immunization of the mother and infants are also availed of. The economically weaker section of the community have 'yellow cards'. They also have ration cards. Though the attitude towards saving is positive yet at times they have to depend on the moneylenders for loans.

SWARAN SINGH

# KUCHBAND

The Kuchband is a small occupational community who trace their origin from Chittorgarh and in due course of time learnt the art of making *kuch* or brush from *changer.* Their women make toys of clay. They are also called Kanjars but they claim themselves to be Gharas. Some of them also prepare *khas-khas* (screen) and *binnas* (cushions), *chinku* (nets for hanging food) (Rose: 1919: 558).

According to their legends, the forefathers of the Kuchband used to prepare *kuch.* The word *kuchband* means, the one who makes weavers' brush. Later on they were engaged in making *tangars,* which is used to collect the *tudi.* Some of them were also engaged in making ropes. About sixty years back they also stopped making *tangars* and preferred to work as shoe shiners. At Dakha-Mullapur, the Kuchbands migrated from Ambala about twenty years ago. They are also addressed as Kanmalia, as they clear the wax from the ears. The Kuchbands were nomads earlier, but now they have settled down. They live in the huts and wear simple *kurta* and *pyjama.* They speak in Hindi (Haryanvi). When they move from one place to another, they carry their luggage on the donkeys. The women wear *ghagra, salwar* and *kameez.* They catch jackal, lizard (*sanda*), hare, and consume the flesh of these animals. The Kuchbands extract curative oil from *sanda* and do blood letting with leeches or by the cupping process. Alcoholic drinks are taken on special occasions, such as the birth of a male child and a marriage ceremony. *Lassi,* tea and curd are also consumed by them. They smoke *bidi.*

They marry within their own community but not in the same *got.* The *gots* are: Soda, Karania, Bains, Madaiya, Gaher, Rari, Gharail. They also avoid marriage between the *gots* of the maternal uncle and aunt; father's brother's wife; and grandmother. They perform the betrothal of their boys and girls between two months to eighteen years. They arrange marriage for their children, when they are of ten to eleven years of age. The *muklawa* takes place at the age of twenty years to twenty-five years. The engagement ceremony takes place with the help of one rupee, which is offered by the relatives of the boy to the relatives of the girl. During another ceremony the boy's relatives also offer three to four hundred rupees in the presence of their traditional caste *panchayat* to the father of the girl as the expenditure for the sweets, in fact as bride price. This ceremony also takes place at the time of engagement. *Bundi* is used as a sweet instead of *laddoos.* All the members of the boy's family visit the house of the girl in order to fix the date of marriage. The girl's father gives a date for the marriage of his daughter, this is known as *kararnama* (agreement).

According to convenience, a time which ranges from two to six months is fixed for the marriage. During this period, they visit once again and a specific date of marriage is arranged. Accordingly, two to four persons of the boy's side along with the boy visit the house of the girl. In the presence of the traditional caste *panchayat,* the rituals of marriage are performed. The expenditure of marriage specially that on food and drinks is shared equally by the parents of the boy and the girl. Marriage ceremony is performed according to the tradition of seven *pheras.* The three items of dress which are a must for the girl are *ghagra, kameez and dupatta.* The marriage party stays overnight during which the ceremony of the *pheras* takes place, at about 4 a.m.

At betrothal, the parents of the bridegroom present five rupees to the bride's family. Two emissaries of the boy's father go to the bride's house and are given liquor. In return they distribute sweet meats and so confirm the betrothal. A marriage letter is sent to fix the date for the shampooing of the hair with *watna.* At the wedding, a pole is fixed-up right in the ground and a burning coal is placed at its foot. A brother-in-law, or sister-in-law of either the bride or bridegroom binds the right-hand thumb of the one to the thumb of the left hand of the other and the couple circle round the pole seven times and afterwards blow seven times on to the coals. Then the bridgroom takes the bride into his thatch or tent and unties the knot informing her that it is his tent and her future shelter.

Widow and widower remarriage is permitted. At the time of birth the post-delivery restrictions on the mother are observed for seven days. Sweets are distributed and there is no special *namkaran* ceremony, however, the old women give a name to the child. The male children wear a black thread with beads and a chain around their waist, it is called *taragari.* Leaves of mango are displayed on the front door, in a ceremony called *sehra,* indicating the birth of a child in the family. After completion of the restriction period, the mother of the newly born child attends to her kitchen, after washing her mouth, face and hands. When a death occurs, the body is carried on a bier of bamboos, shaped like a ladder to the cremation ground.

Three days later the deceased's close relations and those who carried the bier go to the cremation ground and carry with them a small quantity of milk which is sprinkled all around.

*Roti* with *ghee* and *shakkar* is offered to the members of the community on the day of death of an individual. On third and seventh day after death *roti* (which includes *dal*, curd and *phulka*) is also offered to the members of the whole community. The bones of the dead person known as *phul* are immersed into a nearby river or canal.

They have their own traditional caste *panchayat* which is known as Jati Panchayat. They settle all matters related to marriage, breaking of engagement, money transactions and other petty issues. The minimum fine includes the cost of a bottle of alcoholic drink and maximum upto forty rupees. They also excommunicate the individual if the offence is very serious. Serious crimes include adultery, rape, elopement, disrespect for the traditional norms or the insult to the traditional *panchayat*.

The Kuchband worship Ram Deo whose temple is situated in Bikaner. A fair is held twice a year in the months of *Bhadon* and *Magh*, and on these occasions the Kuchband visit the shrine and make offerings. The Kuchband say they are descended from Khizr Pal of Allahbax, in the Aligarh district. There is also a Maharani's shrine of Allahbax and at her shrine a pig is sacrificed. The head is used to make a *palao* while rest of the flesh is cooked separately and thrown into the fire with five loaves and some liquor as an offering to Maharani. They profess Hindu religion and worship all the Hindu gods and goddesses which include the seven *devis*. On the eve of Diwali and Dussehra they clean a place and offer their prayers by *matha tekna*.

They settle at any vacant place and live in huts. They traditionally accept and exchange food with the members of their own community. But the members of other high caste communities do not exchange food with them. They share source of water with others but have separate cremation ground. They participate in various festivals and festivities. The boys and girls do not attend their schools regularly. The Kuchbands visit the primary health centre. They have ration cards to get the essential items. The economically poor individuals have been provided with yellow cards. Handpump is the source of their drinking water. Collected wood is used as a fuel. They are aware of the family planning programme and its various methods. Most of the individuals are self-employed. They find it difficult to save money. However, they attend various social functions with the help and cooperation of their community members.

SWARAN SINGH

# KUMHAR

The Kumhars are also known as Kumar, Ghumar, Kumiar and Prajpati. They are the traditional potters who make earthen pots and utensils. They believe themselves to be the descendants of the creator of this universe—Lord Brahma. According to one legend, Lord Brahma once divided some sugar cane among his sons. Everyone ate his share except the Kumhar who put it in a pitcher and allowed it to grow. Few days later when Brahma asked for the sugar cane none but the Kumhar offered it to the Lord. Bestowing his love and affection, he gave the title of Prajapati to his son Kumhar. Ads one saying goes, *Ram jat ka Rangra, Kishan jat ka Ahir, Brahman jat Kumhar hai, Sheo ki jat faqir*.

They are distributed throughout the country and also in all the districts of Punjab. They speak Punjabi at home, with kin groups and also with others. The scripts used are Gurmukhi and Devanagari.

They take both vegetarian and non-vegetarian food. Taking of eggs, both fertilized and unfertilized, is considered a non-vegetarians diet. Women are normally vegetarians, men consume alcoholic drinks on special occasions; they smoke *bidi*.

They are divided into a number of clans such as, Dab, Dal, Aitan, Solaotre, Mahlotre, Sohal, Sahol, Badial, Dangolia, Nirdhan, Jambe and Tikhan. There is no hierarchy in the clan. The function of these divisions is to regulate marriage alliances and indicate descent and ancestry. The community is aware of the *varna* system and recognize their place as Vaishya. The self-perception of the community is high but other local communities consider them of low status on account of their keeping donkeys, which is considered unclean. They are also deemed as the village menial workers carrying manure, dust, fuel bricks, etc.

They practise endogamy at community level. Village endogamy is allowed but clan exogamy is strictly followed. Marriages are solemnized in adulthood and are negotiated by the elders. Marriage by exchange was practised earlier and this kind of marriage is called *batta-satta* or *phervan. Kanyadan* exists and dowry is given in cash and kind. The patrilocal rule of residence is observed. Divorce may be allowed for reasons of adultery, barrenness and maladjustment.

Both nuclear and extended family types are present. Avoidance relationship is observed between daughter-in-law and father-in-law; husband's elder brother and younger brother's wife. Joking relationship is found between husband's younger brother and elder brother's wife; sister's husband and wife's younger brothers and sisters and grandparents and grandchildren. Rule of inheritance is male equigeniture and succession is by the eldest son. Women's role is mainly confined to the household chores and looking after the family and its needs. They attend and partake in ritual and religious affairs, help in the traditional occupation of the community both in making and selling pots, and contribute to family income. Yet they have a low status and do not have decision-making powers or control over family expenditure.

Rituals at the time of birth, marriage and death are observed. Pre-delivery restrictions are imposed. Post-delivery pollution is observed for thirteen or forty days. It is known as *sootak*. After *sootak* period is over, *chowke-charhna* ritual is performed. Naming and *mundan* ceremonies are informal. Marriage rituals are also performed at bride's residence. Some of the rituals are also performed at the groom's residence. The marriage rituals include *rok*, *mangni*, *shagun*, *barat*, *phere* and *doli*. The actual marriage is performed by *phere* around the sacred fire or *Guru Granth Sahib* and is conducted by the priest. Consummation of marriage is at the groom's residence.

Dead are cremated and the bones, called *phul*, are collected on the fourth day and are immersed in the holy Ganga. *Kirya*, *uthala* or *rasam pagri* takes place on eleventh or thirteenth day. Post-death pollution is observed for eleven days for women and thirteen days for men.

They are traditionlly engaged in making earthen pots and pottery. Transporting bricks, clay, sand, stones, and other such material on donkeys, carts, etc., is the subsidiary occupation. Some have also taken to other occupations such as shopkeeping, hosiery and pulling rickshaw and driving autorickshaw. Transactions are in cash. Child labour exists to augment the income. A few members of the community have acquired land and have taken to settled cultivation. They have unions in the name of Kumhar Sabha to look after their occupational needs. The elders in the family usually sort out the intra-family disputes in the community. Those living in rural areas are governed by the statutory *panchayat* which is heterogeneous and has a role in planning and implementing developmental activities.

They subscribe to both Hindu and Sikh religion. Lohri, Holi, Diwali, Dussehra, Baisakhi, Janamashtami, Shivratri are the common festivals of the community. The services of a Brahman or *gurdwara* priest are availed of for performing birth, marriage and death rites and for religious teaching. They do not exhibit any community specific art and craft. Women are adept in knitting and cloth embroidery. They share Punjabi folk songs, folk tales and folklore with other local communities.

They do not accept and exchange food and water with Scheduled Castes and Muslim communities. From high and other backward class communities they accept water and food but do not exchange with them. However, this rigidity is losing ground particularly in the urban areas. They share cremation ground, religious shrines and water sources with other communities. The number of businessmen, doctors, engineers and white-collar job holders is not large in the community.

Formal education is generally not favoured for both boys and girls. Both boys and girls drop out of school due to economic reasons, poverty and disinterest. Modern methods of family planning including sterilization are used. They use both indigenous and modern medicare. Drinking water is available in the locality and so is electricity. They listen to the radio, watch television and visit the cinema for entertainment. The facilities of banks and ration shop are available to them. They use coal, wood, kerosene oil or even liquified petroleum gas as fuel. The attitude towards saving is positive.

A.K. BHATIA

# KURMI

In Punjab, the Kurmi community is also known as Mali or gardener. The latter name is shared with other castes of same profesions like Kori, Dhanak, etc. A few opinions about the derivation of the term Kurmi or Kunbi were noted by Crooke (1896: 346). According to one opinion it was derived from Sanskrit word *kutumb*, which means family; few others claimed that it was derived from the Sanskrit word *krishi* which's mean cultivation; still others believe that it is derived from the word *kurma* the tortoise incarnation of Vishnu. However, the community is unaware of these derivations. The community is conscious of its national identifications, and the ethnographic accounts testify to these assertions. In Punjab they are a migrant community. Its migration during British times was noted by the ethnographic records, and its current migration is recalled by the community. However, a few members have permanently settled in the state. In the old ethnographic records of Punjab it was described as a 'great caste of cultivators' who was employed in the cantonments of Punjab, like other Purbias, 'cutting grass, weaving and serving as grooms' (Ibbetson 1916: 337; Rose 1919: 572). Ethnographic account of the community exists. In the opinion of Oppert, western Kurmis claimed to have descended from Kauravas of the great Mahabharata war.

However, Crooke pointed out that some Kurmis also claimed their Brahmanical origin. Buchanan had traced out the origins of Kurmi to Gorakhpur Tharus; but Crooke disputed these claims. Dalton regarded the Kurmis of Bihar as the earliest Aryan colonists of Bengal. In his opinion, they were 'a brown tawny-coloured people, of average height, well-proportioned, rather lightly formed, and with a fair amount of good looks. They show well-shaped heads and high features, less refined than the Goalas; but except when they have obviously intermixed with aborigines, they are unquestionably Aryan in outlook. Grey eyes and brownish hair are sometimes met with among them. The women have usually small and well-formed hands and feet.' Risley had challenged their views, which he considered, were confined to Kurmis of Bihar. Even they were not as Aryan in appearance as Dalton made out. He further pointed out that Kurmis of Bengal and Orissa were of different type, where their features resembled Dravidian and Santal tribes. Even Santals considered them as half brothers.

However, Risley himself proposed three hypotheses, which he considered as more tenable—'(1) that the Kurmis are made up of two distinct stocks, one Aryan and other Dravidian; (2) that the entire group comes of an Aryan stock, the type which has been modified to a varying extent by the mixture of blood and vicissitudes of occupation; (3) that the entire group was originally Dravidian, but those portions of it which lay in the way of the Aryan invasion were refined by intercourse with the immigrants, while those settled in remote parts of the country preserved their primitive type' ( Crooke, 1896: 347-8). These accounts, however, do not throw much light on Kurmis of this state. The community in this state has its origin in eastern Uttar Pradesh or Bihar. Morever the community is not aware of its own origin. It seems the account has been modified at least in the memory of the community which migrated to this state.

The community uses dialects of Hindi, within family, its kinship group and with other communities. In addition, it has picked up some knowledge of Punjabi dialects as well. It takes all types of food; women do not take meat, but men take it occasionally. Consumption of vegetables is moderate and fruit is taken occasionally. More rice than wheat is consumed. Gram, *urad*, *moong*, peas, beans, and *masur* are the commonly used pulses. *Vanaspati* and mustard oil are commonly used as cooking medium.

The community is divided into subcastes. There were few endogamous subcastes of Kurmi, viz., Chapria, Singtoria Kharchav, Ghochad, Kunbi and Bakulia. Crooke noted eleven main endogamous groups—Baiswar, Bardiha (bullock men), Gangapari (resident beyond Ganga), Gujrati (resident of Gujarat), Jaiswar (resident of old town of Jais in Rai Bareli district), Kanauji (resident of Kanauj), Khere Ghand (pure Bindis), Patraiha (stone men); Rarh Santhwar (who took name from *senths*, a type of red grass), Singraur (who asserted induction with Porgane or Singrauli) and Mlas (in Azamgarh district) (Crooke 1896: 348-9). There is differentiation at occupational level; a few members work as skilled technicians in auto works but a large number of them work as labour in gardens, canals, rest houses, hospitals, orchards, etc. These differentiations regulate marriage alliances and indicate social status.

In its self-perception, it considers itself of medium status, but others consider them of low status. The community in the state perceives itself as either of Vaishya or Kshatriya origin as they have varying opinion about their origin. The Kurmis are endogamous at community and subcaste levels and exagamous at locality level. Most marriages are still arranged with their kin groups in the places of origin. There is no division of community at *got* levels. However, no marriage is allowed with close relatives. These days adult marriages are arranged by parents through negotiations. They are monogamous and practise *kanyadan.* Dowry is provided in kind.

The usual Hindu symbols of marriage such as vermilion mark, bangles, *bindi,* finger ring, toe ring, earring, nosering and *mangal sutra* are used. *Maur* (headgear) is used by the groom at the time of marriage. Marriage is performed by Vedic rites with five or seven *pheras* around sacred fire. A *pandit* (Brahmin) solemnizes the marriage. Divorce by mutual agreement and with social approval is permitted. Either party can ask for divorce and the aggrieved party is compensated. A sum of rupees five as *chhudwai* is charged for *talaq* or divorce. It is allowed by the village or caste *panchayat.* The children are left to the care of either of the parents as decided by the *panchayat.* Remarriage of both male and female divorcee is allowed. Marriage of widower is also allowed. Marriage rules have changed in favour of adult marriages, and have become more liberal.

The Kurmis live in nuclear families, and are occasionally vertically extended. Male equigeniture is the rule of inheritance and succession rules favour the eldest son. The status of women in the community is inferior as compared to men. They contribute to family income by participating in agricultural activities or as domestic servants. They have role in rituals, religious affairs and have decision-making powers. Birth pollution is observed for seven days. *Namkaran* is done by the family itself or by the *pandit.* Marriage rituals are observed at the bride's residence, and nuptial ceremony is held at the groom's residence. A feast is organized by both sides.

The dead are either buried, cremated or immersed in water. In their place of origin they are immersed in the Ganga, but cases of burial and cremation are also reported. Feast is held after twelve days. One person observes pollution period for twelve days. After a year, *shradh* ceremony is held for the dead.

They are a mainly landless community and traditionally employed as gardeners or *mali* at various places. A few of them are self-employed as *mistries* or mechanics in auto repair workshops. Child labour exists. Payment of wages is received in cash. There is no traditional caste council among them. However, Kurmi Kshatriya Sabha exists at the national level (Verma, 1979). They worship goddess Durga at local Hindu temples. The sacred specialists are the *pandits* who perform the rituals of birth, death and marriage. The main festivals include Holi, Dussehra and Diwali which are of socio-religious significance. It has oral tradition. Folk songs are sung by both males and females at the time of Holi festival. Traditional dance is also performed on that occasion by both males and females.

They traditionally exchange all types of *kachcha*, *sidha* and *pukka* food with other communities. They share water resources, religious shrines and cremation ground with other communities. Cultivator-labour relationship exists, where they are employed in orchard as *mali* or gardener.

Education is partly favoured for both boys and girls. Boys study generally upto seccondry level and drop out because of the need to support the family. The girls study upto primary level and occasionally upto secondary level. They drop out either because there is no school nearby or due to social reasons. Attitute to modern medicare is positive and they make full use of it. Both sexes have accepted modern methods of family planning. Couples prefer one or two children. Drinking water and electricity facilities are available to them. Dissemination of information is through political parties. Firewood and kerosene oil are the most commonly used fuels by the community. They avail themselves of the facilities of public distribution system. Their attitude towards savings is favourable.

VIRINDER SINGH

# LABANAS

Labana was the name given to Banjaras in Punjab. Other names of the community were Gujoria and Jharbella in the Central Provinces, Labhana in Bengal, Laman in Mumbai, Lambadi in Chennai and Labani in Hyderabad and Mysore. Elliot had divided Banjaras into five main sections, which included Labana Banjaras. Other four were Turkya Banjaras, Bayd Banjaras, Mukri Banjaras and Bahru Banjaras. This lends strength to the argument that Banjaras and Labanas are the names of the same community. This view has been confirmed from various accounts of the community given in *Labana Sewak*, a periodical published from Chandigarh. However, many writers have tried to distinguish Labanas from Banjaras, on the basis of distinctive dress of Banjara women. In the opinion of Blunt (1969), although all branches of Banjaras were the carriers of cattle, they were specialized traders as well. Labanas specialized in the trade of salt; while Turkiya, Baids and Bahrup subcastes specialized in carrying grain. Baids were doctors and weavers.

Despite the distinctions drawn, Blunt points out that all Banjaras were commissariat to armies in the field, and were indulging in activities such as cattle lifting (Blunt, 1969: 159). This only show that Labanas are one subgroup of the Banjaras, which is a generic name. Despite this difference of opinion, it can be concluded that Labanas are no different from Banjaras. Two distinct meanings have been assigned to the word *labana* or *lubana*. Firstly, the word is composed of two parts; *loh* which means iron, and *ban* which means arrow. It relates to Lubana, the Rajput ancestors who used bows and arrows in fight. Secondly, the term is derived from *lun* meaning salt and *bana* meaning trade. So Labana means traders in salt. These two meanings have been noted by Ibbetson and Rose. It was derived from the Sanskrit word *vanijya* or *banjya-kara*, which means a merchant (Hutton, 1896: 21, 276). According to Elliot the word *banjara* has originated from the Sanskrit word *banij*, which means a merchant. They speak local dialect of Punjabi language with other communities. However, elderly persons speak Labanki at home. Labanki is more in use among the Labana in the sub-hilly areas of Punjab.

They are regular non-vegetarians. Despite the movement against the use of alcohol, it is still consumed by them. Milk forms a part of their regular diet.

The change in the *gots* of the Labanas becomes obvious if we compare it with the description of Rose. Only Paliah and Thadimyian were noted by him. Marriages are generally endogamous at the community level. However, a few instances of intercaste marriages have been reported by the community. Marriages are exogamous at *got* level. All *gots* are considered equal. But marriage with immediate relatives is avoided. Marriages, which are generally monogamous, are settled through negotiations. Vermilion, bangles, *bindi*, toe ring, earring, nosering, etc., are used as symbols of marriage by women. Dowry is given in kind. After marriage, the rule of residence is patrilocal. Divorce is permitted for various reasons through judicial approval. Both parties can seek divorce. Remarriage of both male and female divorcee is permissible. Even widows and widowers are allowed to remarry.

Families are either nuclear or vertically extended. Joking relationships exist between *sali* and *jeeja*, *dewar* and *bhabi*. Avoidance relationship exists between *noohn* and *sahura*. Family disputes arise mostly due to property problems such as inheritance. Although legally, daughters are entitled to share the paternal property, yet in practice it is male equigeniture which is practised. If some women claim a share it is considered bad. Succession rules favour the eldest son. Women participate in economic, social and religious sphere. They also contribute to family income. Mostly women perform household jobs and in some cases they also control the family expenditure. However, the status of women is low as compared to men.

Marriage is preceded by *thaka* (engagement) ceremony. Marriage is performed by *anand karaj* ceremony in case of the Sikhs and by vedic rites in case of Hindu members of the community. *Muklawa* is a an accepted custom. Consummation of marriage is at the groom's place. Services of the priests to perform birth and marriage rituals are obtained. Pollution is observed at the time of birth and death. *Namkaran* takes place. No food is cooked for three days after death in a family. *Pagdi* ceremony takes place after twelve days.

In the rural areas of Punjab, they are a land-owning community. Land is individually owned. In addition to cultivation they are employed in various services including army, which is considered prestigious in the community. Now, some of them are engaged in industry. However, those having small land holdings also work as agricultural labourers to supplement their incomes. Generally, wages are paid in cash. Traditional caste councils known as Labana *sabhas* exist. A state level Labana Sabha also exists. It also publishes a monthly magazine, *Labana Sewak*, which publishes the community's activities and matrimonial information. In rural areas, the community is well-represented in the statutory *panchayats*. They mainly profess Sikh religion. However, some believe in various Hindu deities.

The community freely interacts with other communities. Food and water are exchanged with other communities. They share festivals and religious shrines with other communities. They are employed in army, industry and judiciary. Leadership has emerged from among them at the state and national level.

The community has benefited from developmental activities. There is a tendency to get good education not only for boys but also for girls. Educational level is better in the urban areas, and boys get better education than girls. Some of them have studied upto graduate and even post-graduate level. The community has favourable response to modern medicare. However, few of them continue to use traditional medicines. Owing to paucity of facilities in the rural areas, the community has to seek medical treatment in the nearby towns. Modern methods of family planning are favoured by both males and females. The community has access to drinking water and electricity supply. In urban areas they get the tap water, but in rural areas, they rely upon tube wells or handpumps. They are exposed to the mass media and communicational facilities. Dissemination of information takes place through the *gram sevaks*. They have made extensive use of modern facilities in agriculture including tractors, chemical fertilizers, tube wells, weed-killers, insecticides, etc. They also avail of the benefits of public distribution system. Their attitude towards saving is positive.

K. GOPALA IYER
VIRINDER SINGH

# LOHAR

The Lohars were considered a member of the group consisting of blacksmiths, carpenters and potters and were divided into two distinct sections. The first were those whose labour was intimately linked to agriculture, such as Lohars, Tarkhans and Chamars. The second consisted of Kumhars, Chuhars, and Nais. They were part of the village *sepi* system (*jajmani* system) and were paid in kind ranging form one-sixth to one-eighth of the gross produce (Bonerjee, 1975: 287). They had to perform certain customary duties such as repairing of agricultural implements like *datari* (sickle), *khurpa* and *hal* (plough). Rose (1919: 36) described the Lohars of Punjab as pure and simple blacksmiths. He observed that in the central states of the eastern plains the Lohars, or blacksmiths and the Khati, or carpenter, are undistinguishable, the same men doing both the kind of work. In Hoshiarpur, they are said to form a single caste called Lohar-Tarkhan. The son of a blacksmith will often take to carpentry and masonry and vice versa. The community traces its descent from Vishwakarma. They believe that the anvil, the bellow, sledge and the hammer were bestowed to them and they were taught to make arrow, trident, horseshoes, sword and war chariot. They believe that the two major subgroups of Vishwakarma were Dhiman and Khati. Dhiman is referred as Dhiman Brahman who consider themselves superior to the Khatis.

However, the current status of these two groups though distinct, yet the occupations seem to overlap. Invariably, a Dhiman Brahman is both a Lohar and carpenter at the same time. The son of a Dhiman Lohar can take up the job of a carpenter and vice versa. They could take the job of a mason as well. This is true of the Khatis as well. The traditional occupation of the Lohar and Khatis is no longer strictly followed. The Sikhs among them are known as Ramgarhias.

The Ramgarhias trace their origin to Dhiman Brahman and claim themselves superior to Khatis. The Ramgarhias perform the job of carpenter, mason and blacksmith interchangeably. The Lohars consider the Sikligar, Gadaliya Lohar and Nalband much inferior in status. They speak Punjabi language. The Ramgarhias use Gurmukhi script whereas the Hindu Lohars use both Devanagari and Gurmukhi scripts.

Lohars take non-vegetarian food occasionally. Wheat is their staple food. They consume milk and milk products.

The social status of Lohars is low and according to description by Rose (1919), they are classed as an impure caste insofar as the Jats and other or similar standing castes will have no social communion with them though not as an outcaste like the scavenger. Rose attributes the low status of this community to impurity similar to that of barber, washerman and dyer which spring solely from the nature of employment. The Ramgarhias have been trying to raise their status and the increasing amount of large-scale building constructions and the manufacture of furniture afforded a good opening for them. In this process they amassed wealth and also acquired large stertches of land. Agriculture in Punjab is not only an assured source of earning but also a symbol of high status. They persistantly attempted to acquire a few acres of cultivable land in the village and there was a slow shift from their ancestral profession to agricuture. But this process of acquisition of land was greatly retarded with the enforcement of the Punjab Alienation of Land Act which did not recognize them as an agricultural community. Consequently, they were virtually debarred from acquiring new land. This anomaly was removed only after Independence. Today they enjoy a much better social status in Punjab.

Their important *gots* are Sohal, Nagi, Chadha, Suri, Bouns, Loyal, Bamse, Vilkhu, Bhardwaj, Rihal, Hatharu, Phallora, Kalsi, Sahota, Dupad, Thanjal, Gill, Raj Bans, Bansal, Panesar, Riat, Kaundal, Bhatti, Adi, Rupray, Gogal, Gujral, Virdi, Sira, Bhullar, Padam, Manku Burji, Sabarwal and Panju.

The *gots* of father and mother are avoided for marriage alliance. The marriage rules are as per the *anand karaj* and Vedic rituals. Marital alliance taked place between Hindu and Sikh sections of the community. They approve marital alliances with castes such as the Jat Sikhs, Aroras, Khatris and Ahluwalias. Divorce is generally not permitted. Widow remarriage is allowed. The range of age at marriage for girls is not below eighteen years and for boys not below twenty-one years. Dowry has become an accepted practice. The practice of *chadar paona* prevails in widow remarriage. Rule of residence after marriage is patrilocal. Joint family system is still strong and the rule of inheritance is male equigeniture. Rituals of the Lohars revolve round their deity Vishvakarma. They celebrate Vishvakarma Day as Govardhan Puja, one day after the Diwali festival.

Observance of the funeral rites includes immersion of the ashes either at Hardwar or Kiratpur Sahib. Women have important role in animal husbandry, household activities and in the decision-making process.

Mandi Gobindgarh followed by Khanna has a high concentration of steel-rolling mills, which are run by Ramgarhias and supply conventional bars, rod, etc., and cater to the needs of north India. It would not be wrong to mention that it is mainly the capabilities of Dhiman Lohars (traditional blacksmiths) that has contributed to the growth and development of the steel-rolling mill of Mandi Gobindgarh.

Therefore, we find that the technology is mainly indigenoulsy designed and over the time, by introducing improvements, it has reached the present heights of perfection and the engineers behind this process of development are mainly the traditionally skilled Lohars or Ramgarhias.

Presently, some of the Ramgarhias are prosperous industrialists in the state as also outside the state. They have among them big industries such as Bharat Tube, and an automobile factory in Ludhiana and they also dominate industries such as machine tools, agricultural implements, flour mills, paper mills, etc., in the state. Many of them have migrated abroad and distinguished themselves as skilled artisans and masons. This community has also produced eminent engineers and one of them was responsible for designing and constructing the Parliament House. Interviews with the Lohars in different districts of Punjab have shown that the *sepidari* system is fast declining. It is only the older generation which is still continuing it and the younger generation is moving out of their traditional occupation. Many of them have taken to service, running flour mills, workshops, factories and industries in towns. Their educational achievements have also made a landmark. They run several important eductional institutions in the state and bring out a regular publication, *Ramgarhia Gazette*.

Their emergence as one of the major economic players in the state has advanced their overall status in the state. Their attitude towards development programme is positive. They avail of loans and facilities for opening industries. They use family planning measures and have easy access to electricity.

RAKESH KUMAR
G. GOPALA IYER

# MADARI

Madaris are also known as Golbaziah in some areas of Punjab. Writings about the community's origins and religious practices are part of the early ethnographic accounts (Rose, 1919; Ibbetson, 1916). The Madaris were the followers of Zinda Shah Madar, a celebrated saint of Oudh. His name was Bazi-ul-din Shah and was a converted Jew. He was born in A.D. 1050 and is said to have died in Makanpur at the age of 383 years, after expelling Deman Makan Deo from that place. It is said that he was given power of living without breathing by the Prophet Muhammad. His followers were secure against venomous snakes and scorpions. Women could not enter his shrine as they were seized by violent pains as if they were burnt by fire. The Madaris were distributed earlier in the districts of Ambala, Ludhiana, Jalandhar, Hoshiarpur, Amritsar, Sialkot and Ferozepur and were unknown in the western parts of Punjab. At that time they belonged to the Beshara section of Islam, who followed no religion, creed or order, but claimed themselves as Muslims (Crooke, 1896: 397-401). The community is distributed at regional and national levels. They keep on migrating from place to place staying at a place not more than six weeks upto a year at a stretch. Due to improvements in the means of communication, frequency of migration in a year has increased. A large number of them migrated to Pakistan in 1947. The eastern districts were earlier the home of this community, but the number has drasatically declined after Partition.

They speak Urdu within the family and kin-group but with others they speak the local dialects of Punjabi, Hindi, Bagdi, Pahadi, etc. Perso-Arabic is the script used by them. They are non-vegetarian and both men and women take non-vegetarian food. Wheat, rice, *jowar*, *bajra* and maize are used as cereals. The pulses taken include gram, *tur*, *urad*, *moong*, peas, *masur* and *moth*. Groundnut oil, mustard oil, sunflower oil besides animal fats and *vanaspati* are used as cooking medium. They prefer *roti* to rice.

They have groups such as Mehtab, Kandewale, Buribothalwale, Sayyad, Puwar, Bhatti, Muthuwale, Suruwale. No differentiation with hierarchy has been reported among the groups. Some of them who are engaged in the business of horse breeding are more prosperous than those who continue with their traditional occupation. Their self-perception is high; but others consider them to be of medium status. They are endogamous at the community and village level. Consanguinity at the level of both cross-cousin and parallel-cousin and maternal uncle-niece exists.

Marriages are generally settled through negotiation and at times by elopement. They are monogamous but polyandry is also not unknown. They neither use vermilion mark nor *mangal sutra*. *Mehar* is payable on demand; and it is also promised for future payment. The rules of residence after marriage is patrilocal. Divorce is permissible with the initiative of males. Maladjustment and want of male child are the main reasons behind divorce. Divorce compensation is given to the wife; sharing the responsibility of children is mutually decided. No divorce by judicial procedure is recognized. Remarriage of widow, widower, male and female divorcees is allowed with full religious rites. There is general liberalization in the rules of marriage and the age at marriage has increased. The community lives in nuclear as well as vertically extended families. Avoidance relationships exist between mother-in-law and son-in-law, and between father-in-law and daughter-in-law. Joking relationships exist with wive's sisters. Inheritance of property follow the rule of male equigeniture and the succesion rules favour the eldest son.

Women in the community have a very low status. They do only household jobs. They participate in the work of animal husbandry, but only at home. The women have to wear *burqa* when outside the home. Some restrictions are imposd on the movement of pregnant women. Post-delivery pollution and restriction on the mother exist. Naming ceremony is performed by the *maulavi* according to Islamic beliefs and on the basis of Quran. The *sunnat* (circumcision) is performed on a male child at the age of two years. *Aqiqa* ceremony is also performed. The dead are buried and pollution is observed. On the third day, a *maulavi* performs the ritual of *jummat*. Marriage ceremony takes place at the bride's place; and both parties arrange a feast at their respective places. *Nikah* is performed by the *maulavi*. The marriage is preceded by the ritual of *sagai*.

Madaris are a landless community and are mainly self-employed and also engage themselves in the breeding and trade of horses. They move from place to place showing *khel tamasha* and perform upto three *majamas* or shows in a day earning upto fifty to one hundred rupees every day. They spend four to five days at a place. A group of three to four male members is always on the move. Children of six to nine years act as a *jamoora* in the *tamasha*. Since the *tamasha* is performed within a circle of spectators, the community is also called Gol Baziah. The present profession is becoming less remunerative at present as a result of which some have already shifted to the profession of breeding and trading horses and ponies. A daily link exists with the local market, which is fully regulated. Child labour exists, both in the performance of *tamashas* and breeding of horses. A traditional *panchayat* of *biradari* with its head office in the village Bhaleda exists. The *panchayat* is an elected body and arbitrates various disputes of the *biradari*. The *panchayat* has unusual powers of sanctioning punishments and rewards. The community believes in Islam and belongs to the Sunni sect. They attend the *mela* of Mukkud in Yamunanagar, and Newal in Karnal, Haryana. Their sacred specialists are from other communities. The festivals of the community are of economic, religious and social significance. They celebrate festivals such as Id-ul-Fitr, Id-ul-Zuha, etc. They participate in all fairs and festivals in which they perform *tamasha*. They have their oral tradition in the form of folk songs which are shared with other communities. A traditional muscial instrument known as *damroo* (a small drum) is used by the community to collect crowds at the place of *tamasha*.

The Madaris exchange food with the Muslim communities. They share water sources and participate in festivals with other communities. However, religious shrines and burial ground are shared with Muslim communities. Leadership has emerged at the village *panchayat* level.

Education for girls is not socially acceptable though it is partly favoured for boys, who study up to the primary or secondary level, but drop out later because of the call of their profession. The community makes use of both traditional and modern medicare. Couples usually have four or more children. Drinking water is available from handpumps. Dissemination of information is through political parties. They use firewood, cow-dung cakes, coal and kerosene oil as fuel. They avail of the benefits of the public distribution system. Their attitude to saving is positive.

VIRINDER SINGH

# MAHASHA

The Mahasha is a new nomenclature for the well-known community Dumna or Domra and Dom. They are said to have emerged as a community out of the group of outcastes from the parentage of the Brahmans, Kshatriyas and Rajputs. A popular legend current among them is that a Brahman family finding no one around to help had to bury a dead cow and thus in this process was made an outcaste. The term 'Mahasha' was coined by the Arya Samajis to upgrade the status of this caste and hence they consider the term 'Dom' or 'Dumna' or 'Domra' as derogatory.

According to the 1971 census they were most numerously located in the district of Gurdaspur (60,803) and also had a sizeable population in the district of Hoshiarpur (6,152). They were also in substantial number in the hill districts of Himachal Pradesh today. Their total population is 1,24,924 individuals (males 66,301, females 58,623) according to the 1981 census.

The term 'Dumna' or 'Mahasha' are more specific to Punjab, Jammu and Himachal Pradesh. After Partition a sizeable section of them had migrated to Gurdaspur district. They have been included in the list of Scheduled Caste communities of Punjab. They are spread all over Gurdaspur district but are more widespread in Pathankot and Batala *tahsils*.

They communicate in the local Punjabi dialect and the script used is Gurmukhi. They take both vegetarian and non-vegetarian food. Wheat and rice are their staple diet; cooking medium is oil and vegetable *ghee*. Alcoholic drinks are occasionally consumed and are mainly purchased from the market.

There are subcaste divisions among them such as Kalotray, Manjotray, Jaswal, Lalotray, Mangotray, Bathnotray, and Bharnaliey, etc. Rose mentions their clans as Kalotra, Manglu, Pargat, Drahe and Lalotray (Rose, 1919: 251). They observe strict *got* exogamy. Some of their important *gots* are Attery, Bhardwaj, Raghuvanshi, etc. They consider themselves superior to some Scheduled Caste communities, e.g. Mazhabi and Ramdasia. They are aware of the *varna* system and are very conscious about being a part of the Hindu system. A study conducted on 'Dumna, Mahasha or Doom' (*Census of India*, 1961) of Himachal and Amritsar make the following observation regarding their 'social status': 'In social status, Dumnas rank in the lower middle zone of social hierarchy of Scheduled Castes. They are reported nearly equal in status to Batwal, Bhanjra, Dagi, Koli, Sanhai, Sansi, Daole or Dauli, and higher than Barad, Dhaya, Gagra, Bangali, Chuhra and Gandhila, who are reported to rank in the lowest zone of hierarchy of castes. They are considered to be much lower in social status than the Brahman, Banias, Kashtriyas, Jats, the so-called clean castes and slightly lower than Ghriths, Lohars, Tarkhans.'

They do not observe subcaste endogamy strictly but observe strict *got* exogamy and also village and caste endogamy. The age at marriage ranges from eighteen to twenty years for both boys and girls. Child marriage is no more prevalent but it was practised in the past. They follow Hindu rituals for performing marriage. Rituals of marriage are performed by the Brahman. The Sikh Mahashas get their marriage rituals performed as per the *anand karaj*. Monogamy is the rule. Marriage symbols are *bindi* and *chura* (red bangles). The *kanyadan* exists and dowry is given both in cash and kind. Divorce is permissible on the ground of adultery and cases of divorce are settled in informal *panchayat*. Junior levirate, known as *chadar paona* is permitted.

Male equigeniture is the rule of inheritance, succession is by the eldest son. Women help their menfolk in agricultural operations and various other related activities. They participate in animal husbandry, collection of fuel and social and religious rituals of the family. Their opinion on selection of mates may, however, be obtained. Women contribute to the family income.

Post-delivery pollution period called *sootak* is observed for one-and-quarter months. The *mundan* ceremony is performed at one, three or five years of age. The main marriage rituals are performed at the bride's residence. The ritual of *rokiya* makes the final settlement of the alliance. This is followed by *sagai*. The ritual of *milni* takes place after the arrival of the groom's party. Marriage rituals are performed around the sacred fire by the priest among the Hindu Mahasha. Consummation of marriage is at the groom's residence.

The dead body is cremated and the bones are immersed in the holy Ganga at Hardwar or at Kiratpur Sahib in Ropar district. On the fourth day the bones are brought from the cremation ground for immersion in water. This is known as *phul chugna*. On the tenth day, the ritual of *rasam pagri* or *uthala* takes place. Birth pollution is observed for thirteen days followed by purificatory bath, known as *guntar*. A big loaf of bread and sweet porridge is prepared and offered to the deity Dewat Siddh.

Since the *shuddhi* movement, introduced by the Arya Samaj, they have given up the work of scavenging and bamboo work. The primary occupation of the community is agricultural wage labour. Large number of them are rickshaw pullers. Some of them have also entered government services and private jobs. Most of them are illiterate. Payment of wage is made both in cash and kind. Statutory *gram panchayat* exists at the village level.

Ibbetson and Rose have indicated in their reports that Dumna is primarily a Hindu and it is hard to find either a Sikh or a Muslim among them. However, the twentieth century has seen a considerable change among them particularly due to the impact of the Arya Samaj movement, Sikhism, and of late, the impact of the Radhaswamis. The study by Sharma (1985) clearly brings out the impact of the *shuddhi* ceremonies of Arya Samaj among Mahashas. Sharma observes, '*Shuddhi* thus was an act of mobilization of untouchables for the cause of Hindus, consequently boosting Hindu consciousness, solidarity and integration' (pp. 93-4). The studies of Ibbetson, Rose and Sharma indicate that this community was socially segregated in the past. The only significant thing experienced by them currently was the shift from traditional 'Dumna' to 'Mahasha' nomenclature. There is a strong tendency among the Mahashas to be identified as part of Hindu community. Sharma's data also indicate that most of the Mahashas had undergone through *shuddhi* ceremony which meant performing of *havan yajna* after their birth following which they were initiated with a sacred thread. This was strongly resisted by caste Hindus. A sizeable section among the Mahasha had some knowledge of the principles and doctrines of the Arya Samaj. The overwhelming proportion of the respondents in Sharma's study have indicated that the stigma of untouchability prompted them to accept *shuddhi* movement. Mahashas now consider their social status to be superior to that of the Scheduled Castes.

The Mahashas worship Nagdevta at the family level. Their major festivals are Lohri, Diwali, Dussehra, Holi, etc. Untouchability is fast declining. They accept water and food from all other local Hindu communities. They share wells and other water sources, crematoria, religious shrines, with other local communities. Landlord-tenant relationship exists. Some of them have taken to white-collar jobs and in defence services. Political leadership among them has emerged at village *panchayat* level and even at the state level.

Boys are taking advantage of formal education but not the girls. Most of them are illiterate or educated only upto the level of primary to middle school. Their attitude towards family planning is not favourable due to their lack of awareness. Facility of drinking water is availabe within the locality through hand-pumps. Electricity is available to them. Cow-dung cakes is their main fuel source. Ration shops are available and sugar and kerosene is supplied to them at controlled rates. They avail of the loans from the banks for purchasing animals, rickshaws and starting small shops.

RAKESH KUMAR
K. GOPALA IYER

# MAHATAM

The Mahatam have a tendency to indentify themselves as 'Rai Sikhs' but the Rai Sikhs who are concentrated in Ferozepur district do not consider the Mahatams as 'Rai Sikhs'. They trace their earlier caste affiliation to the Rajputs. Ibbetson (1916: 203) states that one of their ancestors was a *kanungo* addressed as 'Mahta' by Akbar. The first Mahta settled in Mahatpur in Jalandhar. Here, they adopted the custom of widow marriage, called *chadar dalna* and so became Shudras. Ibbetson confirms that the Jalandhar Mahatams trace their origin from Jammu. The *Punjab District Gazetteer*, Jalandhar Division (1904: 84-5), notes that the Muslim Mahatams were Rajput in origin and became Mahatams by adopting the custom of widow marriage. They communicate in the local Punjabi dialect within the family and with other community memebrs. The script used is Gurmukhi. The term Mahatam has been anathema for them which they want to cast off at any rate. This indicates that their self-perception continues to be low.

They are essentially non-vegetarian though beef is prohibited in the community. Alcoholic drinks are consumed by males only and are purchased from the market. Wheat, pulses, rice, maize and vegetables are their main food ingredients. Locally available fruits such as mango, banana, grapes, papaya, guava, peaches and apple are consumed occasionally. Cooking is done with vegetable *ghee*, oil and *desi ghee*. Milk and milk-products are consumed in plenty. Liquor and sweets are avoided during mourning periods. There is increase in the consumption of meat, eggs and fish these days.

The majority of them have converted to Sikhism and the community has some subcastes and *gots* with no hierarchy among them. The function of the *gots* is to regulate marriage alliances. The Mahatams are aware and recognize their place in society as Rajputs. They consider themselves at par with other Rajput communities, but the Rajputs consider them as socially inferior to them.

Mahatams are endogamous at community level but practise village and *got* exogamy. Age at marriage is around seventeen to eighteen years for girls and twenty to twenty-two years for boys. Marriage symbols are *bindi*, *sindur*, finger ring, toe ring, ear- and nosering. The concept of *kanyadan* exists and dowry is given both in cash and kind. The rules of residence after marriage is patrilocal. Divorce is normally not allowed, but is permissible only on grounds of adultery and moral turpitude. Compensation is given to wife. Either party can divorce with the approval of the village or community elders or the court and the children remain under the care of the father. Remarriage is permitted in case of young widows and divorcees but widowers and divorced male can remarry freely. Junior levirate called *chadar paona* is permitted.

Extended and nuclear family types are prevalent among the Mahatam. Avoidence relationship is observed between father-in-law and daughter-in-law, husband's elder brother and his wife and all the family, village and communty male and female elders. Male equigeniture is the rule of inheritance. Daughters can also claim their rights. Succession goes to the eldest son.

Women help their men in agricultural operations and various other related activities. They not only do the household chores but also actively participate in animal husbandary and carrying potable water. They do not have decision-making powers. On all major issues the final decision is taken by the male members alone.

Post-delivery pollution is observed for one-and-a-quarter month. The naming ceremony is observed in case of male children only. The ritual of first feeding of cereals, *gurti*, is observed. The main marriage ceremony is performed at the bride's residence and a feast is given by her parents. Marriage ceremony is performed by the *gurdwara* priest. They take four *pheras* around the *Guru Granth Sahib*. Consum-mation of marriage is at the bride's residence. The dead are cremated and bones are immersed in the holy Ganga at Hardwar. Death pollution is observed for eleven or seventeen days. This pollution period ends usually in the form of a feast. Agriculture, labour and government and private services are the main occupation of the Mahatams. The land is fertile and well irrigated by tube well and canals. The landless go in for agricultural labour in other's field and some are in *van watna* (rope-making) occupation. Cows and buffaloes are also reared and milk is sold. Statutory *panchayat* exists to implement welfare and development activities.

Sikh Gurus are worshipped by the Mahatams. *Guru Granth Sahib* is the sacred scripture. The sacred shrines and centres of pilgrimage are of the same as of other local Sikh communities. Commonly visited pilgrim centres are Hardwar, Vaishnodevi, Amritsar, Anandpur Sahib and Kiratpur Sahib. Services of the *bhaijee* are availed of for performing the rituals connected with birth, marriage and death. The major festivals observed by them are Dussehra, Diwali, Holi, Lohri, Baisakhi and all the Guruparabs. They are basically converts from

Hinduism. Oral tradition in the form of folk songs, and folk tales exist.

They accept from and exchange water and food with all other local communities but not with some Scheduled Caste communities. They share well and other water sources, cremation grounds, religious shrines and traditional festivals with other local communities. Landlord-tenant relationship is present.

Some of them have taken to white-collar jobs and defence services. Political leadership has emerged at village *panchayat* level. Boys are taking advantage of formal education but only a very few girls are doing so. Most of them are illiterate or are educated upto the level of primary to middle standard. Their attitude towards family planning is not favourable due to lack of awareness. Drinking water is available in the locality through handpumps. They listen to the radio. Only very few of them own television sets. Their fuel source is cow-dung cakes. They avail the facilities of public distribution system. Facilities of ration shops are available and sugar and kerosene oil are supplied at a subsidized price. Banking facilities are available and the Mahatams avail of the loan given for purchasing animals or setting up small shops and for rope-making machines.

RAKESH KUMAR

# MAZHABI

The Mazbi or Mazhabi, is a Chuhra, who has become Sikh. Rose (1919) mentions that Mazhabi means nothing more than the scavenger class converted to Sikhism. The Mazhabis take the *pahul* (Sikh baptism), keep their hair long, and abstain from tobacco, and they apparently refuse to touch night soil, though they perform all the other traditional work of the Chuhra. Their great Guru is Guru Tegh Bahadur, whose body was brought back from Delhi by the Chuhras who were admittted to Sikhism by Guru Gobind Singh as a reward for their devotion. They are good soldiers and some of India's pioneer regiments are wholly composed of the Mazhabis. One of the bravest of the generals of the Gurus was Jiwan Singh, a Mazhabi, whose Samadh is at Chamkaur Sahib. Maharaja Ranjit Singh had a great appreciation for their bravery and enlisted them freely.

The Mazhabi living in Ambala, Ludhiana, and the neighbouring areas consider themselves socially superior to the rest. But it appears that the Rangrethas have abandoned scavenging for better work and this would at once account for their rise in the social scale. The Mazhabis have also social distinctions among themselves. The descendants of the true Mazhabis who rescued Guru Tegh Bahadur's body are the only real Mazhabis but the term is applied commonly to even the more recent converts. Recent converts are looked upon more or less with a critical view and are termed as the Malwais. Until lately the Mazhabis were never found in large numbers in any locality.

According to the *Census of India* (1981), their total population is 13,66,843 individuals which has 7,32,949 males and 6,33,894 females. Amritsar, Ferozepur and Bhatinda districts, have their maximum concentration. They speak Punjabi language and use Gurmukhi script. They have been recognized as a Scheduled Caste. Wheat is their staple food. Pulses used are gram, *urad*, *moong*, *moth* and *masur*. Alcoholic drinks are occasionally used. They do not smoke.

They are divided into different exogamous *gots* and marry within their own community. Intercommunity or interreligion marriages are very rare. They do not carry night soil and occupy a higher position, in the social hierarchy than the Chuhras. They place themselves as

Shudra in the *varna* system. Others consider them inferior due to their past association with the Chuhras. Adult marriage is practised. Marriages are settled through negotiation with the help of a *vichola* or mediator. Monogamy is the prevailing form of marriage. Dowry is given in kind. Rule of residence after marriage is patrilocal. Divorce and remarriage is permitted. Either party can divorce.

Joint families are still common among them, but they are disintegrating into nuclear families. *Purdah* or *ghund* is observed from father-in-law and husband's elder brother. Joking relations are maintained between the *bhabi* and *dewar*, *jeeja* and *sali* and between *sadus* (co-brothers). Most of the conflicts in the family are resolved with the help of elders (*siana*) by mutual compromise. Male equigeniture is the rule of inheritance. All the sons inherit their father's property equally. Eldest son succeeds. Status of women is low.

Women attend to the household activities and take care of the children. They work as agricultural labourers, apart from looking after the domestic animals, collecting fuel and bringing potable water. They play an important role in social functions and rituals of their community. Postnatal restrictions are observed and they start attending to the household activities after seven days. Marriage ceremony is performed according to the Sikh traditions of four *lavan phere*, at the residence of the bride. Consummation of marriage is at the bridegroom's residence. They cremate the dead and death pollution is observed for eleven days; purification ceremony is performed through the recital of *Guru Granth Sahib*.

Their main occupation is agricultural labour, industrial worker or government service. They are landless but expert in agricultural operations. They do not have traditional *panchayat*. Earlier, they were Hindus and were known as the Chuhra but came to be known as the Mazhabi after embracing Sikhism. Some of them have become Nihang Sikhs and wear typical dress of the Nihangs. They accept and exchange food from most of the neighbouring communities. But members of higher social classes do not accept water and food from them due to their past affiliation with the Chuhras. They share road, well, schools, *panchayat ghars* with others. They are employed in defence services, as teachers and in administration.

Boys and girls are encouraged by giving them scholarships to continue their studies. But in spite of favourable educational facilities they are not in a position to avail of the opportunity. The number of drop-outs is still higher among the girls. Medical facilities are available. They generally consult the village *vaid* for medical treatment.

Members of very poor families have been provided with yellow cards to borrow money from the banks. Some of them are employed in government jobs. Radio, cinema, postal services, rail, road and electricity facilities are available. Their attitude towards savings is positive.

SWARAN SINGH

# MEGH

Meghs are also known as Meg or Mihngh.

Rose (1919: 477) states that according to a legend the ancestor of the Megh community used to live in Benaras city and he was a Brahman and had two sons, one of them was very learned and the other was illiterate. The father asked his elder son to teach the younger one, but the elder one disobeyed his father. The father became very annoyed and turned him out of his house. The eldest son left the house and started teaching the children. On one occasion, while performing *aswamedha yajna*, he failed to bring back to life a dead cow, while his father succeeded in doing so. When his father forbade him to eat with him, he became very annoyed and severed all his connections with his father and his descendants are called Mihnghs.

The Meg or Meghs are recognized as a Scheduled Caste and its population according to *Census of India* (1981), is 78,405 individuals; which has 41,861 males and 36,544 females. They are found in all the districts of Punjab, but their major concentration is in the districts of Gurdaspur and Ferozepur.

The Meg or Mong, is the Chamar below the Jammu Hills. But he appears to be of a slightly better standing than the Chamar; and this superiority is due to the fact that the Meg is a weaver as well as a worker in leather, as weaving stands in the social scale a degree higher than shoe-making (Ibbetson 1916). Their concentration is sufficiently high in Jammu and most of the Meghs have migrated either from Jammu or Sialkot (Pakistan). In Hoshiarpur area, they speak Dogri language and use Dogri script. However, at present they speak Punjabi and Hindi and use Gurmukhi and Devanagari scripts. The males wear *kurta*, *pyjama* or *dhoti*, some also wear turban. Their women wear *salwar*, *kameez* and *dupatta*. Those, who have become followers of Arya Samaj are vegetarians and do not take alcoholic drinks. Wheat is their staple food. Rice is taken occasionally. *Makki di roti* and *sarson da sag* is a popular dish during the winter months. Pulses such as gram, *moong*, *masur* or *moth* are also taken by them. Mustard or groundnut oil is used as cooking medium. Milk, tea and curd is also taken. Alcoholic drinks are consumed occasionally by some members. They smoke cigarettes or *bidi*.

When the boys and girls attain adulthood, parents arrange their marriage. The age at marriage varies from twenty years to twenty-five years. They marry within their own community but outside their own *got.* The marriage is simple. The Meghs have the following *gots:* Kushal, Bhardawaj, Uttar, Kaship, Sangarai, Pandam, Kalra and Surajmukhi.

The marriage is performed according to the Hindu traditions. Dowry depends on the financial condition of the girl's parents. Married girls use vermilion, bangles, *bindi* and earring as the symbols of marriage. After marriage the girl goes to stay with her husband. Divorce is allowed with the approval of the court of law. Remarriage is also permitted with the sanction of their traditional caste *panchayat.* Widow remarriage is permitted, but a widow is expected to marry her deceased husband's elder or younger brother. If they are not available she can, with the consent of her guardians, give her hand to any man of the caste, to which the deceased belonged. But if she wishes to marry a man of a different caste from that of her former husband's, he must bear all the expenses of the marriage, or if unable to do so he must give his sister or daughter or any other near relative to some male member of the widow's household in exchange.

Most of the families are joint, but nuclear families are also increasing. The sons equally share the property of their father and the eldest son succeeds his father. The women attend to the household activities. The women have low status. The Meghs, who have become Arya Samajis consider themselves of higher status. But the members of other communities still consider the Meghs to be low status. The post-delivery restrictions on mother and pollution period is observed. The *namkaran* ceremony is performed. The marriage rituals take place at the residence of both the boy and the girl. *Roti* (feast) is given by the girl's parents. Consummation of marriage is at the bridegroom's residence. They cremate their dead. The *shuddhi karan* ceremony is performed and a feast (*roti*) is given to the members of the community. The bones of the dead are immersed in the Ganga at Hardwar. Ancestor worship is also observed.

By occupation, the Meghs are largely weavers and they profess to have learnt this calling from Kabir the *bhagat.* But they also follow various other pursuits, as for example, service as field labourers or domestic. They engage themselves either in business or as labourers in various leather industries. Some of them are engaged in cycle repairing, making saddles, and spare parts of bicycles. They used to be engaged in weaving in the past. They have their traditional caste councils, known as Megh Sabha. They have constructed their own *dharamshala.* They have the Punjab Meg Sabha and the All India Meg Sabha to look into the matters of common interest of the Meghs. The Meg Sabha consists of *pradhan,* secretary, treasurer and the members. Disputes relating to land, water, marriage and engagement are settled by the caste *panchayat.* They belonged to Hindu religion. Later on a large number of them became Arya Samaji. They mostly worship the Vaishno Devi. Few of them are also followers of the Radhaswami sect. They celebrate Lohri, Diwali, and Dussehra. They have their oral traditions including folk songs, folklore and folk tales.

They exchange and accept food and water from other communities. They share source of water, road, school, place of worship with the members of other communities but have their own cremation ground. The community has few educated individuals who are engaged in white-collar jobs as teachers, administrators, etc. Political leadership has emerged at all levels. The educated members of the community are called *bhagat.*

Formal education is favoured for both boys and girls. They study upto college and even university level. They visit hospitals for modern medicare. Their attitude towards family planning is favourable and they generally prefer three children. Drinking water facilities are available within the locality. Coal, cow-dung cakes and kerosene oil are used as fuel. Their attitude towards saving is positive.

SWARAN SINGH

# MIRASI

The Mirasi community derives its name from *miras* which means inheritance. They keep record of the genealogies of various communities such as the Jats, Rajputs, etc., just like the Bhats. Some of the Mirasi are said to claim an Arabic origin. According to one version, the Prophet had once whipped a Akasa (Kassa), a Muslim from Medina and on his death-bed, he asked him to take vengeance on him, in case he had injured any one. Akasa took no revenge but kissed the back of Prophet. One of the descendants of Akasa, obtained the office of a herald after migrating to Persia, and his descendants Quaraishi and Basala (Posla) along with Khwaja Muin-ud-din Chisti came to India and became the Mirasis of the Shaikhs and Sayyids. However according to another version of their origin, Akasa had his son Wahid, who was the jurist of a famous Caliph Umar. Abdulla taught him the law of inheritance and the pedigrees. But the descendants of Akasa restricted their job to the recitation of the pedigrees. Yet another version says that one Asha, who was the servant of the Prophet gave him the title of Mir Asa who was later called the Sultan Mir and whose descendants were called the Miran Sayyids, or the Mirasis (Ibbetson, 1916: 234).

Some Mirasis claim to be the descendants of Kolak Das, son of Brahma. Kolak Das sucked away his father's leprosy and in gratitude Brahma bestowed upon him the boon, that he should be revered by the people and that all he said should be true. So the people trust the Mirasis to this day. The earlier ethnographic account has been found to be true. They speak Punjabi and Urdu languages with the members of their family and use Arabic or Gurmukhi scripts. However, with others they use Punjabi language and use either Gurmukhi or Arabic script. They are non-vegetarians but they avoid consuming pork. Groundnut oil is used as cooking medium. They take tea, *lassi* and milk products, but not alcoholic drinks. However, the Balmiki Mirasi consume alcoholic drinks occasionally. They also smoke.

They are divided into Balmiki, Doom and Muslim Mirasis and have different *gots*. There are also Bhand or Naqqal among them. There are both Hindu and Muslim Mirasis who are musicians. Some of the *gots* of Balmiki Mirasis are, Gill, Kalayana, Shergill, Randhawa, Karu, Kandyara, Bhatti, Sandhu, Nahar, Dhab, Hans, Ghusar, Sahote, etc.

Though they are aware of the *varna* system, they do not recognize their place in the *varna* system. They consider themselves to be of high social status but others consider them of low status. Even the Mirasis of the Rajas consider themselves of higher status than the Mirasis of the Balmiki. Mirasis of different communities do not intermarry. The Mirasis of the Balmiki will marry among themselves, whereas the Muslim Mirasis will observe their endogamy. The Hindus do not marry within the same *gots* but the Muslims do.

Marriage among the Mirasis is arranged by negotiations after the boys and girls attain adulthood. Monogamy is the form of marriage among the Hindus but among the Muslims, polygyny is allowed. Among the Hindus, vermilion, bangles, *bindi* and finger ring are the marriage symbols. Among the Hindus, dowry is given in kind which includes furniture, clothes, bedding, ornaments and utensils depending upon the financial condition of the girl's parents. Among the Muslims, *mehar* is promised for future payment, which varies from ten to twenty thousand rupees. The rule of residence after marriage is patrilocal. Divorce due to maladjustement, barrenness is allowed. Compensation to the wife is given in case of a divorce. Either party can divorce. Children remain under the care of either mother or father. Remarriage is also allowed.

They live either in nuclear or joint families but joint families are more common. Sons inherit the property of their father equally and the eldest son succeed. Women have low status. They attend to household jobs, bring potable water and perform rituals. They neither contribute to family income nor control the family expenditure. There are pre-delivery restrictions. Post-delivery restrictions are observed for forty days. Pollution is also observed after the delivery. Circumcision is performed for the male child among the Muslims and also the *aqiqa* ceremony. The marriage ceremony is performed according to the respective religious traditions of the community such as *nikah* among the Muslims, seven *pheras* among the Hindus and *anand karaj* among the Sikhs. They bury their dead and invite their own community brethren to perform the last rites at the time of death. However, among the Muslims they offer prayers from the Holy Quran after three days of death of an individual and feast (*roti*) is offered to the members of the community. The Hindus cremate and immerse the ashes in water and also worship their ancestors.

They are a landless community who are traditionally engaged by others as musician and *bhand* (*naqqals*). They also beg or work as labourers. They settle all their disputes themselves and nominate their own *pradhan* or *chaudhary* or *nambardar*, according to one's good work. All cases of marriage disputes are referred to the *panchayat*. They impose fines and excommunication on the guilty. Rose (1914: 109-12) gives the following idea of the Mirasi organization.

The Rai Mirasi: They should be compared with the Rai Bhat, he is a man of education and teaches boys Hindi accounts like a Pandha. He is also a poet and composes Kabits. The Rai Bhats are Mirasis of the Jats. Rais claim to have been Hindu Bhats who were converted to Islam but continued to compose and recite Kabits after conversion. Being Brahmans by descent and in former times having been attached to ruling chiefs they stand high in the Mirasi social scale and do not intermarry outside their own group. They get *lags* (commissions) at wedding and on the birth of a son.

Mir Mirasis: The term Mir is applied to any Mirasi out of courtesy. It is also said that the Mir Mirasi is so called because he is Mirasi of the wealthy. But in Ludhiana a Mir Mirasi is defined to be one who taking a *jhanda* (a pole with a pennon) in hand recites verses in honour of their priest *lakhdata*. The Dhadi is one who plays the Dhadh and sings the deeds of heroes dead.

The Kalawant: They are described as the Mirasis of the Rajputs.

The Kumachi Mirasis serve Brahmans. But according to another account they were themselves Bari Brahmans. They say when the Muslim rulers began to convert those Brahmans by force to Islam, one of their ancestors offered himself as a convert on condition that he and his descendants be held in respect by all the Bari Brahmans.

Mir Mangs are Mirasis of the Mirasis, keeping their pedigrees and taking alms from them alone. In Gurdaspur they appear to be called Mir Malang. Naqarchis are Mirasis who play the *nagara* or big drum at weddings. Rababis are Mirasi, who play the *rabab*. They trace their descent from Bhai Mardana, a Mirasi who used to play the *rabab* as accompaniment to Guru Nanak. They are Sikhs and believe in him and recite *shabads* from *Granth Sahib*.

According to *Census of India* (1911: 469), the total population of the Mirasis including Dum, Dhadi, Kalaunt, Kamachi, Mir, Mirzada, Mutrib, Naqarchi, Naqib, Qawal, Sarnai was 2,27,394 individuals, with 1,22,071 males and 1,05,323 females.

They belong to both Hindu and Islam religion and worship according to their respective traditions. The Sikh Mirasis are called Dhadi and Rababis and they worship *Guru Granth Sahib*. They celebrate Lohri, Diwali, Dussehra and Id. Mardana is also worshipped who was one of the disciples of Guru Nanak. The sacred specialists are from other communities, who worship and perform various rites. The community has oral traditions, they sing *qawwalis* and *waran* and folk songs and use all sorts of musical instruments.

They accept and exchange food and water from the members of their own religion. But the members of higher social status do not accept food and water from them. They have separate cremation ground. Patron-client relationship exists. Rose (1914: 112-13) states that the Mirasis are further divided into *gots*. The Poslas are subdivided into four sections, Ghorian, Kharia, Malhar and Gurbal, and these with the Biru, Dedan and Saik are Mirasis of the Sayyids. The Malet, Quraishis and Sohal are Mirasis to the Shaikhs. Dair and Tanor: attached to Rajputs. Kallal, Lalha, Monga and Sanp: attached to Jats, Changar: attached to Brahmas, Barwal: attached to Mahajans, Sohal - attached to Khatris, Lat Kanian: attached to Malis.

The Naqqal Mirasis are found in Ludhiana. With *chamota* (a piece of leather) in their hands they mimic Julahas (weavers) and others. During the time of the Muslim kings, they were made to embrace Islam and soon they learned to play musical instruments. As they adopted singing they had to mix with the Mirasis and learn the art of singing and playing. Since then they are called Naqqal or Bhand, but they do not marry with the Mirasis. They visit their patrons after six months or one year.

Formal education is favoured for the boys and girls. The boys study upto secondary level. There are a few graduates and post-graduates among them. But the girls study upto primary level only because they are poor. Their attitude towards health and medical care is favourable. They prefer four or more children. Drinking water facilities are not available in all the settlements of the community. They are employed in their traditional occupation as Qawwals and Naqqals. They congratulate the client on the eve of marriage and get some money from them as a reward.

They make use of the various media and communication facilities. All the households do not have electric connections. Wood and cow-dung cakes are used as fuel. They have ration card facilities to get sugar and kerosene oil. They approach the landlords or businessmen for loans. They are benefited by the midday meal and immunization programmes.

SWARAN SINGH

# MOCHI

Rose (1919: 123), states that the word Mochi is the name of an occupation and signifies the worker in tanned leather as distinguished from tanner. The Mochi not only makes leather articles, but he also grains leather and gives it a surface colour or stain as distinguished from a colour, dyed throughout. In the west of Punjab however, it is simply used to designate the Muslim Chamar; and are same as the Chamar of the east though his change of religion improves, though only slightly, higher social position. In Hoshiarpur, majority of the Mochis are said to be weavers, and they are not admitted to religious or social com-munion by the other Muslims.

The Mochi deals with cobbler's work. They speak a mixture of Rajasthani and Hindustani dialects at home and Punjabi with others and use Devanagari script. They eat both vegetarian and non-vegetarian food. Pork is eaten. Their staple food is wheat and rice. Alcoholic drinks are consumed by the male members occasionally.

They are divided into a number of *gots* which regulate marriage alliances. Rose (1919: 123) has listed many *gots* of the Mochi, e.g. Bara, Biswan, Chohan, Jabar, Jakhrah, Jhalli, Kuldhar, Khilar, Kilry, Bangar, Mahmau, Ratanpal, Bhatti, Shihmar, Sindhu (in Ludhiana), Balu, Bangarh, Chandhar, Gai, Galhot, Kuler, Mallan, Nagah, Rattu, Sapron, Sarheb, Summan (in Nabha), Banjara Jat, Bhatti Rajput, Bhatti Jat, Chandhar, Daryah, Dhaliwal, Ganere, Gil, Harar, Jat, Kainkar, Kaler Jat, Kantha, Khang Jat, Khokhar Lagah, Lakhi, Mahras, Motle, Salam, Sasan Jat, Shabhmar, Sinh, Soni Khatri, Suman Mochi, Tur (in Kapurthala).

Clan or *got* names are used as surnames. They are recognized as Shudra by self as also by other local communities. They consider themselves as Chamars and practise *got* and village exogamy. Adult marriage is the practice which is settled through negotiation. Monogamy is the rule. The bride price has been replaced by dowry nowadays. Rules of residence after marriage is patrilocal. Divorce is allowed and widow remarriage is permissible. Both nuclear and joint family types prevail. Avoidance relationship is seen between daughter-in-law and father-in-law; *jeth* and younger brother's wife. The traditional joking relationship is seen as in other communities.

All the sons have equal rights in the paternal property and

succession goes to the eldest son. Women have low status in the society. Postnatal pollution is observed and is followed by *mundan* ceremony. The dead are cremated and the bones are immersed in water. Marriage is performed as per the Hindu rites. Consummation of marriage is at the groom's residence.

Shoe-making with processed leather and repairing shoes is their main occupation. They are governed by the modern local civic and judicial systems. They profess Hinduism and worship deities of wider pantheon order. Many have become the followers of Arya Samaj. The Ravidas temple in Varanasi, Garili Nath temple in Alwar and Chamara-di-Gaddi in Bohor village are their sacred shrines. A socio-religious movement has been operating to unite all the communities dealing with leather.

The linkages are strong with the communities dealing with leather. They do not accept water and food from the Chuhras, Deha, Sansi and Dumra. Other communities such as the Brahman, Jat, Khatri and Bania do not accept water and food from them. They have access to the facilities of roads and schools but have separate water sources, cremation ground and places of worship. They participate in political activities and public functions especially in association with other Scheduled Caste communities. They have businessmen in modern intercommunity linkages.

Their attitude towards developmental programmes is positive. Literacy rate is low particularly for girls. Health and medical care facilities are availed of from the government dispensaries or even from private doctors. They are aware of the advantages of a small family and have adopted modern methods of family planning including sterilization. They listen to the radio occasionally, visit the cinema and watch television. Electricity is available for domestic purposes. Facilities of fair price shops are availed of. Banking facility is also available for saving and loan purposes.

A.K. BHATIA

# NAI

The Nai is an occupational community whose members are traditionally engaged in hair-cutting. They are fondly referred to as Rajaji or Ustadji and are distributed throughout the state. They speak Punjabi both with the kin group and in relation to others using Devanagari script.

They are both vegetarians and non-vegetarian. *Roti* with *dal* and *sabzi* forms the staple diet. Cereals consumed are wheat, maize and rice which are their staple food. Locally available pulses and vegetable are consumed. Egg eaters are considered non-vegetarian. Meat eaters consume mutton, chicken and fish. Women are generally vegetarian. *Ghee*, mustard oil and other refined oils form cooking medium. Tea is the most favoured non-alcoholic drink of members of all age groups. They consume roots and tubers in the form of onion, potatoes, ginger, radish and carrot. Men generally take alcoholic drinks. Milk and milk products are consumed in varying quantities. Smoking habit is prevalent and *bidi*, cigarettes and *hookah* (hubble bubble) are smoked.

Social divisions exist in the form of *got*. Some of them are Kalri Phuman, Bhatia, Saddar, Bali, Lakhanpal and Chole. They regulate marriage alliance and indicate descent and ancestry. They are considered of low social standing, just above the Scheduled Castes and are deemed as clean Shudra. They have a high self-perception in as much as considering themselves of Kshatriya origin. Others have a low perception of them due to the nature of their occupation of nail and hair-cutting. In marriage, endogamy is the rule and exogamy is practised at the *got* and village levels. Earlier they used to avoid four *gots* for fixing marriage, that is, of self, mother's and grandmother's (both paternal and maternal). But now only two *gots* are avoided, i.e. of self and mother's.

Marriages are negotiated after the boys and girls attain adulthood. Monogamy is the rule. *Kanyadan* exists and dowry is given in cash and kind, consisting of household articles and jewellery. *Bindi*, bangles and *sindur* form the marriage symbols. Rule of residence after marriage is patrilocal. Divorce is traditionally not permitted. Widow, widower and divorcee remarriage is also not permitted but for willing and young individuals. In changes in the institution of marriage, there is an increase in age at marriage, marriage symbols not being observed strictly, incidences of divorce and liberal attitude towards remarriage. Both nuclear and extended family types prevail. Avoidance relationship is observed between daughter-in-law and father-in-law; husband's elder brother; younger brother's wife. Joking relationships are observed between sister's husband and wife's younger brother and sister; and grandparents and grand childrens. The rule of inheritance is male equigeniture and succession goes to the eldest son. Women's role is mainly confined to the household chores and looking after the family and its needs. They also attend and participate in rituals and religious affairs. At times they take up midwife's services for massaging after delivery. They contribute to the family income yet have a low status.

Life-cycle rituals at the time of birth, marriage and death are observed. Pre-delivery restrictions are imposed. Post-delivery pollution is observed for thirteen or forty days. It is known as *sootak*. After *sootak* period is over *chowki-charna* ritual is performed. Naming and *mundan* ceremonies are performed. *Mundan* is generally performed in the first, third or fifth year. Marriage rituals are performed at the bride's residence and feast is given by the bride's parents. Some of the rituals are also performed at the groom's residence. The main marriage rituals are *rok*, *mangni*, *shagun*, *barat*, *phere* and *doli*. Actual marriage is performed by taking *phere* around the sacred fire conducted by a Brahman priest. Consummation of marriage is at the groom's residence.

The dead are cremated and ashes are immersed in water. Death pollution is observed for eleven days for women and thirteen days for men. The charred bones, called *phul* are collected on the fourth day and are immersed in the holy Ganga. *Kirya*, *uthala* or *rasam pagri* takes place as the last ritual on the eleventh or thirteenth day. Ancestor worship is not observed.

They belong to the occupational category of communities traditionally engaged in hair-cutting against remuneration. Some of them have also taken to other occupations such as dry-cleaning, petty shopkeeping, hosiery and pulling rickshaw and auto rickshaw. Transactions are in cash. Child labour exists to augment family income. Very few are reported to have taken to clerical jobs in private, public and government sectors. Hair-cutting and allied occupations such as shaving, hair-dying, hair-grooming, etc., has become quite lucrative. Traditional caste *panchayat* or *jati-biradari* does not exist but they have unions in the name of barber-union at various levels to look after their occupational interests. Ad hoc *biradari* may also be formed consisting of a few elders and enlightened members of the community for solving community or inter-family disputes. If not satisfied, the aggrieved party is free to approach the court. Those living in urban areas are governed by the local civil and judicial-bodies. Those living in rural areas are governed by the statutory *panchayat* which is heterogeneous and has a defined role in planning and implementing developmental activities.

They subscribe to Hindu religion and Hindu way of life. Fairs, festivals and shrines are the same as of the other Hindus. Lohri, Holi, Diwali, Dussehra, Baisakhi, Janamashtami and Shivratri are the common festivals of the community. The service of the Brahman priests is availed of for performing birth, marriage and death rites and for religious teaching. Women during their spare time do knitting and embroidery. They share Punjabi folk songs, folk tales and folklores with other local communities.

From other communities they accept water and food but do not exchange with them. However, this rigidity is losing ground particularly in the urban areas. They share cremation ground, religious shrines and water-sources with other communities of the region. Formal education is generally not favoured for both boys and girls. Both boys and girls drop out of school due to poverty and disinterest. Their attitude is favourable for modern methods of family planning including sterilization. They visit local government dispensaries, hospitals and private practitioners in case of need. Drinking water is available in the locality and so is electricity. They listen to the radio, watch television and visit the cinema for entertainment. Facilities of banks and fair price shops are available to them. Coal, wood, kerosene oil or even liquified petroleum gas are the fuels used by them. Their attitude towards saving is favourable.

A.K. Bhatia

# NALBAND

The Nalbands had been included in Lohars by Rose (1970: 36) and Ibbetson (1981: 312) in their survey of Punjab castes and tribes. According to Rose 'Nalband' or 'Ferrier' denotes special branches of Lohar community. He also noted that some Lohars have been returned as Nalbands or 'ferriers'. However, Lohars who were interviewed in different districts of Punjab do not include themselves as part of their community nor do they have any occupational or marital relationship with them. After Partition of India in 1947 a large number of Nalband families have migrated to Pakistan. Nalbands were primarily Muslims in Punjab. Only few families of Nalband have been left in Punjab now. They are mostly concentrated in Malerkotla area and in Ropar district or nearby areas. After the migration of the Nalbands to West Pakistan, Lohars (non-Muslim) and other castes have started the occupation of *nalbandi* (fixing horseshoe). Nalbands of Punjab today are Suni Muslim and follow their social and religious practices. Near Malerkotla they observe strict Muslim social customs. In other areas they have been influenced by other social practices. Some of them have adopted Sikh names, for example Ala Rata of Bhiku Majra had his Sikh name as Karam Singh. Sadiq of village Fatehpur has been known as Dyal Singh. Yusuf of Morinda is called Bachan Singh. Even names of women were changed. The Sikh names were adopted in 1947 in the face of possible retaliation by Hindus and Sikhs. There are many changes in their social practices, which took place after 1947. A few of them are noted below.

The member of the community are not able to trace their origin. They remember only one thing that profession of Nalband was followed by their great grandfather also. Although many of them don't attend to the traditional work of Nalband, yet they are very conscious about their caste, its existence and continuation, as is obvious from their marriage practices. In non-vegetarian food they insist upon *halal*, and frequently they have to go to nearby town to procure it. This is the only inhibition in food habits apart from their avoidance of pork and beef. They take all cereals, but mainly take wheat and rice and occasionally maize. All pulses and vegetables are part of their food. Depending upon their economic position they take all fruits and also *desi ghee*. Cooking is done in vegetable oil. They speak dialects of

Punjabi language of the concerned region. Some of them know Urdu language, but the younger generation is not conversant with it since its teaching was discontinued after 1947. However, Nalbands of Malerkotla region know Urdu language because of the facilities available here.

They are all Sunni Muslims. They worship in the nearby *masjids* (mosques) with other fellow Muslims. All Sunni Muslim festivals are celebrated with traditional gaiety. In addition, they go to the nearest *dargah* of Sufi Saints also. Manikpur Sharif and Ranja Sharif are also visited by them. This is shared with other communities. They observe Muslim practices of *sunnat* (circumcision) and *kalama*. Except in Malerkotla and nearby areas, many Muslim customs and practices were diluted or abandoned by them in the wake of 1947 disturbances. *Sunnat* ceremony was being observed at a late age. Now the practice of early *sunnat* has been initiated again. Similarly some of them abandoned the Muslim ceremony of marriage (*nikah*) for short time and adopted the *jaimala* practice. However, the new practice has been abandoned. Inspite of the Sunni practices, they are generally not able to distinguish themselves from Shia Muslims.

Marriage takes place strictly by Muslim rites of *nikah*. There is no consideration of *gotras*. However, now marriage among cousins is being discouraged, inspite of the fact that many in the older generation were married in this manner. The earlier practice was known as *watta* (exchange). They admit having abandoned it due to influence of other communities belonging to Sikh and Hindu religious. The *maulavi* performs the *nikah* ceremony. Brides used to wear green attire, however, now they use red bridal clothes. This is again due to external influences. Bigamy was practised earlier but now more than one marriage is not very frequent. One of the reasons is the economic pressure. Many Nalbands now avoid marriage with those who had followed the *jaimala* practice. Marriages are never arranged outside Punjab.

Similar to other Muslim communities, they also go for the burial of their dead. *Qabristan* (burial grounds) is available for the burial; and wherever it is not available, the village *sarpanch* has provided them with a place of burial. Death rites are observed after three, nine and twenty days of burial; when eatables are distributed among the *biradari*. *Pag* (turban) ceremony takes place after five weeks of the death. These practices are also common with fellow Muslims of other communities. Immediately after 1947 a few cases of cremations were reported in the wake of disturbances and atmosphere of fear; however, this practice did not last long and was discontinued once peace returned to the area.

Nalbands have been exposed to modern trends in society. Children have been going to schools. Some of them could get education even beyond matriculation. However, they are not receptive to good education for girls. Their daughters, get education at the most upto fifth class. This is a reflection of another low status of women in the community. In case of inheritance also, women are not in a position to claim property from their parents. Family planning has been accepted by some families only. Others think it is unethical to limit the number of children. Inspite of low status, their women do not wear *burqa*. Men don't consider it good to live by the earning of women. Hence, employment is traditionally discouraged for women.

They interact frequently with other religious communities like Sikhs and Hindus. They go to their religious places and even participate in their festivals. They say that no untouchability is being practised against them by other communities. This fact has been corroborated by members of other communities.

The community have been exposed to various economic changes. Many of them have left the traditional profession of *nalbandi*. Some have set up cottage industries. However, only few of them have joined the services. They have availed of yellow card facilities and applied for loan, however not for *nalbandi* but other purposes such as rearing buffalo.

VIRINDER SINGH

# NAT

The name of the community Nat is derived from the Sanskrit word *nata*, which means a dancer (Rose, 1919: 163); probably Bazigar is a synonym of Nat. There can be distinction between the two, the Bazigar is a juggler as well as an acrobat, while the Nat is only the latter, and among the Nats, only the males perform, but among the Bazigars both the sexes perform. In the present investigations the community completely dissociated itself from the Bazigar. One of the reasons behind this is that the Bazigars of the area have settled on land. They do not intermarry with the Bazigars and do not like to be addressed as Bazigars. However, the local people refer to them as Bazigar.

A recent study has pointed out that the term Nat which was applied to a number of groups 'of vagrant acrobats and showmen', and Bazigar is a 'section of Nats' (Deb, 1987: 16). Rose has also pointed out that the Nat was a caste, to which Bazigars belonged as an occupational term (1919: 164). Ibbetson had also treated the two as synonymous in 'general parlance', but he agreed that there could be distinction between the two (1916: 285). W. Crooke had perceived this as an intricate problem. In his view, 'The problem of the origin and ethnological affinities of the Nats is perhaps the most perplexing within the whole range of the ethnography of northern India. . . . The real fact seems to be that the name Nat is an occupational term which includes a number of different clans who have been grouped together merely on account of their common occupation of dancing, . . . and performance of various primitive industries' (1896: 56-8).

A few myths about their origin were noted by Rose (1919: 285-7). According to one tradition they were Brahmans of Marwar whose duty was to supply fuel for funeral pyres. In one of the marriages of their own kin, they took fuel along, lest one of them died before it was convenient for Nats to attend their duties. This was considered an ill-omened precaution and their priestly services were dispensed with. They sought the help of a *faqir* (who had a monkey) who taught them the feats of dexterity. In another legend, they were connected with the foundation of the modern state of Sirmur. A *raja* had promised a Natni half of his kingdom if she crossed and recrossed the Giri river on a tightrope. She had almost done it, when the *raja* had that rope cut to evade the promise. The *raja's* capital was swept away by the consequent fury of the river Giri. A *faqir* came to Nahar and disclosed the *raja's* treachery. He was banished from the place and took refuge with a Brahmani. He bade her fly to the other bank of the river, and the town was doomed again. Natni's kindred went to Jaisalmer to get the promised kingdom for one of her sons as successor to the *raja* of Nahar. The *raja* of Jaisalmer gave one of his pregnant *ranis* to the Nats. At Nahar she gave birth to a lion, four monsters and one son. The Nats exercised the lions and banished the monsters named Sotar, Chatan, Baithan, Kharan, and Bhau to the jungle. The son became the first Raja of Nahar. The community does not remember any of these legends. In the opinion of Blunt (1969: 150), this community included all those non- descript vagrants who wander about from country to country, making a living. They were recruited from many strata of the society and were of different social stocks. Amongst the Nats were found 'dancers, tumblers, acrobats of every variety, makers of combs, articles of grass, straw and metal; conjurers, jugglers, snake charmers, tattooers, musicians, thimble riggers and quack doctors. They themselves mentioned that they were rope dancers and now are engaged as labourers. Blunt has pointed out that 'Nat' was a sectional term among Beriyas, Habyras and Kanjar (Blunt 1969: 15). It was also a clan of Jats found in Multan (Rose, 1919: 165).

In 1931 the total Nat population was 3,80,657 in the state, out of which 2,07,245 were males, and 1,73,412 females. There were 1,02,358 Hindu, 41,820 Sikh, and 2,36,104 Muslim members of the community (*Census of India*, 1931, 289). According to 1961 census it was 1,982 out of whch 1,062 were males and 920 were females. Only 95 were returned as Sikhs; and all the rest 1,887 were Hindus (*Census of India*, 1961: 225). According to 1971 census their population was only forty-three and their district-wise distribution was nine in Gurdaspur; four in Amritsar; twenty-three in Ferozpur; two in Ludhiana; two in Patiala; and three in Bhatinda. Out of the total, thirty were returned as males and only thirteen as females (*Census of India*, 1971).

The census of 1961 and 1971 have listed them as Scheduled Caste. The community is widely distributed in many states of India. They, however, perceive their distribution only in Punjab, Haryana and Rajasthan. According to the *Census of India*, 1981, total population of the Nat is 466, with 245 males and 221 females. They speak Bagri dialect with their kin group; and with others they speak Punjabi as well. Being illiterate, they are not able to read or write. Both men and women are non-vegetarian. Wheat, rice, maize and *bajra* are their staple food. *Vanaspati* and mustard oil are used as cooking medium. Both men and women take home-made alcoholic drinks and also purchase them from the market.

Social differentiation exists at the *got* levels. Some of the *gots* are Kals, Muchal, Bhati, Chaohan and Puwar. Their self-perception is of medium level, but others consider them of low standing. In the *varna* hierarchy they recognize their place as Kshatriya. They are endogamous at community level and exogamous at village and *got* level and exclude only the *got* of the father in the settlement of marriage. Most marriages takes place in Bikaner and Alwar ditricts of Rajasthan and are negotiated by the parents. Both child and adult marriages are practised. In case of child marriage, *muklawa* ceremony takes place at the age of nineteen years. In case of adult marriage, the *muklawa* ceremony takes place immediately. They are monogamous. Vermilion, bangles, *mangal sutra*, *bindi*, finger, toe, ear and nose-rings are the marriage symbols. Practice of *kanyadan* exists. Marriages take place by Vedic rites with seven *pheras*. A *pandit* officiates the ceremony.

Rule of residence after marriage is patrilocal. Divorce is permissible with social approval in cases of maladjustment. There is no practice of compensation in divorce. In the case of remarriage of a woman, she is simply allowed to live with another man with social approval. Families are either nuclear or vertically extended. Male equigeniture is the rule of inheritance and the eldest son succeeds the authority. They give equal status to women. Women have decision-making powers and participate in economic activity as wage labourers. They have a role in social functions, rituals and religious matters. They also engage themselves in the collection of fuel and fetching potable water. They contribute to family income and have control over family expenditure. Both men and women work as wage labourers to earn their living.

Post-delivery pollution period is observed for seven days. After this period, a *pandit* is invited to name the child. Marriage rituals take place at a public place near the bride's residence. Both the parties organize a feast on the occasion of marriage. Consummation of marriage is at the grooms place. The dead are cremated and death pollution is observed for twelve days. The bones are immersed in water.

They are a poor and landless community. At present they are mainly engaged as unskilled labourers in urban areas. For social and economic reasons the traditional occupation of rope-dancing by the Natni has been discontinued as it is now considered degrading by other communities because unmarried girls had to display dance on ropes in fairs and festivals publicly. They also gave up their traditional nomadic habits.They have access to daily, fully regulated market. Child labour exists. Payment of wages is made in cash. The community professes Hinduism. The sacred specialists are hired from other communities, to perform birth, marriage and death rites. Local festivals are celebrated, which are of religious and social significance. These include Dussehra, Diwali, Baisakhi, etc. They have an oral tradition, which recalls the experiences of various places by the community.

They exchange all types of *kachcha*, *pukka* and *sidha* food with other communities. They share water, cremationg ground, religious shrines, and festivals with other communities. They have no representation in modern professions or white-collar jobs. They cherish brotherhood with the communities of the Sansi and Bangali living next door.

The community has failed to take advantage of the educational facilities. Both girls, boys, and older generation remain illiterate. They make use of both modern and traditional medicare and have also accepted the modern techniques of family planning as they prefer one or two children.

Drinking water is available within the locality. Firewood is used as fuel, but kerosene is also used occasionally. Their settlements are well connected by roads and railways. They have ration cards and avail of the facilities of public distribution system. They do not have a favourable attitude towards saving of any kind. Informations are disseminated through political parties during election days. The community is too poor to own a place of residence and are threatened with eviction from the places of their settlement.

VIRINDER SINGH

# NATH

The Nath is a Jogi order. They are the descendants of Guru Gorakh Nath and Bharthari. They wear large earrings called *mundra*, however they occupy a lower social position than the *kanpata nath*. They accept articles offered at the death or *kriya karam* of a Brahman. The Nath worship Lord Shiva, which places them very close to the Jogis, who are nothing more than the Acharj, who receive clothes of the dead person. At least one member in each Nath family gets his ears pierced, so they are also called as *kanpata nath* and are of the same social status as the Jogi-Rawals (Rose, 1919: 165).

Another version (Rose 1919: 389), says that the Nath and the Jogi are synonyms. The Jogis include the religious order of the Hindus. In this division are included Augher Jogi and the Kanphata Jogi ascetics, considered to be the followers of Guru Gorakh Nath and they worship Shiva. The Bairagis and Gosains are included in this order. Those who live a married life, called *gharisti* depend upon begging and telling fortunes.

Yet another view is exrepressed in differentiating the Jogi from *yogi*, who are mainly the *sanyasis* and practice *yogabhyas*. This order was founded by Guru Machhendra Nath and Gorakh Nath Sanyasis, who practised *yoga* and attained super power. It is only after attaining certain degree of efficiency in practising *yoga* that they are called *yogis*. The Jogis worship Bhairon, who is another form of Shiva. They are divided into Darshani and Kanphata; those who wear *mudra* are called Nath. Augher do not pierce their ear lobes. Those who carry a *thikar* (broken claypot) for seeking alms include Gudar, Sukkar, Rikhar, Bhukar, Kukar and Ukhar, the snake charmers are called as Kanipas, the followers of the Bhartrihari are known as the Bhartriharis. The other division are Shringihar and Durihar (*Census of India*, 1911: 119).

The Nath are also known as Yogi or Yoginath, and claim their origin from Swami Datta Bhra. There were nine Naths, namely, Gorakh Nath, Ad-Nath, Machhendra Nath, Udai Nath, Santosh Nath, Kambar Nath, Satya Nath, Achambha Nath and Chourangi Nath. Machhendra Nath got his education in *yoga* from its founder Swami Datta Bhra. In addition, there were eighty-four Sidhs, who were the masters of their own subjects of their times, out of whom Gorakh Nath was a very good scientist, and who continued the traditions of the community.

In his account of the origin of the Jogis, Rose (1919: 390), says that: According to the *Tahqiqat-i-Chishti*, a devotee of Shiva desired an offspring, so the god, at Parvati's intercession, gave him some ashes from his *dhuni* or fire and told him, his wife should eat them. The wife however, was incredulous and did not do so, but let the ashes fall on a heap of cow-dung. Eventually the devotee found a child where the ashes had been thrown and took it to Shiva, who said it would grow up a great ascetic and should be given to him. He named it Gorakh Nath, from the place of his birth and instructed him to find a *guru*. As Shiva could find no one worthy, Gorakh Nath set forth to seek a teacher and reaching the sea, offered there a large loaf in a *pipal* leaf. This was swallowed by Rakho, the fish, who twelve years later restored not the loaf, but a child whom Shiva named Machhendra Nath and who become Gorakh Nath's *guru*.

Another version makes Machhendra Nath the issue of Gorakh Nath himself. Shiva then told Gorakh Nath that he must, though an ascetic, have children and advised him to make disciples. Shiva also gave him *dubh* (grass), saying that it should be their clothing and a stick cut from an *ak* tree, saying it should be tied to his garments and used as a *nad*, to be sounded thrice daily: in the morning, in the evening and before the *guru*. He also asked Parvati to pierce Gorakh Nath's ears and place an earthen earring in them. This she did and also mutilated herself dyeing a cloth with the blood and giving it to Gorakh Nath to wear. Gorakh Nath then made twelve disciples: 1. Sant Nath, 2. Ram Nath, 3. Sharang or Bharang Nath, 4. Dharam Nath, 5. Bairag Nath, 6. Darya Nath, 7. Kaik Nath, 8. Nag Nath, 9. Gangai Nath, 10. Dhajja Nath, 11. Jalandhar Nath, and 12. Nim Nath.

Rose (1919: 391) has described—their origin as follows: Bhasmasur, a *rakshasa* had long served Shiva who in return promised him any boon he might claim. So he demanded that, which when placed on anything would reduce it to ashes. Shiva thereupon gave him his bangle. Bhasmasur coveted Parvati, Shiva's wife and he endeavoured to place the bangle on her husband's head. Shiva fled, pursued by the demon and at last hid in a cave on Kailas and locked up its entrance with a stone. Bhagwan now assumed Parvati's form and approached Bhasmasur, but whenever he tried to grasp the vision it eluded his embrace, and at last declared that Shiva used to sing and dance before his wife. Bhasmasur avowed his readiness to learn and while he was dancing as she taught him, she bade him place his hand on his head. In it he held the bangle and was burnt to ashes. Bhagwan then brought Shiva, who was afraid to show himself out of the cave. Shiva's curiosity was now aroused and he demanded that Bhagwan should again assume the form which had enchanted Bhasmasur. This was Mohini, Parvati's double, but even more beauteous than she, and when her shape appeared, Shiva by a process similar to that alluded to above, became the father of Hanuman, who was born of Anjani's ear, and of Machhendra Nath. By a cow he also fathered Gorakh Nath.

The Naths are always said to be nine in number. Their names and titles are variously given. Aungkar Adi Nath (lord of lords), Shiva; Shel Nath (lord of the arrow-shaft): variously said to be Krishna or Ram Chandra; Santokh Nath (lord of gratification); Achalachamba Nath (lord of wondrous immoveability): variously said to be Hanuman or Lakshmana; Gajbali Gaj Kanth Nath (lord of the elephant's strength and neck): Ganesa Gaja Karna, elephant-eared in Sanskrit; Praj Nath or Udainath (lord of the people) said to be Parvati; Mayarupi Machhendra Nath (the wondrous form) *guru* of Gorakh; Gathepinde Richayakari or Naranthar: Shambujaiti Guru Gorakh Nath and Gyansarupe (or Purakh) Sidh Chauranjive Nath, or Puran Bhagat. (Rose, 1919).

The married Naths do not put *mundra* (earring) in their ear lobes. They speak Punjabi language and use Gurmukhi script with the members of their own community and also with the outsiders. Wheat is their staple food. Few of them occasionally take alcoholic drinks. They smoke *bidi* and cigarette. Mutton is taken occasionally. Groundnut oil is used as the cooking medium.

In the past, different people and even rulers took to *yoga* (devoid of passion), hence the *gots* of the other communities such as Rajput, Rathor, Aggarwal, Bathe and Bhati are found among them. They consider themselves of high social status but do not recognize their place in the *varna* system. Members of other communities consider them as of high status. They marry within their own community but not between the same *got.* Adult marriage through negotiation is the practice. Monogamy is the common form of marriage. *Sindur* and bangles are symbols of marriage. Dowry in kind is prevalent.

Rule of residence after marriage is patrilocal. Divorce, though very rare is allowed with the approval of their own *panchayat* or court of law. Maladjustment is one of the common reasons of divorce. Remarriage is also allowed. Nuclear and joint families are common. All the sons equally inherit the property of their father, and the eldest son succeeds the authority. Status of women is low. They attend to various household activities apart from animal husbandry, collection of fuel and bringing potable water. They contribute to the family income but do not have control over the expenditure.

Pre-delivery restrictions are observed and postnatal restrictions on the mother are observed for forty days. Pollution period is observed for seven days, when the ritual of *chowke charhana* is performed and the mother and the baby are first exposed to the sun. Naming ceremony is observed and a feast for the members of the community is offered. Those who have embraced Sikhism, do not observe *mundan* ceremony. The marriage ceremony is performed at the bridegroom's residence through the rituals of four *lavan pheras* or seven *pheras*. Feast is given by the parents of the girl. Consummation of marriage is at the groom's residence. They bury their dead with the head facing towards the north. Of late, they have also started cremating their dead. The bones of the dead are immersed in the Ganga at Hardwar. *Shradh* ceremony is also observed.

The Yogi funeral rites, according to Rose (1919: 399) are: A dying Jogi is made to sit cross legged. After death, the corpse is washed by the deceased's fellow Jogis, a *langoti* tied around its waist and ashes smeared over it. A coffin is then made, if means permit, but a poor Jogi is simply wrapped in a blanket and carried by two men on two poles and the body thrown into a river. A wealthy Jogi is, however, placed on a wooden *chauki*, shaped like a palanquin and upon this flowers are cast. The procession to the grave is called *sawari* and is headed by horses and band playing music. The grave is made deep, with a spacious niche like that in Mohammedan graves and the body placed in it cross-legged and facing the north. The Jogi's *bairagan* is placed before him with a gourd full of water on his right, a loincloth, a *kanak* or staff of Mahadeo, a loaf of wheaten flour and two earthen plates, one full of water and the other of rice and milk. An earthen potsherd is also placed on his head. Then a mound is raised over the grave, and all the Jogis wash their hands with water supplied by the deceased's disciples. They then bathe and the disciples give them sweets. On the third day they are also fed. Later on the *shradh* is, if possible, performed. This is the practice today too.

They are landless but a few of them work on land. Apart from agricultural wage-labour, some of them are engaged in preparing indigenous medicines and in government service for their livelihood. Child labour has been reported. They have a traditional caste council called Bharatiya Nath Biradari Sabha. The members of the *sabha* are elected by voice vote. It deals with matters pertaining to marriage and divorce. The guilty are excommunicated or sometimes cash fines are also imposed. They belong to Hinduism, and some of them have also embraced Sikhism. Those who embraced Islam have migrated to Pakistan.

They traditionally accept and exchange water and food with the members of other communities, such as the Brahman and Bania. They have administrators, doctors and few persons in defence services. Political leaderships from among them has emerged at regional level. Though formal education is favoured for both boys and girls, most of them study only upto primary level. They prefer three children and use methods other than sterilization. Handpump and piped water are the main sources of drinking water. Most of them are self-employed and a few are in government services. They use electricity. Wood and cow-dung cakes are used as fuel. They have ration cards and get sugar from fair price shops. Their attitude towards saving is positive and they do not take loans from moneylenders and shopkeepers.

SWARAN SINGH

# NAV-BUDDHIST

The Nav-Buddhist are those Scheduled Castes who have embraced Buddhism. Dr. B.R. Ambedkar on 14 October 1956 at Nagpur had himself embraced Buddhism and also converted a large number of his followers, who came to be known as Nav-Buddhist or Neo-Buddhist. The Nav Buddhist of Punjab speak Punjabi and Hindi languages and use Gurmukhi or Devanagari scripts with the members of their own community and others.

Wheat is their staple food and they are occasional non-vegetarians. Cooking medium is groundnut oil. They do not consume alcoholic drinks. There are no social divisions but they marry within their religious group, which includes converts from other communities and thus intercommunity marriages do actually take place. They do not recognize the *varna* system but are aware of it. They consider themselves to be of high status but the members of caste Hindus consider them otherwise for their traditional occupation of tanning hides.

Though they marry within their religious group, they avoid marriage between close relatives. Adult marriages are arranged through negotiation or mutual consent. Marriage is performed according to the Buddhist tradition. Monogamy is the common form of marriage. They neither have any symbols of marriage nor dowry. The form of residence after marriage is patrilocal. Divorce though rare is permitted as is remarriage. Both nuclear and joint family types are common. Sons inherit the property of their father equally and the eldest son succeeds. Women take part in social control, religious affairs and have decision-making powers and thus have equal status with men. Yet neither do they contribute to nor control the family expenditure. They observe pre-delivery restriction, post-delivery pollution and postnatal restriction on a new mother. The marriage ceremony is performed in the central hall of the Bodhi society. A feast is given by the parents of the girl at marriage. Consummation of marriage is at the groom's residence. They cremate their dead according to the Buddhist tradition.

They are a landless community, mainly engaged in skin and hide work, as labourers, government servants and a few are in agriculture to earn their livelihood. The mode of payment is in cash. They have their own traditional *sabhas* called Ambedkar Mission Society and Punjab Buddh Maha Sabha with its headquarters at Jalandhar. The society and the *sabha* attend to all the matters related to religion, marriage, death and disputes if any. They profess Buddhism and except the *bhikshu* and *bodhi* nobody is permitted to conduct the proceedings of marriage or any other function. The sacred specialist is from their own community. They celebrate all the festivals associated with the birth, enlightenment and death anniversary of the Buddha.

They have their traditional school of art in Himachal Pradesh where formal training in wall paintings and engraving is imparted to them. They have their own oral traditions. Folklore, folk tales and folk songs are sung separately by both men and women.

There is no restriction among them for accepting and exchanging food and water with the members of other communities at present. They share cremation ground, place of worship, festivals and festivities with the members of other communities. However, the caste Hindus do not accept food and water from those who are engaged in hide and leather work. Modern inter-community linkages exist with those who are engaged in business, in service, in teaching profession, as doctors and in defence services.

They have favourable attitude towards formal education, modern health and medicare. But the family welfare programme is not well-received. Handpump and piped water are sources of drinking water. They take advantage of the media and communication facilities and use electricity, kerosene oil, cow-dung cakes and wood as fuel. They have ration card facilities. Their attitude towards saving is positive. They help each other financially in case of need.

SWARAN SINGH

## NOONGAR

The term Noongar and Shorgar were applied to the same class of person; while the first was salt maker; the latter, saltpetre maker (Ibbetson, 1916). It has been pointed out by Ibbetson that 'Nungar, or as it is often called Nunia or Lunia or Nunari is derived from *nun* (salt) and denotes occupation rather than true caste.' They themselves perceive the origin of their name from their traditional occupational pursuit of salt-making in the past but do not equate themselves with the Shorgar in any way. These days they are more popular as orchard workers than as salt-makers and perceive distribution at regional level. In Punjab, they are found distributed mainly in the tahsils of Rajpura and Kharar of the districts of Patiala and Ropar respectively.

The community has been living in its present location from times immemorial. However, some families have migrated form rural areas to the urban areas in recent years. They speak the local Punjabi dialect among themselves and Hindi with others. Both Gurmukhi and Devanagari scripts are used by them. The Noongar are occasional non-vegetarians but avoid beef and pork whereas consumption of vegetables is moderate. Wheat, rice and maize are their staple food. Mustard oil, groundnut oil and *vanaspati* are their cooking medium. Both home-made and market alcoholic drinks are occasionally consumed, but by the males only. Milk and milk products are consumed by them. Only men smoke *bidis* and cigarettes.

They are divided into a number of *gots* like Khaltia, Kalealia, Jatewadea and Bhogra. Most of them are wage labourers and are economically backward. Majority of them profess Hinduism and a small section of them have embraced Sikhism. Earlier ethonographic records had reported the existence of Muslim sections also who have now migrated to Pakistan. There is a broad territorial differentiation at the occupational level. They are engaged in settled cultivation. They own land, but in Kharar tahsil of Ropar district they continue to pursue their occupation of contract labourers or growing of orchards. Thus a large number of them also work as landless agricultural labourers. These differentiations regulate marriage alliance and indicate social status. The landowning section consider themselves superior to the other sections of the community and claim Rajput status. They recognize the *varna* system and perceive their status as

Kshatriya and of medium status, but others consider them to be of low status. Consequently, a large section have claimed themselves as Rajputs.

They are endogamous at community level but a few cases of inter-community marriages are reported. They are exogamous at village and *got* levels. Adult marriage is the rule. Marriages are settled through negotiation directly or through a *vichola* or mediator. Monogamy is the common form of marriage. Vermilion, bangles, *bindi*, and earrings are symbols of marriage. The ritual of *kanyadan* and dowry in kind prevails among them. Residence after marriage is patrilocal. Either party can divorce with the approval of the community elders or the judiciary. Divorce compensation is given to the aggrieved party and responsibility of the children in such a case goes to either of the parents. Widow, widowers and divorcee remarriages are permitted. There has been a change in rules of marriage. Age of marriage has increased.

They live in both nuclear and vertically extended families. Male equigeniture is the rule of inheritance and though daughters are allowed inheritance by law, they never claim their share because it is considered socially degrading. Succession of authority goes in favour of the eldest son. Women have low status as compared to men. They participate in economic activity and contribute to family income and also control family expenditure. They have a role in agricultural operations, and even work as agricultural labourers. They have a role in animal husbandry and apart from these, they also actively take part in keeping constant watch on the orchards. They have important role in rituals, social functions, religious matters and mechanism of social control and possess decision-making powers. Post-delivery pollution period exists for seven to twenty-one days. The rituals of *namkaran* and *mundan* are performed by them.

Marriage rituals are performed at the bride's place. Marriage take place by the performance of the ritual of seven *pheras* around the sacred fire. Followers of Sikhism among them, however, perform it through the ritual of *anand karaj*. Feasts are organized by both the parties on the occasion of marriage. Consummation of marriage is at the groom's place.

The dead are cremated and the bones are immersed in Ganga at Hardwar. Pollution period after death is observed for seven or seventeen days. Rituals of *satwan* and *satarwan* are performed on the seventh or seventeenth day, as the case may be, after death.

The economy of the community depends upon land and orchards.

For the landowning cultivators, land is the main source of income. The landowning cultivators of Rajpura tahsil are better off than their counterparts in other areas. However, the incident of landlessness is also common in this area. They work as agricultural labourers on the land of others. Under the contractual system prevalent in the area, they take the gardens or orchards of vegetables and fruits from the owners on payment and earn the profit by selling the products in the markets. Sometimes they take on contract orchards and vegetable gardens in flowering stage and remain busy in caring and watching them till the products are matured for sale. In this practice they may also incur heavy losses if the crop fails. Besides this, some of them are shopowners, service holders and cattle owners. They have direct and daily link with fully regulated local market through exchange or cash.

Child labour exists in agriculture and orchard activity. There has been a marked increase in agricultural and daily-wage casual labour. Wages are received in both cash and kind. Modern statutory *panchayat* exists. There are two sections—Hindus and Sikhs—among them. The sacred specialists are from other communities, who perform worship, and rituals of birth, death and marriage. They participate in local festivals such as Dussehra, Diwali, Lohri, Ekadashi, Guruparabs, Janamashtami, and Ramnavami. Both men and women sing local folk songs at ceremonial occasions.

They exchange food and water with other communities. In the older generations there was some reluctance in accepting food from Scheduled Castes, but this tendency is fast disappearing. They share wells and other water sources, crematoria and religious shrines with other neighbouring communities. Cultivator-labour relations prevail in the community. Wages are paid and received in cash as well as kind. A few of them have taken to white-collar jobs as clerks, stenos, etc.

Formal education is partly favoured for both boys and girls who study upto secondary level. Few of them have gone upto the graduate level in education. Both boys and girls drop out of school because of various social reasons and lack of awareness. The attitude of the community to modern medicare is very positive as also towards family planning. They use modern methods of family welfare and prefer two children. They makes use of the facilities of drinking water supply and electricity. They are exposed to modern mass media and communication facilities. Dissemination of information takes place through extension agencies and political parties. Wood, cow-dung cakes and kerosene oil are the fuel used by them. Many of them are self-employed in agriculture, animal husbandry and contractorship in the orchards. The landowners among them avail of the irrigation facilities of tube wells and canals. They use organic manure, chemical fertilizers and insecticides and have access to the public distribution system. Their attitude towards savings is positive and they are not dependent on moneylenders for loans. A few have acquired yellow cards and get loans for purchasing shops and animals.

VIRINDER SINGH

# OD

Ibbetson (1916: 274) had noted that in the western provinces of the united Punjab, Ods were also known as Beldars, a term derived from the vernacular *bel*, a mattock which was used for digging. The community continues to distinguish itself from other labouring communities engaged in digging. The Ods consider themselves unskilled in the job and low in social esteem. According to the *Census of Punjab* (1961: 2), during the reign of Akbar most of them had to flee from Udaipur to save themselves from Muslim atrocities. They became popular by the name of Udee (residents of Udaipur) which got corrupted and was termed as Odd or Od.

Both Rose (1919: 175) and Ibbetson (1916: 275) point out that they are a wandering group whose proper home appears to be in western Hindustan and Rajputana and that at least the Ods of Punjab hail from those parts. Traditional occupation of this community was earthwork which included digging tanks, sinking wells and road and canal construction. It is, however, not proper to use the terms Od and Beldar interchangeably as Ibbetson himself quotes Christie to suggest that there are large communities of professional Beldars who are not Ods and are generally Muslims in Punjab proper and Hindus in the eastern districts.

They claim to have migrated from Hissar and Sirsa region (of the present Haryana) to the eastern and western districts of Punjab in 1947 and settled in various places wherever canal construction was going on. In the reorganized Punjab, they have a small population confined to the districts of Patiala, Sangrur, Ropar and Ferozepur. According to the 1961 census, the Ods numbered 20,829 in the state of Punjab and were more numerous in the districts of Hissar (14,499) and Karnal (3,434). At the time of the 1961 census their population in present Punjab was very few being confined to the districts of Ferozepur (603), Bhatinda (21), and Sangrur (193). However, according to *Census of India* (1981), the total population of the Ods is 6,494, which includes 3,353 males and 3,141 females. They belong to the Scheduled Caste category. They are mainly found in the rural areas and speak Odik and Punjabi languages. They take both vegetarian and non-vegetarian food. Both home-made and marketed alcoholic drinks are consumed.

They consider themselves to be of a rather high status but lower than that of the Brahmans and Rajput. Others, however, assign them lower status. They consider the Ramdasis to be of equal status.

Marriage is performed through the ritual of seven *pheras*. No marriage between immediate cousins is allowed. Some major *gots* of the Ods are Hadola Dao, Hansi, Chitada, Mahdwara, Schore, Tehil, Mikrani. They consider Hadola as the highest and Mikrani as lowest *got*. Adult marriage is the common practice among them. Dowry is given according to the economic condition of parents. Golden *kudki* is the symbol of marriage. No marriage takes place within the same village, because all of them are regarded as relatives.

Women have low status. They do not have decision-making power. Male equigeniture is the rule. Divorce and remarriage is permitted among them. They contribute to the family income by working as agricultural labourers.

Birth pollution is observed for fifteen days. The ritual of *namkaran* is performed through a Brahman. The ritual of *mundan* is performed through either *mami* (maternal aunt) or *bua* (paternal aunt) after five weeks from birth. The dead are cremated. They collect the remains of the bones and ashes from the cremation ground and immerse them in the Ganga at Hardwar. The ritual of *bada* is performed after twelve days of death through a feast (*roti*) to the community people.

They profess Hinduism. Rama, Shiva and Gugapir are some of the common deities worshipped by them.

They are primarily a labourer community and work as canal diggers or as agricultural labourers. Only a few of them have marginal land-holdings. Some of them are small shop-owners and utensil sellers. They borrow money from the local moneylenders. The Ods, working in canals and as agriculture labour, are not getting good wages. Some have consequently shifted to other works such as small village shops or *rehris* (mobile shops) and also sell steel utensils in villages. None of them are in the government service. Despite bad economic conditions, they never availed of loans from government.

Their attitude towards education is positive. They fully make use of the modern medicare system. Drinking water is available within the locality. Many of them make use of the facility of electricity.

K. GOPALA IYER
VIRINDER SINGH

# PASI

Pasi, is a community closely allied to the Khatiks. They are professional watchmen and derive their name from *pasa*, a noose. Their original occupation is climbing the toddy-palm tree by means of a noose and making toddy. They are keepers of pigs and in the cantonments of Punjab are often employed in collecting and selling cow-dung for fuel (Rose, 1919). Another account says 'The Pasis practise either Hinduism or Islam and they are very close to the Khatiks and as they generally keep pigs, hence are close to the Chuhras' (*Census of India*, 1911: 471).

The Pasi is a Scheduled Caste community of Punjab. Total population of the Pasi in Punjab, according to the 1981 census is 5,593, which includes 3,495 males and 2,098 females. The districts of Ropar and Patiala, followed by Ludhiana has the maximum concentration of the community. In Punjab, the Pasis have migrated mostly from the state of Uttar Pradesh. Like the Khatiks, the Pasis are also engaged in rearing pigs and maintaining piggeries is their traditional occupation. The rearing of pigs is often related to the scavenging communities, hence the Pasis are also considered to be one of them.

They speak both Punjabi and Hindi languages and use Devanagari and Gurmukhi scripts.

Wheat is their staple food and they are occasional non-vegetarians. Only men consume alcoholic drinks and smoke *bidi*. The Khatiks and Pasis have the relationship of *roti* and *beti*, i.e. the relationship of interdining and inter-marrying. Adult marriage is the practice and marriages are settled through negotiation with the help of *vichola*. They are monogamous and dowry in kind prevails. Vermilion, glass bangles and earrings are symbols of marriage. Residence after marriage is patrilocal.

Divorce and remarriage is permitted among them and the common reasons for divorce are maladjustment, barrenness, impotency, etc. The compensation in case of divorce is given to the aggrieved party. Either the husband or wife can initiate a divorce. In case of divorce, the children stay with their mother and on attaining adulthood they may stay with their father. Both joint and nuclear families prevail among them.

Sons inherit the property of their father equally. In the absence of male child, daughters inherit the property of their father equally. The eldest son succeeds to the authority of his father. The women attend to the various household activities. Women neither contribute to the family income nor control expenditure. The Pasis observe pre-delivery rituals, post-delivery pollution period and restrictions on the mother after delivery. *Namkaran* ritual is performed by the elderly women in consulatation with the family members. Marriage ceremony takes place at the residence of the bride. The feast is also given by the parents of the bride on the occasion of marriage. Consummation of marriage is at the groom's house.

They cremate their dead and pollution period is observed for eight to eleven days. The *shuddhi kriya* ritual is performed to purify the area and a feast is given to the members of the community on the occasion.

The main occupation of the Pasis is pig rearing and related work. Apart form this, they are also engaged in floor mosaic work and as contract and unskilled industrial labourers. They do not have any caste *panchayat* and are dependent on the court of law for their problems and disputes. As Hindus they worship the Hindu gods and goddesses. The sacred specialists are from other community who perform worship and the rituals of marriage and death. They have oral traditions, folk songs and folklore. The folk songs are sung by the females on the occasion of marriage. The musical instruments commonly used are *dholak* and *chimta*. The Pasis and Khatiks intermarry, they accept food and water from the communities of higher status.

They have their own cremation ground but amicably share shrines and sacred places, water sources, schools, etc., with other communities of the neighbourhood.

In spite of availability of the facility, their attitude towards education is not positive. They make full use of the modern medicare system. They have an unfavourable attitude towards family planning programmes. Drinking water is made available to them within the locality. Firewood and cow-dung cake are main fuel resource for them. They use electricity. Ration cards have been provided to them to procure essential commodities from fair price shops at subsidized rates.

SWARAN SINGH

# PENJA

These days the Penjas and Telis are considered the same. Ibbeston grouped Teli with Penja and Qassab. The synonyms of the Penja include Pinjara, Panjora, Panjwara, Punji or Pinjia, Naddaf, Dhunia, Panbakob, Kalaf Pumba, etc. (Rose, 1919). Some other names of the community were Behna, Katera, Kandera (Crooke, 1896). These days the community in Punjab is known by the name of the Penja or sometimes Kandera or Naddaf. The functional or occupational origins of the community were suggested during British times. Ibbetson had proposed that Penja was a 'Cotton scutcher who, striking with a blow with a heavy wooden plectrum, uses the vibrations of the blow string to separate the fibre of the cotton to arrange them side by side, and part them from dirt and other impurities'. In his opinion only Teli was a caste and Penja was the name of the occupation (Ibbeston, 1916). The occupational origins of word Dhunia, a synonymn of Penja were underlined by Crooke. According to him Hindi word Dhunia is derived from *dhunna*, which means 'to card'. This word *dhunna* is derived from the Sanskrit word *dhu*; which means to agititate. Similarly the Arabic word *naddaf* means 'separator'. A large population of this community now resides in Pakistan. In the Punjab, it mainly resides in the districts of Ropar, Patiala and Sangrur. Ethnographic account as described above exists. It speaks Punjabi language with its kinship groups and with other communities. This language is written in Gurmukhi and Perso-Arabic script. It has no distinctive identification. It wears local Punjabi attire. As Muslim it also avail of the benefits of a religious minority. It is typical Punjabi in its food habits. The consumption of vegetables is moderate. It is occasionally non-vegetarian and it holds true for both men and women. Only *halal* meal is taken. The cereals used include wheat, rice and maize. It takes all locally consumed pulses such as gram, *tur*, *urad*, *moong*, peas, beans, *masur* and *moth*. Only men of the community take alcoholic drinks purchased from the market. The consumption of fruit is occasional.There has been increase in the use of vegetables, fruit and pulses. It now prefers *roti* to rice. Social divisions exist in the community, at social, economic, religious, territorial, occupational and educational levels. It has mainly the followers of Suni sect of Islam. A few followers of Shia sect also exist. It is also differentiated at the occupational level. It has two main traditional occupational divisions, Teli and Penja. The former were involved in the occupations of oil pressing, and the latter were involved in cotton scutching work. This occupational differentiaton still continues. In addition new occupation of agricultural labour, shopkeeper and service have been added. At the territorial level there is a division in this community between the community settled at Malerkotla which continued to observe strict Islamic customs; and those in Ropar district and in some areas of Patiala district, which under pressure had changed their practices. Those two groups do not intermarry. Social divisions exist at *gotra* level.

The *gotras* of the community as available in earlier records include Adi, Alami, Ali, Aman (Ama'n), Arbia, Arli, Baddhar, Badda, Badgujjar, Bagr, Bhalim (Balim, Ba'hlim), Basin (Bhasin), Bathan, Bhand, Bhari, Bharbhunja, Bhatti, Bhehuya, Bhitti, Bhutta, Chahch, Chahil, Chandar, Changar, Channan, Chauhan, Chhalial, Da'har, Dahi' ma, Darema, Deota, Dhawan, Dhia, Dholi Jaddan, Dunga, Gahito, Gala'chi, Ganja, Ganjaur, Gaur, Gendi, Ghaman, Gharia, Gil, Gori, Goria, Gundra, Guiara, Hammi, Hastra, Hindru, Hir, Jadhran, Jaggi, Jaid, Jajuhan Jandan, Jandaraiyan, Januhen, Jathwara, Jatu, Jawam, Jain, Jha,Jhunia Jhala, Jhamain, Jhammat, Jhander (Jhandra'n), Jhiman, Jhuvan, Jindran, Jumditor, Kachhor, Kachhua, Kaith, Ka'l, Kalia, Keljuddan, Kandlot, Kandra, Kali, Kajla, Kale, Kngari, Karim, Ketli (Khetle), Khangru, Kharmshi, Kharse, Khatri, Khetie, Khokhar, Kichchi, Kikkar, Ladu Khel, Langhe, Lare, Lohar, Lund-Datra, Magh Hans, Mahim, Mahindru, Mai, Malak, Malihe, Manda'har, Mange Khel, Manjijh, Marha'ns, Matta, Mehara's Mej, Minha's Mundi, Mural, Nagah, Nuru, Pal, Pillhi, Panji Khel, Pashin, Patha, Pilchi, Phira Khel, Piron, Pua'l, Pundar, Punhar (Punwar), Purana, Puriwal, Quraishi, Ragu, Rahtar, Rajpal, Rathor, Rehrr, Roya, Rura, Sa'hal, Saihna (Sahni), Sainsi, Sakila, Salahan, Samhasi, Samman Khel, Sanga'le, Sarad, Saroha (Saroa), Saundhi, Said, Sayyid (Sed), Siahsaroe, Sabrao, Soda', Sohna, Sotakhni, Sulhare, Sultu keh, Tagaha, Tahim, Taoni, Tarman, Thaddi, Tunar (Tunhar, Tur), Ugan, Wadhan, Warya'h. A few *gotras* such as the Badgujjar, Bhatti, Chauhan, Punwar and Tunwar were extensibly of Rajput origins; Gil was of Jat origins, and a few of Kaiatha and Pathans (Rose, 1970: 464). *Gotras* of Penjas in addition to Telli Gotras were Raunji, Dedan, Phapute, Jand, Hatim, Sohatte, Ahre, Kamboh, Beddhan, Male Hans (Rose, 1970: 464).

These differentiations help to regulate marriage alliances and indicate social status. Its self-preception is of medium level; but others consider it of low status. Marriages take place among Muslim Telis/ Penjas. These marriages are endogamous at the community level. While a preference is given to the same occupation, Teli or Penja; but Teli marrying a Penja is also common. The community is exogamous at village and *gotra* level. Four gotra—father, mother, maternal grandmother and paternal grandmother are excluded, while negotiating a marriage deal. The practice of *gotra* exogamy, excludes any possibility of consangunity at any level. These days most marriages are performed at adulthood. These are contracted by negotiations and are monogamous in nature. The green dress of the bride is a distinctive marriage symbol of the community, which is shared with other communities. The bride also wears toe and earrings. A variable amount of *mehar* is promised for future payment. The amount of *mehar* has increased over time. The rules of residence are patrilocal. Divorce is permissible by social approval, and in rare cases by judicial means. In the earlier practice only the husband was allowed divorce; and in this case compensation was paid to the wife. The custody of the child is given to either mother or father. Although divorce by judicial means is available, there has been no such case reported in the community. The community allows the remarriage of widows, widowers, male divorcees and female divorcees. The age of marriage has increased over time and marriage symbols have become liberal. The community lives in the nuclear and vertically extended families. Joking relationships eixst between *sali* (wife's sister) and *jeeja* (sister's husband), and *bhabi* (elder brother's wife) and *dewar* (husband's younger brother). Avoidance relationships exist between *saas* (mother-in-law); and *jawai* (son-in-law), and *noohn* (daughter-in-law). Disputes arise in families due to matters linked with property. Inheritence is by male equigeniture and the succession rules favour eldest son. There has been an increase in the formation of nuclear families, and decline in the extended family system. The women of the community have a low status. They still have to observe *purdah* at many places, particularly in urban areas such as Malerkotla. The women have a role in the operations of animal husbandry. They have a role in ritual, social, religious matters and mechanism of social control. However, pre-delivery and postnatal restrictions on mother exist. Post-delivery pollution is also reported for a variable number of days. Circumcision of male children is performed at the age of about three years. Marriage rituals take place at the bride's place; and the consummation of marriage is at the groom's place. Feast is organized by both the parties. The dead are buried and observation of pollution of death is also reported. The rituals have become simplified, but have became costlier.

The community is landless. In earlier times the community used to provide edible oils like mustard oil to the community. The oil was extracted with the help of *kohlu* or oil press. The farmers used to bring oil seeds for oil extraction; and the community was provided with food grains for the services done. Oil cake or *khal* was used as cattle-feed. However, the old machines or *kohlus* have became outmoded, due to the installation of new machines. And these are owned by other communities. The earlier machines was operated by water-mills. These can be seen at few places. Many households keep these machines as a mark of the identity of the community. The occupation of cotton scutching among the Penja has also been adversely affected, but it is still not completely outmoded. This has also been affected by the installation of new machines operated by power. They are working as agricultural labour on the land of others. A few have started animal husbandry. There are still other who work as government employees as peons or clerks. Some own small shops in rural areas. The community has daily link with nearby local markets, which are fully regulated; and it exists on the basis of cash. There has been an increase in the number of daily casual labour. In the agricultural operations, child labour also exists. In those operations wages are paid in cash. The community believes in Islam. The predominant section believes in the Sunni sect of Islam. However, the community in Ropar district has a special reverence for Dargah of Manikpur Sharif, which is of some Sufi saint. It is equally revered by all the communities, of the area. Id-ul-Fitr, Id-ul-Zuha are celebrated with enthusiasin at the nearest mosques. It also celebrates Lohri; and greets other communities on the occasion of their festivals. There was some change in religious practices for a few years when the community started burning their dead. Still others started naming their children by Sikh names. But this trend was reversed in 1960s. Now the community adheres to strict Islamic practices.

The Penjas have an oral tradition; and the folk songs are sung by the community. Folklore and folk tales also exist.

These days the community has free interaction with other communities. The burial ground and *masjid* are shared with other brother Muslim. So also the festivals are shared with other communities. However, the cultivator-labour relationship exists in the cases where the community works as agricultural labour, and in such cases the relations between the two are satisfactory.

Education is only partly favoured for both boys and girls. They generally study upto primary level. There are rare cases of boys doing matriculation. While both boys and girls drop-out of school due to social reason, boys drop out because of economic reasons as well. Its attitude to modern medicare is favourable. In few villages dispensaries are available which provide modern medicare. 'Generally, couples have four or more children. But the attitude of the younger generaton is favourable to it, and the situation will change. It has access to drinking water and electricity supply facilities. Drinking water is available from handpumps, tube wells and public supply system. Many Penjas are self-employed in animal husbandry, petty retailing and cotton scutching. It has access to radio and in some cases television as well. Disseminations of information is through extention agencies, and political parties. The places are linked by roads; railways also exist at variable distances. It has access to the post office. It uses firewood, cow-dung cakes kerosene oil as fuels. It has access to ration shops of public distribution system. The attitude to savings is positive, but generally there is little to save. A few have yellow cards, and some have received bans for animal husbandry.

VIRINDER SINGH

# PERNA

The Perna have been described as vagrant gypsies, similar to the Nats or Bazigar. Total population of the Perna according to *Census of India* (1981), is 75 with 36 males and 39 females. Their women are said to be jugglers and generally perform by holding a sword or knife to their throats. Their characteristic occupation was dancing and singing rather than tumbling. Their men merely played the drum for their women to dance. The term 'Perna' refers to the occupation just as the term 'Bazigar' is associated with occupation.

According to Ibbetson (1916: 288) and Rose (1919: 234) the Pernas were divided into two classes, Baratali and Teratali, which were related to dance. *Ali* means beat in music and music with thirteen beats was worth listening to. Traditionally the Pernas like the Kanjars were also nomadic groups. The Bangalis, the snake charmers, are sometimes confused with the Pernas and Kanjars, who keep dogs, donkeys and have their separate dialect. In this regard, the Bangalis are more close to the Sapelas than with the Kanjars and the Pernas.

According to the census of 1911 the Perna population of Punjab consisted of 1,199 males and 1,074 females. It has been reported that most of the Pernas had migrated to Pakistan after Partition. However, a colony at Hari Nagar in Pathankot was identified as a Perna colony by the local inhabitants and their presence was also indicated in some of the local dailies of Punjab. The local inhabitants of Pathankot spontaneously referred to it as the colony of Pernas. According to their accounts the colony existed even before Partition. This was also testified by a Perna leader.

A more systematic account was given by another informer, D. Harish according to whom, in 1934, a society named 'Anjuman Imdad Bahmi Kifayat Sha'ari, Bachat va Karza' was founded. This society purchased land and had forty to forty-five members. The department of criminal tribes was the overall initiator of this move and it was under its close supervision. There were reformatories in some of the prominent cities of Punjab such as Amirtsar, Lahore, etc. The then deputy commissioner was S. Hari Singh and the colony is also named after him as Hari Nagar.

After Partition the Criminal Tribes Act was repealed and all those communities which were enlisted as criminal tribes during the British period were exonerated from this nomenclature. The informer stated that though India became independent in 1947, they became independent only with the repealing of this Act in 1952. The Pernas have had a phase of amity and relative prosperity for nearly two decades. Some of them were also able to build small *pukka* houses with their earnings.

There is a tendency among them to disown their past including their identity as the Perna. The informer also stated that immediately after Partition the Pernas and Bhedkuts had migrated to Pakistan from Hari Nagar colony and those who were left were the Bangalis and not the Pernas. However, the local people had all along identified them as Pernas and not as Bangali.

The observations of Ibbetson and Rose indicate that the Bangalis were engaged as cultivators. Their past history, culture and occupational affiliation place them as distinct from the Pernas.

The Pernas want to be identified with the Bangalis of Kangra district and also to forget their links with the Bangalis and Sapelas of Punjab, whom they include under their border rubric. It appears that the undercurrent of conversion to Christianity is in process. The Church elder is referred to as the *padri.* It has been indicated that they are quite liberal with respect to their religious affiliation. In their daily life they combine religious practices of the Hindus, Muslims and Christians.

About the current marriage practices it was brought home that they marry within their own caste and also with the Bangalis and Sapelas. There are also instances of their women married in upper castes. Their exogamous units are Bambi, Laddar, Karu and Bajjaniye, etc. They follow mainly Hindu marriage ritual of seven *pheras* around a temporary structure which is made for the occasion. The *barat* is feasted as practised among other communities. There is no compulsion for dowry but voluntarily some articles such as clothes, utensils, etc., are given according to the parents' capacity.

They have their common place of worship which is a *mazar* at Khemkaran. They visit that *mazar* occasionally to pray for their well-being and prosperity which they call as *mannat.* People from their own community and also those from Pakistan visit this *mazar.* The dead bodies are buried wrapped in a white sheet of cloth, called *kafan.* Those who accompany the funeral have to take a bath to purify themselves. On the next day after the death close relatives feed the affected members of the family, so that they break their fast. On the third day, there is the ritual of *pani dena* in which all the close relatives, including the local *biradari* are present. On the fortieth day the relatives and the *biradari* are invited for *roti*, at a gathering called to serve food to *biradari* or community and to bring an end to the mourning period.

After marriage the couples form their own nuclear families. Divorce is permitted but thoroughly debated and decided in their own ingenious *biradari* system. The interview with the informants indicated that they marry even close relatives. They also confirm that they worship *devis, devtas, pirs* and Christ. They also visit the Hindus religious places such as Jawalaji. At Pathankot they had their *qabristan* (graveyard). They do not have symbiotic relationship with the Pernas in Pakistan, but some of their erstwhile relatives in that country do visit them occasionally.

They have their own system of resolving disputes and whenever any complaint is received the *biradari* fixes a date for a hearing. Both the parties involved in the dispute have freedom to select their advocate who is called *charava.* After intensive discussion and examining the evidences from both sides, the *panches* (judges) from the *biradari* pronounce their judgement. Both the parties to the dispute have to deposit money as fee ranging from one hundred to two hundred fifty rupees. If the decision is not acceptable then the aggrieved party can file a fresh appeal to next higher court known as *parakh*. The procedure is again the same. Even in this case, if the judgment is not acceptable, the aggrieved party can take recourse to the still higher court of appeal which is called *narakh*. Their highest court of appeal is known as *sarakh*. The *panches* at this stage either give the final verdict or issue remand which would mean any body can initiate the entire process from the lowest to the highest court of appeal. The parties concerned in the disputes are required to bear the expenditure of the advocates (inclusive of their travel cost, lodging, boarding and fees) as also the expenditure as court fees. Direct approach to police or statutory courts is not permissible without *biradari's* permission.

The Pernas, who were dislocated from Pathankot had very high level of illiteracy; only their two prominent leaders were relatively well-educated. One was employed in the army for fifteen years and later on as a welfare officer. Another leader of the community has a bookshop at Amritsar. Some of their women are also educated and employed as nurses. A few of their menfolk are also in service and in petty trades. There are also some graduates among them and the number of matriculates is over twenty. In Punjab the general facilities of free studentship and free books are available to them.

RAKESH KUMAR

# PHARERA

The Phareras derive their name from the word *phera* (encircling). It is said that they used to go round the villages begging, and beating a drum while begging. It is also said that they used to keep a large number of cattle and grazed them for selling milk. The Phareras recall that their forefathers were Hindus, and that they embraced Islam during the reign of Aurangzeb. Many of them migrated to Pakistan after Partition. However, they are still keeping ties with their brethren across the border in that they visit each other on social occasions. They are now turning to Sikhism and have started arranging their marriages according to Sikh *maryada*. They speak Punjabi and use Gurmukhi script. According to the *Census of India* (1981), their total population is 279, having 153 males and 126 females. Some of their titles are Sandhu, Khatra, Dhillon, Randhawa, Cheema and Shergil. Their constitutional status is that of a Scheduled Caste. There are both vegetarian and non-vegetarian among them. Wheat, rice pulses and seasonal vegetables are their staple food. Locally available fruits are consumed. Their cooking is done with mustard oil and hydrogenated vegetable oil. Non-vegetarian items include mutton, chicken (*halal*), fish and eggs but not beef. They also consume milk and milk products. Alcoholic drinks are consumed during marriage and other festive and social occasions. They purchase alcoholic drinks from the market. Because of their conversion to Sikhism most of them avoid smoking.

The Phareras do not observe strict subcaste exogamy. Consanguineous marriages, practised in the past in the cities, are now prohibited in the villages. They consider their community to be inferior to the Sayyads, Sheikhs and Rangars and superior to Mochi, Dogar, Teli, Julaha and the Doom. They regard the Bharai as of equal status. Among them, the age at marriage ranges from eighteen to twenty years for both boys and girls. Parents' consent is necessary for arranging a match before marriage. They follow Muslim tradition for performing marriage, but some perform it through the simple procedure of exchanging garlands in the presence of *Guru Granth Sahib*. Role of a mediator also assumes importance in the settlement of a matrimonial alliance. Marriages in the past were solemnized and legitimized by the *qazi*. They had polygynous form of marriage in the past but now they prefer monogamy. Marriage symbols for the ladies are *mehandi*, *sindur*, earring, nose and toe ring, *jhanjra chura* (red bangles) and red-coloured dress; during social occasions these symbols are strictly in use. *Mehar* is promised for future payment, dowry is paid and rule of patrilocal residence is followed. Divorce rarely takes place, it is allowed only on the ground of adultery or impotency and cases of divorce are dealt with by the *panchayat*. Widow remarriage is permissible; the young widow may be married to her deceased husband's younger brother and this practice is called *chadar paona*.

Both extended and nuclear family types are prevalent among them. Avoidance relationship exists between the father-in-law and daughter-in-law, husband's elder brother and younger brother's wife and between a married woman and all the elderly males of the family, village and community at her in-laws' place. Joking relationship is seen between wife's sister and sister's husband, husband's younger brother and elder brother's wife. Conflict and confrontation crops up on account of property disputes. Male equigeniture is the rule of inheritance, so all sons equally inherit their father's property. Succession is by the eldest son.

Women carry out the household chores and also collect fuel. Earlier they used to work as wage labourers which they have given up. They take part in social and religious affairs of the family, but have limited role in the mechanism of social control besides having decision-making powers. Decisions are taken by the male members of the family. Women at the time of election cast their votes. Their opinion is obtained while negotiating marriage of a son or a daughter, but on all other major issues final decision is taken by the male members only. Pre-delivery rituals are not observed in the community. Circumcision of boys is performed around five to nine years of age. Dead body is buried. A dead body is wrapped in a white cloth and a period of mourning is observed for forty days. On the fortieth day the relatives, community members and friends join to pray for the departed soul, which is termed as *khatam*. After this the family attends to the normal duties.

Earlier their primary occupation was daily wage labour, but now only a few among them work in other's fields; they are mostly in salaried jobs. Very few of them are teachers. Their disputes are referred to either the statutory *panchayat* at the village level or to the law courts for settlement. The traditional method of solving disputes through the elders of the families still continues. They propitiate Pir Lalanwala on happy occasions which is a sacred centre in the vicinity

They offer milk every Thursday to the *pir*. Their major festivals are, Id-ul-Zuha, Id-ul-fitr, Lohri, Baisakhi and Basant and their oral traditions, in the form of folk songs and folklores are in fact shared with other communities of the region. They share wells, and other water sources, religious shrines and traditional festivals with there neighbouring communities.

Some members of this community are in white-collar jobs and political leadership has emerged among them at the village *panchayat* level only. Their attitude towards development programmes is favourable and the impact of these programmes on the community is perceptible. Boys and girls are taking advantage of the formal education facilities and are well-educated generally. Attitude of the Phareras towards family planning programmes is also positive and probably prevalence of formal education among them is responsible for this. Facilities of drinking water are available in the from of wells and handpumps. About 80 per cent of their houses have been electrified. Fuel sources for them are wood, kerosene oil and cow-dung cakes. Medical and social welfare officials often visit their village for necessary help and check-up.

K. Gopala Iyer
Rakesh Kumar

# RACHBAND

The term *rach* stands for the thread used in handloom and this community has derived its name from the term because they spin thread for handloom. The community is distributed in the towns of Jalandhar, Ludhiana, Banga, Nawanshahar, Phagwara, Adampur (district Hoshiarpur) and also in the village of Mahilpur, Badiyan and the village Sanjapind in the district of Hoshiarpur. They speak Punjabi and those who are literate use Gurmukhi script. The male dress consists of shirt, *dhoti*, and *pagri*, while the female dress is *salwar, kameez* and *dupatta*. While *dal-roti* is their staple food, whenever, they can afford, they take non-vegetarian food which comprises mutton, egg, and sometimes pork. They generally take *roti* prepared from wheat and during winter they take *roti* prepared from maize. Consumption of rice is occasional and the pulses taken by them are *moong, moth, masur* and *urad*. Groundnut and mustard oil is the cooking medium. Tea is their most popular non-alcoholic drink. Men take alcoholic drinks on special occasions. Consumption of fruit is very little in this community. They smoke *bidi* and cigarettes. All of them cannot afford to drink milk. However, the children do take milk.

Earlier they were treated as untouchables, but now this social stigma no more exists. They were originally from the state of Himachal Pradesh but migrated to their present habitat more than a century back. Most of their marriage alliances today take place within Punjab only. Some of the important *gots* among them are Heer, Chandle, Kahu, Tomar and Tor. They consider themselves to be of medium social status, but the higher castes consider them to be of low status socially.

They are endogamous and observe exogamy at village and *got* levels. One cannot marry in one's father's and mother's *gots*. Child marriage was in practice among them fifty years back, but at present they marry their boys and girls when they are of eighteen to twenty-two years of age. Marriage alliances are arranged by negotaition with the help of *vichola*. Form of marriage is monogamy. Symbols of marriage among girls are vermilion, earring, nose ring, finger ring and glass bangles. Dowry is not demanded but is paid voluntarily by the bride's parents depending upon their financial condition; poor families sometimes go for marriage by exchange to avoid such payments

The Rachband are patrilocal. Divorce has social sanction and widow remarriage is permissible; a widow can marry her deceased husband's younger brother, which is called *chadar paona* in local parlance. Joint families are prevalent among them; but more and more nuclear families are coming up. Avoidance relationship is observed between *sas* and *jamai*, *bahu* and *saura*, *bharjai* and *jeth*. Joking relationships exists between *bhabi* and *dewar*, *nanad* and *bharjai*, *jeeja* and *sali*. Points of conflict and confrontation in a family are often on issues related to quarrel between children, property, and check on the the freedom of youngsters. All the sons inherit property of their father while the eldest son succeeds his authority. Women of the Rachband community take part in household chores, collection of fuel, economic activities, social and ritual functions. They have a lower status than men. Women help their husbands in their traditional occupation and thereby indirectly contribute to the family income.

Birth of a male child is celebrated with jubiliation. There are no pre-delivery rituals though a period of post-delivery pullution is observed. *Chowki charhana* (sun-worship) is performed after six days of the birth. Some post-delivery restrictions are observed for forty days by the mother of the new born. As they are not economically well-off all the ladies cannot observe such restrictions for the prescribed period. Marriage rituals take place at the bride's residence where the seven *pheras*, the main marriage ceremony, according to the Hindu tradition are performed. A wedding feast is arranged by the girl's parents to the groom's party and the invited members of the community. Consummation of marriage is at the groom's residence. The Rachband cremate the dead and observe a pollution period. Ashes and bones of the dead are immersed in the Ganga at Hardwar. A funeral feast is also hosted for the members of the community by the bereaved family. They feel that the life cycle rituals have become too costly for them and as a result they are curtailing the same.

They still continue with their traditional occupation of making cotton thread for handlooms and also preparing combs. For this they buy raw material from Jalandhar and the finished products are sent to intermediaries at Jalandhar and Banga. From this occupation they can earn only a paltry sum of twenty rupees per head per day. Banga is one of their important marketing centres and some of their people are employed here as teachers, clerks and in other white-collar jobs. Majority of them are still in the traditional profession and now they also prepare bedsheets, *daris* (floor mats), etc.

The Rachband profess Hindu religion and worship all the Hindu gods and goddesses. The sacred specialist or *pujari*, is not from their community. The *pujari* performs the rites associated with birth, marriage and death. Festivals such as Holi, Diwali, Lohri, Dussehra, Janamashtami, Ramnavami are celebrated by them. They share the folklore and folk tales prevalent in Punjab. Women perform *giddha* and men perform *bhangra* on the occasion of marriage; *dhol* or *dholki* are their musical instruments. They maintain good relationship with the neighbours belonging to different communities and these neighbouring communities do not discriminate today either in acceptance of water and food or in their visiting temples. People, both Hindu and Sikh, have a very cordial relationship with them.

Most of them have little or no formal education. Only a few college graduates can be traced among them. They earn enough through their traditional occupation. They get medical care facilities as their attitude is favourable towards modern medicare. Some of them have sterilized themselves in order to control the size of their family. They prefer three to four children. Source of drinking water for them is handpump. They make use of rail, road, and postal facilities and use electricity. Firewood and cow-dung cakes are used by them as fuel. Midday meal scheme is not available to their children. They get immunization facilities for their children and the pregnant women. They have ration cards and get sugar and *atta* at subsidized rates. Few of them have received yellow cards.

K. GOPALA IYER

# RAI SIKH

The community traces its past as Mahatam and Sirkiband. For official purposes however, they are treated differently from the above two groups. The Sirkiband was an occupational term for those who made ropes. The term Mahatam has been assigned two meanings. According to one it has been derived from the word *matam* which means 'grief' caused by death. In its second meaning it is *maha uttam* which means 'best person'. However those Mahatams who have embraced Sikhism are called Rai Sikhs. It is to be noted that Sirkiband was an occupational term applied to the *rassiwat* or *rassibat*, and Mahatam also were engaged in this occupation (Rose, 1919: 49). It was noted that Mahatam were tenants or labourers, who were also engaged in snaring wild pigs.

As recorded in early ethnographic notes, they had migrated from western districts (ibid). Ibbetson considered them a 'low caste' found in foothills along the river Satluj, engaged in hunting animals. At that time a majority of them believed in Hinduism, but a few also believed in Sikhism and Islam. Ibbetson has even claimed the resemblance of this community with the Bahurupias and Bahrup of Banjaras. The community also claimed Rajput origin from a Mahta *kanungo* of Akbar. Their resemblance with Mahatams of Hoshiarpur was also noted (Ibbetson, 1916: 203; Rose, 1919: 50-1). Few of Mahatams were declared as criminal tribes by the British, which included Ikwan, Kashauri, Sirari, Savni (Rose, 1919: 51).

They perceive their identification at regional, interregional, national and international levels. According to few informants, the Rai Sikh have migrated in substantial number from Pakistan, to their present places of settlement in 1947. In Jalalabad the community has migrated mostly from Montgomery district of Pakistan. In Ferozepur district they are claimed to be spread over two hundred villages. The Rai Sikh are numerically predominant in sixty villages in Kapurthala, fifty villages in Jalandhar, fourteen each in Amritsar and Gurdaspur, and fifteen to twenty in Ludhiana. They claim that their kins professing Islam are still living in Pakistan mainly in Lahore, Akada, Saiwal Montgomery areas.

The community feels that since they were declared a criminal tribe in British days and later on acquired the status of Vimukt Jati, or denotified tribe, they should be given the status of Scheduled Tribe. They were also noted as Sirkiband because of their occupation of rope-making, and as Pakhiwara because they used a peculiar net to catch wild boars, which was called *waran*. It may be noted that some of them are also engaged in litigation claiming status of Scheduled Caste as Sirkiband, which has been declared as Scheduled Caste in the state. They speak Punjabi among themselves. To converse with other communities they use Hindi and occasionally English. Gurmukhi, Devanagari and Roman scripts are used by them. They wear typical Punjabi dress, but only a few wear turban. In earlier days, male members wore a peculiar dress, consisting of a long *ghagra* and large earrings.

They have been living in semi-arid plains along the *bet* area of the river Satluj. The area has now been reclaimed by the community as good quality land. The food habits of the community have undergone a great change. In earlier days it was a non-vegetarian community, eating meat of goat, rabbit, fish, chicken, pigs, sheep and whatever else was available. However, consumption of meat and liquor has been completely stopped in a section of the community which has started following Radhaswami sect. Their staple cereal is wheat and rice, maize, *bajra* are also consumed occasionally. They use all pulses mainly gram, *urad*, *moong*, peas, *masur*, *moth*, etc. Mustard oil and *vanaspati* hydrogenated vegetable oil are used as cooking medium. Some are changing from non-vegetarian to vegetarian diet. There has been an increase in the use of pulses, vegetables and fruits.

The community is differentiated at economic, occupational, religious and educational levels. It has agricultural labourers, lawyers, landowners in it. Then, there are followers of Sikhism, Hinduism and Radhaswami Sat Sang religions. Some members of the community are well-educated, some have education upto matriculation while some are illiterate. The community is differentiated into various *gots*. As the community claims its origins from the Mahatam it is necessary to note the *gotras* of that community as noted by Rose (1919: 51), Baksawan, Rai, Bawara, Rawari, Bhatti, Sanora, Bhichar, Sardia, Chauhan, Saroi, Dandal, Seotara, Dilsari, Sirari, Dosa, Sauni, Ghugha, Taur, Jandi, Totum, Kachauri, Tunwar, Karanawal, Vanura, Katwal, Wachwala, Khokhar, War, Madha, Wila Sara, Malhi, Mandal, Manha, Nas, Parbar, Pok (Bok) and Punwar.

These *gots* are also found in this community. The social divisions are used to regulate marriage alliances and to indicate status. The community considers itself of a medium social status, but lower than that of the Jats. On the other hand, other communities consider them to be of low social status. But their status has improved, since they have adopted the occupation of settled cultivation. They trace their origin from the Kshatriya and consider themselves as Rajputs.

Marriages are endogamous in the community. Only one's own *got* is left for the settlement of marriage. A large number of marriages are sororate, levirate or hypergamous. Age of bride and groom is around twenty years. Marriages are settled both by direct negotations as well as through the *vichola* or matchmakers. These marriages are monogamous, but occasional cases of polygamy with the consent of the first wife have been reported. There is no practice of using vermilion or *bindi* at the time of marriage and there is no particular wedding dress. A *chura* (bangle) is worn by the bride as a distinguishing item which was earlier made of silver and now it is of glass. The bride also uses *mehandi* or *gana* on her left leg, which is another distinguishing mark. There is no reported practice of compulsory dowry. However, whenever dowry is given, it is in kind.

Rule of residence after marriage is patrilocal, but generally newly wedded couples establish separate household. Divorce, granted both by the court of law and by the *panchayat* of elders, is recognized by thc community. It is possible for either of the spouses to ask for divorce, and custody of the children and compensation is decided on merit of individual cases and no standard practice exists for this purpose. Remarriage of both male and female divorcees and widows are also accepted. However, it is performed by the simple ceremony of *ardas* and distribution of *prasad.* Some changes in rules of marriage have occurred. Adult marriage has become the rule; solemnizing a marriage by performing *anand karaj* is now a standard practice, even in non-Sikh families. These people mostly live in nuclear families and rarely have vertically extended ones. There exists avoidance relationship between married women and all elder male members of the in-laws' family. Joking relationship exists between *sali* and *jeeja*; between *bhabi* and *dewar.*

Differences arise in families due to various reasons. Most of the disputes are due to matters linked with property. The general practice of inheritance is of male equigeniture. In a few cases women have also claimed a share of their parental property. The succession rule favours the eldest son. Women have low status as compared to the men. But they have definite roles to play in economic activities. They participate in agricultural operations and animal husbandry. They also earn wages as agricultural labourers, contribute to family income, and also control expenditure. They have also role to perform in social affairs, rituals and religious activities. They have a say in the selection of a mate when a young person is getting married.

The mother of a newborn child is not allowed to enter kitchen for twenty-one days. There is a celebration on the the eighth or twenty-first day of birth of a male child. No formal *namkarn* or *mundan* ceremony takes place. Birth of a male child is celebrated on the following Lohri day as well. The dead are cremated. Pollution is observed for seventeen days. On the seventeenth day, *satarwan* is held, when *pagdi* ceremony is performed. Remains of the dead are immersed at Hardwar, or Beas in the case of Radhaswamis. A few members observe *shradh* ceremony. The marriage rites are performed at the bride's place. The consummation of marriage takes place at the groom's house.

The economy of the Rai Sikhs is linked to the land. At present they subsist on cultivation of land and agricultural labour. Their traditional occupation before Independence was of sharecroppers, tenants, agricultural labourers, hunting of wild boar and also in fishing. They also indulged in extraction of illicit liquor near the river-bank. The community also engaged in the occupation of making *sirkis.* They make baskets from reed and grass. However, the profession has gradually changed to the cultivation of land, either as owners of land or as agricultural labourers. The community is considered expert in reclaiming wasteland along the river-bank. It is settled on these lands along the river Satluj in the districts of Ferozepur and Jalandhar. Such areas of settlement are popularly known as *mand,* or *bet.*

Originally the state government had allotted these lands to this community for reclamation. In the Ferozepur district this community cultivates on wastelands in a 70 km belt running between Guru Har Sahai, Jalabad and Ferozepur. The landed property which was transferred to this community was evacuee or custodian property as per documents. Under some laws passed it has been gradually transferred to this community. Earlier the price of this land was five hundred rupees per acre. These days it has increased to twenty thousand rupees per acre, that too of the land which has been under continued cultivation. Even the possession of the unauthorized land, showed in police records as land grabed by the community, is being legalized on payment of ten thousand rupees for one acre. In the 1960s and 1970s the community participated in the struggle launched by the communist parties, to gain ownership rights.

As compared to other communities it was better placed because as Vimukat Jati it had to pay very little land revenue. The other occupation of liquor extraction has declined due to the influence of Radhaswami faith and of late due to police vigilance in the *mand* areas. Since the government has started auctioning fishing rights, their participation in this occupation has also been adversely affected. The community also participates in the agricultural and non-agricultural labour. The other traditional activity, rope making, has declined over the years. However, a large number continues to engage in this activity. The change in the land rights is visible since British times. At that time there were only twenty land-owning families in the village Hazara Singhwala but now in this village only a few families are landless. Other families own about one to ten acres of land. About 50 per cent families have land which is less than two acres. Only a few members have joined the services. The community also has few lawyers. A direct link with the fully regulated market exists. As producers of agricultural commodities, these people have access to nearby grain markets in the towns. Number of agricultural labourers has increased over the years. Child labour exists in the agricultural operations.

There is a state-level *sabha* or association of the community known as the Sikh Secular Welfare Association. There is an All India Rai Sikh Scheduled Tribes Association based in Azadpur, Delhi. Both these associations are demanding Scheduled Tribe status for this community. There are elected *gram panchayats* in the area. In the Ferozepur district there are number of *panches* from this community who are also elected members. In this community, there are believers of both Sikhism and Hinduism. The influence of Radhaswami sect has increased of late. The priest belongs to the other community and performs worship, marriage, birth and death rites. They also impart religious teachings. The community celebrates all the local festivals such as Dussehra, Diwali, Lohri and Baisakhi. However, the community is not deeply religious and their visits to religious places are very formal. The Radhaswami sect has, to a large extent, eradicated the influence of non-vegetarianism and the use of alcohol in the community. There is no specific folklore of the community and the Rai Sikh sing the local folk songs.

The community has good intercommunity relations with their neighbours. They exchange *sidha, kachcha* and *pukka* food with other communities. A few intercommunity marriage have also taken place. They share water sources, cremation ground, religious shrines, fairs and festivals. They work as agricultural labourers on lands owned by the Mahajans and Jat Sikhs. The present status of this community *vis-a-vis* other communities is better than at earlier times. Political leadership has emerged at local and state levels from this community.

The community has experienced variable impact of developmental programmes. Formal education is partly favoured by them for boys and girls. The boys get education upto middle school level, and only in a few cases upto graduation. Girls generally drop out after primary school level. The reasons of dropping out from studies for boys are mostly economic because they are expected to start earning early, while for girls the reasons are mostly social. Remoteness of the schools is one additional reason for dropping out. In case of a few villages across Satluj, in Ferozepur district, the main reason is the non availability of secondary schools. Even those who want to get secondary education for the girls, hesitate to send them to distant places. Some members of the community have even got education upto university level. The attitude of the community to modern medicare is favourable. They have also accepted modern means of family planning. There is tendency for both the sexes to get sterilized. The parents prefer only one or two children. Drinking water is available to them from handpumps and tube wells. A large number of them also get the facility of electric supply. They have access to electronic media.

Cow-dung cakes and firewood are the most commonly used fuels in the rural areas. In urban areas kerosene and cooking gas is also used. They also avail of the benefits of fair price shops. Generally, they procure sugar from these shops. They make use of modern techniques in agricultural operations and use both organic and chemical fertilizers. A few of them also own tractors. Others hire tractors for cultivation. They show mixed attitude towards savings. A few have opened bank accounts. A large number of them have been provided with yellow cards and they have applied for loans mostly to invest in animal husbandry. Some have received loans from the banks for agricultural operations against mortgage of their land. A few take loan from moneylenders in towns.

VIRINDER SINGH

# RAJPUT (HINDU)

Ibbetson (1916: 132) describes the Rajputs of Punjab as fine brave men, who retain the feudal instinct more strongly developed than perhaps any other caste. They are very tenacious of the integrity of their communal property in the village lands, seldom admitting strangers to share it with them. The pride of blood is their characteristic, for pride of blood is the very essence of their Rajputhood. They prefer pastoral to agricultural pursuits looking upon all manual labour as derogatory and upon the actual operation of plough as degrading, and it is only the poorest class of Rajputs who will himself follow the plough.

The community is mainly located in the sub-mountain districts of Hoshiarpur and Gurdaspur. Some of them are also located in the plains of Punjab. There are five subcastes among them which are Dadwal, Naru, Ghorewaha, Charak and Harchand. Traditionally they had a number of superior subcastes and inferior subcastes, the main point of distinction was that the superior subcastes do not touch the plough as it was considered defiling and below status. They would not marry their daughters among the inferior subcastes and would not practise widow remarriage. Most of the Muslim Rajputs migrated to Pakistan and the Hindu and Sikh Rajputs migrated to the present Punjab. One can have a tentative idea of the distribution of the population of this community as per 1931 census in what constitutes present-day Punjab. The total population of Rajputs according to the 1931 census in the united Punjab was 27.90 lakh, of which the Hindus were 10.22 lakh, Muslims 17.21 lakh and the Sikhs, only 51,000.

They speak Punjabi language and use both the Devanagari and Gurmukhi scripts. The male attire is shirt, trousers, *dhoti* and *pagri*; and the females wear *salwar*, *kameez* and *dupatta*. *Dal-roti* is their staple food and they eat eggs, mutton and chicken. Consumption of rice is very little and occasional. The pulses they use are gram, *mah* (*urad*), *moong, moth* and *masur*. Cooking is done with vegetable oil, mustard or groundnut oil or *desi ghee*. Tea and *lassi* are the non-alcoholic drinks consumed by them regularly whereas consumption of alcoholic drinks is occasional among them. Fruits such as mango, banana and oranges are eaten in moderate quantity seasonally. Among changes in their food habits are an increase in the consumption of vegetables and decrease in the consumption of non-vegetarian food and they eat the local Punjabi food. There are both vegetarians and non-vegetarians among them. Milk is an important constituent of their food. The Hindus smoke *bidi* and cigarettes.

Ibbetson (1916: 132) states that the Rajputs of the [old] Punjab may be broadly divided into four groups. First come the Rajputs of the Delhi territory and Jamna valley, for the most part belonging to the two great groups of Chauhan and Tunwar which gave Delhi its most famous dynasties. Next come the Rajputs of the river valleys of the western plains, many of them hardly or not at all to be distinguished from Jats and belonging for the most part of Bhatti of Jaisalmer and Bikaner, and their predecessors, the Punwar. The third group is in the Western Hills including the salt range tract, comprising both dominant tribes of proud position such as the Janjua and Mongral Rajputs from the the Jammu Hills, and descendants either of the Yadubansi (Bhatti) dynasty of Kashmir and the mythical Raja Rasalu of Sialkot so famous in Punjab folklore, or of a group of tribes, apparently of Punwar origin, which now hold the hills on either bank of the Jhelam. Finally we have the Rajputs of the Kangra hills of whom Katoch may be taken as the type, so ancient that their very origin and advent to their present abodes are lost in the past, and the Rajputs of the lower hills which fringe the Panjab Himalayas. . . .

Ibbetson (1916: 100) examined the origin and relationship of Rajputs and Jats and observed 'whether Jats and Rajputs were or were not originally distinct, and whatever aboriginal elements affiliated to their society, the two now form a common stock, the distinction between Jat and Rajput being social rather than ethnic. Those families of that common stock whom the tide of fortune has raised to political importance have become Rajputs almost by mere virtue of their rise, and that their descendants have retained the title and its privileges on the condition, strictly enforced of observing the rules by which the higher are distinguished from the lower castes in the Hindu scale of precedence, of preserving their purity of blood by refusing to marry with families of inferior social rank, of rigidly abstaining from widow marriage, and of refraining from degrading occupation. Those who transgressed these rules have fallen from their high position and ceased to be Rajputs: while such families as attaining a dominant position in their territory, began to affect social exclusiveness and to observe the rules, have become not only Rajas, but also Rajputs or "Sons of Rajas". For the last seven centuries the process of elevation at least has been almost at a stand-still. Under the Delhi Emperors, king-making was practically impossible. Under the Sikhs the Rajput was overshadowed by the Jat, who resented his assumption of superiority and his refusal to join him on equal terms in the ranks of the Khalsa, deliberately persecuted him where ever and whenever he had the power, and preferred his title of Jat Sikh to that of the proudest Rajput." The Rajput community consider themselves in terms of superior and inferior gradation. For example, Dadwal, Harchand, Charak, etc., the subcastes interviewed for this study consider themselves in the superior grade of Rajputs, whereas the two other subcastes Ghorewaha and Naru were considered to be of inferior status. In the past, the superior Rajput caste did not marry with the inferior castes but now such distinctions are gradually disappearing.

They are an endogamous community and observe 'village and *got*' exogamy. Among Rajputs differentiation at social, religious territorial levels occurs. The function of *got* is to regulate marriage alliances. No changes in the surnames, clan and titles have been reported among the Rajputs. They consider themselves superior, while the perception of other communities about them is medium. They are aware of the *varna* system and recognize the same, and place themselves in the *varna* system as Kshatriya. Child marriage has been replaced by adult marriage. Marriage is arranged by negotiation of the parents with the help of either a close relative or *vichola*. Monogamy is the form of marriage. Marriage symbols are vermilion in the hair parting, glass bangles, *bindi*, ear, nose and finger rings.

Dowry in kind is given, and its cost varies with the financial condition of the girl's parents. This dowry includes utensils, ornaments, clothes, furniture, etc. and is given at the time of marriage. They are patrilocal and strictly follow Hindu marriage practices. Widow remarriage was generally not practised by the superior Rajput subcastes in the past, but now it is not so strictly adhered to; the age at marriage for the girls now ranges from eighteen to twenty-one years and for the boys from twenty-one to thirty years. In the past, the marital relationships were purely decided by the elders, but now, the consent, particularly of the boys is being obtained. Divorce was common among subcastes such as Ghorewahas and Narus in the past but the Dadwal, Harchand and Charak did not have any instance of divorce. There is relaxation in this respect also among the latter subcastes.

The pattern of family is generally joint. Avoidance and joking relationships in a family between its various members are maintained.

Mother-in-law and son-in-law; daughter-in-law and father-in-law; sister-in-law (younger brother's wife) and brother-in-law (husband's elder brother) maintain avoidance. However, joking relationships are observed between *bhabi* and *dewar*, a lady and her husband's younger brother, *jeeja* and *sali*, that is a man and his wife's sister; and between the *sadus*. The eldest son succeeds whereas all the sons equally share their father's property. Recently there has been an increase in the number of nuclear families, while the extended ones still continue. The status of woman is still low and they neither control the family income nor do they contribute to the income of the family. Women are consulted on important occasions such as that of a marriage. Primarily the women are engaged in household activities. The daughters also have the right to inheritance of joint property but in practice it is seldom obtained. They are also going for all levels of education including higher education.

A male's birth is celebrated in this community. They observe certain pre-delivery restrictions and the first delivery is always arranged in the house of the would-be mother's parents. They observe postnatal restrictions on mothers, who are not allowed to enter the kitchen for forty days after childbirth. Those who can afford, celebrate the birthday of their son and the *namkaran* is also performed besides holding of *mundan* ceremony. Marriage rituals are performed according to the Hindu tradition of seven *pheras* at the bride's residence. A feast is also given to the members of the *barat*, the groom's friends and relatives by the parents of the bride. Earlier, the *barat* used to stay for two nights. However, the ceremony of marriage is now performed in a single day. One day after the *phera* the girl visits her parents. The consummation of marriage is at the groom's residence. Dead are cremated according to the Hindu ways. The ashes are immersed in the river at sacred places such as Hardwar. Funeral rites are observed on the thirteenth day and purification ceremony on the sixteenth day. First *shradh* ceremony is observed at the end of the first year of the death and subsequently it is observed every fourth year. The pollution after death is observed for fifteen days.

The main occupation of this community in the past was agriculture and it continues to be one of the main occupations even today. However, now they also participate in various non-agricultural occupations. Their representation in the army is very high, and they are also employed in various white-collar jobs in the banks, or government offices, as well as being teachers, professors and engineers. Both the boys and girls of this community acquire higher education. Their traditional caste-councils are no more in common practice though they have a caste association at the state level.

They believe either in Hinduism or Sikhism and worship according to their respective religious traditions. These people celebrate the festivals of Holi, Diwali, Dussehra, Lohri, Baisakhi. They visit sacared places of their respective religion such as temple or *gurdwara*. Sacred specialists who perform birth, marriage and death rites, are not from their community. Various festivals are of social and religious significance for them. In some of the villages the ladies engage themselves in knitting and weaving *daris*.

Members of this community share their oral traditions with other communities of Punjab. The ladies at the time of marriage sing songs and perform *giddha*. The men perform *bhangra* on the occasion of festivals and marriages. Their relationships with other Punjabi communities are very close. Their role in the economic and political development of Punjab has been noticeable. They avoid sharing food and water with the members of those caste communities whom they consider low. The latter may accept water and food from them, but the Rajputs avoid it. The modern inter-community linkages are well developed. Political leadership has developed among these people at the village *panchayat* and regional levels.

Formal education is favoured by them. They have been benefited by the health and medical care services. Handpump is the source of drinking water. Kerosene oil, wood, cow-dung cakes are used as fuel sources. They take advantage of the immunization facilities for the mother and the child. Electricity is available in all the households. They also practise family planning measures. As agriculturists, they use chemical fertilizers, improved seeds and modern agricultural implements such as tube wells and tractors. They also take recourse to bring their produce to the *mandis* or markets for sale. They have ration cards and get sugar, *atta* and rice at subsidized rates. Their attitude towards savings is positive. They help each other on occasions of marriage and death in a family.

K. GOPALA IYER

# RAJPUT (MUSLIM)

For the present study, the Muslim Rajputs were studied in Malerkotla. Here they were employed by the *nawab* to maintain law and order and to settle various disputes. They were brought from Jaisalmer in Rajasthan and recruited in police and armed forces at the time of establishment of the Malerkotla *riasat* (estate). Later on, they embraced Islam. Their various subcastes are Rawat, Baria, Chauhan, Tanwar or Rangar. According to Rose (1919: 287), Shaikh Samail is said to have been the first to convert the Bhattis to Islam. The five *pirs* are Shaikh Samail, Shah Daulat, Shah Fateh Ali, Pir Fateh Khan and Shah Murad—all Bhatti saints.

According to Rose (1914: 298), Rajput element is represented not by those communities who belong to the Rajputs, but some of the Jat also claim Rajput origin apart from Gaurs, Gakkars, Rathis, Thakars, Rawats, Kanets and Ghriths. The Solanki sprang from Brahmanis essence and the Parihars from Devi's. The Chauhans took their origin from fire. The Parihars belong to one of four Agni Kulas and in Punjab they have been replaced by the Sonkla and in Rajasthan they are termed as Rathor. The Tunwars derive their name from Tomara dynasty; who ruled Gwalior in the fifteenth century. The ancestors of Chauhans were the Chapamanas, who had their dynasty in Ajmer around A.D. 950. Punwars can be identified with the Paramaras who ruled Malwa about A.D. 825.

According to Ibbetson (1916: 139): 'Rangar is a term, somewhat contemptously, applied in the eastern and south-eastern district to any Musalman Rajput.' The Muslim Rajputs speak Punjabi and Urdu and use Perso-Arabic script. *Dal* and *roti* are their staple food, while groundnut oil is used as cooking medium. They eat non-vegetarian food including mutton, eggs and fish on special occasions. They take milk and milk products. They smoke and chew *paan*.

The Muslim Rajput are endogamous but allow marriage between close relatives. Their own perception of themselves and the perception of other communities about them is high. Marriage is arranged after attaining adulthood and polygyny is allowed. There are no symbols of marriage, they are patrilocal and divorce and remarriage according to the tradition of Islam are allowed. Nuclear and joint families are common. In a family, avoidance, joking relationship and conflicts are reported. Sons inherit the paternal property equally and the eldest son gets succession. Status of women in this community is low. Certain restrictions on the mother and a pollution period are observed after a birth. Among males, circumcision is performed. Marriage rituals are perfomed at the residence of the bride according to Islamic tradition of *nikah*. They bury their dead.

The less important members of the community were assigned a lower status. With the result the subcastes such as the Rathis and Thakkars have actually been excluded from the Rajputs as the ruling chiefs will marry with their equivalents or of the same social standings, with the result the nucleus of the Rajput community consisted of the descendants of the Kshatriya chiefs. The population of Rajputs according to the *Census of India* (1911: 473) was 16,35,432 individuals.

Chief occupations of the Rajputs were agriculture and defence services. They are now mostly settled agriculturists. Apart from this, they also engage themselves in business, in defence services, government service or labour. Islam is their religion and Id-ul-Fitr and Id-ul-Zuha are their main festival. Traces of pre-conversion religious practices were not observed among them. Folk traditions are shared by them with other communities of Punjab.

They accept and exchange water and food from all the Muslim cummunities. Burial ground and sacred places are shared with other Muslim communities.

Though formal education is favoured by them for both boys and girls, their children generally do not study beyond secondary or graduate levels due to economic or social reasons. They take advantage of modern medicare and family welfare facilities. Handpumps are used for getting drinking water.

They avail of media and communication facilities. Electricity is used for domestic purposes. Wood, cow-dung cakes, kerosene oil or coal is used as fuel. Tube wells are used for irrigation purpose. They use organic manure, chemical fertilizer and insecticide. Immunization facilities for the mothers and infants are available.

SWARAN SINGH

# RAMGARHIA

The Ramgarhia are also known as Tarkhan, Barhai and Khati and are carpenters by profession. The original name of the Ramgarhia community was Thaka that is carpenter. Bansal, Kalsi, Ubhi, Bhanwer, Ghatura, Virdi, Birdi, Jagdev, Matharoo, Saggu, Panesar, Lotey, Riat, Hunjan, Mankoo, Dhiman, Deogan, Nanrey, Sembhey, Salh, Channay, Sohal, Gill, Dhillon, Chadha, Chopra, Sharma, are the major exogamous *gots* of the Ramgarhia.

The ancestors of this community became Sikh, though the exact period of conversion to Sikhism is not known. Their skill and ability to do wood-work with precision and their strong will for work gave them recognition in society. Sardar Jassa Singh, himself a member of this community, changed the name from Thaka to the Ramgarhia. Sardar Jassa Singh was the son of Sardar Bhagwan Singh and was born in 1723. His father was a warrior and helped Zakarya Khan, the then governor of Punjab to win many battles. All his sons were warriors, and fought battles with him. After Zakarya Khan, Mir Mannu was appointed the governor of Punjab and he had a conflict with the Afghans. The Sikhs took full advantage of this and captured many areas of Punjab. During this period Jassa Singh raised a fort at Ram Gauni near Amritsar and was incharge of it. When Mannu died, the administration in Punjab collapsed. The Sikh confederacies built quite strong and autonomus bodies. The Ramgarhias formed one such confederacy under the leadership of Jassa Singh. After Manu's death, the Sikhs confederacies took up the protection of Punjab. The Ramgarhia kingdom was extended upto Kangra, Nurpur, Basohli, and Mandi. A number of important cities of Punjab were also included within the Ramgarhia territory. After Jassa Singh's death, this confederacy was also taken over by Maharaja Ranjit Singh. The Ramgarhias used to work for the landowners. The Lohar (blacksmith) and the Tarkhan (carpenters) used the suffix Ramgarhia to their names.

The term 'Ramgarhia' was increasingly used in the latter half of the nineteenth century. During this period they took up high-skilled works in East Africa and many other parts of the world. Their social status was raised and they became the pioneer industrial entrepreneurs of the Punjab and of many other states of the country.

In this community the gene frequency of (T) is more in case of females than the males. The genotypic frequencies of homozygous tasters (TT) and heterozygous tasters (Tt) is more in the females but homozygous non-tasters (tt) frequency is more in males. The gene frequencies of tasters and non-tasters are 0.4893 and 0.5107 for Ramagarhia females, while these are 0.468 and 0.5320 for the males.

The occurrence of mid phalangeal hair on the corresponding fingers of two hands and sexes shows almost similar trends of variation. Highest incidence is on the digit iv followed by considerable decrease on finger v and least on finger ii. 163 Ramgarhia females were studied and none was found to be colour blind. Out of 156 males 7 were found to be colour blind, giving the frequency of 4.48 per cent. The gene frequency of Hp1 allele has been calculated as 0.138. All the transferrin proteins were normal Tfc type. All albumins were of normal type. Regarding the analysis of transferrin patterns, it was observed that all belonged to normal, type. Similarly there was no variant in the albumin and all were normal types.

The mother tongue of the Ramgarhias is Punjabi. Correspondence with relatives is generally made in Gurmukhi script, though some elders prefer to write in Perso-Arabic script also. The recent trend is to send children to English-medium schools. Children of the present generation prefer to talk in English or Hindi. The staple diet of the Ramgarhia is *dal* and *roti*, made of wheat with vegetables. Rice is used on very special occasions. Those who live in Amritsar and Gurdaspur area take more rice than people in other areas. Earlier, paddy was cultivated in a very small area, but now paddy is grown in plenty covering large areas of cultivable land. This production of paddy has resulted in a change in their food habit and they have started eating rice also. Non-vegetarian food is also consumed.

Ramgarhias constitute a strictly endogamous community. They observe exogamy at *got* level. Earlier the cultural zones tended to be endogamous units. There were three such zones, viz., Majha, Malwa and Doaba. Perhaps this was due to the fact that people of one particular zone used to have cultural practices different from those of another cultural zone. It was not very easy for the Doaba people to get a bride from the Majha area, because the people of Majha considered themselves superior to those of Doaba and Malwa. But such feeling is now almost absent. Previously, professional match-makers used to negotiate marriages. Now friends, and relatives usually do this. Earlier, to contract a marriage for a person, his or her father's and mother's *gots* and six specific *gots* were avoided. Now, only one's father's and mother's *gots* are avoided. There has been a considerable rise in age at marriage probably due to spread of higher education among them. Marriages are performed according to Sikh tenets. The bride and the groom go round the *Guru Granth Sahib* four times. The demand for dowry is not much among the Ramgarhia, whatever is given by the bride's parents is accepted by the groom's side. Actual marriage function is preceded by betrothal ceremony conducted by the priest in the presence of the holy *Guru Granth Sahib*. Majority of the families in this community, specially in rural areas, still follow joint family system. The eldest male member holds absolute authority over the whole joint family. In various rituals of the community, he represents the family. If he ceases to earn due to some reasons, the economic affairs are looked after by the eldest son, but social authority still continues to be with him. The earning members of the family pool their resources and hand it over to the eldest male member, who passes it to his wife or the eldest lady in the house, who also divides the work. But now nuclear families have also come up while joint families are being abandoned. This is due to the fact that members, who go out for better earning and specially those who start their business in the cities or those who are posted elsewhere are compelled to break away from joint families. In the Doaba area, there are villages, where most of the members of the community have gone to foreign countries for earning their livelihood. On coming back they have purchased land in big cities, constructed their houses and have started business. This has also led to a disintegration of the joint family system.

Still, a large number of persons in this community are backward in the field of education which is still not encouraged especially in respect of girls. Owing to this, a large number of women do not have general awareness as compared to some of the other communities in Punjab. As a result of this one does not find Ramgarhia women coming up as entrepreneurs or going for jobs. Regarding their status in social life they are not different from other women of the region.

Most of the rituals such as birth, marriage and death are performed centering around the *Guru Granth Sahib*, as with other Sikh communities. A woman delivers her first baby at her parent's house. Purification of the mother is done after thirteen days of the birth of the child by a Sikh priest. *Namkaran* or naming ceremony is performed in front of the holy *Guru Granth Sahib*. Marriages are also performed according to the Sikh tradition of *anand karaj* in front of the *Guru Granth Sahib*. They cremate the dead. After cremation, all persons who have accompanied the dead body upto the cremation ground go to a nearby *gurdwara*. *Pagri* ceremony is performed on the last day of the mourning period. Duration of this period varies according the age of the deceased. If some older person dies, this is observed between tenth and thirteenth day after death. During these days *sadharan path*, or recitation of the *Guru Granth Sahib* is performed by Sikh priests. Nowadays, *akhand path*, continuous recitation of *Guru Granth Sahib* in forty-eight hours, has become quite prevalent. This makes the mourning period shorter. A turban is tied on the head of the eldest son of the deceased. This is given by the parents of the lady of the house. In case of an infant's death, the dead body is buried.

The community used to be village artisans, mending all agricultural implements, household furnitures, carts, Persian wheels, etc. The Ramgarhias' rise has been, almost entirely, due to their widespread achievements as contractors and as industrial enterpreneurs. They have set up big industries making various machines as well as wooden articles. Some of them have taken to professions of medicine and engineering. In villages many of the community members work as masons. The Ramgarhias of Punjab are all Sikh except a very few Dhimans who are Hindus.

Since they are involved in woodwork, they make various wooden objects engrave sceneries and designs on wooden doors and show-pieces. Their oral traditions are the *shabads* and the *sangeet* recited by the ladies mainly on marriage ceremony. *Giddha* performed by the females and *bhangra* by males, are popular folk dances in Punjab among them.

The Ramgarhia are extremely hospitable people and keep social relations with majority of the communities except the Scheduled Castes. Ramgarhia women may go out, together with the neighbourhood women of other communities, preferably Jats and Rajputs to the fields and market place. However, in matters of marital ties or dining together, the Ramgarhias prefer to stay within the community boundary. Ramgarhias are closely associated with the Lohars, who used to render their services to the *zamindars* by making agricultural implements.

In spite of their backwardness in receiving formal education, the Ramgarhias are quick to adopt any technical innovation. Even in rural areas, they respond positively to the developmental programmes for agriculture, sanitation or health care. This attitude is reflected in the industries established in Ludhiana and Jalandhar and, to some extent, in areas around Amritsar. The entrepreneurs have established some educational institutions to see that members of their community receive formal education and vocational training. Phagwara has a post-graduate college for arts and science, a teacher training college, and a polytechnic. Besides, there are high and secondary schools in Punjab run by a trust of this community.

I.J.S. Bansal
A.S. Bhanwar

# RIAGAR

The Riagars are also known as Raigar, Laskaria Raigar, Rehgar, Regar, Jatia, Sindhi, Jalia and Bola. In Punjab they are also called Bagri. As they are engaged in the tanning of skin, it may so happen that from *rang* they have derived their name Riagar. The Riagars were earlier known as Rangar Rajput and were forced to tan hides by the Sultan of Delhi. Hence according to this belief, the origin of Riagar has been from Rajputs and that they are Sagarbansi. From this belief it is also confirmed that the Raigars have spread from Bhatinda (Punjab) throughout India (Naval, 1986: 21-2). Naval (1986: 22-3) refers to Shri Bajranglal Lohia about the origin of the term Raigar and Raigar community. In the Malwa state, the Raigar people of Madugarh consider their origin from a Raidas caste. Thus the term has originated from Raidas, who are known by this name in Jaipur. In Jodhpur, Marwar and other areas they are called Jatia. Their ladies, as they live among the Jats, wear the dress similar to that of Jat ladies. As they tan the skins of the animals in Bikaner, they are called Rangia. In Mewar they are called Bola. The Raigar of Rajasthan wear *janeu* and marry by the tradition of seven *pheras.*

Naval (1986: 24-5) also refers to Pandit Jawala Parsad and Ramesh Chander Gunarthi, who have proved the origin of the Riagar community about six centuries ago. The stone inscriptions at Hurda are about 980 years old, which proves that this community was known by the name of Raigar and was in existence about two thousand years back. On the basis of the viewpoint of Pandit Jwala Prasad and Ramesh Chander Gunarthi, the community took up the debased profession after A.D. 1408. This community was in existence even before this, but was engaged in better occupations. The views of the above-mentioned were not about the community's origin, but related to the change of their profession. They have also described the attacks of the Mughals in A.D. 1250 and 1408 and show that it was the period related to change of profession and change of religion.

Under those circumstances, the Kshatriyas could survive only by engaging in low professions or by changing their religion. Hence it appears to be more appropriate that during this period these Raigar Kshatriyas, changed their occupation. They speak Rajasthani and use Devanagari script to communicate with the members of their own community and with others, they speak Punjabi and write in Gurmukhi. In Punjab they are found in Bhatinda (100 families), Amarpur, Lal Singh Basti (5 to 7 families), Patiala (2 to 4 families), Jaito, Moga (300 families), Harijan Colony, Mukatsar, Raman Mandi (300 families), Mansa (30 families), Bareta (50 to 60 families), Sunam (150 families), Hall Bazar, Amritsar, Abohar (500 familes) and some other places.

The males of this community wear *kurta*, *pyjama* and trousers, while the females wear *choli*, *ghagri*, *chunni*, *salwar* and *kameez*. They take *dal-roti* as their staple food. Non-vegetarian food and alcoholic drinks are consumed only on special occasions. They cook their food in groundnut or mustard oil. Among non-alcoholic beverages, they take *lassi*, tea and milk products. Fruits are taken in small quantity and seasonally. These people smoke.

They are divided into different *gots*. The names of these *gots* are derived from twenty-one different villages of Bhatinda. They consider themselves to be of high status, but the members of other communities treat them as low status and recognize their position in the *varna* system as Shudra. They marry within their own community but not within the same village and *got*. The boys are married when they are twenty to twenty-five years of age, while the age at marriage for the girls ranges between twelve to eighteen years. Marriages are generally arranged by negotiation with the help of a *vichola*. The ceremony of *mangani* is performed by offering only one rupee. The would-be bride is presented a suit of clothes and fruits by the would-be groom's people. Monogamy is the form of marriage. *Sindur*, bangles, *bindi*, finger and nosering are used as symbols of marriage. Dowry in kind includes *thali*, *lota*, *dari*, ornaments and *peti* (big iron chest).

Cruelty, adultery, maladjustment may lead to a divorce. Both husband and wife have the right of seeking divorce, but generally women do not initiate divorce. Children of divorced parents can stay with their mother if they are young or with their father if they so desire. In case of a divorce, if the husband is found guilty he is made to pay a fine of three hundred and twenty-six rupees, and if the wife is found guilty, the dowry is not returned to her. Nuclear as well as joint families are prevalent among them. Property matters, disregard towards elders or difference in opinion over some petty issues may cause conflict in the family. All the sons inherit property of their father equally, while the eldest son succeeds the father's authority.

The status of women in this community is considered low. They attend to various household jobs, bring potable water and work in the cotton mills as casual labourers. Though they contribute towards the family income, they do not control family expenditure. During the first pregnancy, certain pre-delivery precautions are taken. Postnatal restrictions on the mother are also imposed for forty days. Post-delivery pollution period is observed. When a male child is born, they celebrate it and host a feast to the members of the community. They perform *mundan* ceremony within one year and the parents of the child visit holy shrines for this purpose.

After birth of a child, they ask some Brahman priest to perform the *namkaran* or naming ceremony. *Surya-puja* (sun-worship) is also performed and the Brahman is consulted to fix the date of the *puja*. On the day of *surya-puja* the mother takes a bath and wears new clothes. She sits on a *pat* (stool) in the courtyard of the house facing the sun. *Meetha khana* (sweet food) is prepared and offered to the sun-god. At the time of worship, food grain is placed in a *kalas* (pitcher) filled with water and a branch of *neem* tree. For *sava mahina*, forty days from the birth of a child, on an auspicious day, the mother observes *pujan*. Until the *jalwa pujan* (worship of the god of water) is observed, she can neither touch the pitcher containing drinking water nor can she enter the kitchen. The *pujan* is performed at a pond and is joined by other women.

Marriage rituals are performed at the bride's residence. Groom's friends and relatives are treated to a feast by the bride's parents. The engagement or *sagai* is performed at young age because there are problems of getting a suitable boy if the girl is grown up. On the occasion of *sagai* the people of the locality are invited. The girl's father places on a *thali* one coconut, a little *gur* (molasses) and piece of cloth for a blouse for the boy's mother. The boy's father places coconut and *gur* in another *thali*. Both the boy's and girl's father sit facing each other and exchange these *thalis*. During this exchange, the *thali* of boy's father is kept above the *thali* of the girl's father. Before this exchange the boy's father enquires about the name of the girl, and the girl's father enquires about the name of the boy. After exchanging the *thalis* they feed each other with a small piece of *gur*. The *panch* of the locality is paid one rupee twenty-five paise for *pilai* (purchasing alcoholic drink) and one rupee for *kạmbal chhapai* (printing the blanket). The *panches* keep the amount for purchasing drinks, and the one rupee is given to the mother of the girl. At the end of engagement ceremony, the girl's father sprinkles saffron or pink colour on the bodies of close relatives, which confirms the engagement.

Among the Riagars, dowry is neither demanded nor fixed at the time of engagement. After four or six months, the girl's father asks the boy's father for ornaments and clothes. He also sends clothes for the boy's parents and his family members. This is called *reet*. The *lagan* (auspicous date and hour for marriage) is arranged when the boy and girl reach marriageable age. The bride's and groom's families discuss before fixing a date. Later, the girl's father asks the *pandit* to write down the *lagan*. The date and time of marriage is written on a piece of paper. Yellow rice, *supari* (areca nut), *bindi* (*kumkum*) and a one-rupee coin are placed on this paper. The *lagan* is sprinkled with *kumkum*. The coconut, *lagan* and other articles are tied with *mauli* or *kachcha sut* (a piece of hand-rolled thread). This is sent either through *nai*, *nath* or some relative of the boy's father. The boy's father invites his close relatives and neighbours and accepts the *lagan*.

The other ceremonies performed on this occasion are *path bithana*, *bandaula*, *binayak puja*, *peethi* (*ubatan*), *neot*. The boy's father requests all the neighbours personally to join the *barat*. One day before the departure of the *barat* the boy's father invites to a feast all the relatives and those who will accompany the *barat*. The Brahman priest, conducting the marriage rituals performs *havan* for the bride and bridegroom. Out of the seven *pheras*, during the first four the bridegroom leads whereas the bride leads during the remaining three *pheras* around the *agni* (fire). Consummation of marriage is at the groom's residence.

The Riagar cremate their dead, but saints are buried. Such burial is called *samadhi dena*. They immerse the ashes and bones after cremation in the Ganga at Hardwar within twelve days after death.

The Riagars are a landless community engaged in skin-tanning, shoe-shining, shoe-repairing, shoemaking, or wage labourers and a few are in government service. These traditional skin tanners have not yet adopted the modern techniques of tanning. The youth of the present generation are discarding this occupation and going for government services and other occupations. As a result, this occupation is slowly coming to an end. Leather *juttis* are made by them in rural areas. In the cities, the Riagars are engaged in *chappal* making on a large scale. They have their community *panchayat* at the *mohalla*, state and national levels. The state-level *panchayat* is called Punjab Riagar Maha Sabha, whereas the national-level *panchayat* is called All-India Riagar Maha Sabha. These bodies look after the interests of the community at different levels. The members of the state-level *panchayat* are from the various districts of Punjab and are elected for five years. In the social organization they have the All-India Riagar Maha Sabha on the top. At the state level, Rajasthan State Riagar Maha Sabha, Jaipur, Maharashtra Riagar Maha Sabha, Mumbai and the lower-level *panchayats* deal with local social problems and give their judgements. The Maha Sabhas take up matters related to the upliftment and improvment of their community. These are very important and powerful organizations.

The Riagar profess Hindu religion and worship Bhagwan Ravidas, Lord Shiva, Ramdev Pir, Hanuman, Bhairon and Ganesh. The sacred specialists serving them are from their own community. They have folk tradition and sing songs in Punjabi, Haryanvi and Rajasthani languages.

They accept and exchange food and water from all communities. However, there have been no intercommunity marriages. They can share roads, schools, shrines, but not cremation ground, with other communities. They take part in festivals and festivities but have no specific role to perform. Some of them own business, while a few of them work as administrators, undertake white-collar jobs or are in defence services. Political leadership has emerged in this community at national level. Formal education is favoured by them for both boys and girls.

Modern medicare facilities are available to them. Their attitude towards family planning is positive and most of the couples prefer to have three children. They use methods other than sterilization to plan their families. For these people handpumps are source of drinking water in most of their settlments. They use electricity. Firewood, kerosene oil, cow-dung cakes and liquid petroleum gas, are used as fuel. Immunization programmes for mothers and children serve them. They have ration cards and get sugar, refined edible oil and kerosene oil from the fair price shops. They have yellow cards to get loans from banks on easy terms. On special occasions, if a loan is not available from the banks, the moneylenders or shopkeepers are also approached.

SWARAN SINGH

# SAINI

The Sainis were described in ethnographic literature as a subdivision of the Malis. In some areas, they intermarry but in the state of Punjab there is no such tradition. The Malis or the florists are engaged mostly on the outskirt of the towns in nursery gardening. The Sainis claim a Rajput origin. They may belong either to the Hindu or Sikh religion. The Arains who are also engaged in the same job mostly belong to Islam and are supposed to have no relationship either with the Malis or the Sainis. The Sainis occupy a higher social status than the Malis (Ibbetson, 1916: 188).

The Sainis are also known as Malis outside Punjab. They use Saini as surname. The Sainis in Punjab have their ethnographic and historical accounts. The community traces its origin from the time of the *Mahabharata*. It calls itself Shoor Saini, the brave Saini, and considers itself to have originated from a number of Kshatriya groups. In Punjab, they are mainly settled in the districts of Ropar, Hoshiarpur, Jalandhar and Gurdaspur and have the status of backward class in the state. Both men and women are non-vegetarian, with moderate consumption of vegetable and occasional intake of fruit. They consume cereals such as wheat, rice and maize. All locally used pulses such as gram, peas, *urad*, *moong*, *moth* and *masoor* are consumed. *Vanaspati*, *desi ghee* and groundnut, mustard and sunflower oil are used as cooking media. Only men occasionally use alcoholic drinks. Consumption of fruits, vegetables and pulses has increased in recent years. They smoke *bidi*, cigarettes and a few also chew *paan*.

The Sainis have the clans such as Boli, Pawan, Gaddi, Harmati, Badwal, Alangi, Mangar, Badyal, Barayat and Salahri (Ibbetson, 1916: 189).

The Sainis are differentiated at social, economic, religious, occupational and educational levels. The social divisions help to regulate marriages and indicate social status. Their self-perception is very high; but other communities consider them to be of medium status. They recognize *varna* system and consider themselves to be Kshatriya. They are endogamous at community level, and exogamous at village and *got* level. Marriages are monogamous and are arranged by negotiations. Symbols of marriage include vermilion, bangles, *bindi*, finger rings and earrings. Dowry is paid in a marriage. Rule of residence is patrilocal. Divorce is permissible on various grounds with judicial approval. Either party can seek divorce and divorce compensation is given to the aggrieved party. The community allows remarriage of widows, widowers and divorcees of both the sexes. There has been some liberalization in the rules of marriage.

Families are either nuclear or vertically extended. Avoidance and joking relationships exist in a family. Family disputes often arise on grounds such as inheritance of property or challenge to the authority of elders. Rule of inheritance is male equigeniture, but succession favours the eldest son. There has been rise in the number of nuclear families. Women of this community have low status as compared to the men. They contribute to family income and participate in agricultural operations and animal husbandry. They also have important roles in the rituals, social functions and religious affairs.

The Sainis observe a period of pollution when there is a birth in the family. Postnatal restrictions on the mother exist. Naming ceremony is observed. Marriage rituals are performed at the bride's residence and consummation of marriage is at the groom's residence. A feast is hosted by both the bride's and groom's families at the time of marriage. The dead are cremated and bones are immersed in the Ganga at Hardwar. Death pollution is observed for a fixed period. Rituals are being curtailed.

Land is the main source of economy for the rural section of the community, and this resource is individually controlled. There are landless members as well. The Sainis, these days, are participating in animal husbandry, trade, small-scale industry, government services, private service and self-employment. In the agricultural sector child labour exists. Payment of wages is made in cash. Traditional caste councils known as Saini Sabha also exist. Statutory village *panchayats* are heterogeneous in nature and perform their statutory duties. The community mainly believes in Sikhism and Hinduism. The sacred specialists from other communities impart religious teachings and perform birth, marriage and death rites. The festivals in which the Sainis take part are of economic, religious and social significance for them. The community has its oral tradition, and folk-songs are sung by both men and women.

Sainis maintain good relations with the neighbouring communities. A few intercommunity marriages have taken place as well. They share water sources, cremation ground, and religious shrines and participate in festivals together with the other communities. As cultivators they maintain good relations with labourers. The Sainis who are employed in business, white-collar jobs, or are teachers, administrators, lawyers, doctors and defence services contribute towards establishing and maintaining non-traditional linkages with other communities of the state. Political leadership has emerged from this community at local, regional, and national levels.

The community enjoys all the benefits of development activities. The children of both the sexes get chances for good education, upto the graduation level. The community makes full use of modern medicare and both the sexes have accepted modern family planning methods. It has availed of water supply, electricity supply and public distribution system facilities. Information is disseminated to them through the political parties, extension and voluntary agencies. Some members of this community are self-employed in agriculture, poultry and transport business. Firewood, cow-dung cakes, coal, kerosene oil, and *gobar* (cow-dung) gas are the major sources of fuel. As an agricultural community it makes use of modern irrigation facilities, fertilizers and other modern methods locally available. Its attitude to saving is favourable. The members of the community have ration cards and get sugar, *atta* and rice through the public distribution system.

VIRINDER SINGH

# SANSI

The Sansi are described as the vagrants of the centre of the Punjab, as the Aheris are of its south eastern portions (Rose, 1919). They trace their origin from Marwar and Ajmer, where they still live in large numbers. They are generally a wandering group. They are great hunters, catching and eating all sorts of wild animals. They keep sheep, goats, pigs and donkeys, work in grass, straw and reeds. The men often beg and their women very commonly dance and sing. According to Rose (1919) 'They have some curious connection with Jat of the Central Punjab to most of whom they are hereditary genealogists or bards; and even in Rajputana, they commonly call themselves Dhart or bards. They also act as genealogists to the Dogras of Ferozepur, Rajputs of Hoshiarpur and Jalandhar and the Sodhis of Anandpur.' They trace their descent from one Sansmal of Bharatpur, who they still revere as their *guru* and are said to worship his patron saint under the name of Malangshah.

According to a legend, Sansmal was a singer, and this become a source of income for him. In this way he came across his relatives and tried to uplift their lot. Lord Indra was very impressed and invited Sansmal to ask for a favour. Sansmal asked, '*Hath wich kansa, nahi mangan da sansa*' (My people will be engaged in begging till they get land for cultivation or houses to live in). Lord Indra was happy with this and agreed to mark some villages for them, where they could beg, and declared Sansmal as the *faqir* of the area. The younger brother of Sansmal was Noormal. Sansmal is considered the ancestor of the Sansi. Noormal is the ancestor of the Mirasi. According to Sher (1965), the Sansi are divided into two main moieties of Mahla and Beehdoo after the names of their famous ancestors (sons of Sansmal). Beehdoo had twelve sons and Mahla had eleven. Therefore, the moieties, Mahla and Beehdoo are further divided into twenty-three exogamous units.

The Sansis have now a settled life and they have been declared as a denotified tribe. Earlier the Sansis were covered under the Criminal Tribes Act, as they were engaged in petty crimes, which included small thefts in their own villages. There are two divisions: (a) the Birtwan or Rehluwalas, who derive their name from *rehlus* which is sung by their women as they perform a dance and (b) nomadics. Bhedkut is another synonym of the Sansis and both of them intermarry.

The Sansis are recognized as a Scheduled Caste in the state of Punjab and according to *Census of India* (1981), the population of the Sansi in Punjab is 61,986 individuals, which includes 32,358 males and 29,628 females. The Sansis are found in all the districts of Punjab. Sher Singh Sher (1965) has given an account of the physical characteristics of the Sansis of Punjab: The Sansis are of medium build having average stature of 165.72 cm, with dolichocephalic heads (70 per cent) reptorrhine noses (49 per cent) and brown complexion. The head hair is mostly straight with dark brown or black colour. The eyes are of dark-brown colour (86 per cent) blood group B occurs in higher frequency (42.8 per cent) followed by O (26.7 per cent) A (22.9) and AB (8.6 per cent) blood groups.

The Sansi are non-vegetarian, wheat is their staple food and *dal* and *roti* their common food. Earlier they used to eat meat of such games as wild boar, hare and deer. Alcoholic drinks are also used by them frequently. *Sarson da sag* and *makki di roti* are relished specially during the winter season. Mustard oil is used as cooking medium. Tea and *lassi* are also favoured as drinks by the Sansi.

The betrothal ceremony consists of a visit by the boy's father to the girl's house and presentation of one rupee and some rice to the girl and distribution of sweets. A corresponding visit by the girl's father to the boy's house is also made when a rupee and a little rice are presented to the boy. The date of marriage is fixed in consultation with the Brahman priest. Before the marriage ceremony, the members of the community specially the members of *panchayat* ask the father of the bridegroom, '*From where have you come and why have you come?*'. The very purpose of this is to confirm whether they are true Sansis and the descendants of Mahla and Beedoo.

The marriage procession consists of the bridegroom and four or five persons, who are entertained by the bride's father. The marriage ceremonies are simple and are in conformity with the Brahmanical rites. Seven *pheras* (four led by the boy and three by the girl) are performed round the sacred fire and *mantras* from the Vedas are recited. The father of the bride gives clothings and utensils to his daughter in dowry. Earlier, they used to get their girls married at an age of twelve to thirteen years. At present the age at marriage for the girls varies between eighteen and twenty years and child marriage is no more practised. The children of poor families are married with the help of contributions by the members of the community. The *shagun* (presentation of one rupee and twenty-five paise, coconut and molasses during engagement) is offered to the boy while he sits on a slightly raised wooden platform which is called *chowki.* A feast known as *roti*, which includes *karah*, *puris* and *chhole* are offered by the bride's parents to the members of the community and the groom's party on the day of marriage. Marriages are mostly arranged by negotiation and the services of middleman are not requisitioned. Among the Sansi following the Sikh religion, *anand karaj* is performed in the presence of *Guru Granth Sahib.* The dress of the bride includes *ghagra, chunni, kurti,* anklets, *pajeb, padlea, aule, machli, hasli, tikka, borla.* The married girls use vermilion or *sindur* as a symbol of marriage in the parting of their hair.

According to Rose (1919: 367), 'Whenever a dispute arises between Sansis, the parties call a gathering of their brotherhood and the appointed chiefs of the brotherhood. They lay their case before this assembly and submit to the decision given by the chiefs. The man held to be at fault is punished with a *dand* (a fine imposed by the brotherhood), its amount being fixed by the chiefs. If the parties object to the decision and each still declares himself to be in the right, another custom called *pan bhutti* is observed. Each party gives a rupee to the chiefs who send for two divers. A bamboo is planted in a well and the divers are sent down. They dive into the water and the man whose diver comes to the surface first is deemed to be false and the one whose diver comes up last is considered to be true. Their belief is that water will not allow a false man to remain below its surface. This decision is final'. This practice is still there.

The Sansis have their own traditional *panchayat* which consists of eleven members. The *panches,* i.e. members of the *panchayat* are hereditary or their names are endorsed by the *biradari.* Petty issues are disposed of by the *panchayat* of the clan. In case the matter is serious then decision is taken by the higher *panchayat.* The decision taken by the *panchayat* is binding on both the parties. The Sansis do not approach police or court of law for settlement of their disputes. A person who informs the police or takes side with the police is also punished. The guilty has to take an oath in the temple and is asked to take a dip in a pond. If the person can remain for ten mintues under water, he/she is acquitted. There are other tests too to identify the guilty. Another form of test is to place 1.25 kg of hot iron on seven *pipal* leaves on which is placed *kachcha sut* (handspun thread). In case the thread burns, the person is considered guilty. Another test is to remove the *kaodi* from the hot oil. If a person considers that the *panchayat* has taken a bribe and accordingly has arrived at a decision, then he/she can approach another *panchayat.* The punishment includes excommunication and cash fines which range from twenty to one hundred rupees.

Most of the Sansi profess Hindu religion, but a large number of them have embraced Sikhism. Sansis of hundreds of villages of West Punjab had embraced Islam though they were Hindus upto 1947, the year in which Punjab was partitioned. Sansis have a temple at Sacha Sauda at Ganganagar.They are also the followers of Radhaswami. Hindus worship Lord Shiva. At Ghansal (Rajasthan), there is a temple, built in the memory of their ancestors. Diwali, Dussehra are their main festivals.

The Sansi live in the *jhuggis* (huts). The birth of the first child and specially of a male child is always celebrated after forty days. It is called *chhati*. Close relatives are invited and *roti* is served to the members of the community. Pollution caused by birth lasts ten days. On the tenth day, the *dasuthan* ceremony is performed, which consists of a general cleaning up of the house, the performance of *havan* by the priest, for the purification of the child and mother. The girls of the same *got* are fed on the third or tenth day and *sakkar* (black sugar) is distributed on the birth of a son. For forty days, the mother is not allowed to cook as she is not considered clean. After five weeks, a feast is held and the children are fed sweetened rice. The household is then considered to be free of all impurity. The head of the boy is shaved, when he is two-and-a-half months old. As regards the death ceremonies, the dead body is carried on an *arthi* (wooden bier) or a *charpai* and is cremated. The *kapal kriya* (i.e. the act of breaking the skull) is duly performed. The *phul* are picked up on the third day and on the same day the persons who carried the dead body are fed sweet and rice. The mourning lasts only three days. *Kirya karam* (rites performed after death) is sometimes performed with the help of a Brahman. Earthen pitchers full of water are placed on *dasagatra* and *gaudan* (i.e. cow is given away to some *sadhu*) is performed, if possible.The young girls are also fed. The bones are immersed into the Ganges or in some river or pond. The son gets his head shaved. In case of death of children upto six years of age, the body is buried. On the anniversary of a person's death, the kin and relatives are entertained with non-vegetarian food.

Sansis work as agriculturists, *behrupia*, shoe shiners, collectors of iron dust near the various factories, or work as casual labourers.

*Giddha* and *bhangra* are their folk dances. In the past, generally the Sansis built their houses slightly away from the rest of the village. They never had a close dealing with the Chamars, Mazhabis or

Bhangis. They do not have their own land to construct *jhuggis* and use common village land for this purpose. They do not accept food from Chamar, Mazhabis and Bhangis. They have ration cards for purchasing sugar, kerosene oil and other essential items at reasonable prices. They have their own cremation ground, but share places of worship with other communities. They participate in the festivals and festivities along with other communities.

The Sansis of the Punjab are more advanced than the Sansis living in different parts of the country. In some parts of India, they are still nomads, but the Sansi of Punjab have been leading a settled life for the last hundred years Sher (1965). The Punjab government is also helping the Sansis by offering loans to construct *pukka* houses. Drinking water is available to them through handpumps. Most of them work as daily labourers with the landowners or in the industries. Some of them have radios but none of them own television sets. At some of the localities, electricity is available. Wood or cow-dung cakes are their fuel sources. Those engaged in agriculture, benefit from the irrigation facilities and use fertilizers. They save a portion of their earnings for future use.

SWARAN SINGH

# SAPELA

The term Sapela is derived from *sap* which means snake. They also call themselves Nath. Sapela, Sapera or Sipda is a snake-catcher or -charmer. In the Hill states of former Punjab the Nagalu and Naglu were said to be snake-charmers, like the Sapelas. Sapandi, Sapada, Sapad, Sapahda, Sapiade terms were also used for them. Rose (1911: 409) mentions that, the Sapelas or snake- charmers claim their origin from Kanipa, who was a son of a Jheewar, who caught fish from which emerged Machhendranath and their *guru* was Jalandhar Nath. The Sapelas pierce their ears, wear the *mundra* and brick-red clothes and their social position is lower than the *jogis*. They are nomadic, play the *bin* (gourd-pipe) and carry a snake. *Census of India* (1911: 474), states their total population as 993 individuals, which includes 658 males and 335 females.

According to *Census of India* (1981), their total population is 1,012 individuals which includes 518 males and 494 females. They speak Punjabi language. Males wear shirt, *dhoti*, *pagri* and necklace of beads, whereas their females wear *salwar*, *kameez* and *dupatta*. They have been recognized as Scheduled Caste. They eat *dal-roti* as their staple food. On special occasions, they consume fruits, non-vegetarian food and alcoholic drinks. Groundnut oil is used as cooking medium. They were nomadic earlier and used to hunt wild boar, deer and other wild animals, but now they have a settled life.The males smoke *bidi*.

They are divided into different *gots* such as Marar, Goar, Bhambi, Doom and Ladhu, which are used to regulate marriage alliances. They consider themselves to be of higher status than the Bangala who are also engaged in the same profession. They are aware of the *varna* system and recognize their place as the Shudra. Other communities such as the Brahman, Banias and Jats consider them to be of low status. They marry within their own community. The age at marriage for the males and females is fifteen to eighteen years. The marriage is arranged by negotiations with the help of their traditional *panchayat*. Monogamy is the form of marriage. The *mangani* (engagement) is followed by the marriage ceremony, which is performed according to the Hindu tradition of seven *pheras*. Depending upon the financial condition, girl's parents offer *daj* (dowry) in kind at the time of marriage which includes few ornaments, steel utensils and clothes. The symbols of marriage are bangles of shell, *bindi* and yellow cloth at the time of marriage. After marriage, the girl stays with her husband at her in-laws' house. Divorce is permitted in case of maladjustment. Compensation is given to the wife. Divorce is not allowed, if the woman has children. Widow, widower, male and female divorcee are permitted to marry again.

Family type is joint. Avoidance and joking relationships are observed between the various members of the family. Check on the freedom of youngsters and challenge to the authority of the elders are the points of conflict in the family. Sons inherit the property of their father equally. The eldest son gets the succession. The status of women is low. They are engaged in household activities, collection of fuel, begging and bringing water for drinking purposes. They observe pollution period for five days and the ceremony called, *bahar badhaona* (exposure of the newborn to the outside) and the postnatal restrictions are observed for forty days. When the boys are around twelve to thirteen years of age, the ear lobes are pierced which is called *kan bindhane*. The marriage rituals are performed at the bride's residence. Feast is also offered to the marriage party. Consummation of marriage takes place at the groom's residence. They cremate their dead with head towards the west, the feet towards the east. They also observe pollution period. Bones of the dead are immersed in water. They also worship their ancestors.

The Sapela is a landless community and engaged primarily as snake-catchers and snake-charmers and also collect wild roots and tubers for medicinal purposes. Some work as labourers and collect iron scrap. They visit different villages while playing their *bin* (gourd pipe), they visit households of various villages and collect *atta* (flour). They have their traditional *panchayat*. The members of the *panchayat* are elected by voice vote. There are statutory *panchayats*, which look after the interest of all the communities including the Sapelas. They do not approach police or the court of law to settle their disputes. The *panchayat* of their community imposes fine, ranging from forty rupees to one hundred rupees depending upon the seriousness of the crime. The *panchayat* settles the matters related to marriage, property disputes and divorce. They follow Hindu religion, worship all the Hindu deities and visit different Hindu shrines. They specially worship Shiva, Naina Devi, Googa Pir and Guru Gorakh Nath. Sacred specialist is not from their own community. They celebrate Lohri, Diwali, Dussehra festivals, which are of social, economic and religious significance for them. They have oral traditions and men and women sing folk-songs on special occasions such as marriage ceremony. Their musical instrument is *bin*.

They do not exchange water and food with the Brahman, Rajput, Jat and Bania, but accept food and water from them. They accept and exchange food and water with the Mirasi, who also reside in their locality. They share places of worship. They also take part in various festivals and festivities. They lack modern intercommunity linkages.

Formal education is not favoured for both boys and girls. They make use of both the indigenous health practices and modern medicare. The attitude towards family planning is favoured. They use modern methods of family planning and prefer to have three children. Though all the families do not have their own handpumps, drinking water facilities are available.

Various media and communication facilities are available. They use electricity. Cow-dung cakes and wood are used as fuel. They have ration card facilities and get kerosene oil and sugar when available. They are poor yet the attitude towards saving is positive and they help each other by contributing in times of need.

SWARAN SINGH

# SARERA

Rose (1919) has given other synonyms of Sarera as Sarehra, Sarrahra or as Sadara. He, holds the view that this community is confined to Kangra and adjacent territories. The empirical investigation of this community was undertaken in village Bungal of Pathankot tahsil and the villages of Shahpur Niada and Adamwal of Hoshiarpur district. The study indicated that their ancestors came here five to six generations back from the village Gagrate of Una district in Himachal Pradesh. They migrated to the village Gagrate few generations back. In another village named Adamwal of Hoshiarpur district the informers stated that their grandfathers came to this village from another village of Hoshiarpur district named Janoudhi Dholbaha. The accounts thus testify that the Sarera were mostly located in Kangra and Hoshiarpur districts from where they migrated to the neighbourhood of Pathankot and also spread to the interiors of Hoshiarpur district. The name of the community was closely associated with the nature of their traditional occupation. The term 'sarera' means scutching of cotton which was their traditional occupation. However, the present field investigations both in Pathankot (Gurdaspur district) and villages of Hoshiarpur district have revealed that they call themselves invariably as 'Sarera' and not by the other synonyms. They distinguished themselves from the Salyare caste of Jammu & Kashmir and consider them inferior.

The population of the Sareras was 10,792 in 1881 which only marginally increased to 11,230 in 1931. Their population both in 1911 and 1931 census was more in the district of Kangra and Hoshiarpur. They were also found in Gurdaspur and Jalandhar districts. While in the Kangra district they were overwhelmingly Hindus and in the districts of Hoshiarpur and Jalandhar they were both Hindus and Sikhs. According to *Census of India* (1981) the total population of the Sarera in Punjab is 10,238 individuals with 5,346 males and 4,892 females. The major concentration was in the district of Hoshiarpur and much less in the district of Gurdaspur. In the tahsil of Pathankot they were quite sizeable in the villages of Mammon (40 households), Bungal (22 households), Ahma Chack (14 households), Chhatwal (12 households) and were scattered in very small numbers in three to four villages. In the district of Hoshiarpur they are widely dispersed in several villages but not more than four to five households in any particular village. They were wholly located in the rural areas.

They speak Punjabi dialect. However, Gurmukhi script is used more in Hoshiarpur district and Devanagari script in Pathankot villages. The communities as such did not have any specific identity marker, but the Sikhs among them wear turbans. They have been declared as Scheduled Caste throughout the state of Punjab. One aspect however is clear from Ibbetson's accounts that there is a clear-cut distinction between Sarera and Sarrara. The Sarera were predominantly Hindus whereas Sarraras were mainly Muslims.

They have mixed food habits; there are both vegetarian and non-vegetarian among them. Wheat, rice, pulses and seasonal vegetables are their staple food. They eat locally available fruits such as banana, mango, grapes, papaya, guava and apple. Cooking medium is oil and vegetable oil. Non-vegetarian diet comprises mutton, chicken, fish and eggs. They also consume milk and milk products. Alcoholic drinks are occasionally drunk during festivals, marriage, etc. These are mainly purchased from the market. The Sarera males are fond of smoking. They have increased their meat consumption.

The subcastes among the Sareras of Pathankot villages are very similar to those of Kangra district of Himachal Pradesh. Some of the subcastes' names are Sardial, Malhotra, Pathiaraye, Gangthial, Heer and Bandle. The interaction of the Sareras in Pathankot is more with their brethren in Kangra district, while those in Hoshiarpur confine their interaction with their neighbouring villages in Hoshiarpur district only. They consider themselves superior to other Scheduled Castes such as Ramdasia, Mahasha, Chamar, Batwal, etc. Generally, the Brahmans do not interdine with Sareras. However, nowadays in the schools, the boys belonging to different castes take water from the same pot. In the earlier generations there were lots of restrictions in eating and drinking. In the village of Bungal, there is a temple in which there are no restrictions now. The Sareras of Pathankot consider the Salyares as inferior to them and do not intermarry whereas those of Himachal, Pathankot and Hoshiarpur consider themselves as of similar status. They consider themselves below the Brahmans, Jats and Kshatriya.

They do observe strict subcaste and *got* exogamy and do not marry within close relations from both father's and mother's side. The age at marriage ranges from eighteen to twenty years for both boys and girls. Parents' consent is necessary for marriage. They follow Hindu ritual for performing marriage. Role of a mediator also assumes importance in the settlement of marriage. Invariably, marriages are solemnized and legitimized by Brahmans. Sikhs perform marriage according to Sikh rituals and *anand karaj*. Monogamy is the rule. Marriage symbols are *bindi*, *chura* and red-colour dress. Wearing of ring in finger and ear is common. The concept of *kanyadan* exists and dowry is given both in cash and kind. Settlement of divorce cases is undertaken in informal *panchayat*. Widow remarriage is permissible. The young widow may be married to her deceased husband's younger brother and this practice is locally called as *chadar paona* ritual.

The extended and nuclear family types are prevalent among Sarera. The established interpersonal relations of respect, love and fear of elders exist in the family. Avoidance relationship is observed between father-in-law and daughter-in-law, husband's elder brother and younger brother's wife and all the family, village and community's male elders. Joking relationship is observed between wife's sister and sister's husband, husband's younger brother and elder brother's wife. Conflict and confrontation also creep up on account of property disputes, challenge to the authority of elders and marital disputes.

Male equigeniture is the rule and all sons equally inherit their father's property. Daughters claim no share and leave that to their brothers. Succession is by the eldest son. There is decline of extended families and rise in nuclear ones.

Pre-delivery rituals are not observed. At the advanced stage of pregnancy the women avoid visits to places thought to be haunted with evil spirits like graveyard, etc. The shadow of an issueless woman should not fall on her. The pollution period after delivery is observed for forty days. The naming of the child is not followed by any ritual. The house is purified with cow-dung before she undertakes household work. *Mundan* is performed at the temple of Jawalamukhi in Kangra district. The Sarera's main marriage rituals are performed at bride's residence. After the selection of girl or boy, a ceremony, called *rokiya*, is performed in which the girl's parents give some cash to the boy's parents and other family members. This is followed by *sagai* before actual marriage, when again cash, sweets, clothes are given to the boy and his close relatives by girl's parents. On the marriage day *barat* goes to the bride's residence. The *barat* is received by the girl's side and *milni* takes place. Then the *barat* is entertained. The proper marriage ceremony is performed by the seven *pheras* around the sacred fire amidst the chanting of Vedic *mantras* by the temple priest. The *barat* then returns to the groom's place. Consummation of marriage is at groom's residence.

The Sarera believe that, if death rites are not duly performed, the departed soul finds it difficult to rest in peace. It haunts the other living members of the household. Infants and children below four years are buried, but adults are cremated. On the eleventh day, *kriya* ceremony is observed and *solwan* is performed on the sixteenth day after death. The worship of the *sidh* is supposed to fulfil the wordly desires. The important *sidhs* worshipped are Baba Balak Nath, Bawa Bharthari, Baba Luthru, Baba Polowala, etc. The malevolent spirits manifested are Mata Rani, Googga (god of serpents), Khwaja (god of water), etc. The folk tales about *churel* (female ghost) is popular among the masses. They believe in witchcraft and sorcery. The life-cycle rituals are becoming more expensive.

The primary occupation of the community is labour. Sareras do labour, on daily wages, in fields, on road construction undertaken by military contractors and in small factories. Few of them, who have received some education have also entered in government and private jobs, though mostly the Sareras are illiterate. They also do service in the army. In urban areas they get payments in cash. The daily wages of labour vary according to the area where they work. Earlier they had the community *sabha*. Nowadays either the disputes are referred to statutory *gram panchayat* at village level or to the local courts for settlements. The traditional method of solving any dispute through the elders in the family still continues.

The Sareras at Bungal worship Badhani Baba and gather there once in a year as this is the common Baba of all the communities. The major festivals of the Sareras are Lohri, Diwali, Dussehra, Holi, and Baisakhi. Oral tradition in the form of folk song, folklores and folk tales exist as do in other communities of the region. Untouchability is fast declining.

Some Sareras have members in white-collar jobs and defence services. Political leadership among them has emerged at *gram panchayat* level. Their attitude towards development programme is favourable and the impact on the community is perceptible. Boys are taking advantage of formal education. Mostly Sareras are illiterate or educated at the level of primary to middle. Only a few are receiving college-level education particularly due to economic problems. The attitude toward family planning is not favourable due to lack of awakening. The facilities of drinking water are available in the form of pipe water, which is supplied to them. They listen to the radio, only very few Sarera families own television sets. Electricity is available but only 5 per cent of them have electricity in their houses. Fuel resources are firewood and kerosene oil and cow-dung cakes.

The medical teams and social welfare staff often visit the village for necessary help and check-ups. At the ration shops are available sugar and kerosene oil on controlled rates. The banking facility is available and they avail the loans for small shops and other productive purposes.

They are extremely poor both in Hoshiarpur and Pathankot. They primarily work as labourers in the village Bungal. Only one Sarera boy was a graduate and his brother had a shop manufacturing shawls, etc. In the villages of Pathankot *tahsil* they feel severely constrained by the flow of migrant labour in the construction industry. They feel that it has affected both their employment and wages. In Hoshiarpur villages they are primarily working as agricultural labourers, but in Pathankot they are working as urban labourers particularly engaged in the construcion work of the army, in the loading and unloading of stones and pebbles. One of the severe consequences being felt by the Sareras in Pathankot villages was the acquisition of lands rapidly by the Army Cantonment. In this process they are not only being deprived of their work as agricultural labourers but are virtually being deprived of the source of their livelihood. They are being deprived of their homestead.

Already a number of villages such as Athotharwan, Jakral, Padhotharwan, Halad, Sangad, Barsum, Chhatwal, Jandwal, Bagar, Bargal, Harjal, etc., have been acquired in the process and a large number of poor families have been evicted without provision of alternative homestead. Another predicament being faced by them is that during the British times they were prevented from acquiring any property including land. Even now they can neither acquire land locally nor in Himachal Pradesh. In the case of eviction they are not entitled for any compensation. The Rajputs and Brahmans are the major landowners in the villages. Their poverty is so rampant that an old man physically handicapped is unable to move and cannot take treatment in the absence of money. There were only five matriculates among them in village Bungal and all were unemployed. Their counterpart are better off in Himachal Pradesh. Their percentage of literacy as per 1961 census was 13.81 per cent. They were then mostly employed as labourers on construction sites, in agriculture, households, industry, quarries and transport. The work force participation among them, was 35.67 per cent out of which one-fourth were females. According to the 1971 census they were engaged mainly as labourers in agriculture, construcion, household, industry, etc.

Their literacy rate was around 20 per cent in 1971. There are rarely any officer or advocate or any man of standing in their community. They appear to be conscious of their economic and political backwardness. Yet they find themselves quite incapable of improving their position. They do not have any caste solidarity or even any conscious efforts of getting their castemen into a common fold or in conjunction with other Scheduled Castes. This was invariably the case both in Hoshiarpur and Pathankot.

RAKESH KUMAR
K. GOPALA IYER

# SHORGIR

The Shorgir derived their name from their traditional occupation of extracting saltpetre from the saline agricultural soil. The process of extracting *shora* was a little cumbersome and time-consuming. It takes nearly six months to complete the entire process. This community is spread in a few villages of Patiala and Sangrur districts in the state of Panjab. Their population is also found in the neighbouring districts of Haryana. As per 1921 census their population in Panjab was 1,235. They are also located in parts of Rajasthan and claim a Rajput origin. They are migrants in Punjab where they went from Agra region of Uttar Pradesh after the 1857 mutiny. They communicate in Punjabi language and are also conversant in Hindi. There are both vegetarian and non-vegetarian among them. Wheat, rice, pulses and seasonal vegetables are their staple food. Milk and milk products are also consumed in very small quantity. They use alcohol only during social and festive occasions. Their men folk smoke *bidi.*

Some of their *gots* are: Kotwal, Sarda, Pamar, Skarwal, Shokar, Tanwar, etc. They observe *got* exogamy and do not marry close relations from both the father's and mother's side. Age at marriage ranges from eighteen to twenty years for both the boys and girls. Parents' consent is necessary for marriage. The role of *vichola* acquires importance in the settlement of marriage. Invariably their marriages are solemnized according to Hindu tradition. Monogamy is the rule of marriage. The marriage symbols are *bindi*, *chura* (red bangles) and red-colour *saree.* The Sikhs, who are very few, perform marriage rites according to *anand karaj.* Their women wear finger, ear and noserings. The concept of *kanyadan* exist and dowry is not a compulsion. Divorce is rare and approved only in case of extra-marital relations and objectionable conduct and is settled in their *biradari* or *panchayat.* Widow remarriage is permissible. The young widow may be married to the younger brother of the deceased. This practice is called *chadar paona.* Joint family is found among 50 per cent of the households. Respect for elders is observed by the young ones and avoidance relationship exists between *saura* and *bahu.* Joking relations exists between the *sali* and *jeeja*; *bhabi* and *dewar.* Male equigeniture is the rule of inheritance. Women have limited role in the mechanism of social control, though their opinion on marriage, etc., is taken. Post-delivery pollution called *sootak* is observed for one and quarter months. They perform the *mundan* ceremony of their children before the attainment of the fifth year. It is generally performed at Gurgaon. The first-feeding of the child is performed and is called *gurti.* The dead are cremated and bones are immersed in the holy Ganga at Hardwar. On the twelfth day *rasam pagri* or *uthala* takes place. Relatives and close family friends are invited. They perform the *shradh* ceremony. The first *shradh* ceremony is observed three years after death and subsequently it is observed every year.

Fifteen to twenty years back this community was primarily engaged in extracting saltpetre. They used to take land on fixed tenancy from the local landowners to extract the salt powder. They would start the process in January and the salt powder would be ready by June. All the salt powder thus produced would be sold out to local contractor, who in turn would supply it to the factory owner at Kaithal and other places in Haryana for processing. In the district of Patiala, this community is spread out in nearly fifteen villages (mostly in Samana tahsil) and in the few bordering villages of Sangrur district. The community was dependent for its subsistence on this occupation for nearly six months. They were primarily labourers, who neither had land nor the means of production. They leased in land from the landowners, often on debt. Similarly, they would take an advance from the contractor, who procures the salt powder from them. The contractors are not interested in this activity anymore. As a result this community is now deprived of this occupation which is a basis of their subsistence. Besides this, the landowners also hesitate to lease out land for this purpose. Now the community is primarily working as labourer in agriculture and other allied activities. In the towns of Rajpura and Patiala, they primarily work as labourers doing earth-work, brick-making and as rickshaw-pullers. The occupation of extraction of saltpetre though almost extinct among the Shorgirs in the state of Punjab, still exists in the neighbouring villages of Haryana. There are factories in Kaithal, which still process the raw material extracted from salt-making.

Their main deity is Googa Pir at Bagar in Rajasthan. They perform *puja* of Googa Pir once in a year. The major festivals of the Shorgir are Lohri, Diwali, Dussehra, Holi and Baisakhi. Oral tradition in the form of folk song and folklore exist as in other communities of the region. They share food with 'upper castes', but not their *hookah*,

They share wells and other water sources, cremation ground, religious shrines and traditional festivals with other local communities.

Very few of them are engaged in white-collar jobs and in defence services. Political leadership among them has emerged at village *panchayat* level. Their attitude towards development programmes is favoured and the impact on the community is perceptible. The boys are taking advantage of formal education. Only a few are receiving high school education. The attitude towards family planning is not positive. Facilities of drinking water are available in the form of handpumps and well. Though electricity is available, only few have electricity connections in their houses. Fuel resources are wood and cow-dung cakes. The medical teams and social welfare staff often visit the village for necessary help and check-ups. The facilities of ration shops are available, where sugar and kerosene oil is sold on controlled rates. Banking facilities are available only to those, who live in towns. They avail the loan for milch cattle, *rehri* (mule cart) and other related requirements. Nearly half of them have received yellow cards in the villages.

K. GOPALA IYER
RAKESH KUMAR

# SIKLIGAR

The word *siqligar* is the name of an occupation, and denotes an armourer or burnisher of metal. Many of them probably return themselves as Lohars (Ibbetson, 1916). The Sikligars originally belong to Chittorgarh (Rajasthan) and their occupation was to make various types of weapons used in war. They were not Sikhs at the initial stage. However, it goes to the credit of Shri Ram Singh Ramgarhia who went to Guru Gobind Singh and converted the Sikligars to Sikhism. Guru Gobind Singh invited the Sikligars and requested them to make swords for him, as these people were master craftsmen in polishing *kirpans* (swords) and hence they came to be known as the Sikligars. Slowly, the number of Sikligars, who embraced Sikhism and engaged themselves in making swords, increased and they settled down in Punjab, and the adjoining states. Sikligars in Rajasthan are Hindu, Sikligar of Punjab do not marry with the Sikligar of Rajasthan.

The Sikligars in Punjab are found in all districts. According to the *Census of India* (1981), their total population is 4,321 individuals which includes 2,260 males and 2,061 females. The concentration of the Sikligars is more in the districts of Ludhiana followed by the districts of Bhatinda, Patiala, Jalandhar and Ropar.

They have migrated from Pakistan and have settled at different places, such as Gill Road and Samrala Chowk before occupying their present place in Ludhiana, Preet Nagar, Tajpur Road, where the Government of Punjab has allowed them to settle down by allotting them plots for construction of their houses. Earlier, they used to lead a nomadic life and though now they have been given an opportunity to settle down, they have not yet altogether stopped their old habit of wandering and hunting. During the harvest period, they move out for hunting especially into the districts of Ropar and Hoshiarpur. The game they hunt are pig, deer, hare, partridge, etc. They keep nets to catch their prey and they also have licensed rifles for the purpose. The Sikligar prefer to live in open space and in *sirkis* or *jhuggis.*

However, the Government of Punjab, under its policy of housing to the Scheduled Castes and Backward communities, has given them loans and grants for the construction of *pukka* houses, so that they can have a settled life. The present location of the Sikligars in Ludhiana is at the outskirts of the city, where the Satluj river has retreated itself and is called *Darya-di-Kacher.* They speak Punjabi language with others, but when they talk to the members of their own community, they speak Marwari languages. They are mostly illiterate. The males wear a turban, *kameez* and *dhoti* and their females wear *rangdar* (coloured cloth) which they call *marwari cheet* (type of Marwari cloth), which includes *salwar, kameez* and *chunni* or *dupatta, choli* and *ghagri.*

The Sikligars have been recognized as a Scheduled Caste. They eat wheat as their staple food with pulses. The *roti* made of maize and *bajra* is also consumed and *masur, moong, moth* and gram are the common pulses eaten by them. *Sarson da sag* and *makki di roti* is used during the winter season. Mustard or groundnut oil is the common medium for cooking. Tea and *lassi* are common non-alcoholic beverages. Occasions of marriage and birth are celebrated with country liquor. There is a marked change in their food habits, a change from non-vegetarian to vegetarian diet. The Sikligar are divided into *gots* such as Junni, Dangi, Bhond, Beori (Bhori), Khichi, Tilvithya, Ghor-chare Tok, Jyonimalude, Kalyani, Churi te Biori, Ghor-chare Dangi, Tank-Mundra-de, Sajju, Matharu and Chohan. They are endogamous. The *gots* are used to regulate their marriage alliances.

The Sikligars, due to their Rajput origin and also because of being followers of the tenth Guru of the Sikhs, consider themselves of superior status, but as they work with iron, they are not considered to be a superior caste by the high-caste people. They recognize their status as Shudra in the *varna* system.

The Sikligars maintain endogamy at the community level, but observe clan exogamy. When the two groups of the Sikligars come together they select mates for their children. Both boys and girls get married, when they are around eighteen-twenty years of age. Marriage is arranged thorugh negotiations by the parents of a boy and a girl. The form of marriage is monogamy. Women after marriage use *hansas, hamel* as ornaments for neck, *nath* is used as an ornament for nose and bangles are symbols of marriage. Their marriage ceremony is very simple as they cannot afford elaborate rituals. The dowry generally consists of five to seven suits (*salwar, kameez* and *chunni* form one suit). Two to four utensils are presented at the time of marriage. Rule of residence after marriage is patrilocal. Divorce, though not encouraged, is sanctioned due to maladjustment of the couple, but it is a very rare phenomenon.

The *panchayat* of the Sikligars decides cases of divorce, the compensation, depending upon the merit of the case, is given to the wife's parents. Only the husband can divorce. If the children are young, they remain with their mother and when they attain adulthood, they may or may not return to their father as they choose. Remarriage of the widow or widower and male or female divorcee is permitted with sanction of their traditional *panchayat.*

The child marriage, which was in pratice earlier, has been replaced by adult marriage is the only change in marriage rules. The Sikligars, who have embraced Sikhism, perform their marriage ceremonies according to Sikh traditions.

Vertically extended type of family exists among the Sikligars. Accordingly, avoidance relationship is observed between the mother-in-law and son-in-law; daughter-in-law and the father-in-law; and sister-in-law and elder brother-in-law. Joking relationship is maintained between the sister-in-law and younger brother-in-law; brother-in-law and sister-in-law and between co-brothers. There may be few occasions, when there are conflicts and arguments between the two members relating to the sharing of common source of water, common courtyard, where children may fight while playing. Such scenes of dispute are for a very short time and are resolved without taking up the matter with the elders.

Sons inherit property of their father equally. In case there is no son, the daughters share that property in equal proportions. The eldest son gets the succession. The family has not undergone a change except an increase in the number of nuclear families though the joint family system is very much there in existence. But the increase in the number of the nuclear families is primarily due to non-availablity of residential accommodation otherwise they are having a very good social control over their community and instances of members of the Sikligar community, living separately from their kins, are not yet reported. Also, the males and females work together and women, apart from assisting their husbands in their traditional occupation, look after their families. Women have low status.

Among the Sikligars, various rituals at birth, marriage and death are observed. During the birth of the first child, the mother of a pregnant woman advises her at various stages of her pregnancy as she is generally sent to her parents house for the first delivery. Post-delivery pollution and restrictions are observed. Necessary *puja* is performed, when the child is taken out from its place of birth for the first time. Restrictions on the mother for forty-one days are not possible these days. The mother, after ten or eleven days, may have to look after various household duties and responsibilities.

Elderly women may give any name to the child at the time of birth or at the time of formal registration of birth. Marriage rituals are performed at the bride's residence. The ceremony of *anand karaj* is performed. A feast (*roti*) is given to the marriage party and all the invitees by the bride's parents. Consummation of marriage is at the bridegroom's residence.

They cremate their dead. In case an old man dies, they take out a procession of the dead body known as *baban*. After purification ceremony, a feast is offered to the members of the community. The ashes of the dead person are immersed in the river Ganga at Hardwar. Either some members of their community visit Hardwar or they may request somebody to carry the ashes to immerse there. The Sikligars, perform all the rituals associated with the whole life, from birth to death. But owing to their poor economic conditions, it may not be possible for them to preform all of them due to the increase in prices of all the commodities and services.

Traditionally, the Sikligars are engaged in making swords, knives, daggers, baskets of steel (locally called *tokra*), *taslas* (it is used to carry soil) and buckets (*balti*). They also replace the decayed bottoms of the buckets and *taslas*. Apart from this, they also manufacture other iron implements such as chisels. The articles or implements prepared by the Sikligars are of daily use for the rural people. Today, they do not give much importance to the making of swords, as these are no more in common use as weapon. They maintain their link with the rural masses and sell their implements directly to them. They also visit nearby villages as hawkers for this purpose. The children start learning their traditional occupation from their early childhood and when they have grown up they pick up their profession.

They have their own traditional caste *panchayat*, which is headed by a *pradhan*. The Sikligars settle all of their disputes and conflicts. They do not approach the court of law for this purpose. Depending upon the situation and gravity of the problem, four to five members of the *panchayat* are nominated, who listen to the arguments of both the parties and accordingly give their judgement which is binding on both the parties. The matters disposed of by the Sikligar *panchayat* include cases of loan of money, divorce, engagements and other disputes. If somebody defies the ruling of the *panchayat*, a fine, ranging from five hundred to one thousand rupees is also imposed. The Sikligars do not approach the police. Apart from cash fines, they also excommunicate the defaulter. If the guilty feels repentant and asks for a pardon from the *panchayat* and if the *panchayat* is fully convinced of his pleadings, it sometimes absolves an individual from the fine and punishment. The matter is referred to another *panchayat*, which includes its members from different districts. This *panchayat* enjoys higher powers and status. This is applicable in case an individual defies the ruling of the local *panchayat*. However, such cases are very rare, where the *panchayat* of another area is consulted. There are no rewards, if somebody performs an outstanding feat for his community's benefit. The elderly people, including the members of the *panchayat* give moral support and appreciate his work in public.

The Sikligars follow Sikhism and worship *Guru Granth Sahib*. They visit *gurdwara* and some of them are also Nirankaris. The role of sacred specialists includes religious teachings, performing marriage ceremonies and death rites. The festivals are of socio-religious significance for them. They decorate their walls with paintings and are mastercraftsmen as makers of knives, swords, buckets,.and other iron inplements. On the occasions of birth, marriage and various festivals, the Sikligars sing songs as they have their own folklore tradition. The musical instrument is *dholak*.

The Sikligars exchange food and water with the Bazigar community. It may be mentioned here that the relationship of the Sikligars and the Bazigars is restricted only to taking food together. The Sikligars share wells and other sources of water with other communities. They can visit common religious shrines and *panchayat ghars*. They have their separate crematorium.

Only four children attend the Indrapuri school which is about 2 km from their place of residence. Few can write their signature. They approach a doctor for medical treatment, when it becomes absolutely urgent. They prefer modern medicare. They are aware about the fact that small family can be easily managed. They generally prefer about three children.

Handpumps are the main source of water for drinking and bathing purposes. On an average, five to seven families have to share one handpump under the scheme of providing drinking water to them. The Sikligars have applied for grant of more handpumps. For getting oil and sugar, they have been provided with ration cards to get these at subsidized rates. Most of them are self-employed and work as blacksmiths. A few own transistors. They are likely to get the electric connections soon, as arrangements have already been made in this regard. Cow-dung, coal and wood are used as fuel.

SWARAN SINGH

# SINGHIKAT

The Singhikat are also known as Singhiwala. The term *Singhi* is derived from a word *sing* (horn). The horn, or *sing* of a sheep or goat is used to extract the pus from an infected joint. It is an occupational community and moves from one village to another village to earn livelihood. They migrated from Rajasthan to Punjab about eighty-five years back and live in semi-arid areas adjoining Sirsa district (Haryana) and Rajasthan state. Their concentration in the state of Punjab is not much. They are found at Amarpura Basti, Bhatinda district, Balbir Basti, Faridkot district; Baza Chungi, Jaito Mandi, Kotkapura, Mansa, Budlada, Railline Rampura, etc. They speak Punjabi language with others, whereas Rajasthani and Punjabi languages are spoken within the their own community. Shirt, *dhoti* and *pagri* is the male dress, while the *kameez*, *ghagri* (skirt) and *dupatta* comprise the female dress.

They take such cereals as wheat, maize, *jowar*, and pulses as *moong*, *moth*, *masur*, gram, etc. They take tea and *lassi* as non-alcoholic drinks. Fruits such as mango, orange and banana are consumed seasonally and occasionally. There is a great change in the food habits of the Singhikats. They have now started taking pulses. Earlier they used to hunt wild cats, hare, porcupine and jackal. As there is a ban on hunting, they have been forced to change their food habits accordingly. However, at the time of harvests they hunt hares. They take seasonally available vegetables such as cauliflower, ladies' finger, brinjals, etc. They take rice occasionally. *Dal-roti* is their regular food. They are now also changing from non-vegetarian to vegetarian. They take pork. Groundnut oil is used as cooking medium. They take mutton and alcoholic drinks on special occasions. They smoke *bidi*.

They are divided into different clans, for regulating their marriage alliances. They consider themselves to be of low status, while the members of other communities also consider them low as they engage themselves in skin hides and collection of bones of dead animals. They are not aware of the *varna* system and do not recognize their place in it. They marry within their own community and their marriage alliances also take place in the adjoining Sirsa district of Haryana. Marriage within the same village is also permitted but not within the same *got*. They avoid the *gots* of their father and mother for marriage. Some of the *gots* are Vaid, Sandhu, Sodhi, Athwal, Brar, Luhiya, Attra, Gill, Chohan, Aggarwal, etc. The marriage is arranged by negotiations. The relatives of the boy approach the girl's parents with the help of a *vichola*. They marry their boys and girls when they are about eighteen to nineteen years of age. The ceremony of *mangani* is performed and an amount of sixty to two hundred rupees is presented by the boy's parents to the girl. Earlier, when they were nomads and used to move in group, they used to marry within their own group. Now they have a settled life and this practice has now been stopped. They marry according to the Hindu tradition of seven *pheras*.

Monogamy is the form of marriage. Bangles, ring in the ear, nose and finger are the symbols of marriage. Dowry is given in kind, in the form of ten to eleven utensils, clothes, furniture, etc., depending upon the financial condition of the girl's father. Owing to maladjustment, divorce is allowed. Generally, the husband can divorce and children stay with their mother in case of divorce. Widow, widower, male and female divorcee remarriage is permitted. Some changes in marriage has been observed. They avoid marriage between the close relatives. Village endogamy is allowed, but they search for the mates for their boys and girls outside also. Now there is a change in age at marriage. In the past they married their boys and girls at the young age of five to seven years. On the attainment of adulthood they used to allow consummation of marriage which is called *muklawa*. At present they marry their children, when they are adult and on the next day follows the *muklawa*. They observe the symbols of marriage strictly. The incidence of divorce has slightly increased.

The Singhikats have now started living a settled life. The state government gives loans and financial assistance to the needy individuals either to build their houses or to get their dilapidated houses repaired. They used to live in *kulis* (huts) and some of the Singhikats still continue to do so. However, some of them have either *kachcha* or *pukka* houses to live in. The family is mostly joint, and if the sons are not in a position to live together with their parents, they start living separately in another hut resulting into the formation of a nuclear family. In a joint-family, avoidance relationships are observed between the mother-in-law and son-in-law, daughter-in-law and father-in-law, and other elderly members of the community. Joking relationships are reported between the *bhabi* (sister-in-law) and *dewar* (brother-in-law); *sali* (sister-in-law) and *jeeja* (brother-in-law); and co-brothers. Check on the freedom of youngsters and challenge to the authority of the elders result into conflicts in a family. All the sons inherit the property of their father equally. The eldest son succeeds authority. Changes in family have been observed among the Singhikats. They have now started living a settled life and have abandoned the nomadic life. They used to live in *kulis* and joint families were prevalent. However, now they are settled and though joint families are still prevalent, the nuclear ones are fast coming up.

The status of women is low and they attend to the various household activities, apart from collecting fuel, bringing potable water, begging *atta*, making toys of paper (*damru*) and clay (*ghugu*). Post-delivery pollution and restriction on the mother are observed. Marriage ceremony is performed at the bride's residence. Feast is also given to the marriage party by the bride's parents. Consummation of marriage is at the residence of the groom. They cremate their dead, but a saintly person of their community is buried, and his burial place is called a *samadhi*. The bones of the others are immersed in the nearby river. Feast is also offered to the members of the community after the performance of *puja* for the peace of the soul of the dead. They also worship their ancestors. The rituals have been curtailed.

They are a landless community and work as labourers, collect bones of dead animals, make soap, winnowing fans, and shine shoes apart from their traditional occupation to apply *singhi*. The women visit different villages and sell paper and earthen toys, in addition to begging *atta*. Child labour is reported. They have their own traditional *panchayat*. The elderly and intelligent person of the community is selected by a voice vote as their *panch* or *pradhan*. They settle all their disputes and do not approach police or court of law. They also invite members from other areas. Five to six members form a committee to settle the disputes. The matters related to divorce, marriage disputes and loans are referred to the committee. They impose fine ranging from thirty to two hundred rupees. As they visit different villages and if somebody commits theft, he is fined. They ask the guilty person to jump into the water. The Singhikats presume that if a person is guilty, he will be pushed up by the water. The proceeding of the *panchayat* may continue for two or three days. They invite witnesses also. The guilty are also excommunicated. The expenditure is incurred by the individuals, who invite the committee and it continuous till the members do not arrive at a decision.

They belong to Hinduism and worship Ram Dev Pir. They have a temple at Amarpura Basti at Bhatinda. They also worship the Hindu goddess Mata Rani. In Rajasthan, they have a festival in the month of

*Bhadon* (August) and *Magh* (January). Every Nawami they offer their prayers. The sacred specialists are from their own community. Apart from worship, the *pandit* also performs the rites associated with birth, marriage and death. They celebrate all Hindu festivals such as Lohari, Diwali and Dussehra. They make winnowing fans. They sing local folk songs on the occasion of marriage. The festivals are of religious and social significance for them.

There is no restriction for accepting and exchanging water and food from the Bania, Brahman, and Scheduled Castes or anybody with whom they have relationship of love and affection. However, the caste with whom the Singhikats do not have any intimate relationship, do not invite the Singhikats. They share schools, source of water with other communities. But they have their separate cremation ground. They join the members of other communities on the occasion of festivals and festivities. They lack various modern inter-community linkages.

Formal education is favoured for boys and girls. Most of them study up to primary level. About twenty persons got education under the adult education programme. They follow both the modern as well as traditional medicare. They approach the private medical practitioner at the time of their sickness. The number of children per family is either four or more. Handpump is used for getting water for drinking purposes. They use electricity. Cow-dung cakes, coal or wood are used as fuel. Poor families have been issued yellow cards. They help each other by contribution and do not take loans from moneylenders and shopkeepers.

SWARAN SINGH

# SIRKIBAND

The name of Sirkiband is derived from *sirki* and *band*, which means those who make *sirkis*. The *sirki* is like a mat, which is prepared from grass reed, and used for making the roof. It is also used for making covers for carts. The elephant grass which grows along the sides of rivers also has the habitation of the Sirkibands apart from other communities. The primary reason is that they get in the vicinity the wild grass known as *sarkanda* in abundance which is used for making *sirkis*. Some of them have settled in towns and villages having very close approximity to the river banks such as Satluj and Beas. As land on the river banks is also available, some families of the Sirkibands have also settled down there for agriculture. The Sirkiband is a small community of 14,111 individuals, with 7,335 males and 6,776 females. They have been recognized as Scheduled Caste. Their concentration is mainly in the Ferozepur district (*Census of India*, 1971). Other places having concentration of the Sirkibands are, Jagraon, Sindwabet, Moga, Makhu, Ghurki, Bhatinda, Barnala, Jalalabad, Fazilka, Abohar, Guruharsahay, Mahalam, Jalandhar and Bodowal. They have their own markets to sell the *sirkis*. These markets are known as *sirki bazars* such as at Ferozepur.

In their own way, the Sirkibands consider themselves Rajput Rathors. They have migrated to different places from Chittorgarh (Rajasthan). They hold Jaimal, the grandson of Amar Singh Rathor in high esteem, who had to leave the fort fighting against the Mughal emperor, Akbar. They went to the interior of the jungles and led a nomadic life in search of food and water. As these people moved in different directions, a section of them specialized in making the *sirkis* of grass reed. During their initial stages, they took flesh of all kinds of wild animals which is avoided now.

They speak Punjabi language and use Gurmukhi script. The males wear a turban, *kurta* and *dhoti* or *pyjama*, and the females wear *salwar*, *kameez* and *dupatta*. They still live in *jhuggis* and do not sleep on beds. However, there are a few instances of having *pukka* houses. Some of them are also the followers of Radhaswami sect. They normally abstain from use of alcoholic drinks and non-vegetarian food and their regular food consists of simple *dal* and *roti*. The main cereals are wheat, maize and rice and the pulses are gram, *urad*, *moong*, peas, beans, *masur*, and *moth*. Groundnut oil, mustard oil and *desi ghee* are used as cooking mediums. Some of those who can afford, do eat chicken and mutton but not regularly. Very few people take alcoholic drinks on special occasions. Tea, *lassi* and curd is taken frequently. Rice is used on special occasions, *sarson da sag* and *makai di roti* is relished during the winter season with sufficient quantity of butter. Seasonal vegetables are eaten by them which are ladies' finger, brinjals, peas and cauliflower. Fruits such as mangoes, bananas, etc., are taken occasionally and seasonally. Among changes in food, it has been reported that the Sirkibands presently avoid carrion, few also take pork and consumption of pulses has increased.

They are endogamous and have different *gots*. There are different divisions of the Rajputs such as Jhanaodia, Lakhewale, Labana, Chouhan, Rane, Rathor. They belong to the Rathor category. Their different *gots* are Dhanamsot, Ramana, Bhajhana, Malkana, Panana, Rattarnana, Mahana, Majharawat, Namsot, Lagharana and Diaot. The purpose of the various *gots* is to regulate marriage alliances. Due to their origin from Rajputs, they consider themselves of high status but as they deal with reed and grass, the members of higher social strata consider them as of low status. They are aware of the *varna* system and also recognize their place in it as Kshatriya and claim that they are Rathor Rajputs, though they have now admitted their place as Shudras.

Child marriage was in practice about fifty years ago, when the boys and girls were married at around eight to ten years, which was followed by *muklawa* on the attainment of adulthood. Marriage is arranged by negotiations between the parents of the boy and the girl with the help of a third person called *vichola*, who can be either a Nai, Brahman or a close relative. Monogamy is the form of marriage. Marriage takes place within the same community, but extra care is taken so that *gots* of the mother and father of the boy and girl are not the same. Marriage is arranged, when the boy and girl are adults. First the *mangani* ceremony takes place which is followed by marriage. Earlier they used to marry according to the customs of seven *pheras*, but now the marriage ceremony takes place according to the traditions of *anand karaj* and there are four *lavan pheras*. The feast is offered to the marriage party by the parents of the girl. The marriage ceremony is held in the morning. Dowry, in kind is given, if the parents of the girl can afford it. This may include clothes for all close relatives of the bridegroom. Utensils, *peti*, few ornaments, watch for the bridegroom and furniture constitute the dowry. If husband and wife due to unavoidable circumstances are not in a position to carry on well, the elders try to settle matters. However, if the situation takes such a turn that it is beyond the capacity of elders to arrive at a decision, acceptable to both the parties, both the husband and wife start living separately and the wife approaches the court of law for settlement of dispute. However, if the financial condition of the girl's father is not good, they avoid the long and expensive course of litigation. Remarriage of the divorcee male and female is allowed. In case of death of her husband, the women can marry her husband's younger brother. On the other hand if one's wife dies and he has small children, the choice for remarriage is for the younger sister of his deceased wife.

Divorce and remarriage is permitted. Cruelty, maladjustment, barrenness, impotency, lack of male child may be some of the reasons for divorce. Compensation is given to the aggrieved party. They are patrilocal and live in joint families. Nuclear families are few. Some of the girls may use vermilion after marriage, but they do not continue this practice for a long period. Avoidance relationships exist between mother-in-law and son-in-law, daughter-in-law and father-in-law, sister-in-law (younger brother's wife) and her brother-in-law (husband's elder brother). There are joking relationships between the sister-in-law (elder brother's wife) and her brother-in-law (husband's younger brother), *devrani* (husband's younger brother's wife) and *jethani* (husband's elder brother's wife), *jeeja* (sister's husband) and *sali* (wife's sister), grandparents and grandchildren.

Reasons for disputes in a Sirkiband family may be related to property, distribution of responsibility among the members of the family, the resources of income and challenge to the authority of elders. The sons inherit the property of their father equally and the eldest son gets succession. Recent change in family set-up is marked by rise in the formation of nuclear families. Those who are educated and get either private or government services leave their parental home and stay at the place of their posting. Some of them migrate from the villages or the river banks to the nearby cities and engage themselves either as daily labourers, skilled or unskilled, and as rickshaw pullers. However, the joint families are still prevalent among the Sirkibands.

Women help in the various household activities; they bring water from the handpump, help in agricultural operations, look after the domestic animals and have a role in the performance of various rituals. Pre-delivery restrictions are observed especially during the first pregnancy. Post-delivery restrictions and a pollution period is also observed. The old ladies give a name to the child. In case of death, the pollution period is observed for three to seven days. In case an old person dies, the dead body is taken to the *marian* (burning *ghat*) in the form of a procession. The *sadharan path* or the *akhand path* of *Guru Granth Sahib* is performed for purification and peace of the soul. They immerse the bones of the dead in the Ganga at Hardwar. *Shradh* ceremony is also observed. Among changes in the life-cycle rituals, the post-delivery restrictions on mother and the post-delivery pollution period, which was for forty days earlier, are not strictly observed today. Those women who have nobody to look after them, cannot confine themselves for such a long period. On many occasions they start attending to the kitchen even after ten days. The rituals have been curtailed as they have become expensive.

Most of the individuals have their huts on government land, either on the side of the road, or under the bridge of river. They are engaged in making *sirkis*, *chiks* (curtains), and rope from *munj*. Some of them also work as labourers, rickshaw-pullers, hawkers, *halwais* and *granthis*. Some families of the Sirkibands, who live on the river banks also engage themselves in agriculture. This land is sometimes submerged under floods of the river water and sometimes there are no rains which results in drought and consequently, the yield from a particular crop during a particular season is very low. Agriculture is their secondary occupation as the land is lacking proper irrigation facilities.

The children, from their very early days, start learning the art of making *chiks*, *sirkis* and *tokras* (baskets) and ropes. Mode of payment is by cash. Very few of them are in government services or in business. The traditional *panchayats* are not as much functional as they were earlier. They belong to either Sikhism or Hinduism. The Hindu and Sikh worship, believe and respect each other's religion. At the time of marriage rituals are performed according to their respective religion. They visit both Hindu and Sikh shrines. Change of religion from Hinduism to Sikhism has been reported. They celebrate Diwali, Lohri, Dussehra, Baisakhi festivals along with the members of other communities. The sacred specialist may, or may not, be from the same community. They have folk songs, folklores, and folk tales related to their own community. *Dhol* and *dholki* are used as musical instruments during marriage.

They share water and food with other communities. But they do not marry with the members of other communities. They visit the same religious places. They lack the various modern intercommunity linkages, they have only one inspector in the Food Corporation of India at Abohar.

Though conditions are favoured for formal education but both the boys and girls do not study beyond fifth or seventh standards. They make moderate use of modern medicines and prefer three children. Handpump is the source of drinking water. They listen to the radio. Electricity connections are available to some of them. Those who are engaged in agriculture, use river water for irrigation. They have ration cards to get essential items such as kerosene oil and sugar. The economically weaker families have been provided with yellow cards.

SWARAN SINGH

# SOOD

The Sood or Sud in Punjab has two subgroups known as Uchandia, the Soods of the hills and Newandia, the Soods of plains. In earlier times, according to Ibbetson (1970: 245-6), division in the community was on the basis of permissibility of widow remarriage. Those who permitted remarriage were called Gola, Doghla, or Chichan; and those who did not allow remarriage were called Khara. There is no such division these days, between Khara (pure) and Gola (impure) Soods. However, division on the lines of Uchandia and Newandia Soods still exist. The community is able to establish its identification at regional, inter-regional and national levels. Census data is available about its pre-Independence distribution in the Punjab. The population of the community in the state in 1881 was 19,895, which increased to 21,804 in 1891. It included 21,334 Hindus, 383 Sikhs and 87 Muslim members. In the native state its population was 4,248 and in the British territory it was 17,556. In 1911, the census figures showed their population at 20,647, out of which 11,365 were males and 9,280 were females (*Census of India*, 1911).

There are two main schools of thought on the history of the community. According to the first school of thought the community had its origin in Rajputs; the other school maintains that Soods have descended from Khatris. The first school was advocated by Lala Salamat Rai Sood in 1935. According to this school, the community is descended from the second son of Parmar of Agni Kul, whose name was Sood. Further, back in history they point out that Kadar Rai Sood had fought with Alexander. This school also claimed that word 'Sood' occured in the Veda as well (R.R. Sood, 1979: 12-13). The other school claims the Khatri origin of the community by citing alternative arguments. He points out its *gotras* and subcastes are common with the Khatris, the two castes often intermarry; they have common *purohits*, and religious beliefs (R.R. Sood, 1979: 66-8). Some subcastes of Soods, common with Khatris community has been pointd out by R.R. Sood (1979: 48-9).

The members of the community speak Punjabi, Pahadi and Urdu dialects in its kinship group at house. It uses Gurmukhi and Perso-Arabic scripts for writing purpose. In communication with other communities, it uses Hindi and English as well. Their scripts are

Devanagari and Roman. It consumes both vegetarian and non-vegetarian food. It takes all types of food. There is moderate consumption of fruit and vegetables, which has increased over time. The community prefers *roti* to rice; but consumption of rice has increased. Only male members take alcoholic drinks, purchased from the market. Wheat, rice and maize are the cereals consumed by the community. It uses all locally available pulses such as gram, *tur*, *urad*, *moong*, peas, beans, *masur*, *moth*, etc. The cooking mediums include groundnut, mustard, sunflower oils, vanaspati and animal fats. Fruits consumed include apple, banana, mango, melons, watermelon and oranges.

Social divisions exist in the community at subcaste and *gotra* levels. It is differentiated at social, economic, religious, territorial, occupational and educational levels. R.R. Sood has pointed out fifty-two subcastes each of Uchandia and Newandia Soods (Sood, 1985: 37). He pointed out that these are different from *gotras*. The *gotra* pointed out by him tally with the *gotras* listed by Rose (1970: 431). According to Rose (1919: 431) Soods had following *gotras*:

| | | | | | |
|---|---|---|---|---|---|
| Bahl | Bhulla | Dosaj | Khurpa | Mukandi | Roria |
| Baliggan | Budhi | Dulli | Lau | Nahra | Sallan |
| Barhmi | Daddan | Gach | Mandal | Nandu | Saraf |
| Barnwal | Dewar | Gajri | Mahni | Phakka | Saunl |
| Bassan | Dhalli | Gondal | Mahyar | Pharwaha | Tagala |
| Bawari | Dhanda | Gopal | Makaura | Phassi | Teji |
| Beri | Dhiri | Jari | Midhar | Pura | Udher |
| Bharak | Dhukhi | Kajla | Moman | Rori | Ugal |
| Bhukaha | Dhup | | | | |

Territorial differentiation at the subcaste levels has been pointed out by R.R. Sood. Members of every subcaste have had their pockets in a particular territory, 'Such as Dosajs (formerly Dosans) belonged to a village washed away by the river Satluj. They also settled down in Ludhiana. Kuthualas belonged to Girli, Nehras to Machniware, Burnwals to Samraj, Phassis to Moga, Salhans and Dalits to Morinda (Baganwala), Mohindras (formerly Meedars) to Kot Dalal Khan and Kot Isa Khan, Mehatpur; Phakkas to Sheikhirpur, Gariris to Sultanpur Lodhi, Mayors (formerly Majars) to Mur Mahal and so on and so forth . . . .' (Sood, 1981: 6). In all subcastes of Newandia (plains), the Dosajs is the largest subcaste, followed by Mohindras. The territorial differentiation existed at other levels also. It was between Uchandia (Sood of hills) and Newandia (Sood of plains). This was enforced by the migration of the community to the hills during Aurangzeb's times (R.R. Sood, 1981, Vol. I, p. 11). Both Uchindia and Newandia Sood were prosperous sections of the community The former had much political influence with *rajas* of the hills, to whom they lent the money; and later controlled the sugar trade in plains (Sood, 1986: 18-19). According to information received from the community members, this division between Uchandia and Newandia sections was reinforced by the practice of *watta* (exchange of brides) and bride price in the earlier period by Uchandia sections. And due to this reason Newandias were reluctant to have matriominal relatives with Uchandias. Similarly the division between Gola and Khara existed in the plains. However, in recent times different explanations have been given to this. According to some members of the community Gola Soods practised remarriage of widows; others say they intermarried with other communities. And for these reasons, the Khara Soods did not intermarry with them. A majority of the members of the community are Hindus though there are a small number of Sikhs as well. Most of the Hindu members of the community are Arya Samajis; a few believe in Sanatan Dharma as well.

The community continued to use Sood with their names. In its self perception, the community considers itself to be of very high status. Other communities consider it of medium status. In rural areas, the peasants remember this community for its moneylending activities. Even these days in rural areas the name of the community is derived from vernacular word 'Sood', which means interest paid on the borrowed money.

They are endogamous at community level. However, there is increasing tendency for inter caste marriage. These are mostly with Khatris, but marriage have also taken with Brahmins and Christians in a few cases. The community is exogamous at locality level. There is a tendency to cover large areas in the negotiation of marriage. It is exogamous at *gotra* level. Previously four *gotras* were excluded (Rose, 1970: 471). These days only two *gotras* are exluded, i.e. the *gotra* of mother and father of the bride or groom. All marriages take place at adult age and are monogamous. These are settled by negotiations. However, there is increasing reliance on the newspaper matrimonials to search for the suitable mates. The opinions of boy and girl is taken for the settlement of their marriage. The usual Hindu marriage symbols, e.g. vermilion mark, bangles, *mangal sutra*, *bindi*, finger ring, toe ring, earring, nose stud are used. The practice of *kanyadan* exists. Dowry is generally given in kind. They are patrilocal. Either party is entitled for divorce by judicial approval for various reasons allowed under law. However, in actual practice there are few cases of divorce. The responsibility of children, in case of divorce is decided by the courts, so also the compensation. These days the remarriage of widows and divorcee women is accepted. This is a practice which has changed in past few decades. It should be noted the community has reverence for various *sati* shrines. As in case of female, so also in case of males, marriage of widower and divorcee is allowed. Increase in the age at marriage, liberalization in rules of marriage, acceptance of divorcee, remarriage of divorce women and widows suggest change in the rules of marriage. They live in nuclear or vertically extended families. Joking relationship exist between *dewar*(husband's younger brother) and *bhabi* (wife of elder brother); and *jeeja* (sister's huband) and *sali* (wife's sister). Avoidance relationships exists between *saas* (wife's mother) and *jawai* (daughter's husband), *noohn* (son's wife) and *saura* (husband's father). However, there is lesser practice of *purdah* in the latter case.

Disputes arise in the families due to property matters or challenge to the authority of elders. Although daughters are equally entitled to share in the father's property, the inheritance in practice favours male equigeniture. The succession rules favour eldest son, which are symbolized by the *pagri* ceremony after the death of father. There is rise in nuclear families. The women have a role in control of family expenditure as well. In rural areas they participate in animal husbandry functions as well. Although the practice of *sati* has stopped in the community, they are much respected and even worshipped.

There are few restrictions on the pregnant women before the birth of child. However, after birth her activities are restricted for a period from a week to month. The birth of a child is celebrated with the distribution of sweets. *Namkaran* ceremony is performed by the *purohit. Mundan* (shaving off hair) ceremony in performed in case of male children at the age of three to seven years. Marriage ceremony takes place by seven *pheras* or four *lavan pheras* at bride's residence. *Purohit* is present at marriage. Both the parties arrange feast at the time of marriage. Consummation of marriage takes place at grooms place. It is preceded by *muklawa.* The dead are cremated. Pollution is observed for thirteen days. Then a *pagri* ceremony is held. The bones are immersed in Ganga water at Hardwar. The eldest son usually takes these bones to the place. However, clan deities—*jatheras* and various *satis* are worshipped on the day of Diwali. The rituals are being curtailed and are becoming more expensive.

The community is very sound economically. These days its main occupations are business, white-collar jobs, defence services, etc.

In the rural areas, it is also a landholding community. Wherever it holds land generally it is cultivated by sharecropping. In the state traditionally it was a moneylending and business community. The moneylending profession has become neglible these days. It has entered into small-scale industry as well. Its members are well represented in government and private service, and that too at good jobs. Self-employment exists as doctors, lawyers, accountant, transporters, etc. There is a direct link with fully regulated market. The community participated in the trade of all commodities at retail and at wholesale level. Transaction takes places by cash and at the level of accounts. As a cultivator in rural areas it pays wages in cash. In the rural areas its participation in the statutory *panchayats* is significant.

Traditional caste associations exists in urban areas. These are elected bodies and are called Sood *sabhas*. There is a state level body as well. Its headquarters is at Chandigarh. It has annual gathering and organizes various cultural functions, where various issues relating to community are also discussed. Such gatherings took place at Morinda in 1987. The *sabhas* also charge annual membership fees. It also publishes a magazine called *Sood Sandesh*. The sacred specialists are from other communities. Brahmin performs worship and also inspects religious teachings. The *purohit* is present at the time of birth, marriage and death rites. He also performs the *namkaran*, *phera*, and *pagri* ceremonies in the community. The community participates in the local festivals, which are of religious, economic and social significance. These include Diwali, Dussehra, Holi, Baisakhi, Lohri, Janamashtami, Shivratri, Basant, etc. It remains mainly a Hindu community, with various sects as Arya Samaj, Sanatan Dharm, etc. However, a few members also believe in Sikhism. The community has constructed a number of temples, which include temples of Lord Shiva at Moga, and Dharmkot, Satya Narain temple at Noormahal, and at various other places. Men and women participate in it.

The community in the state interacts freely with other communities. It exchanges water, all types of food—*kachcha*, *pukka*, *sidha*—with other communities. A few cases of intercommunity marriages have been reported.

Being an economically prosperous community, it has benefited from all developmental activities. The education has been extremely favourable for both boys and girls. They have access to all forms of technical and non-technical education, upto college and university levels. The community settled in rural areas is able to get access to education in urban areas. Generally the women get education for better matrimonial prospects though some of them are also in service. The community makes full use of modern medicare.

Both sexes have accepted the modern methods of family planning. All techniques have been accepted for family planning which include occasional abortions as well. Couples generally prefer two children, and occasionally three also. The drinking water and electricity facilities are available. In towns, the supply is from piped water or handpumps; in rural areas it is from handpumps or wells. It also avails of the benefits of modern electronic media such as television and radio. Younger generation of the community enjoy going to the cinema as well. The access to information is throught various extension and voluntary agencies, and political parteis as well. The exposure of the community to newspapers and magazine is good. The places of habitations are well-connected by roads; and frequently by railways as well. All types of fuels are used. which include mainly coal, kerosene oil, cooking gas and solar energy. In rural areas it also uses cow-dung cakes and firewood. As an agricultural community; it has also availed of modern technology in agriculture. It utilizes tractors, tube wells, both organic and chemical fertilizers, various insecticides in the agricultural operations. It has availed of the facilities of food/rations distribution system. Its attitude to saving is very positive. The community itself is not dependent upon moneylender, but traditionally it was itself a moneylending community.

VIRINDER SINGH

# SUNIAR

Sunar, Sonar, Suniar, Saraf or Swarankar is an occupational caste of goldsmiths or silversmiths. The name is derived from the Sanskrit word *suvarnakar* which means 'worker in gold'. They are distributed in all the districts of Punjab having higher concentration in the urban areas than the rural area. However, the Suniars have at least one family in each village. Owing to lack of business prospects at village level, they have migrated to the nearby towns or have taken up some other jobs. In the towns and in the village most of them have their own *pukka* houses. They speak Punjabi language with their family members and use Gurmukhi script. However, those who are educated use the Devanagari and Roman scripts. Males wear *kurta*, *pyjama*, *dhoti* and turbans. The females wear *salwar*, *kameez* and *dupatta*. Men have started wearing pants, shirts, women sometimes wear *saris*.

As observed by us the Suniars have light brown to very fair complexion with straight and fine dark brown hair and brown eyes. The nose has straight nasal bridge and horizontal nasal septum. The face is round with thin lips. Eyes have medium eyebrows.

Most of them are vegetarians. But now, a small section of the community have started taking non-vegetarian food which comprises eggs, chicken or mutton only. But they do not cook non-vegetarian food in their own kitchen; they either go to restaurants or visit the houses of their friends for this purpose. The pure vegetarians avoid the use of even onion, garlic and *masur dal* and bringing in eggs, fish and meat into their houses is strictly prohibited. The non-vegetarians take mutton, chicken and fish. Wheat is their staple food. They take *roti* prepared from the flour of wheat for their breakfast, lunch and dinner. However, during winter season the *roti* prepared from the flour of maize and known as *makki di roti* is eaten along with *sarson da sag*. Pulses include gram, *urad*, *moong*, *masoor*, beans (*rajma* and *rongi*), *moth* and peas are a very good source of protein. Rice is used on special occasions or ceremonies. Mustard and groundnut oils are used as a cooking medium. But *desi ghee* locally prepared or purchased from the market is also taken; it is used for smearing the *roti* and for preparing the *tarka*. Vegetables which are used seasonally are cauliflower, peas, *palak* and brinjal. Mangoes, oranges and citrus fruit and also their juice are taken during the summer season. Milk and milk products are also taken by them frequently. *Lassi* and *dahi* (curd), either home prepared or purchased, are consumed plentifully. Sweets are purchased on special occasions or festivals. Among changes in food habits of the non-vegetarians, consumption of vegetables and fruit has increased. Use of rice is also increasing.

There are two social divisions among the Suniars. These are Tank and Mair. Both these groups are endogamous. Mairs claim to be of Rajput origin and hence they are termed as Mair Rajputs who have learnt the art of making gold or silver ornaments from their forefathers; their's is hereditary profession. The Tank Suniars have learnt making gold or silver ornaments recently and their ancestors were not Suniars. Mair and Tank do not intermarry. Mair include a large number of individuals belonging to Sikh religion. But the Tank group includes persons from all religions such as Hindu, Sikh, Muslim, Jains, etc. Mair Rajputs are divided further into seven groups (Ibbetson, 1916)

The Tank Suniars have the following *gots*: Ajaimal, Bhagal, Dhange, Gurmee, Jogal, Kangali, Mai, Raltra, and Thathre.

Suniar is a endogamous group and marriage within the same *got* is prohibited. Consanguinous marriages are permitted among the Muslims. Junior sororate and levirate marriages are allowed. The age at marriage is eighteen to twenty years among boys and sixteen to eighteen years among girls. Marriage is arranged by negotiation by the parents with the help of *vichola* or *nais*. Form of marriage is monogamy. There are no marriage symbols among the married women belonging to Sikh or Muslim religions. Use of *sindur* in the hair parting is a marriage symbol among the Suniar women. Parents offer gifts to their daughters at the time of their marriage according to their financial position. The gifts may include clothes, furniture, golden ornaments such as necklace, earrings (one set) and bangles.

After marriage, the girl stays with her husband. Divorce is not encouraged, but it is permitted. Remarriage, or *karewa*, is also allowed. Various reasons for divorce are maladjustment, impotency, barrenness, insanity, and adultery. Compensation for divorce is allowed. Both the husband and wife have equal rights for seeking divorce. Before Independence intercaste marriages were not allowed, but due to higher literacy in the urban areas, few cases of love-marriages or intercaste marriages are also reported. Child marriage which was the practice in the past has been replaced by adult marriage.

Extended type of family which includes parents, their married sons and unmarried sons and daughters, is most common among the Suniars. However, it may also happen that due to some conflicts, the married sons may have their separate families and hence generate nuclear type of families. But the occurrence of such nuclear type of families is rare. Avoidance relationships exist between mother-in-law and son-in-law, daughter-in-law and father-in-law. Joking relationship occurs between sister-in-law and younger brother-in-law, brother-in-law and sister-in-law and between co-brothers. There may be some unpleasant happenings resulting into conflict and discord in the family. Most of the conflicts are resolved by mutual discussion for unity and welfare of the family. Boys and girls have equal share in the property of their father. But sisters allow their brothers to have their share of property that they should otherwise inherit from their father, for maintaining good relations with their brothers. The eldest son gets succession. The joint family system is breaking, resulting in the formation of nuclear families. The relationship between the brothers and sisters are sometimes strained due to the inheritance of property.

Women enjoy equal status with men and are free to take part in social functions, rituals, religious and political matters. They also get equal opportunity for education. The delivery of the first child mostly takes place in the house of the girl's parents. When a boy is born, the *nai* or *dai* ties mango and neem leaves, known as *bandarbal* to the front door of the house. When the child is eleven days old, a function known as *chowki charhana* is performed. A feast is given to the members of the community and includes sweets (*ladoo* and *jalebi*), *dal*, *sabji*, and *roti*. New clothes are given to the newly born child after the function of *taragari* (black beads and a coin tied to black thread are put around the waist of the child). Postnatal restrictions and care are observed for forty days. *Mundan*, *dastarbandi* or circumcision ceremonies are performed during childhood among the Hindus, Sikhs and Muslims respectively.

When a boy or a girl attains adulthood, the father mobilizes his influence through his relatives or through a *nai* to find a suitable match for his son or daughter. The girl's father first pays a visit to the house of the boy along with his very close relatives. The *shagun* which includes coconut, dry fruits and a silver coin and sometimes also clothes to the boy and his parents, are offered at this ceremony which is termed as *mangani*. Marriage rituals are performed at the house of the bride. Marriage feast is given to the members of the community by both the parties at their respective places a day prior to the marriage rituals. This feast is known as *roti*. Marriage is solemnized by four *pheras* among the Sikhs, seven *pheras* among the Hindus and by *nikah* among the Muslims. The marriage party arrives in the morning. It takes light refreshment which is followed by actual marriage rituals and then a sumptuous lunch. The marriage party takes the lunch first and later the relatives, parents and other invitees from the girl's side follows them. The marriage party leaves in the evening on the same day. After arrival of the bride at her in-laws' house, a reception party is arranged in honour of the newly married couple. The girl, along with her husband, pays a visit to her parent's house on the next day and they return on the same day. This is known as *phera*. Consummation of marriage is at groom's residence. Among the Muslims, the dead are buried. But among the Hindu and Sikhs the dead are cremated but the bodies of young children are buried. Pollution period is observed for thirteen days. Religious ceremonies are also performed depending upon their economic position. A feast is given to the members of the community after the ceremony. Ancestor worship is observed among the Hindus only. Various rituals associated with birth, marriage and death have become shorter and more expensive.

The Suniars are goldsmith by profession. They prepare gold and silver ornaments. They also prepare ornamants from the old gold or silver ornaments, or supply the fresh gold for the ornaments to others. When they supply new ornaments in exchange for old ones, they deduct 1 gm against every 10 gm (known as *chhot*). Some of them also act as *mahajans* and lend money to the needy persons and keep gold or silver ornaments as security. Owing to lack of business prospects at the village level, some of the Suniars have also started other side-businesses such as shopkeeping, or as *halwais* or vendors selling vegetables. Those who have got an opportunity to get higher education have taken up teaching profession, services as clerks, bank officers, engineers, etc.

They have local, state and all-India level associations for regulating social control. The local *sabha*, has a president, general secretary, treasurer and members. The local *sabha* is mainly entrusted with the charge to attend to the local problems and resolve them without bringing the matter to the police or the court. It may include office-bearers from all the religions which is a very good example of communal harmony.

The state-level association of the Suniars, known as Punjab Swarnkar Sangh, has its head office at Gopal Jewellers, Sarafa Bazar, Ludhiana. The office bearers are from different places of Punjab in order to give wide representation to the area. Punjab Swarnkar Sangh is affiliated to the Akhil Bhartiya Swarnkar Sangh 1626, Dariba Kalan, Delhi 110006. Akhil Bhartiya Swarnkar Sangh, has its sub-office at Patel Chowk, Amritsar. The state-level association attends to the problems not resolved at the local levels. The All India Association takes up the matters of common interest. It may be mentioned here that the members of the Sangh observed a Black Day on 9 January and 9 August every year in order to protest the Gold Control Act of the Government of India. The Act has now been replaced.

A Suniar may be a Hindu, Sikh, Muslim or Jain. The role of sacred specialists may be teaching, performing birth, marriage or death rites. They venerate the holy scriptures of their respective religions and visit their respective religious shrines accordingly. Their common festivals are Lohri, Holi, Dussehra, Diwali, Id-ul-Fitr, Id-ul-Zuha, etc. Various festivals are of socio-religious significance. It may be observed that among the Suniars, the followers of both the Hinduism and Sikhism may be found in the same family. They have firm belief in their respective religions and have equal regards for other religions.

Traditional intercommunity linkages are stronger among the Suniars at village level as compared to the cities. Suniars are invited at the social and religious functions of other communities in a village and vice versa. Suniars depend greatly on the members of other castes and communities. There is no restriction of any kind for the Suniars such as the acceptance of water and food, sharing of water sources, road facilities, school, religious places, *panchayat ghar*, etc., with other communities. Suniars belonging to Hinduism, Sikhism and Islam interact and participate in each other's religious, economic, social and political functions.

Suniar is a business community which also has members in white-collar jobs, as teachers, doctors, engineers and administrators. They frequently come in contact with members of other communities, who are well educated having better economic status. Suniars are more liberal and free in their approach with the members of other communities.

Boys and girls get equal opportunity to go to schools and colleges. They make full use of modern medical care available at the primary health centre or other such dispensaries and or medical colleges and hospitals. Attitude towards family welfare and planning is positive and the couples prefer two to three children. They have their own source of drinking water such as handpumps or piped water.They have ration cards and get suger, *atta* and kerosene oil at subsidized rates. Suniars avail of bank facilities for improving their business and take loans from the banks to start their separate business. They make use of various media facilities such as radio, television and cinema. Network of railways, roads and post and telegraph and telephone facilities have helped them tremendously in improving their business. They have been benefited by electricity. Wood, cow-dung, coal, kerosene oil, or cooking gas are the fuel sources used by them. Cooking gas is used in cities.

SWARAN SINGH

# TELI

The Telis extracts the oil from the oil seeds (*tel*) and also graze the goats and sheeps. Rose (1914: 461), reported that the Telis were divided into three groups namely the Kharasia (millers), Penja (dhunia) or cotton-cleaners; and the Telis proper, who are engaged in extraction of oil. According to another classification in the districts of Patiala and Amritsar, the Telis can be divided into twelve groups (Barhi) and fifty-two groups (Bunjahi or Babanjahi). In different districts this classification has different connotation.

Rose (1919: 462), further states that the Muslim Telis claim their descent from Baba Hassu, who invented the *kohlu* or oil press. According to a traditional story, Luqman, son of Baur, could not extract oil from the oilseeds and it was only on the advice of an oil woman that he could succeed in extracting the oil after mixing water with the oil seeds (*ghani*). According to another story Luqman learnt the art of making oil from a devil in exchange for explanining to him how Luqman kept the cloths dry in an inverted jar. Baba Hassu's son took to cleaning the clothes and he founded the Bunjahis also called as the true Telis. The names of sixty-four *gots* including *als* (*septs*) of the Telis according to Rose (1919: 463) are as follows:

| | | | |
|---|---|---|---|
| Adi | Alami | Ali | Aman |
| Amau | Arbia | Arli | Badda |
| Baddar | Badgujjar | Bagri | Bahlim |
| Basin | Batham | Bhand | Bharai |
| Bharbhunja | Bhasin | Bhatti | Bhehuya |
| Bhittei | Bhutta | Blim | Chahchi |
| Chahil | Chandar | Changer | Chauhan |
| Chaunan | Chhalial | Dahar | Dahima |
| Daroma | Deota | Dhawan | Dhia |
| Dholijaddon | Dunga | Gahlot | Galchi |
| Ganja | Ganjaur | Gaur | Gendi |
| Ghaman | Gharia | Gil | Gori |
| Goria | Gundra | Guzara | Hammi |
| Hans | Hastre | Hindru | Jadhran |
| Jaggi | Jaid | Hir | Jandan |
| Jandarayan | Januhen | Jajuhan | Jatharwa |

| | | | |
|---|---|---|---|
| Jawam | Jhain | Jath | Jhala |
| Jhamain | Jhammat | Jhajhunia | Jhhan |
| Jhimau | Jindran | Jhandar | Kachhor |
| Kachhua | Kail, | Jumditor | Kal |
| Kalia | Kandlot, | Kaith | Kangari |
| Kans | Karim, | Kandra | Ketlj |
| Khangru | Kharmshi | Keljuddan | Khatri |
| khel | Khetle | Kharse | Khokhar |
| Kichchi | Kikkar | Ladhukhal | Langhe |
| Lare | Lohar | Lund-datra | Magh |
| Mahim | Mahindru | Mai | Malak |
| Malhe | Mandahar | Mangekhel | Manj |
| Marhans | Matto | Mehras | Meji |
| Minhas | Mundh | Mural | Nagah |
| Nuru | Pal | Panji Khel | Pashin |
| Patha | Phira Khel | Pilchi | Pillhi |
| Piron | Pual | Pundhar | Punhar |
| Punwar | Purana | Puriwal | Quraishi |
| Ragu | Rajpal | Rathore | Rautar |
| Rehrr | Roya | Rura | Sabrao |
| Sahal | Sahini | Said | Saihna |
| Sainsi | Sakila | Salahan | Samhasi |
| Samman | Sangale | Sarad | Saroha |
| Saundhi | Sayyid | Sed | Siahsaoe |
| Soda | Sohna | Sotakhni | Sulhare |
| Sultukhel | Tagha | Tahim | Taoni |
| Tarman | Thaddi | Tunhar | Tunwar |
| Ugan | Wadhan | Waryah | |

These *gots* or *als* belong to the whole caste, and are not confined to any one branch of it.

In each village there is at least one family of their community. Teli caste is of old standing and of the same status as the Julaha. In the villages, they speak Punjabi language both with the members of their own community and outsiders, while those who are educated use either Gurmukhi or Perso-Arabic script. In the cities they speak Urdu also. They wear local dress. *Dal-roti* is their staple food. They take non-vegetarian food using eggs and mutton. Groundnut oil and pure *ghee* are used as cooking medium. They take milk and milk products. They smoke *bidi*, and take betlenuts. Fruits are taken occasionally, but in moderate quantity.

Some of their reported *gots* are Gauri, Chohan, Khilji, Rajput, Baleem, Sihal, Chander, Sahote, etc. These are considered for marriage alliances. They occupy a position lower than that of the Brahman, Jat, Bania, but equal to that of Julaha and higher position than of Balmiki and Chamar. They are aware of the *varna* system. At present, they observe endogamy at all levels and consanguineous marriages are permitted. They marry outside their village. Marriage is arranged by negotiations, when their boys attain adulthood. Polygyny is allowed. *Nikah* (marriage), is performed according to Islamic traditions. *Mehar* is also announced. The rule of residence is patrilocal. If there is maladjustment and lack of children, *talak* (divorce), is also permitted with religious sacrament. Compensation is to be given in the case of a divorce to the wife. Both husband and wife have the right to divorce. Remarriage is permitted.

Joint families are more prevalent in the village, though the nuclear families are also coming up. Property, disrespect to the elders and petty issues related to check on the younger members of the family, may result in conflict in the family. All sons inherit the property of their father equally, but the eldest son gets the succession. Women attend to the various household activities, and domestic animals. Post delivery pollution period and postnatal restrictions on mother are observed for forty days. *Sunnat* (circumcision) is performed among the boys when they are five to seven years of age. They host a feast to the members of the community.

The marriage is performed at the residence of the bride. *Roti* (feast) is also offered to the marriage party by the parents of the bride, after performance of *nikah*. *Suhagrat* (consummation of marriage) is at the residence of the bridegroom. They bury their dead. After three days, the *maulavi* offers prayers. This is called *kul uthana*. Feast is also given to the community.

The Telis are a landless community. They are engaged in the villages as oil pressers, they have *kohlus* for this purpose. Earlier mustard oil was very commonly used for cooking and ceremonial purposes, which has now been replaced by hydrogenated vegetable oil or sometimes by *desi ghee* or clarified butter. This has adversely affected the primary occupation of the Telis and they have started exploring other areas of their occupation. They keep sheep and goats, works as labourers, agriculture either on contract (*theka*) or share-cropping (*batai*) basis. In the cities they also engage themselves as oil-presses, weaving, animal husbandry, government service, business, small-scale industry (making scissors).

According to Rose (1919: 463), 'The Telis have *chauntra* and subordinate to it are *tappas* at several of the larger villages. The *sarpanch* is hereditary and one or two headmen from each *tappa* assemble at the *chauntra*. The Sarpanch receives a *pagri* at birth, wedding or funeral and exercises the usual functions. Else where they have a system, sometimes without the *chaudharies*.'

In the villages, presently, they do not have their traditional *panchayat*. The village *panchayat* settles their disputes. However, in the cities, the concept of *siana* or *chaudhury* is there and they represent their *panchayat*. They settle matters related to property, marriage and theft, by mutual agreement. They also approach the police and court of law to settle their disputes. They belong to Islam religion and offer their prayers accordingly. The *maulavi* is from other Muslim community and performs various rites associated with birth, marriage and death. In the village, they join members of other communities in celebrating Lohri and Diwali. They visit the nearby *masjid* on the festival of Id-ul-Fitr, Id-ul-Zuha. They sing local folk songs and dance *bhangra* on the occasion of marriage.

They traditionally accept food and water from all the communities of a village except the Chamars and Balmikis. Jats, Brahmans and Banias do not accept their food. They share burial ground with the members of other Muslim communities. They have access to places of worship and can take part in various festivals and festivities. There are a few in business and in service.

Formal education is favoured for both the boys and girls. In the villages, they do not study even upto primary level due to poor economic conditions, but in towns they study upto the college level. They take advantage of hospitals and family welfare schemes. Drinking water is available. They are engaged both in self-employment and government service and take advantage of various media and communication programmes. They use electricity and cow-dung cakes, kerosene oil and wood as fuel. They take advantage of irrigation, chemical fertilizers and insecticides. Immunization facilities are available. They have ration cards and get sugar and kerosene oil at subsidized rates. Attitude towards saving is positive and a few depend on the shop-keepers and moneylenders.

SWARAN SINGH

# BIO-ANTHROPOLOGICAL INFORMATION

The populations of Punjab have been extensively studied by physical anthropologists. Anthropological Survey of India has also covered it under All India Anthropometric Survey (AIAS) as well as All India Bio-anthropological Survey. All India Anthropometic Survey was conducted from May to November, 1969 in seven districts of the state covering six population groups, viz., Brahman, Chamar, Jat Sikh, Khatri, Rajput and Saini (Kumar et al., 1990). In all 1500 individuals were measured. The populations of Punjab on an average are above medium in stature (167.56 cms.), have long head (CI-74.22), medium nose (NI-71.37) and medium to broad face (TFI-83.21). According to Martin's classification around 32 per cent of the population is tall and next 40 per cent of population is medium to above medium in stature. 71 per cent of the population has long to very long head. Broad head is rare (3 per cent). Generally, population of Punjab have medium nose (55 per cent). followed by long nose (39 per cent). However, majority of the population has either broad face (59 per cent of Euryprosopic and Hyper Euryprosopic) or medium face (23 per cent) (Singh, Bhalla & Kaul, 1994).

All India Bio-anthropological Survey (AIBAS) was conducted at six nodal points in Punjab (Ghosh, 1988). Sex ratio shows 118 males per 100 females. Child women ratio indicates low fertility rates as shown by 59 children for 100 females (50 per cent). However category of widowed/separated individuals show greater number of females (5.22 per cent) then males (4.86 per cent). Medium household (6-10 individuals per house) is most prevalent (42 per cent), followed by small household (45 per cent). Around 7 per cent are large households. Females (55 per cent) are less literate than males (47 per cent). Around 12 per cent of the population have above matric education which is relatively quite high to all India average (Singh, Bhalla & Kaul, 1994).

Besides AIAS a number of studies are available on somatometry of Punjab pupulation. These studies support the findings of AIAS. Dermatoglyphic studies indicate preponderence of loops (48-67 per cent) over whorls (33-49 per cent). Ahuja (1974), however reported relatively higher incidence of whorls (48.80 per cent) than loops (47.70 per cent) in Arora population. Punjabi Hindu recorded highest frequency of loops (67 per cent) (Deol, 1954) whereas lowest incidence of loops is found in Arora (48 per cent) (Ahuja, 1974). The frequency of arches varies from 2.43 per cent to 7. 40 per cent. Deol (1954), recorded lowest value of pattern intensity index (12.30) in Punjabi Hindu, whereas highest value (14.50) has been calculated in Arora community by Ahuja (1974).

Incidence of colour blindness is relatively moderate in Punjab population. It occurs between 2.04 per cent to 9.66 per cent in different population. Surprisingly lowest incidence (2.04 per cent) (Shanbag & Bhatia, 1974) and highest incidence (9.66 per cent) (Bansal, 1967) have both been recorded from Khatri population.

Only three communities (Gujjar, Jat & Khatri) have been studied for phenylthiocarbamide tasting ability. Gujjar (Balgir, 1988) have highest incidence of nontaster (t) gene (75 per cent), whereas Jat (Mitter & Bansal, 1975) have lowest occurence of gene (44 per cent)

Occurrence of G6PD deficiency reportedly varies from 2 per cent found in Punjabi Sikh (Bhalla, 1977) to 8 per cent among Punjabi community (Shanbag & Bhatia, 1974). Around 5-7 per cent of the Muslim communities have also been found to be deficient (Bansal et al., 1976).

Around 60 studies are available on ABO blood group system of Punjabi population. Unfortunately most of the studies have concentrated on Brahman, Bania, Khatri, Jat and Rajput groups with a little information on other groups. The studies show that B gene (17.00-36.58 per cent) presonderates over A gene (10.70-30.90 per cent). However Gujjar and Muslim populations seem to be exception where A gene has relatively high frequency than B gene. Ahuja and Siddhu (1981) and Balgir and Sharma (1988) reported relatively high incidence of A gene (58.99 per cent & 20 per cent) over B gene (20.98 per cent & 19.40 per cent) respectively in Gujjars, though lot of variation is noticed in individual gene frequencies in the two reports. Both Muslim Shia and Muslim Sunni have recorded relatively high incidence of A gene (37.16 per cent & 24.14 per cent) than B gene (23.15 per cent & 22.44 per cent) respectively (Bansal et al., 1983). O gene shows lot of variation in its occurrence with least incidence of 21.01 per cent in Gujjar Hindu (Ahuja & Siddhu, 1981) to as high as 71 per cent recorded in Rajput (Mathur, 1959). Incidence of M gene is generally above 50 per cent with a range variation of 55 per cent in Bania (Pal, 1981) to 72 per cent in Jat Sikh (Papiha et al., 1982). In MNSs blood group system, Bhalla (1964) recorded maximum gene frequency for Ms (31.17 37.18 per cent) gene in Arora, Brahmin and Khatri groups studied by him.

Rh blood group system show high incidence of r haplotype (16-33 per cent), but rarely exceeds 33 per cent. On the other hand, $R_1$ haplotype varies from 47 per cent recorded in Jat Sikh (Papiha et al., 1982) to 66 per cent found in Khatri (Shanbag & Bhatia, 1974). Gene d has relatively high occurrence in Gujjar Hindu (35.40 per cent) (Balgir & Sharma, 1988), and Muslim groups (27-32 per cent) Bansal et al., 1983) than other communities (11.20-23.30 per cent respectively.

In serum proteins, Haptoglobin and Transferrin have been extensively studied. The frequency of $Hp^1$ gene varies from 14 per cent reported in Balmiki (Kapur, 1979) to 24 per cent in Brahman (Pal, 1981). The incidence of $Tf^c$ is generally 100 per cent except in Jat group where $Tf^B$ (0.30-3.96 per cent) and $Tf^D$ (0.10-1.04 per cent) have been reported by different investigators (Sunderlal et al., 1976; Kaur et al., 1977; Khanna, 1978).

Biochemical variants have been extensively studied both in Scheduled Caste and other Caste communities. No significant deviation have been reported. The frequency range of different genes in Punjab populations is as follows: $P^a$ (25.00-43.00 per cent), $P^B$ (57.00-74.60 per cent), $PGM^1$ (64.47-76.44 per cent). $ESD^2$ (15.70-24.10 per cent), $GLO^1$ (14.30-37.50 per cent), $Ak^1$ (87.10-92.30 per cent), $PGD^A$ (97.20 per cent) and $ADA^1$ (81.50-90.60 per cent). In addition $PGM^R$ (0.30-1.70 per cent) has also been reported from Jat Sikh (Singh et al., 1974; Chahal & Papiha, 1981).

V. Kaul
N.K. Bagchi

## REFERENCES

Ahuja, Y.R., K. Kant and J.L. Tikoo, 'Genetic investigation among Khatri-Arora Punjabi of India. Dermatoglyphics', *Indian Journal of Heredity*, 6, 1974, pp. 13-18.

Ahuja, S. and L.S. Siddhu, 'Distribution of ABO blood groups and some physical traits among the Gujjars of Punjab', *Indian Journal of Physical Anthropology and Human Genetics*, 7 (2), 1981, pp. 93-6.

Balgir, R.S., 'Demogenetic investigation among the Hindu and Muslim Gujjars: The two breeding isolates of the sub Himalayan and Himalayan regions', Ph.D. thesis (unpublished), Chandigarh: Punjab University, 1983.

Balgir, R.S. and J.C. Sharma, 'Dermatoglyphic studies among the two breeding isolates of Gujjars of North-Western India', *American Journal of Physical Anthropology*, 75, 1988, pp. 391-403.

Bansal, I.J.S., 'Incidence of colour blindness among Punjabis of India', *Journal of Human Genetics*, 16, 1967, pp. 1-5.

Bansal, I.J.S., B. Kaur, P. Singhal and A.J.S. Bhanwar, 'Glucose-6 Phosphate Dehydrogenase (G6PD) deficiency among Muslims of Punjab', *The Anthropologists*, 23 (1 & 2), 1976, pp. 21-5.

Bansal, I.J.S., P. Singhal and K. Kaur, 'A comparative study of blood groups of two groups of Punjab', *Indian Anthropologist*, 4 (1), 1983, pp. 40-6.

Bhalla, N.K., 'A survey of erythrocytic glucose 6 phosphate dehydrogenase activity amongst Punjabi Sikhs', M.D. thesis (unpublished), Patiala: Punjabi University, 1977.

Bhalla, V., 'The genetic analysis of the ABO, MNSs, Rh- Hr and $Fy^a$ blood group systems in three endogamous groups of Punjabi Hindus and the association of blood groups with tuberculosis', Ph.D. thesis (unpublished), University of Delhi, 1964.

Chahal, S.M.S. and S.S. Papiha, 'A population genetic study of the Jat Sikhs, Punjab, India', *Journal of the Indian Anthropological Society*, 16, 1981, pp. 251-60.

Ghosh, G.C., 'All India Bio-Anthropological Survey of India', Calcutta, *Anthropological Survey of India*, 1988.

Mitter, N.S. and I.J.S. Bansal, 'The effect of some social habits on P.T.C. - Taste response in two endogamous groups from Punjab', *Indian Journal of Physical Anthropology and Human Genetics* 1 (2), 1975, pp. 169-73.

Pal, P., 'Genetic distance analysis as based on three ethnic groups of Punjab', M.Phil. thesis (unpublished), Patiala: Punjabi University, 1981.

Papiha, S.S., B.N. Mukuherjee, S.M.S. Chahal, K.C. Malhotra and D.F. Roberts, 'Genetic heredity and population structure in North West India', Annals of Human biology, 9, 1982, pp. 235-51.

Singh, K.S., V. Bhalla and V. Kaul, 'The Biological Variation in Indian populations', National Series, Vol. X, Delhi: Oxford University Press, 1994.

Shanbag, S. and H.M. Bhatia, 'Studies on genetic markers like blood groups, serum groups, G-6PD and abnormal haemoglobin in the castes groups of Saraswats and Lohanas', in *Human Population Genetics in India*, edited by Sanghvi et al., Delhi: Orient Longman Ltd., 1974, pp. 1-10.

Sharma, J.C., 'Blood and P.T.C. studies in Punjabis and the effect of age and certain eating habits on taste threshold', *The Anthropologist*, 6 and 7, 1956-60, pp. 40-6.

Singh, I.P. and D. Singh, 'The study of ABO blood groups of Sainis of Punjab', *American Journal of Physical Anthropology*, 19, 1960, pp. 223-5.

Singh, S., K.N. Sareen and H.W. Godde, 'Investigation of some biochemical genetic markers in four endogamous groups in Punjab, II. Red cell enzyme polymorpisms', *Human Genetics*, 1974, pp. 133-8.

# GLOSSARY

*akhand path* : non-stop recitation of *Guru Granth Sahib*
*amrit* : holy water, prepared with *batasa* made of sugar
*anand karaj* : marriage ritual of circumambulation in sikh religion
*annaprashan* : first feeding of cereal to the child
*arthi* : a wooden bier
*artiya* : commission agent
*asa-di-war* : hymns of *Guru Granth Sahib*, morning sikh prayer
*ashirwad* : blessings
*awa* : kiln
*atta da pedda* : balls of wheat flour (dough)
*babban* : band party that leads the dead body in a procession for last rites
*borla* : ornament of forehead symbolizing wedlock
*bathana/bathona* : widow remarriage
*bandarbal* : a rite associated with birth
*bahar vadhaona/badana* : postnatal ritual of showing the newborn to outsiders
*barat* : marriage party
*barkhi* : ritual held after one year of death
*batai* : sharecropping
*batte-di-shadi/batta satta* : marriage by exchange
*bauli* : deep well approached by stairs
*bhabi/bharjai* : brother's wife
*bhatija* : brother's son, nephew
*bhatti* : oven
*bichola/vichola* : matchmaker, mediator
*bindi* : a symbol of marriage, a round mark put on forehead by married women
*bin* : gourd-pipe
*bundi* : a kind of sweetmeat prepared from gram flour, ghee and sugar
*biradari panchayat* : community council
*chacha* : father's brother
*chachi* : father's younger brother's wife
*chad chadai* : divorce
*chadar paona/chadar prath/ chadar andazi/chadar tanaja* : levirate marriage/ widow remarriage
*challa/chilla* : postnatal restrictions on the mother
*chapati* : unleavened bread prepared from maize/wheat flour
*chati/chhati* : post-birth ritual performed on the completion of six months after birth
*charni lagana* : touching the feet of the lord
*chaturmas* : four months of rainy season
*chavarkhi* : fourth death anniversary

*chhadi* : stick
*chadran* : bedsheet
*chautha* : a ritual performed on the fourth day of death
*chitian* : dried cotton plants
*chogdaar* : secretary
*choti* : tuft of head hair
*choora/chura* : a set of red bangles
*chunni* : ladies head cover
*chunni charhana* : marriage rite associated with betrothal ceremony
*churrel* : female ghost
*churiya jharana* : ceremony held at the time of betrothal
*chowki charhana* : a function held on the eleventh day of childbirth signifying completion of pollution period
*churma* : crumbs of bread pounded with sugar
*dada* : grandfather
*dadi* : grandmother
*dafan karna* : to bury the dead
*dag dena* : cremating the dead body
*dai* : midwife
*dan* : gift
*daj/dahej* : dowry
*dal-roti* : staple food consisting of *chapati* with pulse/lentil soup
*darani* : husband's younger brother's wife
*dewar* : husband's younger brother
*desi ghee* : clarified butter
*dharam bhai* : the one accepted and treated as a brother, a putative kin
*dharamshala* : religious place for all
*dihadi jota* : daily labourer
*dhan* : paddy
*doli* : wedding procession of bride
*gaddi* : seat or place of worship
*garabhadhan* : consummation of marriage
*garbia* : small brass pots associated with death rites
*grishti* : householder
*ghagra* : skirt
*ghani* : extraction of oil from mustard seeds
*ghar jawai* : son-in-law staying in the house of his father-in- law
*goha-kuda* : scavenging
*god lena* : to adopt a child
*ghiya* : pumpkin
*gudana* : tattooing
*gola* : ball
*gaona* : consummation of marriage
*granthi* : Sikh priest
*gurdwara* : Sikh temple
*gurti* : first feeding of the child with something other than milk

*guru-ka-langar* : community kitchen of Sikhs
*guntrala* : cow's urine
*hasli* : neck ornament
*halal* : slaughtering of goat in Muslim style
*jadoo-tuna* : black magic
*janampatri* : horoscope
*janaja* : taking the dead body in a procession for the last rites
*jata* : long hairs
*jadi-buti* : medicinal plants and herbs
*jhopri* : hutment
*janeo/janeu* : sacred thread
*jarda/meetha chawal* : rice cooked with sugar or jaggery
*jata kama* : the birth rite
*jati biradari* : traditional caste council
*jawai* : son-in-law
*jeeja* : sister's husband
*jeth* : husband's elder brother
*jot* : lamp
*jutti* : footwear
*junj/janj* : marriage party
*kabristan* : graveyard
*kachcha* : houses made of unbaked bricks, or uncooked food
*kujia* : death rite
*kanak-ki-roti* : bread prepared from wheat flour
*kanch* : glass
*kandamulas* : roots and tubers
*kangha* : wooden comb
*kanyadan* : the ritual of giving away of the girl in marriage
*kan windhna* : piercing of ear lobes in girls
*kapal kriya* : the ritual of breaking the skull during cremation
*kara* : iron bangle
*karia* : silver anklets
*kararnama* : agreement
*karewa* : widow remarriage
*kashida* : embroidery on cloth
*katcha soot* : handspun thread
*khaddi* : handloom
*khajanchi* : treasurer
*khallar* : wallet
*khalsa* : pure sikh
*khanda* : double-edged dagger
*kharawan* : footwear made of wood
*kharcha* : compensation
*khatam* : death rite held on the fortieth day of the death
*khula path* : recitation of Shri Guru Granth Sahib
*kheer* : rice pudding, cooked with milk and sugar

*kirpan* : sword
*kolhu* : oil-pressing machine
*kriya karam* : post-death ritual
*kudki* : silver ornament worn by an unmarried girl/golden ornament worn by married ladies
*kurmai* : betrothal/engagement ceremony
*kuja* : sugar cup
*kujia bharna* : a post-death ritual
*kulis* : huts
*kumbal* : pitloom
*kurti* : ladies shirt
*lagan* : auspicious date and time for marriage
*lakhnotri* : marriage ceremony
*lande* : a script used to write accounts
*langar* : community kitchen
*lassi* : buttermilk
*lawan* : hymns related to sikh marriage
*luwanchari* : overcoat used in winter
*mahatma* : saint
*makki di roti/makki* : *chapati* made of maize flour/maize
*maklawa/muklawa/muklaba* : consummaion of marriage
*mandir* : temple
*mangani/mangana* : engagement ceremony
*mantra* : hymn
*mrigshala* : deer skin
*masan/masaan* : cremation ground
*masit* : mosque
*matha tekana* : to offer prayer by touching ground with forehead
*mehar* : bride-price to be paid in case of divorce among muslims
*meetha chawal* : sweetened cooked rice
*millani/milani* : embracing/introducing close relatives in marriage ceremony/ ritual welcome
*missi roti* : *chapati* prepared of mixed flour of wheat and gram
*maulavi* : muslim priest
*mudra* : earrings
*munj-da-mujura* : toy made of grass
*machli* : nose ornament
*mundan* : tonsure
*mayan* : sheath of sword
*nagar-khera* : village deity
*namaz* : muslim prayer
*nambardar/lambardar* : head of the traditional panchayat
*namkaran* : naming ceremony
*nanand* : husband's sister
*naria* : ox
*nagara* : kettledrum

*nikah* : marriage according to islamic rites
*noohn* : daughter-in-law
*pargat din* : birthday
*pagri/pag/pugri* : turban ceremony of succession
*pajeb* : anklet
*panjiri* : a sweetend, roasted, flour preparation cooked with sugar, coconut, etc.
*panchayat* : traditional council
*parakh* : higher court
*pardah/ghund* : veil
*peti/petti* : big wooden or steel trunk
*phera pana* : visit of the girl to her parent's house after marriage
*phul* : charred remains after cremation
*phulkari* : embroidary
*pilai* : alcoholic drink
*praya dhan* : other's property, term used for unmarried girls
*pulaw* : a rice dish
*pukka house* : house made of baked bricks
*padlea* : ornament worn in the arms
*qwali* : a group song accompanied with instrumental music
*ragi* : professional/classical singers of *Gurubani*
*rajinama* : agreement
*rand* : widow
*randua* : widower
*rang karna* : tanning of skin
*rasam pagri* : ceremony of succession signifying end of death pollution
*reda/rehri* : cart
*roti* : wheat *chapati*/feast held on special occasions
*riasat* : estate
*ritan* : pre-delivery rite held during the seventh month of pregnancy
*rok/rokana/rokiya/roka* : engagement
*sadharan path* : recitation of *Shri Guru Granth Sahib*
*sadu* : co-brothers
*sagan/shagun* : pre-marriage ritual of offering gifts to the girl/boy
*sagai* : engagement
*saura* : father-in-law
*sali* : wife's sister
*sanda* : lizard
*sandhur* : vermilion
*sant* : saint
*sanji/sanjh* : contract labourer/annual contact for labour work
*sanji* : image of Goddéss Durga worshipped during Dussehra festival
*saral* : python
*sarakh* : court higher than *narakh*
*sarson-da-sag* : a preparation of mustard leaf
*serain* : inn
*shradh* : ancestor-worship

*sas* : mother-in-law
*sati* : the custom of self-immolation at the time of husband's death
*satrawan* : a post death ritual observed on seventeenth day after death
*satwan* : a ritual observed on seventh day after death
*sevadar* : attendant in a sikh shrine
*shehnai* : a reed musical instrument
*shabad* : hymns
*shamlat* : common land
*sehra* : leaves of mango tree tied to a string and displayed on front door; tasselled head-dress
*siana* : village elder/intelligent
*sila* : postnatal restriction on mother
*sindur* : vermilion applied by a married woman as a marriage symbol
*sive/marghat* : crematorium
*sohala* : praise for the dead—a part of death rite
*solwan* : death rite on the sixteenth day after death
*sootak/sutak* : post-delivery pollution period
*sudikaran* : purification
*suhag-de-geet* : marriage songs
*suhagrat* : consummation of marriage
*sunnat* : circumcision
*sur* : home brewed alcoholic drink
*tawiz* : amulet
*tikka* : forehead ornament
*taya* : father's elder brother
*talak/talaq* : divorce
*tanda* : dried maize plants
*tapari* : huts
*taragari* : black beads and a coin tied to a black thread and worn around the waist
*tarka* : seasoning, especially of *dal* preparations
*tasla* : iron bowl for carrying soil
*tirath yatra* : pilgrimage
*theka* : contract
*thobi* : griddle
*tokra* : basket made from the twigs of mulberry tree
*toli* : group of people living in a locality or moving together
*uthala* : purificatory rites, end of the mourning period after death
*vaheda* : ceremony held on the occasion of a child birth
*wadhai* : congratulations
*waran* : a type of song, ballad
*watta* : exchange in marriage
*zamoori/jamoori* : small girls engaged in acrobatics

# SELECT BIBLIOGRAPHY

*Affairs of the East India Company being the Fifth Report from the Select Committee of the House of Commons*, edited with notes and Introduction by Walter Kelly Firminger, 3 vols., Delhi: Neeraj Publishing, 28 July 1812, rpt. 1984.

Ahuja, S., 'Observations on reproductive wastage in the Women in Punjab', M.Sc. thesis, Patiala: Panjabi University (unpublished), 1976.

Ahuja, Y.R., J.L. Tickoo and K. Kant, 'Genetic investigation among Khatri-Arora Punjabi of India-Dermatoglyphics', *Ind. J. Hered* 6, 1974, pp. 13-18.

Anand, B.S., *Guru Tegh Bahadur: A Biography*, Delhi: Sterling Publishers, 1979.

Andreoli and Robbins, *Molecular Biology of Human Proteins with special reference to plasma proteins*, Vol. I, Schultz and Heremons, 1962.

Archer, John Clark, *The Sikhs in Relation to Hindus, Muslims, Christians and Ahmadiyyas: A Study in Comparative Religion*, Princeton: PWP, 1946

Assey, James, *Christianity: Introduction* (Punjab), Batala: CISS, 1976.

Baines, Athelstane, 1976, *Ethnography*, Delhi: Concept Pub. House, 1912.

Bakshi, R., R. Singh and I.P. Singh, 'Secular trend in age at menarche in Punjabis', in *Proceedings of the Xth International Congress of Anthropological and Ethnological Sciences*, Delhi, 1978.

Balfour, Edward, *Encyclopaedia Asiatica: comprising Indian Subcontinent, Eastern and Southern Asia*, Vol. V, Delhi: Cosmo Publications, 1976.

Balgir, R.S. and J.C. Sharma, 'Dermatoglyphic studies among the two breeding groups of Gujjars of North-Western India, *Amer. J. Phys. Anthrop*, Vol. 71, 1987.

Banga, Indu (ed.), *Five Punjabi Centuries: Polity, Economy, Society and Culture, c. 1500-1990*, Essays for J.S. Grewal, Delhi: Manohar, 2000.

Banga, Indu, 'Formation of Sikh State, 1765-1845', in Indu Banga (ed.), *Five Punjabi Centuries: Polity, Economy, Society and Culture, c. 1500-1990*, Delhi: Manohar, 2000.

Bansal, I.J.S., 'Incidence of colour blindness among Punjabis of India', *J. Hum. Genet*, Vol. 16, 1967, pp. 1-5.

Banerjee, Himadri, 'The Kamins of the Punjab (1889-1901)', in *Panjab Past and Present*, Vol. XI, Pt. I, 1977.

Barnes, G.C. and J.B. Lyall, *Report of the Land Revenue Settlement of the Kangra District*, Lahore: Panjab Civil and Military Gazetteer Press, 1850.

Barrier, N. Gerald, 'Sikh Identity in historical and contemporary perspective', in Pashaura Singh and N. Gerald Barrier (eds.) *Sikh Identity: Continuity and Change*, Delhi: Manohar, 2001.

Bhalla, G.S., 'Political Economy since Independence', in Indu Banga (ed.), *Five Punjabi Centuries, c. 1500-1990*, Delhi: Manohar, 2000.

Bhalla, V. 'Ethnicity and Indian origins of Gypsies of Eastern Europe and the USSR: A Bio-anthropological perspective', in K.S. Singh (ed.), *Ethnicity, Caste and People: India and the Soviet Union*, Delhi: Manohar, 1992.

——— 'Blood group distribution pertaining to MNSs and Rh-Hr systems in the Indian subcontinent', *Anthropologist*, Vol. IV, No. 3, 1966.

Bhanwar, A.S., 'Biogenetic Survey of Ramgarhias: An Artisan Caste', Ph.D. thesis, Panjabi University: Patiala (unpublished), 1978.

Bingley, A.H., *History, Caste and Culture of the Jats and Gujjars*, Delhi: ESS Publications, 1978 (1st pub. 1904: Calentt: Superintendent Govt. Printers).

Biswas, N., 'Age at menarche among Punjabi girls of Delhi', *Anthropologist*, Vol. 14, 1976

Blunt, E.A.H., *The Caste System of Northern India*, London: Oxford University Press, 1931 and Delhi: S. Chand & Co, 1969 (rpt.).

Bonarjee, P.D., *A Handbook of the Fighting Races of India*, Delhi: Asia Publishing House, 1975 (1st pub. 1898).

Budha, Prakash, *Glimpses of Ancient Punjab*, Patiala: Punjab University, 1966.

———, *Political and social Movements in Ancient Punjab*, Delhi: Motilal Banarasidass, 1964.

*Census of India*, 1881, Vol. I: Report.

———, 1881, Punjab and its Feudatories, Vol. XIX, Calcutta: Census Super-intendent Punjab.

———, 1891, Vol. XX, Part II.

———, 1901, Punjab and NWFP, Vol. 17A, Parts I and II, Castes, Races and Nationality.

———, 1911, Panjab, Vol. XIX, Part II, Tables, Lahore: Civil and Military Gazetteer Press.

———, 1911, Punjab, Vol. XIV, Part I, Report, Lahore: Civil and Military Gazetteer Press.

———, 1911, *Punjab Census Report 1901*, Vol. XIV, Part II, Tables, Lahore: Civil and Military Gazetteer Press.

———, 1921, Punjab, Vol. 15, Part IV.

———, 1921, Punjab and Delhi, Vol. XV, Part I, Report, Lahore: Superintendent Census Operations, Punjab.

———, 1931, Vol. I, Punjab: Report by Khan Ahmad Hassan Khan, Superintendent of Census Operations, Punjab and Delhi.

———, 1931, Punjab, Vol. XVIII, Part I, Report.

———, 1931, Punjab, Vol. XVII, Part II, Lahore.

———, 1941, Vol. I, Part I, Tables.

———, 1961, Vol. I, India, Part V B (II), A. Mitra, ICS, Registrar General & Census Commissioner.

———, 1961, Punjab, Vol. XIII, Part II C (I) and Part I A (I).

———, 1961, Punjab, Vol. XIII, Part V A, Tables on Scheduled Castes and Scheduled Tribes.

———, 1961, Punjab, Vol. XIII, Part V B (Ethnographic Series)

———, 1971, Ludhiana District Census Handbook.

———, 1971, Punjab, Series 17, Part I A, General Report, Delhi.

———, 1971, Punjab, Series 17, Mother Tongue, Religion, Scheduled Castes and Scheduled Tribes, Part II C (1), Part V A.

———, 1981, India, Series I, Part IV.

———, 1981, Vol. I, Delhi: Govt. of India.

———, 1981, Punjab, Series 17, Parts II A and II B, General Population Tables and Primary Census Abstract, Director of Census Operations, Punjab.

———, 1981, Series 26, Chandigarh.

*Chandigarh Digambar Jain Directory*, 1986, Chandigarh.

Choudhary, Prem, 'Contours of Communalism: Religion, Caste and Identity in South East Punjab', *Social Scientist*, Vol. 24, Nos. 4-6, April-June 1996, pp. 130-63.

Channa, V.C., *Caste: Identity and Continuity*, Delhi: B.R. Publishing Corporation, 1979.

Chhabra, G.S., *Advanced Studies in History of the Punjab*, Jalandhar: Sharanjit, 1960.

Conran, W.L., H.D. Craik, *Chiefs and Families of the note in the Punjab*, Vol. II, Lahore: Govt. Printing Press (revd. edn. by Lepal. H. Griffen), 1940.

Crooke, W., 'Kayasth, Kayastha', in *Encyclopaedia of Religion and Ethics*,

Vol. III, James Hastings (ed.), New York, Edinburgh: T.T. Clark, 1896 (rpt. 1971).

———, *The Tribes and Castes of the North-Western India*, Vol. I, Delhi: Cosmo Publications, 1896 (rpt. 1974).

———, *The Tribes and Castes of the North-Western India*, Vol. II, Delhi: Cosmo Publications, 1896 (rpt. 1974).

———, *The Tribes and Castes of the North-Western India*, Vol. III, Delhi: Cosmo Publications, 1896 (rpt. 1974).

———, *The Tribes and Castes of the North-West India*, Vol. IV, Delhi: Cosmo Publications, 1896 (rpt. 1974).

Cunningham, A., *Ancient Geography of India*, Calcutta, 1966.

Dahiya, B.S., *The Ancient Rulers*, Delhi: Sterling Publishers, 1980

Dardi, Kirpal Singh, *Eh Kamboj Lok*, Jalandhar: Shahid Udham Singh Prakashan, 1979.

Darling, M.L., *The Old Light and the New in Punjab*, London: Oxford University Press, 1930.

Das, Veena, 'Masks and Faces: an Essay on Punjabi Kinship', *Contributions to Indian Sociology* (*NS*), Vol. 10. No. 1, 1976, pp. 3-30.

Datta, R.C., *A History of Civilisation in Ancient India*, Delhi: Vishal Publishers, 1972.

Davies, Collin, *An Historical Atlas of the Indian Peninsula*, Geoffry Cumberlage: Oxford University Press, 1974.

Douie, James Sir, *The Punjab North-West Frontier Province and Kashmir*, Delhi: Seema Publications, 1974.

Deptt. of Social Welfare (Reservation Cell), *Manual of Reservation for Scheduled Castes and Backward Classes in India*, Chandigarh: Govt. of Punjab, 1982.

*District Gazetteer*, 'Punjab', Vol. XIX A, Jalandhar Division, 1904.

———, 'Gurdaspur', Lahore: Govt. Printing Press, 1936.

Eliade, Mircea, *The Encyclopedia of Religion*, Vol. 6, New York: Macmillan Publishing Company, 1987.

Elliot, H.M., *Memories on the History, Folklore and Distribution of the Races of North-Western Province in India*, John Beames (ed. and rev.), Vol. I, London: Trubner & Co., 1869.

*Encyclopaedia of Religion, The*, Vol. XIII, New York: Macmillan Publishing Company, 1987.

Gait, E.A., 'Caste', in James Hastings (ed), *Encyclopedia of Religion and Ethics*, Vol. III, New York, Edinburgh: T.T. Clark, 1971.

*Gazetteer of the Montgomery District*, Lahore: Arya Press, 1883-4.

Ghosh, A.K. and S. Kumari, 'Effect of Menarcheal age on Fertility', *Journal of Indian Anthropological Society*, Vol. VIII, 1973.

Gill, H.S., *Linguistic Atlas of Panjab*, Patiala: Panjabi University, 1973.

Grewal, J.S., *The Sikhs of the Punjab*, (in the New Cambridge History of India Series), Cambridge: Cambridge University Press; Hyderabad: Orient Longman, 1991; Delhi: Foundation Books, 1994.

Grewal, J.S. and I. Banga, *Early Nineteenth Century Punjab*, Amritsar: Guru Nanak Dev University, 1975.

Grierson, G.A., *Linguistic Survey of India*, Vol. IX, Part III, Delhi: Motilal Banarasidass, 1907 (rpt. 1968).

Guha, B.S., *Census of India*, Vol. I, Part III, Ethnographical, Simla: Govt. of India Press, 1935.

Gupta, Hari Ram, *History of the Sikhs*, 'The Sikh Gurus 1469- 1708', Vol. I, Delhi: Munshiram Manoharlal, 1984.

Gupta, P., 'Distribution of ABO, Rh Blood groups and secretor factor among Banias and Brahmans of Patiala (Punjab)', Patiala: Panjabi University (unpublished), 1972.

Gupta, B.R., 'Aggarwals', in *The Illustrated Weekly of India*, 11 March 1973.

Habib, Irfan, *An Atlas of Mughal Empire*, Delhi: Oxford University Press, 1982.

Hershman Paul, *Punjabi Kinship and Marriage*, Delhi: Hindustan Publishing Corporation, 1981.

Hutton, J.H., *Caste in India: Its Nature, Functions and Origins*, London: Oxford University Press, 1896.

Ibbetson, Sir Denzil, C.J., *Punjab Ethnography*, [a reprint of those portions of the report on the Punjab Census of 1981 which dealt with the Religions, the Languages, and the Races, Castes and Tribes of the People], Lahore, 1883.

———, *Panjab Castes*, (Being a reprint of the chapter on 'The Races, Castes and Tribes of the People', in the Report on the Census of Punjab published in 1883 by the late Sir Denzil Ibbetson), Lahore, 1916.

———, *Panjab Castes*, Patiala: Panjabi University, 1916 (rpt. 1970); Delhi: Cosmo Publications, 1916 (rpt. 1981).

*The Imperial Gazetteer of India*, Vols. I-XXV, Delhi: Today and Tomorrow Printers and Publishers.

Izmirlian, Harry, Jr., *Structure and Strategy in Sikh Society: Politics of Passion*, Delhi: Manohar, 1979.

Jain, P.S., *The Jaina Path of Purification*, Delhi: Motilal Banarasidass, 1990.

Jamait, Rai Diwan, *The Domiciled Hindus*, Delhi: B.R. Publishing Corporation, 1974.

Jodhka, Surinder, 'Re Imagining Punjab' (mimeo) at the seminar on 'Punjab Ethnography' held at Amritsar in December 2001 to mark the Golden Jubilee of Indian Sociological Association.

Judge, Paramjit, 'Religion, Caste, and Communalism in Punjab' (mimeo) at the seminar on 'Punjab Ethnography' held at Amritsar in December 2001 to mark the Golden Jubilee of Indian Sociological Association.

Kamboj, Bishan Singh, *Kamboj Prakash*, Patiala: R.M.S. Azad Prakashan, 1980.

Kamble, J.R., *Rise and Awakening of Depressed Classes in India*, Delhi: National Publishing House, 1979.

Kane, P.V., 'A Note on the Kayasthas', in *New Indian Antiquary*, Vol. I, 1938-9, pp. 740-3.

Kalhan, Pandit, *Rajatarangini*, Eng. tr. Sir Aurel Stein, 2 vols., London: Westminster, 1900. Indian edn., Delhi, 1964. Also English tr. R.S. Pandit, Allahabad, 1985.

Kansal, D.K., 'Comparative study of body composition based on Surface Anthropometry in four Punjabi communities', M.Sc. thesis, Patiala: Panjabi University, 1972.

———, 'A study of age changes in physique and body composition in males of two communities of Punjab', Ph.D. thesis, Patiala: Panjabi University (unpublished), 1981.

Karve, Irawati, 'Jat', in *Encyclopaedia Britannica*, Vol. XII, Chicago, 1964.

Kaur, K., 'Bio-chemical Genetic Investigations among the Jat-Sikh', M.Sc. thesis, Patiala: Panjabi University, 1978.

Kaur, S., 'A comparative study of the surface anthropometry and menarcheal age in Jat-Sikh and Bania girls of Punjab', M.Sc. thesis, Patiala: Panjabi University (unpublished), 1974.

Ketkar, S.V., *History of caste in India: Evidence of the Law of Manu or Social conditions in India during the 3rd century A.D.*, Delhi: Motilal Banarasidass, 1996 (rpt.).

Khalsa, Gurudharm Singh, 'The End of Syncretism: Anti-Syncretism in Sikh Tradition', in Pashaura Singh and N. Gerald Barrier (eds.), *Sikh Identity: Continuity and Change*, Delhi: Manohar, 2001.

Khare, R.S., 'A Case of Anomalous values in Indian Civilization', *The Journal of Asian Studies*, Vol. XXV, No. II, 1966

Kler, Swinder, 'A study of some hereditary traits among Jats and Khatris of Punjab', unpublished thesis, Patiala: Panjabi University, 1972.

Kohli, Surinder Singh, *Bulhe Shah*: Maker of Indian Literature, Delhi: Sahitya Akademi, 1987.

Lakshmanna, C., *Caste Dynamics in Village India*, Bombay: Navchetan Publications Limited, 1973.

Lal, Bhai Harbans, 'Sahajdhari Sikh: Their Origin and Current Status within the Panth', in Pashaura Singh and N. Gerald Barrier (eds.), *Sikh Identity: Continuity and Change*, Delhi: Manohar, 2001.

Leef, Murray J., *Information and behaviour in a Sikh village: Social organisation reconsidered*, Delhi: Oxford University Press, 1972.

Lewis, Oskar, *Village life in Northern India*, Urbana: University of Illinois Press, 1958.

Lochlin, C.H., 'The History of Christianity in Punjab', in *Panjab Past and Present*, Vol. VII, Part I, 1973.

Madan, T.N., 'Structural Implications of Marriage in North India: Wife-Givers and Wife-Takers Among the Pandits of Kashmir', *Contributions to Indian Sociology* (NS), Vol. 9, No. 2, 1975, pp. 217-43.

Majumdar, R.C., *History and Culture of the Indian People*, Bombay: Bhartiya Vidya Bhawan, 1966.

Malhotra, Anshu, *Gender, Caste and Religious Identities: Restructuring Class in Colonial Punjab*, Delhi: Oxford University Press, 2002.

Martindale, D. and Gerth H. Max Weber, *The Religion of India*: The Sociology of Hinduism and Buddhism, New York: Noble Offset Printers, 1966.

McLeod, W.H., 'The Turban: Symbol of Sikh Identity', in Pashaura Singh and N. Gerald Barrier (eds.), *Sikh Identity, Continuity and Change*, Delhi: Manohar, 2001.

———, *The Evolution of the Sikh Community*, Delhi: Oxford University Press, 1996.

———, *Guru Nanak and the Sikh Religion*, Delhi: Oxford University Press, 1996.

McMullen, G.O., J.C.B. Webster and M. Cable, *The Amritsar Diocese*, Preliminary Survey, Batala: CISS.

Munshi, K.M., *Glory that was Gurjara Desha (A.D. 550- 1300)*, Bombay: Bhartiya Vidya Bhawan, 1954.

Naval, Chandanmal, *Rigar Jati ka Itihas* (Hindi), Jodhpur: Shyam Printing Press, 1986.

Oberoi, Harjot, *The Construction of Religious Boundaries: Culture, Identity and Diversity in the Sikh Tradition*, Delhi: Oxford University Press, 1994; Chicago: University of Chicago Press, 1994.

Pandit Mohanlal, Shami Potra, *Asli-Twarikh-i-Arorbans*, cf. Rai Diwan Jamait, 1974 (rpt.).

Pathak, Sushil Madhawe, *The Social, Economic and Political problems of the Christian community in Panjab*, Bangalore: Christian Institute for the Study of Religion and Society Publication Trust, 1961

Pathak, Sushil Madhawe, *American Missionaries and Hinduism: A study of their contacts from 1813 to 1918*, Delhi: Munshiram Manoharlal, 1967.

Pettligrew, Joyce, *Robber Nobleman: A study of the political system of Jats*, Delhi: Ambika Publications, 1978.

Pocock, David, F., *Kanbi and Patidar: A study of the Patidar community of Gujarat*, Delhi: Oxford University Press, 1972.

Population Research Centre, 'Source Distribution of Population by Religion and Scheduled Caste', *Census of India*, Series No. XVII, Part II, Chandigarh: Punjab University, 1971.

Powell, B.H. Baden, *A Handbook of the Manufacturers and Arts of the Punjab*, Lahore: Punjab Publishing Co., 1872.

Pradhan, C., *The Political system of the Jats of Northern India*, Bombay: Oxford University Press, 1966.

Ram, Pt. Sant, *Sood Bansawali* (in Hindi, n.d.).

Rampal, R., 'Finger and Palmar dermatoglyphics study of the Banias of Patiala', M.Sc. thesis (unpublished), Patiala: Panjabi University, 1972.

Rapson, E.J, *Cambridge History of India*, Vol. 1, Delhi: S. Chand & Co., 1968.

Risley, H.H., *The People of India*, 2nd edn. by W. Crooke, Calcutta: Thacker & Spink, 1915; Delhi: Oriental Book, 2nd edn., 1969.

Rose, H.A., *Glossary of the tribes and Castes of the Panjab and North-West Frontier Province*, Lahore: Civil and Military Gazette,Press, 1919.

———, *Rites and Ceremonies of Hindus and Muslims*, Delhi: Amar Prakashan, 1983 (rpt.).

Russell, R.V. and Hiralal, *The Tribes and Castes of the Central Provinces of India*, London: Macmillan Co., 1916.

Sabarwal, Satish, *Mobilemen: Limits to Social Change in Urban Panjab*, Delhi: Vikas, 1976.

Samanta, Dipak Kumar, *The Dominant Weak: A Case Study of the Neo-Buddhists of Maharashtra*, Calcutta: Anthropological Survey of India, 1991.

Sangave, A., *Jaina Community: A Social Survey*, Bombay: G.R. Bhatkal, 1959.

Sehgal, I.K., 1979, 'Distribution of the ABO and RH Blood Groups in the Jat-Sikh and Harijans', M.Sc. thesis (unpublished), Patiala: Panjabi University, 1979.

Sharma, S.K., *Social Movements and Social Change*, Delhi: B.R. Publishing Corporation, 1985.

Sharma, J.C., 'Individual variations in physical growth and sexual maturity among Punjabi girls: A study based on Longitudinal data', in *Human Biology Recent Advances*, Vol. I, Delhi: Today and Tomorrow Printers and Publishers, 1982

Sharma, R.S., *Indian Feudalism*, Calcutta, 1965.

Sharma, Satya P., 'Marriage, Family and Kinship among the Jats and the Thakurs of North India: Some Comparisons', in *Indian Sociology*, Series No. VIII, 1973.

Shashi, S.S., *The Shepherds of India: A socio-cultural study of sheep and cattle rearing communities*, Delhi: Sundeep Prakashan, 1978.

———, *Social Structure, Ecology and Economy of Gaddis*, Delhi: Satish Publishing House, 1977.

Shastri, Pandit Radha Prashad, *Arorbans Brivaska*, cf. Rai Diwan Jamait, 1974 (rpt).

Sher, Sher Singh, *The Sikligars of Punjab*, Delhi: Sterling Publishers, 1966.

———, *Sansis of Punjab*, Delhi: Munshiram Manoharlal, 1965.

Sinclair, W.F., 'Notes on Castes on the Dekhan', *The Indian Antiquary*, Vol. III, 1874

Singhal, P., 'Morphological age changes in females belonging to two communities of Punjab (India) with special reference to senescene', Ph.D. thesis (unpublished), Patiala: Panjabi University, 1979.

Singh, Gurusharan, 'Labana Sikhs and Guru-Ghar', *Labana Sewak*, July-September 1985.

Singh, Harbans, *Heritage of Sikhs*, Delhi: Manohar, 1985.

Singh, Khushwant, *A History of the Sikhs*, Vol. I, *1469-1839*, Delhi: Oxford University Press, 1986.

———, 1987, 'Sikhism', in *The Encyclopedia of Religion*, Mircea Eliade, Vol 13, New York: Macmillan Publishing Company, 1987.

———, 'Sikhs', in *The Illustrated Weekly of India*, Annual Issue, 1972.

Sethi, Raj Mohini, 'Is Punjab a developed state or is it a contradiction in terms?' (mimeo) at the seminar on 'Punjab Ethnography', held at Amritsar in December 2001 to mark the Golden Jubilee of Indian Sociological Association.

Singh, I.P., 'A Sikh Village', in Milton Singer (ed.), *Traditional India: Structure and Change*, Philadelphia: American Folklore Society, Biographical Series, Vol. X, 1959.

Singh, Jogindar, 'The Sikh Community: Demography and Occupational Change 1881-1931', in Indu Banga (ed.), *Five Punjabi Centuries: Polity, Economy, Society and Culture, c. 1500-1900*, Delhi: Manohar, 2000.

Singh, Rajpal, *Rise of the Jat Power,* Delhi: Harman Publishing House, 1988.

Sircar, D.C., *Iranians and Greeks in Ancient Punjab*, Department of Punjab Historical Studies, Patiala: Panjabi University, 1973.

Smith, V.A., *The Early History of India*, Oxford: Clarendon Press, 1924.

Sood, Madan Mohan and Ram Rattan Sood, *Origin of Soods: A critical Analysis*, Delhi: Lakhmi Printer, 1979.

Sood, Ram Rattan, *Lest we forget them*, Vol. I (Life and Sketches of Eminent Soods of Past), Delhi: Asia Printing Press, 1981.

———, *Lest we forget them*, Vol. II (Some New Facts, Some Ancestors and Some Families, Some Persons of Present Age), Delhi: Asha Printers, 1985.

———, *Lest we forget them*, Volume III (Some Facts, Some Ancestors, New Families, Some Nobles of Present Age and Sood States), New Delhi: Pawan Printers, 1986.

———, *Lest we forget them*, Volume IV (Sood Monuments and Who's Who), Delhi: Krishna Printers, 1987.

Sood, Ritima, 'Business Elites of Ludhiana: A study of Acquisition and Perpetuation of Elite Status', M.A. dissertation, Deptt. of Sociology,

Sood, Salamat Rai, *Tarikh-e-Soodan* (in Urdu), 1935.

Subrahmanyam, Sanjay, 'Before the Leviathan: Sectarian Violence and the State of Pre-Colonial India', in Basu, Kaushik and Sanjaya Subrahmanyam (eds.), *Unravelling the Nation, Sectarian Conflict and India's Secular Identity*, Penguin Books, 1996.

Tandon, P., *Punjabi Century*, Delhi: Orient Paperbacks, 1961.

Thakur, V., *Some Aspects of Ancient Indian History and Culture*, Delhi: Abhinav Publications, 1974.

Thapar, Romila, *A History of India,* Middlesex: Penguin Books, 1977.

Thind, Harbans Singh, *Kamboj Itihas* (in Punjabi), Jalandhar, 1973.

Tod, James, *Annals and Antiquities of Rajasthan: The Central and Western Rajpoot States of India*, 2 vols., London: Routledge and Kegan Paul, 1957.

———, *Annals of Rajasthan: The Annals of Mewar*, Delhi: S. Chand & Co., 1960.

Uberoi, J.P.S., *Religion, Civil Society and the State: A Study of Sikhism*, Delhi: Oxford University Press, 1996.

Vaidya, C.V., *History of Medieval Hindu India*, Gyan Publishing House, Delhi, 1985 (rpt.).

Verma, K.K., *Changing Role of Castes Association*, Delhi: National Publishing House, 1979.

Wakefield, H.E.A., *Kangra District Gazetteer*, 1893.

Webster, J.C.B., *The Christian Community and Change in Nineteenth Century North India,* Delhi: Macmillan, 1976.

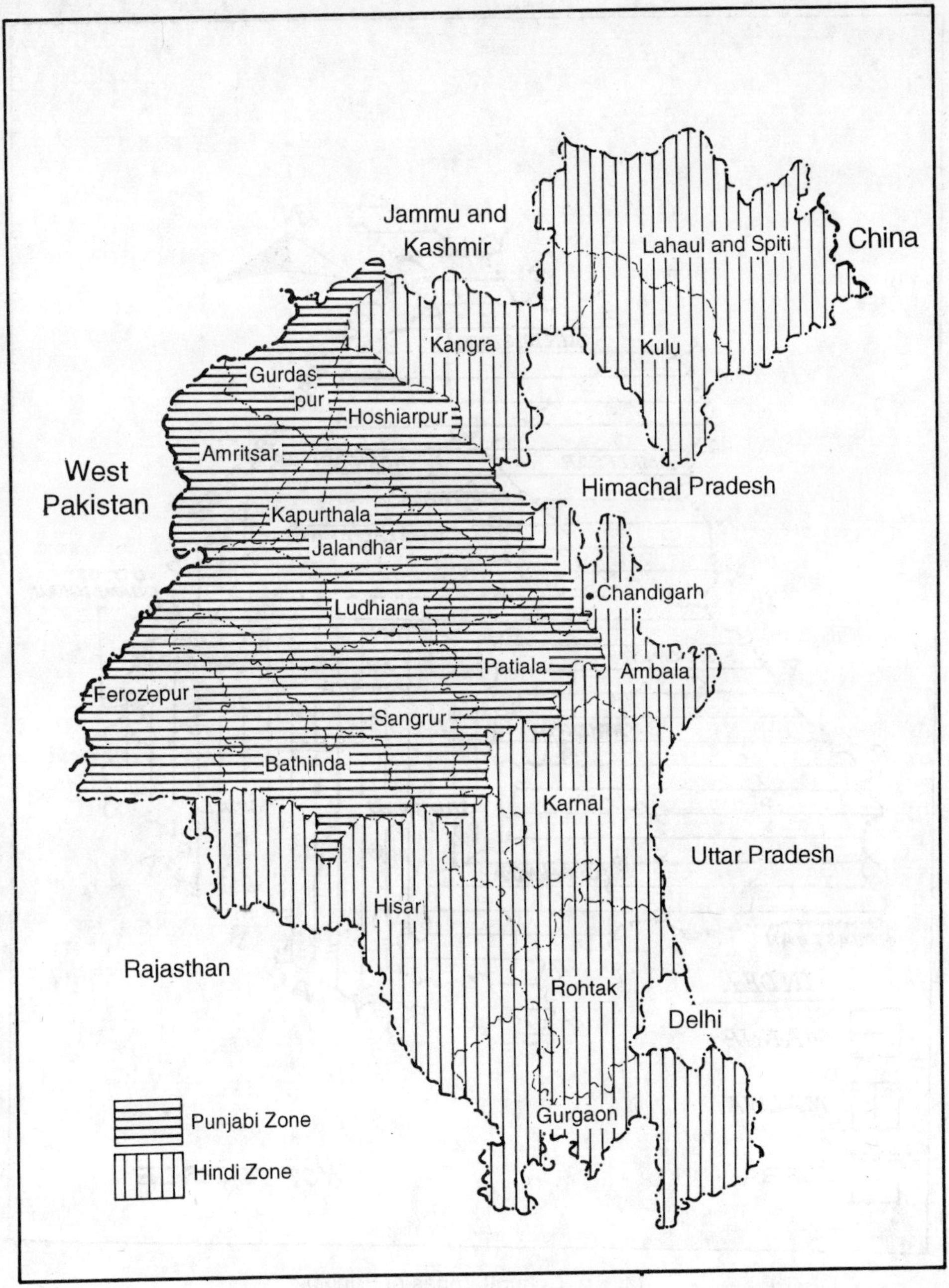


Map 1: The Punjab (1956-66).

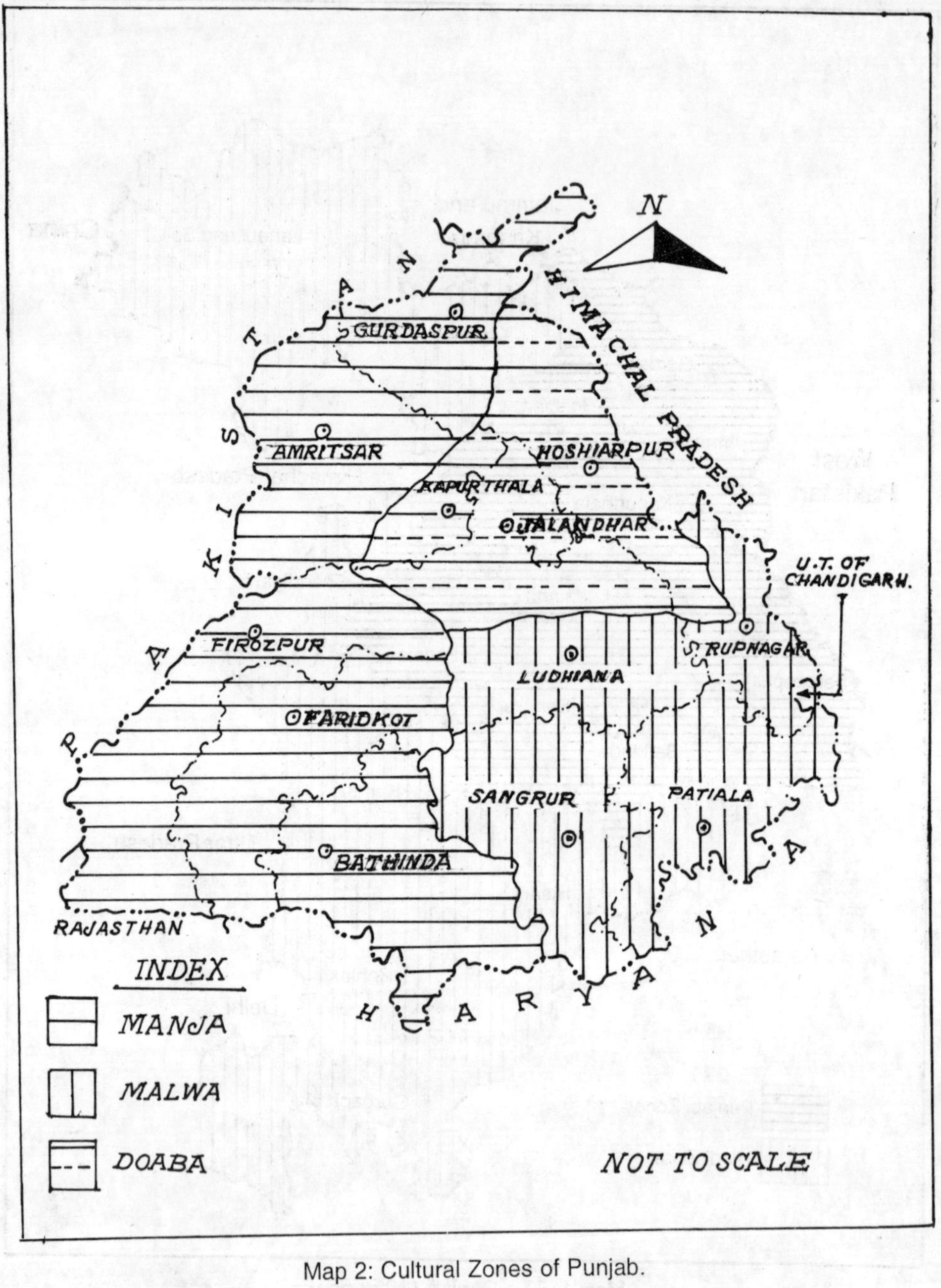


Map 2: Cultural Zones of Punjab.

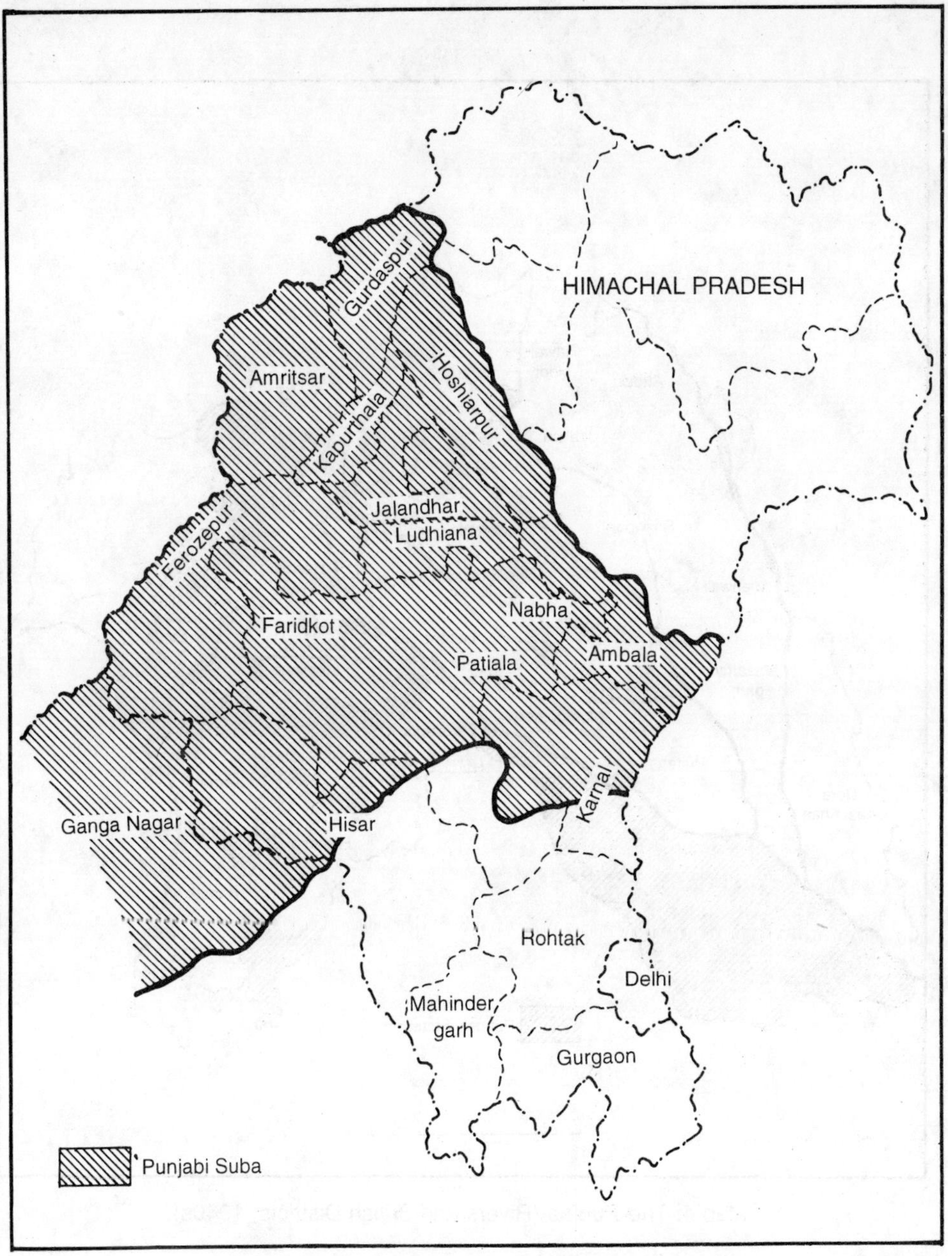


Map 3: 'Punjabi Suba' (Proposed by the Akali Dal).

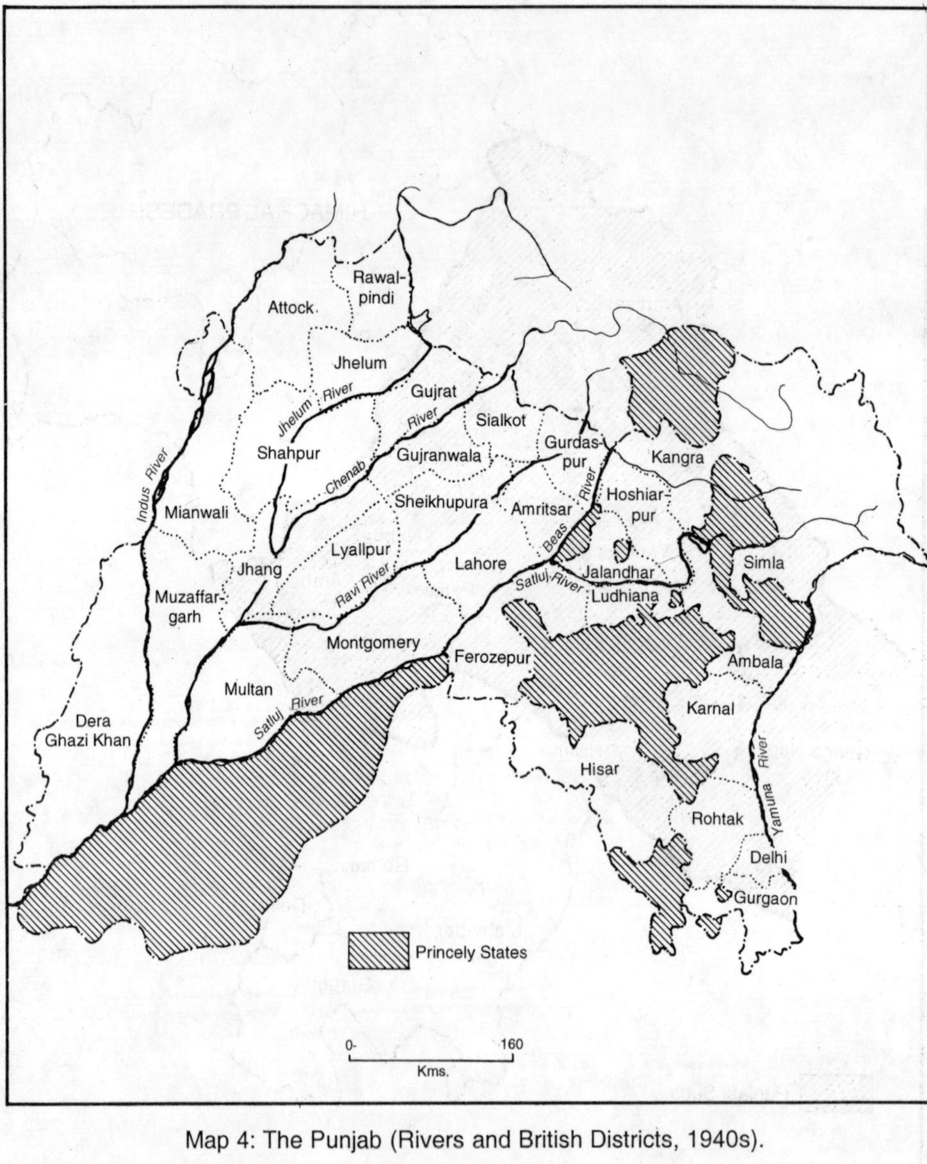


Map 4: The Punjab (Rivers and British Districts, 1940s).

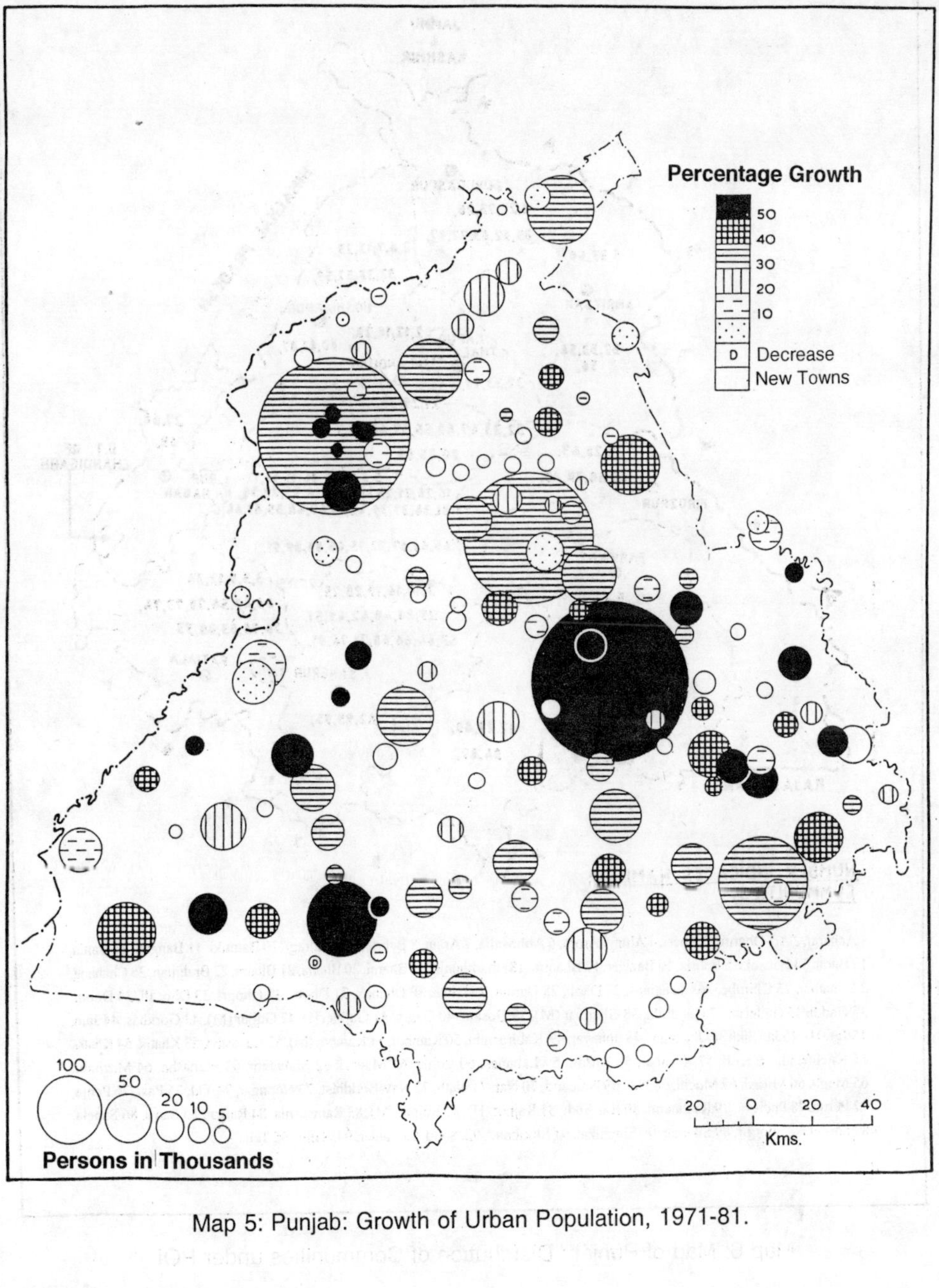


Map 5: Punjab: Growth of Urban Population, 1971-81.

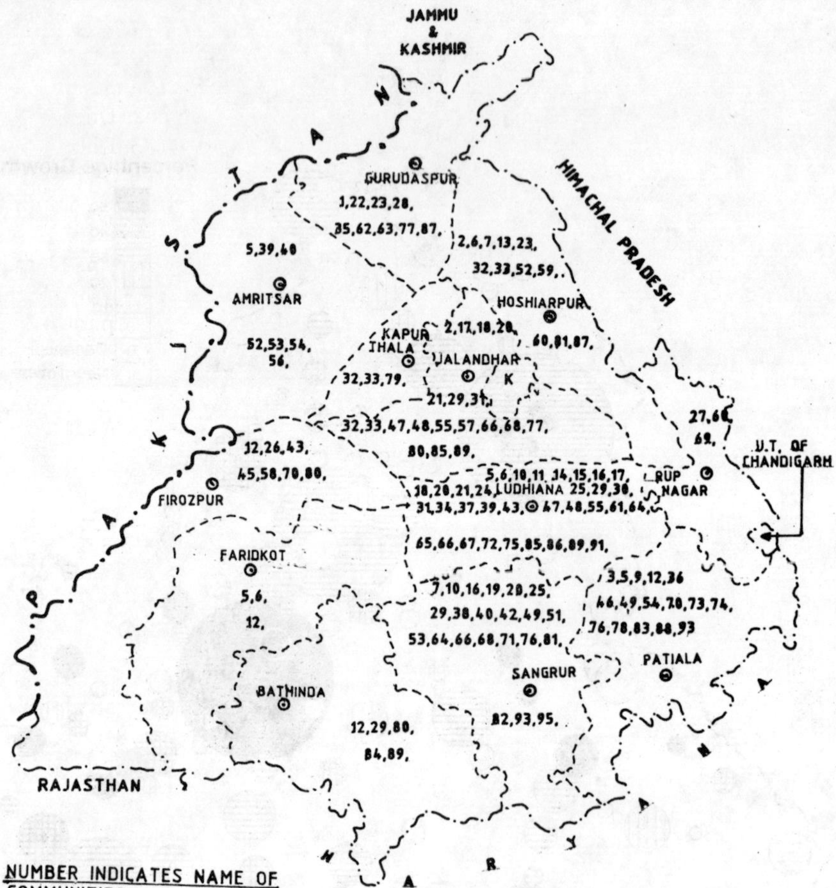


NUMBER INDICATES NAME OF COMMUNITIES.

1 Acharaj, 2 Ad-Dharmi, 3 Aheri, 4 Ahir, 5 Arora, 6 Ahluwalia, 7 Arain, 8 Bahrupia, 9 Bairagi, 10 Balmiki, 11 Bangali, 12 Bania, 13 Barar, 14 Batwal, 15 Bauria, 16 Bazigar, 17 Bhanjra, 18 Bharbhunja, 19 Bharai, 20 Bhatia, 21 Bhatra, 22 Brahman, 23 Chahang, 24 Chamar, 25 Chimbe, 26 Christians, 27 Daoli, 28 Darain, 29 Dhea, 30 Dhanak, 31 Dhobi, 32 Dhogri, 33 Dhosali, 34 Doom, 35 Gaddi, 36 Gaderia, 37 Gandhila, 38 Ghumiar (M), 39 Gosain, 40 Gagra, 41 Gujjar (H), 42 Gujjar (M), 43 Gorkhas, 44 Jain, 45 Jat (H), 46 Jat Sikh, 47 Jhangam, 48 Jhinwar, 49 Kabirpanthi, 50 Kamboj, 51 Kamboj (M), 52 Kayastha, 53 Khatik, 54 Khatri, 55 Kuchband, 56 Koli, 57 Kumhar, 58 Kurmi, 59 Labanas, 60 Lohar, 61 Madari, 62 Mahatam, 63 Mahasha, 64 Mazhabi, 65 Megh, 66 Mirasi, 67 Mochi, 68 Nai, 69 Nalband, 70 Nat, 71 Nath, 72 Nav-Buddhist, 73 Noongar, 74 Od, 75 Pasi, 76 Penja, 77 Perna, 78 Pherera, 79 Rachband, 80 Rai Sikh, 81 Rajput (H), 82 Rajput (M), 83 Ramgarhia, 84 Raigar, 85 Sansi, 86 Sapela, 87 Sarera, 88 Shorgir, 89 Sikligar, 90 Singhikat, 91 Sirkiband, 92 Sood, 93 Suniar, 94 Saini, 95 Teli

Map 6: Map of Punjab: Distribution of Communities under POI

# INDEX